Continuities
in
Structural
Inquiry

Continuities in Structural Inquiry

PETER M BLAU
and
ROBERT K MERTON
Editors

SAGE Publications · London and Beverly Hills

For information address

SAGE Publications Inc, 275 South Beverly Drive,
Beverly Hills, California 90212

SAGE Publications Ltd, 28 Banner Street, London EC1Y 8QE

British Library Cataloguing in Publication Data
Continuities in structural inquiry.
   1. Social structure
   I. Blau, Peter Michael
   II. Merton, Robert K
   301.4   GN478   80-41184

   ISBN 0-8039-9808-2

CONTENTS

III. QUANTITATIVE MODELS

ACKNOWLEDGMENTS

We gratefully acknowledge support from the National Science Foundation — grants SES-7927238 (to Merton) and SOC-7919935 (to Blau). We are indebted to Mary Wilson Miles for aid in monitoring the successive versions of the manuscript, to Gloria Ann Swigert for keeping track of the correspondence with contributors and typing the Introduction, and to Karen Ginsberg for help in proofreading.

In accordance with the request of the editors and contributors, royalties from the sale of this book go to the International Sociological Association.

FOREWORD:
Remarks on
Theoretical Pluralism

Robert K. Merton
Columbia University

When Peter Blau invited me to join him in editing this volume, I agreed for two self-indulgent reasons. The first stemmed from a substantive interest: this would afford an occasion for closely examining once again the varieties of structural inquiry which have been developing in sociology specifically, and in social science, generally. The other reason stemmed from a meta-theoretical interest. That such a diversity of theoretical orientations should turn up within the ostensibly single region of structural inquiry seemed to provide a notable instance of theoretical pluralism, an aspect of the development of science and scholarship which has long interested some of us at work in the sociology of science. The plurality of partly overlapping, partly distinctive theories seems to reproduce in this one region of inquiry the actual and, to my mind, the cognitively appropriate state of sociology at large. For the plain fact is that no single all-embracing and tight-knit theoretical orientation has proved adequate to identify and to deal with the wide range of problems requiring investigation in detail. It seems to be the case, rather, that diverse theoretical orientations are variously effective for dealing with diverse kinds, and aspects, of sociological and social problems. (All this is not to deny, of course, the notorious tendency for theoretical pluralism to degenerate into theoretical fragmentation in which the various theoretical orientations become mutually irrelevant.)

It would only be redundant for me to undertake a substantive analysis of the various modes of structural analysis set forth in this book. For Peter Blau proceeds to do so, systematically and in concise detail, in the Introduction. It is there that he compares their differing imagery of social structure (as social reality or as conceptual construct), their differing ontological and epistemological assumptions, and the problematics generated by each of these orientations. Most in point, he does much to identify a basic commonality amid this diversity of theoretical outlook in the form of an anti-reductionist perspective on the emergent properties of social structure. Finally, he proposes a taxonomy of such properties and of the components of social structure to assist in tracing theoretical connections and disjunctions among the several modes of structural inquiry.

Since Peter Blau provides this substantive cognitive map of the papers in the book, I shall limit myself to a few remarks on theoretical pluralism exemplified in it (thus reiterating and enlarging upon a theme briefly discussed in an earlier paper of mine which, as it happens, appeared in another volume on structural inquiry edited by Blau [Merton, 1975]).

In its most general aspect, the notion of theoretical pluralism is of long standing and has turned up more or less independently in many disciplines. One of its chief exponents, Karl Popper, observed that its importance in the growth of scientific knowledge had been emphasized at the close of the nineteenth century by the geologist T. C. Chamberlin under the heading of 'the method of multiple working hypotheses' (Popper, 1974, pp. 1187, n. 80). We need reach back no further than the 1940s to observe a pluralistic orientation being developed in sociology, economics, biology, and, for that matter, in literary criticism as well. The case for a plurality of theories, paradigms, or conceptual schemes was being developed in opposition to the quest for a single all-embracing theory on grounds which have since been rather fully elucidated by philosophers of science.

In sociology, during the 1940s, this division of opinion derived largely from pro-and-con responses to Talcott Parsons's mode of theorizing. He was anticipating and advocating a theoretical monism in which the then current theories advanced within 'the professional group...should converge in the development of a single conceptual structure' (Parsons, 1948). This monistic orientation was countered in a rather mild-mannered polemic:

> ...when [Mr Parsons] suggests that our chief task is to deal with 'theory' rather than with 'theories', I must take strong exception.
>
>   The fact is that the term 'sociological theory,' just as would be the case with the terms 'physical theory' or 'medical theory,' is often misleading. It suggests a tighter integration of diverse working theories than ordinarily obtains in any of these disciplines. Let me try to make clear what is here implied. Of course, every

discipline has a strain toward logical and empirical consistency. Of course, the temporary co-existence of logically incompatible theories sets up a tension, resolved only when one or another of the theories is abandoned or so revised as to eliminate the inconsistency. Of course, also, every discipline has basic concepts, postulates and theorems which are the common resources of all theorists, irrespective of the special range of problems with which they deal....

Of course, distinct theories often involve partly overlapping concepts and postulates. But the significant fact is that the progress of these disciplines consists in working out a large number of theories specific to certain types of phenomena and in exploring their mutual relations, and not in centering attention on 'theory' as such....

Sociological theory must advance on these interconnected planes: through special theories adequate to limited ranges of social data and through the evolution of a conceptual scheme adequate to *consolidate* groups of special theories.

To concentrate solely on special theories is to run the risk of emerging with *ad hoc*, unrelated speculations consistent with a limited range of observations and inconsistent among themselves.

To concentrate solely on the major conceptual scheme for deriving all sociological theory is to run the risk of producing twentieth-century equivalents of the large philosophical systems of the past, with all their suggestiveness, all their architectonic splendor and all their scientific sterility. (Merton, 1948, 1978)

At much the same time, the economist Wassily Leontief was independently complementing the advocacy of theoretical pluralism *within* a discipline by advocacy of *inter-discipline* pluralism in the interpretation of historical development. There he was, in the late 1940s, noting the distinctive cognitive contributions of diverse disciplinary perspectives which, even when incommensurable in their internal logics, could be complementary:

...we face the choice between obdurate insistence on some *monistic interpretation* — which means overtaxing the analytical resources of one, chosen discipline and neglecting the capacities of all the others — or *practical pluralism*.

The pluralistic character of any single explanation reveals itself not in simultaneous application of essentially disparate types of considerations but rather in the ready shift from one type of interpretation to another. The justification of such *methodological eclecticism* lies — and this is the principal point of the argument that follows — in the limited nature of any type of interpretation or causation (I use the two terms interchangeably). Neither the economic, nor the anthropological, nor, say, geographical argument can, in the present state of the development of the respective disciplines, lead to the statement of uniquely defined necessities. Considering any given sequence of events *alternatively in the light of each one of such different approaches*, one can at best assign it to as many different ranges of 'possibilities.' Although the internal logics of the respective disciplines are *incommensurable*, the various ranges of possibilities thus derived are *comparable*, since all of them are described in terms of alternative developments of the same particular processes. (Leontief, 1948, pp. 618-19; my italics)

Leontief thus centers on the idea central to theoretical pluralism: that though theoretical orientations may differ in their cogency when directed toward the same problems, their very difference of perspective typically leads them to focus on different rather than the same problems. As a result, the theories are often complementary or unconnected rather than contradictory. Failure to recognise this possibility often results in the mock controversies that recurrently pepper the history of the sciences. That this is not at all peculiar to sociology, or specifically to alternative modes of structural analysis, appears clear from the observations of the biologist-polymath Paul A. Weiss on the plurality of concepts, theories and orientations in various disciplines:

> Science has a good record of success in resolving *tenacious sham controversies by proving opposing tenets to be not mutually exclusive, but rather validly coexisting alternatives.* Scientific history abounds with scientific verdicts in which, on unassailably 'objective' evidence, cases of supposedly irreconcilable contradictoriness were adjudicated by showing the conclusions of both contenders to have been valid. The complementarity principle of Bohr, affirming the right of coexistence of both a corpuscular and a wave concept of light; the duplicity theory of von Kries, establishing that both of two theories concerning the function of the retinal elements in color vision, formerly thought to be in conflict, were correct; the perennial fight between the embryological credos of preformation versus epigenesis — whether the whole array of organs in an adult organism is preformed as such in the egg in miniature form or whether all development is *de novo* to both concepts; all these are classical illustrations. . . . (Weiss, 1973, p. xii)

Nor is the concept of pluralism as involving complementary rather than inevitably contradictory theories limited to the sciences. In the domain of literary criticism during the 1940s and afterward, the Chicago Neo-Aristotelians also argued the case for pluralism. As Ronald S. Crane, one of the chief architects of that school, put it in his introduction to one of their composite manifestoes-and-examplars:

> These essays. . .are as much an essential part of the program of the Chicago group as their essays in 'Aristotelian' poetics. And *the only critical philosophy that underlies them all* is contained in the very un-Aristotelian attitude toward criticism, including the criticism of Aristotle, *which they have called 'pluralism.'* The term may be unfortunate: what they meant it to convey was simply their conviction that *there are and have been many valid critical methods, each of which exhibits the literary object in a different light, and each of which has its characteristic powers and limitations.* (Crane, [1952] 1970, p. iv)

And in his exemplifying 'Outline of Poetic Theory', Elder Olson, another of the same critical persuasion, went on to note:

> If a *plurality of valid and true kinds of criticism* is possible, choice must still be exercised, for it is impossible to employ all methods simultaneously. . . . Choice is determined by *the questions one wishes to ask and the form of answer one requires* and by the relative adequacy of given systems. (Olson, [1952] 1970, p. 9)

This small sampling of pluralist perspectives could of course be easily enlarged — most easily by turning to the prime, disputatious discussions of pluralism and monism which have lately gathered force in the philosophy of science. But in these remarks, it must be enough only to refer to a few works by some of the principals in that ongoing energetic debate: the practically ubiquitous Popper (1974) and Kuhn ([1962] 1970, 1977), along with Naess (1972), Lakatos (1978), and the extreme formulations of Feyerabend (1975), with some notice of the useful overviews of this clash of philosophical opinion which have been provided by Radnitsky (1971) and Klima (1971).

The few formulations by workers in various disciplines quoted here are perhaps enough to suggest that, however much the disciplines differ in other respects, they are alike in perforce taking a single all-embracing theoretical orientation which unifies the postulates of the discipline as an ultimate ideal rather than as a description of the actual state of the field. It is being proposed here that the plurality of current theories, paradigms, and thought-styles are not a mere happenstance, simply incidental to the development of each field of inquiry. Rather, it appears to be integral to the socially patterned cognitive processes operating in the disciplines. With the institutionalization of science, the behavior of scientists oriented toward norms of organized skepticism and mutual criticism works to bring about such theoretical pluralism. As particular theoretical orientations come to be at the focus of attention of a sufficient number of workers in the field to constitute a thought collective, interactively engaged in developing a particular thought style (Fleck, [1935] 1979), they give rise to a variety of new key questions requiring investigation. As the theoretical orientation is increasingly put to use, further implications become identifiable. And, in anything but a paradoxical sense, newly acquired knowledge produces newly acquired ignorance. For the growth of knowledge and understanding within a field of inquiry brings with it the growth of *specifiable and specified ignorance*: a new awareness of what is not yet known or understood and a rationale for its being worth the knowing. To the extent that current theoretical frameworks prove unequal to the task of dealing with some of the newly emerging key questions, there develops a composite social-and-cognitive pressure within the discipline for developing new or revised frameworks. But typically, the new does not completely crowd out the old, as earlier theoretical perspectives remain capable of dealing with problems distinctive of them.

This sort of process seems to have been at work to produce the diversity of theoretical orientations advanced in this book. Each account of particular modes of structural inquiry is in effect both a cognitive and social announcement. Cognitively, it announces the critical rationale of a more or less coherent set of structural problems, concepts, analytical procedures and findings. Socially, it announces the commitment of a group of scholars to the particular theoretical orientation and, with or without the author's intent, it attempts to make a case for others in the discipline to adopt that orientation in their own work.

This twin cognitive-and-social character of such expositions is once again taken as integral, not incidental, to the development of a field of inquiry. The public adoption of one rather than another theoretical orientation is at the least a tacit (and often, an explicit) claim that it is more powerful and consequential in solving the cognitive problems it is designed to solve and more fruitful in raising new significant problems than rival orientations. After all, in terms of a cognitive rationale, why else would a scholar adopt a structural orientation to begin with and, within that generic frame of structural thought, why else adopt a Lévi-Straussian, Marxist, Weberian, or other orientation? So it is that this volume provides yet another concrete case of knowledge-claims that exemplifies the problem of the determinants of theory-choice and problem-choice in science (Zuckerman, 1979); a problem still not well understood which has remained on the agenda of the sociology of scientific knowledge since at least the early, perceptive, and long neglected monograph by Ludwik Fleck, *Genesis and Development of a Scientific Fact* ([1935] 1979).

It is also not sociologically incidental that theoretical pluralism should make for controversy and cognitive conflict. Sociologists are scarcely alone in appearing to be forever engaged in hot dispute. Whether they are more so than the generality of other scholars and scientists is not clear and, to the best of my knowledge, comparative rates of cognitive conflict among disciplines have yet to be investigated systematically. At any rate, the tribe of sociologists seems no more controversial than the articulate, internecine tribe of today's philosophers of science, with its clans engaged in vigorously announcing their own claims to sound knowledge while cheerfully denouncing the claims of others. To the extent that members of a thought-collective claim exclusive access to sound knowledge about a given region of phenomena they deny that there is truth in the ideas being advanced by cognitively opposed thought-collectives. This is a condition admirably calculated to produce increasingly passionate cognitive conflict and ensuing cognitive segregation. The process is somewhat as follows: deepened cognitive conflict leads to progressive alienation in which members of each thought-collective develop selective perceptions of the theoretical orientation being advanced by the others. These perceptions harden into self-confirming stereotypes. This, in turn, leads to reciprocal (and often well-founded) claims to having been misunderstood and, accordingly, misrepresented. In due course, full cognitive segregation sets in, with members of rival thought-collectives no longer making an active effort to examine the work of cognitively opposed collectives. No doubt this is the sort of thing which led Alfred Marshall, in properly ironic mood, to propose the 'general rule that in discussions on method and scope, a man is nearly sure to be right when affirming the usefulness of his own procedure, and wrong when denying that of others.'

It is the merit of even the most severely critical papers in this volume that they give no evidence of such theoretical segregation of the several modes of structural inquiry.

REFERENCES

BLAU, Peter M. (ed.) (1975) *Approaches to the Study of Social Structure*. New York: Free Press.

CRANE, R. S. (ed.) ([1952] 1970) *Critics and Criticism*. Chicago: University of Chicago Press.

FEYERABEND, Paul (1975) *Against Method: Outline of an Anarchistic Theory of Knowledge*. London: NLB.

FLECK, Ludwik ([1935] 1979) *Genesis and Development of a Scientific Fact*. T. J. Trenn and R. K. Merton (eds.), Chicago: University of Chicago Press.

KLIMA, Rolf (1971) 'Theorienpluralismus in der Soziologie', pp. 198-219 in A. Diemer (ed.), *Der Methoden- und Theorienpluralismus in den Wissenschaften*. Meisenheim: Hain.

KUHN, Thomas S. ([1962] 1970) *The Structure of Scientific Revolutions*. Chicago: University of Chicago Press.

KUHN, Thomas S. (1977) *The Essential Tension: Selected Studies in Scientific Tradition and Change*. Chicago: University of Chicago Press.

LAKATOS, Imre (1978) *The Methodology of Scientific Research Programmes*. Cambridge: Cambridge University Press.

LEONTIEF, Wassily (1948) 'Notes on the Pluralistic Interpretation of History and the Problem of Interdisciplinary Cooperation', *The Journal of Philosophy*, XLV (November 4): 617-24.

MERTON, Robert K. (1948) 'The Position of Sociological Theory', *American Sociological Review*, 13: 164-68.

MERTON, Robert K. (1975) 'Structural Analysis in Sociology', pp. 21-52 in P. M. Blau (1975).

NAESS, Arne (1972) *The Pluralist and Possibilist Aspect of the Scientific Enterprise*. Oslo: Universitetsforlager.

OLSON, Elder ([1952] 1970) 'An Outline of Poetic Theory', pp. 546-66 in R. S. Crane (ed.) (1970) [see above].

PARSONS, Talcott (1948) 'The Position of Sociological Theory', *American Sociological Review*, 13 (April): 156-64.

POPPER, Karl R. (1974) 'Replies to My Critics', pp. 961-1197 in Paul A. Schilpp (ed.), *The Philosophy of Karl Popper*. LaSalle, Ill.: Open Court.

RADNITZKY, Gerard (1971) 'Theorienpluralismus-Theorienmonismus', pp. 135-84 in Alwin Diemer (ed.), *Der Methoden- und Theorienpluralismus in den Wissenschaften*. Meisenheim: Hain.

WEISS, Paul A. (1973) *The Science of Life*. Mt Kisco: Future Publishing Co.

ZUCKERMAN, Harriet (1969) 'Theory Choice and Problem Choice in Science', pp. 65-95 in Jerry Gaston (ed.), *Sociological Perspectives on Science*. San Francisco: Jossey-Bass.

INTRODUCTION:
Diverse Views of Social Structure and Their Common Denominator

Peter M. Blau
*Columbia University and State University
of New York at Albany*

'Varieties of Structural Inquiry' was the topic of three sessions at the World Congress of Sociology in Uppsala, Sweden, in 1978, and most of the papers in this volume were originally presented there.[1] The collection represents, as its title indicates, 'Continuities in Structural Inquiry', inasmuch as it succeeds an earlier collection of papers on the same general subject (Blau, 1975). The different chapters in this book, as well as those in the earlier one, are very diverse not only in their conception of social structure but also in their method of analysis. They range from purely qualitative discussions of conceptual issues to quantitative models of structural analysis based on empirical data. Some compare and critically evaluate different theoretical orientations in the study of social structure. Others present conceptual analyses and refinements. Still others develop formal theoretical models and apply them to quantitative empirical data.

The questions arise whether such diverse discussions have any common denominator and whether there is any reason to combine them in one book. Some social scientists interested in the theoretical debates in the first part may well not be particularly interested in the quantitative models in Part III, and vice versa. Nevertheless, there are good grounds for including these very different modes of structural interpretation in the same book, because only by doing so can the book convey the great diversity of structural analyses being practiced today. Such diversity and pluralism of approaches in a discipline tend to be a main source of advances in systematic knowledge, as my fellow editor noted in his paper in the earlier collection (Merton, 1975).

The question remains, however, whether there is anything distinctive about these analysts of social structure with so greatly differing viewpoints. Is there any common denominator in their approach that distinguishes it from that of other social scientists? I shall suggest an affirmative answer, after first presenting an overview of the contents of this volume.

OVERVIEW OF VOLUME

The discussions in the first part of the book deal explicitly with different structural orientations, centering attention on the major and most widely known forms of structural analysis. In particular, the structuralism of Lévi-Strauss and Marxist structuralism are discussed and compared with structural-functional analysis in anthropology and sociology. Lévi-Strauss's theoretical scheme is analyzed in relation to those of Radcliffe-Brown, Parsons, Weber, and others. Althusser's and Wallerstein's Marxist structural approaches are critically examined. The papers in Part II dissect the concept of social structure, specifying various dimensions and elements, and draw some implications from the analysis of structures of interdependence. In the last part, three quantitative models of social structure are constructed and applied to empirical data.

The first two papers contrast Lévi-Straussian structuralism with structural-functionalism, the theoretical tradition derived from Durkheim and represented particularly by British anthropologists and by Parsons in American sociology. Leach compares it with the structural orientation in British anthropology, as most notably represented by Radcliffe-Brown and Meyer Fortes. He stresses that for these British anthropologists the term 'social structure' refers to empirical reality — to observable groups and hierarchies dividing a population and 'actually existing in the world out there.' For Lévi-Strauss, in sharp contrast, social structure is a mental construct devised by the theorist to explain empirical observations and only roughly reflected in the various empirically observed patterns of social positions and relations. To be sure, British structuralists realize that the empirical data they see out there depend on their conceptual framework, and Lévi-Strauss does note that his structural constructs embody the central features, though not every detail, of the empirical patterns observable in different systems or cases. Yet it makes an all-important difference for the nature of a theory and its falsifiability, to use Popper's (1959) term, whether or not its core concepts are assumed to refer to empirical patterns that are exogenous to the theoretical formulations and thus furnish independent tests of them. This difference between British and French structuralism engendered disputes about the importance of empirical evidence in the anthropological study of kinship, and it led to even sharper controversies when Lévi-Strauss focused his attention in recent years primarily on the study of myths. For his interpretative scheme for myths is less precise, further removed from objective empirical conditions, and less amenable to testing in research than his theory of kinship, yet it is his mythology that Lévi-Strauss considers his major theoretical contribution. Leach concludes his essay by attempting to reconcile these differences.

Rossi compares the transformational structuralism of Lévi-Strauss with various forms of empirical structuralism in sociology, especially with Parsons's structural-functionalism. Whereas Leach's aim is to present a balanced view of alternative structural approaches, Rossi — in this paper and in his other writings — explicitly considers himself a spokesman for Lévi-Strauss, and his objective is to criticize other orientations to the study of social structure in terms of transformational structuralism. For example, he chastizes empirical structuralism for lack of epistemological sophistication, empiricist preoccupation with observable data, and mechanistic theorizing based on statistical models, juxtaposing Lévi-Strauss's opposite tendencies in all these respects. Rossi's spirited defense of Lévi-Strauss and his attack on other versions of structural analysis in sociology bring into high relief the difference between Lévi-Strauss's approach and what Rossi calls the empirical structuralism in American sociology.

Both authors invited to discuss Marxist structuralism, whose papers constitute the next two chapters, are critical of it, and both criticize it not from a conservative but from an alternative Marxist perspective. The one makes this criticism in general theoretical terms, the other rests it on the significance of particular historical conditions and bases it on a case study of a specific revolution.

Heydebrand presents a general conceptual analysis and critique of Marxist structuralism, with special emphasis on Althusser's formulation. He starts with an original analysis of the homology between Saussure's concept of linguistic structure and Marx's concept of economic structure, noting the parallel between the linguistic duality of signified and signifier and the economic duality between labor and wages. Raising the sociology-of-knowledge question of why Marxist structuralism emerged, he sees it as an outgrowth of the conflict between the growing anti-Stalinism of leftists after World War II and the reaction against this 'infantile leftism' of the New Left, with its utopianism, its anti-authoritarianism, and its emphasis on the writings of the young Marx, whose discussion, as exemplified by that on alienation, is still more influenced by ideological residues of Hegelian dialectics than by a systematic model of economic determinism. Building such a scientific model of Marxist social structure is precisely Althusser's aim. In the process, he transforms Marx's distinction between economic infrastructure and superstructure into a three-level structure by distinguishing an intermediate political structure from both the ideological superstructure and the economic base. In terms of the sociology of knowledge, a theory that gives the political structure a special role is compatible with a movement that is dominated by the state socialism of the Soviet Union. A major objection of Heydebrand's against Marxist structuralism is that it neglects the importance of practical criticism as an inherent part of dialectical analysis. Another criticism he advances is that Marxist structuralism is in many respects akin to traditional structural-functional analysis in sociology, as has also been noted by representatives of the latter (see, for example, Lipset, 1975). Both make the assumptions of order, determinism, and functionality. Both assume that an orderly social structure exerts, and needs to exert, external constraints on individual. Finally, instead of continually criticizing existing social conditions and seeking to improve them, as a critical sociologist should, Marxist structuralism as well as structural-functionalism implicitly accepts existing political structures (albeit not the same structure: Stalin's Russia in one case; Nixon's America in the other) as inevitable and perhaps even the best possible.

Zeitlin develops his historical argument on the basis of a thorough case study of the unsuccessful bourgeois revolution against large landowners in Chile in the middle of the nineteenth century. One question raised in this Marxist case study is why Chile, despite this defeat, became a stable democracy lasting over a century, and Zeitlin stresses that such a question cannot be satisfactorily answered without taking into account the distinctive historical circumstances governing class formation and class conflict. In ninetenth-century Chile, the independent power bases of various classes prevented any one from imposing an oppressive regime on the rest, thereby furthering the development of democracy. Zeitlin is primarily concerned with the theoretical implications for Marxist analysis of his historical investigation, on the basis of which he severely criticizes Wallerstein's (1974) world-system theory as making false inferences because it entirely ignores the effects of particular historical conditions on national developments. His argument is that socioeconomic developments cannot be explained by theoretical generalizations, at least not without specifically taking into consideration the influences of distinctive historical circumstances. He also criticizes Wallerstein's theory for being functional and resting on teleological assumptions, and he extends this criticism to Althusser's and to dependency theory.

The theme of Eisenstadt's chapter is that Max Weber not only anticipated Lévi-Strauss's basic principle but actually went beyond it, and specified, as Lévi-Strauss did not, the social processes that mediate the influences of this principle. The principle is that social patterns must be explained in terms of a deep structure composed of codes of symbols and myths. The structural thesis that the symbolic dimension of social life is what explains it poses a question that it never answers, namely, what the specific institutional mechanisms are through which cultural symbols and values affect the overt social organization. Eisenstadt suggests that the answer is implied by Weber's concept of 'Wirtschaftsethik' generally and by his theoretical analysis of the role of the Calvinistic ethic in the development of capitalism particularly. The Protestant ethics, and religious dogmas generally, are symbolic codes of social values which govern people's orientations, legitimate authority, and consequently affect the concrete organization of social life.

The next two papers analyze the concept of social structure by distinguishing several levels or dimensions. Warriner uses as differentiating criterion what the elements are whose interrelations delineate the structure. On the basis of this criterion, he distinguishes three levels of social structure. The interpersonal level refers to the structure of social relations among persons, for example the sociometric network in a small group. The interpositional level describes the structure of relations among social positions (which are often confused with the persons who are their incumbents), for instance the kinship system in a tribe. The inter-organizational level depicts the structure of relations among formally organized collectivities, such as the patterns of trade among firms in a community or the interlocking directorates among corporations in a society.

Wallace also stresses the importance of conceptualizing structure as a hierarchy of successive levels of more encompassing structure. On every level, we must distinguish the aggregates constituting the structures and the elements composing these aggregates, although the elements of a wider aggregate can in turn be treated as aggregates composed of narrower elements in the study of the next-lower level of structure. Wallace's main point, however, is that these differences in structural scope can be analyzed in three distinct dimensions. The number of organisms can range from a small group to a large society; the social behavior being examined can vary from a single act, such as a greeting, to a complex syndrome of action, such as a marriage; and the regularity being under investigation can pertain to a narrow time and space — hourly productivity in one factory — or to broad ones — a nation's annual rate of economic growth. These three dimensions refine the analysis of successive levels of structure, and they can be alternatively employed to delineate an eight-fold property space of social phenomena. First, a study may deal with human or with nonhuman organisms; in either case, it may be concerned primarily with their physiological or their psychological behavior; each of the resulting four categories may entail investigations focusing on spatial or on temporal regularities. Cross-classification of these three dichotomies yields eight types of pure social phenomena, any combination of which may be involved in a particular analysis. Wallace concludes that various social theorists tend to concentrate on different combinations of social phenomena and generally leave out some aspects of social structure in these terms.

Kadushin's chapter deals with networks of circular or indirect social exchange. Direct exchange is necessarily limited to those persons who have direct social contact. Large structures of social exchange, therefore, inevitably entail much indirect exchange. Direct exchange is sustained by personal obligations, the need to reciprocate for services lest they be discontinued, and social disapproval for ingratitude, but these factors do not generate rewards for those who 'cast their bread upon the waters' in the hope of some future returns from third parties. This poses the problem of the conditions that do promote indirect exchange, the problem discussed in Kadushin's paper.

Boudon analyzes a variety of paradoxical consequences that structures of interdependence generate. If the actions of individuals are interdependent, they often have aggregate results that are contrary to what any of the individuals intended or desired. A simple illustration with which Boudon introduces his discussion is that long waiting lines to buy theater tickets make it rational for every person to come earlier to the box office, which increases the average waiting time and reduces the chances to get tickets, contrary to everybody's interest. A more complex example is a meritocracy where occupational chances largely depend on education. This makes every person interested in obtaining as much schooling as possible, raising educational levels, reducing educational inequality, and enhancing educational mobility. But Boudon shows that these changes will not appreciably improve chances of occupational mobility or diminish inequality in occupational status if the occupational distribution is exogenously determined by industrial conditions and economic demand. On the contrary, the result is that more education than before is required to achieve a given occupational status, contrary to the interests of job applicants, although it continues to be in the interest of every applicant to maximize her or his education, since doing so improves occupational opportunities, which repeats the process in the next generation by further raising the education needed to have the same occupational chances as one's parents. Boudon concludes from the numerous cases he examines that structures of interdependence tend to be at the roots of the external social constraints that individuals experience in collective situations, because such structures imply that the aggregate actions of many persons often have results that are neither anticipated by them nor in their interests and that they experience as an externally imposed change in social conditions.

The three papers in the last part of the book develop formal theoretical models and apply them to empirical data. Mayhew and Schollaert present a baseline model of social structure, continuing Mayhew's interest in such models in which structural conditions are derived from probabilities based on the size or another quantitative property of a collectivity. In the model here, the probable degree of rank differentiation in a social structure is predicted from its size and wealth alone, which makes it a purely sociological model that completely ignores any influences of personal attributes of individuals. The number of persons in a collectivity, the total wealth, and the per capita wealth exert independent positive influences on the expected rank differentiation. Although a collectivity's diversity of ranks, and its inequality, in the sense of concentration of resources (as measured by the Gini index), are not necessarily related, the authors claim that their model predicts the latter as well as the former strictly on the basis of size and wealth.

McPherson formulates quantitative procedures for analyzing the contribution voluntary associations make to a community's social integration and the significance that class differences have for mobilizing power. He estimates from sample data important parameters of the rectangular matrix, persons by voluntary associations. His calculations indicate the extent to which associations are linked through their members, the extent to which persons are linked through common memberships, and the extent to which the community is integrated through participation in voluntary associations. The class differences in organizational participation that research has consistently demonstrated have a multiplier effect on organizational linkages, and the more class-homogeneous organizations are, the greater are the class differences in linkages produced by this effect. Thus, the class differences in participation and the homogeneity of voluntary associations interact to multiply the advantages that a dense network of organizational linkages gives the upper strata for mobilizing resources in political conflicts.

In the final paper, Breiger uses a block-model — originally developed for studying networks in small groups — to test Wallerstein's (1974) theory about the economic relations among nations in a world system. He notes that this procedure is particularly appropriate for such a test, because it classifies units not by their own characteristics but by their relations with others, just as Wallerstein conceptualizes a country's place in the world system in terms of its relations with other countries. An earlier block-model analysis of international trade (Snyder and Kick, 1979) essentially confirms Wallerstein's thesis that these economic relations reflect the difference between a core of economically dominant and a periphery of exploited nations (a third intermediate category seems to be not so clearly manifest in the empirical data). Breiger finds a parallel pattern within the group of core nations: a central core and countries on the periphery of the original larger core. However, he raises the question whether the total trade, on which both his and the earlier empirical analyses are based, does not reflect primarily the economic resources and strength of a nation, whereas the theory demands that nations be classified by their relations with others, not by their own attributes. To answer it, he uses a refined procedure to control for total trade and thereby for economic strength. The resulting residual patterns of import and export relations reveal not a monolithic structure with a single central core, but several competing centers.

EMERGENT PROPERTIES

The conceptions of social structure explicated or implicit in these papers differ greatly and even contain contradictory elements. Some juxtapose social structure and culture, whereas for others cultural symbols and ideas are the very crux of deep structure. Some conceptualize the structure as the theory that postulates patterns and thereby makes sense out of empirical observations, whereas others consider the social structure to exist out there in empirical reality and to constitute the explicandum to be explained by the theory, not the theory itself. Some define structure in terms of differences in positions or ranks which influence social relations, whereas others define it in terms of patterns of social relations from which they derive distinctions among positions. In the eyes of some, structural sociology abstracts the purely formal aspects of social life — size, differentiation, hierarchy — and ignores all substantive content, but in the view of others, macrosociological structural inquiry centers attention on the distinctive character of historical social systems at particular times and places. Integration, order, and consensus are the defining attributes of social structure emphasized by some; differentiation, contradiction, and conflict are those stressed by others.

Yet one can discern a common denominator underneath all these different views of social structure. It is that social structure refers to those properties of an aggregate that are emergent and that consequently do not characterize the separate elements composing the aggregate. In any structure we can distinguish the elements composing it and the aggregate they compose, but analytically we must also distinguish the aggregate from the structure. The aggregate is merely the sum of the elements, but the structure depends on their relationships, in the broadest sense, including under relationships relative positions and indirect influences as well as direct connections. This distinction is ignored if one cannot see the forest for the trees. The sum of many trees is the same whether each stands in a different yard or they all are crowded together, but only in the latter case do they make a forest. Water differs from hydrogen and oxygen not in the elements composing them, but in the connections between the elements, whether the two kinds of atoms are linked in one molecule or in two different ones. The structure of a group differs from the aggregate of its members similarly by those properties that cannot be used to describe individual members because they characterize relations or combinations of members and hence describe the group as a whole. Centering attention on emergent properties of collectivities, structural analysis is inherently anti-reductionist.

The distinction is not merely one between human individuals and collectivities, however. Emergent structural properties can be observed on numerous levels of aggregation. The criterion of emergent property is formally the same on all levels, and this means that the nature of these properties does not remain the same. The criterion, to repeat, is that the property can describe only the aggregate as a whole and not its component elements. In terms of this criterion, average IQ or median education are not attributes of group structure, although they do describe the aggregate of group members. Sociometric networks and group cohesion, on the other hand, are attributes that cannot distinguish individual group members and that therefore constitute emergent properties of group structure. Organizations also have emergent properties, that is, properties that differ from any characterizing the work groups and other subunits composing the organization. The shape of the hierarchy of authority, the degree of centralization of decision-making, and the division of labor illustrate emergent structural properties of organizations. Nations have emergent properties that differ from the aggregate characteristics of their communities, organizations, and regions. The form of government in a country and its economic institutions are examples.

Emergent social structures are often depicted with broad strokes in vague and even mysterious terms. Scholars speak of the spirit of an age, the configuration of a culture, the decline of a civilization, the 'Volksgeist' or national character of a people, the 'Gestalt' of a social system. The imprecise ways in which emergent properties and the phrase embodying them — 'the whole is more than the sum of its parts' — have been used are undoubtedly the reason that rigorous philosophers of science have criticized them (see Nagel,

1955). But emergent properties can be defined in strictly operational terms, and even the more abstract theoretical concepts used in structural analysis can be — and must be, in my opinion — conceptualized with sufficient precision so that their implications are operational and can be empirically measured. Several categories of operational emergent properties will be noted presently. But first something needs to be said about the components of social structure, the connections that link them, and the levels of structural inquiry.

The components of social structures may be conceptualized as persons, roles, statuses, positions, groups, places, or any other subunits of some encompassing collectivity. Initially, the components are usually described by unique labels, either their names or symbols substituting for names. Thus, in a sociometric study of small groups, individuals are identified by names, letters, numbers, or similar distinctive symbols; in a study of the occupational structure, occupations are identified by their names; in macrosociological studies, cities are described by their names, or nations are. But as long as cases or their subunits are identified by distinctive labels, they can be described only one at a time, and it is impossible to analyze them systematically to develop generalizations about social structure, not even limited and tentative generalizations. Systematic analysis requires substituting ordered analytical properties for the unique labels (Przeworski and Teune, 1970). In survey research, for example, respondents are categorized by various attributes of theirs in order to ascertain the relationships between these analytical properties of people, such as that between education and voting preference. In structural inquiry, the procedure is in principle the same, except here we must first substitute analytical properties of the structure for the unique labels of the subunits. For example, the names or symbols by which individual group members are designated are replaced by various characteristics of the group's sociometric network in a study of small groups, or the names of occupational groups are replaced by an index of the division of labor in a comparative study of nations.

In macrosociological studies, the components of social structure are themselves large collectivities with their own social structure. This raises the question of how the direct connections between collectivities should be conceptualized. For example, should interdependence be considered a direct connection, even in the absence of any communication? Should unilateral dependence?

Should common values and norms? Of course, these are mere questions of definition, but my preference is to give a negative answer to all of them and define direct connection or social relation (as distinguished from abstract relationship like being larger or having more resources than another group) in terms of actual social interaction and communication, which may be fleeting (a single transaction) or lasting (a marriage), sociable or economic, cooperative or entailing conflict, between peers or between superior and subordinate. However, some social contacts, such as sociable ones, can occur only between individuals, not between groups, and not all members of large groups can be in direct contact. Accordingly, the indications of direct social relations between different groups are usually rates of social interaction between their members, for instance, rates of inter-ethnic marriage or rates of interracial friendships or rates of dating between members of different social classes. It was Durkheim who first emphasized that social facts can often be represented by rates of individual behavior — marriage rates, divorce rates, suicide rates.

Social structures are nesting series with successive levels of more and more encompassing structure, as analyzed by Simon (1965) in a pioneering paper and further elaborated by Wallace and Warriner in this volume. Thus — reversing the order and starting from the top — nations consist of regions subdivided into provinces or states, which comprise counties and cities, and these are composed of neighborhoods divisible into blocks containing buildings in which families and other households live. The investigator decides which level of structure to examine, which will be her unit of analysis about the structure of which generalizations can be advanced. Whatever scope of structure is selected, it can be analyzed in relation to its two adjacent levels. The next higher level is the social context that influences the structure under investigation. For example, if the structure of work groups is studied, conditions in their department are the most immediate social context; if the structure of firms is studied, conditions in the market are. It is evident that contextual influences cannot be systematically traced unless structures in a substantial number of different contexts are analyzed. The next lower level consists of the component elements of the aggregate whose structure is being studied, for instance a work group's members, a city's ethnic groups, a company's departments and branches. However, the analysis of the social structure itself differs fundamentally from the study of its components and their internal structure, because the former focuses on the emergent properties of the aggregate that characterize not its component elements individually but only their composition and relations.

Let us finally examine four basic kinds of emergent properties. The first one is the size or number of component elements of a social aggregate. For a small group, this is always the number of individual members. But for a society or other large aggregate, there are two ways of counting number of components. One is, as with small groups and collectivities of any size, the number of individual members. Another is the number of larger components, for example the number of incorporated communities of a state, the number of establishments of a corporation, the number of independent firms in a market, the number of lineages in a clan. Size (or number of individuals) and number of sub-collectivities, several kinds of which may be considered, are indicative of two different kinds of emergent properties of the aggregate. Size is not strictly speaking a property of the social structure (though it may be considered the foundation of all structural properties that refer to various forms of differentiation), whereas number of components clearly is an attribute of the social structure. However, a collectivity's size is the prototypical emergent property of a social aggregate of elements: it has unambiguous operational meaning; it would not exist were it not for the elements; yet it does not characterize these elements taken separately, but only in the aggregate. The size of groups or societies is often ignored or treated as of no theoretical interest. I think that, on the contrary, size is a concept of major theoretical significance in structural sociology, because it is a generic emergent property of all social aggregates, including not only all types of collectivity whose structure is under study but also the groups in any dimension that constitute the structural components into which any collectivity can be divided.

A second kind of emergent property pertains to the social relations between people, which constitute the direct connections among elements that give the aggregate its structure. The social relations of individuals in small groups entail direct social interaction and communication. The group structure — more precisely, one aspect of it — can be graphed as a sociometric network and is usually represented in a who-to-whom matrix, from which a variety of measures of structure can be derived. In macrosociological analysis of entire societies or other large collectivities, the structural components are combinations of individuals in various dimensions (lest relations between millions of components must be examined) — groups of all types, places of varying scope (neighborhoods, communities), and strata along various lines of hierarchical differences. All these subunits of a population may be subsumed under the concept of social position, using the term in its broadest sense to refer to all differences among people on the basis of which they themselves make social distinctions. Indicators of the direct connections between different positions, as has been mentioned, are the rates of social relations or interaction between their incumbents, for example the rates of social contact between persons occupying different ranks in an organization. However, there are also other direct connections between the large components of a society, such as trade or other exchange transactions between firms, coalitions or conflicts between political parties. Concepts referring to the social relations among people identify evidently emergent properties of the structure of an aggregate, which would not exist were its component elements examined separately.

Another emergent property is the composition of the aggregate reflected in the differences among its elements. Whether the component elements are unordered nominal categories and can only be labeled or are ordered classes that can be ranked, one can determine the differences among them and the degree of diversity they represent. How distinct are various institutions, and how many separate institutional spheres are there? How great is the industrial diversity, division of labor, or ethnic heterogeneity? Do most people have the same religion or is there much religious heterogeneity? Differences in the size of various components as well as in their number must be taken into account in ascertaining diversity or heterogeneity. Assume that the same 10 religious denominations are represented in two communities; but in one 90 percent of the population belong to the same denomination and only 10 percent to any others, whereas in the second about 10 percent belong to each denomination; clearly there is less religious heterogeneity in the first community where the population is unevenly divided among denominations than in the second where it is evenly distributed among them. For components that refer to variations in some resource — wealth or income or power or education — the unevenness of the distribution indicates the degree of inequality (specifically, the difference between the population distribution and the resource distribution does). The various forms of inequality are aspects of an aggregate's composition. Compositional characteristics also meet the criterion of emergent property of referring unambiguously to the structure of an aggregate without being manifest in the individual elements composing the aggregate.

Finally, two types of higher-order structural properties should be noted. One consists of the global characteristics (Lazarsfeld and Menzel, 1969) of society's infrastructure that are assumed to underlie and explain the observable patterns of social life. The approach to the study of social structure emphasizing these properties gives rise to quite different and even contradictory theories, depending on the fundamental nature the substructure is assumed to exhibit, notably whether it is considered to comprise objective economic conditions or subjective cultural values. For Marx the infrastructure consists of material economic conditions — productive forces, relations of production, and the dialectical interplay between them. For Lévi-Strauss, the deep structure is the realm of cultural symbols and meanings; and for Parsons, too, cultural values and norms constitute a substratum that ultimately governs social action, people's relations, and society's institutions.

The other type of higher-order structural property constitutes abstractions derived from lower-order properties, from the patterns either of social relations among elements or the combination of elements. Thus, network analysts have called attention to a variety of more complex factors, based on combinations of simpler ones, in terms of which social networks can be characterized and analyzed (Mitchell, 1969; Barnes, 1972). Block-modeling utilizes similarities in patterns of social relations to derive images of structures of social positions (White et al., 1976), as illustrated by Breiger's investigation of trade among nations. A different kind of abstraction can be derived from the composition of an aggregate, which refers to its internal differences, specifically to the distributions of the population among different positions. Since numerous dimensions of internal differences can be distinguished, one can raise the question to which extent the differences along various lines intersect rather than nearly (or completely) coincide, as empirically indicated by their positive correlation. For instance, how strongly are differences in occupation, education, and income related? The degrees to which differences in various dimensions cross-cut are precise higher-order emergent properties of social structures, which have important implications for social relations and integration (Blau, 1977).

Emergent properties are the source of the external structural constraints individuals experience, and their operation indicates that such contraints are not incompatible with free will. Take the influence of the composition of a community on social relations as an illustration. Although every Christian American is free to establish a close friendship with a Jew, most Christians do not have a Jewish close friend and could not possibly have one, because there simply are not enough Jews in the country to go around, so to speak. Although individuals are free to establish any social relations, they are not free to determine what others are available in their environment for them to establish social relations with, and this characteristic of the social structure inevitably constrains the aggregate choices of individuals. Another illustration, from Boudon's discussion, is that everybody is free to take his money out of the bank or leave it in, but if most others start taking their deposits out it constrains the rest to take theirs out too, thereby hastening the day when the bank no longer has the resources to pay its depositors, which is surely not what they wanted to accomplish. The individual is helpless and must participate in this process lest she loses her money. The underlying principle is that emergent properties are characteristics of social structures over which individuals have no control, even when these characteristics are the aggregate results of their own actions, and these conditions of the social environment necessarily restrict what people's free will can realize.

DIFFERENCES IN CONCEPTION
OF SOCIAL STRUCTURE

Recognizing the significance of emergent properties of social aggregates appears to me to be the minimal common denominator of structural sociology. The contrasting approach is the psychological reductionism of methodological individualists like Homans (1974), who seek to explain social aggregates in terms of their elementary properties, that is the psychological concepts and principles governing individual behavior. Otherwise, however, the conceptions of structural sociologists differ greatly, as mentioned earlier and illustrated by the papers in this volume. Lévi-Straussian and Marxist structuralism focus on different emergent properties and differ in other ways, and the theoretical orientations of both differ from that of network analysts and that of structural-functionalism. Let us briefly examine some of the major differences.

The scope of structural inquiry can range from the microsociological study of the sociopsychological processes and social networks in small groups to the patterns of social positions and relations in entire nations or even the world system of international relations. (On a more abstract level, microsociology deals not with small groups but with the microprocesses and - structures that pervade society, such as impression management, social exchange, and status-sets and role-sets, analogous to microeconomics.) A problem of many comparative studies of nations is that they are confined to very few countries, which diverts attention from the analysis of the structure of societies, as there are too few cases, and encourages treating societies as given social contexts and analyzing the behavior and attitudes of individuals as influenced by their societal context. The study of the structure of society cannot proceed in this manner but must make societies, not their individual members, the units of analysis, whether data on a sufficient number of societies are collected to permit making reliable generalizations, or whether ideas to be tested later must be based on case studies of a few.

Another difference, pertaining to scope in a more analytical sense, is whether the analysis is confined to the social structure, however circumscribed, or extends to external forces considered to be the determinants of conditions in the structure and of structural change. Such exogenous causes of structural conditions and changes may be but are not necessarily part of a conception of an infrastructure. This is a difference between Parsons and Lévi-Strauss, if I interpret them correctly. For Parsons the culture is analytically distinct from, and a major exogenous influence on, the social structure (though Wallace notes that Parsons is inconsistent regarding the distinction between culture and social structure), but for Lévi-Strauss cultural symbols and meanings are the essence of the social structure itself. Evolutionists from Spencer to Lenski (1975) have treated technological change as the force that governs the evolutionary development of increasing structural differentiation. For Homans as well as for Freud, the psychological principles of human behavior are the exogenous determinants of social structure. Recently, biosociologists (for example Wilson, 1975) have suggested that the structure of social life has its ultimate roots in the biological makeup of human beings.

The conception of social structure may be grounded in a subjective or objective ontology. The difference between Hegel's idealistic interpretation of history and Marx's materialistic one illustrates this contrast. The basic issue is whether social structure is conceptualized as a symbolic mental construct or as an objective empirical reality manifest in distributions of resources and positions. Wallace's distinction between the psychological and the physiological dimension of social phenomena refers to this dichotomy, as does the difference between psychoanalysis and behaviorism in psychology and that between the Parsonian and the ecological approach in sociology. The structuralism of Lévi-Strauss represents the subjective view (as pointed out by Leach, Rossi, and Eisenstadt); Marxist structuralism, the objective.

Accepting the principle that theories must go beyond summarizing empirical findings in order to explain them (Braithwaite, 1953, pp. 50-87), structural analysts still differ in the extent to which their most abstract theoretical terms refer to a realm of structure beneath empirical observations and only roughly reflected in them, or are derived from empirical observations and have logical implications for operational terms that can be measured in research. A conception of social structure as an underlying substratum modeled by the theorist as an ideal type that is not fully manifest in any actual historical case tends to entail concepts that are not of sufficient precision to have unequivocal empirical implications, as Leach notes for Lévi-Strauss's concept of deep structure. Whereas the latter's model of kinship structure does imply actual marriage rules, his discussions about the meaning and underlying structure of myths, though they may be admired for their insights, are not precise enough to allow other investigators to classify myths unambiguously in terms of the conceptual distinctions that Lévi-Strauss suggests.

On the other hand, when theoretical terms are abstractions from combinations of empirical observations, it is less difficult to conceptualize them both abstractly and precisely. For example, the conception that a nation's position in the world-system depends on its pattern of exports and imports with other countries independent of its economic strength is quite an abstract idea, since various exports and imports exhibit different patterns and all of them actually do depend on a nation's strength, but Breiger's block model captures the main empirical implications of this theoretical idea. Similarly, Boudon's paradoxical consequences of systems of interdependence are abstracted from the purposeful actions of individuals, yet his illustrations show that their empirical manifestations are observable. To define social structure as a multidimensional space of lines of differentiation, as I do (Blau, 1977), is an abstraction that is derived from and finds expression in empirical relationships between various lines of differentiation.

Another difference in approach to structural analysis is whether the concept of social structure is closely tied to assumptions about social function and functional requirements. Thus, Parsons's conception of social structure has its foundation in his theoretical assumptions that all social systems must meet four functional needs and must do so by becoming differentiated into four spheres of institutional structure, which serve, respectively, the functions of adaptation, goal attainment, integration, and pattern maintenance. As the subsystems must meet the same functional requirements, they become further subdivided along parallel lines, and evolutionary development consists of increasing differentiation in the form of recurrent fission. Merton's recent theoretical writings provide a contrast. In his earlier work, his study of social structure was also linked to his functional analysis. More recently, however, he has moved toward a more distinct form of structuralism, as noted by Barbano (1968), and as most clearly evident in his analysis of status-sets and role-sets (Merton, 1968, pp. 422-38). A similar divergence in the development of two social scientists occurred a generation earlier. Malinowski remained primarily a functionalist, whereas Radcliffe-Brown (1940, pp. 188-204) moved toward a structural analysis that was at least somewhat skeptical of functional inferences and assumptions.

Simmel distinguishes the forms of social life from its content, and he stresses that the subject matter of sociology comprises the forms of social association ('Vergesellschaftung') abstracted from their content, although the concrete expressions of social forms are always through or in some substantive contents. By content Simmel refers to two kinds of factors: the psychological orientations of individuals that motivate their conduct, such as envy or greed; and the institutional area under consideration, such as economic or political life. The residual concept of forms of social association refers primarily to processes of social interaction, like competition and conflict, focusing on the common features of each kind regardless of whether it is motivated by jealousy or ambition and whether it takes place in sociable intercourse or in the course of work. But forms of social life also refer to patterns or structures of different social positions, such as the role of stranger, the division of labor, or the distinction between the status of pauper and merely being poor.

Social structure may be conceptualized in terms of its formal properties, as Simmel does, or in terms of its substantive content, as Weber does. Whereas Simmel examines triads independent of whether they are composed of three persons or three nations and whether they are involved in economic or military contests, Weber is concerned with the substantive significance of the Calvinistic ethics for social conduct and institutions. In macrosociology, a focus on forms often deals with the shapes of people's distribution — whether most are in the same or distributed among different positions — whatever the contents of the positions, as illustrated by studies of the division of labor and of stratification — and a focus on content tends to examine the import of cultural value orientations — their substantive meaning and its influence, as exemplified by studies of religious beliefs or political ideologies.

However, this is not the only way in which the distinction between form and content can be applied to macrosociological studies. Another contrast in these terms, which could be alternatively described by Windelband's dichotomy of nomothetic and ideographic conceptions, is whether attention centers on formal theoretical abstractions or on distinctive historical conditions. Do we look in our explanations of socioeconomic developments for generic characteristics of class structures and systems of international relations, or for the particular historical circumstances in the various countries, which is the issue Zeitlin raises in his criticism of Wallerstein and Althusser? Are there general formal properties and principles underlying the diverse empirical contents of kinship rules and myths, which is the issue that distinguishes Lévi-Strauss from British anthropologists, as Leach notes? Should one construct theories about inequalities in general, regardless of the substantive nature of the inequality, or should social theories deal specifically with economic inequality or some other particular kind, which is a difference between my and Marxian structural theory? The formal approach is more abstract and general; concern with content is more historical and empirical. In terms of this distinction, Lévi-Strauss's theory and mine are more formal, Weber's and Marx's have more content. Generality is achieved at the cost of specificity. Social forms leave out historical contents. Marx's theory has more empirical content than mine — in Popper's (1959) technical sense of 'empirical content' — inasmuch as my propositions do not distinguish the implications of various kinds of inequality whereas his specify implications of economic inequality.

A final difference in structural analysis to be mentioned is whether the most primitive concepts are social relations, social positions, or neither. They are neither for theories that conceptualize structure in cultural terms of symbols and values and meanings, as Lévi-Strauss does. But most structural sociologists distinguish the cultural realm of ideas and ideals from the structural realm of different positions and patterns of relations. For some, the patterning of social relations is the starting point of the analysis, the assumption being that the relations among people are what differentiated their roles and positions. For others, the starting point is the difference in socially recognized positions, the assumption being that people's social positions greatly influence their social relations. The former orientation is most prevalent in microsociological studies, the latter in macrosociological studies, which is quite appropriate because the primary direction of causal influence in the two is probably in opposite directions. When small groups are first formed the social relations that become established in the course of processes of social interaction differentiate the roles of group members, but in lasting organizations or societies persisting differences in social positions rooted in ascribed attributes or available resources govern most social relations. The first approach is illustrated by research using sociometric techniques or block-modelling procedures to analyze social relations in a fairly small group and using the patterning of these relations to classify individuals by social role or position. These methods have been originally developed in the study of small groups of human beings, but they have been adapted to examine the relations among groups of collectivities, as illustrated by Breiger's analysis of trade among nations. The second approach is exemplified by empirical investigations that first classify individuals by social positon into a limited number of categories — on the basis of religion, ethnic affiliation, industry, or occupation, for instance — and then analyze the patterns of relations between persons in proximate and those in distant social positions. McPherson's paper on voluntary associations uses a variant of this procedure.

The combination of an objective ontology, an emphasis on form rather than content, and a macrosociological assumption that differences in social positions are a major influence on social relations

— this combination invites a concern with size of groups, number of groups, and size distribution among groups in sociological inquiry. For size is the most formal objective property of social aggregates and their components. Although size is not, strictly speaking, an attribute of social structure, a population's size distributions among components and positions, which indicate its heterogeneity and inequality in various respects, are prototypical emergent properties of its social structure. This stress on the quantitative dimension of social structure represents my own view, which is, of course, not shared by all analysts of social structure. Only four of the contributors to this volume — Boudon, Mayhew and Schollaert, and McPherson — similarly center attention on the significance of size and numbers for structural inquiry.

NOTE

1. The versions published here are largely much revised and expanded. Four papers that had not been presented at the World Congress were added to make the collection more representative of the major forms of structuralism; the four added papers are those by Leach, Heydebrand, Zeitlin, and Boudon.

REFERENCES

BARBANO, Filippo (1968) 'Social Structures and Social Functions,' *Inquiry*, 11: 49-84.
BARNES, John A. (1972) *Social Networks*. Reading, Mass.: Addison-Wesley.
BLAU, Peter M. (1975) *Approaches to the Study of Social Structure*. New York: Free Press.
BLAU, Peter M. (1977) *Inequality and Heterogeneity*. New York: Free Press.

BRAITHWAITE, Richard B. (1953) *Scientific Explanation*. Cambridge: University Press.

HOMANS, George C. (1974) *Social Behavior: Its Elementary Forms*. New York: Harcourt Brace Jovanovich (first published 1961).

LAZARSFELD, Paul F., and Herbert MENZEL. (1969) 'On the Relations Between Individual and Collective Properties,' pp. 499-516 in A. Etzioni (ed.), *A Sociological Reader in Complex Organizations*. New York: Holt, Rinehart, and Winston (first published 1961).

LENSKI, Gerhard (1975) 'Social Structure in Evolutionary Perspective,' pp. 135-53 in P. M. Blau (ed.), *Approaches to the Study of Social Structure*. New York: Free Press.

LIPSET, Seymour M. (1975) 'Social Structure and Social Change,' pp. 172-209 in P. M. Blau (ed.), *Approaches to the Study of Social Structure*. New York: Free Press.

MERTON, Robert K. (1968) *Social Theory and Social Structure*. New York: Free Press (first published 1957).

MERTON, Robert K. (1975) 'Structural Analysis in Sociology,' pp. 21-52 in P. M. Blau (ed.), *Approaches to the Study of Social Structure*. New York: Free Press.

MITCHELL, J. Clyde (1969) 'The Concept and Use of Social Networks,' pp. 1-50 in J. C. Mitchell (ed.), *Social Networks in Urban Situations*. Manchester: University Press.

NAGEL, Ernest (1955) 'On the Statement "The Whole is More than the Sum of Its Parts",' pp. 519-27 in P. F. Lazarsfeld and M. Rosenberg (eds.), *The Language of Social Research*. Glencoe, Ill.: Free Press.

POPPER, Karl R. (1959) *The Logic of Scientific Discovery*. New York: Basic Books (first published 1935).

PRZEWORSKI, Adam and Henry TEUNE (1970) *The Logic of Comparative Inquiry*. New York: John Wiley.

RADCLIFFE-BROWN, A. R. (1940) 'On Social Structure,' *Journal of the Royal Anthropological Institute*, 70: 1-12.

SIMON, Herbert A. (1965) 'The Architecture of Complexity,' *General Systems: Yearbook of the Society for General Systems Research*, 10:63-76.

SNYDER, David and Edward L. KICK (1979) 'Structural Position in the World System and Economic Growth, 1955-1970,' *American Journal of Sociology*, 84:1096-1126.

WALLERSTEIN, Immanuel (1974) *The Modern World-System*. New York: Academic Press.

WHITE, Harrison C., Scott A. BOORMAN, and Ronald L. BREIGER (1976) 'Social Structure from Multiple Networks,' *American Journal of Sociology*, 81: 730-80.

WILSON, Edward C. (1975) *Sociobiology*. Cambridge, Mass.: Belknap Press.

I

DIVERSE ORIENTATIONS

1

BRITISH SOCIAL ANTHROPOLOGY AND LÉVI-STRAUSSIAN STRUCTURALISM

Edmund R. Leach
Cambridge University

As late as 1953 the word 'structuralism' denoted for British social anthropologists what has now come to be known as 'structural-functionalism'; that is to say, it was the brand label for the particular style of anthropological practice that had been developed at Oxford under the auspices of Radcliffe-Brown from 1936 onwards. The prototypical exemplars of work in this vein are Evans-Pritchard (1940), Fortes and Evans-Pritchard (1940), and Fortes (1945; 1949), but numerous very high-quality monographs produced by Gluckman and his pupils at a somewhat later period are in the same style, and indeed nearly all monographic studies of particular societies produced by British social anthropologists during the past 40 years have been 'structural-functionalist' in some degree.

British social anthropologists first became aware of the existence of a rival style of 'structuralist' social anthropology (namely that of Lévi-Strauss) in the early 1950s, but although Leach (1952) and Richards (1952) both recognized that Lévi-Strauss (1949) was a work of major significance, neither of them appreciated the extent to which Lévi-Strauss was prepared to break away from the empiricist conventions that his British colleagues took for granted. What was at issue became more apparent with the publication in Tax et al. (1953) of a letter from Radcliffe-Brown to Lévi-Strauss in which Radcliffe-Brown tried to spell out the difference between his own use of the term 'structure' and that employed by Lévi-Strauss. Not long after this event Lévi-Strauss himself delivered a lecture, both at Oxford and in London, that was an early version of his important essay, 'The Structural Study of Myth' (Lévi-Strauss, 1955). Later still a different aspect of Lévi-Strauss's innovation was highlighted in the polemical debate between Homans and Schneider (1955), who were criticizing Lévi-Strauss, and Needham (1962), who was defending him.

In 1963 the Association of Social Anthropologists devoted its annual meeting to a discussion of the work of Lévi-Strauss, which by that time included his re-evaluation of totemism and *La Pensée sauvage* (Lévi-Strauss, 1962a, b), but when I edited the proceedings of the symposium I was forced to emphasize that most of the British social anthropologists who were in attendance showed very little understanding or sympathy for Lévi-Strauss's position (Leach, 1967, Introduction).

Today the understanding is considerably greater, and it is now becoming rare to encounter a PhD dissertation in British social anthropology that has not been influenced at least in some marginal degree by ideas derived at first or second hand from Lévi-Strauss's structuralism. But structuralist ideas have been assimilated and adapted rather than accepted. Parisian structuralism dressed up in English clothes is, from Lévi-Strauss's point of view, entirely heretical.

BRITISH AND FRENCH VIEWS OF STRUCTURE

The research tradition of British social anthropology which derives from the work of Malinowski and Radcliffe-Brown remains emphatically empirical and particularistic. 'Social structure' in this tradition refers to the immediate articulation of directly observable social groups — for example, households, lineages, age-sets, sub-castes — and to the consciously recognized hierarchy of offices and office-holders within a directly observable community of quite modest scale; 'social organization' refers to the way that directly observable individual members of such a system conduct their day-to-day affairs within the framework of jural constraints provided by the 'social structure.' Social structures are thought of as actually existing in the world out-there, external to man; and the principles of their articulation are imagined as being closely analogous to the mechanical principles by which man-made structures such as buildings and natural organisms are held together.

Analogies of this sort have a long history in Western thought but in the case of British social anthropology they derive directly from Radcliffe-Brown's interpretation of Durkheim's 'mechanical' and 'organic' solidarity as described in *The Division of Labour* (1893), with some infiltration of ideas derived from Max Weber by way of Talcott Parsons. Radcliffe-Brown in particular supposed that social structures in this objective sense exist as species types, and he argued that the first task of a scientific social anthropology must be to establish a taxonomy of such species based on comparative morphology.

The underlying schema in Lévi-Strauss's thinking is quite different, though it likewise has a long history. Vico (1744) repeatedly emphasized that, while we can never hope fully to understand the world of nature out-there, because it was made by God and the mind of God is beyond our comprehension, we can emphatically hope to understand human society because society was made by man and its characteristics must necessarily reflect characteristics of the human mind of which we have direct experience. Lévi-Strauss does not refer to Vico, but his assumptions concerning the data of comparative social anthropology are similar. The social anthropologist's ultimate task is to gain insights into the operations of 'the human mind,' considered as a vehicle of thought that is common to all humanity. Cultural and social phenomena — material, verbal, organizational — are to be thought of as projections onto the world out-there of structured patterns generated by human minds. It is further postulated that, at the most basic, abstract level, the variety of such patterns is very limited. The diverse structured patterns discernible in directly observable cultural phenomena are all transformations of a narrow range of mentalist structures which are common to all humanity.

When viewed in this way the empirical social structures that Radcliffe-Brown considered to be examples of fixed species types become transformed into transient representations of patterns of ideas. Even so, we can hope to discover the deep structure in the human mind of which these transient patterns are expressions by observing what is common to the manifest structures of whole sets of cultural phenomena in which each individual member is considered to be a partial transformation of each of the others.

This assumption that the structures manifest in culture are projections of unconscious structures in 'the human mind' clearly derives from the Freudian assumption that the manifest discourse of a patient with his psychoanalyst contains unconscious structures which are symptomatic of the patient's neuroses. The purpose of structuralist analysis in social anthropology is likewise to demonstrate that manifest (cultural) materials incorporate messages that ordinarily are recognized only at an unconscious level of the human psyche.

The argument is not as 'idealist' and 'metaphysical' as this summary presentation might suggest; it is simply that there is a difference of metaphor. Where Radcliffe-Brown, in line with Hobbes and Durkheim, found his prototypes for social structure in buildings, machines, and biological organisms, Lévi-Strauss borrows his analogies from structural linguistics. The binary oppositions that feature so prominently in structuralist analyses of the Lévi-Straussian sort derive from the distinctive features of Jakobson's phonology and ultimately from de Saussure's concept of the linguistic sign. Likewise, the notion that sets of cultural phenomena incorporate transformations of a shared basic structure belongs to the same style of thinking as that which underlies the transformational-generative grammars of Noam Chomsky. This is true despite the fact that direct interaction between structuralists of the Lévi-Straussian sort and structuralist grammarians of the Chomsky school has been minimal.

DE SAUSSURE'S SCHEMA
AND LÉVI-STRAUSS'S THEORY

It may be helpful at this stage to present de Saussure's original scheme in simplified form.

Any ordinary word of an ordinary spoken language operates at a variety of different levels. We may distinguish: (i) an empirical level in the world out-there, in which a word is a *cultural object*. This object may exist in a variety of forms — for instance as a segment of sound pattern imposed on the breath, as a pattern of ink marks imposed on a piece of paper, as a pattern of magnetism imposed on a piece of magnetic tape — and the patterns in each case are transformations of each other; they share a common structure. It is only because they share a common structure that the patterns in these different media can all be said to represent the same word; (ii) a subjective level in the mind of the speaker or listener or reader, in which the word exists as a *sound image*, that is, as a mental construct of the word as it might be uttered in sound; (iii) a deeper subjective level, in which the word exists as a *concept or idea*.

The crucial points in de Saussure's argument all derive from this distinction between the sound image, which we can label S (the 'signifier' or 'signifying') and the concept s (the signified). In any one language S and s are combined into a single whole, 'the linguistic sign', which we can write $\frac{S}{s}$. In this form of the word the relationship between S and s which we have written as '-' is arbitrary. That this is so is evident from the fact that the English word 'dog' and the French word 'chien' clearly 'mean the same thing.' In other words, the concept s embodied in each of these very different linguistic signs is the same.

But since the sound images ('S') are quite different, it follows that the relationships ('-') between S and s are also different. Hence it is the relationship that converts the sound image into a concept or the concept into a sound image, and this leads to the perhaps unexpected conclusion that it is the relationship that really carries the 'meaning' of the sign as a whole.

To the uninitiated this kind of argument may seem to make mountains out of molehills, but the underlying purpose of the exercise can be illustrated by a phonological example.

When the human ear interprets verbal sound patterns as sequences of words it does so by discriminating contrasts such as: vowels (V) vs consonants (C); voiced stops (b, d, g,) vs unvoiced stops (p, t, k); labial sounds (b, p) vs dental sounds (d, t) and guttural sounds (g, k); and so on. The discriminating distinctive features are paired oppositions (vowel/consonant, voiced/unvoiced, etc.). For example, the decision as to whether a particular sound pattern is to be heard as 'pat,' 'bat,' 'bad,' 'pad,' 'pet,' 'bet,' 'bed,' or 'ped' rests on no more than two such distinctions — the voicing of the consonants which distinguishes 'p' from 'b' and 't' from 'd', and the vowel position which distinguishes 'a' from 'e'. Different speakers of English do not pronounce their p's and b's, t's and d's, a's and e's in exactly the same way; but we recognize what they are saying by noticing contrasts — that is, relationships between similar sounds. Furthermore, we are able to assemble these sound patterns into 'words' by recognizing relationships between the relationships.

The crucial point here is that, as individual speakers and listeners, we are quite unaware of the kinds of discrimination that are necessary if we are to encode or decode speech.

Lévi-Straussian structuralists claim that the same is true of non-verbal cultural communication. All assemblages of cultural data incorporate messages. At an unconscious level the participant members of the cultural system in question interpret the messages without being aware that they are doing so. But the social anthropologist who seeks to make these unconscious messages conscious must approach his problem as a linguist and start by looking for the distinctive features of the cultural 'phonology.'

A good example of this aspect of structuralist methodology is provided by Lévi-Strauss's concept of 'the atom of kinship', which he first presented many years ago (1945), when he was closely associated with the linguist Roman Jakobson, but has only very recently defended against criticism (Leach, 1977; Lévi-Strauss, 1973, 1977). I shall discuss the original formulation at some length because it exemplifies very clearly the divergence between Lévi-Strauss's thinking and that of the structural-functionalists.

At the heart of the matter lies the fact that, although Lévi-Strauss and his British colleagues use many of the same technical terms — in particular 'kinship,' 'descent,' 'filiation,' 'marriage' — they attach quite different meanings to these words without, as a rule, being aware that they are doing so.

For example, in the article in question Lévi-Strauss declares categorically: 'What is generally called a "kinship system" comprises two quite different orders of reality..,the system of ter-minology...[and] the system of attitudes.' But as he develops his argument it becomes clear that his real interest is in the abstract structure that ties together the concepts that lie at the back of the terminology. What he calls the 'system of attitudes,' as manifested in behavior, is of interest only as a symptom of this postulated unconscious structure. The structural-functionalists see matters exactly the other way round. Kinship is a matter of empirically observable behavior operating within a framework of specifiable jural rules. It may be of interest to note the degree to which the categories of the kinship terminology make discriminations that are consistent with observed kinship behavior, but it is the behavior, not the terminology, that is the focus of interest.

Similarly, in the language of the structural-functionalists, the words 'filiation,' 'descent,' 'marriage' refer to relationships that link actual individuals to other individuals or to social groups considered as corporations, whereas in Lévi-Strauss's usage they denote contrasted ideas which form part of the technical language of social anthropology but to which the ethnographic facts on the ground are only loosely related.

One consequence of this is that Lévi-Strauss uses the terms 'patrilineal' and 'matrilineal' in a much looser sense than do the structural-functionalists, who (at least in their more cautious moments) restrict such terminology to societies that contain objectively observable patrilineal or matrilineal descent groups as the case may be. In the context of the 1945 article this is highly relevant, since two of the specimen societies that Lévi-Strauss lists as examples of patrilineal systems (Tonga and Lake Kabutu) would not be reckoned by the structural-functionalists as having unilineal descent systems at all!

But, indeed, it is characteristic of the whole of Lévi-Strauss's anthropological writing that the details of enthnography play only a secondary illustrative role. The basic argument is built up a priori by reasoning from elementary axioms — such as that human society could not exist without an incest taboo between brother and sister. The ethnographic evidence is then 'shown to fit' the preconstructed structural pattern. In this regard the 1945 paper was unusually explicit. Lévi-Strauss emphasized right from the start the high level of abstraction at which he was operating: 'a kinship system does not consist in the objective ties of descent and consanguinity between individuals. It exists only in human consciousness. It is an arbitrary system of representations, not the spontaneous representation of a real situation'; and ' "kinship systems" like "phonemic systems" are built by the mind in the level of unconscious thought.' But the mind ('l'esprit') that engages in these building activities seems to be viewed as a metaphysical entity which is a law unto itself. Although Lévi-Strauss has sometimes written as if this 'mind' were a universal attribute of actual human brains — a propensity to think in a particular way complementary to the universal propensity of human children to acquire a spoken language — he has also written as if it were a kind of group mind capable of making intentional decisions independently of the operation of any particular human brain.

Here again the British empiricists find themselves at a loss. But to return to the 'atom of kinship': Lévi-Strauss presented his paper as a critique and extension of the then prevailing theories concerning the 'avunculate', that is concerning the special relationship that has repeatedly been reported by ethnographers as existing between mother's brother and sister's son. In matrilineal systems the sister's son is the mother's brother's heir so a special relationship is only to be expected; but in many patrilineal systems also the sister's son possesses rights vis-à-vis his mother's brother even to the extent of being entitled to steal his property without redress. An earlier generation of anthropologists had explained such customs as a cultural survival from an earlier period when matrilineal inheritance had been the rule. A celebrated paper by Radcliffe-Brown (1924) had proposed quite a different explanation: in a patrilineal system the mother's brother is a kind of 'male mother'; his indulgence toward the sister's son reflects this contrast of roles vis-à-vis the authoritarian father.

Radcliffe-Brown himself later retracted parts of this argument, but the implied distinction between relationship to the father by virtue of common membership of a unilineal descent group and relationship to the mother's brother by virtue of the 'individuating' tie of 'complementary filiation' through the mother was of great significance for the later development of structural-functionalist thinking. Fortes's (1953) definitive essay on 'The Structure of Unilineal Descent Groups' derives ultimately from Radcliffe-Brown's 1924 essay, just as Lévi-Strauss's massive *The Elementary Structures of Kinship* (1949) derives directly from his 1945 critique of Radcliffe-Brown.

The crux of this criticism is that all previous theories about the avunculate were much too narrow in range. The avunculate is incomprehensible if viewed in isolation; it becomes somewhat more comprehensible if, like Radcliffe-Brown, we contrast the mother's brother-sister's son relationship with the father-son relationship, but we will see what is involved only if we realize that all empirical cases of ethnography are just isolated manifestations of parts of a much more general abstract structure. To understand the avunculate in the general case we need to consider not just uncle-nephew and father-son but also brother-sister and husband-wife, and it is the structural permutations of the relations between these relationships that will show us what is involved quite independently of any particular empirical evidence.

Lévi-Strauss goes about it in this fashion. He takes it as axiomatic that the incest taboo (the nature of which is not specified but is assumed to include a veto on sex relations between full siblings of opposite sex) is a human universal which somehow marks the transition from animality (nature) to humanity (culture). Since men may not marry their own sisters or daughters it follows that they must seek mates elsewhere. Exogamy is thus the correlate of the incest taboo. Furthermore, the necessity to find a sexual mate from among 'the others' is the basic source of ideas concerning exchange. In the later work (Lévi-Strauss, 1949) this theme is expanded, in that a major distinction is drawn between systems in which a woman is exchanged for another woman (restricted exchange) and systems in which a woman is exchanged for commodities of some other kind which are in turn, either directly or indirectly, exchanged for another woman (generalized exchange). Thus from Lévi-Strauss's point of view the intricacies of international trade and the domestic arrangements of empirical families are alternative expressions of the same abstract principles that are ultimately reducible to the same 'elementary structure of kinship.'

In the 'atom of kinship' argument this ultimate elementary structure is formulated (with a wholly male orientation!) as follows.

Assume that A and B are two adult males and that b is sister to B and wife to A, and that C is the son of A and b and therefore sister's son to B. Assume further that all empirical person-to-person relationships are reducible to expressive behaviors which are the reciprocal opposites to alternative expressive behaviors, thus: close/distant, affectionate/hostile, supportive/authoritarian, etc. In other words, assume that behaviors that are thus described always exist in pairs and carry significance like the distinctive features of a phonological system. If we accept this proposition, then each pair may be further reduced to a simple binary opposition which we can denote as $+/-$. Bear in mind that it was taken as axiomatic that marriage is the obverse of the incest taboo between siblings of opposite sex. Hence brother/sister is always the opposite of husband/wife; so if brother/sister is $+$, husband/wife must be $-$ and vice-versa. Derivatively mother's brother/sister's son is always the opposite of father/son. This gives us a matrix of possibilities.

	brother/sister	husband/wife	father/son	mother's brother/ sister's son
1	+	−	+	−
2	+	−	−	+
3	−	+	+	−
4	−	+	−	+

According to Lévi-Strauss, Radcliffe-Brown's empiricist arguments apply to the second alternative only with respect to certain patrilineal systems and to a less marked degree to the third alternative with respect to certain matrilineal systems. But according to Lévi-Strauss all four alternatives are discernible in the reports of the ethnographers, but since the 'patrilineal' Tonga fall into alternative 4 and both the 'matrilineal' Suiai and the 'patrilineal' people of Lake Kabutu into alternative 1 the issue of patrilineal or matrilineal descent is irrelevant. It is rather that

> the avunculate [is] one relationship within a system [which] must be considered as a whole in order to grasp its structure. This structure rests upon four terms (brother, sister, father, and son), which are linked by two pairs of correlative oppositions in such a way that in each of the two generations there is always a positive relationship and a negative one...This structure is the most elementary form of kinship that can exist. It is, properly speaking, *the unit of kinship* [Lévi-Strauss, 1945; in 1963 version].

In the latter part of his article Lévi-Strauss elaborates his thesis that units of kinship of this kind are the building blocks out of which kinship systems as wholes are constructed, and he reiterates his theme that kinship systems are 'symbolic systems' analogous to linguistic systems rather than structures of empirical objects. He also reiterates his assertion that the universality of the incest taboo is basic to the whole enterprise.

FROM KINSHIP TO MYTH

Over the years the reaction of empirically minded British social anthropologists to this kind of argumentation has been very mixed. On the positive side most of them would now agree that that any particular small-scale element of social structure is likely to be just one of a number of variant possibilities, and that important insights may be gained by making cross-cultural comparisons not just between phenomena that are clearly repetitions of the same pattern, but also between phenomena that, though sharply contrasted at the manifest level, can yet be shown to be transformations of a common underlying structure. On the other hand, the British have been almost unanimously highly critical of Lévi-Strauss's attitude toward ethnography. What worries them is not so much Lévi-Strauss's abstract rationalizations as his claim that the 'idealist' schema that results is in fact compatible with the empirical evidence. For example, there is a fallacy right at the very heart of the matter; we now know for certain that in ancient Egypt, certainly for several centuries and probably for several millennia, quite ordinary people regularly married their full sisters. And sceptical anthropologists are repeatedly coming up with other comparable cases in which there is the widest possible deviation between the doctrine and the recorded facts. Moreover, although Lévi-Strauss often backs up his illustrative examples with considerable ethnographic detail, his choice of evidence is highly selective. It often seems that the evidence has been made to fit, rather than shown to fit, the rationally calculated abstract structure. Furthermore, Lévi-Strauss always manages to brush aside the numerous awkward cases in which the empirical evidence does not fit with the theory at all.

Committed Lévi-Straussian structuralists usually reply to criticisms of this sort by emphasizing that the ultimate object of their inquiry is not the diversity of structures that occur empirically in recordable ethnographic situations, but the structure of the human mind which generates the phenomena of culture as projections of itself. The structures inherent in operations of the human mind are, by axiom, universal. Discrepancies between the theory and the evidence tend to be explained away (i) by questioning the veracity of the ethnographer; (ii) by postulating that historical accident has distorted an earlier more compatible state of affairs; (iii) by introducing the catch-all thesis that the structuralist argument applies only to 'elementary' (primitive) cultural systems and cannot be expected to be manifested in data from 'complex' (sophisticated) systems. However, the precise principle according to which an 'elementary' system is to be distinguished from a 'complex' one is left conveniently vague.

The uncompromising stance adopted by the senior protagonists in this debate, Fortes and Lévi-Strauss in particular, has made it difficult for their followers to suggest that perhaps there may be merit and deficiency on both sides. For example, as regards kinship, Lévi-Strauss's abstract structuralist theory would certainly have been improved if he had paid closer attention to what is involved in Fortes's distinction between 'descent' and 'complementary filiation.' But correspondingly, the generality of Fortes's structural-functionalism was from the start severely limited by a persistent refusal to recognize that marriage rules, operating within a context of unilineal descent, may, in certain circumstances, generate alliances that are every bit as much as a part of the ongoing empirical social structure as the unilineal descent groups themselves.

Again, it is only now, 30 years after the first publication of *Les Structures élémentaires de la parenté*, that the empiricists are beginning to realize that Lévi-Strauss's 'idealist' distinction between 'restricted' (reciprocal) exchange and 'generalized' (asymmetrical) exchange was possibly more significant as a contribution to exchange theory as such than as a perhaps rather misguided contribution to the analysis of kinship. Professional anthropologists and economists alike continue to be fascinated and puzzled by the peculiarities of the Kula Ring first described by Malinowski nearly 60 years ago and only recently the subject of renewed intensive research. Some of the difficulties of this classic anthropological mystery might appear less intractable if we paid closer attention to the fact that the asymmetries of the Kula correspond to those of Lévi-Strauss's 'generalized exchange,' and that the people who are involved in these exchanges themselves mix up the language of kinship and marriage with the language of economic trade.[1]

But all this has an air of 'déja vu.' The negative attitude that British social anthropologists have adopted toward the whole body of Lévi-Strauss's kinship studies derives from the academic battles of an earlier generation. This is no longer what structuralist argument seems to be all about. It is the Lévi-Strauss who wrote *Le Totémisme aujourd'hui* (1962a), *La Pensée sauvage* (1962b) and *Mythologiques* (1964-72) who now arouses interest among British anthropologists, rather than the author of *Les Structures élémentaires de la parenté* (1949). At the same time it needs to be emphasized that most would-be English readers of this corpus have been completely overawed by the sheer bulk and density of the four-volume *Mythologiques*, parts of which even now remain untranslated. In consequence the British view of what Lévi-Strauss was trying to say during this phase of his career is derived mainly from the English-language versions of his 'The Story of Asdiwal' (1958), which is a far better exposition of the structural study of myth than the earlier essay (Lévi-Strauss, 1955), the essay on totemism (1962a), parts of *The Savage Mind* (1926b) and parts of *The Raw and the Cooked* (1964), especially the section on 'The Culinary Triangle,' which had been published separately (1966).

As was the case with the earlier work of kinship, these writings

build on a body of structuralist theory which derived from de
Saussure and Jakobson, but they emphasize a different aspect of
that theory, namely those sections in which de Saussure (1916)
distinguishes between syntagmatic chains and paradigmatic
associations and where Jakobson distinguishes between metonymy
and metaphor (Jakobson and Halle, 1956). The crux of the argument is that, in linguistic discourse, signs (that is, words considered
as combinations of sound image and concept) are fitted to meanings by virtue of two non-exclusive principles. On the one hand
words and sentences are linked together in sequential chains,
building up meaning by virtue of contiguity (metonymy); on the
other, ideas and sets of ideas are linked together by perceived and
asserted similarity (metaphor). Lévi-Strauss's major insight has
been to recognize that, typically, in the institutions that have been
grouped under the label 'totemism' and in the sorts of myth where
animals and birds converse as if they were humans, a whole set of
creatures — say, the class of birds — is being linked by metonymy
while at the same time metaphor is being used to make the mythical
actions of these creatures serve as prototypes of the actions of
human beings. The empirical data of totemism are thus generalized
and made to appear as a special case of an all-pervading human
propensity to make orderly sense out of the world of culture by
drawing on categories that serve in the first place to impose human
order upon the world of nature.

In *Le Totémisme aujourd'hui* (1962a) Lévi-Strauss once again
emphasized his disagreements with the British empiricists. The
British, he claimed, tended to give a functionalist utilitarian twist to
their theories of totemism. Totemic species of animals and plants
were given ritual value *because* they had economic value, whereas
according to his own argument totemic animals were 'good to
think' rather than 'good to eat.' Unfortunately, when translated into English this much-quoted quip is either nonsense or a misleading
verbal trick; for, after all, foods that are 'good to eat' are material
substances, whereas animals that are 'good to think' might be just
ideas about animals rather than animals as such. And Lévi-Strauss
never makes it entirely clear as to which of these two alternatives is
intended. There are places where he seems to be saying that it is the
very essence of 'thought in the wild' ('la pensée sauvage') that
abstraction should be handled concretely, as would be the case
when one works out the result of an arithmetical calculation by
means of an abacus rather than by mental arithmetic. In that case

the animals that are 'good to think' should perhaps be 'goods to think with.' If on the other hand the 'good-to-think' animals are just the species names of animals, much of what is written about the categorization of the world in *La Pensée sauvage* seems to lose its point. Certainly I myself would argue that structuralist doctrine becomes fully convincing only when it can be applied to specific materializations of ideas, for example, to directly observable patterns as they occur in the layout of settlements, the structure of buildings, the sequences of ritual performance. By contrast, the structural study of myth, though highly seductive, is potentially so elastic that it evades criticism. Lévi-Strauss's own view is' just the reverse. It is the structural study of myth that can lead us to general truths concerning the structure of the human mind; empirical examples of this structure as exemplified in ritual performances and material edifices are, by comparison, trivial and uninteresting.

These differences of view, though deep rooted, are not necessarily irreconcilable. The first concern of the empiricist anthropologists is with cultural facts as they can be directly observed on the ground. And here the ecological relationship of society to the environment necessarily comes first. At a subsistence level, men must eat to live rather than live to eat. The manifest social structure of a society must be such that the production and reproduction of both human beings and resources is sustainable over a period of generations at a fair level of efficiency. The forms that human society and culture exhibit at any particular time and place are certainly not determined by the environment; indeed, they often appear singularly ill-adapted to environmental circumstance. But even so, the environment sets limits on what is culturally possible. By contrast, Lévi-Strauss would emphasize that the myth-making imagination can transcend all consideration of what is physically possible.

But these are not all-or-nothing arguments. Even if it be conceded that some aspects of human social behavior represent practical adaptations to environmental necessity, most of the empiricists would agree that the details of culture can never be fully explained in this way. Human action in a cultural context not only 'does' things; it 'says' things. Even if at times Lévi-Strauss seems rather pointedly to ignore the practicalities, this is only because his primary interest is in the analogy between the way things are 'said' in cultural action and the way things are 'said' in human speech. He would like his structural social anthropology to have the same generality as linguistics. It follows that his prime concern is with what is general to all kinds of cultural patterning rather than with particular cases. By contrast, the empiricist anthropologists *are* interested in particular cases. Like Lévi-Strauss, they may be interested in understanding how patterns in culture may convey messages, but for them the infrastructure comes first.

But the difference of view stems from a difference of interest rather than from disagreement over methodology. Even the most thoroughgoing empiricist, who insists that man, like any other species of animal, must eat to live, has to recognize that it is characteristic of mankind everywhere that when men eat they do not eat like animals. All kinds and conditions of men, in all parts of the world, make a ritual of eating; mealtimes everywhere are complex performances conducted according to elaborate conventions which determine when we shall eat, with whom we shall eat, what we shall eat at what time and on what sort of occasion, and even the sequences in which different kinds of food and drink are served up. The more elaborate these conventions become, the less animal we feel ourselves to be.

Lévi-Strauss's generalizations in this area are once again only partly compatible with the empirical evidence, but they are provocative. He suggests that different treatments of food constitute a code of distinctive features, such as cooked/raw, boiled/roast, smoked/rotten. Further, he argues that the cooking of food is a marker by which men distinguish themselves from animals (who eat their food raw) and that the boiling of food, which, more than any other process, converts natural raw food into a cultural product, is especially appropriate for food that is to be eaten in the privacy of the home away from strangers. The details need not concern us here but the general idea is clear enough: in order to live comfortably in the sociocultural world that men build around themselves, they have to make maps of that world by the use of categories of persons, places, animals, things. 'We' are at the center of that world; 'we' are the prototypical representatives of civilization; everything around us is tame and disciplined. By contrast, wild nature is far away on the periphery of 'our' world. And so too of 'the others.' The further away that 'they' are, the less they are like us and the closer they become to wild beasts. So among men we distinguish members of the household, neighbors, enemies, strangers...; among animals we distinguish pets, farm animals, predators, wild monsters...; among foods we distinguish boiled food, roast food, smoked food, raw food...Each system is metaphoric of each of the others.

At first such ideas may seem far-fetched, and in the early 1960s when Lévi-Strauss was engaged in writing *La Pensée sauvage* (1926) and *Le Cru et le cuit* (1964) he was certainly inclined to exaggerate the extent to which human beings everywhere recognize a sharply defined opposition between Nature and Culture and also the degree to which particular binary oppositions, like raw/cooked or boiled/roast, carry the same semiotic significance in all cultural circumstances; but there are striking continuities. For example, it has recently been demonstrated that a classification of animal/human relationships derived from contemporary English social practice and linguistic usage can be applied directly to categories employed by fourteenth-century Occitans-speaking peasants living in the Pyrenees! (Ladurie, 1979)

But now let me say something about the structural study of myth, for it is particularly in this area that it is commonly thought that Lévi-Strauss has made really significant innovations.

If we ignore recent adaptation to Lévi-Strauss's ideas, it can be said that the British social anthropologists still maintain a Malinowskian view of myth. Social structure consists of an ongoing integrated set of rule-bound institutions. Every such institution necessarily possesses a charter of legitimacy, a traditional history that purports to record how the institution came into being and why the rules are as they are and have been like that since time immemorial. Myths are the sacred tales that embody such charters; for the teller and for the hearer myths are true because they are sacred. Conversely, from the viewpoint of the anthropologist, it is the sacredness of the tale that makes it a myth. In this schema mythical stories need not necessarily be impossible or even wholly false as history. For example, Magna Carta is a genuine historical document which functions as myth in the education of British and American schoolchildren. Its mythical quality lies in the fact that it is made out to be the fountainhead of representative parliamentary institutions. From the point of view of British social anthropologists, a story that ceases to have this kind of 'sacred' practical application will cease to be a myth and become a mere fairytale.

THE HARMONY OF MYTHOLOGY

Lévi-Strauss's use of the concept 'myth' is very different. He has not, so far as I am aware, ever committed himself to a formal definition of what the term means, but it may be inferred that, in his view, all myths contain elements of the fanciful; they transcend what we know from experience to be normally possible; thus, in myth, men converse with birds and animals, they fly like birds, they die and come to life again, they visit lands above the sky and below the sea, and so on. There is thus a radical contradiction between the truth of myth and the truth of history — as we in the West now conceive of history.

Lévi-Strauss does not, I think, deny that myths, when recounted within their indigenous cultural context, may function as charters in the Malinowskian sense, though he would probably claim that only a minority of myths operate in this way. But this is not what interests him. His concern rather is with mythology as a form of language; the four volumes of *Mythologiques* are supposed to provide a sort of mytho-linguistics. To achieve this end he pays only minimal attention to the use of particular myths in particular cultural contexts; instead he compares myths and myth systems cross-culturally with a view to discovering what is generally true of such systems when considered in isolation from their cultural contexts.

The approach is similar to that employed in *Les Structures élémentaires de la parenté* (Lévi-Strauss, 1949) in that myth systems are assumed to consist of patterns of segmental elements of stories (sequences of words), just as kinship systems were assumed to consist of patterns of kinship terms (individual words). In the case of myth, Lévi-Strauss's most important innovation is his recognition that myths and segments of myths operate as sets rather than in isolation. We gain insight into the meaning of such a set by superimposing the individual segments one on top of the other and treating each as a metaphoric transformation of each of the others. Lévi-Strauss himself has suggested an analogy with music.

In a musical work such as Bach's *Goldberg Variations*, each section is a permutation of each of the earlier and later sections, but the musical 'message' of the work is in the combination of the individual sections into a single totality. Although the sections are heard one by one, one after another, they are combined into a unity in the mind of the listener. And comparably, in an orchestral work the individual instrumentalists play quite separate melodic sequences, no one of which is 'meaningful' by itself, but the listener hears the music as construed by the conductor with all the different melodic patterns combined into a harmonic whole. It is the melody combined with the harmony that makes the music.

Just how this kind of theory can be applied to actual ethnographic data is not at all easy to expound. If Lévi-Strauss is to be believed, the harmonics of myth-making turn on variations of very fine-grain detail, and since none of the materials that he uses is likely to be familiar to the ordinary reader of this paper, it is difficult to explain what is involved. However, although Lévi-Strauss himself has repudiated the suggestion that his theories can be properly applied to biblical materials, the structure of the New Testament gospels can serve to illustrate the general idea. There are four gospels, not one; each gospel purports to tell the same story but in fact the details vary very considerably; in some instances the accounts in the different gospels are flatly contradictory. In the traditional style of Christian New Testament scholarship the object of the exercise is to discover the true history that lies at the back of the contradictions; the significance of the contradictions is minimized and eventually explained away altogether. If however the corpus of the four gospels were to be seen as a set of myths in Lévi-Straussian terms then the existence of several versions of 'the same' story would be given the utmost significance, for it would be assumed that it was precisely in such points of disagreement that the crux of the story really lies.

For Lévi-Strauss the meaning of a body of mythology is to be found not in the melodic story-line of any one tale, but in the harmonic combination of metaphors implicit in stories that do *not* fit tidily together. To arrive at these shared meanings which unconsciously underlie manifest discrepancies it is necessary to resort to a drastic form of reductionism, and it is here of course that Lévi-Strauss and his critics are liable to drift far apart. The meanings that Lévi-Strauss extracts from his mythological systems depend once again upon the ingenuity with which he converts symbolic images into binary oppositions and then extracts from such pairings transformable sequences of relationships between relationships.

In very broad terms myth is represented as a special form of illusion in that, under the guise of manifest stories that are psychologically acceptable, it masks deep-seated logical contradictions that are psychologically intolerable.

Again I will illustrate by means of a biblical example rather than by reference to any of the intricate patterns that Lévi-Strauss himself has used. Death is the binary opposite of life, but in myth death becomes another form of life. In Lévi-Strauss's schema the structured opposition brother-sister, husband-wife is basic. But if a wife can never be a sister, the parents of a wife can never be the same as the parents of her husband, and there is a 'contradiction' about how things were 'in the beginning.' So Adam and Eve's 'original sin,' which (in myth) is the causal origin of death, is 'really' incest but is transformed, by the equivocations of Genesis 1:26-28; 2:21-25; 3:1-24, into a story about the craftyness of a talking serpent, the opposition between good and evil, and the moral instability of women.

It should be emphasized however that Lévi-Strauss is not particularly concerned with what myths 'mean' in any straightforward sense. His point rather is that all moral rules are human inventions, built up out of mental concepts, and that every system of moral (that is, cultural) rules will necessarily contain basic internal contradictions. He is concerned to show how 'the human mind' copes with such contradictions. Bodies of myth are to be understood as externalizations of mental process attempting to resolve the irresolvable. His concern is with the working of the mental process rather than with the particular resolutions that may (or may not) be reached.

For the empiricist British much of this argument seems to be far up in the sky. The French reflexive tense allows Lévi-Strauss to write as if myths thought out their problems for themselves without the aid of human thinkers, and to some degree he probably feels that this is really the case. A musical performance requires the prior existence of a composer, a conductor, and an orchestra, but, granted all that, there is still a sense in which the music generates itself!

Yet the empiricists cannot help but be beguiled. The fact that, in the flesh as well as in myth, sisters and wives may be confused does not contravert Lévi-Strauss's thesis that at the level of conceptual models, the terms sister/wife form a binary opposition out of which innumerable patterns of molecular scale structure can be built up. Furthermore, over the whole field of cultural activity, when you look at the facts, 'texts' of the most diverse kinds — literary sequences, ritual sequences, architectural forms, settlement patterns, domestic arrangements, elements of costume, and many others — do seem to have many of the repetitive, transformational characteristics that Lévi-Strauss discusses, so perhaps the 'human mind' really does impose its universal patterning proclivity on the diversity of human culture.

I do not myself see the issue as one of either/or. Empiricists will in any case continue to be primarily interested in the holistic details of particular cases, but they can benefit from the insights that flow from the reductionist 'Gedanken' experiments of structuralist rationalism. But structuralism is certainly not the golden key which will solve all the riddles of the anthropologist's universe. Just as the empirical details of the DNA/RNA genetic code are turning out to be a great deal more complicated than the Nobel laureate theorists at one time imagined, so also the structuralist theorists of the human mind will one day have to come to terms with all those irritating details of empirical social structure that fail to fit in with their universalist theories.

It is easy enough to see where the difficulties lie.

Structural-functionalists and Lévi-Straussian structuralists share a static, photographic conception of how things are. At any given point of time a structure 'exists' as an articulation of decomposable elements. Both groups have long recognized that there is an arbitrariness about how the anthropologist takes his postulated structure to pieces for the purposes of analysis. What are the principles that distinguish one 'element' from another? If one sequence of 'text' is metaphoric of the next sequence of 'text,' how do you distinguish the beginning and end of a sequence? What is the principle of 'découpage'? And what if one adopts a far-out Heraclitan view of reality in which everything is flux and all events and things are transient illusions?

According to some influential critics, the fatal defect of both structural-functionalist and structuralist anthropology as systems of interpretation is that they ignore the time dimension — they are applicable only to 'societies without history.'

I cannot agree. History conceived of as a sequence of clearly defined events is illusory since the events in question are arbitrarily selected and arbitrarily distinguished and the mere statement of sequence inevitably creates the impression that the most recent items were 'caused by' the earlier ones.

History conceived of as a continuous melting of inchoate circumstance into later inchoate circumstance may resemble the truth of experience but is devoid of meaning.

History conceived of as a sequence of transformations of an holistic episteme — as in the writings of Michel Foucault and Thomas Kuhn — is simply structuralist analysis all over again, even if the authors concerned reject the suggestion that they are structuralists.

All the same, I would agree that it has been a persistent weakness both of structural-functionalism of the British type and of the more orthodox forms of Lévi-Straussian structuralism that the authors concerned have been too anxious to demonstrate simply that structures persist or are repeated transformations of the same persistent deep structure. These demonstrations have provided many novel insights into hitherto bewildering congeries of social and cultural facts. But the parallel problem of how structures change, not just in their superficial appearance but at the most abstract basic level, has so far been largely neglected. And this is despite the fact that Radcliffe-Brown declared himself to be a devoted admirer of Heraclitus while Lévi-Strauss has from time to time posed as a disciple of Marx.

NOTE

1. A major conference designed to review our present understanding of the Kula was held in Cambridge, England, in July 1978.

REFERENCES

DURKHEIM, E. (1893) *De la division du travail social*. Paris: Alcan.
EVANS-PRITCHARD, E. E. (1940) *The Nuer*. Oxford: Clarendon Press.

FORTES, M. (1945) *The Dynamics of Clanship among the Tallensi*. London: Oxford University Press.

FORTES, M. (1949) *The Web of Kinship amonng the Tallensi*. London: Oxford University Press.

FORTES, M. (1953) 'The Structure of Unilineal Descent Groups,' *American Anthropologist* (n.s.), 55:17-41.

FORTES, M. and E. E. EVANS-PRITCHARD (eds) (1940) *African Political Systems*. London: Oxford University Press.

HOMANS, G. C. and D. M. SCHNEIDER (1955) *Marriage, Authority and Final Causes: A Study of Unilateral Cross-Cousin Marriage*. Glencoe, Ill.: Free Press.

JAKOBSON, R. and M. HALLE (1956) *Fundamentals of Language*. The Hague: Mouton.

LADURIE, E. le R. (1979) *Montaillou: The Promised Land of Error*. New York: Vintage Books (abridged English translation of *Montaillou: village occitan de 1294 à 1324*. Paris: Gallimard, 1975).

LEACH, E. R. (1952) 'The Structural Implications of Matrilateral Cross-Cousin Marriage,' *Journal of the Royal Anthropological Institute*, 81 (1951):23-55 (published 1952).

LEACH, E. R. (1966) 'Anthropological Aspects of Language: Animal Categories and Verbal Abuse,' in E. Lenneberg (ed.), *New Directions in the Study of Language*. Cambridge, Mass.: MIT Press.

LEACH, E. R. (ed.) (1967) *The Structural Study of Myth and Totemism*, Association of Social Anthropologists. Monograph no. 5. London: Tavistock.

LEACH, E. R. (1977) 'The Atom of Kinship, Filiation and Descent: Error in Translation or Confirm of Ideas? *L'Homme*, 17:127-9.

LÉVI-STRAUSS, C. (1945) 'L'Analyse structurale en linguistique et en anthropologie,' in *Word: Journal of the Linguistic Circle of New York*, 1 (2):1-21. (English translation with modified text published as Chapter II of *Structural Anthropology*. New York: Basic Books, 1963).

LÉVI-STRAUSS, C. (1949) *Les Structures élémentaires de la parenté*. Paris: PUF (the second edition was substantially revised. The English language translation (1969) is based on the second edition but contains further revisions).

LÉVI-STRAUSS, C. (1955) 'The Structural Study of Myth,' in T. Sebeok (ed.), *Myth: A Symposium Journal of American Folklore*, 78 (270):428-44.

LÉVI-STRAUSS, C. (1958) 'La Geste d'Asdiwal,' *Ecole Pratique des Hautes Etudes* (Section Sciences religieuses), Paris, pp. 3-43. English translation: 'The Story of Asdiwal,' in E. R. Leach (ed.), *The Structural Study of Myth and Totemism*. London: Tavistock, 1967.

LÉVI-STRAUSS, C. (1962a) *Le Totemisme aujourd'hui*. Paris: PUF (English translation *Totemism*. Boston: Beacon Press, 1963).

LÉVI-STRAUSS, C. (1962b) *La Pensée sauvage*. Paris: Plon (English translation *The Savage Mind*. Chicago: University Press, 1966).

LÉVI-STRAUSS, C. (1964) *Le Cru et le cuit*. Paris: Plon (English translation *The Raw and the Cooked*. New York: Harper & Row, 1969).

LÉVI-STRAUSS, C. (1964-72) *Mythologiques*, 4 vols. Paris: Plon.

LÉVI-STRAUSS, C. (1966) 'The Culinary Triangle', *New Society* (London), 22 December: 937-40.

LÉVI-STRAUSS, C. (1973) 'Réflexions sur l'atome de parenté,' *L'Homme*, 13:5-30.

LÉVI-STRAUSS, C. (1977) 'Reponse à Edmund Leach,' *L'Homme*, 17: 131-3.

NEEDHAM, R. (1962) *Structure and Sentiment: A Test Case in Social Anthropology*. Chicago: University Press. (This was a prize essay which existed in mimeograph form several years earlier.)

RADCLIFFE-BROWN, A. R. (1924) 'The Mother's Brother in South Africa,' reprinted in *Structure and Function in Primitive Society*. London: Cohen and West, 1961, pp. 15-21.

RADCLIFFE-BROWN, A. R. (1957) *A Natural Science of Society*. Glencoe, Ill.: Free Press (a mimeograph version was widely known among British social anthropologists from 1948 onwards). The text is a verbatim transcript of lectures delivered in Chicago in 1937.

RICHARDS, A. I. (1952) Review of Lévi-Strauss, C., *Les Structures élémentaires de la parenté* (1949), *Man*, 52:12-13.

de SAUSSURE, F. (1916) *Cours de linguistique générale* (edited posthumously by C. Bally, A. Sechehaye, A. Riedlinger) (English translation *Course in General Linguistics*. New York: Philosophical Society, 1959).

TAX, S. et al. (eds.) (1953) *An Appraisal of Anthropology Today*. Chicago: University Press.

VICO, G. B. (1744) *The New Science of Giambattista Vico*. Translated from the 1744 edition by T. G. Bergin and M. H. Fisch, Ithaca (NY): Cornell University Press, 1948.

2

TRANSFORMATIONAL STRUCTURALISM: LÉVI-STRAUSS'S DEFINITION OF SOCIAL STRUCTURE

Ino Rossi
St John's University

The intent of this paper is to clarify the precise nature of the theoretical premises of Lévi-Strauss's structuralism and to show that they offer a valid alternative to the empiricist premises that have led traditional sociological paradigms to an impasse between an empiricist or a formalistic mode of sociological theorizing. Given the familiarity of the Anglo-Saxon audience with traditional, or empirical, structuralism, I shall use it as a contrasting point of reference to introduce the reader to the new form of structuralism I call 'transformational structuralism.' The latter is based on a conception of scientific explanation alien to the 'scientific' standards that have prevailed in our sociological tradition. Therefore, the significance and importance of transformational structuralism can be understood only by first examining its criticism of the traditional conception of scientific explanation.

VARIETIES OF EMPIRICAL STRUCTURALISM

A terminological clarification is, first of all, in order. What do I mean by 'empirical' and 'transformational' structuralism? Empirical structuralism is not synonymous with structural-functionalism — the sociological tradition rooted in organism analogies and Durkheimian ideas applied with different emphasis in anthropology by B. Malinowski (1936, 1944, 1948) and A. R. Radcliffe-Brown (1940, 1965), and in sociology notably by Talcott Parsons (1951, 1961), Robert K. Merton (1968) and Marion Levy (1952, 1966).

Under the label of 'sociological structuralism' Walter L. Wallace (1969) lists the functional structuralism of Kingsley Davis and Merton, the exchange structuralism of Peter M. Blau, J. W. Thibaut and H. H. Kelley as well as the conflict structuralism of Lewis A. Coser and Ralf Dahrendorf. Blau (1975) distinguishes three structural perspectives: first, the holistic, ahistorical and all-inclusive perspective of Parsons and Gerhard Lenski; second, the behaviorist, elemental and ahistorical perspective of George Homans and James S. Coleman; lastly, the multiple paradigm approach of Merton. There is no agreement among authors on how to classify and label the various forms of structuralism, or even on whether the label of 'structuralist' or that of 'functionalist' is more appropriate to characterize certain sociological approaches. For instance, Parsons has argued in a recent essay that his own approach should be called 'functionalism' rather than 'structural-functionalism' as the notion of 'function' has in his theory of action a greater analytical power than the notion of 'structure' (1975). Jonathan H. Turner seems to follow Parsons's suggestion when in the second edition of his text on sociological theory (1978) he presents Parsons, Merton and Coser as representatives of as many types of functionalism, whereas he labels Blau as an exchange structuralist.

These classificatory controversies do not relate to the focus of this paper, which is designed to undertake a critical evaluation of the empiricist assumptions shared by all forms of previous structural or functional or structural-functional paradigms. George Ritzer has reviewed various definitions of the term 'paradigm' offered by Thomas Kuhn and has proposed his own definition in the following terms:

> A paradigm is a fundamental image of the subject matter within a science. It serves to define what should be studied, what question should be asked, how should it be asked, and what rules should be followed in interpreting the answers obtained [Ritzer, 1975, p. 7].

This is a clear-cut definition but one that reflects the limitations of traditional sociology. The focus of this definition is on substantive (subject-matter) and methodological aspects of the paradigm, and ignores (or perhaps takes for granted) epistemological considerations, that is the way in which the subject matter is conceptualized. Here lies a first key difference between what I have called 'empirical' and 'transformational' structuralism. Transformational structuralism holds that the way in which social scientists define their scientific object of analysis is of crucial importance, since that definition delimits the range and aspects of data they are sensitized to as well as the conceptual and methodological apparatus they will employ. Everyone agrees on calling any sociologist who selects 'social structure' as providing the unity of scientific analysis a 'structuralist' and, perhaps, as a main explanatory variable or perspective on the basis of which explanatory variables are selected. The focus on social structure, for instance, distinguishes structuralists from interpretative sociologists whose selection of data and methods derive from their concern with the 'meaning' of social interaction. However, transformational structuralists introduce a crucial distinction when they label as 'empirical structuralists' all those sociologists who use a definition of social structure based on behaviorist, positivist, or other variants of empiricist presuppositions. Tentative, and perhaps debatable, as the classifications of sociological structuralism may be, they are useful for delimiting the range of sociological theories that I include under the term of 'empirical structuralism,' because in my judgment they all share, in one form or another, an empiricist definition of social structure.

As I have said, in this paper empirical structuralism is contrasted with transformational structuralism. The latter term includes those recent versions of structuralisms that reject the empiricist conception of social structure; this is the case of the semiotic structuralism of Claude Lévi-Strauss (1963, 1976), the genetic structuralism of Jean Piaget (1970), and the transformational linguistics of Noam Chomsky (1957, 1965), to mention a few leading exponents of the anti-empiricist orientation.

My explicit task is to focus on Lévi-Strauss's version of structuralism, a task I consider quite central, since Lévi-Strauss has pioneered and directly or indirectly influenced the various applications of transformational structuralism in social sciences. Some attention will also be given to Piaget, especially in the discussion of structural epistemology, because Piaget has dealt with structural epistemology more extensively and clearly than any other structuralist in psychological or social sciences.

Lévi-Strauss has been heavily influenced by Ferdinand de Saussure, the Geneva linguist who revolutionized the study of linguistics and proposed the science of semiology, or the formal study of the life of signs in society (1966). Lévi-Strauss has defined culture as a system of signs, and has conceived the social sciences as semiological disciplines (1976, p. 9). The term 'sign' is used by Lévi-Strauss in the semiotic or Saussurean sense rather than in the traditional sense of the term 'symbol.' In traditional sociology the term 'symbol' is defined in terms of the meaning (content) it conveys; this is true in symbolic interactionism, in the theory of social action and so on. On the contrary, for de Saussure a sign consists in the structural relationships between the 'sound-image' (the signifier) and the concept expressed by the sound-image (the signified). Neither the signifier nor the signified have meaning outside their relationship in the sign. Similarly, the meaning of each 'sign' is merely relational, that is, determined by its relationships of difference with other signs, and not by its 'substance' or content. In this sense Lévi-Strauss's structuralism is properly called semiological (according to the early French terminology) or semiotic (according to the Anglo-Saxon and now internationally prevailing terminology).

On the contrary, Jean Piaget has derived his theoretical orientation not from linguistics, but from mathematical and biological disciplines, and, therefore, his structuralism cannot be called semiotic structuralism. However, both Lévi-Strauss and Piaget share the notion of social structure as a system of transformations, this being the key notion required to understand their shared theoretical and methodological principles. Their notion of transformation derives from the mathematical notion of 'group' and the algebraic notion of 'transformation,' these being notions also fundamental to Chomsky's concept of 'deep structure.' There are, to be sure, differences among these three thinkers on various aspects of the concept of social structure, and especially on the concept of 'transformation' which, in Chomsky's works, has assumed a specific and technical meaning (see Rossi, forthcoming). However, all these thinkers adopt a meta-empirical notion of social structure. The same is true of the so-called 'structural Marxists,' such as Louis Althusser (notwithstanding his protest against the label of 'structuralist'), Lucian Sebag, Maurice Godelier, and other thinkers in philosophical, linguistic, and social disciplines that have been inspired by their works. Notwithstanding various differences among structural Marxists and between them and transformational structuralists, all of them make a distinction between empirical, or directly observable, structures and the logic underlying the various possible combinations of the elementary components of empirical structures; such a logic is alternatively conceptualized as the constitutive grammar governing the actualized and possible alternative kinds of realization or composition of empirical structures. The distinction between the two levels of structure entails rejection of the empiricist assumption that only what is empirically observable is a legitimate object of 'scientific' investigation and that no theoretical explanation can ever reach the stage of established 'scientific' knowledge unless it can be falsified through empirical or sensory-based observations.

I have repeatedly used the term 'meta-empirical' and 'anti-empiricist' to underscore the radical break introduced in the social sciences by transformational structuralists (and structural Marxists) with their rejection of the empiricist criterion of scientific knowledge. That the two types of structuralism are in sharp contrast is shown by the conflicting claims that their respective exponents make about their own intellectual tradition. For instance, both Blau (1975, p. 1) and Merton (1975, p. 16) list Durkheim and Marx among the main intellectual antecedents of sociological structuralism. At the same time Merton (1975, p. 1) dissociated structuralism from the more recent structuralist thinking of de Saussure, Jakobson, Lévi-Strauss and Piaget. Blau concurs with Merton on this point and even adds that Lévi-Strauss's structuralism has been rejected by most American sociologists and anthropologists (Blau, 1975, p. 3) (because, he should have added, they share an empiricist orientation). Yet, transformational structuralists, and especially Lévi-Strauss (see Rossi, 1974, pp. 7-30), reserve a prominent place for Durkheim and Marx among their intellectual antecedents. At one point in his career Lévi-Strauss stated that he was closer to the Durkheimian tradition than any of his colleagues (1965, p. 63), and that he intended to continue what is valid in Durkheim's sociology (1945). Some interpreters of Lévi-Strauss's works also state that Durkheim laid the foundations of modern transformational structural analysis (Glucksman, 1974, p. 25) together with Marx, Freud, de Saussure (de George and de George, 1972, p. xiii). Are empirical and transformational structuralists making contradictory claims, or do they emphasize different aspects and adopt different interpretations of Durkheim's and Marx's thought? I firmly believe the latter to be the case.

To explain why representatives of empirical and transformational structuralisms often reject each other's approach outright and make these claims about their intellectual ancestry, we must first understand their different epistemological orientations.

EMPIRICIST BIAS OF TRADITIONAL STRUCTURALISTS: EMPIRICIST AND FORMALIST ANALYSIS AS IMPASSE

Transformational structuralists have the merit of having grounded their theoretical and methodological approach on explicitly analyzed epistemological assumptions, in contrast to empirical structuralists who hardly ever discuss epistemological issues or analyze the theoretical basis of their notion of social structure. By epistemology, I mean explicit discourse about the source and validity of scientific knowledge. Such discourse must deal with the scientific definition of the object studied. It might be objected that in defining the object to be analyzed before carrying out its scientific analysis, one inevitably alters or twists the data in the direction of one's particular theoretical orientation. Conventional sociologists might claim that the term 'data' can only indicate the 'objective' characteristics of what is studied, that is, characteristics that any social scientist can and should perceive regardless of theoretical presuppositions. Against this contention, transformational structuralists argue that the terms 'data' and 'objective characteristics' are scientific concepts, and no scientific concept is independent of theoretical presuppositions.

The scientist's theoretical orientation inevitably determines the kind of data that are worth studying and the characteristics that must be considered as 'objective' or scientifically valid. For instance, positivist sociologists claim that the notion of 'social fact' is scientifically valid because it entails an objective or unprejudged attitude toward the data. On the contrary, this notion is a positivistic construct, based on the arbitrary principle that social facts must be analyzed as if they were 'natural' phenomena. Such a conception of social facts deprives social phenomena of meaning and betrays a positivistic theory of scientific knowledge and experimental method.

I do not claim that all forms of traditional structuralism can be labelled as 'positivist,' only that they all share the empiricist notion of scientific explanation. My claim can be easily substantiated by a brief examination of the definitions of social structure proposed by a few leading exponents of empirical structuralism.

In 1964, Peter Blau had distinguished the theory of social action from his own approach by defining the latter as 'the study of the actual associations between people and the structures of their associations' (1964, p. 13). The issue is, of course, what is meant by 'structures of association.' Recently Blau has distinguished three definitions or 'mental images,' as he has called them, of social structure. For Coleman, Homans, and Merton, structure refers to the 'configuration or arrangement resulting from social relations among people or the intersecting of statuses and roles relations' (Blau, 1975, pp. 10-11). For Parsons, Lipset, and Bottomore, social structure refers to 'a fundamental substratum that molds social life and history.' According to Blau, these three authors conceive social structure as 'a substratum *abstracted* from people's conduct and relations' (my italics), although the substratum is conceptualized differently by the three thinkers, either as institutionalized norms and values that govern people's orientations (Parsons), or as expected behavior (Lipset), or as the substratum of objective conditions and contradictions governing actual relationships (Bottomore). To these two kinds of images of social structure, Blau opposes his own, Coser's and Lenski's usage of social structure, which is defined as 'the study of the forms and degrees of social differentiation among people that are *reflected in their social relations*' [my italics]; the attention of these sociologists is on 'multiple levels of status differences *observable* in complex societies' (Blau, 1975, pp. 14-15, my italics; see also Blau, 1974, p. 616).

The italicized terms 'abstracted' and 'observable' indicate the underlying dimension of Blau's classification. The first two types of definitions of social structure refer to 'abstract' properties of social relations (that is, 'configurations' or 'substrata' of social relations), whereas Blau's definition refers to 'observable' characteristics of social differentiation. In Blau's formulation, then, the differences among the various definitions of social structure come down to a difference between an 'empirical' or an 'abstract' level of conceptualization; this distinction is in line with traditional sociological thinking, but it fails to do justice to Lévi-Strauss's position. Blau draws an explicit parallel between Lévi-Strauss's notion of deep structure and Marx's notion of infrastructure, on the one hand, and Parsons's, Lipset's, and Bottomore's concern with the 'underlying substratum abstracted from observable social life' (Blau, 1975, p. 13) on the other hand. In his 1974 presidential address, Blau differentiated his own structuralism

from that of Lévi-Strauss since for Lévi-Strauss 'social structure
has nothing to do with empirical reality but with models which are
built after it.' According to him, Lévi-Strauss's definition is a
theoretical construct, 'a system of logical relationships among
general principles which is not designed as a conceptual framework
to reflect empirical conditions but as the theoretical interpretation
of social life' (Blau, 1974, p. 615).

The precise meaning of Blau's criticism is not quite clear. Any
structural (or, for that matter, sociological) formulation entails a
'theoretical interpretation' of social phenomena by definition.
What does it mean to say that a conceptual framework should
'reflect' empirical conditions? Lévi-Strauss's notion of social structure does reflect empirical conditions but not mechanically, that is,
not as a one-to-one correspondence; his mechanical ('structural')
models are not isomorphic with statistical models but are
hypothetical formulations of relational constants (or systemic
tendencies) underlying the empirical regularities expressed by
statistical models. The latter are based on frequencies of empirical
events which are the results of the combined interaction of systemic
tendencies and contingent factors, psychological, historical,
ecological, and so on (Rossi, 1973). The lack of distinction (not opposition) between the statistical and structural level of analysis is at
the roots of the criticism levelled at Lévi-Strauss by Blau and a long
list of empiricist critics (see Rossi, 1977a, 1978).

We have seen that Blau has likened Lévi-Strauss's and Parsons's
conceptions of social structure. Does Blau, then, mean that Parsons's definition of social structure does not reflect 'empirical' conditions of social relations? The answer depends on how Blau uses
the term 'reflection.' If he means that a definition of social structure, such as his own, should contain the whole content and
nothing but the content of what is 'observable,' then he assumes a
one-to-one correspondence between his definition and observable
reality. But, then, what is the heuristic and explanatory value of
sociological concepts, if they are supposed to replicate the complexity and heterogeneity of social relations? If this theoretical position
is rejected, then one concedes that sociological concepts inevitably
entail some form of 'abstraction'; and then either one accepts Parsons's level of conceptualization or, at least, one must propose a
satisfactory answer to the problem of correspondence between concepts and social reality.

This dilemma is intrinsic not to Blau's positions per se, but to the traditional way of using statistical models and conceiving the process of theory formation. The latter has been understood to entail a process of 'abstraction' in line with the positivistic, and ultimately Cartesian, dichotomy posited between object and subject, mind and matter, 'observable' empirical regularities and 'theoretical' concepts. If the empirical and theoretical levels of explanation are dichotomous or heterogeneous, theoretical concepts are inevitably based on an 'abstraction,' that is, selection of the essential, objective 'elements' of empirical social relations with the neglect of others not deemed essential. Parsons, for instance, explicitly notes that theorizing entails an analytical separation of essential from nonessential 'elements' of social relations (1961, p. 730). The outcome of this dichotomous view is that only a two-fold choice is open to a sociologist: theoretical conceptualization must be directly related to 'observable' aspects of social relations (as Blau proclaims he is doing) or based on theoretical constructs which are 'abstracted' or separated from observable reality (as Parsons does). My argument is that both alternatives are intrinsically faulty, as they lead respectively to an empiricist and a formalist approach.

That this is the inevitable outcome of the traditional dichotomous perspective can be shown by brief examination of the position formulated by Parsons, who is one of the few 'traditional' sociologists who have tackled this issue systematically. We remember that in *The Structure of Social Action* he rejected empiricist realism, on the one hand, and nominalism and intuitionism, on the other (Parsons, 1961, pp. 728-30, 773), and proposed instead a position he called 'analytical realism.' In reality, Parsons rejected the exaggerated version of empiricism according to which any science must give 'a full complete explanatory account of a given sector of concrete reality' (Parsons, 1935, p. 470). The reason is that such a position implies the 'fallacy of misplaced concreteness' or, as Parsons explained more recently, the notion that scientific knowledge is 'a total reflection of reality out-there' (Parsons, 1970b, p. 830).

However, Parsons still remains anchored to the more moderate version of the empiricist conception of explanation which is shared by interpretative and structural sociologists of traditional orientation. In fact, he defines social structure as 'any set of relations among parts of a living system which on empirical grounds can be shown to be stable over a period of time' (Parsons, 1975, p. 69). Social structure, then, refers to empirically observable patterns of interaction. Similarly, 'function' is defined as 'the consequences of the existence and nature of certain empirically observable structures and processes in such systems' (1975, p. 70). These definitions of structure and function are based on the empiricist assumption that only sensory-mediated information is a 'legitimate' object for scientific analysis. Consequently, a level of intelligibility arrived at by a logical analysis would not constitute a 'scientifically' acceptable datum because it could not be falsified through empirical observations. (And so most of Parsons's analyses would not be acceptable.)

Parsons's definitions of 'structure' and 'function' appear to be in line with Blau's principle that· 'social structure' must refer to 'observable' properties of social relations. We remember, however, that Blau's definition of social structure does not include the whole content of the 'multidimensional space of the differentiated social positions,' but only 'the forms and degrees of social differentiations among people that are reflected in their social relations' (Blau, 1975, p. 14). Were a sociologist to follow literally the stringent requirement that only what is directly 'observable' can be included in sociological concepts, he could formulate only 'empirical' rather than 'conceptual' explanations. Empirical explanations are those based on 'observable' concepts which have as immediate referents sensory-mediated observations. These kinds of concepts contain a very low level of abstraction and permit the formulation of explanations based on observable empirical regularities. In D. Willer and M. Webster's opinion, sociological knowledge has not been cumulative because it has remained anchored to 'observables' rather than using 'theoretical' concepts as exact natural sciences have done (1970, p. 756).[1]

Parsons is directly or indirectly aware of this problem. As soon as he has set out 'empirical' social structure as an object of analysis, he immediately adds that sociological theory 'does not refer to empirical generalizations about certain classes of concrete phenomena but to an abstractly analytical conceptual scheme' (1975, p. 73). Abstract concepts, however, must be related in a systematic and precise way to empirical generalizations, if one wants to avoid a formalistic theory. Parsons is clearly aware of this danger also:

> the most important single proposition [about functional analysis is that it] will become intolerably confusing if there is not the best possible clarification of

system references. This obviously has to be a problem concerning data about the objects of investigation 'out there.' At the same time, however, it must concern the theoretically defined cognitive system with which the investigator is working. [Parsons, 1975, pp. 71-2]

The issue, then, to be clarified is how one can be sure that the two different levels of analysis are consistent with each other. Parsons admits that sociology has been caught for a long time in the dilemma of defining the subject matter either in 'analytical terms' or in 'concretely empirical terms' (1977, p. 335). He argues that the 'theoretical' order must be congruent with the 'socio-empirical order,' but such a congruence must 'not be interpreted to imply a one-to-one correspondence' (1977, pp. 338-9). However, if a one-to-one correspondence is excluded, how and when, and between which elements of the two levels of explanation, does the 'congruence' occur? Parsons does not deal with these questions, or, rather, he concedes that 'there is simply no way of making the two [levels of explanation] match neatly so that it is possible to have the best of both worlds' (1977, pp. 335-6). There is a basic gap in Parsons's position. The notion of 'generic' congruity between the two levels of theorizing is incompatible with the principle of empirical verification or falsifiability, since this principle implies the possibility of establishing a direct link between theoretical concepts and empirical generalizations. Parsons never makes clear what he substitutes for the positivistic notions of verifiability or falsifiability which he resolutely (and I may add, rightly) rejects (1977, p. 338).

In defense of his own position Parsons refers to Chomsky's position (and so he joins Blau in likening the notion of social structure held by Parsons and Chomsky). He states that his analytical theories are as unfalsifiable as 'the "deep structures" of a language [which] cannot be demonstrated to be either "grammatical" or "ungrammatical"; they are components on the basis of such judgments, not themselves constitutive of them. The judgments apply to sentences, not to deep structures' (Parsons, 1977, p. 338). Here, Parsons confuses his own position with that of Chomsky's. Chomsky's notion of deep structure is not a concept 'abstracted' from the observable linguistic behavior of speakers. On the contrary, it refers to the competence that speakers have in determining the correctness of an indefinite number of sentences they can both produce or understand. The linkage between deep structures and

surface structures is provided by transformational rules. Consequently, in Chomsky (and in Lévi-Strauss and Piaget) there is never
a separation or a dualistic dichotomy (typical of positivistic
thinkers) between deep structure and surface structures, subject-
object, empirical (observable) regularities and theoretical (abstract)
concepts; on the contrary, there is a transformational and constitutive relationship between the two orders of reality. There is no
priority or relationship of causal influence between one order and
the other, since the two orders are correlative and simultaneously
constitute each other. (This is what goes under the term of 'structural causality' we shall discuss shortly.)

The conclusion is quite clear. The dualistic view of the relationship between knowledge and external reality, subject and object,
which Parsons has inherited from positivistic thought has trapped
him and traditional sociology into the insoluble dilemma of choosing between empirical and analytical levels of theorizing. Once a
dichotomy between the two levels is posited, one cannot effectively
link them any longer. Only in transformational structuralism can
one find a satisfactory solution to the 'correspondence' problem
between social reality and theoretical explanation. This is to say
that the notion of transformational relationships of Lévi-Strauss,
Piaget and Chomsky offers the only viable alternative to the
positivistic notion of 'correspondence rules.' It is the notion of a
transformational relationship between mind and external reality,
theoretical (structural) concepts and empirical regularities that
permits us to relate knowledge of the universal and the particular
and to avoid both the empiricist and formalistic postures that have
remained an insoluble dilemma in traditional sociological theory.
We must now consider the theoretical and scientific basis of the
alternative proposed by transformational structuralists.

THEORETICAL AND SCIENTIFIC FOUNDATIONS
OF TRANSFORMATIONAL STRUCTURALISM

The notions of deep structure and transformational relationships
are not arbitrary and mentalistic notions but are, rather, concepts
based on carefully examined epistemological presuppositions as
well as on recent research developments in mathematics, linguistics,
neurophysiology, and physics.

Epistemological Presuppositions of
Transformational Structuralism

Transformational structuralists are opposed not to the scientific or experimental method but to the empiricist interpretation of external and internal 'experience,' that is, respectively, the behavioral and subjective aspects of social phenomena. Empiricist social scientists conceive 'experience' as a reading or registering of already organized and immediately discernible characteristics which are presumed to exist in external objects or within the conscious states of the individual. Lévi-Strauss has strongly rejected the 'dull' and 'naive' empiricism and objectivism of those who accept as a reliable object of investigation what is immediately given in sense perception. He also refuses to accept consciousness as a reliable source of knowledge and prefers to 'understand Being in relation to itself and not in relation to oneself' (Lévi-Strauss, 1965, p. 62).

Transformational structuralists find not only naive but false the positivist and behaviorist assumptions that people's conscious explanations and overt behavior are to be taken at their face value as objects of scientific analysis. It is well known that verbal explanations may hide ideological and material interests, or can be a product of rationalizations or reflect a poor understanding of social processes; moreover, the explanations of certain people at times contradict the explanations of others. For these reasons, transformational structuralists argue that we have to go beyond surface structures to find the deep and real structures that account for the variety of observable phenomena or conscious explanations and their apparent contradictions. This is accomplished through a scientific analysis which consists of breaking the data down into their basic components. Those units are basic that occur repeatedly in a variety of contexts in combination with other changing units. Not the elementary units, but the relationships among them are the object of scientific analysis, which is designed to determine the set of relationships that remain constant in the various combinations and recombinations of the elementary units. The grammatical rules governing the recombinations and transformations of the constant relations are the deep structures or generative matrices of which observable data are as many manifestations and particular realizations. These external manifestations or realizations of deep structures are only a few of the many other possible realizations. Durkheim pioneered this type of explanation in *The Elementary*

Forms of the Religious Life, when he stated that we can understand recent religions only through historical analysis because historical analysis 'alone enables us to resolve institutions into its constituent elements' (1961, p. 15). Durkheim wants to distinguish between the essential and the secondary constituent elements: 'Everyone of these [complex religions] is made up of such a variety of elements that is very difficult to distinguish what is secondary from what is principal, the essential from the accessory' (1961, p. 17). Durkheim seems to anticipate also the relational aspect of transformational structuralism when he asserts that, 'since the facts there [in primitive religions] are simpler, the relations between them are more apparent' (1961, p. 19). This relational and combinatory view of the social reality constitutes the ontological perspective underlying structural epistemology.

Scientific Support for the Epistemological and Ontological Views of Transformational Structuralism

Empirically oriented social scientists have criticized the notion of deep structure because in their opinion such a notion defies the scientific criteria of empirical validity and falsification. For instance, in arguing against my position, the anthropologist Ronald Cohen has defined the notion of 'deep structure' as unacceptable 'mumbo jumbo' (1977), just as Rodney Needham of Oxford has attacked me for having maintained that positivist and empiricist criteria are not applicable in the evaluation of structural analysis (Needham, 1978; see also Rossi, 1978a).

However, there is enough evidence to prove that contemporary scientific research is not reconcilable with empiricist assumptions but strongly supports the structural perspective. Empiricist epistemology is based on a philosophical interpretation of classical physics which assumes the existence of universal laws and a precise measurability of directly observable data: moreover, physical phenomena are considered to be located in a fixed space and time. However, the theory of relativity has shown that the laws of classical physics do not have universal applicability and that empirical observations are not the same in different spaces and times. Moreover, quantum physics has revealed a degree of indeterminacy between the 'observer' and 'observed' such that physical matter cannot be described in terms of ordinary experience, but only indirectly, intuitively and through a mathematical language. 'Mathematical abstractions grasp beyond experience, a realm of the possible instead of the factual, of the unobvious instead of the obvious. It is a realm of structures, of patterns of connectedness which replaces the world of things' (Schwannenberg, 1976, p. 36). This interpretation of modern physics is explicitly confirmed by the renowned physicist W. Heisenberg, who in a recent interview has stated that the substance of reality seems to consist of mathematical structures (Sullivan, 1974, p. 21).

The relational and mathematical perspective is pervasive also in contemporary biology and linguistics. For instance, the biologist Gunther S. Stent explains that the genetic code involves 'a language in which a triplet of successive nucleotide bases in the DNA polynucleotide chain stands for one protein amino acid' (Stent, 1970, p. 926). The combination and recombination of small genetic elements into larger and larger units follows fixed mathematical ratios. Similarly, Roman Jakobson hypothesizes that there is a basic set of invariant distinctive features (sound features in binary oppositions) in each language which through a set of transformations constitute the whole phonological system of language.

Were more space available, we could show that contemporary scientific thinking is permeated by the following notions. First of all, the emphasis is on the study of relationships among the 'constituent elements' of facts rather than on the facts themselves, as simple as these may be. Second, the attempt is made to formulate in mathematical and logical terms the set of relationships that remain constant throughout the many combinations of the elemental units; the combinatory rules of these elementary units function like algebraic matrices which govern the constitutive processes of reality.

Such a relational and mathematical perspective is central in the works of transformational structuralists who maintain that the scientific object of investigation must be defined through a scientific language or a system of forms constructed to understand the composition of the data under consideration. The intent of transformational structuralists is to build a system of mathematical relationships which codify the relational constants among the basic components of social facts and permit us to relate the systems of relationships formulated in various disciplines in order to build a universal scientific language. Jean Piaget, a prominent exponent of this view, has proposed a 'constructive' definition of structure as the totality of relationships of logical and natural processes which constitute a concrete phenomenon and govern the transformations that the system can be subjected to; the transformations are governed by cybernetic laws of self-regulation. It is not surprising, then, to read the following defense of the structural perspective by a leading molecular biologist:

> Neurological studies have indicated that, in accord with the structuralist tenets, information about the world reaches the depth of the mind not as raw data but as highly processed structures that are generated by a set of stepwise, preconscious informational transformations of the sensory input. These neurological transformations proceed according to a program that pre-exists in the brain. The neurological findings thus lend biological support to the structuralist dogma that explanations of behavior must be formulated in terms of such deep programs and reveal the wrong-headedness of the positivistic approach which rejects the postulation of covert internal programs as 'mentalism'. [Stent, 1975, pp. 1055-6].

Relational and Constructivist Mode of Explanation

The conceptualization of social reality and cognitive activity proposed by transformational structuralists has opened the way to a new type of scientific explanation. We have seen that the positivistic and dichotomous perspective has led empiricist sociologists to conceptualize the process of theory formation as a process of 'abstraction' and that such conceptualization has led to a dilemma of choosing between empiricist or formalist types of explanation. As I have explained elsewhere (Rossi, 1974, pp. 74-6), transformational structuralists hold a relational and 'constructive' view of explanation which, consistently with a Galilean view of the universe, focuses on the relationship among the components of a phenomenon and formulates the laws of their combination, variation and transformation. This view is antithetical to the classifactory mode of explanation, which, consistently with an Artistotelian view of the world, formulates concepts by abstracting the essential properties from the objects. Not only Parsons but all empirical structuralists implicitly or explicitly follow the Aristotelian and essentialist way of thinking: they 'abstract' types or 'forms' of social interactions and differentiation from 'observed' (Blau) or 'objective elements' (Parsons) of social relations.

One should add that the constructive mode of explanation is consistent with, if not demanded by, the cybernetic perspective, so fundamental in Parsons's formulation of the cybernetic hierarchy of control among the four subsystems of the General System of Action (Parsons, 1965, pp. 30-8) and in the more recently proposed notion of generalized media of interchange (Parsons, 1970, 1975). Upon close examination, it becomes clear that the cybernetic perspective implies a decisive break with the empiricist and dualistic perspective, as the focus of cyberneticians is on context and not on content. Gregory Bateson has explained that the focus on relationships among data rather than on data themselves (content) gives a new meaning to the inductive and dialectic approaches. What is crucial in cybernetic explanation is 'the relationship between context and content.' For instance, the meaning of the phoneme derives from its relationships of difference with other phonemes; similarly, the meaning of the word derives from its relationship of similarity and/or difference with the other words of the utterance. The cybernetic perspective entails a switch from 'content' to 'context' and a focus on the 'hierarchy of context' (Bateson, 1967, p. 30). The notion of 'context' must not be understood according to the empiricist perspective which conceives the relationship between system and environment as an interaction or adaptation between two separate entities. On the contrary, the system-environment relationship must be understood in terms of a mathematical function, that is, as a relationship between variables. For cyberneticians, the relationship between system and environment is governed by a program, or, to use an existentialist term, by meaning. Seen in this light, then, the existence of a phenomenon is a function (in the mathematical sense) 'of the relationship between the organism and the environment' (Watzlawick, Beavin and Jackson, 1967, p. 259).

This switch from the notion of subjective meaning (content) to a mathematical and cybernetic view of meaning (program) or from an empiricist to a mathematical notion of function, is what is missing in Parsons's use of cybernetics, as I demonstrate elsewhere (Rossi, forthcoming).

It remains to consider the analytical and/or methodological advantages of the transformational notions of social structure and scientific explanation over the traditional ones.

THE NATURE OF STRUCTURAL EXPLANATION

The notion of deep structure implies a distinct mode of theoretical analysis consisting of the following elements: priority of cultural explanations; usage of an explanatory and predictive notion of social structure; and substitution of the notion of structural causality for the traditional notion of social causality and deductive reasoning.

Analytical Priority of Cultural Over Structural Explanations

Since empirical structuralists are interested in external and observable patterns of interaction, they subordinate the symbolic component of social facts to a consideration of social structure or they neglect it altogether. By 'symbolic component' I mean ideas, beliefs, values. In the positivisitic phase of his work, for instance, Durkheim explained collective representations on the basis of morphological or structural factors. But toward the end of his career, and especially in *The Elementary Forms of the Religious Life* (1961), he considered collective representations as organizing principles of the cultural system and as partially constitutive principles of social structure.

Radcliffe-Brown continued the structural orientation of Durkheim when he explained cultural institutions, such as kinship and religion, in terms of their contribution to the maintenance of social solidarity. A minimum of social integration was assumed by Radcliffe-Brown as essential for the survival of society, and 'society' is considered as a reality in and by itself.

According to Malinowski's functional theory of culture, culture exists because of its contribution to the fulfillment of the needs of society or individuals. In this teleological and reductionist view, culture is subordinated to social structure and the interdependence and interrelationship of social elements (structure) is assumed and not explained.

Merton's structuralism remains faithful to this structural-functionalist framework. The direct focus and first step of functional analysis consists in the analysis of patterns of interaction discernible in the activities of individuals and groups. For Merton anything can be an item appropriate for functional analysis as long as it is 'standardized, that is patterned and repetitive.' He explicitly states that not only social roles, processes, and structures, but also 'cultural patterns' are items for functional analysis (Merton, 1968, p. 104). He explains, however, that the functional analysis of the Hopi rain ceremony, a typical cultural phenomenon, consists in analyzing the actions oriented toward obtaining rain and the persons who participate in the patterns of behavior and in describing the participants in structural terms. By the latter expression he means that the functionalist has to locate the position of the participants in the interconnected network of roles, statuses and affiliation groups. Functionalists may argue that Merton's paradigm pays adequate attention to the 'cultural element,' because the analysis is explictly extended to the cultural 'meanings' ascribed to people's behavior. However, these meanings are understood as subjective dispositions, motives, purposes, or as behaviors having 'cognitive and affective significance' for the participants (1968, p. 112). Clearly, then, culture is reduced either to a structural description of the behavior of people who participate in the event or to a psychological reality; consequently, culture becomes a dependent variable at odds with the symbolic perspective of the later works of Durkheim and the position of Parsons.

In 1964, Peter Blau started his analysis from small interaction processes and then went on to analyze the basic exchange processes of attraction, competition, differentiation, integration and opposition, first in micro-social systems and later in macro-social ones. When he analyzed macro-social systems, Blau introduced the notion of shared values as 'media of social transactions' in so far as values set the standards of appropriate performance for social exchanges. This notion seems related to Parsons's notion of 'generalized symbolic media of interchange.' However, from Blau's perspective, culture is analytically subordinated to structural considerations. He explicitly states that, although structures of social relations are deeply influenced by common values, social structures have significance of their own and 'must be investigated in their own right.' Blau goes on to state that interest in the structure of social associations distinguished his own and Simmel's concerns from the Parsonian concern with the structure of social action and Weber's explanation of social action in terms of subjective meaning rooted in common social values (Blau, 1964, p. 13). In principle, one could not quarrel with the legitimacy of the analytical distinction between 'culture' and 'structure,' except when it is tantamount to a de facto neglect of the symbolic principles which, according to Durkheim, 'constitute' social facts and, according to transformational structuralists, regulate the structure of various social exchanges.

In Blau's more recent book (1977a), the structural focus of analysis is even more explicit. There Blau proposes a 'deductive theory of the structure of social associations which rests on the quantitative conception of social structure' (Blau, 1977a, p. 26). The last phrase refers to such quantitative properties as the number of people occupying different social positions, the frequency distribution of social positions, the frequency of associations among people in these social positions, and so on. The intent is to discuss 'the implications of the number and distribution of people (the quantitative dimension of social life) for their social relations' (1977b, p. 26). Blau himself distinguishes his 'Simmelian,' — I would call it 'behaviorist' — explanation of social relations from the 'cultural' and 'psychological' explanations proposed respectively by Parsons and Homans.

To understand the full implications of the epistemological and methodological differences between empiricist and transformational structuralism, we must now consider the issue of the descriptive vs the explanatory use of the term 'structure.'

Descriptive Use of the Term 'Structure'

Not all empirical structuralists agree on the components of social structure, but all seem to agree on three basic ideas. First, social phenomena must be explained in terms not of psychological but of social characteristics which are objective, that is, external to the individual. Second, these objective social characteristics are interrelated in patterned ways, that is, they are structured. Third, these patterns of stable interrelationships impose structural constraints on the behavior of individuals. All three ideas are least implicitly contained in Durkheim's notion that social facts are external and constraining 'facts,'[2] and in Marx's oft-quoted statement, 'It is not consciousness that determines life, but life that determines consciousness' (Marx and Engels, *The German Ideology*).

The second idea is alternatively explained as referring to the interrelationship, interconnectedness and interdependence of the components of a given set of phenomena; this idea has been central to the often vague usage of the term 'structure' in the sociological literature. The notion of interconnectedness also implies the idea of forms or patterns of interrelations, which are relatively enduring and stable. Such an interrelationship or interdependence often explains better than historical or geographical or other contingent factors why the components of a social structure are found together.

The word 'structure' often implies integration and the notion that what is integrated is slower to change than what is not. This may or may not be true, depending on which part of the socio-cultural system is affected by social change, and on the cause of social change. Some authors also imply that what is structured is basic, and therefore that it is the most important aspect of social phenomena to be explained. Furthermore, the notion of structure can be used to explain or predict change. In fact, if one component of structure is affected by change, we can predict the consequence of this change on the other components that are interrelated with it.

These usages of the term 'structure' do not entail great analytical specificity or explanatory power. They do not, in fact, tell us anything about the particular features of the social structure or why social structure should exist at all, as Homans concedes (1975, p. 56). Simply stated, to speak of social structure in this way is the same as saying that one wants to study stable and fundamental aspects of social facts without saying anything about the nature and relationships of their components and the laws by which they come into existence.

Structure as an Explanatory Notion

A few examples taken from Lévi-Strauss's structural analysis will serve to show why transformational structuralists claim that their notion of structure is explanatory rather than vaguely descriptive. In the area of totemism and kinship systems, Lévi-Strauss has been able to account for a variety of empirical data on the basis of the variation of the fundamental relationships among the few basic constituents of the aspects of the culture under study. Before Lévi-Strauss, anthropologists had offered a variety of explanations of totemism, each of them accounting for only certain types of totemism and not others. By extending and reversing Durkheim's perspective, Lévi-Strauss has shown that the apparently irrational use of many insignificant insects or animals as totems is explained by an underlying logic of the natives who use them conceptually to organize the social world. Totemic species are used as intellectual devices through which not only differences but also basic similarities and complementarities among different social groups are clearly conceptualized, concretely expressed, and, thereby, reinforced. For instance, the totemic animals are often pairs of animals, such as eagles and hawks, which belong to the same species. This allows expression of the notion that just as the eagle and the hawk are two different birds, so the eagle clan and the hawk clan are two different clans; thus, one can understand why they are unrelated and in exogamic relationship. At the same time, the two clans belong to a same tribe just as the two animals belong to the same category of birds; we can, then, understand why the two clans exchange marriage partners with each other. Moreover, the variety of totemic systems themselves are shown to be generated by the combination of the natural order with the social order, both of which are dichotomized, the first into animal category and particular animals, and the second into social category and persons. When a natural species is combined with a social group (clan, moiety, etc.) we have social totemism; when a natural category is combined with a person we have individual totemism; and so on. All the known forms of totemism are expressions of one or another of these possible combinations (Lévi-Strauss, 1967, pp. 16-17).

In the realm of kinship, Lévi-Strauss has shown that the great variety of kinship systems is best explained not in terms of particular and ad hoc historical explanations or contingent factors, but as concrete manifestations of an elementary symbolic structure, which he calls the 'atom of kinship'. Any system is one possible combination of a few basic relationships among the four terms, brother, sister, father and son (Lévi-Strauss, 1963, p. 72). Similarly, Lévi-Strauss has shown that a previously unexplained variety of heterogeneous marriage systems can be explained as empirical instances generated from two elementary structures of exchange, which he calls restricted and extended exchange (Lévi-Strauss, 1969, pp. 122-5). He has resolved apparent contradictions among explanations of observable structures given by different social actors by showing that social systems, which on the surface appear to be a dualistic type, are in reality based on an underlying tripartite structure (Lévi-Strauss, 1963, p. 161). He has also refined Durkheim's symbolic orientation by showing that collective representations are well-structured systems, built out of a few logical principles. At the same time, he has shown that a variety of systems of marriage exchanges are based on the perception of relationships of similarities and differences and on isomorphic forms of structuring the natural and social world.

The Concept of Structural Causality

Jean Piaget states that transformational analysis replaces causal analysis, or, we should rather say, causal analysis as traditionally understood. All social scientists must face the challenging task of explaining patterns of social relations or mythical stories and the differences among various patterns emerging from comparative and historical analysis. However, transformational structuralists maintain that to explain one pattern in terms of the causal influence of other patterns is unsatisfactory because this amounts to explaining data by other data external to them and, therefore, not to explain them at all. Aside from the issue of its applicability in sociological analysis, the notion of causality has been traditionally understood as 'a relationship of antecedence and consequence between two data, or sets of data,' without explaining how the structure of the antecedent phenomenon originates or changes the consequent phenomenon. In contrast, when transformational structuralists explain that one pattern has transformed into another, they must specify the basic components of the phenomenon and the rules by which those components have combined to generate the phenomenon.

We have to caution the reader that, at these early stages of their endeavor, many practitioners of transformational analysis, Lévi-Strauss included, use the notions of combination, permutation and transformation somewhat loosely and often as synonymous notions, whereas in linguistics and mathematics these notions have a precise, technical meaning. Transformational linguists state that a given meaning (deep structure) can be expressed through a variety of sentences (surface structures) as in the cases of passive, active, or interrogative sentences which are produced ('generated') according to precise syntactical rules.[3] The rules that govern the connection between the deep structure and the large variety of surface sentences derived from it are called transformational rules. Transformational grammarians show, for instance, that only certain permutations, or the rearranging of the linear order of the

basic elements of a sentence, are grammatically correct and produce meaningful sentences. Transformational linguists have formulated some transformational rules and are trying to formulate
others with the hope of accounting for the whole structure of
language.[4] Not all linguists agree with Chomsky's explanation of
language, and this is especially true of the representatives of
'generative semantics' (see Fillmore and Langendoen, 1971; Chafe,
1970). However, even the representatives of generative semantics
hold a relational view of language because they understand the
sentence as being composed of elements, each one of which plays a
specific role in interrelationship with the roles of the other
elements. Lévi-Strauss's transformations consist in a logical ordering and reordering of data to determine their essential components.
If changing the position of a unit within a patterned set of elementary components or substituting one unit for another alters the
nature of the datum, the unit is taken as an essential component of
the datum.

We can now understand why Piaget maintains that the law of
variation is a basic analytical tool for relational (in his terms, 'con-
structivist') structuralism. Piaget also states that the procedures by
which the whole is formed from the relationships among the
elements have priority over the whole itself and that combinatory
laws structure the system by governing its transformations (Piaget,
1970, p. 9). By transformational analysis one can move in an orderly
way from one pattern of social relationships to another so that the
various patterns are seen in a relationship of transformation to
each other. In Piaget's terms, causal explanation is to be
understood not as the formulation of statistical relationships
among observable variables but as the discovery of systematic
transformations among various levels of culture, including
language, and social organization. For transformational structuralists the issue is not only to formulate the rules that govern the
internal transformation of the structure of a system, but also to
provide rules that coordinate the deep structural rules of the system
with patterns of observable behavior or surface structures.

The formulation of transformational rules is one of the most
challenging tasks to be undertaken by sociologists if the ideas and
tools of transformational structuralism are to strengthen and widen
the analytic scope of sociological analysis.

Predictive Power of Structure

Once we have discovered the deep structures of social patterns we can predict empirical structures and social change in so far as they are determinable on the basis of the structural components or relational constants of the system. The deep structures are arrived at by formulating mechanical models (Lévi-Strauss, 1963, pp. 283ff) which differ from the statistical models used by empirical structuralists. Statistical models are formulated on the basis of modal frequencies of empirically observable events, while mechanical models consist of hypothesized constant relationships or deep structures which delimit the range of the possible transformations of the system. These relational constants are isolated through a mental operation from observable events which are produced by the interaction between relational constants among components and contingent components of historical and psychological character. By isolating the deep structures of social systems, mechanical models permit us to relate various systems to each other through transformational operations as well as to predict what changes are produced in the system when one or more of its elements are modified (Lévi-Strauss, 1963, p. 279).

Raymond Boudon has suggested a clarifying distinction between the 'intentional' and 'effective' use of the notion of structure. In the intentional sense, the term 'structure' indicates that the object of study has a systematic character and must be studied as a system because it is composed of interdependent parts. The 'effective definition' is equivalent to what I have called 'explanatory definition' since it accounts for the systematic character of the object. Boudon translates the 'effective' notion of 'structure' into a deductive formula composed of a threefold component: (1) an axiom, (2) structural rules, and (3) empirical rules of behavior. He also gives concrete applications of his formula (Boudon, 1968).

George Homans deserves credit for being one of the very few behavioral and empiricist sociologists who has entered into a dialogue with transformational structuralists on this very point. The problem is that empiricist and psychological assumptions keep him from doing thorough justice to Boudon's argument. Homans argues against the distinction between deep and surface structures on the ground that both must be ethnographically documented

(Homans, 1975, p. 61). No one can deny that latter statement, but the basic issue is whether his behaviorist assumptions make him reject the existence of deep structures a priori, an attitude that is contrary to the contemporary thinking in physics, biology, psychology, and linguistics, as we have noted. Homans adopts the empiricist notion of deduction in stating that deduction should explain both the general tendencies as well as exceptions in the system and ignores the difference between statistical and mechanical models. Since mechanical models are based on the structural tendencies of the system as a system, they cannot be used to predict observable events since these are the results of the interaction between the structural tendencies of the system and contingent factors (see Rossi, 1973, 1977a).

Homans also reveals a psychological bias when he states that the axioms should not be arbitrary like those of geometry, but should be contingent and based on the nature of things, actions of people and data provided by 'behavioral psychology' (Homans, 1975, p. 6). This amounts to assuming that social phenomena are outcomes of wholly contingent facts. Psychological data are contingent when they are explained in terms of learning and association mechanisms, but Gestaltists and Freudian psychologists as well as Piaget have shown the existence of structural principles that underly psychological processes.

CONCLUDING REMARKS

We have discussed the epistemological and scientific assumptions of the structural approach as well as key elements in its paradigm. At this point one might raise the question about the structural approach as a 'scientific' method and how it meets the criteria of scientific verification. I have discussed elsewhere the notion of 'science' and 'verification' proposed by transformational structuralists (Rossi, 1973), as well as the operational procedures of the structural method (Rossi, 1974, pp. 82-96). A still more challenging task would be to explore the contribution that the structural paradigm can make to the strengthening and extension of the traditional critical, interpretative, and 'natural science' paradigms, to use H. Wagner's typology (1963). This issue is amply discussed elsewhere (Rossi, forthcoming).

NOTES

A few sections of this paper were read at the session of the 'Theoretical Section' of the 1978 American Sociological Association meeting and have later been modified and amplified. Key ideas of the fourth part of the paper were the subject of debate at the panel on 'Varieties of Structural Inquiry' organized and presided over by Peter M. Blau at the 9th World Congress of Sociology (14-18 August 1978) in Uppsala, Sweden. I thank Peter Blau for inviting me to his panel and for the challenging questions he raised during the debate,and the ACLS for having provided a travel grant.

1. One could argue that Blau uses truly 'conceptual' explanations, as is evident from his usage of the concepts 'forms,' 'social differentiation' and so on. It is precisely the usage of 'theoretical' concepts that enables him to formulate truly 'conceptual' and deductive explanations (see Blau, 1977b, p. 26). However, here I am discussing only Blau's (and Parsons's) programmatic position.

2. Parsons has recently stated that Durkheim's notion of social environment as 'factually' given to the individuals was a profound insight in the history of the social sciences. Durkheim expressed this insight through the notions of 'social environment' and 'social facts' conceived as properties of a given set of objects present in the world external to the individual (Parsons, 1975, p. 72).

3. In this essay I refer mainly to the linguistic usage of 'transformational' rules. For a discussion of 'transformation' in mathematics, see the essays by Marc Barbut in Lane (1970), by Robin Gandy in Robey (1973), Lorrain (1975), El Guindi and Read (1979).

4. For an essential and clear exposition of transformational linguistics see Chomsky (1957, 1965, 1968) and Langacher (1972).

REFERENCES

BATESON, Gregory (1967) 'Cybernetic Explanation,' *The American Behavioral Scientist*, 10:29-32.
BLAU, Peter M. (1964) *Exchange and Power in Social Life*. New York: John Wiley.
BLAU, Peter M. (1974) 'Parameters of Social Structure,' *American Sociological Review*, 39 (October): 615-35.
BLAU, Peter M. (ed.) (1975) *Approaches to the Study of Social Structure*. New York: Free Press.

BLAU, Peter M. (1977a) *Inequality and Heterogeneity*. New York: Free Press.
BLAU, Peter M (1977b) 'A Macrosociological Theory of Social Structure,' *American Journal of Sociology*, 83 (1):25-54.
BOUDON, Raymond (1968) *A Quoi sert la notion de structure?* Paris: Gallimard.
CHAFE, Wallace L. (1970) *Meaning and the Structure of Language*. Chicago: University Press.
CHOMSKY, Noam (1957) *Syntactic Structures*. The Hague: Mouton.
CHOMSKY, Noam (1965) *Aspects of a Theory of Syntax*. Cambridge, Mass.: MIT Press.
CHOMSKY, Noam (1968), *Language and Mind*. New York: Harcourt, Brace Jovanovich.
COHEN, Ronald (1977) 'The Emperor's Clothes: Review of a Review,' *American Anthropologist*, 79 (1): 113-14.
DURKHEIM, Emile (1961) *The Elementary Forms of the Religious Life*. New York: Collier Books (first published 1912).
EL GUINDI, Fadwa and Dwight W. READ (1979) 'Mathematics in Structural Theory,' *Current Anthropology*, 20(4):761-90.
FILLMORE, Charles and D. Terence LANGENDOEN (eds) (1971) *Studies in Linguistic Semantics*. New York: Holt, Rinehart and Winston.
de GEORGE, R. T. and F. M. de GEORGE (eds) (1972) *The Structuralists: From Marx to Lévi-Strauss*. Garden City, N Y: Doubleday.
GLUCKSMAN, Max (1974) *Structuralist Analysis in Contemporary Social Thought*. Boston: Routledge & Kegan Paul.
HOMANS, G. C. (1975) 'What Do We Mean by Social Structure?' pp. 53-65 in Blau (1975).
JAKOBSON, R. and M. HALLE (1956) *Fundamentals of Language*. The Hague: Mouton.
LANE, Michael (1970) *Introduction to Structuralism*. New York: Basic Books.
LANGACHER, Ronald W. (1972) *Fundamentals of Linguistic Analysis*. New York: Harcourt, Brace, Janovich.
LÉVI-STRAUSS, Claude (1945) 'French Sociology', pp. 503-37 in *Twentieth Century Sociology*, G. Gurvitch and W. E. Moore (eds). New York: The Philosophical Library.
LÉVI-STRAUSS, Claude (1963) *Structural Anthropology*. Translated from the French by Claire Jacobson and Brooke Grundfest Schoepf. New York: Basic Books (French original 1958).
LÉVI-STRAUSS, Claude (1965) *Tristes Tropiques*. New York: Atheneum (French original 1955).
LÉVI-STRAUSS, Claude (1967) *Totemism*. Translated by Rodney Needham. Boston: Beacon Press (French original 1962).
LÉVI-STRAUSS, Claude (1969) *The Elementary Structures of Kinship*. Translated by J. H. Bell and J. R. Von Sturmer under the editorship of Rodney Needham. Boston: Beacon Press (French original 1949).
LÉVI-STRAUSS, Claude (1976) *Structural Anthropology*, vol. II. Translated by M. Layton. New York: Basic Books.
LEVY, Marion J. Jr (1952) *The Structure of Society*. Princeton: University Press.
LEVY, Marion J. Jr (1966) *Modernization and the Structure of Societies*, 2 vols. Princeton: University Press.

LORRAIN, Francois (1975) *Reseaux sociaux et classifications sociales: essai sur l'algebre et la geometrie des structures sociales*. Paris: Hermann.

MALINOWSKI, Bronislaw (1936) 'Anthropology', *Encyclopedia Britannica*, Supplement, vol. 1.

MALINOWSKI, Bronislaw (1944) *A Scientific Theory of Culture*. Chapel Hill: University of North Carolina Press.

MALINOWSKI, Bronislaw (1948) *Magic, Science and Religion and Other Essays*. New York: Free Press.

MERTON, R. K. (1968) *Social Theory and Social Structure*. New York: Free Press (first published 1949).

MERTON, R. K. (1975) 'Structural Analysis in Sociology,' pp. 21-52 in Blau (1975).

NEEDHAM, Rodney (1973) 'Pronouncement in Competence,' *American Anthropologist*, 80(2):386-7.

PARSONS, Talcott (1935) 'Sociological Elements in Economic Thought, I,' *Quarterly Journal of Economics*, 49 (May):414-53.

PARSONS, Talcott (1951) *The Social System*. New York: Free Press.

PARSONS, Talcott (1961) *The Structure of Social Action*. New York: Free Press (first published 1937).

PARSONS, Talcott (1970a) 'Some Problems of General Theory in Sociology,' pp. 27-68 in *Theoretical Sociology*, John C. McKinney and Edward A. Tiryakian (eds). New York: Appleton-Century-Crofts.

PARSONS, Talcott (1970b) 'On Building Social System Theory: A Personal History,' *Daedalus,* 99(4):826-81.

PARSONS, Talcott (1975) 'The Present Status of Structural-Functional Theory in Sociology,' pp.67-84 in *The Idea of Social Structure*, Lewis A. Coser (ed.). New York: Harcourt, Brace, Joranovich.

PARSONS, Talcott (1977) 'Comment on Burger's Critique,' *American Journal of Sociology*, 83(2):335-9.

PARSONS, T., E. SHILS, E. D. NAEGELE, J. R. PITTS (eds) (1965) *Theories of Society*. New York: Free Press (one-volume edn) (first published 1961).

PIAGET, Jean (1970) *Structuralism*. Translated and edited by Chaninah Maschler. New York: Basic Books (French original 1968).

RADCLIFFE-BROWN, A. R. (1940) 'On Social Structure,' *Journal of the Royal Anthropological Institute*, 70:1-12.

RADCLIFFE-BROWN, A. R. (1965) *Structure and Function in Primitive Society*. New York: Free Press.

RITZER, George (1975) *Sociology: A Multiple Paradigm Science*. Boston: Allyn and Bacon.

ROBEY, David (ed.) (1973) *Structuralism: An Introduction*. Oxford: Clarendon Press.

ROSSI, Ino (1973) 'Verification in Anthropology: The Case of Structural Analysis,' *Journal of Symbolic Anthropologies*, 1 (2) (September): 27-56.

ROSSI, Ino (ed.) (1974) *The Unconscious in Culture: The Structuralism of Claude Lévi-Strauss in Perspective*. New York: Dutton.

ROSSI, Ino (1977a) 'Reply to Cohen,' *American Anthropologist*, 79(1):114-15.

ROSSI, Ino (1977b) 'On the Notion of Social Structure: A Mental or Objective Reality?' *American Anthropologist*, 79 (4):914-16.

ROSSI, Ino (1978a) 'On Theoretical and Technical Incompetence: The Case of Needham,' *American Anthropologist*, 80(3):675-6.

ROSSI, Ino (1978b) 'Toward the Unification of Scientific Explanation: Evidence from Biological, Psychic, Linguistic, Cultural Universals,' in *Discourse and Inference in Cognitive Anthropology*, Marvin D. Loflin and James Silverberg (eds). The Hague: Mouton.

ROSSI, Ino (forthcoming) *Structural Sociology*. New York: Columbia University Press.

de SAUSSURE, Ferdinand (1966) *Course in General Linguistics*. Edited by C. Bally and A. Sechehaye; translated by W. Baskin. New York: McGraw-Hill (French original 1916).

SCHWANNENBERG, Enno (1976) 'On The Meaning of the Theory of Action,' pp. 35-45 in Loubser et al. (eds), *Explorations in General Social Science. Essays in Honor of Talcott Parsons*. Vol. 1. New York: Free Press.

STENT, G. S. (1970) 'DNA,' *Daedalus*, 39(4):909-37.

STENT, G. S. (1975) 'Limits to the Scientific Understanding of Man,' *Science*, 187 (4181): 1052-7.

SULLIVAN, W. (1974) 'Experimental Findings Challenge Accepted Theories on Atomic Physics and Cause Confusion in Science,' *New York Times*, 29 April; 21.

TURNER, Jonathan H. (1978) *The Structure of Sociological Theory*, 2nd ed. Homewood, Ill.: Dorsey Press.

WAGNER, Helmut R. (1963) 'Types of Sociological Theory,' *American Sociological Review*, 28 October: 735-42.

WALLACE, Walter L. (ed.) (1969) *Sociological Theory*. Chicago: Aldine.

WATZLAWICK, P., J. H. BEAVIN and D. D. JACKSON (1967) *Pragmatics of Human Communication: A Study of Interactional Patterns, Pathologies and Paradoxes*. New York: W. W. Norton.

WILLER, David and Murray WEBSTER, Jr (1970) 'Theoretical Concepts and Observables,' *American Sociological Review*, 35(4):748-57.

3

MARXIST STRUCTURALISM

Wolf V. Heydebrand
New York University

As one of the major postwar intellectual perspectives, Marxist structuralism has attracted considerable attention in the social sciences. Its impact has been comparable to that of phenomenology and, to a smaller extent, existentialism. Marxist structuralism is commonly associated with the writings of Louis Althusser, Nicos Poulantzas, and Maurice Godelier in France, Galvano Della Volpe and Lucio Colletti in Italy, Perry Anderson, Robin Blackburn, and Gareth Stedman Jones in England (all three have been editors of *New Left Review*), and Goran Therborn in Sweden. This list is incomplete; nor would all of these writers identify themselves necessarily as 'structuralist' since it is 'the nature of an intellectual quest to be undefined' (Sartre, 1968, p. xxxiii). Nevertheless, structuralism refers to a coherent set of methods and ideas. French structuralism in particular has attained a fairly high degree of intellectual dominance and theoretical articulation, perhaps because of the original 'dialectical' debates between structuralists, existentialists, and phenomenologists (Lévi-Strauss, 1966, p. 245; Sartre, 1976; Merleau-Ponty, 1973; see also Poster, 1975) in the 1950s and 1960s, and because of the controversies surrounding the theoretical and political 'practice' of Louis Althusser.

In the following, I shall trace briefly the background of structuralism in structural linguistics and structural anthropology, and the adaptation of Marxism to structuralism. Then I want to focus on the main concepts in the work of Althusser, and to point out the parallels and differences between his conceptions and empirical social science. Finally, I will offer a critique of the notions of

Author's Note. I want to thank Beverly Burris and Katherine Stone for their critical comments and helpful editorial suggestions.

theoretical, ideological, and political practice because they exemplify the inherent contradictions of Marxist structuralism and its incapacity to confront criticism of its own limitations. This is particularly important in view of the uncritical acceptance of Marxist structuralism by many social scientists and the tendency to equate Marxist structuralism with Marxism in general.

THE STRUCTURALIST BACKGROUND

At the beginning of this century, Ferdinand de Saussure introduced a number of methodological innovations into the study of language. In his *Course in General Linguistics*, de Saussure (1966) treated language as a system of conventional signs rather than tracing isolated linguistic phenomena in terms of their historical development or focusing on the cultural variations of substantive meanings. De Saussure (1966, p. 67) views the linguistic sign as a holistic combination of two structural elements: a form which signifies (the signifier, such as the word 'arbor'), and an idea or concept to which the form refers (the signified, the concept 'tree').

The relationship between signifier and signified is not natural or fixed but social and, hence, infinitely variable. Therefore, the nature of the sign itself is completely arbitrary. Since signifier and signified can take any form, and since signs can be combined into an infinite variety of languages, the proper focus in the study of language is on the relational and structural characteristics, rather than on fixed, essential, or universal meanings associated with either the signifier or the signified. De Saussure detaches the study of language from its historical, cultural, psychological, or metaphysical matrix and shifts the analytic focus from such concepts as 'objects,' 'reality,' or the 'thing-in-itself' to the formal properties and the internal structural relations of sign systems (Culler, 1977, pp. 25, 126). Linguistic units are meaningful, not because they constitute a nomenclature that refers to fixed, autonomous entities, but because of their capacity to produce identity-in-contrast, binary oppositions, formal distinctions. Thus, the essence, content, and use-value of symbols and objects are subordinated to their relational identity, their position and function within a given system, their exchange-value.

The analysis of the role of linguistic value as exchange-value suggests a new perspective on the origin of linguistic structuralism in the categories of the capitalist economy. The term 'value' as used by de Saussure does not refer to the idea of merit or to normative acts that are desirable or intrinsically worthy. Value refers to positional equivalence in a system of exchange, in short, to exchange-value which, like money, reduces all use-values with different contents, meanings, identities, and origins to a common denominator. De Saussure's new conception of linguistics counterposes language as a system of exchange and circulation of 'pure values' (1966, p. 80) to a process of historical production of signs where linguistic values are 'somehow rooted in things and in their natural relations, as happens with economics' (p. 80). This latter type of use-value, or 'natural value,' can

> to some extent be traced in time if we remember that it depends at each moment upon a system of co-existing values. Its link with things gives it, perforce, a natural basis, and the judgments that we base on such values are therefore never completely arbitrary; their variability is limited. But we have just seen that natural data have no place in linguistics. [de Saussure, 1966, p. 80]

De Saussure did not invent structuralism merely as a new scientific method of analyzing language. While innovative in its own right, the new method was in line with a new way of thinking about, and generalizing from, the realities of the economic system. This new categorical order represents the structure and processes of the capitalist political economy in terms of its own self-understanding, that is, from within its own categorical and theoretical horizon. As Alfred Sohn-Rethel puts it, 'In commodity-producing societies the significance and historical necessity of the exchange abstraction in its spatio-temporal reality is that it provides the form of the social synthesis' (1978, p. 35).

The dualism of linguistic structuralism can be called a naive dualism since, unlike bourgeois economics, it does not seek to hide or mystify the relation between use-values and exchange-values. Marx's justly celebrated analysis of commodity fetishism exposes capitalism's ideological tendency to mystify the contradictory character of the capitalist exchange process, as revealed in 'the material relations between persons and social relations between things' (Marx, 1906, p. 84). Thus, de Saussure openly asserts the radical inner duality of 'all sciences concerned with values' (1966, p. 79). He suggests that the duality between system and history

> is already forcing itself upon the economic sciences...; political economy and economic history constitute two clearly separated disciplines within a single

science...; proceeding as they have, economists are — without being well aware of it — obeying an inner necessity....A similar necessity obliges us to divide linguistics into two parts, each with its own principle. Here as in political economy we are confronted with the notion of *value*: both sciences are concerned with *a system for equating things of different orders* — labor and wages in one and a signified and signifier in the other. [de Saussure, 1966, p. 79]

Thus, the 'inner necessity' of objective, scientific analysis creates an homological relationship between linguistics and economics, a clear case of the social determination of the new structuralist language by the language of capitalism. Indeed, 'the study of language has opened the route to an understanding of mankind, social history, and the laws of how a society functions' (Coward and Ellis, 1977, p. 1; see also Lévi-Strauss, 1967, p. 54; Balbus, 1977; Baudrillard, 1972; Lefebvre, 1966). For de Saussure,

values

all values are apparently governed by the same paradoxical principle. They are always composed: (1) of a dissimilar thing that can be *exchanged* for the thing of which the value is to be determined; and (2) of *similar* things that can be *compared* with the thing of which the value is to be determined. [de Saussure, 1966, p. 115].

One could hardly find a more lucid statement of the abstract, formal principles of capitalist exchange and circulation which an 'inner necessity' obliges Saussure to apply to linguistics to reveal 'the secret identity of commodity form and thought form' (Sohn-Rethel, 1978, p. xiii).

Here is the origin of a fundamental flaw in Marxist structuralism: the contradiction between the systemic imagery of circulation, and the phenomenology of exchange relations, on the one hand, and the Marxian critique of exchange and circulation as an ideological veil that masks the crisis-ridden nature of capitalist production, on the other. De Saussure clearly articulates the connection between his new linguistic method and the bourgeois categorical order when he says:

Instead of pre-existing ideas, then, we find in all the foregoing examples *values* emanating from the system. When they are said to correspond to concepts, it is understood that the concepts are purely differential and defined not by their positive content but negatively by their relations with the other terms of the system. Their most precise characteristic is in being what the others are not. [de Saussure, 1966, p. 11]

Even more significantly, de Saussure assimilates the idea of a substantive, concrete, historical identity to that of exchange-value: 'We see, then, that in semiological systems like language, where elements hold each other in equilibrium in accordance with fixed rules, the notion of identity blends with that of value, and vice versa' (1966, p. 110). Such is the fetishism of language and the secret thereof.

De Saussure's distinction between language, as a code, and speech, as the performance or execution of the code, emphasizes the separation of 'what is social from what is individual, and what is essential from what is ancillary or accidental' (1966, p. 14; see also Barthes, 1964). Furthermore, we can see now that the language system plays the role of a deterministic conceptual model, with its own internal structure and determinate rules of transformation, whereas speech, the actual 'behavior' of language, is a probabilistic model subject to infinitely many individual influences and variations. As Jonathan Culler puts it,

> The distinction between [language] and [speech] has important consequences for other disciplines besides linguistics: for it is essentially a distinction between institution and event, between the underlying system which makes possible various types of behavior and actual instances of such behavior. Study of the system leads to the construction of models which represent forms, their relation to one another, and their possibilities of combination, whereas study of actual behavior or events would lead to the construction of statistical models which represent the probabilities of particular combinations under various circumstances. [Culler, 1977, p. 27]

An important consequence of the arbitrary nature of signs and the constant flux of speech activity is the distinction between the diachronic study of language, that is, the way it changes and evolves historically, and the synchronic analysis of a linguistic system at one time. This distinction between system and history, structure and process, being and becoming is instituted precisely in order to counteract the continuous flux, relativity, and historicity of linguistic phenomena. It gives rise to the methodological imperative of having to understand the code before the application, and entails an epistemological priority of the synchronic system state over historical evolution, of structure over origins. *code*

The historical reconstruction of transitions must focus on changes in forms and relations rather than on changes in substantive meanings; on the social, objective, structural, systemic fact rather than on the individual, the subjective, the isolated event. 'The linguist who wishes to understand a state must discard all knowledge of everything that produced it and ignore diachrony' (de Saussure, 1966, p. 81). Most importantly, 'historical change originates outside the linguistic system. Change originates in linguistic performance, in [speech], not in [language]. . . . Changes do not occur in order to produce a new state of the system. . . . Changes are part of an evolutionary process to which the system adjusts' (Culler, 1977, pp. 36-7). Hence, historical change is neither teleological nor meaningful in any total sense; historical facts are of a different order from systemic or structural facts, and historical change, instead of being produced by human praxis, involves merely the displacement of one form or structure by another. History becomes event-less history.

The affinity of these ideas with forms of structural analysis other than linguistics is striking. Jean Piaget (1970) has traced some of the linkages between the underlying structural 'model' and its manifestations in biology, anthropology, and psychology, especially with respect to Gestalt psychology and Piaget's own brand of 'genetic structuralism,' which views structure as a system of transformations. However, even though 'structures consist in their coming to be, that is, their being "under construction",' they nevertheless depend on higher level structures, 'on a prior formation of the instruments of transformation — transformation rules or laws' (Piaget, 1970, pp. 140-1).

Piaget's model of structure emphasizes three key elements: the idea of 'wholeness,' in contrast to an atomistic composite of independent elements; the idea of structured wholes as determined ('structured') by internal rules of transformation, construction/reconstruction, and reproduction; and the idea of self-regulation of structures, that is, their 'relative autonomy' with respect to other structures and their self-maintenance of internal rhythms, operations, balances and boundaries.

Claude Lévi-Strauss's (1966, 1967) structural anthropology, influenced by structural linguistics through Roman Jakobson and the phonological school of Prague (Pingaud, 1965; see also Rossi, 1974) constitutes an application and elaboration of linguistic structuralism in the immediate vicinity of sociology. In his attempt to formulate a method for producing a model of social reality, Lévi-Strauss develops a 'systemic' concept of social structure. It involves not only such system characteristics as internal interdependence of elements but also the idea of formal structural homology — the reproducibility of the structure on different levels such that a series of transformations can produce a group of models of the same general type, ascending from the 'order of elements' in the social structure to the 'order of orders' and ultimately to some universal order (Lévi-Strauss, 1967, pp. 302-9). For Lévi-Strauss, the advantage of structural models is that they make it possible to arrive at general laws and to specify the internal logic of social systems such that all the observed facts are immediately intelligible, an assumption shared with Gestalt psychology and other approaches based on a coherence concept of truth.

The search for general laws leads Lévi-Strauss to shift his attention from the study of conscious phenomena (opinions, ideology, speech) to the study of the unconscious infrastructure (basic codes, cognitive forms, myths, language, scientific models). Indeed, the formal structure of the unconscious mind serves as an ultimate reference point or matrix (Lacan, 1966; see also Mitchell's [1974] defense of the Oedipus complex). This psychological absolute is surpassed among structuralists only by Chomsky's (1965, p. 19) bio-linguistic suggestion 'that a particular grammar is acquired by differentiation of a *fixed innate scheme*, rather than by slow growth of new items, patterns, or associations.' Finally, Lévi-Strauss once again asserts the primacy of synchrony over diachrony, and the futility of the search for origins. This 'structuralist assault on history,' as the critical theorist Alfred Schmidt (1969, p. 263) points out, is one of the hallmarks of contemporary social science, leading to a fundamentally pessimistic attitude of resignation expressed in such notions as 'eternal recurrence,' 'there is nothing new under the sun,' and 'plus ça change, plus c'est la même chose.' Ultimately, Lévi-Strauss takes structural anthropology back not only to the agnostic dualism of Kant's a priori categories, but to the pre-Socratic belief that reality can be found only in changeless, eternal 'Being' and that it is logically absurd to see change as 'real' or as anything other than recurrent rearrangements of internal relations and structural building-blocks (Lévi-Strauss, 1966, pp. 16-36; see also Genette, 1965; Lefebvre, 1966b, Derrida, 1972).

The epistemological consequence of Lévi-Strauss's position is that myths and symbols constitute raw material to be deciphered and structured by scientists whose logical procedures and models ensure the creation of true knowledge which, in turn merely confirms the changeless nature of Being, the ultimate order of the universe that reveals itself in myths and symbols. Q.E.D.

THE ADAPTATION OF MARXISM
TO STRUCTURALISM

The immediate textual sources for the adaptation of Marxism to structuralism are not so much the writings of Marx, old or young, but Engels's formulation of historical materialism in terms of the complex interaction between base and superstructure and his conception of socialism as a scientific theory of society. For example, in his letters to Joseph Bloch and C. Schmidt (erroneously collapsed by Tucker [1978, p. 762] into a single letter to Bloch), Engels (1978) sets out a number of ideas which are crucial to Marxist structuralism. First, there is an ad hoc distinction between three levels of social structure: the economic (the base), the political, and the ideological (both part of the superstructure). This distinction, a wholly arbitrary trinity of structural elements listed merely for the purpose of illustrating the complexity of the base-superstructure dichotomy, reappears in Mao-Tse-Tung's notion of economic, political, and ideological practices as constituting a social formation and is taken over by Althusser and Poulantzas as a central conceptual structure with deep ontological implications. This three-level structure tends to reappear in the writings of Marxist structuralists without any reflection on its origin, theoretical significance, or implication: it is a form of logical or 'conceptual empiricism' (Glucksmann, 1977, p. 285), and it functions almost as dogma. Engels (1978) explains to Bloch that the 'ultimately determining element in history is the production and reproduction of real life,' usually rendered as the 'economic' element. Removed from the 'economic' level, the 'political forms of class struggle' and the 'ideological' elements 'also exercise their influence upon the course of the historical struggles and in many cases preponderate in determining their *form*' (Engels, 1978). From this tripartite distinction, then, Marxist structuralists conclude that there are three separate 'regions,' each with its own form of 'practice' and each 'relatively autonomous' of the others. Nevertheless, as Engels explains further, 'there is an interaction of all these elements in which amid all the endless hosts of accidents...the economic movement finally asserts itself as necessary' (1978). After depicting history loosely as 'arising from conflicts between many individual wills,' Engels describes what Althusser later is to give a more 'scientific' connotation and to call 'overdetermination': 'Thus there are innumerable intersecting forces, an infinite series of parallelograms of forces which give rise to one resultant — the historical event' (1978). Still speaking in the manner of someone who must explain a complicated matter in simple terms, Engels goes on to say: 'This may again itself be viewed as the product of a power which works as a whole, *unconsciously* and without volition,' (1978; emphasis in original). Here Engels formulates the historical process in almost structuralist terms: the subjection of individual wills and events to a social, objective whole which moves with the unconscious force of a natural process.

It should be noted that Engels clearly does not use the Freudian idea of the 'unconscious' but merely the notion that historical actors are typically not aware of the consequences of their actions, that their consciousness is limited, and that it becomes accessible through praxis, through the historical development of scientific socialism. The historicity of consciousness is central to Marx's and Engels's thought but is negated, as we shall see, in the structuralist concept of 'theoretical practice.' Engels's letters to Bloch and Schmidt, as well as many of his other later writings, must be seen in the context of the emerging simplification and reification of Marxist ideas, especially the intellectual straightjacket of technological and economic determinism that academic social scientists are so fond of putting on Marx. In the process, Engels often simplified himself, a fact that Althusser and others have used in order to proclaim the need for turning the ideological and philosophical material contained in the masters' thoughts into true science (Thompson, 1978). Indeed, Engels himself talks of the need to transform ideology into science. 'The history of science,' says Engels, 'is the history of the gradual clearing away of this nonsense or of its replacement by fresh but always less absurd nonsense' (1978, p. 764). As if anticipating Althusser's 'generalities' and Poulantzas's 'regions,' Engels states that 'the philosophy of every epoch, since it is a *definite sphere in the division of labor*, has as its presupposition certain definite thought material handed down to it by its predecessors, from which it takes its start' (1978, p. 764; emphasis added). And further: 'Here economy creates nothing anew, but it determines the way in which the thought material found in existence is altered and further developed' (1978, p. 764). In defending himself against a mechanistic conception of dialectics, Engels describes dialectics not in terms of simple cause-and-effects, but as a complex process that goes on in the form of interaction among levels of the social structure. This notion is later used by Althusser as a reference point for attacking 'empiricism' and turning Marxian historical dialectics into a deterministic scientific model of 'contradiction and over-determination.' But it is precisely against mechanistic conceptions of economic determinism, that Engels throws up his arms and declares:

> What these gentlemen all lack is dialectics. They always see only here cause, there effect. That this is a hollow abstraction, that such metaphysical polar opposites exist in the real world only during crises, while the whole vast process goes on in the form of interaction — though of very unequal forces, the economic movement being by far the strongest, most primeval, most decisive — that here everything is relative and nothing absolute — this they never begin to see. Hegel has never existed for them [Engels, 1978, p. 765].

While it must be soothing to structuralist ears to hear that 'everything is relative and nothing absolute,' it surely cannot be very comforting to learn that 'metaphysical polar opposites exist in the real world only during crises' and that Engels states, disapprovingly, that 'Hegel has never existed for them.' But, then, Engels himself is being cast as merely one of those predecessors whose thought material has to be cleansed of philosophical and ideological impurities (see Thompson, 1978, pp. 50-5). It should be clear that I am not arguing for a dogmatic, 'correct' interpretation of Marx's and Engels's writings; the point is that using Engels as a philosophical source while putting him down for ideological ambiguity is a form of intellectual 'bricolage,' an arbitrary scholastic exercise where what is selected and what is rejected are determined by the analytical needs of the moment, not by the theoretical adequacy of the concept to its object or by a critical interpretation of the Marxist project as a whole. One must ask, therefore, what kinds of motives animate the adaptation of Marxism to structuralism? While it is notoriously difficult to impute motives to intellectual construction, some political and historical answers are suggested in the writings of Althusser and, generally, in the pessimistic 'metaphysical pathos' of structuralism (see also Mayrl, 1978).

After World War II, Marxist intellectuals and politicians had to confront a number of new realities. While Marxism had to be disentangled from the embarrassment of Stalinism, it was also felt to be necessary to counter the resurgent idealist-voluntarist inter-pretation of Marx which was seen as embedded in the early writings (Fromm, 1961) and was ascribed to a lingering Hegelian influence on Marxist thought (as in Lukács, 1967). Moreover, the Eastern European 'revisionist' movement, centered paradoxically around both Titoism and the Praxis group in Yugoslavia, and the critique of the Stalinist state apparatus began to be perceived as a real threat to the legitimacy of state socialism and the success of the 'socialist' project (Thompson, 1978). Internally, many Western Left party politicians began to be threatened by the 'subjectivist' notions of spontaneity and individualist politics of post-World War II existentialism, socialist humanism (Fromm, 1966; Thompson, 1978, p. 129), 'infantile leftism' — the anti-authoritarianism of the New Left — and the re-emergence of utopian, anarchist, and critical visions of Marxism with a state-less socialist future in both East and West. Few on the Left could overlook the remaining inner contradictions of state socialism or the unexpected temporary resilience of advanced capitalism. This crisis in Marxist theory and politics is well expressed in both Lukács's 'Preface to the New Edi-tion' (1967) of his *History and Class Consciousness*, and in Althusser's note 'To My English Readers' and his 'Introduction: Today' to his essay collection *For Marx* (1970). Both are moving and eloquent statements by two Marxist intellectuals who were deeply involved in the party politics of their time. It is against this historical and political background that one may perhaps best understand the perceived need for a new theoretical framework for Marxist theory and politics, one that would de-emphasize the im-mediate relevance of specific historical events such as the Stalinist suppression of revolutionary and critical Marxism, or the 'ideological' rather than 'scientific' character of much left-wing political praxis and, conversely, would accentuate the complexities of advanced capitalism, the structural persistence of previous in-stitutions and modes of production into current social formations, and the problems of reproduction, hegemony, and dominance fac-ing any state apparatus — capitalist or socialist.

Althusser, a philosopher and Communist Party theoretician in postwar France, saw structuralist and materialist elements as pro-viding the raw materials for such a new theoretical framework. He rejects the label 'structuralist,' condescendingly referring to struc-turalism as a 'very French specialty' and 'not a completely worked-out philosophy, but a jumble of vague themes which only realizes its ultimate tendency under certain definite conditions' (Althusser, 1976, pp. 128, 129). It is nevertheless abundantly clear that Althusser proceeded to merge Marxist and structuralist ideas, that he began to re-interpret Marx and Engels in the light of structuralist methods of 'reading' a text (Althusser and Balibar, 1970), that he 'cleansed' Marxism of its Hegelian, ideological, and prescientific traces (hence he wrote 'for Marx'), that he took seriously the idea of a scientific (read: 'structurally determined') socialism, and that he succeeded in making Marxism respectable for a wide variety of scientifically oriented academic audiences. The link between structuralism and Marxism had been forged and the union was to beget a vast progeny of scholarship: critical, epistemological, theoretical, and even empirical (see, A. Glucksmann, 1977; M. Glucksmann, 1974; Schmidt, 1969; Blackburn and Stedman Jones, 1972; Geras, 1972; Lewis, 1972; Ranciere, 1974; Vilav, 1973; Veltmeyer, 1975; Lecourt, 1975; Therborn, 1976; Zimmerman, 1976; Poulantzas, 1973, 1974, 1975, 1976; Callinicos, 1976; Hindess, 1977; Ruben, 1977; Coward and Ellis, 1977; Thompson, 1978; V. Burris, 1979 Appelbaum, 1979). Among the early critical analyses, André Glucksmann's (1977) is easily the most brilliant and the most disillusioned. Among the latest critiques, Thompson's (1978) is probably the most comprehensive, the most passionate, and the most devastating.

Before presenting the main tenets of Marxist structuralism, a fundamental difference between philosophical dualism and Marxist dialectics must be noted. Without a grasp of this analytical distinction it is difficult to understand structuralism, and impossible to understand Marxist structuralism.

X   Philosophical dualism is the doctrine of the existence of two independent and mutually irreducible metaphysical substances or forces, an absolute duality of the principles that govern reality, including social reality. Ontological dualism posits the dichotomy of matter and mind, moral and religious dualism the radical separateness of good and evil, epistemological dualism that of the real object and the datum immediately present to the knowing mind. In the history of philosophy, these dualisms are represented by Plato's distinction between sensible and intelligible worlds; Aristotle's binary logic and his dualistic distinctions between essence and accident as well as between form and content; Descartes' dichotomy of thinking and extended substances (mind and body), which are later subsumed by Spinoza under the seemingly monistic concept of substance and the associated notions of immanent effectivity and synchronic causality. The line of dualistic descent continues with Leibniz's notion of actual and possible worlds, and culminates in Kant's categorical dichotomy between the noumenal (the 'thing-in-itself') and the phenomenal.

Dualism is the most pervasive and dominant perspective in Western philosophy, especially in philosophical idealism, up to Hegel. Logically, it is possible to counterpose dualism, on the one hand, to monism (the doctrine that there is but one fundamental reality) and, on the other hand, to pluralism (the assumption of the existence of many ultimate substances). But the more crucial contradistinction to be made here is the one between dualism and dialectics. It is the dialectical perspective, especially since Marx's critique of Hegel's idealism and Feuerbach's materialism, that introduces a number of new conceptions, such as those of reality as social and historical processes, rather than determined substances; historical contradiction and mediation rather than inevitable conflict of opposites; the notions of collective, human praxis, self-transformation, and self-determination rather than either arbitrary voluntarism or mechanical determinism. These conceptions transcend both monism and pluralism. The only dialectical concept that might possibly suggest a throwback to Spinoza's monism is that of the totality, the concrete unity of the socio-historical whole within which, through human practical activity, contradictions and mediations are articulated and constitute the historical process. But on closer examination, the Marxian concept of totality has little to do with Spinoza's substance, however structured or differentiated, or with Hegel's absolute spirit, which works itself out through an idealist dialectic of self-active, self-contradictory thought (Bernstein, 1971, p. 11; Lefebvre, 1968, p. 46). These brief philosophical considerations are presented here mainly for the purpose of providing a conceptual baseline for the comparison between dualism and dialectics in the ensuing discussion. Marxist structuralism, as I will show, takes a profoundly dualistic approach to social reality, even though it seeks to combine the binary terms of each duality under a structured unity such as de Saussure's sign or Althusser's real object in which production and being are united (A. Glucksmann, 1977, p. 310). As Bernard Pingaud puts it, quoting Lévi-Strauss, 'Structuralism denies all dualism. It is the union of the emotional and the intellectual' (Pingaud, 1965, p. 2). But, however unified, the dualism persists. Thus, Maurice Cornforth observes that 'Althusser specializes in antitheses...one of his chief antitheses concerns "science" and "ideology." He simply opposes one to the other without relating them', (Cornforth, 1973, p. 139).

In its dualism, Marxist structuralism is, therefore, unwittingly tied to the traditions of Aristotelian logic, Cartesian ontology, Kantian epistemology and transcendental metaphysics, and Rousseauean ethics (see, for example, Lucio Colletti's [1972]appropriation of Rousseau on behalf of a Marxist-structuralist ethics; see also Della Volpe, 1962). Marxist dialectics, on the other hand, may well be seen as an altogether new philosophical tradition which, following Hegel's break with Kant, is oriented toward the transcendence of philosophy itself. Thus, Marxian dialectics seeks to transcend the duality of idealism and materialism in Western philosophical history, as well as the endemic dualism within each of these two traditions. Hence, the assimilation of Marxism to structuralism is a highly problematic endeavor and has, in my view, not only distorted the Marxian view of praxis and history (the so-called materialist conception of history), but has also reduced Marxian dialectics to dualistic, pre-dialectical categories. It is because of this philosophical regression to traditional philosophical positions that Marxist structuralism dovetails significantly with that theory of science (viz. logical positivism) which to this day informs both the natural sciences as well as much of academic social science, especially the varieties of structural-functionalism and of systems theory (see Appelbaum, 1979; Heydebrand, 1972; Piccone, 1969; Schmidt, 1969). It is also for this reason that structuralism — even in its Marxist variety — has considerable attraction for academic social scientists who believe in the utility of theoretical integration, if not in accumulation. I myself shall take a critical position with respect to the possibility and utility of theoretical integration between structuralism and Marxian social theory.

MAIN TENETS OF MARXIST STRUCTURALISM

The central analytical contribution of Marxist structuralism takes the form of categorical distinctions rather than theoretical propositions. It is, therefore, useful to look at some of the main concepts developed by Althusser in his 'reading' of Marx, Engels, Lenin, and Mao-Tse-Tung. Since the concepts form a framework of highly interrelated definitions, it is not necessary to begin with a particular baseline of primitive concepts or first principles: any concept will do as a starting point and will, in time, lead us through the whole edifice, returning us in the end to the arbitrary beginning. Let us start with the notion of 'reading' a text.

For Althusser, reading a text is always symptomatic reading, a diagnostic process of producing its underlying, unconscious structure and constructing its problematic. The uncovering of the underlying problematic is similar to Freud's deciphering a patient's symptoms and their verbalizations within the theoretical framework of psychoanalysis, or Marx's deciphering capitalism's deep structure from the ideological materials of previous economists within the paradigmatic framework of historical materialism. The problematic is itself structured in such a way that both presence and absence of symptoms and problems are indications of its operation. For this reason, only a fully developed science (viz. historical materialism in Marx's case) has the capacity to reveal the problematic of the capitalist mode of production. A 'science,' in turn, emerges from pre-scientific and ideological elements by means of a theoretical breakthrough, a kind of intellectual mutation or 'epistemological break.' This epistemological break or rupture, a concept adapted from Bachelard (Lecourt, 1975), is tantamount to a leap from pre-scientific, ideological materials to the logically ordered world of science. As Althusser's translator Ben Brewster puts it, 'this leap involves a radical break with the whole pattern and frame of reference of the pre-scientific (ideological) notions, and the construction of a new pattern (problematic)' (Althusser, 1970, p. 249). Hence, the conjecture that the young Marx had some kind of 'eureka' experience which allowed him to leave behind the remains of Hegelian idealism and dialectics and to enter into the more mature, scientific phase of *Capital*.

Reading Capital (Althusser and Balibar, 1970) is therefore a process of re-tracing Marx's scientific analysis of the capitalist problematic after his epistemological rupture, and producing an even more scientific, logically structured account of the underlying problematic. But lest we think that an epistemological rupture can be empirically identified, we must conceptualize it as an ongoing, continuous separation between ideology and science, which in the last analysis can be diagnosed and overcome only by the theoretical practice of subsequent agents of knowledge production. 'Ideology' is, therefore, merely the ' "lived" relation between men [sic] and their world, or a reflected form of this unconscious relation, for instance a philosophy...it is distinguished from a science not by its falsity, for it can be coherent and logical (for instance, theology) but by the fact that the *practico-social predominates in it over the theoretical*, over knowledge' (Althusser, 1970, p. 252; emphasis added). Because the epistemological break signifies an inherent structural instability in our capacity to *know* on the basis of scientific theory, in contrast to mere ideology or practice (shades of Plato's dualism of knowledge vs opinion and being vs becoming), ideology and theoretically unguided practice may continue to coexist with science (historical materialism) even in future socialist and communist societies. In other words, it is scientific theory and its agents that determine the truth of socialism, not the other way around. As Althusser puts it in a deliberate swipe against pragmatism, 'Marxism is not true because it is successful, but successful because it is true.' What, then, is theory?

For Althusser, theory is theoretical practice, the transformation of ideology into scientific knowledge.

> *Theoretical practice* is...its own criterion and contains in itself definite protocols with which to *validate* the quality of its product, i.e., the criteria of the scientificity of the products of theoretical practice. This is exactly what happens in the real practice of the sciences: once they are truly constituted and developed they have no need for verification from *external* practices to declare the knowledges they produce to be 'true', i.e. to be knowledges. At least for the most developed of them and in the areas of knowledges they have sufficiently mastered, they themselves provide the criterion of validity of the knowledges — this criterion coinciding perfectly with the strict forms of the exercise of the scientific practices considered. [Althusser and Balibar, 1970, p. 56]

The epistemological implications of this position do not change much when Althusser, as a result of his 'self-criticism,' declares that 'philosophy is, in the last instance, class struggle in the field of theory' (1976, p. 37). Since theoretical practice involves language, logic, and scientific procedures, it is outside the base-superstructure dichotomy. The latter comprises, following Engels's remarks to Bloch, the 'external practices' such as economic, political, ideological practice. Theoretical practice, however, is a special kind of structured activity that is subject only to its own determinations and is therefore prior to, and independent from, the base-superstructure problematic. This conception is in line with structuralism's assignment of language to a superior and privileged place in the order of things. But as a political strategy, it follows directly from Stalin's critique of the Soviet linguist Marr as treating language too simplistically as part of the superstructure, and Stalin's theoreticist decision to view language, logic, and the neutral observation language of science as independent of, and prior to, processes of interpretation, theorizing, and philosophizing (Stalin, 1972; see also Gouldner, 1970, p. 453, and Geras, 1977, pp. 264-5). It must be noted here parenthetically that, while Gouldner's account of the linguistic controversy between Marr and Stalin is insightful, his discussion is itself impaired a by dualistic interpretation of 'classical Marxism.'

Within Althusser's theoretical practice, then, scientific practice takes a middle position between philosophy (dialectical materialism, the theory of theoretical practice as such) and scientific knowledge, the product of scientific practice in the form of scientific concepts. Althusser refers in this context to three levels or 'Generalities' involved in the process of knowledge production or theoretical practice. The raw materials of science are Generalities I, the substratum of ideological, philosophical, and previously conceptualized but as yet underdeveloped products of previous 'scientific' activity. Generalities II are the means of theoretical production, the paradigm within which scientific-theoretical activity occurs, in the present case, historical materialism as a scientific theory of history. The application of Generalities II to Generalities I produces Generalities III, the outcome or product of theoretical practice. Generalities III are the scientific concepts that constitute concrete knowledge, the result of transforming abstract, unformed, half-baked thought-material into concrete, more adequately formed, more certain knowledge of the real world.

But since Althusser is an epistemological dualist, the process of cognition and knowledge production can never reach the thing-in-itself: the sense datum immediately present to the knowing mind and the real object known must necessarily remain separate. 'The process of knowledge "ends" as it "begins" entirely without thought' (Geras, 1977). Thus, the 'concrete-in-thought' (Generalities III) is irreducibly distinct from reality, the real object, the 'real-concrete' which exists outside and independently of thought. (Althusser, 1970, p. 186.) This radical epistemological dualism of Althusser leads him to question the traditional distinction between the knowing subject and the object known, and to reject all epistemologies involving a subject-object interaction as 'empiricist,' including pragmatism, voluntarism, idealism, and positivism. Since all of these 'positions,' according to Althusser, involve a process of abstraction by the subject of the essence of the object, they must necessarily remain 'ideological,' just as the subject-object problematic itself is an ideological remnant of idealism. By contrast, Althusser holds that the knowledge of the real object is part of the object itself, a view that comes, paradoxically, close to epistemological realism. In this view there is no need to assume the existence of a thinking or practicing subject (individual or collective) in order to understand the process of knowledge production: the object reveals itself — indeed, inscribes itself — on the 'reader' in the objective, scientific process of theoretical practice, the production of knowledge.

Just as de Saussure had attempted to unify signifier and signified (thought and object of thought) within the concept of the sign, thereby seemingly solving the problem of subject-object duality, so Althusser seeks to unify subject and object under the extra-historical umbrella of theoretical practice, an intellectual coup d'etat which earned him the label 'idealist' (Thompson, 1978, p. 13; Geras, 1977, pp. 264, 266). The social character of science, its existential determination and historical evolution, is not treated as problematical, just as the synchronic character of language as a system of relations had been given priority over the socio-historical development of speech activity. Althusser never makes clear why an epistemological rupture needs theoretical practice to see the light of day. Thus, the relation between practice and rupture is a genuine logical contradiction: it would seem to be understandable only from the contradictory notion of theoretical practice itself, that is from the notion of a practice that occurs simultaneously within the real historical object (viz., as the impersonal, subject-less production of scientific concepts) and outside it (viz. as an a priori practice which is independent of base and superstructure — see A. Glucksmann, 1977, p. 306). The very model for the concept of 'practice' is, of course, not the Marxian 'praxis' — human-sensual-critical-revolutionary activity — but a habitual, recurrent, repetitive, reified, institutionalized form of productive activity. Althusser's choice of terms is significant here since 'practices' are customs, conventions, established procedures. Praxis may give rise to practices, but the two concepts are clearly not the same (see also B. Burris, 1980; Tomich, 1969).

So far we have seen Althusser at work as a student of epistemology and the theory of science, an identity that Althusser later seeks to shed as being the result of a 'theoreticist error' (1976, p. 119). Let us now take a look at Althusser's 'object of knowledge,' such as it is, starting with the concept of 'structure,' by Althusser's own definition a scientific concept that belongs to the level of Generalities III. This tells us that we are not to look for an empirical entity such as a pattern of recurrent social interaction among persons or groups, the historical actions of human collectivities, or 'population distributions among. . . differentiated positions' (Blau, 1977, p. 3). Rather, we are to look for a conceptual model of empirical reality. And here we learn that a 'structure is always the co-presence of all its elements and their relations of dominance and subordination — it is an "ever-pre-given structure" ' (Althusser, 1970, p. 255). This means that we are always dealing with a 'decentered structure in dominance' (p. 256). It is de-centered because it 'is never separable. . . from the elements that constitute it, as each is the condition of existence of all the others; hence it has no center, only a dominant element, and a determination in the last instance' (p. 255). But the dominant element is not fixed for all time; it varies according to the overdeterminations of the contradictions and their uneven development.

In the social formation this overdetermination is, in the last instance, determined by the economy. The economy is ultimately determinant in that it governs which of the instances of the social structure will occupy the immediately determinant place. This structural topography

> signifies that the determination in the last instance by the economic base can only be grasped within a differentiated, therefore complex and articulated whole (the 'Gliederung') in which the determination in the last instance fixes the real difference of the other instances, their relative autonomy, and their own mode of reacting on the base itself. [Althusser, 1976, p. 177]

In other words, that set of elements of the structure usually called the superstructure 'is *relatively autonomous* but the economy is *determinant in the last instance*' (Althusser, 1970, p. 255; see also Poulantzas, 1967).

It is clear from this 'definition' of structure that we must first understand the various other concepts contained in it in order to grasp its meaning. One way to do this is to examine, with

Althusser, the pre-scientific, ideological material that Althusser, through his theoretical practice, endeavors to transform into scientific concepts. One such piece of raw, pre-scientific rock is the Hegelian concept of 'totality.' 'The Hegelian totality presupposes an original, primary essence that lies behind the complex appearance that it has produced by externalization in history; hence it is a structure with a center' (Althusser, 1970, pp. 254-5).

> This concept has become confused by its use by all theorists [sic!] who wish to stress the whole rather than the various parts in any system. However, the Hegelian and the Marxist totalities are quite different. The Hegelian totality is the essence behind the multitude of its phenomena, but the Marxist totality is a de-centered structure in dominance (q.v.). [Althusser, 1970, p. 256]

(Note that 'theorists' are being given real objective status here in contrast to being merely 'readers' or 'bearers' of a structure.)

This rather scholastic, if not dogmatic, distinction between Marxian (structured) and Hegelian (expressive) totalities has been adopted fairly uncritically by much of the sociological scholarship inspired by Althusser and Poulantzas (see Therborn, 1976, p. 399; Burawoy, 1978; Wright, 1978, pp. 11, fn. 2, 14, 30). Its basis is not a critical analysis of Hegel and Marx but an essentially undocumented 'reading' of Hegelian and pre-Hegelian ideas in the light of an already given set of structuralist concepts such as 'structural causality,' 'structural determination,' and 'structural effectivity' (Althusser and Balibar, 1970, pp. 186-90, where there is not a single textual reference to Hegel). In fact, there is no such thing as an 'expressive totality' in Hegel; instead, there is an idealist conception of reality as spirit which, through a dialectical movement of self-activity and self-contradiction, progressively externalizes and objectifies itself in history (see Bernstein, 1971, ch.1). Unlike Marx's careful critique of Hegel's idealism and Feuerbach's materialism (or rather, inverted idealism), Althusser's 'reading' of Hegel and pre-Hegelian idealist influences only succeeds in throwing out the dialectical baby with the idealist bath (cf. Althusser, 1970, pp. 90ff, 161ff). But let us return to the concept of structure.

We saw that the dominant element in a 'social formation' (read: society, the concrete complex whole comprising economic, political, and ideological practices) is 'not fixed for all time but varies according to the overdetermination of the contradictions and their uneven development' (Althusser, 1970, p. 255). The term 'contradiction' refers here to 'the articulation of a practice into the complex whole of the social formation.' It involves the way it contributes to a particular balance of forces, to a concrete constellation of dominant and subordinate structures, to a specific historical conjuncture. The conjuncture of forces in a particular historical moment denotes a state of overdetermination of contradictions such that they are either fused or condensed into a revolutionary rupture, or displaced and thus neutralized in periods of stability. Hence, 'the overdetermination of all contradictions in a social formation means that none can develop simply; the different overdeterminations in different times and places result in quite different patterns of social development', in short, in uneven development (1970, p. 250). But one must not think of the concept of overdetermination in terms of multivariate, empirical-causal imagery, but rather in terms of structural causality or specific effectivity, since the elements that constitute a given social formation are themselves the condition of existence of all the other elements, and 'each has its precise influence on the complex totality, the structure-in-dominance' (1970, p. 251; also Althusser and Balibar, 1970, p. 186). The relationship between structures is therefore not contradictory in the sense that one emerges out of the other and comes to stand against it as its alienated outcome, as for example in the notion that the growth of the productive forces gives rise to the social relations of production. Rather, contradiction is conceptualized as a specific, concrete conflict between two structures, where one is dominant and the other subordinate. This dualistic conception of 'contradiction' is well expressed by Godelier when he says: 'The basic contradiction appears... between production and consumption and between production and circulation of commodities.... It is not a contradiction within a structure, but *between two structures*' (Godelier, 1972, p. 351; emphasis in original). And in a discussion of the 'problem of determination' that leads beyond Althusser and closer to structural-functionalism, Godelier states:

> For a social activity... to play a dominant role in the functioning and evolution of society... it is not enough for this activity to assume a variety of functions: it must also, over and above its explicit finality and functions, directly and from within assume the function of a relation of production.... This hypothesis should be understood as positing the universal existence of a hierarchy among the functions which must be assumed by social relations if a society is to exist as such and reproduce itself [Godelier, 1978, p. 90].

Moreover, 'the distinction between infrastructure and superstructures is not a distinction between institutions. It is essentially a distinction between functions' (1978, p. 85). Here, we are clearly in the theoretical vicinity of Parsons and Smelser and the notions of structural differentiation and adaptive capacity as central to the evolution of social systems.

It would be possible at this point to go on to the voluminous writings of the late Nicos Poulantzas and to show not only Althusser's influence but also the more or less subtle ways in which Poulantzas has modified and to some extent concretized the structuralist heritage. But enough has been said to give a flavor of some of the basic concepts of Marxist structuralism, both as a particular approach to theorizing and as an analytical apparatus applied to the political economy of capitalism. What is striking about Althusser's Marxist structuralism is that it has maintained itself in relative conceptual purity, notwithstanding his self-justification with respect to the problems of science, ideology, philosophy, and theoretical practice (Althusser, 1976, pp. 101-61). Significantly, there is no provision in Marxist structuralism for a critical self-understanding in the sense of critical theory which is rejected as 'idealist' (Therborn, 1977, p. 87). Hence, there is a rather universal defensive stance which rejects most criticisms as based on misunderstanding, or else as animated by speculative rationalism, empiricism, positivism, or any of the other 'most threatening forms of bourgeois ideology: humanism, historicism, pragmatism, evolutionism, philosophical idealism' (1977, p. 146). Criticism can only take the form of a critical discourse *within* theoretical practice. Critique, therefore, remains a sort of logical bricolage and reconstruction, such as the re-definition of concepts, rather than self-transformation by means of removing the conditions of limited, constrained, or distorted consciousness (Connerton, 1976, p. 19; see also Paul Ricoeur's distinction [1970, p. 26] between restoration of meaning and de-mystification of illusion). It is for these reasons, then, that Althusser's 'self-criticism' cannot be anything but self-justification, just as Hindess and Hirst's 'auto-critique' (1977) is a retrenchment rather than a critique. The point is significant because I believe that the suppression of critique is intimately connected with the reification of consciousness in structuralism and positivism, an intellectual atrophy which Lukacs (1971, pp. 110-48) has identified with 'the antinomies of bourgeois thought' and of the capitalist political economy (see also Lenzer,

1975). My own critical stance toward Marxist structuralism does not signify an uncritical acceptance of Lukács's 'Hegelian Marxism,' or an orthodox interpretation of Marx, or a dogmatic suppression of diverse viewpoints within Marxism. Rather, it is a reaffirmation of the need for practical criticism and for the possibility of criticism as central elements of Marxian dialectics.

Given the strict separation between science and ideology, then, it is not surprising that Marxist structuralism has been more or less successfully adapted to a Marxist-scientific version of systems theory which in many ways echoes the fundamental assumptions of structural-functional 'empirical' theory and its associated theory of science (Bridges, 1974; Frankel and Trimberger, 1976; Bernstein, 1978, Part I; Plaut, 1978; Appelbaum, 1979). Let us take a closer look at the similarities and differences between Marxist structuralism and empirical social science.

THE ADAPTATION OF MARXIST STRUCTURALISM TO EMPIRICAL SOCIAL THEORY

One of the central elements of the sociological concept of social fact since Durkheim has been its sociological realism, anti-reductionism, and hard determinism — in short, the practice of describing social phenomena in collective terms and explaining them in terms of social laws (Brodbeck, 1968, p. 239). Similarly, Marx occasionally used a concept of social structure that had a definite anti-reductionist ring. For example, 'in the social production which men carry on they enter into definite relations that are indispensable and independent of their will' (Marx, 1904, p. 11); or: 'Society does not consist of individuals, but expresses the sum of interrelations, the relations within which these individuals stand' (Marx, 1973, p. 265); or again: 'I paint the capitalist and the landlord in no sense couleur de rose. But here individuals are dealt with only in so far as they are the personifications of economic categories, embodiments of particular class relations and class interests' (Marx, 1906, p. 15). A more 'structuralist' translation of the last phrase, sponsored by *New Left Review*, renders it as 'personifications of economic categories, the bearers (Traeger) of particular class relations and interests' (Marx, 1976, p. 92).

These notions of social structure can, indeed, be interpreted as 'structuralist,' but only if one separates 'structural constraints' from a dialectical conception of human social praxis where 'men make their own history' even though 'they do not make it just as they please' (cf. Appelbaum, 1978). Sociological determinism has long been exposed as harboring an 'oversocialized conception of man' (Wrong, 1961) and being in need of 'bringing men back in' (Homans, 1964). Anti-reductionism and the phobia of methodological individualism, then, clearly unite classical sociology and Marxist structuralism.

Another common element is anti-historicism. Here it was the specific contribution of functionalism that sought to replace the search for historical origins by an analysis of the consequences of social patterns for the maintenance and reproduction of social structures and for the integration and adaptation of social systems (Merton, 1957; Parsons, 1950; Godelier, 1972). Thus, the varieties of structural-functionalism and of systems theory provide perhaps the most telling basis for comparison with Marxist structuralism. Not only is there a common conception of needs, functions, and structures as universal and trans-historical features of all societies, but the conceptualization of social change as recurrent process, and of conflict and exchange as functional for social integration, is remarkably similar in both functionalist and structuralist social theories. Both types of theories go far in describing the functions of different institutions (including the state) for the reproduction of society, but fail to deal with the limits of reproduction, legitimation, and adaptation. It must be noted that 'limits' in structuralist terminology does not refer to the historically finite failure of dialectical mediations and the collapse or resolution of contradictions, but to structural limits 'within which some other structure or process can vary and [which] establish[es] probabilities for the specific structures or processes that are possible within those limits' (Wright, 1978, p. 16).

Thus, structures and social systems are conceptualized in terms of relatively autonomous levels, sub-systems, or 'regions,' and social causation is replaced by a binary concept of evolutionary 'anchorage' and cybernetic 'control' (Parsons, 1967), not to mention the generalization of functionalist analysis to all forms of sociological analysis under the disclaimer of 'the myth of functional analysis' (Davis, 1959). Clearly, among functionalists, Parsons here comes closest to Lévi-Strauss's dissociation of system and history. Finally, the sociological concepts of value-neutrality and objectivity resonate well with Althusser's separation of science and ideology. Moreover, the criteria for adequate scientific theorizing inspired by Popper and codified by Nagel, Braithwaite, and others have entered sociological theorizing through the work of Merton (1957), Blau (1977, pp. 11-17), Galtung (1967, pp. 315, 458), and others. Adequate scientific procedures must include a provision for different levels of abstraction and for a broad explanatory scope of theories, a precise and determinate definition of concepts and hypotheses, which, in turn, permits the identification of negative evidence and allows for a high degree of testability (falsifiability). Good theories must be simple and parsimonious, must integrate interrelated propositions, and must entail a systematic, formal hypothetico-deductive model to permit both logical derivation and empirical testing of specific propositions. Except for the 'empiricist' criterion of testability and its related elements of explanatory and predictive capacity, these are scientific procedures on which both empirical social theorists and Marxist structuralists could agree, and even testability is beginning to be admitted to Marxist structuralism, albeit only in the form of 'empirical studies,' 'relationships of determination...between categories and the appearances of empirical investigation,' or simply 'illustrations' (Wright, 1978, pp. 10, 15, 17).

To guard against naive empiricism, empirical generalizations must, of course, themselves be interpreted in terms of higher-level theoretical generalizations. Social theories must provide scientific explanation of the determinate and invariant (though not necessarily invariable) elements of social structure. And Merton and Althusser would squarely agree on the importance of separating the history of theory from the systematic structure of scientific theory, since there is an ideological, pre-scientific substratum in the historical raw materials which leads to an 'attractive but fatal confusion of utilizable sociological theory with the history of sociological theory' (Merton, as quoted in Bernstein, 1978, p. 14). Just as the 'lore' of social theory can and must be separated from its scientific content, so the utilizable elements in Marx's social theory can be operationalized, propositionalized, and thus 'made relevant to contemporary social-science inquiry' (Zeitlin, 1967, p. 155; see also Coser, 1979; Szymanski, 1973; Rodinson, 1969, p. 67).

However, the adaptation of Marxist structuralism to contemporary social science inquiry is neither complete nor without its problems. Ultimately, Althusser's concept of science shares more with Parsons's anti-positivism than with the neo-positivism of empirical theory. One must not, therefore, overlook the important differences that continue to exist beneath the analytic and programmatic parallels.

At the outset, it is crucial to understand that the language of science in Marxist structuralism is different from the terminology of either empirical theory or Marxist historical-dialectical analysis. Similar terms may be used, but they have different meanings. Concepts such as empiricism, positivism, theory, explanation, and causation are defined in different ways, and there are also fundamental differences with respect to the definition of such Marxist categories as dialectic, contradiction, mediation, ideology, critique, and practice.

It is for these reasons that Althusser claims to be anti-empiricist and anti-positivist while at the same time clinging, in the notion of theoretical practice, to a highly formalized concept of science and of self-correcting scientific procedure. This is, of course, already contained in the structuralist notion that 'language bears within itself its own critique' (Derrida, as quoted by Lemert, 1979, p. 101). How can Marxist structuralism be scientific, yet non-positivist and non-empiricist? The answer lies largely in Bachelard and Lévi-Strauss's conceptions of science as constructing models rather than theories, although Althusser and Lévi-Strauss differ with respect to fine points of epistemology (M. Glucksmann, 1974, pp. 115, 139). Thus, a model can be understood as a conceptual framework, a way of defining reality which is more or less useful and adequate for understanding and insight (see Brodbeck, 1968, p. 579). In its simplest form, a model is a replica, a reproduction, an isomorphic reconstruction of different aspects and levels of reality. But a model is, of course, also an intentional, 'interested' way of reproducing reality (Barthes, 1963). Nevertheless, as a model it is true by definition; that is, it has the truth-value of logical or tautological statements.

By contrast, a theory can be viewed as a set of interrelated propositions that, while having logical coherence, can also be tested empirically by means of correspondence between observable empirical regularities and theoretical explanations. It is this latter notion of an 'analytical theory of science' that is typically defined as 'positivist' (Habermas, 1976, p. 131) and rejected by both Althusser and Habermas as a bourgeois concept of science. But instead of subsuming analytic and interpretive elements under a higher-level conception of critical social science with practical intent (Horkheimer, 1972; Habermas, 1976), Althusser unwittingly regresses to a primitive notion of science as a spontaneous recognition of preformed, 'ever-pregiven structures' which must, paradoxically, be produced through theoretical practice. As Lévi-Strauss puts it, 'The social structure has nothing to do with empirical reality but with models built after it' (as quoted in Blau, 1977, p. 2). Or, in Godelier's words,

> For Marx, as for Claude Lévi-Strauss, 'structures' should not be confused with visible 'social relations' but constitute a level of reality invisible but present behind the visible social relations. The logic of the latter, and the laws of social practice more generally, depend on the functioning of these hidden structures [as quoted in M. Glucksman, 1974, p. 145].

The structuralist theoretician, then, is like a fifteenth-century alchemist, mixing structural elements in the laboratory of abstractions and distilling ever-new structural concoctions. Somehow, theoretical practice strikes one as magic rather than science. Althusser's arsenal of theoretical concepts and their specious definition is a good starting point. For Althusser, 'empiricism' refers to the naive empiricist belief in the cognitive relevance of immediate sense data, and 'positivism' to the naive, vulgar one-dimensionality of empirical regularities which are generalized to the level of universal laws. Both notions are largely caricatures of social science research, especially of critical sociology. They constitute, in Thompson's words, a 'continuous, willful, and theoretically-crucial confusion between "empiricism" (that is, philosophical positivism and all its kin) and the empirical mode of intellectual practice' (Thompson, 1978, p. 10).

A theory, for Althusser, is not a set of interrelated, testable propositions to be confronted by empirical evidence, but an a priori conceptual model that is neither true nor false, but only more or less diagnostically adequate for the symptomatic reading of a given problematic. Althusser functions here as the political clinician who diagnoses a case, then recommends treatment, rather than as a self-critical researcher with questions and hypotheses. Explanation is based not on an assessment of temporal-causal relationships but on an explication of a priori determinations. As Lemert puts it, following Umberto Eco, 'Explanation is the analysis of relations between structures and between structures and actions at a given historical moment, Eco, 1976, 125-129' (Lemert, 1979, p. 107). Hence, causality always refers to *structural causality* or effectivity, the pre-given relation between levels of structure (deep structure vs surface structure) or between dominant and subordinate structures; hence, it refers to synchronic determination at a given point in time. Following Althusser and Poulantzas, Wright (1978, p. 15) has recently decomposed the concept of structural causality into six basic modes of determination: structural limitation, selection, reproduction/non-reproduction, limits of functional compatibility, transformation, and mediation. But here, too, the analytical has precedence over the empirical in that these modes of determination are organized into

> models of determination, that is, schematic representations of the complex inter-connections of the various modes of determination involved in a given structural process. Such models of determination can be considered symbolic maps of what Althusserians have generally referred to as 'structured totalities'. [Wright, 1978, p. 15]

The priority of the analytical over the empirical was, of course, always a hallmark of Parsons's conception of systems and sub-systems; hence his proverbial insistence on the development of a conceptual framework as a precondition for the evolution of general theory, which was essentially equated with systems theory. Explanation and testing, similarly, were seen as an application of conceptual models after the fact, rather than as a future-oriented or, at least, contingent test of the explanatory power of a theory. Needless to say, both conceptions of explanation fail to take into account the emergent qualities of social construction as part of a dialectics of practice. Hence, the disjuncture between explanation and prediction in both Marxist structuralism and systems theory.

By the same token, however, the definition of Marxist categories by Marxist structuralists differs significantly from their use by Marx or from critical interpretations of their meaning within the overall framework of Marxian social theory. For example, dialectics is not seen as a historical process of development of contradictions and mediations, but is either rejected as a Hegelian 'dialectic of consciousness' or reified in the concept of overdetermination. Contradictions are seen not as a historical-dialectical process of development from activity to outcome and its potential alienation

(Heydebrand, 1977), but as a dualistic relation of conflict between a particular 'practice' (economic, political, ideological) and the total constellation of practices in a social formation. Mediations are seen not as the temporary suspension (not resolution) of historical contradictions, but as a kind of ' "contextual variable": processes of mediation determine the terrain on which other modes of determination operate' (Wright, 1978, p. 23). Ideology is seen not as a form of limited consciousness (see Block, 1978, p. 212; Ollman, 1978, pp. 239; 1973), but as lived experience, the 'lived relation between men and their world, or a reflected form of this unconscious relation, for instance a philosophy' (Althusser, 1970, p. 252). Hence, ideology or ideological practice is part of the superstructure and must be strictly distinguished from science which stands outside base and superstructure. As I have already indicated, critique is dealt with either as ideology (interpretation) or as scientific rectification of ideology. There is no such thing as critique of science or theoretical practice, hence the ridicule heaped on the idea of a critical theory of society (Therborn, 1977, p. 83).

Most significantly, the concept of praxis in Marx is decomposed into different practices and levels of practical consciousness, an important point of contact between Althusser and Habermas. Here, the dialectical element in 'human sensuous, practical activity' (Marx, in Tucker, 1978, p. 143) is reduced to dualistic, pre-dialectical constructs: base and superstructure in Althusser, labor and interaction in Habermas (1974, p. 142). As a result, human collective activity, including class struggle, is first de-activated and cleansed of its ideological and spontaneous elements, then theoretically revived and reconstituted under the auspices of science and the guidance of the party. This procedure is similar to the structuralist treatment of social and historical change. The image I have of the structuralist treatment of social change is one of heavy movers who, instead of seeing a river in flux, freeze it, cut the ice into blocks, carry them downstream, and re-assemble them. It is not accidental that systems theory has had similar problems in dealing with historical change (Nisbet, 1969, p. 265; Frankel and Trimberger, 1976; see also the structuralist problems of dealing with historical transformations and the transition between modes of production; for instance, Hindess and Hirst, 1977).

EVALUATION AND CONCLUSION

In the preceding pages I have discussed the origins of structuralism
in structural linguistics and anthropology, the adaptation of Marxism to structuralism, the main concepts of Althusser's Marxism,
and the similarities and differences between Marxist structuralism
and academic social science. In evaluating Marxist structuralism as
an intellectual and ideological phenomenon, it must first be
acknowledged that it has played an important role as a theoretical
catalyst in the discussion and clarification of Marxian ideas.
Precisely because of their analytic rigor and their preoccupation
with exact concepts, precise definitions, and determinate meanings,
Marxist structuralists have forced others into the clarification of
their own ideas, the questioning of fundamental assumptions, and
the discussion of Marxist ideas even by non-Marxists. This is a
positive contribution of considerable significance and has caused
Marxist ideas to be taken seriously in their theoretical import, not
just as a curiosum of nineteenth-century intellectual history. Marxist structuralist writers have exhibited a very high level of intellectual productivity and have put out a voluminous body of literature
touching on a vast array of issues in the social sciences, art, politics,
and philosophy.

However, Marxist structuralism is an internally contradictory
amalgam of two radically opposed intellectual and ideological notions: the reification and universalization of the structural
categories of the capitalist political economy and, emerging from it
and ultimately opposing it, the Marxist dialectical critique of the
reification and of its stifling political consequences. We have seen
that structuralism embodies a search for an absolute reference
point, an arrest of history, a search for permanent order that an-
ticipates the technocratic ideology of control functions, levels,
structure, and system as inevitable — indeed, as ever pre-given
features of social formations. Structuralism thus reveals itself not
only as an ideology, but as 'ideology of non-ideology' (Schiwy,
1969, p. 27; see also Habermas, 1970). The methodological search
for unchanging, precise categories has turned into the formulation
of 'theoretical' principles which impose a certain fixed ontological
order on the 'real object' by means of a reified 'object of
knowledge.' This is not accidental, since structuralism began as a
methodology, yet ended up as a disembodied, content-less
metaphysical schema. Most crucially, Althusser's absolute

reference point, theoretical practice, functions as an ultimate arbiter of truth and is, therefore, immune to historical change, above and beyond the reach of critical interpretation, and independent of practical transformation. This is an attempt at thought control and suppression of dissent which is profoundly at variance with the Marxist conception of dialectical critique and praxis as the social and historical sources of knowledge and science (see Sohn-Rethel, 1978; Thompson, 1978; Tomich, 1969).

Moreover, the structuralist emphasis on the synchronic functioning of a system tends to hold constant the parameters of its production, construction, and transformation. Like all forms of systems analysis, it tends to focus instead on the internal dynamics of the system, namely the interchange between the structural parts of the system, or in the language of *Capital*, on the sphere of circulation. One could argue that it may well be the task of the moment to understand the resilience of capitalism; hence there may be some value in focusing on the superstructural functioning of the capitalist system, its mechanisms of control, integration, and adaptation. However, we do not want to disregard the historical changes in capitalism, the articulation of its internal contradictions, and the practical possibilities of its transformation. Structuralists do not even raise the question of whether systems conceptions of social structure can logically accommodate such notions as contradictions and historical dialectical change. The answer is that they cannot. This is true quite apart from the fact that there is an a priori methodological decision to exclude diachronic or historical analysis from consideration, or to treat it as secondary or subordinate to synchronic analysis. Basically, the fundamental dualism of structuralism precludes a dialectical analysis. Social systems can, of course, be analyzed in terms of such concepts as strain, stress, tension, selection, regulation, incompatibility, conflict, condensation, fusion, displacement, dominance, or their synonyms. The problem is that Marxist structuralists, just like sociological conflict theorists, tend to use the words 'dialectics' and 'contradiction' to refer to any or all of these concepts, but their meaning is often limited and distorted since 'dialectics' and 'contradiction' are silently defined in dualistic, conflict-theoretical, or systems-theoretical terms. According to Godelier, the notion of internal contradictions as the source of change must be abandoned; 'change has to be thought in terms of "variable contradictions between invariant structures" ' (Zimmerman, 1976, p. 78).

At the beginning of this essay I raised the question of possible reasons for the adaptation of Marxism to structuralism. I suggested that the historical constellation of political forces after World War II had triggered a certain ideological crisis within Marxism, a crisis that has been widely acknowledged and documented (Althusser, 1978; Howard and Klare, 1972; Claudin, 1979; Sartre, 1968; Sweezy, 1979; Thompson, 1978). However, the ideological crisis in Marxism may be seen as but a temporary phase in the ongoing and deepening crisis of capitalism as a world-historical system. The pessimistic 'metaphysical pathos' of structuralism is shared by most ideological and philosophical trends that have emerged since the nineteenth century. This pessimism characterizes not only classical sociology (see Gouldner, 1955) and the later forms of the Frankfurt School of critical sociology — for example Horkheimer's turn to the pessimistic philosophy of Schopenhauer — but also the two other intellectual movements most closely related to structuralism, viz. phenomenology and existentialism. In all three movements this pessimism appears as a crisis of meaning, as a crisis of understanding and authenticity and, most importantly, as a crisis of political commitment. The significance of this brief and discursive comparison is that each of the three movements constitutes an attempted ideological solution to the underlying but differentially experienced problems of bourgeois capitalism in delivering on its promises.

The responses to the political and ideological problems of liberal democracy, apart from libertarian and critical Marxism, have been remarkably similar and read like a Freudian case study. First, there is a retreat from the flux and uncertainty of history, a denial of meaningful historical change. Sisyphus-like repetition of activities is seen as inevitable; change as eternal recurrence. This goes hand in hand with a denial of meaningful historical identity, a retreat from authentic subjectivity and community into the determined objectivity of language, logic, and science (structuralism, positivism), into transcendental essences (phenomenology), or into pure existence (existentialism). In each of these alternatives, a compulsive search for an absolute reference point animates the attempt to 'overcome' the fatal, dualistic dissociation between the emotional and the intellectual, between existence and essence, form and content, science and ideology, subject and object, theory and praxis. Each starts out as a radical rejection of metaphysics; yet all end up as ontologies. Each denies the necessity or even the possibility of historical self-transformation, of individual or collective praxis. Hence, each is a-critical or anti-critical with respect to its own ideological limitations or, worse, with respect to the historically finite movement of the capitalist political economy. Since there is 'no exit,' no way to confront the historical movement of capitalism or to regain control over a system that seems out of control, there are few alternatives; either 'waiting for Godot' ('the hour of determination in the last instance never comes'), or the hedonistic immersion into the isolated, sensual self, or political bricolage (including Eurocommunism and technocracy), or the ultimate self-negation: depression and suicide (Durkheim's fourth 'fatalistic' type due to over-integration or over-determination). In Foucault, a former disciple of Althusser, this nihilism becomes a 'structuralism without structures' (Piaget, 1970, p. 128). Foucault's gloomy resignation is rooted in the presumed self-liquidation of structuralism through the abstraction and generalization of language to the point of a mathematical a priori:

> by stretching its possibilities to the breaking point [structuralism] spells the end of man. In reaching the summit of all possible speech, man does not attain to its heart but to the boundary of what limits it: death roams about in this region, thought becomes extinguished, the original promise indefinitely remote. [Piaget, 1970, p. 129]

Thus, phenomenology, existentialism, and structuralism appear as the three great products of bourgeois self-alienation and self-hatred, the modern indicators of a deep ideological malaise, of epistemological despair (are we real, are you real?), existential anxiety, and ethical nihilism (what is to be done? or undone?). Hence, they are not only infinitely adaptable to different ideologies such as idealism, materialism, Christianity, Marxism and positivist social science; but they also permit various forms of intellectual recycling and substitution among themselves: phenomenologists become structuralists, existentialists become phenomenologists, structuralists become existentialists (see Mayrl, 1978, on the affinity between structuralist and phenomenological Marxism and, generally, Poster, 1975). It appears as if Nietzsche's tragic vision of 'eternal recurrence' and his call for the 'transvaluation of all values' are heeded today not only by the 'new philosophers,' sociobiologists, and technocratic system planners, but by all true believers turned cynics.

Marxist structuralism, in general, and Althusser's 'metaphysical passion for a system' (A. Glucksmann, 1977, p. 314), in particular, exemplify the search for an answer in an especially contradictory way. Hence, on the one hand, the emphasis on insulated theoretical practice, science, relative autonomy, and determination in the last instance, and, on the other hand, the relegation of ideology, politics, and class struggle to a netherworld of mere historical existence. From a critical Marxist perspective, however, the most problematic consequences of this ideological dead-end are its convergence with the widespread manifestation of political passivity and apathy, and the bleak pessimism as to the possibility of political praxis, a phenomenon that Alan Wolfe and others have described as alienated politics (Wolfe, 1977, p. 288). Thus, it is precisely with respect to politics that Marxist structuralism has had its most serious internal problems, epitomized first by Althusser's silence vis-à-vis the French workers' and student revolt in May 1968, and then by his self-castigation for having placed theory above the class struggle without really changing his basic theoretical position. And it is here that Marxist structuralism tends to feed directly into the systemic needs for order, stability, and popular acquiescence of both the capitalist and the state-socialist societies. The politically most damaging element of Marxist structuralism is that it provides the basis for a theoretical justification of technocratic state — administration — rather than for a dialectical critique and transformation of all reifying and alienating forces in recent history, starting with the class structure and the state apparatus of contemporary capitalism.

REFERENCES

ALTHUSSER, Louis (1970) *For Marx*. New York: Vintage.
ALTHUSSER, Louis (1976) *Essays in Self-Criticism*. London: New Left Books.
ALTHUSSER, Louis (1978) 'The Crisis of Marxism,' *Theoretical Review*, 7 (September/October): 1-10.
ALTHUSSER, Louis and Etienne BALIBAR (1970) *Reading Capital*. New York: Pantheon Books.

APPELBAUM, Richard (1979) 'Born-Again Functionalism: A Reconsideration of Althusser's Structuralism,' *Insurgent Sociologist*, 9, 1 (Summer): 18.

BALBUS, Isaac, D. (1977) 'Commodity Form and Legal Form: An Essay on the "Relative Autononmy" of the Law,' *Law & Society Review*, 11(3) (Winter): 571.

BARTHES, Roland (1963) 'L'Activite structuraliste,' *Les Lettres nouvelles* (February): 13-37.

BARTHES, Ronald (1964) *Elements of Semiology*. London: Cape.

BAUDRILLARD, Jean (1972) *Pour une Critique de l'economie politique du signe*. Paris: Gallimard (*The Mirror of Production*, translated by M. Poster. St Louis: Telos Press, 1975).

BERNSTEIN, Richard J. (1971) *Praxis and Action*. Philadelphia: University of Pennsylvania Press.

BERNSTEIN, Richard J. (1978) *The Restructuring of Social and Political Theory*. Philadelphia: University of Pennsylvania Press.

BLACKBURN, Robin and Gareth STEDMAN JONES (1972) 'Louis Althusser and the Struggle for Marxism,' in D. Howard and K. E. Klare (eds), *The Unknown Dimension: European Marxism since Lenin*. New York: Basic Books.

BLAU, Peter M. (1977) *Inequality and Heterogeneity: A Primitive Theory of Social Structure*. New York: Free Press.

BLOCK, Fred (1978) 'Class Consciousness and Capitalist Rationalization: A Reply to Critics,' *Socialist Review*, 8 (4-5):212.

BRIDGES, Amy Beth (1974) 'Nicos Poulantzas and the Marxist Theory of the State,' *Politics and Society*, 4 (2) (Winter): 161.

BRODBECK, May (ed.) (1968) *Readings in the Philosophy of the Social Sciences*. New York: Macmillan.

BURAWOY, Michael (1978) 'Contemporary Currents in Marxist Theory,' p. 16 in S. McNall (ed.), *Theoretical Perspectives in Sociology*, New York: St Martin's Press.

BURRIS, Beverly (1980) Review of Pierre Bourdieu, *Outline of a Theory of Practice, Insurgent Sociologist*, 9(4) (Spring): 89-91.

BURRIS, Val (1979) 'Structuralism and Marxism,' *Insurgent Sociologist*, 9 (1) (Summer — special issue on Marxism and Structuralism): 4-17.

CALLINICOS, Alex (1976) *Althusser's Marxism*. London: Pluto Press.

CHOMSKY, Noam (1965) 'Persistent Topics in Linguistic Theory,' *Diogenes*, 15 (Fall): 19.

CLAUDIN, Fernando (1979) 'Some Reflections on the Crisis in Marxism,' *Socialist Review*, 45 (May/June): 137.

COLLETTI, Lucio (1972) *From Rousseau to Lenin: Studies of Ideology and Society*. New York: Monthly Review Press.

CONNERTON, Paul (1976) 'Introduction,' *Critical Sociology: Selected Readings*. New York: Penguin.

CORNFORTH, Maurice (1973) 'Some Comments on Louis Althusser's Reply to John Lewis,' *Marxism Today* (May): 139.

COSER, Lewis (1979) 'Is it Time to Bury Karl Marx?' Annual Meetings of the American Sociological Association, Boston.

COWARD, Rosalind and John ELLIS (1977). *Language and Materialism: Developments in Semiology and the Theory of the Subject*. London: Routledge & Kegan Paul.

CULLER, Jonathan (1977) *Ferdinand de Saussure*. New York: Penguin Books.

DAVIS, Kingsley (1959) 'The Myth of Functional Analysis,' *American Sociological Review*, 24 (December): 757.

DELLA VOLPE, Galvano (1962) *Rousseau e Marx*. Rome: Riuniti.

DERRIDA, Jacques (1972) 'Structure, Sign, and Play in the Discourse of the Human Sciences,' p. 247 in R. Macksey and E. Donato (eds), *The Structuralist Controversy*. Baltimore: Johns Hopkins University Press.

de SAUSSURE, Ferdinand (1966) *Course in General Linguistics*. New York: McGraw Hill.

ECO, Umberto (1976) *A Theory of Semiotics*. Bloomington: Indiana University Press.

ENGELS, Friedrich (1978) Letter to Joseph Bloch and to C. Schmidt, p. 760 in R. C. Tucker (ed.), *The Marx-Engels Reader*. New York: Norton. (Letter first published in 1890.)

FRANKEL, Linda and Ellen Kay TRIMBERGER (1976) 'The Limitations of Marxist-Structuralism as a Theory of Social Change,' Annual Meetings of the American Sociological Association.

FROMM, Erich (1961) *Marx's Concept of Man*. New York: Ungar.

FROMM, Erich (ed.) (1966) *Socialist Humanism: An International Symposium*. New York: Doubleday Anchor.

GALTUNG, Johan (1967) *Theory and Methods of Social Research*. New York: Columbia University Press.

GENETTE, Gerrard (1965) 'Structuralisme et critique litteraire,' *L'Arc*, 26:30.

GERAS, Norman (1972) 'Marx and the Critique of Political Economy,' in R. Blackburn (ed.), *Ideology in Social Science*. New York: Pantheon.

GERAS, Norman (1977) 'Althusser's Marxism: An Assessment,' in New Left Review (eds), *Western Marxism, A Critical Reader*. London: Verso.

GLABERMAN, Martin (1969) 'Lenin vs. Althusser,' *Radical America*, 3(5) (September): 19.

GLUCKSMANN, André (1977) 'A Ventriloquist Structuralism,' in New Left Review (eds.), *Western Marxism, A Critical Reader*. London: Verso.

GLUCKSMANN, Miriam (1974) *Structuralist Analysis in Contemporary Social Thought: A Comparison of the Theories of Claude Lévi-Strauss and Louis Althusser*. London: Routledge & Kegan Paul.

GODELIER, Maurice (1972) *Rationality and Irrationality in Economics*. New York: Monthly Review Press.

GODELIER, Maurice (1973) 'Structure and Contradiction in Capital,' in R. Blackburn (ed.), *deology in Social Science*. New York: Vintage.

GODELIER, Maurice (1978) 'Infrastructures, Societies, and History,' *New Left Review*, 112 (November-December): 84.

GOULDNER, Alvin W. (1955) 'Metaphysical Pathos and the Theory of Bureaucracy,' *American Political Science Review*, 49: 496.

GOULDNER, Alvin W. (1970) *The Coming Crisis of Western Sociology*. New York: Basic Books.

HABERMAS, Juergen (1970) 'Technology and Science as "Ideology",' in J. Habermas, *Toward a Rational Society*. Boston: Beacon.

HABERMAS, Juergen (1974) 'Labor and Interaction,' in J. Habermas, *Theory and Practice*. Boston: Beacon.

HABERMAS, Juergen (1976) 'The Analytical Theory of Science and Dialectics,' in T. W. Adorno et al. (eds), *The Positivist Dispute in German Sociology*. New York: Harper Torchbooks.

HEYDEBRAND, Wolf (1972) Review of Talcott Parsons, *The System of Modern Societies*. *Contemporary Sociology*, 1 (September): 381.

HEYDEBRAND, Wolf (1977) 'Organizational Contradictions in Public Bureaucracies: Toward a Marxian Theory of Organizations,' *Sociological Quarterly*, 18 (Winter): 83.

HINDESS, Barry (1977) *Philosophy and Methodology in the Social Sciences*. Atlantic Highlands, NJ: Humanities Press.

HINDESS, Barry and Paul HIRST (1977) *Mode of Production and Social Formation: An Auto-Critique of 'Pre-Capitalist Modes of Production'*. Atlantic Highlands, NJ: Humanities Press.

HOMANS, George C. (1964) 'Bringing Men Back In,' *American Sociological Review*, 29 (December): 808.

HORKHEIMER, Max (1972) 'Traditional and Critical Theory,' in *Critical Theory: Selected Essays*. New York: Seabury Press.

HOWARD, Dick and Karl E. KLARE (eds) (1972) *The Unknown Dimension: European Marxism since Lenin*. New York: Basic Books.

LACAN, Jacques (1966) *Ecrits*. Paris: Ed. du Seuil.

LECOURT, Dominique (1975) *Marxism and Epistemology: Bachelard, Canguilhem, Foucault*. London: New Left Books.

LEFEBVRE, Henri (1966a) *Le Language et la société*. Paris: Gallimard.

LEFEBVRE, Henri (1966b) 'Claude Lévi-Strauss ou le nouvel Eleatisme,' *L'Homme et la société*, 1 (July-September), 21.

LEFEBVRE, Henri (1968) *The Sociology of Marx*. New York: Random House, Vintage Books.

LEFEBVRE, Henri (1971) *Au-dela du Structuralisme*. Paris: Anthropos.

LEMERT, Charles (1979) 'Structuralist Semiotics and the Decentering of Sociology,' p. 96 in S. McNall (ed.), *Theoretical Perspectives in Sociology*. New York: St Martin's Press.

LENZER, Gertrude (ed.) (1975) *Auguste Comte and Positivism: The Essential Writings*. New York: Harper.

LÉVI-STRAUSS, Claude (1966) *The Savage Mind*. Chicago: University Press.

LÉVI-STRAUSS, Claude (1967) *Structural Anthropology*. New York: Doubleday Anchor.

LEWIS, John (1972) 'The Althusser Case,' *Marxism Today* (January): 23.

LUKÁCS, Georg (1971) *History and Class Consciousness*. London: Merlin Press.

MARX, Karl (1904) *A Contribution to the Critique of Political Economy*. New York: Charles H. Kerr (first published 1859).

MARX, Karl (1906) *Capital*, vol. I. New York: Charles H. Kerr (first published 1867).

MARX, Karl (1967) *Writings of the Young Marx on Philosophy and Society*, edited by L. Easton and K. Guddat. New York: Doubleday.

MARX, Karl (1973) *Grundrisse*, translated by M. Nicolaus. Harmondsworth: Penguin (first published 1939-41).

MARX, Karl (1976) *Capital*, vol. I. New York: Vintage (first published 1867).

MAYRL, William W. (1978) 'Science and Praxis: The Epistemological Foundations of Structural and Phenomenological Marxism,' San Francisco: Annual Meetings of the American Sociological Association.

MERLEAU-PONTY, Maurice (1973) *The Adventures of the Dialectic*. Evanston, Ill.: Northwestern University Press.

MERTON, Robert K. (1957) *Social Theory and Social Structure*, rev. ed. Glencoe: Free Press (first published 1949).

MITCHELL, Juliet (1974) *Psychoanalysis and Feminism*. London: Allen Lane.

NISBET, Robert A. (1969) *Social Change and History*. New York: Oxford University Press.

OLLMAN, Bertell (1973) 'Marxism and Political Science: Prolegomenon to a Debate on Marx's Method,' *Politics and Society* (Summer): 491.

OLLMAN, Bertell (1978) 'On Teaching Marxism,' in B. Ollman and T. M. Norton (eds), *Studies in Socialist Pedagogy*. New York: Monthly Review Press.

PARSONS, Talcott (1950) *The Social System*. Glencoe, Ill.: Free Press.

PARSONS, Talcott (1967) 'Evolutionary Universals in Society,' in T. Parsons, *Sociological Theory and Modern Society*. New York: Free Press.

PARSONS, Talcott (1971) *The System of Modern Societies*. Englewood Cliffs, NJ: Prentice-Hall.

PIAGET, Jean (1970) *Structuralism*. New York: Harper Torchbooks.

PICCONE, Paul (1969) 'Structuralist Marxism?' *Radical America*, 3(5) (September): 25.

PINGAUD, Bernard (1965) 'Comment on Devient Structuraliste,' *L'Arc*, 26:1.

PLAUT, Martin (1978) 'The Problem of Positivism in the Work of Nicos Poulantzas,' *Telos* 36 (Summer): 159.

POSTER, Mark (1975) *Existential Marxism in Postwar France: From Sartre to Althusser*. Princeton: University Press.

POULANTZAS, Nicos (1967) 'A Propos de la theorie marxiste du droit,' *Archives de Philosophie du droit*, tome XII: Marx et le droit moderne, M. Villey (ed.). Paris: Editions Sirey.

POULANTZAS, Nicos (1973) *Political Power and Social Classes*. London: New Left Books.

POULANTZAS, Nicos (1974) *Fascism and Dictatorship*: London: New Left Books.

POULANTZAS, Nicos (1975) *Classes in Contemporary Capitalism*. London: New Left Books.

POULANTZAS, Nicos (1976) *The Crisis of the Dictatorships*. London: New Left Books.

RANCIERE, Jacques (1974) *La Lecon d'Althusser*. Paris. Gallimard.

RICOEUR, Paul (1970) *Freud and Philosophy: An Essay on Interpretation*. New Haven, Conn.: Yale University Press.

RODINSON, M. (1969) 'Sociologie marxiste et ideologie marxiste,' p. 67 in International Social Science Council, *Marx and Contemporary Scientific Thought*. The Hague, Mouton.

ROSSI, Ino (ed.) (1974) *The Unconscious in Culture: The Structuralism of Claude Lévi-Strauss in Perspective*. New York: Dutton.

RUBEN, David-Hillel (1977) *Marxism and Materialism: A Study in Marxist Theory of Knowledge*. Atlantic Highlands, NJ: Humanities Press.

SARTE, Jean-Paul (1968) *Search for a Method*, New York: Vintage

SARTRE, Jean-Paul (1976) *Critique of Dialectical Reason*. London: New Left Books.

SCHIWY, Guenther (1969) *Der franzoesische Strukturalismus*. Hamburg: Reinbek.

SCHMIDT, Alfred (1969) 'Der strukturalistische Angriff auf die Geschichte,' p. 194 in A. Schmidt (ed.), *Beitraege zur marxistischen Erkenntnistheorie*. Frankfurt: Suhrkamp.

SOHN-RETHEL, Alfred (1978) *Intellectual and Manual Labor: A Critique of Epistemology*. London: Macmillan.

STALIN, J. V. (1972) *Marxism and the Problems of Linguistics*. Peking: Foreign Languages Press.

SWEEZY, Paul (1979) 'A Crisis in Marxist Theory,' *Monthly Review*, 31(2) (June): 20.

SZYMANSKI, Al (1973) 'Marxism and Science,' *Insurgent Sociologist*, 3(3) (Spring): 25.

THERBORN, Göran (1976) *Science, Class, and Society: On the Formation of Sociology and Historical Materialism*. London: New Left Books.

THERBORN, Göran (1977) 'The Frankfurt School,' in New Left Review (eds.), *Western Marxism, A Critical Reader*. London: Verso.

THOMPSON, E. P. (1978) *The Poverty of Theory and Other Essays*. New York: Monthly Review Press.

TOMICH, Dale (1969) 'The Peculiarities of Structuralism,' *Radical America* 3(5) (September): 34.

TUCKER, Robert C. (ed.) (1978) *The Marx-Engels Reader*, 2nd ed. New York: Norton.

VELTMEYER, Henry (1975) 'Toward an Assessment of the Structuralist Interrogation of Marx: Claude Lévi-Strauss and Louis Althusser,' *Science and Society*, 38: 4.

VILAR, Pierre (1973) 'Marxist History, a History in the Making: Towards a Dialogue with Althusser,' *New Left Review*, 80 (July-August): 65.

WOLFE, Alan (1977) *The Limits of Legitimacy: Political Contradictions of Contemporary Capitalism*. New York: Free Press.

WRIGHT, Erik Olin (1978) *Class, Crisis, and the State*. London: New Left Books.

WRONG, Dennis (1961) 'The Oversocialized Conception of Man in American Sociology,' *American Sociological Review*, 26 (2) (April): 183.

ZEITLIN, Irving M. (1967) *Marxism: A Re-Examination*. Princeton: Van Nostrand.

ZIMMERMAN, Marc (1976) 'Polarities and Contradictions: Theoretical Bases of the Marxist-Structuralist Encounter', *New German Critique*, 7 (Winter): 69.

4

CLASS, STATE, AND CAPITALIST DEVELOPMENT: THE CIVIL WARS IN CHILE (1851 AND 1859)

Maurice Zeitlin
University of California

The rivalries and often internecine clashes between large landowners and capitalists, as well as their struggles with the direct producers, were crucial in shaping the tortuous development of capitalism in Europe. These rivalries were critical not only during the transitional epoch, when aristocracy and bourgeoisie, as more or less separate classes, contended for social supremacy and political hegemony, but even after the merger of landed property and capital and the formation of a 'coalesced bourgeoisie' (Marx, 1963, p. 48). Despite their coalescence, landowners and capitalists might (depending on the specific historic circumstances) still have differential locations in the productive process and, as a result, form distinct *class segments*, divided by contradictory interests and political requirements (Zeitlin et al., 1976). The general historical question is how the rise and remanence of such a coalesced dominant class, split, as Marx put it (1963, p. 48), between the 'two great interests...of landed property and capital,' affected capitalist development and the nature of the bourgeois state.

This question is the focus of our analysis of the mid-nineteenth-century civil wars (1851 and 1859) in Chile. The historical collision between land and capital was replicated here, once again, with its own peculiar twists and decisive impact on the development of capitalism and democracy. The analysis of these intraclass struggles and of the abortive bourgeois revolution in which they erupted is not only of intrinsic historical interest (especially, as we now know, because they were premonitions of the even sharper class conflicts that were to come in our own time): it is also of theoretical relevance for our understanding of the determinants of development and underdevelopment and of the form taken, authoritarian or democratic, by the bourgeois state. In a theoretical reprise following the substantive historical analysis, I offer a critique of a contrasting, and opposed, 'world-system' conception of development, so as to explicate further the general method and theory underlying this study.

LAND AND CAPITAL IN MID-NINETEENTH-CENTURY CHILE

A prolonged and ascending arc of internal capital accumulation and the concomitant transformation of social relations of production in town and country began almost abruptly in the 1830s and 1840s with the discovery and exploitation of rich silver and copper veins, followed quickly by a mid-century breakthrough in coal production and copper smelting and a rapid increase in agricultural and livestock production spurred by the burgeoning coastal trade for the mining camps and the sudden opening up of major new export markets for cereals and flour in Australia, California, and, later, England and Europe. In the 1850s, Chile became the world's leading producer of copper, accounting for roughly a third of total production in the next few decades; Chile all but monopolized the Pacific grain market, and export prices rose to a level never reached before or since in its history. At mid-century, Lota, the coal mining center, had a population of 5,000, and visitors from Great Britain could easily believe that they had been transported back to a corner of their own blackened coal country. Extensive copper smelters were already operating at Lota, Huasco, Copiapó, Caldera, and Guayacun in 1858. Chilean copper ores, hitherto exported almost entirely 'en bruto,' were now largely transformed into bars and ingots in the Chilean smelters and foundries. Linked to the coal and copper production were brick and tile works, glass and bottle factories, brass foundries, machine shops, boiler works, and workshops for copper utensils and equipment. Breweries, carriage and cartmaking works, cement plants, sugar refineries, paper mills, and factories using machinery in the manufacturing process were producing woolen textiles, rope, twine, boots and shoes, soap and candles, and tackle, rigging and cordage; by the 1870s many such factories would be exporting to the United States. In 1857, steamships owned by national capital joined Chile's large 200-vessel merchant fleet, composed until then of sailing ships.

At the same time, Chileans established major banks, their capital originating mainly in copper financing and trade and in grain exporting. Insurance companies and brokerage houses competing with the English were also founded during the 1850s, and as early as 1840 the first stock exchange was opened in the seaport city of Valparaíso. In 1854, statutes to govern the formation of corporations ('sociedades anónimas') were enacted into law, signaling the ascent of the corporate form as a critical mode of capital accumulation, particularly in banking, insurance, mining, and, above all, railroad companies, although it was not until the later nitrate boom in the 1870s that the corporate form and stock exchange were to become central features of 'the credit system' and large-scale investment in Chile.

Chile's large landed estates were engaged in export production almost from their beginning three centuries earlier. Throughout the eighteenth century, while juridical encumbrances on the direct producers in agriculture were progressively eliminated, the process of land encroachment and concentration had gradually resulted in the domination of the countryside by the large estate; and various 'free' forms of settlement on the land and smallholding were increasingly converted into explicit tenancy arrangements and were directly incorporated into the manorial system of production, in order to assure the provision of sufficient labor to produce for growing export markets. At the same time, the types and amount of labor service required of the emerging agrarian tenantry were also increased: in fact, the eighteenth and early nineteenth centuries had witnessed the creation, out of the formerly relatively independent producer or renter, of a specifically Chilean-coerced form of tenant labor, 'inquilinaje,' which was to continue to be the characteristic form of estate labor almost until the present. This protracted change was now, at mid-century, to be suddenly heightened in response to the vast new export and internal coastal markets for agricultural products and processed foodstuffs. Not only these 'markets,' but specifically capitalist relations of production, were at the root of these changes.

From the 1850s on, there was a dramatic rise in migration from the countryside toward the cities and mining districts; 'péones' were also increasingly drawn off to be employed as wage laborers in the construction of roads, canals, irrigation works, and, most heavily, railroads, as well as in the new smelting works and growing manufacturing industries. Financed and constructed entirely by national capital, and predominantly by the mine owners, the railroads were the major employers of wage labor on a large scale. The peak of floating rural population was reached in the 1840s. The rapid population movement from the countryside, just when high profits were to be had by expanded agricultural production, when competition for new markets was intense, and when the demand for agricultural labor was rising, now made 'labor scarcity' and the fear of rising agrarian wages a pressing problem for the landlords. Their response was to cut 'inquilino' perquisites, lengthen the working day and reduce the number of holy days, increase labor rents and service obligations, and increase and extend (by raising the number of supervisory and surveillance personnel) their direct control of the labor process. In short, they were able to radically reinforce and consolidate seignorial relations of domination and to intensify exploitation of the agrarian tenantry.

Buttressing and reinforcing these 'extra-economic' relations of coercive appropriation was a rural 'credit system' controlled by the large landowner who was virtually the only source of loans for the smallholder, sharecropper, and tenant. This 'economic nexus' extended the large estate's direct control of the surrounding peasant production, subordinated the peasantry and tenantry even more fully to its dominion, and compelled them, as neither surveillance nor supervision could, to expend themselves in production. Unlike the 'usurer's capital' that weighed heavily on landlord and peasant alike in medieval Europe, and ruined them both (cf. Marx, 1967, vol. III, pp. 593-99), the asymmetry of debt merely strengthened the existing agrarian relations in Chile. Yet also in the midst of the antiquated historic forms being reproduced in the Chilean countryside, there appeared, especially in the granary works and flour mills, specifically capitalist relations of production. Employing large numbers of wage workers, as well as technicians (many foreign) and mechanics, the mills constructed in Chile at mid-century were 'technologically equal to any mills in the world at the time' (Bauer, 1975, p. 66). Though most large estates retained traditional methods of production, some landowners were known as 'agricultores progresistas' because they introduced mechanical threshers, reapers, and other farm machinery, fine cattle, new seed lines, etc. Still, mechanization was quite limited at mid-century, though not much less than in European cereal-producing countries of the time, 'with large and stable rural labor systems,' like Germany and France (Bauer, 1975, p. 105).

What is distinctive about this process of 'modernization of agriculture,' and has to be underlined, is that, limited though it was, it was largely the work of the new mining magnates: 'they bought lands to form great estates in the central valley, irrigated them... acquired modern machinery and implanted new types of cultivation' (Encina, 1955). It was here, above all, in its most direct form that the coalescence of land and capital took place; that, in fact, landed property became agrarian capital, and landlord and capitalist were one. It is precisely this segment of the dominant class that consummately personifies the development of Chilean capitalism; it is this newly created class segment that is not only 'dynamic and innovative,' but also politically democratic, combative, and even revolutionary. It is this capitalist segment, above all, that constitutes the bearer of radical ideas in mid-nineteenth-century Chile and strives, even in armed struggle, for class hegemony and political power.

CLASS AND STATE

In 1851 and again in 1859, civil war divided the class from within; but, in contrast to the even bloodier conflict under Balmaceda as the century drew to a close, it also drew important elements of other classes — artisans, smallholders, and miners — into its orbit, threatening momentarily to become transformed into a genuine bourgeois revolution. These intraclass conflicts were partial and contingent reflections of the rivalry between land and capital. They were partial because other critical elements undoubtedly entered into the causal process and set the revolutionary struggles in motion; they were also contingent to the extent that it was the unique combination of these elements — regional consciousness, church-state conflict and the example and force of European bourgeois revolutionary ideology — that overdetermined the entire process and, perhaps, made it possible; without these interrelated elements, the interests and aspirations of mining capital might not have taken on revolutionary social content or erupted in armed struggle for state power.

What was the nature of the state against which bourgeois radicals and liberals declaimed and organized? In its origins and nature it was the product of the mixed temporalities, Chilean and European, in which it was fashioned: its inception, of course, was in the early nineteenth-century wars of independence that displaced Spanish dominion. This meant that, at the outset, the traders, artisans and mine owners (and notably few 'revolutionary artistocrats') who constituted the main ramparts of the new state, just as they had of the independence movement itself, were to strive to erect it as an anti-royalist and republican structure, heir on the one hand to the models — political, legal, and juridical — present in the bourgeois and post-Napoleonic era, and on the other to its architects' own exigent needs: unification of the country under a central administration without re-imposition of the dominion of the large landowners on which the royalist political order had rested. There were, however, no amalgams of property and sovereignty, no specifically feudal jurisdictions and boundaries, no warring principalities and petty states, no autonomous sovereignties of urban corporations, which formed the prehistoric stage of bourgeois society in Europe, whose destruction or unification was necessary to establish the new post-colonial state in Chile. On the contrary, to this extent Spanish royalism had itself prepared the ground for the modern state. This is not to say, of course, that, in practice, intendant, magistrate and landowner jurisdictions did not coincide (as they did and were to continue to do), but that, in principle and in law, the writ of the state was neither confined nor impeded by pre-capitalist political forms. In this sense, then, the political options of the new revolutionary 'statesmen' were relatively open: though there were, certainly, disparate social relations underlying the contrasting 'constitutional' theories that guided their efforts to fashion new state forms, social 'interests' and political consciousness were variably coincident precisely because the struggles in Chile were fought in an international bourgeois historical context. Therefore, in one form or another, it was a *republican* state that each post-independence Constitution (1812, 1823, 1828) framed. The unavoidable question at issue throughout the first decades of independence as successive regimes rewrote their state principles was, therefore, 'merely' whether the state was to be not only republican but democratic as well. In the course of these struggles, what emerged was, as its first chief of state aptly named it, an 'autocratic republic.' Its legal, juridical, and political principles were embodied in the 1833 Constitution. And, with scarce modification, this was the form of state at mid-century.

The executive of the state, not Parliament, was vested with the main attributes of sovereignty: the chiefs of state, not Parliament, decided the budget, fixed all public officials' salaries, appointed and promoted military officers, and named the members of the Supreme Court, and neither he nor his Council of State were subject to parliamentary censure or prerogative, and could, in fact, veto the Congreso's legislation. The intendants, governors, and prefects who ran the provincial, local, and municipal administration were the appointees, agents, and direct representatives of the executive, as were trial judges and justices of district courts. Senators and deputies to the bicameral national Congreso were elected by limited suffrage (men, propertied, literate, aged twenty-five and over), and senators, though not deputies, from candidates nominated by the president and his ministers and approved by the appointed provincial and municipal officials of the state. In short, Chile's mid-nineteenth-century state was a highly centralized, unitary, and hierarchical political apparatus; yet it was also a state in which were inscribed the legal and juridical principles of the inviolability of private property and equality before the law, of freedom of movement and travel (that is, of a free labor market), and of freedom of contract and of trade. No prohibitions excluded any social category of individuals from trade, landownership or industry, or bound the immediate producer to the land. A Civil Code (enacted in 1855), constituting a systematic codification of the national jurisprudence, provided the 'calculable adjudication and administration' in the state necessary to secure contracts, ensure property ownership, and standardize taxation and fiscal obligations. It was, in fact, a capitalist 'rational legal order' with neither patrimonial, monarchical, nor feudal encumbrances. In a word, it was, contrary to most Chilean historians who consider it a 'feudal conservative state' (Jobet, 1955, p. 47), a hierarchical and authoritarian form of capitalist state governing a social formation in which large landed property and capital were in uneasy 'balance,' in which the former was neither feudal nor 'fully' capitalist, and the latter was still in the throes of incipient development.

This was the conundrum of the 1850s struggle between landowners and capitalists: it took place on the terrain of a political and legal order that, while bourgeois in 'structure,' ensured the hegemony of large landed property in class and state. To lay hold of it and use it was an abstract possibility for the mine owners and their allies: to turn its hierarchic, centralized apparatus against the landed and utilize it to enforce their own interests. Abstract it was and is, because in the concrete historical circumstances, and the conditions of the state's formation, it stood as the incarnate representative of an antiquated past: what emerged, then, as the supreme political demand of the liberal and radical activists of the class was a federalist, decentralized, and parliamentary democratic state. They called for the limitation of executive powers, enlargement of manhood suffrage and direct popular election of the Senate as well as Chamber of Deputies, provincial and local autonomy and popular election of intendants, prefects, governors and judges. In short, they demanded the abolition, not amendment, of the 1833 Constitution, and with it, the authoritarian state structure it represented. Not through the state but against the state, in a 'Constituent Assembly' of the people, was the new Constitution to be written and the old discarded.

That the political hegemony of the landowners rested on their social dominion in the countryside and their enhanced control of the agrarian tenantry was also clear to capital's most advanced political 'theoreticians.' They understood, in the words of Santiago Arcos (one of the principal organizers, with Fransisco Bilbao, of the Society of Equality that brought artisans and bourgeois intellectuals together in Santiago and played a pivotal role in the 1851 revolt), that, 'so long as *inquilinaje* endures in the *haciendas...*, so long as that omnipotent influence of the *patrón* over subaltern officials persists... no [political] reform will be solidly established' (Segall, 1953, pp. 266-7). Only an 'energetic...revolution to cut out the roots of all these evils,' and end 'poverty as the normal state...of the plebe in the cities and the laborers, *inquilinos*, and servants in the countryside,' Arcos wrote in 1852, could establish 'a stable government that guarantees social peace, and security for the laborer, the artisan, the miner, the merchant, and the capitalist' (Amunátegui Solar, 1946, p. 84; Segall, 1953, p. 268).

Thus, precisely at a historic moment when the transformation of smallholders and renters into a subordinate agrarian tenantry was being consummated and the large landowners of Chile were coming to regard 'inquilinaje' as their own 'peculiar institution,' these unwonted forms of social domination were to be tested, in a struggle for state power, by an emergent and aspiring capitalist segment of the dominant class itself, at the head of armed artisans and mounted peasant detachments. This movement's ideas were at once the expression of an epoch in which profoundly new social relations were appearing in town and country, and the direct articulation of the meanings seen in them by their participants and bearers.

At their root, as well, were the historically specific contradictory interests and political requirements of large landed property and capital, which became more sharply defined as the state, under the hegemony of the Central Valley landowners, 'postponed their aspirations' (Vitale, 1971). The most immediate contradictions between them were manifested in the taxation and fiscal policies of the state. In 1851, on the eve of the first of the abortive mid-century revolutions, public revenues came almost exclusively from taxes on mining and its exports. Throughout this and subsequent decades, not only were taxes on large landowners infinitesimal while their burden rested almost entirely on mine owners, but 'landowners enjoyed an ever decreasing tax burden' (Bauer, 1975, p. 118).

On 30 December 1858, on the eve of the 1859 revolt, *El Curicano* editorialized:

> The Constituent Assembly embodies the aspirations and desires of the provinces...to govern themselves, to elect their own judges and intendants, to serve the interests of their localities...to be represented in accordance with the taxes they pay rather than have to beg from the general Government... Once we were exploited by the Spanish Court...now by the court of Santiago. The general government does not invest a tenth of the revenues in our Department that we contribute annually to the national treasury. [Vitale, 1971, p. 252]

One of the first acts of the revolutionary regime of Pedro León Gallo in Copiapó, on 11 January 1859, was to cut in half the taxes on ores and metals exported abroad (despite the need to finance its own rebel army). The mines were 'developed despite state policy that increased the costs of production with immeasurable taxes' (Bunster, 1965, p. 137).

The mid-century financing of railroad construction, essential to the expansion of mining production, was disproportionately borne by major mine owners. The first line — in the north, from Copiapó to Caldera — was built by Chilean mining capital without state financial assistance, and a recurrent theme in congressional debate was the copper capitalists' lament that the mining provinces of the north were abandoned to 'private initiative' while the regime spent millions in the Central Valley (Przeworski, 1974, p. 10). The same pattern was repeated in other state capital investments in infrastructure: irrigation canals, roads, and bridges were built throughout the Central Valley, with scarce attention to the south central milling zone from Talca to Concepción. Yet at this time, 'most of the flour shipped from Valparaiso as exports or coast trade to the northern mining region or consumed in the port was from the mills of Constitución, Tomé and Concepción' (Oppenheimer, 1976, p. 51). Without this direct access to the Santiago-Valparaíso line, the south central millowners would be put at a major competitive disadvantage, as their spokesmen argued in the senate debates over the railroad's construction.

As is evident, the contradictory interests of land and capital had a specifically regional expression: mining and agrarian capital on the one hand, large landed property on the other — each had its relatively distinctive and compact geographical areas of development. Consequently, the contradictory impact of state policies on these segments of the class was rendered transparent: the contradictions between land and capital were transformed into social cleavages and expressed in sharp political conflict. It was precisely in the emergent capitalist areas that radical democratic ideas and revolutionary conspiracies flowered in 1851 and again in 1859, and where the centers of armed struggle against the state were located. What distinguished them, though, was not merely their contradictory interests, but, and perhaps above all, the fact that they contained, especially in the northern mining towns, quite divergent 'societies within a society,' with qualitatively different class relations at their core.

From Talca to Concepción, smallholders, independent millers and farmers, and large mechanized flour mills employing wage workers, rather than the large estates of the Central Valley based on a subordinate agrarian tenantry, were apparently preponderant. Of the 145 large estates in the country in 1854, for example, only 4 were located below Curicó. It was here that several of the fiercest battles of the 1851 and 1859 revolts were fought, often led by the same men, whom Encina, Chile's leading conservative historian, mistakenly calls 'revolutionary aristocrats' (Encina, 1949, p. 316). The main leaders of the armed struggle in the south central area were not 'revolutionary aristocrats,' but large mill owners and mining capitalists (such as Juan Antonio Pando and Juan Alemparte Lastra).

Another agricultural zone in which there were organized uprisings both in 1851 and 1859 was in and around San Felipe in the Valley of Putaendo (to the north-east of Valparaiso). Long 'an obstinate center of liberal agitation,' here, too, armed artisans and smallholders fought regular troops. Lying in a nook to the north of the Central Valley, the Department produced dairy products, fruit, and vegetables for neighboring and Santiago markets, and had a relatively 'equitable distribution of land,' supporting independent 'yeoman farmers' (Bauer, 1975, pp. 126-7). San Felipe itself was a principal center of artisan production, and in 1851 the Society of Equality (in the only base it had outside Santiago) led a 'popular mutiny' that deposed the intendant and established a Committee of Neighbors to govern this provincial capital, until they were defeated by Los Andes and Putaendo civic guards (Edwards Vives, 1932, p. 657). Again in 1859, artisans and laborers, 'indoctrinated by the Society of Equality since 1851,' and led by bourgeois 'youth imbued with the doctrines' of the Constituent Assembly, took over the local garrison of the Civic Guard, 'requisitioned money and fiscal specie' from the Department's treasury, installed their own intendant, recruited troops in the neighboring countryside, and went on to take Putaendo. After five days of 'obstinate and bloody resistance,' the combined troops of the Los Andes Civic Guard and a regular division of the line defeated the insurrectionaries on 18 February 1859 (Edwards Vives, 1932, pp. 28-82).

The epicenter of the revolutionary movement in 1859 was in the northern mining provinces of Atacama and Coquimbo, a relatively compact and remote region of the country where the class relations unique to capitalism were pre-eminent if not exclusive in the entire production process. On this basis, and the region's 'geo-economic' distinctiveness as silver and copper miner to the world, there was erected a distinctive 'frontier' society of free men with a strong democratic strain, where the distinctions between 'master and man,' 'patrón' and 'peón,' landlord and tenant were 'foreign' to the new men of rough vigor, hard work and boundless ambition, 'drawn from all social classes' and, indeed, from many nations, who had come there in recent years. While some of the silver and copper mines were highly mechanized and worked by over a hundred miners, most were small establishments typically employing less than a dozen men. Production relations in the mines and foundries were based, not only or mainly on a mass of wage workers employed by capital, but on a variety of mixed forms of production involving (as, in fact, it still did in England during the same period) intermediary contracting and sub-contracting relations between capital and labor. The 'pirquinero' typified the northern miner.

Usually the owner of his own equipment, he worked either independently or in association with others, as equal producer with the same right in the final product; or, if he was the legal owner of the claim, he might, while working with the men, retain a special share of the product and the right to hire or fire new workers and exert his authority in the labor process. Still other 'pirquineros' were dependent on merchant capitalists or incipient bankers, the so-called 'habilitadores,' who supplied them with equipment and foodstuffs as an advance against a share of production; often these miners became — in the course of such transactions — transformed into wage workers in all but name. The immediate employer of many miners was often another miner, who was at once boss, technician, and fellow worker, and, in turn, employee of the mineowner.

Outside of mining but thoroughly integrated with it were the small production units that abounded in the region, some being workshops employing several craftsmen and artisans under the direction of the shop owner himself or contractor of the capitalist, others simply one-man artisan shops, where proprietor and worker were one — all producing or repairing the array of tools, supplies, equipment, and machinery involved in mining, smelting, and transporting the ores. Here was the objective basis for a sense of identity between workmen and capitalist, small mineowner and large — conditioned also by the quick change of fortune mining made possible. In such a world was nourished the bourgeois individualist, the 'self-willed and intractable workman,' whom capital was later destined to subordinate and transform into its mere appendage, as it had largely done already in the coal mines at Lota and Coronel in the south of the country. For now, however, the mutuality of interest between them and the clarity with which their fate depended on the same industry, whose fluctuations and fortunes determined their own, was more sharply defined than the inherent class contradictions that were soon to divide labor and capital.

It was in this enclave of bourgeois civilization that mining capital came to be the bearer and personification of radical democratic consciousness — even utopian socialist ideology — in mid-nineteenth-century Chile. Throughout the 1850s, the intelligentsia who led the struggle for democratization of the state were predominantly mine owners or their scions. But because they were an intelligentsia, the ideas they held, the doctrines they debated, and the principles they espoused had a relative autonomy of their own. Their commitments and passions were no less real for being explicable. They moved in a milieu in which ideas counted and conscious choice became necessary between the rationalist, humanist and democratic currents of that revolutionary bourgeois epoch in Europe and the clerical and reactionary justifications of inequality and authoritarian rule.

Yet it has to be emphasized that, not only did ascendant capital determine the direction of the democratic movement by the underlying social relations it was bringing into being, but also the movement's most active and conspicuous leaders and participants were themselves members of the bourgeoisie.

Certainly, we must be wary of attaching decisive importance 'to the class background of *individuals* participating in revolutionary events. Too many random factors influencing the decisions and behavior of individual members of different classes are at work for a close relation to be found,' as Baran rightly remarks, 'between the *class content* of a historical movement and the *class origin* of possibly even significant numbers of its participants and leaders.' This observation may apply especially to bourgeois revolutions, as Baran argues: 'Traditionally, bourgeois as *individuals* have nowhere taken active part in *revolutionary politics*' (Baran, 1957, p. 153).

But whatever the general validity of this proposition, it is *not* borne out in Chilean experience, as I have been emphasizing. On the contrary, the young bourgeoisie of Chile did *not* substitute 'their money for their persons in the struggle for freedom' (Baran, 1957, p. 153), as their counterparts may have done elsewhere. Rather, they personally fought and bled, and suffered imprisonment or deportation, in the insurrectionary struggles of the 1850s — perhaps precisely because of their specific 'economic and ideological habitat' in mid-nineteenth-century Chile. Indeed, the roll-call of the liberal and radical democratic agitators, organizers, and insurrectionaries of the 1850s reads almost like a 'Who's Who' of the Chilean mining bourgeoisie at the time: of the 38 names that have come down to us (and on which appropriate data were found) as among the most active and conspicuous leaders of these struggles, 20 were from mine-owning families and 6 more were from the industrial, mill-owning, merchant or banking families; 3 were intellectuals and 2 were state officials (both judges); 2 were from large landed families (with no identifiable mining or industrial connections); 4 were artisans and 1 was a smallholder. Of the 22 who actually led and engaged in armed insurrection, 10 were from mining capitalist families, 4 were mill-owners, merchants or industrialists, 2 were professionals, 1 was a landowner, 4 were artisans, and 1 was a smallholder. In short, this was a bourgeois revolutionary insurrection led and participated in directly by the bourgeoisie themselves. Their decisive defeat came on 29 April 1859 at Cerro Grande.

In a nation of less than a million and a half citizens, the civil war of 1859 took 5,000 lives, and 'few families remained untouched by dead, wounded or imprisoned' during the four months of insurrection against the state. In its wake, the regime deported 2,000 people, and meted out death sentences in absentia to hundreds of alleged conspirators and revolutionaries whose names were publicly posted everywhere. In fact, no leading bourgeois revolutionaries were executed, though most were imprisoned or deported, or escaped into exile. But countless 'obscure and nameless men' — artisans, miners, and peasants — were summarily executed. As the editor of *El Mercurio* wrote, 'Execution is the price the people pay, because they have no voice and their sacrifice leaves no trace' (Tornero, 1861, pp. 190-4; 304-6).

THE MEANING OF THE CIVIL WAR

Is it true that their sacrifice left no trace? What were the historical consequences of these insurrectionary struggles, for whom artisans and smallholders provided the mass base and the mining bourgeoisie the resolute leadership? In that question inheres the answer. Above all, because the young Chilean bourgeoisie was not content to trade its right to rule for the right to make money, and to subordinate itself and society to retrograde and repressive political forms, the civil wars of the 1850s were to have enduring significance as a momentous contribution to the advancement and consolidation of civil liberties and political rights in Chile. The clashes between mining capital and the hegemonic agrarian elements reinforced the political divisions within the dominant class and provided the basis for the formation of a democratic capitalist state. Despite their defeat in armed confrontation, and precisely because the nascent bourgeois elements twice demonstrated their readiness and capacity for insurrection on behalf of their democratic aspirations, they were soon to enter the lists as organized political parties, and to invigorate a hitherto docile Congreso with their continuing struggles to democratize the state. They thereby laid the basis for the relatively durable and vital parliamentary democracy that was to replace the authoritarian and hierarchical state against which their insurrections were aimed at mid-century.

The immediate result of the insurrection's defeat was not only severe repression, but also the juridical expansion of the executive powers of the state, and the virtual abolition of legal limits to arbitrary arrest, search and seizure, dissolution of assembly, closure of the press, etc. The suffrage was also even further restricted by new and increased property and income qualifications for the vote. But in the course of the next decade, the struggle for democratization was renewed, as many erstwhile revolutionaries, granted amnesty by the new president in 1861, returned to active intervention in the political arena, some winning seats in the Chamber of Deputies and Senate. Indeed, in 1866 Pedro León Gallo, former commander of the revolutionary army of the north, ran unsuccessfully for the presidency, as did one of the major spokesmen and conspirators of the 1850s, Benjamin Vicuña Mackenna, in 1875, as the 'people's candidate.' In fact, in 1870, when one of the original democratic partisans of the 1850s, Federico Errázuriz Zañartu, was elected president, it was as the conservative and landed candidate, opposed by a coalition of liberal and radical democrats behind the candidacy of mining magnate José Tomás Urmeneta, whose electoral support came almost exclusively from the northern mining and south central milling provinces.

The tendency toward the political ascendance of the democrats was undergirded by a renewed burst of capital accumulation during the 1870s, based mainly in the exploitation of new silver mines near Caracoles and nitrate plants in the Peruvian territory of Antofagasta. These years also witnessed the growth of a host of new manufacturing industries to supply the growing internal market, many using steam-driven machinery. Concomitant with this accelerated growth of mining and manufacturing capital was a relatively rapid transformation of the state structure, and the increased expansion of civil liberties and political freedoms during the early 1870s.

Successively, the presidency was restricted to one five-year term of office; the freedoms of press, assembly and association were guaranteed; a system of proportional representation in parliamen-

tary elections was instituted; the executive authority of the state
was increasingly hedged in, its extraordinary powers all but
abolished; the Chamber of Deputies and Senate gained a majority
of the seats in the Council of State, hitherto a docile instrument of
the presidency, and measures were enacted to assure the responsibility of the president's ministers to Parliament; intendants and
governors, and other officials of the state, were prohibited from
simultaneously holding legislative office; senators were now elected
directly by the provinces; administration of provincial elections and
candidate approval was taken from the intendant and lodged in a
local board of 'major taxpayers'; and other prerogatives of intendants and governors (and thereby of the executive of the state) were
abolished. Finally, suffrage was extended to all men without property or income qualifications. In short, the old authoritarian
capitalist state went through a swift metamorphosis into one
possessing the most basic features of bourgeois democracy.

But if it is unquestionable that the insurrectionary struggles of
the 1850s had these lasting effects in the impetus it gave and the
bases it laid for political democracy, the defeat of the insurrection
also mattered profoundly: it restricted Chile's chances for relatively
independent capitalist development. It paved the way for a later
decline of productive capital in the Chilean social formation and
what we may term its 'subordinate coalescence' within the dominant class. This, of course, cannot be 'empirically demonstrated,'
but the specific historical circumstances in which Chile's abortive
revolution occurred indicate how crucial its real triumph might
have been.

These mid-century insurrections, as we have seen, reflected and
embodied emergent capitalist relations, and the subsequent
modifications in the structure of the state in the 1870s were also
conditioned by the continuing economic ascendance of capital.
However, these were years in which the vulnerability of Chilean export capitalism also became increasingly evident. British commercial capital had long since established itself securely in the international brokerage and trade of Chile's mineral and grain exports,
much of which went directly to English ports; and during the 1870s,
and especially after Chile wrested the nitrate territories of
Tarapacá and Antofogasta from Bolivia and Peru in the War of
the Pacific (1879-83), English capital took increasing hold of
nitrate production itself, erecting its own plants and construc-
ing its own railroads to carry these products to the sea for export to in-

ternational markets; and it was to become heavily involved, if not pre-eminent, in Chile's own coastal trade for the mining areas of the north.

Simultaneously, the penetration of capitalism in the countryside meant, as I have emphasized, the accelerated incorporation of the peasantry into the large estates, and their transformation into an agrarian tenantry. Thus, the paradox and problem of Chilean historical development is that the so-called 'commercialization of agriculture' reinforced the dominion of the large landowners in the countryside precisely when the development of capitalism also was creating, in the mine owners, a rich and thoroughly bourgeois adversary for social supremacy and state power. Put differently, capitalist development led simultaneously to the landowners' successful imposition of new forms of social domination, in the guise of 'pre-capitalist' and 'archaic' seignorial relations, and to the expansion of civil liberties and political freedoms and the establishment of the democratic state. Chilean history took, as Lenin (1934, pp. 180ff; 254ff) might have said, the 'Prussian road' in the countryside and the 'American road' politically. What might have happened if the insurrection of 1859 had won, and the armed artisans, miners, and smallholders, led by bourgeois democrats, had actually conquered direct political power? What difference would it have made for Chilean historical development if its bourgeois revolution had not been aborted?

To suggest an 'answer' to these questions, we have to glance back, first, at the competitive position of Chilean capital at mid-century, and, second, at the potential class content of the revolutionary movement. From the late 1840s on, Chilean capital both increasingly threatened and was threatened by British capital on its own soil. Major Chilean copper and coal magnates and south central mill owners competed directly with British producers. In fact, in the late 1850s they had considerably displaced British coal from its dominant position in Chilean markets and had gained, through various cartel arrangements, clear ascendance in flour milling and exporting. The establishment of major copper smelting plants, purchased from the United States and Germany, directly competed with British smelters in Chile and in Wales that had hitherto monopolized the industry. Some advocates of national capital also sought self-consciously to enlist the state in their competition with the British: 'it is well known,' Atacama mining capital's newspaper, *El Copiapino*, proclaimed as early as 8 October 1857, that 'three or four English houses control the market in copper and create a rise and fall [in prices and demand] when they want' (Ramírez Necochea, 1960, p. 87).

Of the state policies proposed to deal with this situation, one was widely discussed among Chilean capitalists: a proposal for the establishment of a State Bank, to provide the necessary loans and credits for Chilean mining investment independent of the English houses, and to reduce their preponderant role in the credit system as a whole. One of the leading advocates of the State Bank, and of political measures to protect Chilean manufacturing from British competition, was copper mine owner and newspaperman Pedro Felix Vicuña Aguirre, 'the author of the revolution of 1851' (Encina, 1949, pp. 55; 285) and, again, a leading participant, with his son Benjamin Vicuña Mackenna, in the 1859 insurrection. His line, continued by his successors at *El Mercurio* throughout the 1860s and by *El Ferrocarril* as well, was that Chilean 'products cannot compete with European imports' effectively without 'laws to prohibit foreign manufacturer' (cited in Ramírez Necochea, 1960, p. 89). *El Mercurio* — whose owner, Santos Tornero, was also a leading partisan of the 1859 insurrection — urged that

> Chile can be industrial, since it has the capital, the labor and activity, but it lacks the decided will to want to be. There is strong foreign capital representation in the importation of manufactured products. Foreign capital is and will always be disposed to put any and every obstacle in the way of the establishment of industry in the country... Protectionism has to be the mother's milk of every nascent craft or industry... Without protectionism, every nascent advance remains exposed to the furious and coordinated assaults of foreign imports, represented in 'free trade'. [*El Mercurio*, 4 May 1865; cited in Ramírez Necochea, 1960, p. 90]

The British response to Chilean capitalist development was a continuing, and finally successful, effort to roll back whatever incipient protectionist measures were already being taken. As early as 1845, even before the advanced smelters were installed in Chile, the British Embassy reported to its government that the recently opened Chilean foundries and smelters would be 'a great detriment' to British mining and shipping interests in Chile; and the next year, 39 English commercial and mining firms solicited their government's assistance: 'As a consequence' of the Chilean smelters, they argued, 'instead of raw copper ores, large quantities of ingots and bars are being sent to Europe to supply copper and bronze manufacturers there, to the detriment of British smelting and manufacturing interests.' Similarly, in 1859, at the behest of English coal mine owners in Chile, their embassy urged that the special import taxes on English coal be rescinded, since these would have 'disastrous results for all British interests' in Chile (Ramírez Necochea, 1960, pp. 65, 68). In fact, Britain's coal industry also dumped its exports in the northern mining districts at a loss in order to stymie Chilean coal production, with only momentary success.

The question that now has to be asked is whether a regime established in Chile by a successful revolution in 1859 under the aegis of the mining and agrarian bourgeoisie would have possessed a heightened nationalist animus and imposed protectionist state policies that could have resisted the penetration of British capital and provided the impetus for rapid industrialization. We have no need to endow their consciousness with unwarranted retrospective coherence, in order to understand that it might have made an enormous difference for the development of capitalism in Chile if the revolutionaries had taken state power in 1859. For, as we have seen, it was precisely some of the leading participants and partisans of the revolutionary movement who had the clearest understanding of how decisive was Chilean capital's historic choice. Certainly, as Anderson (1974, p. 55) has rightly emphasized, 'no class in history immediately comprehends the logic of its own historic situation; in epochs of transition, a long period of disorientation and confusion may be necessary for it to learn the necessary rules to its own sovereignty.' In possession of state power, those who had such a comprehension, albeit inchoate, might well have imposed their hegemony on their class and enforced the state policies necessary to establish the sovereignty of national capital in Chile.

Closely bound up with this was the revolutionary potential inherent in the armed struggles in the countryside. We do not know, from the available sources, if the agitation and organization of the peasantry by their social 'superiors' provided the main impetus to their participation in the insurrectionary movement, or if their participation was impelled by the momentum of their own class needs and grievances. That the latter was present is indicated by the fact that the armed 'montoneras' arose in the 1850s precisely in the areas where a relatively independent smallholding segment of the peasantry, not yet subjected directly to the manorial regime, still existed. There were certainly armed guerrilla bands made up of artisans, laborers and smallholders that acted independently and were not commanded by bourgeois revolutionaries. There were also spontaneous risings triggered by these organized struggles, especially in and around Talca.

Whatever the relative independence of the insurrectionary movement in the countryside, though, the bourgeoisie certainly found willing allies in the rural population. The combination of an increase in the number of men seeking work in the mines, or in construction of the railroads, canals, irrigation works, and roads, with the simultaneous acceleration in the impositions on the peasantry, the encroachments on its customary prerogatives and the incorporation of lands previously loosely attached to the large estates within their domains, certainly gave resistance and revolt its own independent agrarian wellsprings. What cannot be doubted is the insurrectionary alliance of artisans, laborers, smallholders, and miners, their armed seizure of towns and cities and several large estates, the spontaneous risings sparked as a consequence, and the active participation and leadership of many 'representatives' of the bourgeoisie in these armed struggles, who had the conscious aim of taking state power. And, as we saw earlier, specifically agrarian demands were articulated by several of these bourgeois revolutionaries — enough, in fact, to provoke *El Correo del Sur* (19 April 1859) to denounce the 'huasos' who were ready to 'surrender themselves to socialism and communism' (Vitale, 1971, p. 282). Indeed, barely two years after the defeat at Cerro Grande, *El Mercurio* (29 May 1861) again raised the issue of the division of the large estates:

> We consider the division or break-up of agrarian property necessary, both because this would work in favor of creditors and debtors as well as permit small capitalists to become proprietors; it would also increase production as the result of the more direct and detailed care that can be given to a small farm. At the same time, this measure would result in a peaceful revolution in landed property. [Ramírez Necochea, 1955, p. 93]

Here, clearly, these advanced political leaders of the Chilean bourgeoisie intuitively grasped the decisive place of a 'revolution in landed property' in the development of capitalism: it was essential to ensure rising labor productivity in agriculture and the growth of an internal market, both in agricultural equipment and consumer goods, for domestic manufacturing — which, in turn, would tap Chile's mining resources for fuel and raw materials, and end mining capital's dependence on foreign markets.

What social forces might have been tapped, what real impetus there might have been to the break-up of the large estates and the transformation of smallholders into independent farmers and agrarian capitalists, if the revolutionaries had gained state power in 1859 — in short, what the real potential was for a so-called 'bourgeois democratic agrarian revolution' in mid-nineteenth-century Chile — is the tantalizing and unanswerable question posed by the defeat of the revolutionary bourgeoisie in these almost forgotten struggles over a century ago. Instead, the old agrarian relations were reinforced and the internal market for manufacturing restricted — which, in turn, heightened the speculative and unproductive nature of Chilean capital, through preponderant investment in landed property, in trade, and in financing the export of raw materials. Simultaneously, and in the absence of protectionist state policies, British imports competed directly and with increasing success against domestic products for even that small market, thereby also strengthening these self-same tendencies, and paving the way for Chile's stunted and distorted capitalist development.

Thus, the 1859 civil war was a decisive turning point in Chilean history. The defeat of the revolutionary bourgeoisie represented the suppression of an alternative and independent path of capitalist development for Chile — a realm of objective historic possibilities unfulfilled because the bourgeois revolution was aborted. The subsequent pattern of development in Chile, that is, Chile's so-called underdevelopment, was essentially determined by these specific processes of class formation and of class and intraclass struggle. The eventual subordination of productive capital to landed property in the political economy was the outcome of capital's failure to gain hegemony within the dominant class at a critical historic moment when the emergent capitalist forms of production and their concomitant class relations required the effective use of state power to buttress and consolidate them. Instead, the dominion of the large landowners and mercantile/financial capitalists in the state was secured. Under their aegis, the state facilitated the subsequent penetration of foreign capital in nitrates (and, much later, in copper) and the eventual displacement of Chilean by foreign capital. This was to occur, however, only after another momentous civil war three decades later, provoked by a final attempt from within the dominant class itself to stem foreign capital's ascendance.

THEORETICAL REPRISE

In Chile, as elsewhere, the pattern of development and underdevelopment for an entire epoch hinged 'upon the outcome of specific processes of class formation, of class struggle' (Brenner, 1977, p. 91) — in particular, as I have argued, the class and intraclass struggles that erupted in civil war and abortive bourgeois revolution in the middle of the nineteenth century. It was in and through these struggles that both the enduring pattern of capitalist development and the structure of the bourgeois state in Chile was produced.

Put in more general terms, the political form of the bourgeois state, either democratic or authoritarian, is the relatively contingent historic product of specific social struggles between classes and class segments (especially the bourgeois and landed segments of the dominant class itself) in determinate circumstances. At the same time, these struggles determine not only the political form but also the social content of the state, for they are crucial in deciding which of the contending segments of the dominant class — land or capital — actually gains hegemony within it and is able to impose its particular interests as class (and national) interests through the state. Once established, the specific class relations and their concomitant state policies thereby determine (within given material limits) the country's potential for capitalist development (and underdevelopment) and, as a result, its vulnerability to the expansion and penetration of foreign capital and, in turn, its relative location in and effect on global political economic relationships.

The historic situation in which Chile's bourgeois democratic state was originally forged, and its vitality for the century of its continuing existence until it was recently smashed, reveals again that capitalist democracy is the fragile flower of a specific constellation of class relations and social struggles. The historic peculiarity of Chile's bourgeois democratic state lay in the anomaly that the social formation it governed never became quite bourgeois itself: rather, in its agrarian social relations, the large estate, using extra-economic coercion, or 'labor repressive means' (Moore, 1966), to extract the surplus product of the agrarian tenantry ('inquilinos'), remained the preponderant unit of production. The social supremacy of the large landowners in the countryside was not seriously challenged again, after the risings of the 1850s, until the Left's successful penetration and organization of agrarian labor a century later. The large estate continued to dominate the Central Valley, where the bulk of both the peasantry and of agricultural production were centered, though independent farming took root, mainly through foreign settlement, in the near south, and cattle-raising enterprises employing wage labor were established in the southernmost areas several decades later. A century after the radical bourgeoisie's call for a 'revolution in landed property,' Chile still had one of the highest concentrations of landownership in the world (Sternberg, 1962, p. 34). The large estates closely approximated a patriarchal system of social control internally well into the 1930s if not beyond, while the apparatus of force and violence in the countryside as a whole was essentially regulated by the large landowners, and alternative sources of information were prohibited and independent associations forbidden. The landowners had control of both the vote and the labor power of the tenantry and dependent smallholders, and this was the sine qua non of their continuing hegemony.

Such class relations certainly provided 'an unfavorable soil for the growth of democracy' (Moore, 1966, p. 435). There was in Chile neither a prolonged period of agrarian struggles in which the peasantry gradually freed themselves of the dominion of the large estates nor a sudden moment of revolutionary convulsion that broke the base and smashed the state of the large landowners, thereby sealing politically the emergent capitalist relations and laying the basis for a democratic republic. Rather, as we know, the so-called bourgeois revolution, which in one way or another historically encompasses these transformations, was aborted by the defeat of the revolutionaries in the civil wars of the 1850s in Chile. Contrary, for instance, to the historic developments in England and France, 'the political hegemony of the landed upper class [was not]...broken or transformed' in Chile, nor were the peasantry turned into independent farmers producing for the market. These specific preconditions for the emergence of European capitalist democracy (as discerned again in a penetrating comparative analysis by Moore [1966, p. 430], and long argued by Marxian scholars) were not established in Chile.

Yet, as we know, Chile for over a century, despite the unshaken dominion of the large estate, was to be one of the world's few stable parliamentary democratic states. How was this possible?

An adequate answer requires analysis of the historical prelude to, and the causes and consequences of, the final intraclass civil war of 1891; but its essentials, I think, are already set out in our analysis of the historic meaning of the 1850s' struggles and their aftermath. For, as we have seen, the struggles of the mining and agrarian bourgeoisie against the political dominion of the Central Valley landowners continued after the civil war. These radical democratic capitalists retained for many decades an independent and growing economic base, and they were gradually able to abolish, through continuing political clashes, the most repressive and authoritarian features of the bourgeois state against which they had rebelled, and to construct a relatively democratic parliamentary state in its place. These struggles prevented the consolidation in Chile of a bourgeois state ruling by means of a powerful repressive apparatus and thus one that would have imposed, to borrow Moore's words in another context, a whole climate of political and social opinion 'unfavorable to human freedom' (1966, p. 421). The Chilean bourgeoisie of these decades was neither tame nor timid in its attacks against the old regime. It launched its own serious intellectual assaults on the bastions of that regime, probed them with an oppositional though inchoate theory aiming to transform both the state structure and agrarian property relations, and fought the bloody civil wars of the 1850s to make a democratic revolution. And then, with an independent economic base still growing, it continued the political struggles despite its revolutionary defeat.

The struggles of the bourgeoisie took place, moreover, at a phase of capitalist development, as we saw, when the working class — as a class of wage laborers rather than artisans — was still incipient and therefore posed no independent challenge to the reign of property, whether land or capital. The radical bourgeoisie fought sharply for their own independent interests, mobilized subordinate classes on their behalf, and identified their particular interests with the general expansion of individual freedoms and political rights. The violent class struggles between labor and capital were still decades in the offing, scarcely discernible in these mid-century battles, in which artisans, miners and mine owners, smallholders and mill owners, fought side by side under the banner of democracy. As a result, the bourgeoisie had neither the temptation nor the need to cement a reactionary alliance with the landowners and to forge a repressive state to contain and discipline the workers. The historic option remained, however, and might well have been chosen, once the mass working-class struggles, especially in the nitrate fields, from the 1880s onward began to threaten capital at the end of the century. That this path was not 'chosen' is another peculiarity of Chilean history, which would require another analysis to explain. What can be said here, however, is that, paradoxically, when several decades later the Balmaceda regime (1886-91) attempted to put through a revolution from above, and to utilize the executive power of the state to enforce it, even against Parliament, liberal elements of the bourgeoisie allied with reactionary and clerical land-owners to resist and overthrow that regime. This, too, was a decisive, but contradictory, watershed in Chilean history, for it both buttressed bourgeois freedoms and stymied capitalist develop-ment — but that is another story.

The emergence and development of capitalist relations of produc-tion within Chile in the middle of the nineteenth century, as well as the subsequent development of Chilean capitalism, was unques-tionably bound up with — and I use that ambiguous phrase pur-posely, for reasons that should become clear in a moment — the ex-pansion of capitalism on a world scale. The mid-nineteenth century was, in fact, precisely a period of rapid growth of world trade in Europe without precedent — it increased from 1840 to 1850 by 70 percent, a rise whose rapidity 'was unsurpassed in the whole of the nineteenth century' (von Braunmuhl, 1979, p. 207). The specific process of accelerated capital accumulation within Chile at mid-century, through the production of commodities (cereals, flour, minerals) for exchange on the world market and solely as a means of realizing surplus value, could not have occurred if international capitalism, and with it 'a world-embracing commerce and a world-embracing market' (Marx, 1967, vol. I, p. 146), had not already reached a relatively high level (although, of course, both agriculture and manufacture in Chile were also spurred by the transformation of productive relations in the north, the appearance of masses of working men in the mines and on the railroads, which provided a burgeoning home market). In this sense, and to this ex-tent, it is unquestionable that the so-called integration of Chile into the world market is historically inseparable from the development of capitalism there.

Thus, Chile exemplifies the important methodological precept that not only the existence, but also the particular shape and historical development of particular nation states can be understood adequately only through an analysis of the relation between the state, the national capital and the *international* development of the contradictions of capital accumulation. [Holloway and Picciotto, 1979, p. 29; original emphasis]

Clearly, in every country that developed in the wake of development of capitalism in Europe and England, and especially in the aftermath of the latter's industrial revolution, 'class relations and the relation of the state apparatus to society bear in a specific manner the imprint of that country's position on the world market' (von Braunmuhl, 1979, p. 171). But, of course, the empirical question, and with it the theoretical meaning of such a generalization, is precisely, what does it mean to say: 'bears the imprint in a specific manner'? What that 'imprint' is, and how it is stamped into the specific historic development of a particular social formation, is exactly what is at issue, both on a generic theoretical level and in specific empirical cases. The critical question is how the important observation that states and classes and nations 'develop... within the context of the development of the world system' (Wallerstein, 1974a, p. 67) is translated into specific theoretical propositions and concrete hypotheses about the real connections between the so-called world economy and class relations, the nature of the state (and political power), national identity, and the pattern of development and underdevelopment in a given country or region.

For the world-system theory and some variants of 'dependency' theory, it is more than an important heuristic methodological precept, with which I certainly agree, to emphasize the need to investigate carefully the close and, I must add, *reciprocal* interconnections between the 'world market context' and the political relations and historic development of particular social formations.

Rather, this is the mere preface to the overarching theoretical assertion, which I reject (and which my concrete analysis of mid-nineteenth-century Chile clearly contradicts), that the 'world market' plays the '*dominant* role... in the determination of the particular form of development of the productive forces, of class relations and, last but not least, the specific configuration of the state apparatus, its function and its perception of its function as much as its position in the context of a class society' (von Braunmuhl, 1969, p. 167). So, what is supposedly primary, antecedent, causal, if we must, in the determination of the specific class relations and form and role of the state in a given country or region, is the world market or the world-system itself. *It*, supposedly, constitutes the 'totality' of which specific states and national political economies are merely the 'individual instances' or 'integral components' (von Braunmuhl, 1979, p. 172). Indeed, apparently, not only is the world-system the primary determinant of historic development or social change within particular social formations, but it forms a veritable ontological principle in the theory: it is, this world-system, the one and only reality: 'world-systems,' so it is said, 'are the *only real* social systems' (Wallerstein, 1974, pp. 384, 351; my emphasis)! The consequence of this rather extraordinary contemporary mix of nominalism and idealism is that classes and their contradictory interrelations and real struggles in the specific social formations they constitute historically now become merely the phenomenal form of a self-unfolding world-system. To name that world-system is thereby to discover, without empirical investigation, the reality of all its constituents; by naming the world-system a 'capitalist world-system,' we transform all other coexisting productive forms and class relations into merely variant forms of 'capitalism': 'The point is,' says Wallerstein, 'that the "relations of production" that define a system are the "relations of production" of the whole system and the system... is the... world-economy' (1974a, p. 127). Indeed, 'the modern world-economy is, and *can only be* [!], a capitalist world-economy. It is for this reason that we have rejected the appellation of "feudalism" for the various forms of *capitalist* agriculture *based on coerced labor* which grew up in a world-economy' (1974a, p. 350; my emphasis).

Quite clearly, I agree that the various repressive adaptations of agrarian relations of production to the development of capitalism from at least the sixteenth century on were not in any meaningful historic sense 'feudal'. I have emphasized the same point frequently in my work,[1] and in the present historical analysis, where I argued that capitalist development 'led to the landowners' successful imposition of new forms of social domination, in the guise of "precapitalist" and "archaic" seignorial relations in mid-nineteenth-century Chile.' But it is precisely the specific historical contradictions inherent in the development of 'pre-capitalist' forms of exploitation (including even the construction of new slave civilizations in parts of the Americas and the United States), as the result of the development of capitalism, that requires substantive analysis. To conceptualize them as 'capitalist,' despite the profoundly different class relations, internal dynamics, and state forms they involve in contrast to the relations between free wage labor and capital, results in the neglect of the most significant questions: how, in fact, do such class relations arise, or how are they resisted and free labor forms established? What class struggles between the agricultural producers and large landowners — and between the latter and capitalists — occur, under what conditions, with what long-term consequences for the development of the particular social formations resulting from these struggles? These are precisely the sort of questions I have had to grapple with in trying to understand the conundrum of the specific historic development of Chile; and, without an answer to these questions, the pattern of development of any particular social formation — and, indeed, as Brenner (1976) has persuasively argued, the original historical emergence of capitalism in England and Europe — is incomprehensible. By assuming the prior existence of capitalism, the world-system theory never has to address precisely that central question: what explains the origins and consolidation of distinctively capitalist relations of production?

By an unwitting conceptual sleight of hand that gives the same name to different realities or sees them as merely 'individual instances of the totality,' world-system theory's supposed attention to the 'whole system' makes the specific social realities that really constitute it historically disappear. The result is that an ostensibly historical theory is, in practice, un- and even anti-historical. By its ontological assumption that only the 'world-system' itself is 'real,' and by its focus on market relations alone, the theory obscures rather than reveals the concrete internal social relations that underlie that so-called 'capitalist world-economy' and propel its contradictory historical development. Within the theory, there is no way to analyze how the potential for capitalist development is determined by the emergence of a specific historic ensemble of class relations, based on specific methods of production and appropriation of the surplus product, in a particular social formation. Such critical questions as the following must go begging theoretically, for within the parameters of 'world-system theory' they can neither be asked nor answered. How does the specific historical configuration of class relations in a given social social formation affect its internal development? How did this class configuration originate historically? Why did class relations take this determinate historical form, and what were its developmental consequences? What are the specific internal dynamics of accumulation peculiar to these class relations, and how do they determine the impact of the 'world market' on the social formation's development? What is the relative impact of the 'world market' vs specific types of penetration and expansion by various units of capital, themselves affected by their internal relations with labor, on the pattern of development? — and what determines, on the one hand, the types of penetration and expansion of capital, and on the other, their consequences for a specific social formation?

Above all, the pattern of development of the world-system, or world market, the source of the so-called core/periphery, metropolis/satellite structure, etc., is simply assumed by the theory, taken as a given, and left unexplained. Or, in place of explanation, there appear tautologies: 'the historical development of this world-system' ('of this metropolis-satellite monopolist structure'), we are told, 'generated the development of the monopolizing metropolis and the underdevelopment of the monopolized satellites' (Frank, 1969, p. 240). Within the theory, there is no way that the absolutely central and critical question can be posed: what are the effects on the world-system itself of the actual class and intraclass struggles, state activities, and types of development in particular social formations, under specific historical cricumstances? What are their transformative consequences for the nature and structure of global political economic relations? How do class and interclass struggles within nations and states, and national struggles within, between, and against states, by radically realigning or transforming these class, state, and national relations, thereby also profoundly alter the global reality itself?

Rather than grappling squarely with these primary theoretical questions, generalizations bereft of historical content, such as the following, are offered:

While the advantages of the core-states have not ceased to expand throughout the history of the modern world system, the ability of a particular state to remain in the core sector is not beyond challenge. The hounds are ever to the hares for the position of top dog. Indeed, it may well be that in this kind of system it is *not structurally possible* to avoid, over a long period of historic time, a *circulation of the elites* in the sense that the particular country that is dominant at a given time tends to be replaced in this role sooner or later by another country. [Wallerstein, 1974a, p. 350; my emphasis]

This usage of a crucial notion from elitist theory is no mere semantic lapse. For, despite its historical trappings, world-*system* theory has no *historical* theory — no theory, that is, to explain the real historic development of the constituent social relations that actually structure the so-called world-system. It is, in fact, not a theory of historical development, of the origins and transformations of social relations, but of moving equilibrium, of stasis, of altered appearances but unchanging realities, of a system within which states mysteriously slip in and out of a pre-given categorical division between core, semi-periphery and periphery, a system which, as Wallerstein, not accidentally borrowing from Parsons, assures us, has 'a strong trend toward self-maintenance' (1974a, p. 350).

What explains this division? How did the so-called core, periphery and semi-periphery originate historically? The generic answer, in world-system theory, is that

> the capitalist world-economy was built on a worldwide division of labor in which various zones of this economy (that which we have termed the core, the semiperiphery, and the periphery) were *assigned* specific economic roles, developed different class structures, used consequently different modes of labor control, and profited unequally from the workings of the system. [Wallerstein, 1974a, p. 162; my emphasis]

But this is no answer at all. It does not even point toward an answer, and cannot because it both reifies the so-called capitalist world-economy and inverts the real historic process in which these global relations were created. The world economy itself, we are told, apparently 'assigned specific economic roles' within itself to its own 'zones,' and these 'zones' then 'used different modes of labor control...' etc. What has happened here, unfortunately, is that the theory's atemporal categories have imperceptibly been given a life of their own, and have imposed (whatever their author's intentions) on the social reality that was meant to be understood by them, so that now the categories make that reality fit their a priori selves.

Such a formulation, almost unnoticed, substitutes itself for historical explanation, and thereby begs the question that is most crucial: what explains the relative development of particular countries and areas, and how do they not only become located vis-à-vis each other within, but actually shape the global political economic relations in which they are involved?[2] Instead of disclosing how and why these global relationships eventuated as they did, an unwitting historical teleology assures us that this is what they had to become:

> The world economy was based precisely on the assumption [whose?] that there were in fact these three zones and that they did in fact have different modes of labor control. *Were this not so*, it would not have been possible to assure the kind of *flow* of the surplus which *enabled the capitalist system to come into existence.* [Wallerstein, 1974a, p. 87; my emphasis]

Just so; the world economy originated because of its consequences, because its inner purpose was realized in the birth of capitalism.

The reified categories and teleological arguments of the theory are inherent in its structure, because it displaces classes and their interrelations, and therefore the specific productive relationships that encourage rising labor productivity and compel the continual reinvestment of labor's surplus product, from the center of the analysis of development and underdevelopment. Indeed, despite the many references to 'classes' and 'class formation' in the metropolis/satellite or core/periphery world-system model, what appears, instead, are strata differentiated by their place in the world-system's 'hierarchy of occupational tasks,' having differentiated values, and receiving unequal 'rewards,' in accordance with their 'productive tasks' or 'levels of skill,' à la functionalist stratification theory.

> The division of a world-economy involves a hierarchy of occupational tasks, in which tasks requiring higher levels of skill and greater capitalization are reserved [how? by whom or what?] for higher ranking areas. Since a capitalist world-economy essentially rewards accumulated capital, including human capital, at a higher rate than 'raw' labor power, the geographical maldistribution of these occupational skills involves a strong trend toward self-maintenance....The social system is built on having a multiplicity of value systems within it, reflecting the specific functions groups and areas play in the world division of labor. [Wallerstein, 1974a, pp. 350, 356]

This stratification model conceals the real nature of class relations and mystifies their historical origins, and thereby also turns the real connection between the division of labor and class relations topsy-turvy. Within it, there are no relations of compulsion, coercion and exploitation, no relationship between producers and appropriators, oppressors and oppressed, dominant and subordinate classes. Slaves, serfs, tenant farmers, yeomen, artisans, and workers become merely 'occupational categories' (Wallerstein,

1974a, pp. 86-7); the real historical relations in which they are involved, the exploitation and domination to which they are subject by slaveowners, landlords and capitalists, simply disappear from the model, replaced by 'productive tasks' to which 'rewards' are distributed by some invisible hand.

Absent from the *model*, the historic origins of specific class relations almost disappear from the substantive analysis also. Despite the considerable (and correct) attention given to the discussion of slavery and other 'extra-economic' or coercive forms of exploitation that are erected anew as a consequence of the development of capitalism, even these real historic relations tend to appear only in a peculiarly disembodied form in the analysis itself. The impact of conquest, pillage, subjugation, and exploitation (and decimation) of populations in the Americas, India, and Africa by the armies of the various states of Europe and their merchants, slave traders, mine owners and adventurers from the sixteenth century onwards are certainly noted,[3] but they appear, nonetheless, as if they were the result of some self-expanding world-system. Thus, their real historical origins become obscured: 'Why different modes of organizing labor — slavery, "feudalism," wage-labor, self-employment — at the same point in time within the world economy? Because each mode of labor control is *best suited* for particular types of production' (Wallerstein 1974a, p. 87; my emphasis). And why are they 'best suited'? Because of the level of skill required. For example, since slaves will do only what they are compelled to do, 'once skill is involved, it is *more economic* [sic] to find alternative methods of labor control, since the low cost is otherwise matched by very low productivity' (Wallerstein, 1974a, p. 88). Thus, 'slavery was not used everywhere' (by whom?), primarily because certain types of production (grain, cattle-raising, and mining) 'required a higher level of skill among the basic production workers...These workers therefore had to be compensated for ['rewarded'?] by a slightly less onerous form of labor control' (Wallerstein, 1974a, p. 90). So, as in the functionalist stratification model, and even when confronted by historical realities entirely opposed to its basic assumptions and propositions, we find that the various historical forms of exploitation dissolve themselves into 'occupational categories' differentially rewarded (with a little bit of freedom) in accordance with their level of skill. So, slaves are slaves because what they produce makes them so; the objects produce their subjects; and the system provides its own rewards.[4]

That, in reality, the various forms of coercive class relations created in different areas of Asia, Africa, and the Americas were the unintended historical consequence of bloody struggles between colonial conquerors and native peoples, and the capacity the latter had to resist their subjugation and exploitation, given their material conditions and the nature of their own social formation before it was attacked and penetrated — these real historic origins of particular types of class relations in the so-called periphery all but vanish analytically. The nature, origins, and consequences of these class relations are not integrated in any systematic fashion into the analysis of development and underdevelopment, and of the historical division of the globe into its so-called core and periphery.

Shorn of systematic analysis of the historical potential of classes, based on the specific exploitative relations between them and their struggles to subvert and eliminate or to preserve and reinforce these relations, through which they make history (though not as they please), the historic process of development and underdevelopment is mystified. It takes on the appearance of a unilinear process of unexplained increasing social differentiation within the world-system, of system-expansion, or of the result of 'turbulence' in the value-system that disturbs the system's self-equilibration. What accounts for the development of the world-system? Its 'multilayered complexity provided the possibility of multilayered identification and the constant realignment of political forces, which provided at one and the same time the underlying turbulence that permitted technological development...' (Wallerstein, 1974a, p. 86).

Attributing development to turbulence in the system is a logical consequence of the analytical focus of the theory on the 'flow of surplus,' on the system's distribution of 'rewards,' rather than on the production and appropriation of the surplus product. We have been told, remember, that somehow 'the capitalist world-economy essentially rewards accumulated capital... at a higher rate than "raw" labor power' (Wallerstein, 1974a, p. 350), as a consequence of which comes the system's inequalities. The 'system' itself rewards its components (such as 'zones' and 'occupational skills'); but whence cometh these 'rewards,' what is their origin, how is wealth produced, what is the source of the 'surplus' that 'flows' within that world-system? How is the social product, by the very way in which it is produced socially, by the relations of production in which it is produced, already divided within the productive process between producers and appropriators? Within world-system theory, as in functionalism and bourgeois political economy, these questions go unasked.

What is the relationship between so-called 'accumulated capital' and ' "raw" labor power'? Now, a class theory of historical development puts such questions at its very center, and it attempts to explain rather than assume these relations. Capital is produced by labor power; it is the embodied productive capacity of the workers themselves; it is their surplus product, which under capitalism has been converted into the commodity form, appropriated from them over and above the product necessary for their own continued laboring existence. Under capitalism, the workers must produce for capital to produce for themselves, and capital cannot survive or expand otherwise; but the process takes on the appearance of free and equal exchange precisely because the class relationship is mediated by the commodity form, by the market, in and through which capital realizes the surplus value incorporated within the commodities labor produces. It is this class relationship within which capital is accumulated.

The way that the surplus product of the direct producers is extracted and appropriated by the dominant class(es) — and the struggles it involves — impels the development and underdevelopment of specific social formations. Once capitalism has already become ascendant historically, the critical question becomes: how are the various pre-capitalist social formations fitted into this exploitative process, whether through foreign conquest, colonial rule, and capital penetration, or through incorporation into the 'world market,' with what consequences for these social formations and their own development, and, in turn, with what consequences for the development of global relations?

If these class relations are not analyzed, the reasons for the historical origins of particular social formations, and the specific relations of production compelling or impeding accumulation within them, cannot be explained. Without such analysis, the sources of development and underdevelopment of particular countries or areas, and, as a consequence, of the so-called international division of labor in which they are located, remain a mystery. At best, and only in a highly limited way, only the question of 'unequal exchange' can be addressed; the question stays at the level of distribution of what is produced, as if it were preternaturally given, rather than attempting to discover, as any theory of development must, how and why it is produced. It is 'slapping history in the face to want to *begin* with the division of labor in general,' or with the market, as Marx once put it (1976, p. 183), so as to arrive at the class relations that actually underlie and determine it.

Thus, the capitalist world market and international division of labor appear upside down; they appear as the source of class relations in the 'world-system' model, rather than, as they are in reality, as the refracted historical product of class relations. The result of 'specialization of tasks' in the world division of labor, Wallerstein says, are 'differing forms of labor control and different patterns of stratification' (1974a, p. 84). In short, 'the different roles [in the division of labor] led to different class structures which led to different politics' (1974a, p. 157). The almost identical formulation appears in Frank's metropolis/satellite theory of underdevelopment.

> The colonial and class structure is the *product* of the introduction into Latin America of an ultraexploitative export economy, dependent on the metropolis, which restricted the internal market and created the economic interests of the lumpen bourgeoisie producers and exporters of raw materials. [Frank, 1972, p. 14; my emphasis]

In other words, 'the relations of production and the class structure...developed in response to the predatory needs of the...metropolis' (1972, p. 23).

These formulations, as I think my substantive historical analysis of Chile demonstrates, invert the actual historic process by which, because of specific processes of class formation and of class and intraclass struggle and state policy, productive capital becomes subordinated to landed property within the political economy, as well as to mercantile and speculative capital, so that the development of capitalism is stymied. To argue, as Frank does, that the 'introduction' of an 'ultraexploitative export economy' leads to underdevelopment, or that underdevelopment is the 'result,' as Wallerstein puts it, 'of being involved in the world economy as a peripheral raw material producing area' (1974a, p. 392), is to beg the main historical question entirely: What were the specific historic circumstances and the class relations and state activities in a given social formation that either allowed its conversion into a so-called satellite and its condemnation to 'peripheral raw material' production or, on the contrary, compelled the development of its productive forces and, therefore, determined its place in, and its impact on, the international division of labor or world market?

Even using this imagery of satellite/metropolis, core/periphery tends to becloud the analytical question. Because, of course, these are mere metaphors, which, as we have seen, when hardened before our eyes into realities of their own detract our attention precisely from the question just posed. Put differently, the question is two-fold: on the one hand, what determines the location and impact of a particular social formation on the so-called world-market? On the other, what produces that world market, what determines its division of labor and types of 'specialization,' between countries or regions producing mainly raw materials for export to others whose production is geared both to domestic and foreign markets for manufactured production and consumption goods (as well as agricultural commodities)? The answer to both sides of the question is the same. It is only because specific types of productive relations are established in a state or region (with determinate material conditions of production) in the first place that 'it' — that is, its dominant class(es) — can 'specialize' in certain types of production; and it is the reciprocal interaction between countries and regions, based on their internal class relations and material conditions and mediated through 'world market' exchange, that creates the division of labor between them on a global level. It is the class relations within nations that determine the global relations between them.

But our conclusions here, stated as general theoretical propositions, are already dangerously abstract — already too far removed from their necessary and only valid basis in the historically specific analysis of these interrelations in the concrete historical development of particular social formations. Only through such analysis (which I have attempted in my own assessment of the meaning of the mid-nineteenth-century struggles in Chile between landed property and capital and the shaping of the form and content of its specific bourgeois state) can the fruitfulness and validity of these propositions be assessed. What is more, in my effort to re-place the theoretical emphasis on the primary source of development, the class relations between producers and appropriators and the nature of the state under given material and historical circumstances, the generalizations have emerged, perhaps, in too linear a form. These are not linear, but dialectical relationships, in which the class relations and patterns of development within states (or regions) and the global political economic relations established between them (as I think the preceding substantive analysis of Chile demonstrates) have reciprocal effects on each other. In a real sense, these relations not only reciprocally affect each other; they interpenetrate.

No analysis of the historical development of Chile, as I have emphasized, can possibly be adequate that does not take into account the impact on it of Chile's place in global political economic relations, and of the specific form taken by foreign penetration in Chile. What happens in the 'world market' at this time (mid-nineteenth century) necessarily reverberates throughout Chilean society. Chile's capitalists thrived on foreign demand for copper, grain, and flour, in the finance and sale of which English (and some German) capitalists and bankers in Chile as well already had a significant role (a role, however, that was to become of primary significance in actual production, especially nitrates, only later, in the decades following the abortive revolution).

Moreover, not only did foreign capital at this time already have a role (mainly indirect) in the exploitation of Chilean labor, through the appropriation in interest charges and commercial profits of a share of Chilean capital's profits; but Chilean capital, also, was beginning to exploit not only Chilean, but foreign, labor. Within decades, major Chilean capitalists would have direct investments in railroads and mines in Bolivia and Peru; and would fight an imperialist war to annex successfully these countries' territories in the altiplano. They would also manipulate so-called world market prices for their own primary products from their seats on the London exchange and Paris Bourse, form partnerships with English bankers, traders and nitrate capitalists, and participate with them in organizing the control of world nitrate production and marketing, through cartels and other 'nitrate combinations,' and so on. Finally, in still another decisive historical turning point, the relationship within the dominant class, between elements of Chilean banking and nitrate capital on the one hand and British capital on the other, as well as the role of British and French state policy, was to be crucial in the defeat of the revolution from above attempted under Balmaceda's leadership.

Thus, 'internal' and 'external,' national and foreign, class and global relations intrude on and interpenetrate each other at critical points, in their historical development and in contemporary reality. But we must be clear that — to put it with perilous abstraction — this is an asymmetrical dialectic of historical development: it is, in the first instance, the particular ensemble of class and class-state relations formed historically within a given social formation that determines how and to what extent global relations will affect their development.[5]

'World-system' theory has borne the brunt of the present critique as a way of clarifying further the general method and theory of the preceding substantive historical analysis; but it was not selected arbitrarily. It is, first of all, a theory with basic assumptions and propositions which directly contradict my own; and it appears, in particular, as the underlying intellectual structure of a recent important and very influential historical sociological study. Yet, despite the immense scholarship and rich intelligence displayed in that work, it is flawed critically by its author's theory — a theory that hobbles the understanding of the very historical social realities the work is aimed at analyzing. World-system theory also bears the brunt of my critique because, despite the radical political commitments of its advocates, the theory itself is the latest influential variant of what has long been the dominant mode of bourgeois thought here. It is regnant today in one form or another in every social science discipline in the United States, whatever the name attached to it (neoclassical synthesis, cliometrics, modernization theory, or structural-functionalism), and now is also put forth here and abroad as 'Marxism' (structuralism).

It is an idealist mode of thought in which, as Marx long ago put it, 'fixed, immutable, eternal categories' masquerade for social reality. It is a mode of thought in which, in place of real men and women making the social relations that make them, 'the social system' appears as a structure bereft of any subject other than its own self-moving 'market' or functional sub-systems. Men and women make rare appearances only as evanescent systemic epiphenomena: as Parsonian 'actors' or 'concrete units' whose 'interaction' is determined by the constituent 'regulatory patterns' of the social system's 'value system,' in conformity with its own 'goals' and 'functional requirements,' or as Althusserian 'supports of functions,' and, above all, as *never anything more* than the occupants' or 'agents' of 'places and functions' (Althusser and Balibar, 1970, pp. 112, 180; my emphasis). Society, as the ensemble of the real social relationships in which men and women are involved, and that they make and are made by, becomes instead a 'social system [that] has the characteristics of an organism,' and their history becomes merely a tale told of how, over its 'life span...its characteristics change in some respects and remain stable in others...in terms of the internal logic of its functioning' (Wallerstein, 1974a, p. 347).

In contrast to such notions, our own substantive analysis reveals, on the most general level of abstraction, how thoroughly 'social structures' are partially contingent historical products, actively created and recreated by real men and women, involved in determinate social relations that were themselves produced historically, by prior human activity. Of these social relations it is the contradictory relations in which men and women produce and transform their own conditions of existence, through which they thereby also reproduce and transform the ensemble of social relations between them, that we call 'society.' Classes form themselves in the struggle to reduce or intensify the exploitative process inherent in the relations of production in which they are involved. This struggle, in turn, enters into and shapes these relationships and the process of class formation itself. It simultaneously structures the relations within classes and the relations between them. Class relations, and class 'interests,' in short, are both 'objectively given' and are themselves the dialectical historic product of these relations.

Classes, indeed, are distinguished precisely by their history-making potential. The productive relations in which classes make themselves set objective limits to potential historical development and, as Przeworski has put it well, simultaneously constitute 'a structure of choices given at a particular moment of history. Social relations are given to a subject, individual or collective, as *realms of possibilities*...a set of conditions that determine what course of action has what consequences for social transformations' (1977, p. 377). In this way, the consciousness of classes, however inelegant, inchoate or 'false,' enters into class relations as an intrinsic and constitutive characteristic of these relations. The consciousness that classes have of themselves is the consciousness expressed in their practical political activity, which in turn conditions and transforms their consciousness and, in consequence, the very nature of the classes and their relations. In this sense, class conflict and class formation are moments of the same social process; neither follows as an 'effect' or is necessarily prior. Rather, they reciprocally interpenetrate in real historic development. Classes are shaped by and in specific struggles and by the consequences (intended and unwitting) of these struggles, as well as by unique circumstances and events (including decisive defeats) that, as Max

Weber once remarked, 'load the historic dice.' Classes are determined both by their objective location in a historically specific
ensemble of production relations and by their self-activity, through
which they constitute and transform these relations and their location within them. In this sense, and to this extent, classes and class
relations, and the social formations they define, possess an inherent, relatively contingent, historicity. This, in a phrase, sums
up my conception of society and its development. It is a conception
put far better by Marx, in words everyone who is committed not
only to understanding the world, but to changing it, should take as
a guide:

> Men make their own history, but they do not make it just as they please; they do
> not make it under circumstances chosen by themselves, but under circumstances
> directly found, given and transmitted from the past. [Marx, 1963, p. 15]

NOTES

1. See, for instance, Petras and Zeitlin (1968), especially the articles by Rodolfo
Stavenhagen, Luis Vitale, and Anibal Quijano, in which the myth of 'feudalism' in
Latin America is systematically attacked (a myth that until then was accepted by
most liberal and Marxian theorists of development) and the significance of mercantile capitalism and the integration of Latin America in the world market in the
origins of class relations is emphasized. Also see Zeitlin (1969; 1972).

2. Extensive evidence appears in the work whose theoretical meaning is ignored,
especially in the lengthy footnote quotations from various historical sources.
Wallerstein's own account, together with these footnotes, of the emergent and
changing roles of Spain, France, the Netherlands, and England in early capitalist
development suggests strongly, contrary to his own theory, that it was the internal
class and class-state relations in these countries — struggles between the 'mesta,' the
Catalan bourgeoisie and the crown in Spain; specific historical forms of agrarian
production and tenure relations in England and France and their effect on the cohesion of the landed in their relation to the state; and the lengthy anti-feudal struggles
culminating in the Netherlands revolution — that explain their development and
determined the nature and extent of their impact on and place within global
political economic relations. See Wallerstein (1974a, pp. 166-67; 181-4; 192-5;
201-11; 227-35).

3. One difficulty in critically examining world-system theory, as in this instance,

is that it is the underpinning of a study in which, as just noted, there are a host of citations and lengthy footnote quotations of arguments and evidence from various historical studies, whose analytical relevance and theoretical meaning are not explicated but, on examination, are often inconsistent with world-system theory. Limitations of space, and the fact that this is not a review of Wallerstein's book, but of the theory in it, precludes detailing them. One egregious example of this might be given, though. There are numerous references in the book, as there should be, to the works of such outstanding Marxian historians as Maurice Dobb and R. H. Hilton. The main evidence and theoretical reasoning of their own works on the development of capitalism directly contradict world-system theory. But Wallerstein never grapples explicitly with their central thesis (enunciated sharply in their debate with Paul M. Sweezy and, by extension, with Henri Pirenne) concerning the transition from feudalism to capitalism: that it was in the internal contradiction between petty production and coercive extraction of the direct producer's surplus product under feudalism, and not in trade originating 'outside the feudal system' that capitalist production relations emerged historically. As Hilton put it:

> The economic progress which was inseparable from the early rent struggle and the political stabilization of feudalism was characterized by an increase in the total social surplus of production over subsistence needs. This, *not* the so-called revival of *international trade* in silks and spices, was *the basis for the development of commodity production*. [My emphasis]

This quotation appears at the end of a lengthy footnote (Wallerstein, 1974a, pp. 41-2) in which other quite relevant quotations from Pirenne and Sweezy on the one side and Dobb on the other precede it. But Wallerstein's only comment relating to these quotations is to say that it was probably trade in staples rather than trade in luxuries that accounted for 'the expansion of European commerce' (1974a, p. 41). So the question is converted into what sort of trade leads to expanded trade; and the production relations on which that trade rested and which made its expansion possible disappears as a question, despite its appearance in a footnote. Even when it appears that this question is obliquely being addressed, the proposed answer is circularly contained by the theory. So the expansion of trade, it is argued, required the expansion of production, and this took place through 'technological innovation...precisely where there was dense population and industrial growth...which were the very places where it became more profitable to turn the land use to commercial crops' (Wallerstein, 1974a, p. 42). But, of course, this ignores the basic question, as to why in some places where it was 'profitable to turn the land use to commercial crops,' the result was not at all 'technological innovation' or 'industrial growth,' but, on the contrary, the reinforcement of coercive means of surplus labor extraction and the stagnation of technique. The question is what relations of production, what relations between the peasantry and the landowners, made an absolute growth of production possible, not on the basis of existing techniques in agriculture and heavier burdens on the peasantry, but, on the contrary, through technical innovations and rising labor productivity by relatively independent cultivators? As Brenner has put it precisely, 'To account for capitalist economic development is, therefore, at least to explain the basis for this conjunction between the requirements for surplus extraction and the needs of the developing productive forces' (1977, p. 68); and this, in turn, means to discover the class relations produced historically, as the unintended consequence of class struggles in which the peasantry freed themselves from extraeconomic coercion by the landlords, that made accumulation through rising labor productivity possible.

4. Again, this 'explains' the origins of class relations by their consequences, and inverts the historic process. It may be true that slave labor was relatively less productive than free labor, in other words that slavery impeded labor productivity. But it certainly was not low labor productivity that led to slavery. Quite apart from the theoretical issue, the fact is that many skilled craftsmen were slaves in both ancient Greece and Rome and in the American South, where their planter masters often rented them out for employment by others, even as factory workers.

5. One of the problems haunting any theoretical discussion of development and underdevelopment and its relationship to the so-called world market is precisely the absence of historical specification, or the tendency to state relationships as if they are not themselves historically produced and historically determinate. So we must be wary of projecting contemporary global relationships, or even those established during the imperialist era of accelerated territorial annexations and conquests in the last quarter of the past century, into the preceding historical epoch when capitalism had not yet become the ascendant mode of production. How the disparate areas of the globe and the class and class-state relations within them were related at the dawn of the capitalist era, how they became related under late nineteenth-century imperialism, and how they are related in the present may have quite different answers with quite different theoretical implications for our understanding of development and underdevelopment. The essentials can be disclosed only through historically specific analysis. Certainly, a critical theoretical and social issue today is how the various countries fit into contemporary international capitalism, and how they affect and are affected by the global political economic relations now dominated by multinational corporations based in a few of the advanced capitalist countries. These corporations now command labor, administer production, and accumulate capital throughout the globe, as their singular theater of operations; and the competitive struggle between them, conditioned by and conditioning their relations with labor nationally and internationally, is of unquestionable importance in shaping contemporary realities. But, again, it is not the 'world market' but the internationalization of class relations and class struggle that has to be the focus of our theoretical inquiry and political practice.

REFERENCES

ALTHUSSER, Louis, and R. Etienne BALIBAR (1970) *Reading Capital*. London: New Left Books.

AMUNÁTEGUI SOLAR, Domingo (1946) *La Democracia en Chile: Teatro Politico (1810-1910)*. Santiago: Universidad de Chile.

ANDERSON, Perry (1974) *Lineages of the Absolutist State.* London: New Left Books.

BARAN, Paul (1957) *The Political Economy of Growth.* New York: Monthly Review Press.

BAUER, Arnold J. (1975) *Chilean Rural Society from the Spanish Conquest to 1930.* Cambridge: University Press.

BRENNER, Robert (1976) 'Agrarian Class Structure and Economic Development in Pre-Industrial Europe,' *Past and Present,* no. 70 (February): 30-75.

BRENNER, Robert (1977) 'The Origins of Capitalist Development: A Critique of Neo-Smithian Marxism,' *New Left Review,* no. 104 (July-August): 25-92.

BUNSTER, Enrique (1965) *Chilenos en California: Miniaturas Historicas,* 3rd ed. Santiago: Editorial del Pacifico.

EDWARDS VIVES, Alberto (1932) *El Gobierno de Manuel Montt, 1851-1861.* Santiago: Editorial Nascimento.

ENCINA, Francisco A. (1949) *Historia de Chile: desde la Prehistoria hasta 1891,* vol. XIII. Santiago: Editorial Nascimento.

ENCINA, Francisco A. (1955) *Nuestra inferioridad ecónomica: sus causas, sus consequencias,* 9th ed. Santiago: Editorial Universitaria (originally published 1911).

FRANK, Andre Gundar (1969) *Latin America: Underdevelopment or Revolution.* New York: Monthly Review Press.

FRANK, Andre Gundar (1972) *Lumpenbourgeoisie: Lumpenproletariat. Dependence, Class, and Politics in Latin America.* New York: Monthly Review Press.

HOLLOWAY, John, and Sol PICCIOTTO (eds) (1979) *State and Capital: A Marxist Debate.* Austin, Texas: University of Texas Press.

JOBET BÚRQUEZ, Julio Cesar (1955) *Ensayo Critico del Desarrollo Economico Social de Chile.* Santiago: Editorial Universitaria.

LENIN, Vladimir (1934) *Selected Works,* vol. III. Moscow and Leningrad: Cooperative Publishing Society of Foreign Workers in the USSR.

MARX, Karl (1963) *The Eighteenth Brumaire of Louis Bonaparte.* New York: International Publishers (originally published 1852).

MARX, Karl (1967) *Capital,* vols. I-III. New York: International Publishers (originally published 1867-79).

MARX, Karl (1976) *The Poverty of Philosophy,* pp. 105-212 in Karl Marx and Frederick Engels, *Collected Works,* vol. 6. New York: International Publishers (originally published 1847).

MOORE, Barrington, Jr (1966) *Social Origins of Dictatorship and Democracy.* Boston: Beacon Press.

OPPENHEIMER, Robert Ballen (1976) 'Chilean Transportation Development: The Railroads and Socio-Economic Change in the Central Valley, 1840-1885,' Department of History, UCLA, unpublished PhD dissertation.

PETRAS, James, and Maurice ZEITLIN (eds) (1968) *Latin America: Reform or Revolution?* Greenwich, Conn.: Fawcett.

PRZEWORSKI, Adam (1977) 'Proletariat into Class: The Process of Class Formation from Karl Kautsky's The Class Struggle to Recent Controversies,' *Politics & Society,* 7 (4): 343-401.

PRZEWORSKI, Joanne Fox (1974) 'The Responses of Chilean Entrepreneurs to Changing Copper Prices, 1874-1887. A Preliminary Analysis,' paper presented at forty-first Congress of Americanists, Mexico, D.F., September.

RAMÍREZ NECOCHEA, Hernan (1955) *Historia del Movimiento Obrero*, Siglo XIX. Santiago: Empresa Editora Austral.

RAMÍREZ NECOCHEA, Hernan (1960)   *Historia del Imperialismo en Chile*. Santiago: Empresa Editora Austral.

SEGALL, Marcello (1953) *Desarrollo del Capitalismo en Chile*. Santiago: privately published; distributed by Editorial del Pacifico.

STERNBERG, Marvin (1962) 'Chilean Land Tenure and Land Reform,' Unpublished PhD dissertation. University of California at Berkeley.

TORNERO, Santos (1861) *Cuadro Historico de la Administración Montt escrito segun sus propios documentos*. Valparaíso: Imprenta i Libreria del Mercurio.

VITALE, Luis (1971) *Interpretación Marxista de la Historia de Chile*, vol. III. Santiago: Prensa Latina.

VON BRAUNMUHL, Claudia (1979) 'On the Analysis of the Bourgeois Nation State Within the World Market Context. An Attempt to Develop a Methodological and Theoretical Approach,' pp. 160-77 in Holloway and Picciotto (1979).

WALLERSTEIN, Immanuel (1974a) *The Modern World-System: Capitalist Agriculture and the Origins of the European World-Economy in the Sixteenth Century*. New York: Academic Press.

WALLERSTEIN, Immanuel (1974b) 'The Rise and Future Demise of the World Capitalist System: Concepts for Comparative Analysis,' *Comparative Studies in Society and History*, 16 (January): 387-415.

ZEITLIN, Maurice (1969) 'Cuba — Revolution without a Blueprint,' *Trans-action*, 6 (6) (April): 38-42; 61.

ZEITLIN, Maurice (1972) 'Camilo's Colombia: The Political, Economic, and Religious Background to Revolution,' pp. 1-46 in Father Camilo Torres, *Revolutionary Writings*, edited by Maurice Zeitlin. New York: Harper and Row.

ZEITLIN, Maurice, W. Lawrence NEUMAN, and Richard E. RATCLIFF (1976) 'Class Segments: Agrarian Property and Political Leadership in the Capitalist Class of Chile,' *American Sociological Review* 41 (December): 1006-29.

5

SOME OBSERVATIONS ON STRUCTURALISM IN SOCIOLOGY, WITH SPECIAL, AND PARADOXICAL, REFERENCE TO MAX WEBER

S. N. Eisenstadt
The Hebrew University

TRADITIONS OF STRUCTURAL ANALYSIS IN SOCIOLOGY

The most recent vogue of structuralism in sociology and anthropology has been connected, above all, with the work of Lévi-Strauss (1963, 1966, 1967, 1968, 1969, 1970, 1971a, b) and his followers (for example, Needham, 1960; Leach, 1967, 1970) and of some of the Marxists — such as M. Godelier (1973, 1978; see also Sebag, 1964) who tend to combine Marxism with structuralism. But this is only one aspect or dimension of 'structuralist' approaches and controversies in social sciences in general and in sociology in particular; to understand those issues fully it is worthwhile to put them into a somewhat broader historical context.

The structuralism of Lévi-Strauss has stressed, as we shall see in greater detail later on, the importance of the symbolic dimension of human experience as against the institutional-organizational aspects of social life, claiming that the structure of the latter is derivable from the rules of the former. But, as is well known, the terms 'structure' and 'structural analysis' in sociology derive first of all through the emphasis on social structure. These analyses have developed in opposition to what we have identified elsewhere as the 'discrete' approach to the analysis of sociological phenomena — be they behavior of individuals, structures of groups, or the like — the most important characteristic of which is that it views such phenomena as relatively separate and discrete entities or traits which tend to coalesce either randomly or in terms of some external forces which are not social but physical, biological, or spiritual (see Eisenstadt and Curelaru, 1976). As is well known, such an approach was predominant in the first stages of development of sociological theory and has persisted to this day.

It is against such approaches that there gradually developed in sociological theory and analysis a much stronger emphasis on the emergent quality of (different aspects of) social structure and the view of such structures as having relatively autonomous properties, major aspects of which shape the more concrete patterns of behaviour or features of organizations and without reference to which these patterns or features cannot be fully understood.

From this point of view, we can discern three major 'structuralist' traditions in the history of sociological analysis. One, connected above all with the work of Karl Marx and later with the functional (English) school of anthropology and with the structural-functional school in sociology, as represented by Talcott Parsons, has laid the main stress on the systemic qualities of social groups and societies. It has maintained that different concrete patterns of behavior and social organization can be understood only in terms of their 'place' or contributions to the working of such larger systemic entities, in other words, by their functions in the working of such systems (Parsons, 1964; Parsons and Shils, 1956; Parsons and Smelser, 1965).

The second structural tradition, most fully epitomized in Merton's (1963, especially chapter XI) work in general and in his analysis of roles, role sets, status, and status-sets in all their rich manifestations, has focussed on what may be called the major mechanisms that organize the emergent structural properties of social structure, and that influence — often in unexpected ways — the behavior of individuals and shape many specific details of the structuring of concrete social organization.

The third structural tradition — which to some degree overlaps the second one — has crystallized in the school of formal sociology in Germany in general, and in the work of Georg Simmel (1908) in particular (Wolf, 1950; see also Eisenstadt and Curelaru, 1976), and has been more recently developed in Blau's work on *Inequality and Heterogeneity* (1977). This tradition has particularly emphasized the analysis of the formal characteristics of social interaction — such as the social distance or proximity between individuals and groups, the structuring of social interaction in terms of hierarchy and equality, the patterns of distribution of individuals among social positions — and of the constraints they exert on the activities of individuals.

It is interesting to note that, with the partial exception of Merton's work, there has been little direct confrontation between these different models of traditions of structural analysis and only a few attempts to analyze their interrelations and the mutual constraints that the dimensions of structure emphasized by these approaches exert on one another.

Neither was there, until recently, much confrontation between such structuralist or structural approaches and those — such as the works of Dilthey in Germany or the culturologists in American anthropology — that emphasized the primacy of the cultural or spiritual dimension of human life. Indeed, one front against which the structural approaches developed has initially been that of such culturalistic approaches.

RECENT CONTROVERSIES IN SOCIOLOGY AND THE EMERGENCE OF SYMBOLIC STRUCTURALISM

The relative novelty of the recent (above all, Lévi-Straussian) structuralism resides in searching for the structural principles that shape social organization and structure, not in the sphere of social organization but in that of the symbolic dimension of human activities.

The claims of the (symbolic) structuralists can be seen as part of the more general criticism directed against the structural-functional model which began to be vocal since the mid-1960s. These criticisms comprised, in addition to the structuralists, such schools as the 'conflict' school represented by Dahrendorf (1961), Bendix (1968), and Collins (1975); the exchange school, represented by Homans (1961), Blau (1967), Coleman (1966, 1979); the symbolic interactionist and ethnomethodology models, with their emphasis on the construction by individuals in their social interaction of the meanings of the definition of situations in which they interact (Blumer, 1969; Goffman, 1959; Garfinkel, 1967; Cicourel, 1973); the Marxist model or models which were revived in the late 1960s; and the 'systems,' or 'secondary cybernetic' approach to the analysis of social systems, developed above all by Walter Buckley

(1967), Margoroh Maruyama (1968) and Karl Deutsch (1963).

The discussions developed around these various models and counter-models, the continuous confrontation of the counter-models with the structural-functional model, and with each other, constituted the focus of theoretical discussions and controversies in sociology from about the middle 1950s onwards.

Perhaps the theme common to all these schools or approaches has been the non-acceptance of the 'natural' givenness of any single institutional order in terms of its organizational needs or prerequisites. Any institutional arrangement — be it the formal structure of a factory or a hospital, the division of labor in the family, the critical definition of deviant behavior, or the place of a ritual in a given social setting — was no longer taken for granted, as given and derivable from its functional place in the broader social system. The different patterns of behavior that developed in connection with it were no longer examined only or mainly in terms of their contribution to the workings of such a setting. The very introduction and continuity of such institutional arrangements was transposed from a given into a problem to be studied.

The various models differed in their proposals for coping with this problem of how to explain concrete institutional orders. One proposal emphasizes the point that any institutional order develops, is maintained, and is changed through a process of continuous interaction, negotiation, and struggle among those who participate in it. Within this broad approach, the conflict and exchange schools emphasized the elements of power and bargaining over resources in such negotiations, while the symbolic-interactionists and ethnomethodologists focussed on the definition of the meaning of these situations and especially on the basic codes of the language of social interaction.

In contrast, the (symbolic) structuralists, and to some degree the Marxists, provided a seemingly contradictory answer to the problem. They emphasized the search for some principles of 'deep' or 'hidden' structure of social structure akin to the kind that, according to linguists such as Chomsky, provide the deep structure of language. In attempting to identify the principles of this structure, the Marxists stressed a combination of structural and symbolic dimensions — such as the dialectic between forces and relations of production, alienation, class struggle and class consciousness — as providing the principles of the deep structure of societies that explain their crucial institutional features and dynamics.

THE BASIC PREMISES OF
SYMBOLIC STRUCTURALISM

The symbolic structuralists, on the other hand, stressed the importance of the symbolic dimension of human activity, of some inherent rules of the human mind.

Lévi-Strauss's own emphasis on the autonomous characteristics
of the symbolic sphere and on its inherent internal structure was to
no small degree derived from a dissatisfaction with the derivation
or development of Durkheim's work in (above all English) social
anthropology which tended to explain the symbolic sphere in terms
of contributions to the workings of the social system. Instead, he
stressed the high degree of autonomy and dimension of human
nature, culture, and also of social order.

But structuralism, as developed by Lévi-Strauss, goes beyond the
mere emphasis on the autonomy, importance, or even
predominance of the symbolic dimension in the construction of
culture and society. The crux of the structuralist claim (Macrae,
1968; Godard, 1965) is, first, that there exists within any society or
culture some 'hidden structure' that is more real, permeating the
overt social organization or behavioral patterns; second, that the
rules that govern such structure are not concrete rules of organization and are not derived from organizational or institutional needs
or problems but are crystallized code-wise in the rules of the human
mind; third, that it is these rules that are the constitutive element of
culture and society, and they provide for deeper ordering principles
of the social and cultural realms; fourth, that the most important
of these rules (according, at least, to Lévi-Strauss and his followers)
are those of binary opposition, which are inherent givens in all
perceptions of the world by the human mind, and the rules of
transformation which govern the ways in which the contradictions
that are supposedly inherent in the working of human minds are
resolved; and, fifth, that it is these principles that constitute the real
models of the society — that is, the models according to which
society is structured — which need not be identical with the conscious models represented in the minds of its participants or symbolized in various concrete situations.

Lévi-Strauss, and especially his followers, continuously stressed
that their method was applicable to the explanation not only of
cultural creations, and output — symbols, myths, and the like —
but also to social phenomena and to social life (for example,

Maranda, 1972), thus continously impinging on the work of 'conventional' social anthropologists and giving rise to animated and vociferous discussions between the two camps.

Given that the structuralist position was a combination of sociological or anthropological and philosophical analysis (Scholte, 1966; Lepenies and Ritter, 1972; Rossi, 1973; Rotenstreich, 1972), and that most of the structuralists dealt with the system of rules that governs or explains various symbolic creations (for instance, Maranda and Maranda, 1971), while most of the 'conventional' anthropological analyses were concerned with problems of organization and institutional aspects of social systems, the discussions between them turned into heated controversies. In these controversies, theoretical axioms and empirical levels of analysis were often intermixed in such ways that they did not facilitate the development of fruitful confrontations or hypotheses or specification of the types of data through which the different approaches could be tested and validated.

STRUCTURALIST CHALLENGES FOR SOCIOLOGICAL ANALYSIS

Yet in principle, the confrontations that developed in sociological and anthropological research in relation to these controversies can be of great interest for the further development of sociological analysis. Such potentially fruitful confrontations have developed, as Eisenstadt and Curelaru (1976) have shown elsewhere in detail, in studies of modernization, development, and convergence of industrial societies. In these studies, the dissatisfaction with the initial 'classical' models of modernization, with their strong neo-evolutionary orientations and the close relations to the structural-functional school, has given rise to a strong emphasis on cultural traditions, as manifest in symbolic systems or orientations which are at least one important factor that shapes the institutional development of these societies.

The initial emphasis on the importance of tradition in shaping the institutional contours of modernizing societies, which has been in principle close to the structuralist approach, was indeed, on the one hand, persuasive. However, it has also indicated the weak points of this approach, points that at the same time are of great importance for the further development of sociological analysis, a development that would incorporate the structuralist challenge in the mainstream of sociological analysis.

They have indicated that the structuralists (and the upholders of 'tradition' in studies of modernization) have failed to come to grips with several crucial questions and problems inherent in their assumptions or approaches. The most important of these problems is to determine which aspects of the symbolic realm, of 'culture' and of the human mind are indeed of importance in providing the possible principles of deep structure of societies. Besides, they failed to indicate the concrete institutional and organizational loci and derivatives of these symbolic rules, of the so-called general rules of the human mind; in other words, they failed to indicate the ways through which these rules impinge on the actual workings of societies, that is the institutional areas that are shaped by the symbolic dimensions of human activities. Finally, they failed to identify the carriers and social mechanisms through which such orientations, the principles of deeper structure, are activated within institutional frameworks.

SOME POSSIBLE RESPONSES:
THE CONTRIBUTION OF MAX WEBER

The delineation, in the framework of these controversies, of the problems raised by the structuralist approach, and the consequent confrontation between the major theoretical approaches in sociological analysis, made some constructive meetings between them possible.

One such constructive meeting, which focused on the central problems stemming from confrontations and from the study of comparative civilizations in general and of modernization in particular, brings us back to Weber. To my mind, Weber's work on comparative religions provided important indications about possible answers to these problems, although this has often been forgotten in the substantive controversy about the Protestant Ethic (see Eisenstadt, 1968). To understand that full impact of his work it is best to come back to this major starting point in his comparative studies of religion and especially to the role of the Protestant Ethic thesis in the general theory (Weber, 1951, 1952a, b).

As is well known, these studies have shown that many of the organizational aspects of capitalism had developed in all great civilizations, whether China, India, or ancient Israel — often much beyond what can be found in Europe of the sixteenth or seventeenth century. Yet it was only in Europe that a full-fledged capitalist economic order or civilization developed. The clue to this unique development in the West lies, according to Weber, in Protestantism. But it is not just general characteristics of Protestantism that are of crucial importance in this analysis. Rather it is certain specific aspects of Protestant belief and of the social structure of its carriers that provide clues to some of the problems posed by the structuralist controversy in general and to its possible impact on studies of comparative civilizations and modernization in particular.

The starting point of such an analysis is the examination and elaboration of one of the central analytical concepts developed by Weber, namely, that of 'Wirtschaftsethik' (see Eisenstadt, 1973, 1978). A 'Wirtschaftsethik' neither connotes specific religious injunctions about proper behavior in the economic field nor is just a logical derivative of the intellectual contents of the theology or philosophy predominant in a religion. Rather, as above all Weber's analysis of the non-European religions indicates, 'Wirtschaftsethik' has to do with a general mode of 'religious' or 'ethical' orientation; with the evaluation of a specific institutional sphere based on the premises of given religion or tradition about the cosmic order and its relation to human and social existence, and consequently, to the organization of social life.

Thus, 'Wirtschaftsethik' is, in a sense, a 'code,' a general 'formal' orientation, a 'deeper structure,' which programs or regulates the actual concrete social organization.

Although most of Weber's work dealt explicitly with the relation of such 'codes' to the economic sphere, his work throughout, in general and notably in the discussion of non-European civilizations or religions, contains extremely important analyses of what may be called the 'Status Ethic' and the 'Political Ethic' of the great religions, that is, the religious evaluation of different dimensions of status or of the political sphere (see Eisenstadt, 1968). The analysis of the non-European religions especially showed how the codes of a religion exert their influence on the institutional setting of the society or civilization within which the religion operates, and on the direction of change in it.

Such codes are indeed given, for Weber as for Lévi-Strauss, in the very nature of the human situation, but not as abstract categories of the human mind. Unlike many modern structuralists, Weber did not conceive a symbolic code as a purely 'formal' category of the human mind which organizes only a set of abstract, symbolic categories. Rather, it is rooted in the symbolic expression of the existential nature and problematics of man. Weber conceived of such codes as the key to the unlocking of the basic symbolic structural and organizational elements of human and social existence in his analysis. For him, they are the guide in the search for salvation and for the different possible solutions to the existential problem, a search and solution given in the very construction of symbolic reality by man.

Weber's analysis also specifies the direction in which to look for the carriers and mechanisms of such codes, above all among the articulators of cultural and social models in general and among religious activists in particular.

In his analysis Weber identified the movements of 'orthodoxy' and 'heterodoxy' both as carriers of continuity of the basic codes of these civilizations and as indicators of possible changes in their range. He showed how out of different constellations of such carriers there developed in specific institutional settings the potentialities of change of the major religions, and he indicated the different concrete ways in which such potentialities were actualized.

His analysis also points out — most explicitly in the studies of the Chinese literati and Hindu Brahmins — that it is the control over communication, over the use of resources and of access to control positions, that constitutes the most important mechanisms through which these carriers institutionalized such codes or orientations.

Moreover, implicit in Weber's work is the specification of the areas of social organizations that are shaped by such codes. Even here, however, his analysis indicates that among the most important are the patterns of authority and legitimation of regimes; the major models of political economy and of relations between state and economy that are prevalent in them; the structuring of social hierarchies; and the character of class and status conflicts.

It is these different institutional patterns that are related to some of the basic conceptions and premises prevalent in their respective societies — derivable from their basic codes. It is by shaping these aspects of the institutional structure that these conceptions can be seen as providing the principles of deeper structure of societies. These are the principles that shape the specific characteristics of the different societies beyond those of their characteristics that can be explained in terms derived from the more sociological traditions of structural analysis, such as levels of structural differentiation (see Eisenstadt, 1978).

Thus we see that Weber's work provides indications, however preliminary, of answers to the problems posed by the structuralist challenge. These are indeed only indications, which have to be, and have begun to be more systematically explored and analyzed. They raise many new problems, among them, from the vantage point of the structuralist premises, that of the relations between the principles of the symbolic dimension of human life and those that shape institutional structure. But they raise these problems constructively. They point the way to the broadening of sociological analysis by facing up to the challenges of the structuralist approach through their incorporation in institutional analysis. The constructiveness of these indications is also evident in the fact that they make it possible, through the analysis of the carriers of codes and of the mechanisms through which these are institutionalized, to bring together the two major themes of contemporary controversies in sociology, namely, the analysis of social structure in terms, first, of negotiated order and, second, of deep structure.

REFERENCES

BENDIX, R. (1968) *State and Society*. Boston: Little Brown.

BLAU, P. (1964) *Exchange and Power inn Social Life*. New York: John Wiley.

BLAU, P. (1977) *Inequality and Heterogeneity: A Primitive Theory of Social Structure*. New York: Free Press.

BLUMER, H. (1969) *Symbolic Interactionism*. Englewood Cliffs, NJ: Prentice-Hall.

BUCKLEY, W. (1967) *Sociology and Modern Systems Theory*. Englewood Cliffs, NJ: Prentice-Hall.

BUCKLEY, W. (ed.) (1968) *Modern Systems Research for the Behavioral Scientist*. Chicago: Aldine.

CICOUREL, A. (1973) *Cognitive Sociology*. Harmondsworth: Penguin.

COLEMAN, J. S. (1966) 'Foundations for a Theory of Collective Decision,' *American Journal of Sociology*, 71(6): 615-27.

COLEMAN, J. S. (1979) 'Political Money,' *American Political Science Review* 64(4): 1074-87.

COLLINS, R. (1975) *Conflict Sociology: Toward an Explanatory Science*. New York: Academic Press.

DAHRENDORF, R. (1961) *Class and Class Conflict in Industrial Society*. London: Routledge & Kegan Paul.

DEUTSCH, K. (1963) *The Nerves of Government*. New York: Free Press.

EISENSTADT, S. N. (ed.) (1968) *The Protestant Ethic and Modernization*. New York: Basic Books.

EISENSTADT, S. N. (1973) *Tradition, Change and Modernity*. New York: John Wiley.

EISENSTADT, S. N. (1978) *Revolution and the Transformation of Societies*. New York: Free Press.

EISENSTADT, S. N. and M. CURELARU (1976) *The Form of Sociology: Paradigms and Crises*. New York: John Wiley, pp. 89-101, 121-5.

GARFINKEL, H. (1967) *Studies in Ethnomethodology*. Englewood Cliffs, NJ: Prentice-Hall.

GODDARD, D. (1965) 'Conceptions of Structure in Lévi-Strauss and in British Anthropology,' *Annual Reiview of Anthropology*, 1: 329-49.

GODELIER, M. (1973) 'Horizons,' *Trajets Marxistes en Anthropologie*. Paris: Maspero.

GODELIER, M. (1978) 'Infrastructures, Societies and History,' *Current Anthropology*, 19 (December): 763-71.

GOFFMAN, E. (1959) *The Presentation of Self in Everyday Life*. New York: Doubleday.

HOMANS, G. C. (1961) *Social Behavior: Its Elementary Forms*. New York: Harcourt Brace Jovanovich.

LEACH, E. (1967) *Genesis as Myth and Other Essays*. London: Tavistock.

LEACH, E. (1970) *Lévi-Strauss*. London: Fontana.

LEPENIES, W. and H. RITTER (eds) (1972) *Orte des Wilden Denkens*. Frankfurt: Suhrkampf.

LÉVI-STRAUSS, C. (1963) *Structural Anthropology*. New York: Basic Books.

LÉVI-STRAUSS, C. (1966) *The Savage Mind*. London: Weidenfeld & Nicolson.

LÉVI-STRAUSS, C. (1967) *Totemism*. Boston: Beacon Press.

LÉVI-STRAUSS, C. (1968) *Mythologiques: L'origine des manieres de table*. Paris: Plon.

LÉVI-STRAUSS, C. (1969) *The Elementary Structures of Kinship*. Boston, Beacon Press; London: Fontana/Collins.

LÉVI-STRAUSS, C. (1971a) *Mythologiques: du miel aux cendres*. Paris: Plon.

LÉVI-STRAUSS, C. (1971b) *Mythologiques: L'homme Nu*. Paris: Plon.

MACRAE, D. G. (1968) Introduction to R. Boudon, *The Use of Structuralism*. London: Heinemann.

MARANDA, P. (1972) 'Structuralism in Cultural Anthropology,' *Annual Review of Anthropology*, 1: 329-49.

MARANDA, P. and K. MARANDA (1971) *Structural Models in Folklore and Transformational Essays*, The Hague: Mouton.

MARUYAMA, M. (1968) 'The Second Cybernetics: Deviation-amplifying Mutual Causal Processes,' in W. Buckley, *Modern Systems Research*. Chicago: Aldine.

MERTON, R. K. (1963) *Social Theory and Social Structure*. New York: Free Press.

NEEDHAM, R. (1960) 'A Structural Analysis of Aimol Society,' *Anthropologica*, 116: 81-102.

PARSONS, T. (1964) *The Social System*, New York: Free Press (first published 1951).

PARSONS, T. and E. SHILS (eds), *Toward a General Theory of Action*. Cambridge, Mass.: Harvard University Press.

PARSONS, T. and N. J. SMELSER (1965) *Economy and Society*. New York: Free Press (first published 1956).

ROSSI, I. (1973) 'The Unconscious in the Anthropology of Claude Lévi-Strauss,' *American Anthropology*, 20: 20-49.

ROTENSTREICH, N. (1972) 'On Lévi-Strauss' Concept of Structure,' *Review of Metaphysics*, 25(3): 489-526.

SCHOLTE, R. (1966) 'Epistemic Paradigms: Some Problems in Cross-Cultural Research on Social Anthropological History and Theory,' *American Anthropology*, 68: 1194-1200.

SEBAG, L. (1964) *Structuralisme et Marxisme*. Paris: Petite Bibliothèque Payot.

SIMMEL, G. (1908) *Soziologie: Untersuchungen über die Formen der Vergesellschaftung*. Berlin: Duncker & Humblot.

WEBER, M. (1951) *The Religion of China*, translated and edited by H. H. Gerth. Glencoe, Ill.: Free Press.

WEBER, M. (1952a) *Ancient Judaism*, translated and edited by H. H. Gerth and D. Martindale. New York: Free Press.

WEBER, M. (1952b) *The Religion of India*, translated and edited by H. H. Gerth and D. Martindale. New York: Free Press.

WOLF, K. H. (ed.) (1950) *The Sociology of Georg Simmel*. New York: Free Press.

II

CONCEPTUAL ANALYSIS

6

LEVELS IN THE STUDY
OF SOCIAL STRUCTURE

Charles K. Warriner
University of Kansas

Of all the problematic terms in the sociological lexicon, 'social structure' is perhaps the most troublesome. There is little agreement on its empirical referents and there are continuing arguments as to whether it is anything more than a metaphor for the analysis of social processes. Those who wish to keep the use of 'structure' close to its etymological origins (from L., to arrange, heap together; akin to E. *strew*) define it as the demographic distribution of persons in physical space. This usage excludes direct reference to the social processes of relationship and interdependency. At the other extreme, social structure refers to postulated or analytical and hidden relationships underlying the manifest observables of social life as in Chomsky's and Lévi-Strauss's 'deep structures,' a use that makes it a part of the 'composite intellectual and social movement known as "structuralism" ' (Merton, 1975, p. 32; also see De George and De George, 1972).

TERMINOLOGICAL DIVERSITY

The more frequent sociological use of the term, and its major utility for sociology, lies in its reference to social units standing in some sort of recurrent social relationship to each other; that is, as identifying and describing an observable social phenomenon involving 'the interrelation or arrangement of "parts" ' (Nadel, 1957, p. 4). It is in this sense that 'social structure' is often paired with 'social organization,' the two terms together referring to social actors in a regular interdependency created and maintained through inter-actor action. 'Structure' usually focusses attention upon the actors and their differentiating identities, while 'organization' emphasizes their 'functional' or processual interconnections. In this paper I focus upon the use of 'social structure' in the latter sense.

Because of the metaphoric origins of this use of the term 'structure' we must continually reaffirm two basic facts about social phenomena in order to avoid major arguments over its use. That is, we must continue to remind ourselves (a) that the units whose relationships constitute social structure, unlike units in physical structures, are not autonomous entities whose character is fixed by processes antecedent to and independent of the structural processes themselves; and (b) that the relationships of those units are not static, spatial dimensions, but activity processes between the units. That is, social 'space' is defined by what the units do in relation to each other. Thus, it is quite a different idea from that of physical space. An additional issue relates to the distinction between 'the system of "ideal" relations [i.e, the prescriptive, normative or cultural descriptions]...and the system of actual relations' (Bottomore, 1972, p. 115; see also Park, 1974, pp. 12ff; Blau, 1977, p. 1). I assume here that our data are observations of action, not statements of belief or norms.

CONCEPTUALIZATIONS OF SOCIAL STRUCTURE

Social structure, so conceived, has utility for two quite different kinds of sociological inquiry. One use is for describing the relevant contextual and situational factors in individual human behavior. In this use structure is described as the categorical identities of persons that affect, channel, or constrain what they do and how they interact in particular inter-actor situations. Thus, gender is a categorical as opposed to an individual identity, as is social class, age grade, ethnicity, occupation, or organizational office. When we describe persons in these terms we are defining their 'social personalities' (Warner and Lunt, 1941, pp. 26-8). If we know the categorical identities of the person that are relevant in his or her society we then, as Warner often asserted, 'know all we need to know about the person as a member of the society,' that is, we have defined the major contextual variables that affect his or her behavior in social situations.

The second utility of the idea of structure lies in its use as a description of the nature of the society, as a map of the social territory, as describing the positions or locations within which people act and the interconnections between them without concern for the occupants per se. This use emphasizes the identities as social positions. Unfortunately, the first usage, combined with a reductionist strategy of explanation and a voluntaristic view of social forces (Park, 1974, pp. 213-14) has led to a focus upon individuals as the constituent units of society, a focus upon interpersonal interaction as the basic process of structure, and a focus upon personal biography as the locus of explanations of structure. These attitudes confuse the use of the idea of structure as context with the use of the idea of structure as describing the society. The second usage of the idea of structure involves a shift in the focus of our attention from the explanation of individual behavior to an explanation of structure itself.

Preoccupation with the use of structure for describing the context of individual behavior vitiates the use of structure for explaining society. Furthermore, the concepts of structure developed for the explanation of individual behavior are unable to deal with the structural phenomena of contemporary societies or with the structural characteristics of the large economic, political or other bureaucracies of which they are in major part constituted.

The literature on social structure reveals two major conceptualizations of social structure that have become fairly well established; but a third orientation, not yet given conceptual recognition or consensual validation is emerging from the research literature. I shall identify these as (I) the interpersonal, (II) the interpositional, and (III) the inter-organizational views of social structure. Each is based on a different exemplar social situation used as the empirical reference for developing structural concepts and testing structural propositions. I shall argue that these views represent and reflect successive emergent levels of structural reality (cf. Edel, 1957), and that each view has a unique utility for dealing with its own level of structural phenomena, but cannot be usefully applied for the description and analysis of the other levels.

If Warner (1962) is correct, we are experiencing the development of a new form of social organization, a 'national primary society' in which organizations are replacing communities as the units of national organization (see also Chandler, 1969, 1977). If so, it is not surprising that the inter-organizational view of social structure has not been clearly developed. We have not yet become accustomed to this exemplar situation.

Accepting the utility and legitimacy of each of these three views of social structure recasts a number of issues and problems in the study of social structure, especially those that have to do with 'bridg[ing] the micro-macro gap' (Merton, 1975, p. 34). In particular, each successive formulation redefines the problem of the relation of individuals to society, and each identifies new problems in the empirical transformation processes by which these levels are related to each other.

The Interpersonal Concept of Social Structure

The interpersonal (level I) conception of social structure is uniquely sociological and American at that (perhaps because of the heavy individualistic, homocentric, and nominalistic bias of American social thought). It takes as its exemplar situation the primary group, such as the family (vide Burgess's 'a unity of interacting personalities'), the very small stable society, or the small ad hoc experimental group. In these situations personal biography and personal identity in the group are the locus of the factors that account for the structural character — the personal identities in terms of which persons act and relate to others. Sociometric approaches to structure especially illustrate this orientation.

In the primary group and small society the interdependency of persons hinges upon their 'social' relations rather than upon the division of labor (cf. Durkheim, 1964) and as a consequence the essential structural process is symbolic interaction which builds personal identities and networks of relationship. The interaction may be analyzed in terms of exchange (Homans; Blau), as subordination and domination (Simmel), as presentations of self and confirmations (Mead, Blumer, Goffman), or as the sharing of cultural typifications (Berger and Luckmann) without affecting the essential fact of the network and its identification, because all of these are involved in the undifferentiated interaction in primary relations.

Traditionally this approach has emphasized the ever-changing process of such relationships and thus structure is viewed as a temporary end result (Buckley, 1967, p. 19, describing R. E. Park's view), as a 'snapshot' of a particular moment in time, and hence as an abstraction (Nadel, 1957, p. 12; Blau, 1977, p. 244; Berreman,

1978, p. 226), an 'artificial observation' (Buckley, 1967, p. 21) or arbitrary 'fixing' of what is a dynamic process, not a concrete form.

The micro-structural problems of the interpersonal approach are those concerned with the aspects of personal biography and the ways in which these become incorporated into the actions of these persons in their relationships (Blau, 1977, p. 2). The mediate-structural problems are those of describing the network of relationships and the characterization of nature of the interdependency (as defined by the 'role' of each in the network) that develops. Finally, the macro-structural problems of this approach concern questions of the interconnections of networks and the flows of influence or other interdependency materials through these connections.

The Interpositional Concept of Social Structure

The interpositional (level II) view of social structure is generally attributed to the social anthropologists, especially Radcliffe-Brown (Bottomore, 1972, p. 113; Nadel, 1957, p. 3; Blau, 1977, p. 2) although bows are sometimes made in the direction of Durkheim, Marx, and others. As this origin suggests, the exemplar situations used for conceptual validation and empirical exploration are the so-called 'primitive' tribes, societies of such a size and elaboration that persons are frequently related to each other in terms of categorical identities rather than personal identities, that is, through identities that they share with others as members of a class, a moiety, a kinship position, or other category.

In these cases it was not possible to describe efficiently and effectively the networks of relationship — that is, to deal with structure — in terms of persons, but required the use of the idea of social position or role. (A whole series of arguments incidental to our present concerns revolves around the preference for the use of the term 'role' as opposed to 'position'; cf. Nadel, 1957, p. 29.) Thus, the unit of structure becomes the social position, not the person, and the process of structure is the patterns of relations between positions, not the interactions between persons. A major characteristic of this approach is its recognition that the relationships between positions involve more than 'social' relations conceived in terms of symbolic interaction. Positions may be related in terms of division of labor (or other workflow connections), in terms of power and authority through flows of directives, and symbolically. (Each of these kinds of interconnection involves questions of interdependence of actors.) This conception of relationships lies at the heart of Durkheim's idea of the division of labor as leading to organic solidarity and to Marx's conception of classes as involving different relations to the mode of production and hence different interests.

Many scholars such as Nadel (1957) and Blau (1977) have had difficulty in coming to terms with this conception of structure. Part of the difficulty may be ascribed to Radcliffe-Brown, who in his formal theoretical statements spoke in terms of 'persons in relationships' (Radcliffe-Brown, 1968, p. 9; 1957, p. 55), but in his descriptive and analytical procedures dealt with categorical identities or social positions ('mother's brother' and 'sister's son'). Afraid of losing the person and thus ceasing to be humanists and judging secondary relations to be 'inauthentic,' or so accustomed to the idea that 'groups are composed of persons' that we cannot use other terms, we feel it necessary continuously to assert the presence of human actors and personal biography by speaking of 'persons in positions,' and thus find ourselves unable to deal clearly with the position as the unit of structure or with interpositional relations as more than interaction. As a consequence we confuse the problem of structural description with that of accounting for the processes by which this new level of structural phenomena became possible.

It is both cumbersome and unnecessary to continue repeating the formula that persons are the only agents of action. Where the actions ('inter-actions') are patterned with respect to position rather than personal biography, we can appropriately speak of the position as the unit of structure. To be comfortable with this formulation, either as individual scholars or as a discipline, requires that we re-examine our conceptions of the relation of personality to social structure. The interpersonal point of view has been closely connected with the notion of 'structural constraints' as the formula for the relation between persons and structure. This voluntaristic view of action sees the actor as constructing and initiating 'his' actions with the 'structure' placing constraints upon his choices. Quite a different interpretation is that which views social structure as being the source of the structuring of acts and their initiation while the actor's choice at best is among structurally given alternatives (Merton, 1968). Gerth and Mills (1953), in my estimation a sadly neglected book, is one of the best expositions of this view of the relation between personality and social structure, and I have treated this in *The Emergence of Society* (Warriner, 1970). A theory of action thus becomes central to the problems of structural analysis, as Coleman (1975) asserts, but not always in the terms he argues for.

The interpositional conception of structure introduces several important changes in our general conception of structure. First, where the interpersonal approach speaks of social structure in the singular and treats society as if it had one structural system, the interpositional view almost universally asserts that societies have multiple structures, whether these are identified as 'institutions' (Ginsberg, 1939; Bottomore, 1972; Gerth and Mills, 1953), 'parameters of structure' (Blau, 1977), 'dimensions of structure' (Warner and Lunt, 1941), or 'role systems' (Nadel, 1957). That is, positions exist in a system of related positions (uncle with mother, grandfather, etc.; doctor with patient, nurse, etc.), and in most societies there are several such systems in operation (age grades, gender, kinship, ethnicity, occupation, rank, etc.), so that a person may be occupying several positions at the same time. This idea has fundamental consequences for our analysis of the relation of individuals to social structures and to society as a whole, for it suggests that in such societies (or their communities) the individual participates in a segmented way, rather than as a continuous single biographical entity.

A second major change in our conception of structure is the challenge that the positional view makes to the notion of structure as an arbitrary fixing of what is a continuous process. The positional conception implies that there is a stability of units and of relationships both through time and across persons and situations such that it is now appropriate to view structure as a less arbitrary interpretation of the data. (This does not imply that there is any necessity for continuity, but merely reflects the observation of frequent continuity of positions and relationships between them.)

Within this framework micro-structural analysis focusses upon the problems of the occupancy of positions by persons, especially those of access to positions and of the extent to which persons become involved in structurally induced role conflict through occupying incompatible positions in two structures at the same time. The mediate structural problems are those of describing the positions in each structure and of the ways in which those positions are interconnected through relationships, whether of power, prestige, division of labor, symbolism, or communion. Finally, the macro-structural problems are those of the conditions of origin and differentiation of the several structural systems in societies and of their interconnections (cf. Lenski, 1970, 1975).

The Inter-organizational Concept of Social Structure

The inter-organizational (level III) conception of social structure is nascent in a variety of research endeavors rather than a conceptually established position. Nevertheless, we can identify the major outlines of the position. Illustrative contributions to this approach are found in Warner's (1962, 1967) essays on the emergent American society, Lehman's (1975) attempt to characterize the structure of health-care delivery systems in terms of inter-organizational relations, and Turk's (1973) description of community structure in similar terms.

The exemplar situation for this approach is the 'organizational society' (Presthus, 1962), in which the interdependency of persons is mediated by a variety of corporate groups such as economic organizations, governmental agencies, unions and other large-scale organizations which have replaced communities as the nexus of interdependencies. The units of societal structure are organizations, and the structural process (relationships) consists of the transactions between organizations through which flow (a) power (in the form of directives and agreements), (b) goods, services, and money or other material values, (c) personnel, and (d) 'cultural' materials ('facts,' norms, values, or ideologies).

The mediate structural problems of the inter-organizational approach are those of describing the various ways in which organizations are interconnected in differentiated networks and of tracing the inderdependencies involved in various types of networks. Over the past few years increasing attention has been given to the conceptual and methodological problems of describing these networks, especially of distinguishing the several kinds and their consequences.

The micro-structural problems of this level are two-fold: (a) those of intra-organizational structure, and (b) the micro-micro problems relating to the participation of persons in the organization and their occupancy of positions. The macro-structural problems can be defined only in general outline as those of the inter-connections of various kinds of organizational networks. Little has been done on the nature of the interconnections between the net-works of organizations of, for example, higher education and those of financial, governmental or industrial organizations.

The interorganizational perspective introduces a fundamentally new structural idea: the introduction of a new kind of actor. In the interpositional view the actors are still individuals (but not persons), although their acts are constructed by the units of struc-ture, positions. That is, units of action are still performed by and are coterminous with the acts of individuals, even though these acts are structured by and triggered into performance in terms of the positions the actor is in. With the introduction of the inter-organizational perspective we recognize that positions have become embedded in an organized system, in which unit acts in transactions (a corporate take-over for example, or accrediting a hospital) are coterminous not with what a single individual does, but rather with the articulation of activity of several individuals. A new form of in-tegration of action has come about in which what individuals do is often meaningless except as embedded in a program of action in-volving many others within the corporate entity.

The organization is the acting unit, and its activity systems are the acts that are observed. This implies that societal structure at this level is no longer conceived in terms of the interrelationships of per-sons or of actors in positions, but rather of actors in positions embedded in organized acting units. As a consequence the fatefully crucial interdependencies of individuals are mediated by (a) the positions they occupy, and (b) by the organized systems in which those positions are embedded.

CONCLUSION

In this paper I have taken the position that these approaches to social structure — the interpersonal, the interpositional, and the inter-organizational — represent not three perspectives on one reality (Blau, 1975, pp. 3-7), but rather three different levels of structural reality, each described in its own terms. Unless we wish to argue that all societies are structurally alike, and thus to reject the facts of societal evolution, we are forced to treat these approaches as equally valid though concerned with different emergent levels of phenomena.

The 'one-reality' conception views 'macro-structures' as complex expressions of interpersonal relations and, as Coleman (1975, p. 86), for example, asserts, 'must be ultimately analyzable in terms of relations between individuals.' This dictum implies that the activities in which actors in organizations are engaged are the voluntary creations of individual biography 'constrained' by 'structural' forces. In contrast, it is not only easier, but also more consistent with the data to argue that all regular actors in positions in organizations are alike (in other words, that personal biography makes little difference in what they do). Consistent with this is the emerging 'population ecology' view of organizations (Aldrich and Pfeffer, 1976; Hannan and Freeman, 1977) which takes the position that what organizations do and what they are like internally is a function not of their personnel composition, but of their social environments, especially their relations with other organizations.

In contemporary complex societies each of these levels of structure is present and a full description of societal structure would consider each level and the interconnections between the levels. However, in terms of the most fateful interdependencies of persons, the most critical for the fate of the society is the interorganizational level. It may well be, as Homans (1947) has argued, that civilizations degenerate only so far as the interpersonal (small-group) level before they are rebuilt, and it may well be that the particular form of organizational society that has developed is not viable, so that its destruction is inevitable; but in the meantime it behooves us to pay attention to this level of structural phenomena.

REFERENCES

ALDRICH, Howard E. and Jeffrey PFEFFER (1976) 'Environments of Organizations,' pp. 79-105 in *Annual Review of Sociology*, Alex Inkeles (ed.). Palo Alto, CA: Annual Reviews Incorporated, 1976.

BERREMAN, Gerald D. (1978) 'Scale and Social Relations,' *Current Anthropology*, 19 (2) (June): 225-37.

BLAU, Peter M. (ed.) (1975) *Approaches to the Study of Social Structure*. New York: Macmillan/Free Press.

BLAU, Peter M. (1977) *Inequality and Heterogeneity: A Primitive Theory of Social Structure*. New York: Macmillan/Free Press.

BOTTOMORE, T. B. (1972) *Sociology: A Guide to Problems and Literature*. New York: Random House/Vintage.

BUCKLEY, Walter (1967) *Sociology and Modern Systems Theory*. Englewood Cliffs, NJ: Prentice-Hall.

CHANDLER, Alfred Dupont (1969) *Strategy and Structure: Chapters in the History of Industrial Enterprise*. Cambridge, Mass.: MIT Press.

CHANDLER, Alfred Dupont (1977) *The Visible Hand: The Managerial Revolution in American Business*. Cambridge, Mass.: Harvard University Press.

COLEMAN, James S. (1975) 'Social Structure and a Theory of Action,' pp. 76-93 in P. Blau (ed.), *Approaches to the Study of Social Structure*. New York: Macmillan/Free Press.

de GEORGE, Richard and Fernande de GEORGE (1972) *The Structuralists from Marx to Lévi-Strauss*. New York: Doubleday Anchor.

DURKHEIM, Emile (1964) *The Division of Labor in Society*. New York: Free Press (first English translation, 1933).

EDEL, Abraham (1957) 'The Concepts of Levels in Social Theory,' pp. 167-95 in L. Gross (ed.), *Symposium on Sociological Theory*. Evanston, Ill.: Row, Peterson.

GERTH, Hans and C. Wright MILLS (1953) *Character and Social Structure: The Psychology of Social Institutions*. New York: Harcourt Brace Jovanovich.

GINSBERG, Morris (1939) 'The Problems and Methods of Sociology,' pp. 436-78 in F. C. Bartlett et al. (eds), *The Study of Society*. London: Routledge & Kegan Paul.

HANNAN, Michael T. and John FREEMAN (1977) 'The Population Ecology of Organizations,' *American Journal of Sociology*, 82 (March): 929-64.

HOMANS, George C. (1950) *The Human Group*. New York: Harcourt Brace Jovanovich.

LEHMAN, Edward W. (1975) *Coordinating Health Care: Explorations in Interorganizational Relations*. Beverly Hills: Sage.

LENSKI, Gerhard (1970) *Human Societies: A Macrolevel Introduction to Sociology*. New York: MacGraw-Hill Book Company.

MERTON, Robert K. (1968) *Social Theory and Social Structure*. New York: Free Press (first published 1949).

MERTON, Robert K. (1975) 'Structural Analysis in Sociology,' in P. Blau (ed.), *Approaches to the Study of Social Structure*. New York: Macmillan/Free Press.

NADEL, S. F. (1957) *The Theory of Social Structure*. New York: Free Press.

PARK, George (1974) *The Idea of Social Structure*. Garden City, NY: Doubleday Anchor.

PRESTHUS, Robert (1962) *The Organizational Society: An Analysis and a Theory*. New York: Alfred A. Knopf.

RADCLIFFE-BROWN, A. R. (1957) *A Natural Science of Society*. Glencoe Illinois: The Free Press.

RADCLIFFE-BROWN, A. R. (1968) *Structure and Function in Primitive Society*. New York: Free Press (first published 1952).

TURK, Herman (1973) *Interorganizational Activation in Urban Communities: Deductions from the Concept of System*. Washington, DC: American Sociological Association.

WARNER, W. Lloyd (1962) *The Corporation in the Emergent American Society*. New York: Harper.

WARNER, W. Lloyd (1967) 'The Emergence of the National Society,' Chapter 1 in W. L. Warner et al. (eds), *The Emergent American Society*. New Haven, Conn.: Yale University Press.

WARNER, W. Lloyd and Paul S. LUNT (1941) *The Social Life of a Modern Community*. New Haven, Conn.: Yale University Press.

WARRINER, Charles K. (1970) *The Emergence of Society*. Homewood, Ill.: Dorsey Press.

7

HIERARCHIC STRUCTURE IN SOCIAL PHENOMENA

Walter L. Wallace
Princeton University

The basic idea of hierarchic structure is the successive aggregation of elements into levels of greater and greater inclusiveness — as exemplified by the notion that under specificable conditions two or more individual organisms may be described as a 'small group,' two or more small groups as an 'organization,' two or more organizations a 'community,' two or more communities a 'society,' and so on.

Note that hierarchic structure is here regarded as a purely descriptive concept, associated with no particular explanatory hypothesis or evaluative judgment. Thus, by itself, the concept does not imply that more inclusive levels control, initiate, or sustain less inclusive ones, or vice versa; it does not imply that middling (meso-) levels dominate extreme (micro- and macro-) ones, or vice versa; and it does not imply that any level is better or worse than any other. Such hypotheses and evaluations, of course, may be parts of empirical or normative theories of given hierarchic structures, but they are not essential to the description of such structures as hierarchic.

This paper tries to explicate the concept of hierarchic structure, to demonstrate its consistently pivotal but too often unconscious

Author's Note: Sarane Spence Boocock, Peter M. Blau, Marvin Bressler, and John I. Kitsuse have my appreciation for their stimulating comments and queries regarding the subjects of this paper (and Professor Blau also for the invitation to prepare it in the first place). Blanche Anderson and Barbara Weik provided cheerful and expert typing assistance. Most of my work for this paper was carried out during 1974-75 at the Center for Advanced Study in the Behavioral Sciences, and I am grateful for its support.

and incomplete role in describing the structure of social phenomena, and to suggest ways of systematizing that role.

Our first step takes Simmel as point of departure for identifying four variants of hierarchic structure in social phenomena. In the next two steps, the principle of hierarchic structure and a generic definition of social phenomena are specified. Then the principle and the definition are brought together and some descriptions of social phenomena advanced by Parsons and by Blau, respectively, are analyzed as illustrations of that conjunction. Lastly, the principle of hierarchic structure is specifically applied to the description of complex social phenomena by taking into account the four variants identified in our opening discussion of Simmel.

SIMMEL AND FOUR VARIANTS OF HIERARCHIC STRUCTURE

Consider Simmel's images of 'concentric' and 'juxtaposed' relationships between subgroups of a society. In the concentric relationship, the individual's 'participation in the smallest of... groups already implies participation in the larger groups' (1955, p. 147); participation in these groups implies participation in still larger groups; and so on up to the society as a whole. The picture is clearly hierarchic; Simmel describes a single nesting series of subgroups such that any given subgroup is composed of smaller subgroups (or, in the case of the smallest subgroup, of individuals), and is also a member of a larger subgroup or group.

In the juxtaposed relationship, Simmel argues that the organizing principle is not one of successive whole inclusion of subgroups but of chainlike sharing by one subgroup of another subgroup's members. Thus, a given individual 'may belong, aside from his occupational position, to a scientific association, he may sit on a board of directors of a corporation and occupy an honorific position in the city government' (1955, p. 150);[1] another individual may belong to the same scientific association but otherwise have a different set of subgroup memberships; a third individual may belong to the same board of directors but otherwise have still another set of memberships; and so on. The result, from the viewpoint of the subgroups, is linkage via shared membership rosters, and we may therefore refer to this relationship as concatenated.[2] Concatenated structure is the image underlying Merton's 'status set' and 'role set' (1957, pp. 368-84), and Blau's 'multiform heterogeneity' (1977; pp. 83-90). Note that hierarchic and concatenated structures may coexist and be complementary, as Simmel indicates when he claims that 'the individual *adds* affiliations with new groups to the singular affiliation which has hitherto influenced him in a pervasive and onesided manner' (1955, p. 151; emphasis added).

Thus, in the hierarchic relationship, subgroups share their membership, as subgroups, in the larger groups that they themselves constitute; in the concatenated relationship, subgroups share the members (whether these are regarded as smaller subgroups or as individuals) who constitute them. Now let us infer two other types of subgroup relationships which, although not mentioned by Simmel, complete the logical possibilities suggested by his conceptualization and help illuminate their joint implication.

The types in question may be called 'integrated' and 'segregated.' In the integrated case, subgroups share membership in larger groups and also share their own member elements. The extreme here is represented by Durkheim's concept of the primeval 'horde' (1933, pp. 174-5) and by Toennies's concept of 'Gemeinschaft' (1957, pp. 37-42). In the segregated case, subgroups share neither membership in larger groups nor their own member elements. This case seems represented by Toennies's apocalyptic vision of the denouement of Gesellschaft (1957, pp. 228-35), by Sumner's separation of 'in-group' and 'out-group' (see Coser, 1978, p. 297), and by Sorokin's notion of 'independent congeries' (1947, p. 58).[3] Figure 1 presents the integrated, hierarchic, concatenated, and segregated subgroup relationships for direct comparison.[4]

The essential conclusion here, for present purposes, is that in all four relationships elements are aggregated into levels of greater inclusiveness, and it is on this ground that we regard them all as variants of hierarchic structure. One of these, however, is the pure type-case and is therefore called 'hierarchic.' Because this case epitomizes what all four variants have in common we concentrate our attention on it, returning briefly to differences among variants toward the end of this paper.

Not only do we concentrate here on the pure type-case of hierarchic structure, but we also concentrate on problems of sociological description rather than explanation. This is because description is logically prior to explanation, and without something

FIGURE 1
Hierarchic Structure

Members   Membership
Shared   Shared

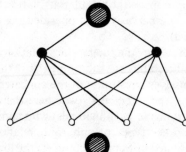

Integrated: Yes   Yes

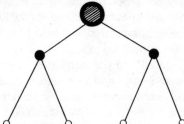

Hierarchic: No   Yes

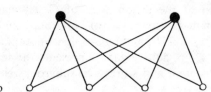

Concatenated: Yes   No

Segregated: No   No

● Four types of subgroup
○ Relationships via shared members and/or
⬗ Shared membership in larger groups

well defined as its object, explanation soon degenerates into mere verbiage.

THE PRINCIPLE OF HIERARCHIC STRUCTURE

If we define an 'element' as any phenomenon treated as though it were unitary, homogeneous, indivisible, then a 'hierarchy' may be defined as two or more levels in which elements at any lower level are grouped into several aggregates and then these aggregates are treated as elements at the next higher level.[5]

The distinction between 'element' and 'aggregate' is obviously crucial to this principle, and an 'element' is defined as any concept or phenomenon treated as though it were homogeneous and indivisible, while an 'aggregate' is defined as any concept or phenomenon treated as though it were heterogeneous and divisible. It is important to emphasize that it is one's 'treatment' of a phenomenon and not what that phenomenon 'actually is' (whatever that may mean) that counts. Thus, the very same phenomenon may be treated as an element in one analysis and as an aggregate in another. For sociological example, note that the individual organism is often treated as an element making up a larger aggregate in which the analyst is interested. In this tradition, Hawley argues that 'life viewed ecologically is an aggregate rather than an individual phenomenon. The individual enters into ecological theory as a postulate and into ecological investigation as a unit of measurement' (1944, p. 403). But the individual may also be viewed as an aggregate composed of its own elements, as Parsons suggests: 'actors are conceived as systems: they are never oriented to their situations simply "as a whole," but always through specific modes of organization of independent components' (1960, p. 471). Thus also we find Adorno criticizing 'empirical sociology' (chiefly survey research) for giving 'primacy of significance to human beings as individuals, instead of defining socialized man today first and foremost as a moment — and, above all, the object — of the social totality.' Empirical sociology, says Adorno, makes the error of regarding individually experienced 'subjective facts [such as opinions, attitudes] as if these things existed in themselves and not, as they really are, reified' (1976, p. 242). But in sharp contrast with this view, Collins argues that 'only real people can do things....''Organizations,'' ''classes,'' or "societies" never do anything' (1975, p. 12), and insists that all such collectivities (presumably including the 'social totality' to which Adorno refers) are mere 'hypostatizations.'

In short, one theorist may regard society as real and the individual as 'reified,' while another regards the individual as real and society as 'hypostatized.' The principle of hierarchic structure, however, calls on us to regard no level as intrinsically any more or any less real than any other, to regard all designations of levels as hypothetical and not self-evident, and to seek empirical tests for them.

In this connection it may be noted that, as Nagel says, 'The doctrine of emergence is sometimes formulated as a thesis about the hierarchical organization of things and processes, and the consequent occurrence of properties at "higher" levels of organization which are not predictable from properties found at "lower" levels' (1961, p. 366), and that the doctrine of holism is closely associated with emergence (see 1961, p. 380).[6] But as both Nagel and Hempel (1965, pp. 259-64) argue, predictability is a function of theories about properties rather than the properties themselves, so that what is 'emergent' or 'holistic' to a theory that accepts one hierarchic level as 'real' may not be so to a theory that accepts another level as 'real.'

Not only do we take no position here regarding the reality of given levels within a hierarchy; we also take no position regarding the reality of hierarchies per se. Here too there is a controversy — between those who regard hierarchies as (real) aspects of the way things exist independently of our observation of them, and those who regard hierarchies solely as observers' (nominal) techniques for describing things. On the realistic side, Simon argues that 'Scientific knowledge is organized in levels...because nature is organized in levels...and nature is organized in levels because hierarchic structures...provide the most viable form for any system of even moderate complexity' (1973, p. 27). On the nominalistic side, Smith argues that

Nature itself comprises all levels and knows not our distinctions.... The new structures that seem to emerge as aggregates when seen on a larger scale are partly illusory: it is less a characteristic of the structure itself than of the limited resolution of our perception (whether visual or conceptual). Each 'level' is what we see at certain resolutions. [Smith, 1969, p. 80]

Neither side of the controversy over whether hierarchies are real or nominal[7] seems to deny the scientific utility of hierarchic concepts — even the nominalistic side recognizes its heuristic value — and my avoidance of the issue here is grounded on this common acceptance. Accordingly, it cannot be overemphasized that the principle of hierarchic structure is here regarded as setting forth neither the only way phenomena 'are' (in some absolute, realist, sense) nor the only way they can be described.[8]

But it also cannot be overemphasized that, given an appropriate definition of the kinds of observations necessary and sufficient to define a social phenomenon, the principle of hierarchic structure points directly to empirical tests that can differentiate the utility of alternative designations of levels within such phenomena. In order to see how this may be so, let us first consider a generic definition of social phenomena and then consider how that definition may lend itself to hierarchic conceptualizations and to empirical tests of substantively significant differences between hierarchic levels.

GENERIC DEFINITION OF SOCIAL PHENOMENA

We define a social phenomenon, generally, as any interorganism behavior regularity. According to this definition, a social phenomenon will be said to exist if and only if at least one behavior of a given organism[9] is observed to be regularly accompanied by at least one behavior of at least one other organism. More exactly, we need to observe that, whenever and wherever organism A manifests a behavior, organism B regularly (not necessarily always or everywhere, but satisfying some arbitrarily set criterion level of relative frequency) manifests a behavior. B's behavior may be temporally or spatially ordered in any way with respect to A's behavior (at the same, or at a different, time or place); it may or may not be the same behavior throughout the regularity (B may systematically change the nature of his/her behavior); and the behavior may be literally anything within each organism's repertory. Incidentally, A and B may be of the same or different biological species, and neither organism need be human.

'Interorganism behavior regularity' is proposed here as a minimal, generic, definition of any and all social phenomena.[10] By emphasizing the generic nature of the definition, I mean to stress two important implications: first, analysts are free to add any

number of qualifying restrictions to the definition without disturbing its status as common denominator for all the resulting variations; and second, the analysis of such variations may be carried
out by comparing them, not only directly with each other, but to
the generic definition itself.

Thus, the generic definition leaves analysts free to specify
reference to certain organisms and not others, to certain behaviors
and not others, to certain regularities and not others, to certain
combinations of organisms, behaviors and regularities and not
others. In addition, analysts are free to concentrate only on those
interorganism behavior regularities that are characterized by that
sustained behavioral alternation between participants that the term
'interaction' always indicates (I suggest below that, unfortunately,
an a priori explanation is likely also to be implied by the term). The
generic definition of a social phenomenon as 'interorganism
behavior regularity' does not in any way rule out such special
restrictions; it only asserts that they are measurably special rather
than generic. The generic definition subsumes, and provides the
criterion for systematically differentiating, all such special definitions. To illustrate, consider the following examples from classical,
and modern, theorists.

Marx and Engels say: 'By social we understand the cooperation
of several individuals '(1947, p. 18); Durkheim says: 'in order that
there may be a social fact, several individuals, at the very least,
must have contributed their action' (1938, p. lvi); Weber defines a
'social relationship' as 'the behavior of a plurality of actors in so
far as, in its meaningful content, the action of each takes account
of that of the others and is oriented in these terms' (1947, p. 118),
and Simmel says: 'Society merely is the name for a number of individuals, connected by interaction' (1950, p. 10). All these definitions are subsumed by the generic one offered here, although the
former typically, but differentially, require more than the latter.
Thus, Marx and Engels seem to impose the additional requirement
that the behavior in question must be cooperative;[11] Weber requires
the coincidence of psychological (that is, orientational) behavior as
well as physiological behavior; Simmel requires behavioral
reciprocity ('interaction'); and Durkheim's further explication of
his definition of a social fact requires that the joint activity have a
particular effect.[12] The common denominator underlying these
various special requirements, however, seems to be the observation
of at least one behavior regularity across at least two individual

organisms — with the regularity component, unfortunately, remaining only implicit.

Several modern definitions may also be cited, but from the viewpoint of the generic definition being advanced here they all include either too little (they omit mention of one or more components of social phenomena), or too much (they risk tautology by incorporating explanations as parts of their definitions),[13] or both. Here are some examples of the 'too little' type. Davis omits explicit mention of the behavioral and regular nature of 'relations,' but clearly specifies their interorganism character: 'Like an organism, a society is a system of relations, but relations between organisms themselves rather than between cells' (1949, p. 26). Inkeles's definition, on the other hand, specifies the behavioral and regular qualities but does not explicitly mention the interorganism quality of social phenomena:

> When we say that there is a social system, we refer to the coordination and integration of social acts which permit them to occur in a way that produces order rather than chaos; and when we speak of 'order' we mean that events occur in a more-or-less regular sequence or pattern.... [Inkeles, 1964, p. 25]

At one point, Homans seems to permit a single idiosyncratic event to be called 'social' ('social behavior is simply behavior in which the action of one man causes the action of another' (1974, p. 77)), but elsewhere he stresses the regularity component of social phenomena ('The usual descriptions of groups connsist of statements of customs, that is recurrences, in human behavior at different places or at different intervals' (1950, p. 28)).

Now here are some examples of the 'too much' type. Parsons says: 'A social system consists in...individual actors interacting with each other...[that is] actors who are motivated [by] the "optimization of gratification" and whose relation to...each other is defined and mediated in terms of a system of cultural...symbols' (1951, pp. 5-6). This definition seems doubly excessive: once in its requirement of 'interaction' and again in its requirement of 'motivation' and 'symbols.' It will, of course, be noticed that the generic definition is less restrictive than Parsons's insofar as the former permits one-way 'action' as well as two-way 'interaction' to be called 'social.' But more important, for reasons to be specified below, the generic definition deliberately avoids including either action or interaction as requisites for the identification of social phenomena and leaves them both to explanatory hypothesis rather than pre-empting them by conceptual definition. The latter objection is also ground for regarding Parsons's requirement of motivations and symbols as excessive; these requirements are properly hypotheses that may (or may not) explain social phenomena, and their inclusion in the conceptual definition of those phenomena both asks us to accept those hypotheses prior to empirical test and threatens any theory built on this definition with tautology. Merton, too, specifies interaction: 'the sociological concept of a group refers to a number of people who interact with one another in accord with established patterns' (1957, p. 285). And if by 'in accord with' Merton means that the 'established patterns' regulate and thus explain the group, then his definition, like Parsons's, risks tautology. Blau and Scott much more clearly risk it when, after saying 'Social organization refers to...the observed regularities in the behavior of people,' then go on to require that these regularities be 'due to the social conditions in which [the people] find themselves' (1962, p. 2).

The important thing about the 'too little' definitions is that they all appear to be orbiting, so to speak, an implicit center of gravity whose location none of them, taken singly, indicates precisely. Taken together, however, one definition's inclusions compensate for another's omissions, with the result that that location (namely, the generic definition of social phenomena) stands revealed — by triangulation, as it were. The 'too much' definitions point in the very same direction when they have been stripped of explanations. One of these explanations (namely, interaction), however, recurs often enough to warrant specific justification for barring it from the generic definition.

Interaction

The essential idea of 'interaction' (whether implicating the use of symbols or not) is that some action of entity A causes, and thus explains, the reaction of entity B, and that some reaction of entity B causes, and thus explains, the next reaction of entity A, and so on, back and forth, with the emanation of causes (and effects) alternating between entity A and entity B. By requiring only a descriptive, probabilistic, 'regularity' of behavior between entities, the generic definition of social phenomena acknowledges that that regularity may be explained in this way, but it may not — indeed, the regularity may conceivably be explained by causes emanating from sources randomly distributed throughout the universe but be no less 'social' for that or any other explanation.[14] Therefore, the idea of interaction (and, of course, its close relative, 'interdependence') is barred from the generic definition because that definition seeks unbiasedly to reserve this and all other possible explanations for testable hypothesis rather than pre-empting any of them by arbitrary definition.

Thus, when Weber denies that the simultaneous opening of umbrellas by people caught in a sudden shower is social because the people are reacting to rain and not to each other (1947, p. 113), he pre-empts the empirical comparison of that hypothesis with others by defining 'social' so as to rule it out from the start. An empirical test might well reveal, for example, that all but the first people to open their umbrellas during a shower (analogous, say, to all but the first physicians who adopt a new drug during an outbreak of disease (see Coleman et al., 1957)) are oriented to each other as well as to rain. Such revelations, of course, can never occur if they are ruled out by definition. But even should there be no such revelation — even if we should find that a given instance of umbrella-opening is really only a response to rain — still, equifinality (von Bertalanffy, 1956, p. 4)[15] holds that any given outcome may be accomplished in several different ways. There does not seem to be any good reason to rule out the study of certain instances of a given outcome simply because they are not accomplished in some preferred way; the very differences in ways to skin a cat seem fit sources of knowledge about cats — and about their skinners.

Now, having tried to account for the exclusion of 'interaction' from the generic definition of social phenomena proposed here, let us examine the range of observations that that definition includes.

Scope of the Generic Definition

First, by referring merely to 'organisms,' the definition includes non-humans as well as humans. It therefore registers the fact that the way has always been more or less open (though rarely well-trod) to treating biological species as a variable rather than a constant in sociology, and thus open to a 'comparative sociology'[16] that will be the peer of comparative psychology, comparative physiology, comparative anatomy, and genetics. Moreover, the definition includes aggregates or 'collectivities' of any number of organisms, of the same or different biological species, as participants in social phenomena, provided only that there are identifiable behavior regularities within and between such collectivities. Accordingly, we refer to 'individuals' or 'collectivities' (or 'entities,'[17] as inclusive of both) as participants in social phenomena. Bearing in mind that the ultimate constituents of all entities in which sociology takes interest are individual living organisms, and noting also that the constituents of higher organisms seem themselves to have evolved from organisms that could at one time live independently of one another, it becomes reasonable to reverse the Spencerian organismic analogy that 'societies are like organisms' and suggest, instead, that 'higher organisms are like societies.' We would thereby extend the potential relevance of sociological principles to biological realms in which they are presently relative strangers.[18]

Second, by referring simply to 'behavior,' the definition embraces literally all behavior whether it be called 'economic,' 'political,' 'educational,' 'religious,' 'cognitive,' 'affective,' 'attitudinal,' 'cooperative,' 'conflictful,' or whatever. And most emphatically, *both* physiological (roughly speaking, skeletal-muscular, motor, or 'body') behavior and psychological (roughly speaking, neuroendocrine, dispositional, or 'mind') behavior are included, separately and in all their possible combinations. Thus, in contrast to Weber, it is not required (but it is permitted) here that physiological behavior be 'oriented' by psychological behavior,[19] or that it be psychologically endowed with 'meaning' by the manifesting entities, in order to constitute a social phenomenon. And in contrast with Marx, it is not required (but it is permitted) here that psychological behavior be expressed in physiological behavior in order to constitute a social phenomenon.[20] From the standpoint of the definition being offered here as generic and inclusive, the defining regularity between two or more entities may involve any variety of behavior described as physiological on both sides, any variety described as psychological on both sides, any variety of one on one side and of the other on the other side, or any mixture of both on either or both sides.

For example, there seems to be widespread agreement that human 'social institutions' like the family, the polity, the economy, the church, the military, represent combinations of particular shared physiological behaviors (or ways of doing things) and shared related psychological behaviors (ways of thinking and feeling about the indicated ways of doing things). Thus, Parsons defines 'institutionalization' as consisting in 'the integration of...values and norms with elements of the motivational systems of individuals in such ways as to define and support systems of social interaction' (1961, p. 35); Blau defines it as 'the emergence of social mechanisms through which social values and norms, organizing principles, and knowledge and skills are transmitted from generation to generation' (1964, p. 25); and Berger and Luckmann define it as 'a reciprocal typification of habitualized actions by types of actors' (1966, p. 54). All these formulations denote combinations of shared physiological and psychological behaviors, and such combinations are embraced by the generic definition.

Note, once more, that *any* variety of behavior may be involved in social phenomena according to the generic definition. Parsons and Shils, in a more exclusive definition, argue that the 'physics-chemical interchange between organism and environment...is not action, or behavior....Action involves not a biochemical conceptual scheme but an "orientational scheme"' (1951, p. 542). Sorokin concurs in this exclusion: 'stripped of their meaningful aspects, all phenomena of human interaction become merely biophysical phenomena and, as such, properly form the subject matter of the biophysical sciences' (1947, p. 47). The present point of view, however, holds that all behavior (including of course subjectively meaningful behavior, but not limited to it) falls within the scope of sociology. That organisms may blink, breathe, perspire, eliminate, open umbrellas, be born, get up in the morning, hunt, fish, rear cattle, criticize, get together in time or space seems surely to provide foci for our disciplinary interest, whatever the limits of our personal specialties.

Third, by referring simply to 'regularity'[21] and thus requiring, at minimum, only a non-zero conditional probability,[22] the definition denotes merely a joint occurrence sometime/somewhere in time or space, such that interorganism behaviors may be regular — or 'patterned,' 'structured,' 'organized,' or 'ordered' — in time only (thus, one organism's behavior may be observed regularly to precede the other's, or they may occur simultaneously), or in space only (thus, the behaviors may be observed in some regular spatial juxtaposition — east-west, near-far, above-below, central-peripheral, etc.), or regular in both time and space (say, every 14

July in Paris, or 4 July in Boston, or 7 May in Evanston). And perhaps needless to add, the regularities in question may be observed across any distances in space and time (for example, across the 10,000 years since the start of the Neolithic Age, or across the 240,000 miles between earth and moon).

Note that, in addition to being inclusive in all the senses just indicated, the generic definition proposed here is open. Thus, the questions of what constitutes an 'organism' (are viruses organisms? will computers, robots, and other artificial — or other natural — entities eventually be regarded as organisms?); what constitutes an 'inter'-organism versus 'intra'-organism phenomenon (which sort of phenomena occur in colonial organisms?); and what constitutes 'regularity' (what level of conditional probability is satisfactory for a given purpose?) seem likely to be permanently moot questions. Their answers at any given moment seem only conventional working definitions that are perpetually subject to change.

Equivalent Formulations

The definition of social phenomena proposed above may be regarded as having three equivalent formulations, such that a social phenomenon may be defined as: (1) entities between which behavior regularly occurs; (2) behaviors regularly occurring between entities; and (3) regularities in behaviors occuring between entities.

The equivalence of these formulations arises from their common reference to all three of the conceptually required components of social phenomena; the differences among them arise from their emphases among these components. According to these emphases, then, sociologists may pursue: (1) interests in social collectivities when the entities component is emphasized (here we employ concepts ranging from the two-person dyad and 'small groups,' through crowds, masses, associations, and communities, to societies and 'blocs' of societies; (2) interests in social relations when the behaviors component is emphasized (here we employ concepts regarding status, role, values, norms, conflict, exchange, communication, coercion, personal influence, and the like);[23] and (3) interests in social stability and change, and in social spacing, when the component of temporal or spatial regularity is emphasized (here we employ concepts referring to progress and retrogression, to cycles, rhythms, evolution, decline, revolution, and catastrophe, and referring to spatial longitude and latitude, zones, gradients, density, and distance).

Property-Space For Social Phenomena

Figure 2 portrays the property-space implied by what we have said so far, and we give the three basic dimensions or components of this space some elementary detail by partitioning 'organisms' into human and non-human types; 'behaviors' into physiological and psychological types; and 'regularities' into temporal and spatial types. This property-space asserts that every interorganism behavior regularity — that is, every social phenomenon — is describable as some combination of human or non-human organisms manifesting some combination of physiological or psychological behaviors with some combination of temporal or spatial[24] regularities.

FIGURE 2
Social Phenomena: Property-Space for Describing
their Components

Regularity	Organisms			
	Human		Non-human	
	Behavior			
	Physiological	Psychological	Physiological	Psychological
Spatial	a	b	c	d
Temporal	e	f	g	h

Thus, in cell (a) we locate descriptions of interorganism behavior regularities in which the organisms are said to be human, the behaviors of interest are regarded as mainly physiological, and the spatial aspect of the regularities is of primary interest (for instance, descriptions of students' talk and other actions in the classroom, rural-urban voting differences; suicide rates in France and Germany). In cell (b) we locate descriptions of interorganism behavior regularities in which the organisms are said to be human, the behaviors are regarded as mainly psychological, and the spatial aspect of the regularities is primary (descriptions of students' attitudes in the classroom; rural-urban political opinion differences; anomie in France and Germany).

Descriptions of interorganism behavior regularities in which the organisms are said to be human, the behaviors are regarded as mainly physiological, and the temporal aspect of the regularities is primary are in cell (e) — for example, description of students' talk and other actions during class hours, voting changes from early to late twentieth century, suicide rates during spring, summer, fall, winter. And descriptions of interorganism behavior regularities in which the organisms are said to be human, the behaviors are regarded as mainly psychological, and the temporal aspect of the regularities is primary are located in cell (f) — like descriptions of students' attitudes during class hours, political preference changes between early and late October, anomie during spring, summer, fall, winter.[25]

Note that each cell shown in Figure 2 may be internally differentiated to any desired degree — such that, to take cell (a) as an example, human organisms may be differentiated by sex, age, race, height, weight, etc.; physiological behaviors may be differentiated by the anatomical subsystems (arms, legs) that manifest them and by their objects (the natural environment, other people); psychological behaviors may be differentiated according to whether they are cognitive, cathectic, or conative; spatial regularities may be differentiated by their latitude, longitude, distance above or below sea level; temporal regularities may be differentiated according to whether they are diurnal, monthly, seasonal, annual, and so on, ad infinitum. Thus, some descriptions of interorganism behavior regularities may offer many more details which, although not specifically indicated by Figure 2, are logically encompassed by it.

On the other hand, other descriptions of interorganism behavior regularities may offer less detail than Figure 2 indicates by combining two or more of its cells. Thus, the behavior in question may be described as both physiological and psychological; the regularities may be described as spatio-temporal; and some of the organisms in question may be described as human while others are described as non-human (and, conceivably, they may all be described as both human and non-human, as in the case, say, of the last common ancestors of humans and apes).

Important though the aim of encompassing a wide variety of specific descriptions having greater, and lesser, detail may be, Figure 2 has an even more important objective: it seeks to differentiate and interrelate the four most widely used general concepts in describing social phenomena.

The Social, Cultural, Spatial, and Temporal Structures of Social Phenomena

Kroeber and Parsons claim that

> it is useful to define the concept *culture* [as referring to] transmitted content and patterns of values, ideas, and other symbolic-meaningful systems.[26] ...On the other hand, we suggest that the term *society* — or more generally, *social system* — be used to designate the specifically relational system of interaction between individuals and collectivities. [Kroeber and Parsons, 1958, p. 583; see also Ogles, Levy, and Parsons, 1959]

Somewhat more indeterminately, Merton indicates the same distinction: 'cultural structure may be defined as [an] organized set of normative values...[while] by social structure is meant [an] organized set of social relationships' (1957, p. 162).[27] In line with these claims, and in an effort to make their distinction more determinate, we suggest that cells (a) and (e) in Figure 2 represent human *social* structure, while cells (b) and (f) represent human *cultural* structure. In other words, the first pair of cells represent descriptions of people doing things together in space and time (that is, interorganism physiological behavior regularities), while the second pair represent descriptions of people perceiving, thinking, or feeling things together in space and time (that is, interorganism psychological behavior regularities).

If we disregard the type of behavior involved in a given social phenomenon (whether it is physiological or psychological) and focus on the type of regularity involved (whether it is spatial or temporal), two additional pairs of cells are derived. The first pair, cells (a) and (b), then represent descriptions of what is somewhat misleadingly called human 'ecology'[28] (that is, spatial structure in interorganism behaviors), as Hawley indicates when he argues that the sociological specialty called human ecology is concerned with 'the spatial pattern of the activities that make up a community' (1950, p. 235). The second pair, cells (e) and (f), represent descriptions of what is usually called human social 'change,' 'stability,' or 'process' (temporal structure in interorganism behaviors). Unfortunately, the more repetitive temporal regularities are often left undifferentiated from ecological structure. Thus, Hawley includes temporal as well as spatial patterning among ecological concerns on the ground that 'A temporal pattern is implicit in each and every spatial pattern' (1950, p. 288);[29] but Sorokin's (1947) treatment of temporal patterning independently from spatial patterning should be noted, in contrast.

Finally, it should be noted that cells (c), (d), (g), and (h) — and their own cross-cutting pairs of cells that refer to the social, cultural, spatial, and temporal structure of non-human social phenomena — have been largely ignored by sociologists so far. Descriptions that lie in these cells have come overwhelmingly from ethologists, ecologists, entomologists, primatologists, and comparative psychologists. Figure 2 and the basic ideas behind this paper, however, would include all these descriptions as sociological — whether or not they are also claimed by other disciplines.

HIERARCHIC STRUCTURE IN SOCIAL PHENOMENA

After everything that has been said up this point it is a relatively simple task to add the hierarchic dimension to the descriptive framework. We need only note that the generic definition of social phenomena (as elaborated above) permits individual organisms to be aggregated and re-aggregated into collectivities of increasing complexity; it permits behaviors to be aggregated and re-aggregated into subsystems, systems, and super-systems of behaviors; it permits regularities to be aggregated and re-aggregated into patterns of longer and longer duration, more and more complex rhythm, and broader, deeper, span. And it follows, of course, that the social structure, cultural structure, spatial structure and temporal structure of social phenomena — as discussed above — may be similarly aggregated and re-aggregated.

We have, in short, what we shall call 'componential hierarchies' — hierarchic structure in each component of social phenomena taken separately. And it is this conceptualization that enables us to suggest general criteria for identifying substantively significant differences between levels.[30]

Substantively Significant Levels

In a word, we know that a substantively significant discontinuity (that is, a difference between levels) in any one of the componential hierarchies has been identified when that discontinuity is correlated with discontinuities in the other componential hierarchies.

This criterion of 'substantive significance' in level distinctions rests on the claim that no phenomenon may be declared 'real' until its boundaries have been confirmed in more than one of their properties (and also each property has been confirmed through more than one measurement procedure — see Campbell and Fiske, 1959). Thus, Campbell quotes Rice to the effect that, if a jazz concert patron visually sees a saxophone, ' "Corroboration would be required in the form of other sense impressions. . . emanating from or relating to the saxophone" ' (1958, p. 16) before the patron could safely say his/her vision of a saxophone is not an hallucination. Campbell concludes that:

> for the more 'real' entities, the number of possible ways of confirming the boundaries is probably unlimited. . . . 'Illusions' occur when confirmation is attempted and found lacking, when boundaries diagnosed by one means fail to show up by other expected checks. . . . It might well be alleged that any scientifically useful boundary must be confirmable by at least two independent means. [Campbell, 1958, p. 23]

The pursuit of 'substantively significant,' correlated discontinuities in the componential hierarchies of social phenomena, however, is persistently and seriously hampered (but not altogether prevented) by an inconsistency in the metrics applied to the various componential hierarchies. Thus, on the one hand, sociologists have long been unanimous in treating the individual human being as the irreducible element of the entity componential hierarchy — even though every one of us probably also accepts the view of the anatomical sciences that the individual human being may also be treated as an aggregate of smaller entities ranging from, say, the respiratory, digestive, nervous, and motor system level through the organ level to the cell, organelle, molecular, etc., levels. Moreover, we also seem to possess fairly wide consensus on units of the regularity hierarchy — received, in the main, from statistics, chronology, and geography.

However, we remain very far from agreement on the sociological units of physiological and psychological behavior. As a result, one analyst may locate an inter-hierarchy correlation that other analysts find difficult to replicate partly because they may employ different units (and therefore describe different hierarchies of behavior). If sociological description — as well as the explanation that depends on it — is to become more testable, replicable, and cumulative, we must eventually remove the current metrical inconsistency between hierarchies by developing conventional behavior units just as we now accept conventional entity and regularity units.[31]

Descriptive analysis in sociology, of course, continues to make progress despite this inconsistency — partly because of agreement on the entity and regularity units, and partly because we do at least have consensus on the basic, albeit still gross, distinction between physiological and psychological behavior and therefore between social and cultural structure. Such analysis takes, or should take, the form of searches for answers to three questions:

(1) What are the behavior and regularity properties of entities at different levels? Most of the descriptive side of specialty literatures in sociology — those devoted to dyads, triads and other groups, families, schools, social movements, organizations, bureaucracies, cities, communities, societies, etc. — addresses this general question. Here we want to know something about what 'goes on' in these different collectivities; specifically, we want to know the physiological and psychological behaviors that members typically share, or exhibit in complementary or conflicting fashion, and we want to know the temporal and spatial regularities (including change and stability, dispersion and concentration) that typically mark these joint behaviors.

(2) What are the entity and regularity properties of social behavior at given hierarchic levels? Here we inquire about the

various entities (sometimes called 'structures') that perform given behaviors (sometimes called 'functions') at different times and places. We would like to know whether certain social behaviors (say, 'economic,' 'political,' 'educational,' 'adaptive,' 'normative,' or 'fiduciary') are typically carried out by certain collectivities and with certain spatiotemporal patterns.

(3) What are the behavior and entity properties of social regularities at different hierarchic levels? This question focusses attention on one of the least developed aspects of sociological description. Here we want to know whether certain temporal and spatial regularities are associated with certain entities and with certain behaviors. If a fast tempo (for example) is observed in a given behavior, we want to know whether we can expect only small collectivities to be involved and whether only certain kinds of behaviors will be involved.

Needless to say, the identification of properties is an important variety of theoretic hypothesis and empirical research in every scientific field, and we may indeed think of all investigation into the properties of a given level in a given hierarchy as searches among conceptually related hierarchies for the empirical correlates of that level.

It follows that descriptive analyses of entity, behavior, and regularity componential hierarchies in sociology are highly interdependent and potentially self-correcting insofar as hypotheses concerning differences between levels in one componential hierarchy are testable against correlated differences in the other componential hierarchies. ' "What is the difference between an atom and a molecule? An atom interacts at one energy level and molecules interact at the other, and that is how we tell the difference" ' (Simon, 1973, p. 9, quoting Melvin Calvin). Similarly, Wilson points out that

> What we call the "natural interfaces" [between levels] are identifiable either by the occurrence of a steep decrement in the number or strength of linkages crossing them, as developed by Simon...in the concept of near-decomposability, or through the existence of some form of closure. [Wilson, 1969, p. 118][32]

It appears, then, that our notions about entities of all kinds and at all levels are perpetually subject to revision by the correlated continuities and discontinuities that we discover between them, on the one hand, and behaviors and regularities, on the other. Similarly, our notions about behaviors undergo revision as we learn more about the entities that manifest them and the regularities with which they are manifested. And finally, our notions about regularities are revisable under the impact of new knowledge about the entities and behaviors that manifest them.

On the strength of this argument, the question of how many levels may properly be designated within any given componential hierarchy is here left open in order to permit one analyst to distinguish only micro- and macro-levels; another to distinguish micro-, meso-, and macro-levels; still another to distinguish 10 or 20 different levels — all depending, first, on showing that the discontinuity between any two adjacent levels within the hierarchy of concern is empirically associated with a discontinuity in one or more of the remaining hierarchies, and, second, on the precision required by the analysis, since greater precision is likely to require more levels.

At this point we have set forth, roughly, what may be regarded as a two-dimensional scheme in which the 'horizontal' dimension consists of the components of social phenomena and the 'vertical' dimension consists of the principle of hierarchic structure. Let us now see whether this scheme actually works for descriptive systematics, parsimony, and comparability by applying it to two images of social phenomena that are already in the literature. The images I have chosen (set forth by Parsons and Blau, respectively) will be seen to complement each other, and to illuminate related images described by Weber and Marx, respectively. Parsons and Blau both manifest interest in the physiological behavior hierarchy, but they each relate that hierarchy to a different one of the remaining componential hierarchies.

Parsons and the Subsystems of Action

Parsons has distinguished between social structure and cultural structure as follows:

> The social system focus is on the conditions involved in the interaction of actual human individuals who constitute concrete collectivities with determinate membership. The cultural system focus, on the other hand, is on 'patterns' of meaning, e.g. of values, of norms, of organized knowledge, and beliefs, of expressive 'form'. [Parsons, 1961, p. 34]

Unhappily, however, the distinction thus forcefully drawn (not only here but elsewhere as well — see Parsons et al., 1951, p. 7; Ogles et al., 1959, p. 249) is at once abandoned when Parsons asserts that 'the structure of *social* systems...*consists in* institutionalized patterns of normative *culture*' (1961, p. 36; emphasis added; see also pp. 37, 43). The abandonment is underscored when Parsons describes 'the interaction of individuals' (the social system, by the definition just quoted) in terms of 'role' and 'collectivity,' defining them, respectively, as the '*normatively regulated* participation of a person in a concrete process of social interaction,' and as 'the system of such interaction of a plurality of role-performers...*so far as it is normatively regulated* in terms of common values and of norms sanctioned by those common values' (1961, p. 42; emphasis added). Finally, the social-cultural distinction seems completely undone by Parsons's assertions that 'the role component *is* the normative component' and 'the collectivity component *is* the normative culture' (1961, p. 43; emphasis added)[33] — thereby reducing social system to cultural system.

However, suppose we take Parsons not at his second but at his first word; suppose we 'distinguish social systems from cultural systems' in the manner discussed above; and suppose we apply that distinction strictly and consistently to the following description:

> The basic subsystems of the general system of action constitute a hierarchical series of such agencies of control of the behavior of individuals or organisms. The behavioral organism is the point of articulation of the system of action with the anatomical-physiological features of the physical organism and is its point of contact with the physical environment. The personality system is, in turn, a system of control over the behavioral organism; the social system, over the personalities of its participating members; and the cultural system, a system of control relative to social systems. [Parsons, 1961, p. 38]

As just indicated, our first step in understanding this picture is to re-draw Parsons's own distinction between 'social system' and 'cultural system.' This serves as the basis for the second step: understanding the relationship to these systems, and to each other, of 'behavioral organism' and 'personality system.'

Parsons gives us one important clue in the following passage from a somewhat earlier publication:

> A social system is a system generated and constituted by the interaction of two or more individual actors, whereas a psychological [i.e., personality] system is a

system of action characterized by the fact that all the behavior belonging to it is behavior of the same living organism. . . . As a generalized mode of orientation, a cultural pattern is at least potentially applicable to more than one object and characteristic of more than one actor. [Parsons, 1959, p. 614; emphasis removed; see also pp. 635, 645]

From this, it seems clear that, in addition to the social-versus-cultural dimension, a second dimension is needed to describe logical relations between cultural system, social system, and personality system, such that the first two will refer to behavioral properties of collectivities of several actors, while the third will refer to psychological properties of one actor only.

The 'behavioral organism,' however, presents a special interpretive problem. Here is what Parsons says:

The organism is that aspect of the physiologically functioning system which interacts directly with the personality and the other systems of action. . . . For many purposes, only part of the total concrete organism should be treated as part of the system of action. Later we will refer to this part as the 'behavioral organism.' [Parsons, 1959, p. 615]

Note that, of all the systems of the general system of action, only this one is not consistently called a 'system' (except when it is significantly, though only momentarily, re-named the 'behavioral-organic system' (Parsons, 1970, p. 44), or the 'physiological system' as against the 'psychological system' (Parsons, 1959, p. 632)). This terminological inconsistency is not trivial; it signals the conceptual problem: does 'behavioral organism' refer primarily to behavior or primarily to organism? If it refers primarily to behavior, then it is a system of action like the other systems of action (personality, social, and cultural), and we may then proceed to inquire about its distinctive kind of behavior. But if it refers primarily to organism, then we are dealing with an entity in which a given kind of behavior may be problematic — that is, at any given moment the entity may or may not perform that behavior. In other words, if we read, literally, 'behavioral organism,' then a specific kind of entity, not a specific kind of behavior, is indicated, and the 'behavioral organism' thus appears anomalous among the other systems of action. But if we read 'organismic behavior,' then a specific kind of behavior is indicated, and the 'behavioral organism' therefore appears consistent with the other systems of action.

In trying to answer this question, note that, in addition to writing, sometimes, simply of 'organism,' Parsons describes it (see above) as a '*part* of the total concrete organism,' rather than, say, as a 'behavior' or 'process' of the total concrete organism. And, perhaps with some equivocation, he says, 'The total concrete organism is not an action system in our sense' (1970, p. 44). Such remarks seem to suggest an entity, rather than a behavior, referent. And in apparent consistency with an entity referent, Parsons's definition of the personality system leaves no behavioral room for 'behavioral organism': 'The *total* system of behavior of one organism is its personality' (1959, p. 645; emphasis added). But on the other hand, Parsons argues forcefully that

> *behavior* is the empirical subject matter of the theory of action. The properties of a behaving organism, independent of its behavior in actual situations, are of interest to that theory only insofar as they condition or are otherwise involved in the behavior. [Parsons, 1959, p. 614; emphasis in the original]

And this suggests a behavioral rather than entity referent. The tendency toward a behavioral connotation also seems supported by Parsons's mention (quoted above) of that system as 'physiological' (rather than anatomical).

Now suppose we somewhat arbitrarily resolve Parsons's ambiguity in favor of consistency with the other action systems and interpret 'behavioral organism' to have a behavioral rather than entity referent — as organismic *behavior*. Then Parsons's references to it as the 'physiological system' in contradistinction with the 'psychological system' seem clearly to indicate physiological rather than psychological behavior.[34] And on this basis, it immediately becomes clear that Parsons's 'basic subsystems of the general system of action' describe the individual and society in terms of a two-level hierarchy of physiological behaviors ('behavioral organism' and 'social system') and a two-level hierarchy of psychological behaviors ('personality system' and 'cultural system'), each implying a two-level hierarchy of entities (individual and collectivity).[35]

Thus interpreted, Parsons's subsystems of action help illuminate the hierarchic components underlying the conceptualizations of 'social action' and 'social relationship' that are most essential to Weber's sociological theorizing. 'Action is social,' says Weber, 'in so far as, by virtue of the subjective meaning attached to it by the acting individual...it takes account of the behavior of others and is thereby oriented in its course' (1947, p. 88). Note that this definition is cast at the individual and not at the collective level; it takes only one 'acting' individual to constitute social action insofar as the other individuals — the ones toward whom the first, socially acting, individual is oriented — may be oriented and behaving toward something else entirely. Note also that the definition requires both physiological 'acting' and psychological attachment of 'subjective meaning' on the part of the first individual. It therefore seems fair to regard Parsons's 'behavioral organism' and 'personality system' as explications of Weber's definition of 'social action.'

Now let us note that from 'social action' Weber constructs 'social relationship': 'the term "social relationship" will be used to denote the behavior of a plurality of actors in so far as, in its meaningful content, the action of each takes account of that of the others and is oriented in these terms' (1947, p. 118). Here Weber clearly refers to the collective level of physiological and psychological behaviors when he indicates that 'a plurality of actors' is both objectively behaving toward, and subjectively oriented toward, each other; and this image seems explicated by Parsons's 'social system' and 'cultural system.'

It may be noted, in passing, that Parsons's explanatory hypotheses (which he refers to in the quotation above as 'a hierarchical series of...agencies of control') selects a causal path toward which Weber himself seems to be ambivalent. In the path Parsons chooses, psychological behavior shared within a collectivity determines the collectively shared physiological behavior; the latter determines the individual's psychological behavior; and such behavior then determines the individual's physiological behavior.[36]

Note that the entity hierarchy remains implicit in Parsons's description of the subsystems of action — although his occasional interpretations of the 'behavioral organism' subsystem as an entity may well be signs of an irresolute awareness of the need to explicate that hierarchy. By contrast, Blau's discussion of 'the division of labor and the distribution of power' (1977, p. 185) includes clear and explicit emphasis on the entity hierarchy. This inclusion, however, is counterbalanced by an exclusion that Parsons would surely never tolerate: Blau drops the psychological behavior hierarchy from consideration.[37]

Blau and the Division of Labor

Blau begins his discussion of the division of labor by asserting that
'how society's work is organized can be looked at from two
perspectives: that of the *occupations* among which work is divided,
and that of the *organizations* among which work is divided' (1977,
p. 185; emphasis added). Already behavior and entity referents
may seem to be indicated by 'occupation' and 'organization,' but
that is not the case, as Blau immediately points out: 'the term ['occupations'] is usually reserved for the distribution of [individuals
in] the labor force among occupations, and it is used in this
restricted sense here' (1977, p. 185). Thus, by 'occupations' Blau
means not the behaviors performed, but the performers of
behaviors — the occupiers of occupations, so to speak — a reversal
of meaning which is the converse of that in Parsons's 'behavioral
organism,' as discussed above. We must therefore regard Blau's
two 'perspectives' on 'how society's work is organized' as referring
to two hierarchic levels of entities which can perform that work: individuals ('occupations') and collectivities ('organizations').

Now here is how Blau conceptualizes behavioral 'work' itself.
First, for Blau, as for Marx and Durkheim, 'work' and 'labor'
clearly connote externalized, *physiological*, behavior (even where
that behavior is only the expression of psychological behavior). Second, Blau differentiates two types of work: 'The two major forms
of division of labor are the subdivision of work into repetitive
routines and its subdivision into expert specialties' (1977, p. 188).
Thus, eschewing the substantive distinctions in work (distinctions
in *what* is done) that are implied by the behavioral notion of 'occupations' (because he has already elected to use that term in the
'restricted sense' quoted above), Blau employs a formal distinction
in work (*how* it is done). The latter distinction hinges on defining as
'routine' tasks that are 'repetitive' (that is, constant) over time and
as 'specialty' tasks that are 'variable' over time (see 1977, p. 187).
However, since Blau does not indicate the time interval he has in
mind, and because what is constant over a short time interval may
be variable over a longer time interval, and vice versa, his definition
is indeterminate.

But as information theory, linguistics, genetics, particle physics,
astronomy, cytology — indeed, the entire corpus of natural science
— seems to indicate, complex and specialized processes (not ex-

cluding the division of labor) may be usefully regarded as aggregates of shorter and simpler routines. Accordingly, Blau's 'routinized' versus 'specialized' distinction may be regarded as specifying a two-level hierarchy of behavior attributed to the social phenomenon called 'the divison of labor' such that that division is said to occur between elemental behavior 'routines' or between complex aggregates of these routines — that is, 'specialties.'

Viewed in this light, it therefore appears that, in describing the division of labor, Blau implies two componential hierarchies whose levels are correlated: there is a two-level hierarchy of entities ('occupation' and 'organizations'), and by its side there is a two-level hierarchy of physiological behaviors ('routines' and 'specialties').

Although he does not say so explicitly, it seems that Blau believes these two hierarchies have undergone parallel evolutions from micro toward macro. Thus, he refers to '*modern* societies, wheɩe so much of the total work is carried out in large *organizations*' (1977, p. 203; emphasis added; see also p. 197), and he refers to '*Earlier* industrial developments [as having] promoted large-scale *routinization*' (1977, p. 194). Blau thereby implies that division of labor entities were once only (or mainly) individuals and the division of labor behaviors performed by them were once only (or mainly) routines; the modern division of labor, however, is between large organizations that perform specialties.[38] This hierarchic and evolutionary image helps illuminate an application of the principle of hierarchic structure to components of social phenomena which is central to the classical Marxian image of human history.

Thus, during what Marx calls 'primitive communism,' the individual was a generalist who produced all needed goods and services and was, in this behavioral sense, indistinguishable from the whole society. In terms of Figure 1, the relationship, behaviorally speaking, was integration: the micro- and macro-entity levels encompassed the same macro range of behaviors; behaviorally, the individual was a little society and the society was a big individual.[39] With the development of handicrafts production, however, the individual became a behavioral specialist — producing only one commodity but producing that commodity in its entirety. In our terms, this means that a meso-level in the behavior hierarchy emerged and was allocated to the micro-entity level. In the next, manufacturing, stage a meso-level entity (the factory and, more generally, the privately owned business firm) emerged and took over the meso-level behavioral specialties that had developed in the previous stage. To this end, however, the micro-entity level was further downgraded to performing micro-behavior.

Marx looks upon the successive demotion of individuals from behaviorally macro-generalists, to meso-specialists, and finally, to micro-routinists as a central feature of the long but ultimately transitory process of individual 'estrangement,' 'alienation,' and degradation. The emergent meso-level factory and firm, however, does not seem to be regarded as transitory by him. Marx expects them to persist long after the proletarian revolution restores the individual to the generalist level by substituting machines for human beings in routines and specialties (a substitution already nascent, says Marx, in the present industrial stage of the division of labor), and otherwise making it 'possible for [the individual] to do one thing today and another tomorrow, to hunt in the morning, fish in the afternoon, rear cattle in the evening, criticize after dinner' (Marx and Engels, 1947, p. 22).

In differently partial but overlapping ways, then, Parsons and Blau (as well as Weber and Marx, their acknowledged intellectual forebears) illustrate the intersection of what this paper terms the principle of hierarchic structure and the generic definition of social phenomena: Parsons concentrates on correlations between hierarchic levels in the psychological behavior and the physiological behavior components of social phenomena, while Blau concentrates on correlations between hierarchic levels in the physiological behavior component and the entity component of social phenomena.

It should be noted that neither Parsons's nor Blau's concentrations (in the description cited) includes reference to the spatial or the temporal regularity componential hierarchy. Although both Parsons and Blau do refer to these hierarchies elsewhere (see, for example, Parsons, 1961, pp. 70-9; 1966; Blau, 1977, pp. 90-3, 155ff), the theorist who has written most extensively on temporal regularities and their correlates in other componential hierarchies is Sorokin,[40] and among those who have written most extensively on spatial regularities and their correlates are Park (1936, 1952; Park and Burgess, 1920), and Hawley (1944, 1950, 1971). Unfortunately, we do not have space here to analyze details of various approaches to the temporal and spatial regularity hierarchies but it may be said that in general the problems appear to be very much the same as with the analysis of the other componential hierarchies and their relationships.

In our discussion so far, however, we have kept our promise of dealing with only the simplest and most direct variant of hierarchic structure in social phenomena. It is time to recall all four variants of that structure and take them explicitly into account.

COMPLEX SOCIAL PHENOMENA

All descriptions of complex social phenomena seem to hinge on identifying parts that are segregated from one another in certain respects and integrated with one another in certain other respects. Thus van den Berghe refers to social systems as consisting of 'subsystems which are functionally unrelated and structurally discrete and disparate, but which are interlocked because they share certain elements in common' (1963, p. 702), and Gouldner describes organizational structure as 'shaped by a tension between centrifugal and centripetal pressures' (1959, p. 423). The evolution of such complex systems generally appears to involve hierarchic structure:

> The time required for a complex system, containing k elementary components, say, to evolve by processes of natural selection from those components is very much shorter if the system is itself comprised of one or more layers of stable component subsystems than if its elementary parts are its only stable components.... Hence, almost all the very large systems will have hierarchic organization. [Simon, 1973, pp. 8, 9]

As 'elementary components' become fitted together into 'component subsystems,' and the latter then become fitted into 'a complex system,' properties are often said to emerge in the subsystems and systems which were not manifest in the elementary components. Thus, Durkheim argues that 'a whole very often has very different properties from those which its constituent parts possess' (1978, p. 76); Simmel observes that 'increasing quantity results in entirely new phenomena' (1950, p. 116); and, more generally, Blau defines emergent properties as 'essentially relationships between elements in a structure...relationships [that] are not contained in the elements' (1964, p. 3).

It appears, then, that the concepts of complexity and emergence depend on the more elementary notions of system integration and segregation. But exactly what relationships are indicated by system

FIGURE 3
Hierarchic Structure and Social Phenomena:
Property-Space Cross-Classifying their Variants
and Components, Respectively

Variants of Hierarchic Structure	Components of Social Phenomena				
	Entity	Behavior		Regularity	
		Physio-logical	Psycho-logical	Temporal	Spatial
Integrated					
Hierarchic					
Concatenated					
Segregated					

'integration' and 'segregation,' and where may these relationships manifest themselves? Figure 3 is the answer indicated by the present analysis.

Thus, our analysis leads us to suggest that the 'integration' and 'segregation' of social phenomena may take four principal forms, and that each form may be manifested at any of five points, independently. With this suggestion we seek to make more systematic the general observation that two or more social phemonena may be related to each other at certain points in certain ways and in other ways at other points. We would thereby permit more systematic empirical investigation of the distinctive consequences of each possible combination of relationships across all five points. By way of illustration, consider two classical, and instructively different, analyses of divisions of labor.

Durkheim's (1933) description of 'lower' societies, with their 'segmented' social structure (hence, minimal division of labor) and 'mechanical' cultural structure, may be interpreted as positing integrated relationships across all components. The emergence of 'higher' societies, with their 'organized' social structures (hence high division of labor), may then be interpreted as representing a shift to concatenated relationships (product differentiation, process fragmentation, and exchange) in the physiological behavior component. At this point, it is important to note Durkheim's emphatic distinction (drawn explicitly only toward the end of his book and in the 'Preface' to the second edition) between the 'normal' and 'abnormal' forms of societies in which this shift takes place. The distinction emphasizes his belief that concatenated relationships in the physiological component cannot be self-sustaining but must be sustained by other relationships in other components.

Thus, in order to constitute the normal form, at least three hierarchic levels of psychological behavior relationships must be present (society-wide, occupation-wide, and job-specific levels of normative regulation — 'organic solidarity'), and at least three hierarchic levels of entities (the society as a whole, occupationa. 'corporations,' and individuals) must be correlated with them. In addition, Durkheim indicates that temporal and spatial regularities must be 'coordinated' across physiological behaviors, and the temporal and spatial regularity with which different individuals (and presumably also occupational corporations) come to perform such behaviors must be in accord with the distribution of 'natural talent' among them (in other words, the division of labor must be 'spontaneous' and 'free').

In the abnormal forms, however, one or more of these mainly hierarchic relationships does not develop. Instead, they all tend toward segregation (manifest in 'anomie,' selfish individualism, and 'incoherence and disorder') and eventually drag physiological relationships down with them.

Thus does Durkheim describe three types of societies: one in which integrated relationships predominate in all components of social phenomena; a second in which concatenated relationships in one component are combined with hierarchic relationships in the others; and a third, degenerate, type in which the latter combination fails and all relationships deteriorate toward segregation.

Our second illustration also refers to a division of labor, but where Durkheim refers to the appearance of that division in all realms of social life (with perhaps more emphasis on the economic realm), Weber's discussion of 'legitimate authority' refers specifically to its appearance in the political aspects of life — the division of labor between those who command and those who obey (Weber, 1947, pp. 324-407; see also pp. 124-132). A more important difference for our present concerns, however, is that Durkheim stresses concatenation between the physiological behavior of one entity and the physiological behavior of another, while Weber' stresses what may be called cross-concatenation between the physiological behavior of one entity and the psychological behavior of another. Thus, Weber conceptualizes one entity's physiological issuance of 'commands' as belonging to the same sociocultural subsystem as another entity's psychological attribution of 'legitimacy' to those commands, and he conceptualizes the second entity's physiological 'obedience' as belonging to the same sociocultural subsystem as the first entity's psychological imputation of its 'right' to issue further commands.[41]

Together, then, Durkheim and Weber provide complementary illustrations of the flexibility offered by Figure 3, and with that in mind we propose it as a simple instrument for understanding, comparing, and devising sociological descriptions of great complexity.

CONCLUSIONS

We have tried to do three main things here. We proposed a principle of hierarchic structure and four variants of that structure (Figure 1); we proposed a generic definition of social phenomena and three components of those phenomena (Figure 2); and finally, as a comprehensive guide to descriptions of social phenomena, we proposed a cross-classification of hierarchic structure variants with social phenomena components (Figure 3).

NOTES

1. Note that Simmel's use of 'may' here means that, although the various subgroups must be overlapping in order to constitute a juxtaposed relationship, exactly which individual participants will manifest that overlap is to some extent indeterminate.

2. I prefer 'concatenated' to 'juxtaposed' because the specifically chain-like (or, better, chainmail-like) metaphor implied by concatenation seems to capture the linked positioning of subgroups that Simmel indicates better than does 'juxtaposition,' which indicates only side-by-side positioning, without any necessary overlaps.

3. Sorokin, indeed, mentions all but one of the four subgroup relationships shown in Figure 1:

> the total sociocultural world appears as an enormous arena of millions of systems, now subordinated to one another and yielding sometimes the vastest supersystems; now coordinated with one another [as 'partners' without subordination of one to the other]; now being independent congeries in regard to one another. [Sorokin, 1947, p. 58]

4. These four relationships should be regarded as ideal-typical, with many transitional points between types. Thus, subgroups may share few or many of their member elements and may share few or many of their memberships in higher groups. In addition, any complex society may combine these relationships in various ways — such that the relationship between some of its subgroups may be described as approximating, say, the segregated type, while the relationship between other subgroups approximates the concatenated, or the hierarchic, or the integrated relationship — and these relationships may contend with one another within the same complex organization or society (see Gouldner's discussion of 'organizational tensions'; 1959, pp. 413-26).

5. Herbert A. Simon's trailbreaking paper, first published in 1962, forms the basis for this definition, although Simon uses more restricted descriptive terms (i.e., 'system' and 'interrelated') than I think are necessary: 'By a hierarchic system, or hierarchy, I mean a system that is composed of interrelated subsystems, each of the latter being, in turn, hierarchic in structure until we reach some lowest level of elementary subsystem' (1965, p. 64). Mesarovic and Macko's definition, however, requires neither 'system' nor 'interrelationships' (but permits them, of course), and is thus more strictly in accord with the definition used here: 'An object on a given stratum becomes a relation on a lower stratum and an element becomes a set. A subsystem on a given stratum is a system on the stratum below' (1969, p. 34). And so is Grobstein's: 'Hierarchical order refers to a complex of successively more encompassing sets' (1973, p. 31).

6. Edel uses the term 'emergence' to mean simply occurrence, but the phenomenon he describes seems to be emergence in Nagel's sense:

the behavior of lower-level elements after the emergence of the higher-level phenomena may follow different laws from what it did when the higher-level phenomena had not yet existed, or from what it does in areas where they are not present. This may be loosely described as the interference of the higher-level entities in the lower level, or the assertion of higher-level causality, or the denial that the higher-level phenomena are epiphenomenal. [Nagel, 1959, p. 169]

We return to the problem of emergence toward the end of this paper.

7. One way of resolving the dilemma has been proposed most explicitly by Pattee, but adumbrated by Simon (1965). The latter points out that two kinds of self-descriptions are present within the living organism, in the forms of DNA and RNA ('state descriptions'), and proteins ('process descriptions'). Pattee argues more generally that in certain inorganic as well as organic hierarchies, real description of their own behavior are formed. (See 1969, pp. 167, 177). Such internal descriptions would seem to include culture in social phenomena; and culture may therefore be viewed as but one of a family of 'real' self-descriptions of complex systems.

8. Simon, however, argues that 'if there are important systems in the world that are complex without being hierarchic, they may to a considerable extent escape our observation and our understanding' (1965, p. 72).

9. The problem of defining 'organism' belongs to the discipline of biology; I, at least, am prepared to accept whatever definition is current there at any given moment (just as, presumably, biologists are prepared to accept whatever definition of 'molecule' is current among chemists) in token of the hierarchic structure of scientific lexicons. Behavior may then be defined as any event occurring in an organism.

10. Note that our definition coincides reassuringly with notions about the general nature of 'organization' per se — whether social and cultural organization, biological organization, physical organization, or whatever — and thus provides a basic conceptual link to all other scientific disciplines. Thus, Ashby argues that

> The hard core of the concept 'organization' is, in my opinion, that of 'conditionality.' As soon as the relation between two entities A and B becomes conditional on C's value or state then a necessary component of organization is present...the converse of 'conditional on'...occurs in mechanical forms, in hardware, when what looks like one machine proves to be composed of two (or more) sub-machines each of which is acting independently of the others....If 'conditionality' is an essential component in the concept of organization, so also is the assumption that we are speaking of a whole composed of parts. [Ashby, 1968, p. 108]

The three components of Ashby's 'organization' are 'conditionality,' 'action,' and 'parts,' and in this light, a reasonable reformulation of his definition of organization might be 'inter-part action conditionality' — an exact, but more abstract, conceptual parallel to the present definition of social phenomena as 'interorganism behavior regularity.'

11. But we know, from all their writings on class struggle, that they did not intend to rule out conflict behavior. Indeed, their term 'Zusammenwirken,' here translated as 'cooperation,' may be rendered more literally and more inclusively as 'joint activity.' See also Marx's letter to Annenkov, where society is called 'The product of

men's reciprocal action' (Marx and Engels, 1969, p. 518) and the nature of the 'action' is left open and inclusive.

12. At one point, Durkheim requires that a social fact be 'capable of exercising on the individual an external constraint' (1938, p. 13).

13. I say such definitions risk tautology without necessarily being tautological because tautology lies in the explanation that is applied to a given definition, not in the definition itself. Thus, it is non-tautological to define a given phenomenon by the presence of certain explanatory causes if one then seeks either to explain these causes with other causes, or to add other causes to the explanation of the phenomenon. However, there appear to be at least two great (though not insuperable) problems with this procedure. First, it is not easy to meet its analytical requirements. The analyst is always required, of course, to show that his/her sample of observations fits its conceptual description (the process of achieving this fit is called 'interpretation' or 'operationalization'; see Wallace, 1971, pp. 66-8) before any explanatory analysis can begin. But when an explanatory cause is part of the conceptual definition, that cause must be shown actually to be true for the sample. Needless to say, this is no small preliminary requirement and one that, at least in sociology, is rarely if ever met. The second problem arises from the possibility that one's inclusion of a hypothetical explanation in a definition may be unintentional as such; one may simply be expressing the strength of one's a priori conviction that that hypothesis will actually be upheld by empirical test, without realizing that the expression itself renders the hypothesis tautological and therefore sets it beyond reach of such a test.

14. As Marvin Bressler (private communication) points out, claiming that all social phenomena must be due to interaction is similar to claiming that all cases in which the same culture trait occurs in different times and places must be due to diffusion (and not to independent invention).

15. Durkheim says: 'To arrive at the same goal, many different ways can be and actually are followed' (1938, p. 94). See also Merton on 'functional alternatives' (1957, pp. 36, 52).

16. Note the implied distinction from 'sociobiology'. The latter seems currently to emphasize the importance of certain traditionally 'biological' variables in accounting for social phemonena across species; the comparative sociology I have in mind would hold no brief for any particular explanatory variable a priori but would stress the exploration of systematic variations as well as constancies in such phenomema and in their explanations.

17. I avoid the term 'actor' because the behavior selected for sociological analysis may be defined analytically as entirely psychological and therefore 'thought' or 'feeling' rather than 'action.' Even the Weberian and Parsonian definitions require the presence of physiological behavior (see Weber, 1947, p. 88; Parsons and Shils, 1951, p. 53).

18. Not complete strangers, of course. Durkheim says: 'Not without reason has it been said that the self is itself a society, by the same right as the organism' (1938, p. iii; see also p. xlviii).

19. 'Action is social insofar as, by virtue of the subjective meaning attached to it by the acting individual (or individuals), it takes account of the behavior of others and is thereby oriented to its course' (Weber, 1947, p. 88). Parsons echoes this view by describing his own theoretic scheme as concerned with 'acts,' defined as 'behaviors to which their authors and those who significantly interact with them at-

tribute, in Weber's phase, a "subjective," which is to say cultural or symbolic, meaning' (1970, p. 29).
20.

> From the start the 'spirit' is afflicted with the curse of being 'burdened' with matter, which here makes its appearance in the form of...language. Language is as old as consciousness, language is practical consciousness, as it exists for other men, and for that reason is really beginning to exist for me personally as well. [Marx and Engels, 1947, p. 19]

More recently, Berger and Luckmann reassert the requirement that psychological behavior must be expressed in physiological behavior by claiming that, although 'internalization' of meaning is 'the begining point' of every human being's 'induction into participation in the societal dialectic' (1966, p. 129), every 'human being *must* ongoingly *externalize* itself in activity' (1966, p. 52; emphasis added).

21. We hold, of course, that the natural sciences — including sociology — can describe and explain only regularities and never singularities. Thus, Cohen and Nagel assert that 'Scientific explanation consists in subsuming under some rule or law which expresses an invariant character of a group of events, the particular events it is said to explain' (1934, p. 397); thus, particulars must be shown to be parts of regularities in order to be explained by science. Description and explanation select and construct those attributes or aspects of a particular observation — entirely unique in its totality — that subsume and regularize it. The fact that scientific description and explanation are rigorously communicative (owing to a normative commitment to replicability and intersubjective reliability) is the prime assurance that that subsumption and regularization will occur.

22. Weber grounds the definition of a social relationship and of social power in such conditonal probabilities (1947, pp. 119, 152), and Parsons refers to a non-zero conditional probability as 'factual order' ('The antithesis of [factual order] is randomness or chance in the strict sense of phenomena conforming to the statistical laws of probability' — 1937, p. 91) and asserts that 'a social order is always a factual order' (1937, p. 92).

23. Durkheim expresses the difference between the first and the second interests when he notes that social and cultural phenomena 'could be examined from two different points of view.' One could study them as 'a number of *actions* coordinated in view of a goal...Or one might prefer to study the *entity* charged with accomplishing these actions' (1978, p. 63; emphasis added). Levy's 'distinction between concrete and analytic structures' seems to echo Durkheim — but with greater ambiguity, partly because Levy defines analytic structures only residually:

> *Concrete structures* are...at least in theory capable of physical separation (in time and/or space) from other units of the same sort...[and include] membership units involved in social action***Analytic structures* are...not even theoretically capable of concrete separation from other patterned aspects of action...the economic and political patterns are analytic structures. [Levy, 1952, pp. 88-9; for an interpretation of Levy's discussion similar to the present one, see Moore, 1978, p. 337]

Merton also draws the distinction between social collectivities and social relations when he defines a 'group' as 'a number of *people* having established and characteristic social relations,' and then defines 'social relations' as 'patterned forms of social *interaction*' (1957, p. 285; emphasis added).

24. Reference here is to conventional physical space with its dimensions of length, breadth, and height. 'Social' space is here constituted by organisms, behavior, and regularity dimensions and may thus be regarded as a 'hyperspace' which includes another space (i.e., physical) in one of its dimensions. The general term 'space' is taken to indicate an abstract concept applicable to the set of loci defined by the coordination of any two or more dimensions, and one's choice of dimensions is a matter of entirely arbitrary definition. Once the space is constructed, however, its usefulness becomes subject to other, non-arbitrary, criteria. What becomes crucial then is the ability of the space in question to order observations descriptively, to permit the application of explanatory-predictive principles to them, and to do all this in ways not inconsistent with other, better established, spaces and the principles applied to them. Therefore, no 'ineluctability,' no 'reality,' no 'concreteness' can be inherent to any space whatever; all spaces (including physical space) have reality socially *conferred* on them (or revoked from them, or refused to them) by their perceived usefulness — which, of course, is always subject to change from many quarters. In one sense, this entire paper seeks to explicate the usefulness of social space as defined below by Figure 3.

25. Note that Figure 2 is meant to classify only what things are 'said to be'; how things are 'regarded;' what aspect is of 'primary interest.' These phrases indicate that we are dealing here with descriptions of social phenomena and not with social phenomena themselves (again, whatever that may mean).

26. However, Kroeber and Parsons depart from the present usage by stipulating that cultural systems are 'factors *in shaping of* human behavior' (1958, p. 583; emphasis added) — thereby seeming to restrict culture to the analytical role of explanans rather than establishing it as one of the principal explananda of sociological analysis. In a second departure from the present usage, Kroeber and Parsons include 'the artifacts produced through behavior' as parts of culture. By contrast, I prefer to regard such artifacts as intermediate between purely human social phenomena and purely non-human non-social phenomena. This status makes them crucial to the explanation and preduction of human social phenomena but they play no part whatever in the definition of those phenomena.

27. The indeterminancy lies in the definition's silence on the question of what is 'social' about either social structure or social relationships.

28. 'Somewhat misleading' because the concept 'ecology' covers all environing resources for life; space is only one of these.

29. The ground seems erroneous because any given spatial pattern can be produced by impingments that are random (i.e., non-patterned) in their temporal occurrence, and vice versa.

30. Note that we continue to refer here only to how social phenomena are described, not to how they are explained. Blau merges these two problems when he says

> microsociological theory seeks to explain human relations in terms of the psychological and social processes underlying them, such as processes of symbolic communication, of competition and cooperation, of social exchange. . . . Macrosociological theory, on the other hand, seeks to explain the relations among various parts of entire societies in terms of the differentiation of these parts. [Blau, 1977, p. 2]

The view adopted here sharply distinguishes the description of the thing-to-be-explained from the 'terms,' to use Blau's word, in which it is explained (see Wallace, 1971, p. 95). We therefore regard one's designation of explanandum as logically independent of one's designation of explanans — excepting only that the two must not be identical or else the theory will be tautological (an eventuality, incidentally, that Blau defends — 1977, p. 12). Thus, a given theory may well apply micro-explanantes to macro-explananda, while another theory applies macro-explanantes to micro-explananda. Blau himself seems to rely on this independent variability insofar as his 1977 book proposes to account for micro-explananda (e.g., interpersonal contacts across group boundaries) with more macro-explanantes (such as size differences between the *groups* in question), while an earlier book accounts for macro-explananda with micro-explanantes in proposing 'to derive the social processes that govern the *complex* structures of communities and societies from the *simpler* processes that pervade the daily intercourse among individuals and their interpersonal relations' (1962, p. 2; emphasis added).

31. A similar urging may be found in Adler (1960), except that he makes behavior the *only* unit required in sociology when he 'reduces' entities to behavior (without also 'reducing' behavior to entities), and includes regularity as a necessary part of behavior (without also including behavior as a necessary part of regularity). Another, more generalized, plea for measurement consensus may be found in Gibbs (1972).

32. Wilson identifies two kinds of closure that correspond to the spatial and temporal types of regularities discussed here: 'topological closure [involving] closed surfaces of a spatial neighborhood,' and 'temporal closure [involving] a neighborhood in time' (1969, p. 54). He adds that 'the properties of space and time are closure properties of structures, bringing to mind the basic idea of Leibnitz that space and time have no independent existence but derive from the nature of structures' (1969, p. 55). The converse may also be true (i.e., entity and behavior structures may have no independent existence apart from space and time).

33. One possible explanation of Parsons's apparently unknowing reversal of his original policy seems to be his overwhelming (and perhaps blinding) personal conviction that

> society is *not understandable* apart from its relations to a cultural system. This is to say that the actions of individual persons in their capacities as members of a social system *must* be oriented in terms of the meanings of cultural symbol systems, of what is sometimes called patterns of culture. [Parsons, 1973, p. 35; emphasis added]

It may, however, not be so; there appear to be other ways of understanding society and other ways of constraining the actions of individual persons into social structure (see Wallace, 1969, pp. 1-59).

34. Indeed, at one point he does identify this system with 'body' and the personality system with 'mind' (Parsons, 1959, p. 651).

35. Such a recasting helps account for the rise in prominence, within Parsons's theory, of the concept 'behavioral organism.' The 'action frame of reference' initially comprised only 'three configurations' (personality, social system, and culture), wherein 'personality' was ambiguously described as both a 'system of orientation and motivation' and 'physiological organism' (1951, p. 7); as being, vaguely,

'organized around the biological unity of the organism' (1951, p. 75); and as being similar to social systems insofar as they — but not cultural systems — were said to be capable of overt behavior ('action') (1951, p. 76). In 1959, however, Parsons stresses the separate introduction of

> behavioral organism: it will be noted that, compared to previous publications, we speak of four rather than three primary subsystems of the general theory of action; the organism, in certain respects, has been added. . . . This represents a definite theoretical innovation. [Parsons, 1959, p. 613]

And in 1970 he claims that this addition has 'rounded out' the action frame of reference — although not for the reasons being stressed here but because it enables him to identify that frame's now four subsystems with the four functional imperatives (see Parsons, 1970, pp. 43-4). Parsons does not tell us *how* the addition enables him to make this identification, but considering the emphasis he gives to 'a striking set of numerical relations' involving the number four (1970, p. 38) it seems just possible that the presence of fourness in the form of both schemes is his principal criterion of substantive identity here.

36. Weber's ambivalence toward this causal path (which he does seem, in the main, to accept) is evident at at least two points. First, he claims that the distribution of objective power in a collectivity can determine the distribution of subjective orientations in it (see his discussion of the legal order: 1947, pp. 127-30, 329ff). Second, he claims that 'charismatic' individuals can affect the collectivity in ways at least different from if not also stronger than, the ways it affects them (1947, pp. 358-63). Parsons himself argues for causation in both directions along the indicated path, but he claims that 'The more important [direction] for *our* purposes' (1966, p. 113) is the one specified here. Parsons calls this more important causal direction one of 'cybernetic control' and calls the reverse direction one of 'necessary conditions' (see 1966, pp. 28, 113).

37. Blau says: 'I consider my focus on group structures and status structures, and explicitly not on culture [defined by Blau as values and symbols, rules and myths'], to be in the tradition of Marx' (1977, p. 16). In striking and unexplicated contrast, however, Blau has also claimed that 'Value consensus is of crucial significance for social processes that pervade complex social structures' (1964, p. 24).

38. Blau also argues that 'the trend has been toward increasing concentration of [power] in giant organizations, and their top executives" (1974, p. 633), and that this concentration is 'incompatible with democracy in the long-run' (1977, p. 241) because it endangers 'the integration of the diverse parts in industrial society and the counteracting forces permitting gradual change in democracy***[and thereby threatens] to replace democratically instituted recurrent social change with alternate periods of social stagnation and revolutionary upheaval' (1974, pp. 633, 634). In a similar line of argument, Coleman says of 'corporate bodies' in modern society that 'what was once a hard shell of protection for men, shielding them from the state and giving them the strength of collective action, has. . .come to develop power on its own' (1974, p. 35) and to exert that power against individual freedom. Thus, both Blau and Coleman challenge and qualify Durkheim's hierarchic structural hypothesis that 'A nation can be maintained only if, between the State and the individual, there is intercalated a whole series of secondary groups near enough to the individuals to attract them strongly in their sphere of action and drag them, in this

way, into the general torrent of social life' (1933, p. 28). Blau, and Coleman, assert
that at least some of the meso-entities (namely, secondary groups) to which
Durkheim refers may not maintain but destroy a democratic nation by emergent
behavior regularities which do indeed drag individuals into the torrent of social life
— but binding and drowning them there.

39. Durkheim, refuting this Marxian image, most aptly says it portrays the individual as 'an empire embedded within another empire' (1978, p. 69).

40. Sorokin describes his four-volume principal work, entitled *Social and
Cultural Dynamics*, as 'an investigation of the nature and change, the dynamics of
integrated culture: its types, its processes, its trends, fluctuations, rhythms, tempos'
(1937, p. x). Elsewhere, he describes 'dynamic general sociology' as an investigation
of '(a) recurring social processes...(b) recurring cultural processes...(c) rhythms,
tempos, periodicities, trends and fluctuations in social and cultural processes in persons, and how and why persons change' (1947, p. 16). For other treatments,
beholden to Sorokin, see Moore (1963a, b).

41. It may also be noted that where Durkheim's image of the 'normal' division of
labor portrays the equal subjection of all entities and all physiological behaviors to
the same society-wide level of the psychological behavior (i.e., normative) hierarchy,
Weber describes an ultimate inequality in this respect. Thus, the entities at the sum-
mit of legitimate authority only issue and never obey commands, while the entities at
the bottom only obey and never issue commands. Simmel proposes to remove this
'onesidedness' with temporal or spatial alternation between an entity's issuing and
obeying commands (1950, p. 285).

REFERENCES

ADLER, Franz (1960) 'A Unit Concept for Sociology,' *American Journal of
Sociology*, 65:356-64.
ADORNO, Theodor W. (1976) 'Sociology and Empirical Research,' in Paul Con-
nerton (ed.), *Critical Sociology*. New York: Penguin.
ASHBY, W. Ross (1968) 'Principles of the Self-Organizing System,' in Walter
Buckley (ed.), *Modern Systems Research for the Behavioral Scientist*. Chicago:
Aldine.
BERGER, Peter L. and Thomas LUCKMANN (1966) *The Social Construction of
Reality*. New York: Doubleday.
BLAU, Peter M. (1964) *Exchange and Power in Social Life*. New York: John Wiley.
BLAU, Peter M. (1974) 'Parameters of Social Structure,' *American Sociological
Review*, 39:615-35.
BLAU, Peter M. (1977) *Inequality and Heterogeneity*. New York: Free Press.
BLAU, Peter M. and W. Richard SCOTT (1962) *Formal Organizations*. San Fran-
cisco: Chandler.

CAMPBELL, Donald T. (1958) 'Common Fate, Similarity, and Other Indices of the Status of Aggregates of Persons as Social Entities,' *Behavioral Science*, 3:14-25.

CAMPBELL, Donald T. and Donald W. FISKE (1959) 'Convergent and Discriminant Validation By the Multitrait-Multimethod Matrix,' *Psychological Bulletin*, 56:81-105.

COHEN, Morris R. and Ernest NAGEL (1934), *An Introduction to Logic and Scientific Method*. New York: Harcourt, Brace & World.

COLEMAN, James (1974) *Power and the Structure of Society*. New York: W. W. Norton.

COLEMAN, James, Elihu KATZ, and Herbert MENZEL (1957), 'The Diffusion of an Innovation Among Physicians,' *Sociometry*, 20:253-70.

COLLINS, Randall (1975) *Conflict Sociology*. New York: Academic Press.

COSER, Lewis A. (1978) 'American Trends,' in Tom Bottomore and Robert Nisbet (eds), *A History of Sociological Analysis*. New York: Basic Books.

DAVIS, Kingsley (1949) *Human Society*. New York: Macmillan.

DAVIS, Kingsley (1959) 'The Myth of Functional Analysis as a Special Method in Sociology and Anthropology,' *American Sociological Review*, 24:757-72.

DURKHEIM, Emile (1933) *The Division of Labor in Society*. Glencoe, Ill.: Free Press (first published 1893).

DURKHEIM, Emile (1938) *The Rules of the Sociological Method*. Glencoe, Ill.: Free Press (first published 1895).

DURKHEIM, Emile (1978) *On Institutional Analysis*. Chicago: University of Chicago Press (first published 1900).

EDEL, Abraham (1959) 'The Concept of Levels in Social Theory,' in Llewellyn Gross (ed.), *Symposium on Sociological Theory*. New York: Harper & Row.

GIBBS, Jack (1972) *Sociological Theory Construction*. Hinsdale, Ill.: Dryden Press.

GOULDNER, Alvin W. (1959) 'Organizational Analysis,' in Robert K. Merton et al. (eds), *Sociology Today*. New York: Basic Books.

GOULDNER, Alvin W. (1960) 'The Norm of Reciprocity,' *American Sociological Review*, 25:161-78.

GROBSTEIN, Clifford (1973), 'Hierarchical Order and Neogenesis,' in Howard H. Pattee (ed.), *Hierarchy Theory*. New York: George Braziller.

HAWLEY, Amos (1944) 'Ecology and Human Ecology,' *Social Forces*. 22:398-405.

HAWLEY, Amos (1950) *Human Ecology*. New York: Ronald Press.

HAWLEY (1971) *Urban Society: An Ecological Approach*. New York: John Wiley.

HEMPEL, Carl G. (1965) *Aspects of Scientific Explanation*. New York: Free Press.

HOMANS, George C. (1950) *The Human Group*. New York: Harcourt Brace Jovanovich.

HOMANS, George C. (1974) *Social Behavior: Its Elementary Forms*. New York: Harcourt Brace Jovanovich (first published 1961).

INKELES, Alex (1964) *What Is Sociology?* Englewood Cliffs, NJ: Prentice-Hall.

KAPLAN, Abraham (1964) *The Conduct of Inquiry*. San Francisco: Chandler.

KROEBER, A. L. and Talcott PARSONS (1958) 'The Concepts of Culture and of Social System,' *American Sociological Review*, 23:582-3.

KUHN, Thomas S. (1964) *The Structure of Scientific Revolutions*. Chicago: University Press.

LEVY, Marion J., Jr (1952) *The Structure of Society*. Princeton: Princeton University Press.

MARX, Karl and Friedrich ENGELS (1947) *The German Ideology*. New York: International Publishers (first published 1846).

MARX, Karl and Friedrich ENGELS (1969) *Selected Works*, vol. I. Moscow: Progress Publishers.

MERTON, Robert K. (1957) *Social Structure and Social Theory* (revised and enlarged). New York: Free Press (first published 1949).

MESAROVIC, M. D. and D. MACKO (1969) 'Foundations for a Scientific Theory of Hierarchical Systems,' in Lancelot Law Whyte et al. (eds), *Hierarchical Structures*. New York: American Elsevier.

MOORE, Wilbert E. (1963a) *Man, Time and Society*. New York: John Wiley.

MOORE, Wilbert E. (1963b) *Social Change*. Englewood Cliffs, NJ: Prentice-Hall.

MOORE, Wilbert E. (1978) 'Functionalism,' in Tom Bottomore and Robert Nisbet (eds), *A History of Sociological Analysis*. New York: Basic Books.

NAGEL, Ernest (1961) *The Structure of Science*. New York: Harcourt Brace Jovanovich.

OGLES, Richard H., Marion J. LEVY, Jr, and Talcott PARSONS (1959) 'Culture and Social System: An Exchange,' *American Sociological Review*, 24: pp. 246-50.

PARK, Robert E. (1936) 'Human Ecology,' *American Journal of Sociology*, 42:1-15.

PARK, Robert E. (1952) *Human Communities: The City and Human Ecology*. Glencoe, Ill.: Free Press.

PARK, Robert E. and Ernest W. BURGESS (1920) *Introduction to the Science of Sociology*. Chicago: University Press.

PARSONS, Talcott (1937) *The Structure of Social Action*. Glencoe, Ill.: Free Press.

PARSONS, Talcott (1951) *The Social System*. Glencoe, Ill.: Free Press.

PARSONS, Talcott (1959) 'An Approach to Psychological Theory in Terms of the Theory of Action,' in Sigmund Koch (ed.), *Psychology: A Study of a Science*. New York: McGraw-Hill.

PARSONS, Talcott (1960) 'Pattern Variables Revisited: A Response to Robert Dubin,' *American Sociological Review*, 25:467-83.

PARSONS, Talcott (1961) 'An Outline of the Social System,' in Talcott Parsons et al. (eds), *Theories of Society*. New York: Free Press.

PARSONS, Talcott (1966) *Societies: Evolutionary and Comparative Perspectives*. Englewood Cliffs, NJ: Prentice-Hall.

PARSONS, Talcott (1970) 'Some Problems of General Theory,' in John C. McKinney and Edward A. Tiryakian (eds), *Theoretical Sociology*. New York: Appleton-Century-Crofts.

PARSONS, Talcott (1973) 'Culture and Social Structure Revisited,' in Louis Schneider and Charles Bonjean (eds). *The Idea of Culture in the Social Sciences*. Cambridge: University Press.

PARSONS, Talcott, et al. (1951) 'Some Fundamental Categories of the Theory of Action: A General Statement,' in Talcott Parsons and Edward A. Shils (eds), *Toward A General Theory of Action*. New York: Harper.

PARSONS, Talcott and Edward A. SHILS (1951) 'Values, Motives, and Systems of Action,' in Talcott Parsons and Edward A. Shils (eds), *Toward A General Theory of Action*. New York: Harper.

PATTEE, Howard H. (1969) 'Physical Conditions for Primitive Functional Hierarchies,' in Lancelot Law Whyte et al. (eds), *Hierarchical Structures*. New York: American Elsevier.

SIMMEL, Georg (1950) *The Sociology of Georg Simmel*. Glencoe, Ill.: Free Press (first published 1908).

SIMMEL, Georg (1955) *Conflict, and the Web of Group Affiliations*. Glencoe, Ill.: Free Press (first published 1908).

SIMON, Herbert A. (1965) 'The Architecture of Complexity,' in General Systems: Yearbook of the Society for General Systems Research, vol. X:63-76 (first published 1962).

SIMON, Herbert A. (1973) 'The Organization of Complex Systems,' in Howard J. Pattee (ed.), *Hierarchy Theory*. New York: George Braziller.

SMITH, Cyril Stanley (1969) 'Structural Hierarchy in Inorganic Systems,' in Lancelot Law Whyte et al. (eds), *Hierarchical Structures*. New York: American Elsevier.

SOROKIN, Pitirim (1937-41) *Social and Cultural Dynamics*, 4 vols. New York: American Book.

SOROKIN, Pitirim (1947) *Society, Culture, and Personality*. New York: Harper.

STINCHCOMBE, Arthur L. (1968) *Constructing Social Theories*. New York: Harcourt, Brace Jovanovich.

TOENNIES, Ferdinand (1957) *Community and Society*. New York: Harper (first published 1887).

VAN DEN BERGHE, Pierre L. (1963) 'Dialectic and Functionalism: Toward a Theoretical Synthesis,' *American Sociological Review*, 28:695-705.

VON BERTALANFFY, Ludwig (1956) 'General Systems Theory,' in *Yearbook of the Society For The Advancement of General Systems Theory*, vol. I.

WALLACE, Walter L. (1969) 'Overview of Contemporary Sociological Theory,' in Walter L. Wallace (ed.), *Sociological Theory*. Chicago: Aldine.

WALLACE, Walter L. (1971) *The Logic of Science in Sociology*. Chicago: Aldine.

WEBER, Max (1947) *Theory of Social and Economic Organization*. Glencoe: Free Press (first published 1925).

WILSON, Albert (1969) 'Closure, Entity, and Level,' in Lancelot Law Whyte et al. (eds), *Hierarchical Structures*. New York: American Elsevier.

8

NOTES ON EXPECTATIONS OF
REWARD IN *N*-PERSON NETWORKS

Charles Kadushin
City University of New York

> Cast thy bread upon the waters: for thou
> shalt find it after many days.
>
> Eccles. 11:1

This paper offers some first steps in a theory of expectation in networks. While there are a number of theories about mutual expectation in dyads, relatively little attention has been given to situations in which objects or symbols circulate among three or more social units. In such a situation, unit A passes something to B, which in turn passes something to C, which passes something on to A, which began it all. As we shall see, what is passed may be material or nonmaterial. The units can be individuals or social aggregates of one kind or another, though for present purposes the focus will be on individuals.

One aspect of such a system is the expectation, noted in the epigraph of this paper, that one will eventually get something in return from someone, somewhere, even though it may not be from the person or social unit to which something was originally passed. For present purposes, then, let us define trust as the expectation that one will eventually receive a reward from some other unit in the social system, though not necessarily the same unit with which one has had the original transaction. Observe that one trusts not necessarily a particular person or social unit, but rather the entire

Author's Note: Jeffrey C. Alexander, Bernard Barber, Morton Deutsch, Robert K. Merton, Stanley Milgram, and Noel Tichy have commented on various drafts of this paper, though none of them, of course, are responsible for its present form.

system. In fact, trust in the other would be misplaced, since in the system described the other cannot guarantee the bread's return. Thus our theory is not about dyadic trust but about some causes and consequences of trust in social systems.

To be sure, circular exchanges have been noted before. Lévi-Strauss (1969) has developed an important theory about them, and some implications of his theory for exchange theory have been developed more recently by Ekeh (1974). Early in this century, Frazer (1919 discussed the exchange of women from one lineage to another and Malinowski analyzed the Kula ring (1922). But a modern theory of expectations in networks has still to be adequately developed, in part, perhaps, because we believe that circular exchanges are outmoded or limited to peculiar Polynesians or ancient Africans.

In the first part of this paper, we will therefore attempt to convince the reader that there are many situations in which contemporary actors delay gratification not only over time, a process that has been well studied, but also, in a less observed but equally important way, over social space. We will show that in certain familiar situations we are indeed prepared to give to another but to expect our reward, if any, from some other third party who may at the time of the initial 'gift' be unspecified and unknown. The situations we will describe involve at least three persons. Following Lévi-Strauss (1969) and Ekeh (1974), we note at least three types of such networks: net generalized exchange, which is the true circle — A gives to B, who gives to C, etc. until A becomes a recipient; individual-focused net generalized exchange, in which the group as a whole benefits each member in turn; and group-focused net generalized exchange, in which each member in turn gives to the group. We will show how these situations differ fundamentally from the two-person situations analyzed by traditional exchange theory, even though some aspects of exchange remain at least heuristic.

Our theory attempts to specify some of the conditions under which a person in a potentially N-person exchange network will be likely to risk passing something on, and will 'trust' that the network will afford some reward. A major feature of N-person exchange networks, however, is indeterminancy. In light of these indeterminancies, we will discuss some factors that determine costs, rewards and the degree of trust in different types of N-person networks. We will also note in passing how the theory developed is related to similar ideas about 'faith,' 'commitment,' and 'trust.'

EXAMPLES OF *N*-PERSON NETWORK EXCHANGES

Here are examples of *N*-person network exchanges intended to make the concept more homely. The examples are not systematic but we hope to demonstrate that the phenomenon of network exchanges is a general one. The examples will be drawn from each of four major institutional areas: integrative, cultural, adaptive or instrumental, and power and political institutions. The reader is encouraged to add examples; in particular, as we hope will become apparent, the field is wide open to the construction of one's own situations, that is, to laboratory experimentation.

First, integrative institutions. The dinner party is referred to by Ekeh (1974, p. 53) in his discussion of exchanges in which a single person benefits a group — or 'net generalized exchange.' An individual reciprocates a dinner party by simultaneously inviting his set of friends to a dinner party. Each member of the set in turn does the same. To me this sounds more like the American institution of the weekly poker game rather than a dinner party circuit, but be that as it may. Let us relax the model a bit. Let us suppose that a dinner party consists of more than one guest. The guests are expected to reciprocate, eventually, or they may not be asked to another party. On the other hand, not all guests will reciprocate immediately, nor all at once (since this is logically impossible). But in most cases the persons who attend a dinner party are socially tied to one another. The ties may be indirect and operate via a social circle (Kadushin, 1976). The reciprocity of the dinner party is thus the reciprocity of the entire circle. Some guests at the party will invite the host and other guests (but not all the other guests), and the entire process will be repeated in serial fashion until there is some measure of equity in the giving and receiving of parties. Full reciprocity is unlikely to occur, though all members of the circle will eventually be invited to some parties, some of which will be given not by the original guests but by their friends or their friends' friends. As every social climber knows, the way to get invited to parties at the homes of people one has never met is to invite to one's home people who have large and effective networks. The network itself, as it were, eventually reciprocates. To understand the motivation of giving dinner parties, we must understand their place in maintaining a particular social circle. And to be sure, as is true of all the examples we shall give, motives are always mixed — there are obvious immediate rewards in a dinner party including deference behavior on the part of guests. But we are here focusing on expectations of future rewards.

A less anecdotal and more carefully studied integrative situation is 'helping behavior' (Hornstein, 1976). For example, given an underlying value system which supports such acts, persons are more likely to return experimentally 'lost' objects such as wallets, contributions to charity, and so on, if they perceive a similarity between themselves and the 'loser.' Moreover, both subjects in field experiments and subjects in laboratory gaming situations are apparently more likely to have their 'we-ness' or solidarity impulses enhanced or strengthened if they are exposed to a benign social environment than to an unpleasant or dangerous one. Thus, subjects in laboratories are more likely to be biased in favor of those like themselves if they hear simulated 'good news' rather than 'bad news.' Persons in field situations are more likely to mail 'lost' contributions to charity if they are exposed to good reports about their community than if exposed to bad reports (Holloway, 1978). If the community is a nasty one, then one can expect a lower probability that, should one lose one's own wallet (or whatever) it will be returned, or the act one was engaged upon (making a gift to charity via the mails) completed. A lower expectation of a return of one's own wallet leads to a lower probability of acting in N-person exchanges (our interpretation — not Holloway's or Hornstein's).

Within the cultural sphere, persons in scientific circles often engage in a form of indirect reciprocity which Ekeh calls 'chain generalized exchange,' in which A gives to B who gives to C, etc. until the gift returns to A. Unlike Kula ring exchanges, the items passed around by scientists have instrumental as well as ritual values. Giving and asking for references are such items. A reference will be given to a colleague who may or may not immediately reciprocate. Eventually, the giver of the reference may get a reference from someone else when and if it is needed. To understand 'invisible colleges,' one needs to understand the motivation to exchange information.

There is perhaps nothing so instrumental as having or getting a job. Chain-generalized exchange is characteristic of job-finding in professional, technical, and managerial employment, as we see from Granovetter's study (1974). Most persons in these fields find their jobs not through the *New York Times* but through a network of friends or 'Old Boys.' Moreover, the network is indirect, since it is friends of friends that are most effective, rather than one's direct acquaintances. It seems, that, for many jobs, persons are quite willing to pass along information to others they do not know if the other is vouched for by a friend.

In power institutions, the phenomenon of doing favors for others who are not well known to the donor is well documented. The power broker operates, it is true, on a direct quid-pro-quo basis, but power brokers also tend to amass generalized credit to be called upon in ways unknowable and even from persons not directly known. Indeed, it is this aspect of brokerage that produces 'profit' for the broker (Boissevain, 1974, chapter 6).

In these examples we have not rediscovered altruism. Rather, we have rediscovered the following.

(1) All transactions, including market transaction, require mutual trust (Deutsch, 1973).

(2) As Barber (1977) has pointed out, despite the ideological dominance of the theory of the market, some if not most transactions do not take place in a purely market situation. The major difference, in our view, is that they involve trust in a third party who is often unknown and unknowable at the time of the transaction.

(3) The amount of trust, which we have defined as the subjective calculation of the probability of receiving a reward, depends upon the shape of the network (Ekeh, 1974). In this paper we do not explore the issue of network shape.

(4) It is obvious in a number of examples that the performance of an exchange act may lead to immediate, and not only delayed, gratification. While one gives dinner parties in the hope that someone else will return the favor, giving the party is in itself pleasurable. Generally, being consulted by others, for example in giving a scientific reference or in passing on job information, is an act of deference. Most of us enjoy high rank as a pleasure in and of itself. Thus, there is immediate gratification in being able to fulfill a request because the request implies our superiority. Many of these immediate gratifications, however, come close to confusing input with outcome; as Deutsch (forthcoming) has pointed out, acting in conformity with one's values also conveys pleasure. This entire matter deserves further attention.

(5) In the examples given, much has been made of the eventual return to donors of the same commodity they have given; that is,

they eventually get to eat someone else's dinner, get a reference from another scientist, or hear of a job from another person. There are also situations in which one thing is given in exchange, and the bread comes back in a different form. A person gives a dinner party and eventually some member of that circle offers a job to the original party-giver. Though we have noted the symbolic media aspect of exchanges, this is again a complex matter which deserves much attention and which cannot be handled within the confines of this paper.

(6) There is a special category of network integration which may be similar to other forms of immediate or delayed gratification but which has a special place in sociological theory. Performing any of the acts in the examples above may, either immediately or later, promote the actor's integration into the circle or network. This integration may be perceived as gratifying or it may not, but in any case it is an important consequence of the exchange. Again, this is something worthy of attention, but not here.

SOCIAL AND CULTURAL ELEMENTS IN EXCHANGE AND THE PROBLEM OF INDETERMINANCY

We are hardly the first to observe the differences between two-person situations and those with more than two. As both Simmel (1950) and Durkheim (1949) have pointed out, third parties impose an entirely different dimension on exchange. Durkheim also showed that, even in two-party contracts, there is always an extra-contractual element consisting of the rest of society and of the cultural values of that society. Since exchange theory has been worked out for dyadic situations, it is very important for our argument to review the nature of exchange theory, point out its limitations, and show that N-person exchange systems require trust not in the other person but in the entire system of exchange. This trust in systems — that is, a belief or an expectation that the system will offer a reward — inevitably involves consideration of values. Thus, N-person exchanges involve not only some expectations about the actions of others, with whom one is not now in contact, but also some consideration of one's own and others' values. Finally, N-person systems are more indeterminate than two-person systems, and this fact, curiously, gives them their power.

There are a number of exchange theories. Here we present the most influential offspring of these theories: equity theory and its revision, expectancy theory.

Equity theory is a set of assumptions and propositions that attempt to show under what conditions people consider an exchange to be equitable and to predict what they will do if they do not consider it equitable. The theory seems to require at least four assumptions.[1]

(1) Actors are motivated by the desire to maximize their 'outcomes,' that is, their 'rewards minus their costs' (Adams, 1965; Walster, Berscheid and Walster, 1976).

(2) Actors tend to follow the principle of 'distributive justice' (Homans, 1961). That is, in two-person situations, the ratio of one person's outcome to input should equal the other person's ratio of outcome to input. Various versions of how this balance is to be calculated have been proposed, but the basic idea of people getting out of a situation what they put into it remains.

(3) Should assumption (2) of distributive justice not hold true in a situation, then actors are motivated to restore equity.

(4) Equity is not objective but holds true in the minds of the actors. Thus actors look for reference groups with which to compare their outcomes. So-called 'comparison level' theory is invoked by researchers. Other 'cognitive tricks' are possible, such as denigrating the victim: a person receives less than his or her fair share because in some ways they 'deserve it.'

Equity theory has generated much impressive experimental work which we do not go into here. Nevertheless, there are serious problems with the approach. Deutsch (forthcoming) offers a series of trenchant objections. For example, the notion of maximizing outcome runs counter to the third principle of feeling discomfort at the lack of equity. Deutsch feels that socialization, social pressure, or both may be the cause of the discomfort. Distributive justice is difficult to measure since it assumes a common currency of rewards, costs, and inputs, and yet the classic nineteenth-century problem of interpersonal comparison of utility is not directly addressed in the equity literature. Further, experimental data show that different forms of reward are important to different people. Then, too, a given behavior can be, at the same time, both input and outcome, for we need merely apply the commonsense notion that some acts are pleasurable in themselves regardless of their consequences. Finally, Deutsch points out that equity theory is purely individual in that it focuses attention on what goes on in an individual's head without considering strategic moves to anticipate what someone else might be doing to maximize their gains.

Expectancy theory (Lawler, 1973) meets some of the issues of interpersonal comparisons of utility by focusing even more on intrapersonal process. Motivation is said to be the outcome of several complex semi-rational decision processes. First, the actor 'calculates' the subjective probability that his effort will lead to a satisfactory performance. Expectancy theory allows for the actor to take into account in his calculation his ability and his situation. (Actually, there is no reason for not introducing a more complex 'theory of action,' though expectancy theorists generally have not seen fit to do so.) The second step in calculating motivation is for the actor to list several possible outcomes which might result from the performance, and to rate the subjective probability that they would result. Finally, the actor assigns valences to these different outcomes. Motivation, then, is the sum of the probabilities of different efforts leading to different performances times the sum of the probabilities that different performances lead to different valued outcomes. Among the many consequences of this approach is the idea that different persons are motivated by different rewards, thus basically undermining the very notion of any simple situation of 'distributive justice.'

Expectancy theory 'solves' the distributive justice problem only by implying with even greater clarity than equity theory that there are additional factors in any two-party situation. These factors may consist of third parties who directly affect the amount of effort actors expend and/or the quality of their performances. Third parties may indirectly affect effort and/or performance by serving as comparison groups. Actors evaluate their efforts, their performances and their expected outcomes in terms of comparable efforts, performances, and outcomes of others. Finally, culture enters as a 'third party' in that some actors may apply different standards than other actors in evaluating outcomes because they have different values. These values may have been long ago internalized or may be more recently acquired in response to surrounding culture. Both equity theory and expectancy theory view these various social and cultural factors as essentially random. Deutsch's query about what others will do in a situation incorporates one more element in the calculation of subjective probabilities of performance and outcome, but it does not hold a special or honored place in the theory.

For present purposes, we do not wish to abandon the notions

that persons somehow calculate their efforts, performances, and outcomes; that they look around to what others are doing and getting in order to evaluate their rewards; and, further, that their motivation to engage in any given effort is in some way, explicitly or more often implicitly, related to these calculations. This seems altogether reasonable and a proper base for theorizing. What is needed is a more explicit and careful articulation of cultural and social elements in exchange situations, and it is to this articulation that the remainder of this paper is devoted.

CULTURAL AND SOCIAL ELEMENTS IN EXCHANGE

The cultural element, as we have said, is trust. To the extent that trust is a special case of generalized commitment, in Parsons's (1967) sense of the term, to that extent it seems unalterable by any immediate set of rewards or punishments. Honor implies that one does something because it must be done, not because one will be sanctioned for the performance or non-performance of the act. On the other hand, if commitment or trust is indeed a medium that circulates, as Parsons suggests, then various circumstances are going to lead to its banking or accumulation, while other circumstances will lead to its loss or expenditure.

It is difficult to articulate the two opposing notions of commitment as a fundamental value and commitment as contingent on performances in the two-person situation because there is little room in two-person systems for the 'slippage' or indeterminancy that characterizes the real world. In dyads, when alter does not perform according to ego's expectations, this fact is immediately noted. It does not take too many 'trials' for ego to cut down its input to alter. There is much more possibility for indeterminancy in circular networks with at least one third party. In such situations, one can have both the belief that an act ought to be performed for its own sake and the belief that one will receive, eventually, a valued outcome for effort expended. The reward may not be directly in kind, and may come not from the original party to the exchange but from some other party in the social network. That is the meaning of 'Cast thy bread upon the waters for thou shalt find it after many days.' Third-party reward and 'many days' create the indeterminancy. Thus, one can hold to a commitment without an apparent reward for a long time before one's trust declines. The effectiveness of this erratic reinforcement schedule has been noted by Skinner (1953) as well as by many religious systems which establish altruism as a fundamental value ('virtue is its own reward'), while at the same time noting that altruistic behavior may result in a positive outcome, if not in this world than perhaps in the next.

This aspect of trust may indeed be implied by Ecclesiastes, and in some cultures may be of considerable importance in certain exchange situations; rewards in the world to come will not, however, figure in our present analysis. Whether we take this view literally or with tongue firmly in cheek, we have the common situation in which there is an expectation that one will eventually receive a reward, and in which this expectation is a relatively stable and noncontingent component of an entire system of beliefs. One can act as if one is strategizing about an eventual reward and at the very same time hold to a belief in the ultimate value of the act.

In the systems we are describing, trust, as we have said, is not in a single other individual but rather in the entire social system. In the following analysis we shall be interested in those aspects of the social system that lead individuals to develop trust in the system and thus increase their commitment to it and, conversely, in those aspects that lead individuals to decrease their trust and thus decrease their commitment to the system. The motor for change is obviously in the mutable aspect of the system — the calculation of ultimate rewards and punishments.

CALCULATING THE PROBABILITY OF AN ACT IN *N*-PERSON EXCHANGES

Let us focus on the nature of the indeterminancy. It is easy enough to specify the elements that produce the probability that an act will take place in an *N*-person network system:

$$P = \frac{V + T + R}{C} - K$$

where P is the probability of an action, V is the value placed on the act (the cultural component), T is the trust in the social system, R is the discounted value of the reward (a cognitive psychological component), C is the perceived cost of the action (also a psychological component), and K is a constant which must be exceeded for the action to take place.

K has both psychological and social-system components. R is discounted in the sense that a reward of a given value is preferred if it is expected in the short run rather than in the long run. Because of discounting, R is not entirely independent of T. If T is very great, then the long-term value of R rises, since it is discounted less than an R over an equal length of time, which is believed less likely to occur at all.

The difficulty with this equation should be frankly stated: under many conditions, the coefficients are either indeterminate or else vary within a range that, given the value of K, makes it unknown whether an action will or will not take place.[2] Further, the equation expresses things as they are at time $1(t_1)$. But as we learn from expectancy theory, feedback loops are possible, so that the expected situation at t_2 changes the value of some of the elements in the equation. This notion has been systematically built into the equation by borrowing the notion of discount from economic theory, but other feedback loops are possible.

In the type of network under discussion, there are actually two components to trust. One is the general faith in the efficacy of the social system, a faith that Klausner (1978) has suggested is a necessary precondition for any action, but especially for those accompanied by some degree of risk. The development of the generalized form of trust has fascinated psychologists since William James (see James, 1956) and has been more recently specified by Deutsch (1973). We do not attempt to add to the discussion of generalized trust. We focus rather on the component of trust that is specific to circular networks, namely the belief that one will eventually receive a reward, or what we have more generally called the 'Cast thy bread...' principle, for this belief is one of the more important reasons for indeterminancy in the system.

In general, as Deutsch has shown, trust is the result and the cause of a cooperative stance. Many experimental data have suggested that trust can be built up over a number of experimental trials, and is in general an orientation that is sensitive to experience. Since trust in an eventual reward cannot by definition be vindicated by any given experimental trial, its relationship to experience is more problematic. It seems to be the case that a fairly rare random reward in circular network situations is sufficient to 'restore one's faith in human nature,' that is, to demonstrate that the bread eventually returns. Rare irregular rewards are effective only if, prior to any situation or set of 'trials,' there is already a fairly high level of trust.

Some preconditions of trust will be reviewed below. The point is that experience affects the kind of trust we are talking about only in relatively indeterminate ways. Obviously, faith in an eventual reward can be extinguished, but only an occasional reward is sufficient, under given conditions, to maintain the faith (Skinner, 1953). Thus, the crucial element of two-person exchange systems, people's observation that their efforts result in a clear outcome, occurs only intermittently in N-person exchanges, though in many situations this intermittent reward is sufficient to keep the system going. It is this fact that above all makes an N-person exchange different from two-person exchanges and makes these N-person exchange systems heavily, though not exclusively, dependent on prior cultural and social-system components.

SOME FACTORS DETERMINING THE VALUES OF COST, REWARD, AND TRUST

A full theory of expectation in N-person networks requires a systematic exploration of all the factors in our equation for action. Among these, values probably have received the most attention elsewhere, and will not be dealt with here. Threshold phenomena are exceedingly important and vary, most likely, not only with the personality of the actor but systematically with the characteristics of the social system. 'We-ness,' for example, refers to a threshold. The greater the sense of 'we-ness' in a situation, the greater the probability of action — not because 'we-ness' calls for any particular action or gives a value to any particular set of choices, but rather because 'we-ness' lowers the threshold.

It is useful, in my opinion, to separate the general sense of belongingness from a more specific sense of trust in the social system. The more we feel part of a social situation, as in 'we-ness,' the more vulnerable we are to all of its aspects, including the sense of trust. Vulnerability heightens the effect of the other elements in the equation and hence affects the threshold for action. Since integration and 'we-ness' have been extensively reviewed elsewhere, the full implications of the relationship of integration to the threshold will be explored in future work.

This leaves trust, cost, and the value of a reward as the elements I begin to discuss here. There are two reasons for beginning with these variables. First, equity theory and expectancy theory have been highly developed and have much to say about costs and outcomes or rewards. Second, trust is the variable that most clearly links theoretically the psychology of dyadic relations with the sociology of *N*-person networks.

Four situations in *N*-person network exchange systems involving these variables will be sketched: (1) costs are low and rewards are high; that is, there is a high probability of action; (2) costs are low regardless of other factors: (3) high trust levels are created by a social system which then leads to a high probability of action even in the face of high costs; (4) trust is differentially distributed in a social system. It is obvious from our equation that we only begin to explore the many different combinations of variables and levels of variables.

Low Cost and High Reward

From both equity theory and expectancy theory, we derive the hypothesis that an action is likely to occur if the cost to the donor is perceived to be low and the discounted outcome is highly valued. Expectancy theory, in combination with network theory, introduces a further feedback loop and an additional variable that relates costs to outcome. The additional variable is the likelihood of a successful performance of the act. If costs (or effort) are low, there is a high expectation of a successful performance; the outcome or reward is highly valued, then the outcome receives a low discount. Merely because the outcome will take place in an uncertain future is, in this situation, no reason to discount it heavily. Thus action is highly probable.

In terms of our examples, the cost of giving information about a job if a person already has a good one is quite low. The performance is easy enough. There is a high hope that, if the giver of information would eventually need a job, then other persons, at the moment unknown, would spring to help him. The value of a job is very great and, in this situation, it is certainly not discounted merely because it is in the future. On the other hand, suppose jobs are scarce. We might expect different behavior. Indeed, when during a time of recession, Jacobson (1975) re-studied the very same city

Granovetter (1974) had observed during a time of relatively full employment, Jacobson found that, rather than pass along jobs to persons they did not know at all, men tended to keep the word within the circle of their intimates — the very opposite of weak tie behavior. The difference between the two situations is obviously one of cost. First, a man might need a job himself very soon, and any long-term prospects of receiving help would be heavily discounted. Second, one might receive immediate negative sanctions from the circle of intimates if the job were passed on to third parties. The laws of dyadic reciprocity rather than the laws of circular networks seem to apply in this situation. Similarly, the cost of giving a research reference is low if one has the information, but the potential outcome of getting information if one does not have it is very high. The information is not needed now, so it is not discounted. Finally, in the 'lost object' studies, the cost to the returner was very low. When costs were high, the rate of return was much lower.

What Structural Facts Tend to Make for Low Costs?

The issue of costs is obviously crucial in N-person network exchange. Though some 'Cast thy bread...' situations thrive in spite of high costs (dinner parties, some altruistic behavior, many power brokerage situations, and others), it is apparent that low costs are very important to the maintenance and establishment of circular network exchange systems. By and large, costs are low when symbols are exchanged rather than material objects having value in and of themselves. This is one of the reasons why Parsons places so much emphasis on the development of symbolic media of exchange.[3] Of course, not all symbolic exchange is low cost, as we well know from the example of money, but symbolic exchange at least makes it possible to give something away and yet still retain it. Costs are inevitably low when the giver of the symbol does not lose it by virtue of having given it away. Thus, giving someone an idea or a reference or love need not be costly since the giver still retains the idea or the reference and the self-esteem. When ideas, references, or self-esteem are exchanged in a competitive situation, however, there is the possibility that the giver may suffer some loss as a result of the exchange. A scientist working in an area on the cutting edge in competition with others may hesitate to aid another scientist in the same field. Some fields have scarcer resources than others. Historians of ancient times with their limited sets of documents may hesitate to share a newly discovered manuscript, while a social scientist may be quite willing to share survey data that are in principle easily obtained. The norms of historians with regard to reference-giving may thus be less generous than those of social scientists. These norms intervene to some extent to force persons to give their behavior the appearance, if not the reality, of altruism. It is in this area of assessed costs that we find many of the cognitive tricks that people play on themselves, which have been called to our attention by equity theory.

Different institutional areas tend to exchange different things, as noted above. Cultural and integrative spheres more often have some set of symbols as their main exchange, while power and adaptive spheres more likely emphasize the exchange of objects and goods with intrinsic value. The exchange of the latter in dyadic situations of short duration poses no particular problem. Persons part with a good in return for another good of equal or greater value to them. With symbols, people can sometimes eat their cake and have it too, a situation that makes them more likely to wait for their eventual return. Hence we are more likely to find net generalized exchanges in cultural and integrative spheres than in others, though we have given examples from all spheres. Whether we can then say that net generalized exchanges cause integration or are the result of it is not now clear.

How Is Trust Maintained in High-Cost Situations?

For an action to take place, as we learn from equity theory, there must be expectations of high outcome if there are also high costs. As we see from expectancy theory, however, the expectation of outcome can be divided into two components: the outcome itself is of high value, and/or the probability of getting any outcome at all may be very high. If I am absolutely sure to get some reward, I may engage in high-cost behavior more often than if I have a low probability of getting a potentially high reward, for then the reward is heavily discounted. The probability of getting an outcome is related to our old conceptual friend, trust. Thus, in situations where trust is high, persons will be more likely to engage in high-cost giving. In network exchange, trust is an attribute not of the immediate exchange dyad, but of the entire system. Other things equal, the greater the visibility of the network or circle, the greater the trust. Thus, one may be more willing to give elaborate dinner parties for a circle of friends whom one knows well than for a set of guests one hardly knows. The exception is the case of social climbing noted above, in which the expectation of reward may be high not because there is a high probability of getting it but because the reward itself is highly valued.

We are talking about trust in the system, or the system itself, rather than about trust in any one individual. For example, the Holloway-Hornstein experimental manipulation, cited above, that makes the social environment seem more worth trusting produces higher rates of altruism. Many social scientists have argued that trust in a system is in fact more stable and more powerful than trust in particular individuals. Note that 'we-ness' can also be separately manipulated from creating the sense of a trustworthy environment. High 'we-ness' also produces altruistic behavior by lowering K, as explained above.

Another kind of trust in the system in high-cost situations is institutionalized altruism. Merton and Gieryn (1978) 'define altruism generically as behavior which benefits others at the expense of the benefactor...in the short run.' In their terms,

> Institutionalized altruism is the special form of altruism in which structural arrangements, notably the distribution of rewards and penalties, promote behavior that is beneficial to others. Institutionalized altruism focusses attention on alternatives of action that are weighted by social structures to increase the rates at which individuals choose altruistic actions beyond what would otherwise be the case (if based upon human nature, prior socialization, or other dispositional tendencies). [Merton and Gieryn, 1978, p. 319]

Furthermore, as the following passage makes plain, this type of reciprocity is a structured expectation that operates in the general 'Cast thy bread' model:

> An important feature of institutionalized altruism is the mechanism through which rewards are returned to the initial benefactor. When altruism is institutionalized, it operates beyond the bounds of friendship specifically, and of dyads generally. Unlike cases of pure altruism, where the rewards (if any) pass back from the original beneficiary to the benefactor, in the institutionalized arrangement, the benefactor's rewards are more likely to come from *other individuals* in the social system of which he is a part. To jump ahead to the special example discussed in this paper, it is the professional's peers, in the first instance, who

determine whether his behavior is in accordance with preferred and not merely prescribed patterns, and indirectly it is they who determine the rewards the professional is to receive by way of standing in the field. [Merton and Gieryn, 1978, p. 320, emphasis added]

Successful institutionalization, it can be seen from Merton and Gieryn, structures all the devices we have observed in high-cost situations. Again, it is important to see that we are talking not about the norm of altruism, or even about situations that make the norm more salient, but about ways in which altruism seems to be positively or negatively sanctioned by third parties to the original transaction.

Further, if institutionalization is also defined as the structured perception that 'everybody is doing it," and if persons are motivated to act because others are doing it, then, as Granovetter (1978) implies, norms or rewards may be irrelevant. 'Cast thy bread' behavior is thus an overdetermined behavior in institutional situations.

Differential Distribution of Trust

It has often been noted that those with higher rank or more power in a system are likely to regard it more highly and to have more faith in it; hence, 'noblesse oblige.' Persons of higher rank are more likely to give in accord with the 'Cast thy bread' principle than persons of lower rank. This is obvious in the examples cited of dinner parties, reference-giving, job referral, and power brokerage. The latter situation rests almost entirely upon this principle. This situation leads to the typically observed imbalances in exchange situations in which the more powerful create a sense of obligation (and resentment) on the part of the less powerful and the less well endowed. Both high- and low-power individuals therefore engage in cognitive distortions of the situation, behavior that becomes instituted as myth, and which Marx refers to as 'ideology.' Without the ideology that people get what they deserve, long N-person circular exchanges might tend to break down. Ideology is thus 'derived' from the third and fourth general principles of equity theory.

A BEGINNING

These notes on expectation in networks are obviously preliminary. The very concept of seriously considering individuals' motivations to participate in network behavior on other than a direct quid pro quo basis has yet to engender serious research. In the interest of focusing attention on this problem, we have given some examples of network behavior which involve the principles of 'Cast thy bread upon the waters': persons give something to another but expect to gain their outcome from the transaction only at some later time from some other person. Although principles of equity and expectancy theory may rest on inadequate or contradictory assumptions, by placing these theories within the context of univocal exchange, and adding values and trust to the equity equation, we have been able to speculate about some of the conditions under which persons will be likely to exchange different types of goods and symbols. Some preliminary suggestions have been offered showing how these theories can be altered to take account of network realities. In turn, we begin to understand the workings of expectation in networks.

NOTES

1. The discussion in this section on equity theory has been informed throughout by Deutsch (forthcoming).
2. Granovetter (1978) shows that small variations in the distribution of individuals' thresholds can have enormous consequences in highly linked networks if K is a function of the perceived number of others taking the action. I have not yet been able to incorporate this finding in a general theory of N-person networks except to note that small differences in the level and distribution of K may make the values of the other factors inconsequential in determining the state of the entire network. Thus, if one thinks that 'everybody' is engaged in 'cast thy bread' behavior, and if it takes but one or two others to overcome K, and if the system is highly observable, then R can be very small or C very big. Of course, K is dependent not only on the motivation to act if others act but on many complex factors, and Granovetter considers other consequences of varying thresholds.

3. Parsons (1967, pp. 208; 347-54) distinguishes four symbolic media of exchange between systems and subsystems: commitment, influence, power, and money. Commitment controls the processes of influence, which in turn control power, which in turn controls money. In the reverse order, each medium of exchange is the necessary but not sufficient condition for the preceding medium. Thus, power requires money, influence requires power, and commitment requires influence. In our terms, trust, as the eventual expectation of a return or reward, is a special form of generalized commitment. Parsons (1967, p. 364) defines commitment as a generalized appeal to a subjective sense of obligation without any threat of situational sanctions. Commitments involve the honor of the actor or social unit, and thus always imply a reference to basic norms and values (p. 367). Because commitment rests on these basic standards, it falls within the category of Parsons's 'pattern-maintenance' functions. The analysis of trust in his system therefore requires an analysis of the statics of a particular value system, a different task than the one we have chosen.

REFERENCES

ADAMS, J. S. (1965) 'Inequity in Social Exchange,' in L. Berkowitz (ed.), *Advances in Experimental Social Psychology*, vol. 2. New York: Academic Press.

BARBER, Bernard (1977) 'The Absolutization of the Market,' in G. Dworkin, G. Bermant and D. Brown (eds), *Markets and Morals*. Washington, DC: Hemisphere.

BOISSEVAIN, Jeremy (1974) *Friends of Friends: Networks, Manipulators and Coalitions*. Oxford: Basil Blackwell.

DEUTSCH, M. (1973) *The Resolution of Conflict*. New Haven, Conn.: Yale University Press.

DEUTSCH, M. (forthcoming) 'Justice,' Chapter II in *Social Psychological Perspectives on Distributive Justice*.

DURKHEIM, Emile (1949) *The Division of Labor in Society*, translated George Simpson. New York: Free Press (first published 1902).

EKEH, Peter (1974) *Social Exchange Theory: The Two Traditions*. Cambridge, Mass.: Harvard University Press.

FRAZER, Sir James G. (1919) *Folklore in the Old Testament*, vol. I. London: Macmillan.

GRANOVETTER, Mark (1974) *Getting a Job: A Study of Contacts and Careers*. Cambridge, Mass.: Harvard University Press.

GRANOVETTER, Mark (1978) 'Threshold Models of Collective Behavior,' *American Journal of Sociology*, 83 (May):1420-43.

HOLLOWAY, Stephen (1978) 'The Influence of Social Context on Social Categorization and Discrimination,' PhD dissertation, Columbia University.

HOMANS, G. C. (1961) *Social Behavior: Its Elementary Forms*. New York: Harcourt Brace Jovanovich.

HOMANS, George C. and David M. SCHNEIDER (1955) *Marriage, Authority and Final Causes: A Study of Unilateral Cross Cousin Marriage*. New York: Free Press.

HORNSTEIN, H. H. (1976) *Cruelty and Kindness: A New Look at Aggression and Altruism*. Englewood Cliffs, NJ: Prentice-Hall.

JACOBSON, David (1975) 'Fair Weather Friends: Labor and Context in Middle Class Friendships,' *Journal of Anthropological Research*, 31:225-34.

JAMES, William (1956) *The Will to Believe, and Other Essays in Popular Philosophy and Human Immortality*. New York: Dover (first published 1897).

KADUSHIN, Charles (1976) 'Networks and Circles in the Production of Culture,' *American Behavioral Scientist*, 19 (July):769-84.

KLAUSNER, Samuel (1978) 'The Societal Stake in Stress-Seeking.' Philadelphia: Center for Research in the Acts of Man, mimeo.

LAWLER, E. (1973) *Motivation in Work Oraganization*. Monterey, California: Brooks Cole.

LÉVI-STRAUSS, Claude (1969) *The Elementary Structures of Kinship*, rev. ed. Boston: Beacon Press (first published 1949).

MALINOWSKI, Bronislaw (1922) *Argonauts of the Western Pacific*. London: Routledge & Kegan Paul.

MERTON, Robert K. and Thomas F. GIERYN (1978) 'Institutionalized Altruism: The Case of the Professions,' pp. 309-44 in T. Lynn Smith and Man Singh Das (eds), *Sociocultural Change Since 1950*. New Delhi: Vikas Publishing House.

NEEDHAM, Rodney (1962) *Structure and Sentiment: A Test Case in Social Anthropology*. Chicago: University Press.

PARSONS, Talcott (1967) 'Pattern Variables Revisited: A Response to Robert Dubin,' and 'On the Concept of Influence,' in *Sociological Theory and Modern Society*. New York: Free Press.

SIMMEL, Georg (1950) *The Sociology of Georg Simmel*, translated Kurt Wolff. Part II. New York: Free Press (first published 1908).

SKINNER, B. F. (1953) *Science and Human Behavior*. New York: Free Press.

WALSTER, E., E. BERSCHEID and G. W. WALSTER (1976) 'New Directions in Equity Research,' in L. Berkowitz and E. Walster (eds), *Advances in Experimental Social Psychology*, vol. 9. New York: Academic Press (first published 1973).

9

UNDESIRED CONSEQUENCES AND TYPES OF STRUCTURES OF SYSTEMS OF INTERDEPENDENCE

Raymond Boudon
Centre National de le Recherche Scientifique,
Paris

When a doctor issues a prescription or an academic writes an article, they are acting within the context of a role. When a young person chooses to study music or mathematics, this choice is still an action, but this action is not carried out within the context of a role. By definition, we will call those systems of interaction where individual actions can be analyzed without reference to the category of roles 'systems of interdependence.'

To illustrate the distinction, let us take a very simple example. I am observing the flow of a line in front of the cashier in a movie theatre. The customers all perform the same sequence of actions: they announce the film they wish to see and pay the price of the ticket. These actions are carried out within the context of a system of customer-cashier interaction. This system clearly defines the role of the two protagonists. The cashier would be quite astonished if the customer asked for his opinion about the film, and the customer would be quite surprised if the cashier intervened in his choice. Now, let us consider the aggregate of potential customers forming the line. These customers constitute a system of interaction: the possibility of each entering the theatre and the waiting time of each are determined by the others. Thus, the fact that X has chosen to see the same film as Y and arrived earlier than Y has the

This chapter has been translated by Jodi Ellen Brodsky, Columbia University, with the assistance of Robert K. Merton.

consequence that X imposes an additional wait on Y. X and Y are, therefore, really in a situation of interaction, but not in a relation of roles. To distinguish this second situation from the first, we shall speak of 'systems of interdependence.'

For the sake of clarity, it is useful to speak of the individual *actor* in the case of functional systems and of the individual *agent* in the case of systems of interdependence. The notion of 'actor,' like that of 'role' is borrowed from theatrical language. Likewise, actor and role are two correlative concepts of sociological theory. The word 'agent' clearly designates the individual bearer of action without referring to the category of roles.

Systems of interdependence are often characterized by the fact that actions emitted by agents of the system produce collective phenomena as such unintended by these agents. An example of this case in point is represented by the Mertonian analysis of the racism of American workers after World War I (Merton, 1957). The white workers who were opposing the admission of blacks into unions had not explicitly, or even implicitly, the intention of excluding blacks from the job market. Nor did they have the desire to contribute to the reinforcement or racism. They simply did not believe that blacks could demonstrate union loyalty and, as a result, were loath to admit them in the name of union interests that can be considered neither illegitimate nor misunderstood. The system of interdependence creates an 'overshooting' effect here: the local effects of individual actions are amplified on the global level, by the interdependence among agents. On the local level, a black does not succeed in joining the union that would grant him access to the job market. The recurrence of the same phenomena at multiple points in the system leads to a collective phenomenon, namely the reinforcement of racism, and consequently the growing difficulty of blacks to enter the job market through the main door of the union.

A classic example of the amplification effect is that of financial panics such as those that we saw develop at the time of the great crisis of the 1930s. A rumor spreads on a possible insolvency of the banks. Each client individually appears at the teller's window to withdraw his fortune before his bank goes bankrupt. The aggregate of these individual actions obviously has the effect of *actually* placing the bank in a state of insolvency. The *belief* in the truth of the rumor has the consequence of bringing on its realization. Of course, this result in itself has not been sought by any of the agents. Merton gives this type of effect the name of 'self-fulfilling prophecy' (Merton, 1957). In certain cases, faith *can* effectively move mountains.

From now on, we will designate these types of effects as aggregate effects or emergent effects. An aggregate effect or emergent effect is thus an effect that is not explicitly sought by the agents of a system and that results from their situation of interdependence.

Let us immediately remark that emergent effects are not restricted to systems of interdependence. Tocqueville showed, in *L'Ancien Régime*, that the stylistic difference between French and English eighteenth-century political philosophy could be considered as what we are calling an emergent effect. In the same way, in Crozier's analysis of the monopoly, the dominating character of the administrative director and the submission of the department head are emergent effects resulting from the structure of the system of interaction linking the two actors. The transformation of the patient, the third outsider of Goffman's analysis of asylums, and the feelings of overdetermination and manipulation felt by students in mass universities, are, likewise, emergent effects.

But systems of interdependence are no doubt richer in emergent effects. The reason for this is simple. Actually, the transition from an unorganized system to an organized system is often due to the manifest will of social agents to eliminate undesirable emergent effects. On the other hand, it is clear that a process of organization inevitably implies the introduction of norms and constraints which restrict the margin of individual autonomy and, therefore, include certain categories of actions in *roles* (Buchanan and Tullock, 1965).

Let us consider a very simple case. When, for example, in the event of a strike of the French national electric company, traffic lights no longer function in Paris, the driver can no longer interpret his role correctly. He is like an actor who has forgotten his lines confronting the failure of the prompter. An emergent effect then occurs: traffic jams, which clearly do not result from the will of the actors and which each would wish to avoid.

SOME CLASSICAL EXAMPLES OF EMERGENT EFFECTS

The sociological tradition is particularly rich in the analysis of systems of interdependence and in making manifest the emergent effects they produce. To state the same proposition more interestingly, many phenomena that hold or have held the attention of sociologists appear to be or have been implicitly or explicitly analyzed as emergent effects of systems of interdependence.

We recalled the example of Merton's analysis of racism. The work of Tocqueville reveals numerous emergent effects. Let us content ourselves with a single example. Even today, when we compare a map of France and a map of England, we notice at first glance that the frequency of small towns is much greater in France. This difference was already evident in Tocqueville's day. In *L'Ancien Régime* he interprets this as the result, obviously unsought by the agents, of differences between the two social systems. The greater importance of the state in the case of France is reflected in the fact that it can distribute a greater number of 'places' and that these are more coveted, and consequently valued. The supply of places thus creates a demand which tends to reinforce the supply. This is why numerous landowners leave their land and come to occupy royal posts, contributing to the multiplication of the number of small towns.

The Hegelian and Marxist tradition, for its part, provides numerous examples of emergent effects. Indeed, one could justifiably defend the thesis according to which the notion of 'contradiction,' in the Hegelian and Marxist sense, and the notion of 'dialectic' itself cover, in large part, the notion of emergent effects (Schneider, 1971). Hegel no doubt made an unfortunate choice when he borrowed a classical term from logic, that of 'contradiction,' to explain a fundamental proposition, namely that the will of individuals can turn against itself. Such a distortion of meaning could only be a cause of confusion. This confusion was so overwhelming that Hegel himself was taken in by it and believed that he had discovered a new logic. Be that as it may, the notions of contradiction and dialectic point to a profound discovery, namely that the interdependence among agents of a system can produce unintended effects sometimes contradictory to their objectives. Such, for example, is the significance that must be granted the famous dialectic of the master and slave in the *Phenomenology of Mind*. It shows how power can be transformed into impotence and, under certain conditions, impotence into power.

Such is also the importance of several of Marx's analyses and particularly of the famous law of the 'falling rate of average profit.' This law is so well-known that it is sufficient to review it in a few words. All other things being equal, capitalists appropriate ever-increasing profits as total production increases and as the proportion of 'fixed' capital (machines) to 'variable' capital (salaried work) increases. However, there is a 'contradiction' between the two variables determining overall profit. Indeed, it is in the capitalist's interest to increase his productivity, that is, to reinvest a part of his profit to acquire more efficient and more rapid machines permitting production in less work time. But doing this, he contributes to lowering the rate of profit, since in Marx's theory profit is a result of the discrepancy between the value produced by the labor of the worker and the salary he receives (Marx, 1956).

It is of little importance whether the law of the falling rate of average profit is true or false. It illustrates a case in point where agents are placed in a system of interdependence the structure of which is such that they are stimulated to contribute to producing a result that they surely did not seek. A capitalist cannot help seeking to invest. Investment has *offensive* value: if I am the first in my field to arrive at an increase of productivity, I will be in a position to offer my product at a lower price and deprive my competitors of a portion of their customers. But it also has *defensive* value: it protects me from the risks that come from investments by others. A privileged strategy of simultaneously offensive and defensive value is likely to be adopted by all. However, in doing so capitalists, according to Marx's analysis, do a disservice to capitalism. Indeed, all increases in productivity lead the system toward a virtual limit-state where production costs would include only the smallest fraction of wages and where the rate of profit would consequently be practically nil. In a system of fully automated production, the capitalist would not, by definition, be able to levy any profit since the profit results from an under-payment of workers' labor. The source from which investment is financed would thus be exhausted and the capitalistic machine should then cease to function.

This scheme is clearly overly mechanistic. To the extent that it neglects the capacity of social agents to modify the structure of systems of interdependence leading to undesirable emergent effects, it is certainly not applicable to reality. Hence the weakness of Marx's materialism. Revealing a limit-state does not imply the necessity of its realization. But the mechanistic aspect of Marx's analysis makes it interesting didactically. It shows that certain systems of interdependence induce social agents to undertake actions leading to what are, from their point of view, undesirable effects. It also indicates — this point is of particular importance — that, in certain situations, social agents can be aware of the undesirable effects that they incur, while at the same time being incapable of avoiding them. Assuming that Marx's capitalist knows and accepts the Marxian analysis of the tendency toward a falling rate of profit, this does not result in the ipso facto elimination of the undesirable effect. On this point, a 'materialistic' interpretation is justified. It is no longer justified if it leads to the conclusion that the actors are irremediably incapable of modifying the tendency toward an indefinitely extended fall in the rate of profit.

We will now consider some more nearly contemporary examples of analyis where sociologists analyze important social phenomena as emergent effects of systems of interdependence.

My first example is taken from a book by the German sociologist Georg Simmel (1958), *Philosophie des Geldes* ('The Philosophy of Money'). There, Simmel develops a hypothesis that will often be taken up again after him, namely that the form of economic exchanges affects the form of relations among social agents. Thus, the substitution of money for the barter economy produces a multitude of emergent effects. Its character as an instrument of the precise measure of value, its divisibility, the ease with which it can be accumulated and transferred, encourages individuals to place their relations with one another under the insignia of rational calculation. More generally, the quantitative character of money has the effect of accentuating the depersonalization of the relations among social agents in modern societies where its use is highly developed.

A useful parenthesis may be opened here. One can reinterpret Simmel's analysis, in a 'free' yet faithful manner, with the aid of *the famous* polarities to which Parsons gave the name 'Pattern Variables' (Parsons, 1951). Actually, formalizing Simmel's hypothesis in *Philosophie des Geldes*, one would be able to say that the transformation of economic exchanges resulting from the use of money had the effect of crystallizing these distinctions on the one hand, and of considerably increasing the frequency of specific, universalistic, affectively neutral, achievement-oriented interactions on the other.

Parsons himself offered several examples of emergent effects. The best known is perhaps that of the nuclearization of the modern family. Why, asks Parsons (1951), are the most advanced industrial societies characterized by a situation in which members of the same family living together in the same household tend to be more and more strictly reduced to the couple and their young children?

Essentially, this results, he tells us, from the nature of the system of the division of labor in modern industrial societies. The complexity of the system makes occupation an essential dimension of status. In other words, the income, the prestige, the power, and, in a general way, the material and symbolic resources of which the individual disposes are largely determined by the nature of his occupational activity. On the other hand, an individual's occupational status is generally the consequence of a long process of investment and trial and error. After a certain point, the family is generally no longer of any help to the individual in this respect. Even in the case where it continues to bring him financial support, it is unable to guarantee him access to a multitude of occupations. The merchant or the artisan may, under certain conditions, transmit his socio-occupational status to his son or daughter. But even a high-ranking executive has only very limited opportunity to intervene in locating his son or daughter in the socio-occupational status system. Compared with traditional societies, industrial societies are thus characterized by a weakening of the average capacity of the family to control the process of placing individuals into the socio-occupational system. This has the effect of distancing and autonomizing ['d'entraîner une distanciation et une autonomisation'] of the individual in relation to the family. Thus, the nuclearization of the family is interpreted by Parsons as a consequent emergent effect of the system of interdependence created by the supply and demand of occupational statuses in modern industrial societies.

In drawing upon the analyses of Tocqueville, Marx, Simmel and Parsons, I deliberately kept illustrations located on the macrosociological plane. In fact, these analyses all concern phenomena located on the plane of entire societies. They show that the sociologist can choose a very general level of analysis without having to relinquish an analysis of actions. In all the cases reviewed, the emergent effect is analyzed as the result of an aggregate of individual actions within the context of a system of interdependence.

These systems of interdependence are not necessarily situated on the macrosociological plane, in other words on the plane of societies taken as a whole.

Union conflicts provide sociology with the opportunity to analyze systems of interdependence of a more accessible size. Here, briefly stated, is an example that to me, seems of great interest

(Ord, 1959). It deals with knowing why American unionism seems to have positive effects on the productivity of the economic system, giving the outside observer the impression that there is an understanding between unionists and industrialists.

The increase in productivity obviously cannot be considered an objective deliberately sought by unionists, either as end or as means. A realistic description must ascribe quite another principal objective to the unionists, or more precisely the union apparatus: to maintain the support of its membership, and if possible to enlarge it, by trying to obtain such varied advantages as increases in wages, increased job security, etc. In sum, the quasi-cooperative character of the relations between industrialists and unions must be considered not as a result of the agent's will but as an emergent effect of the system of interdependence.

The key to the mystery is brilliantly provided by a team of English trade unionists. In England, as in France, increases in wages result very largely from negotiations on the national level. In contrast, negotiations in the United States usually occur at the level of the enterprise. This permits unions to employ a strategy of a sequential type. In general, the union first attacks the most dynamic enterprise of the industrial branch. Being the most dynamic, this enterprise is also the most prosperous. But, by the same token, it is the most vulnerable. This is because, on the one hand, it can bear the effects of an increase in wages more easily than the others and, on the other, a protracted strike would expose it to the formidable risk of losing the lead that it holds over its competitors as well as the advantages resulting from this lead. This vulnerability makes the dominant firm a special target of unionist attacks. Once that firm yields, the union attacks the less prosperous firms. At the end of the negotiation process, the least prosperous firms concede wages that will either be equal or be slightly lower than those of the dominant firms. The gradual nature of unionist pressures has the unintended effect of stimulating all firms to economic efficiency while avoiding exposure to brutal and unanticipated pressures that would risk threatening their equilibrium.

Another interesting meso-sociological example is provided in an analysis conducted by Nieburg (1969). This author asks why violence in American black ghettoes ceased abruptly toward the middle of the 1960s. A superficial analysis would attribute this change to measures in favor of blacks instituted by the administration. Actually, according to Nieburg, it is due rather to the fact that, blacks having accumulated considerable supplies of arms during the tense period at the beginning of the 1960s, the police began to adopt an attitude of circumspection and prudence in their relations with the ghettoes. The aggravation of tensions between the white and black communities also had the unanticipated effect of putting an end to the violent confrontations.

In the works of authors like Coser (1964, 1967), one will find processes of reversal comparable to those described by Nieburg, where actions instituted by the agents of a system of interdependence transform a situation — the case of German unionism, for example — or result in institutionalized conflict.

The several preceding examples permit us to put our earlier distinction between types of systems of interaction into concrete form. In some cases — functional systems — interaction is carried out within the context of roles. In other cases — systems of interdependence — the notion of role holds little value for the analysis. However, interdependence may take different forms: direct interdependence, such as union negotiations confronting industrialists, the German government confronting the English government on the eve of World War I; indirect interdependence, such as Marx's capitalists or Tocqueville's landowners who, while they never actually meet at any time, 'cooperate' in the production of emergent effects — the fall in the rate of profit and the creation of an urban network dominated by small towns.

These illustrations also allow us to measure the diversity of systems of interdependence. As a consequence of this diversity, it hardly seems useful to try to state them in terms of general propositions. Here the sociologist is still dedicated to the analysis of the singular. At best, that analysis of singular systems of interdependence may reveal several typical fundamental structures. '

Certain emergent effects, for example, take the form of *reinforcement* effects, for example the case of the amplification of anti-black racism of American workers (Merton, 1957). Others take the form of *reversal* effects; for example, the French revolutionary government requisitions grain to avoid scarcity in the cities but in doing so brings about the virtually complete disappearance of grain from the markets; by arming themselves, ghetto blacks contribute to easing ethnic relations. Others take the form of *contradictions* (in the dialectical sense); according to Marx, for example, the capitalist cannot simultaneously achieve his short-term objective of making profits and his long-term objective of avoiding a situation where he would no longer be able to reap profits. Still others take the form of social *innovation* effects, provoking the appearance of phenomena never before seen, such as the nuclearization of the family. Yet others take the form of *stabilization* effects, effects of the type discussed by Coser or Touraine regarding the institutionalization of conflicts.

One could extend this list. It is also undoubtedly possible to systematize the list further by substituting a more elaborate classification for the simple enumeration that we have just presented. But this is not the place for developing our framework in that fashion.

In the sections that follow, we have chosen to present, in some detail, several examples of systems of interdependence leading to interesting emergent effects. A detailed examination of these examples will complete the overview just outlined.

STRUCTURE WITH NEUTRALIZATION AND DIVERGENCE EFFECTS

In certain cases, one observes that individual changes are neutralized on the collective level. The stability of the collective phenomenon of public opinion can result in a marked instability of individual opinions. When such an effect appears, let us call it a 'neutralization effect.'

Lipset and Bendix (1959) aroused considerable surprise when they showed that the structure of integenerational mobility did not vary notably among countries otherwise as different as France, Japan, Germany, the Scandanavian countries and the United States. The levels of economic development of these countries, a decade after World War II, could not be considered identical: they differed in terms of social politics. Historically, some of these countries had had a system of legal stratification — for example the 'etats' of the 'Ancien Régime' in France, the 'Stände' in Germany — another, the USA had not. Sociologically, barriers between classes were more marked in Europe than in North America. Strangely, however, the sum of these differences exercised no notable effect on the structure of intergenerational mobility. The extent of the flow from one social category to another over the course of a generation appears comparable in industrial countries as a whole.

One's surprise is intensified by the fact that, to the extent that information was available (Glass, 1954; Carlsson, 1958; Girod, 1971; 1975; Müller, 1975; Blau and Duncan, 1967), the structure of intergenerational mobility also appears to be remarkably stable over time for each of these societies. In Great Britain, Sweden and the United States, the structure of social mobility appears to be slightly affected by the considerable changes that industrial societies have undergone over the course of half a century. Neither economic development nor considerable educational development appears to have had a notable effect on the structure of intergenerational mobility.

I only add that the results presented by Lipset and Bendix in 1959 remain largely true 20 years later.

It can be shown that this stability of mobility has the status of an emergent effect. It results from the aggregation of individual behaviors and decisions but is not among the ends that social agents have chosen for themselves. This emergent effect occurs in the form of a neutralization effect. Individual behaviors change over time; likewise, certain distributions resulting from these behaviors change over time. Hence, the average educational level rises. Nevertheless, certain collective effects of these individual changes appear to be remarkably stable. This is particularly the case with the structure of intergenerational mobility, which we shall now examine.

To show that some effects of this type may occur in spite of their counter-intuitive character, let us consider a simple model. Imagine that, in an industrial society which we shall not seek to identify, we can distinguish a system of stratification composed of three social classes: C_1, upper; C_2, middle; C_3, lower. In this society, between two periods which we shall call t_1 and t_2, the average educational level rose sharply. Moreover, there occurred a democratization of access to the educational system (see Boudon, 1975; as well as Fararo and Osaka, 1976; Rogoff, 1975; Useem and Miller, 1975; Elster, 1976; Alker, 1976; Andorka, 1976). Table 1 gives the educational level achieved by members of one cohort of individuals distributed by social class of origin for the periods t_1 and t_2.

It will be noticed that this table shows a rise in the average educational level. On the other hand, the disparity between the classes is attenuated. Therefore, in t_1, 33 percent of upper-class adolescents pursue higher education as compared with 10 percent in the middle

TABLE 1
Level of Education as a Function of Social Class of Origin and Period (fictitious data)

Educational Level Achieved	Social Class of Origin and Period					
	C_1 (Upper)		C_2 (Middle)		C_3 (Lower)	
	t_1	t_2	t_1	t_2	t_1	t_2
	%	%	%	%	%	%
(1) Completed higher education	23	31	5	9	1	2
(2) Higher education not completed	10	10	5	7	2	3
(3) Completed high school education	6	6	4	5	2	3
(4) High school education not completed	17	16	15	17	8	12
(5) Completed junior high school education	26	22	36	34	33	36
(6) Primary school education	18	15	35	28	54	44
Total	100	100	100	100	100	100

class and 3 percent in the lower class. In the second period, these percentages rise to 41, 16, and 5 percent respectively for the three classes. Thus, the coefficient of disparity between the upper and middle class changes from 3.3 to 2.5, the coefficient of disparity between the upper and lower class from 11.0 to 8.2, and the coefficient of disparity between the middle and lower class from 3.3 to 3.2. Table 1 therefore simulates a system where individual educational behaviors by social class or origin seem to be changing through time. These individual changes engender collective changes. Thus, the average educational level rises; the disparities between classes are attenuated. Is this change necessarily translated into a change in the structure of intergenerational mobility? This is the question we will now examine.

Reasoning intuitively, one may be tempted to give an affirmative response to the question. Educational level has a determinate importance in the acquisition of socio-professional status. If the equality of educational chances increase, if in other words the social class of origin exercises a less determinate effect on educational level, one 'deduces,' by an apparently legitimate deduction of the syllogistic type,[1] that the equalization of educational chances must have the effect of attenuating the degree to which social origins determine socio-occupational status. In short, intuition tells us that the equalization of educational chances must involve an increase in intergenerational social mobility.

To test the validity of this argument, we shall complete the simulated model that we began to construct. To do this, we will introduce the hypothesis that the educational level achieved by individuals represents a sort of 'priority ticket' of varying value. The most desirable social positions are allotted, in priority, to adolescents equipped with the best educational level until the supply of positions or adolescents is exhausted. As soon as a social category is filled or a category of adolescents exhausted, one passes to the next category. The process is represented in Table 2. We assume that 10,000 positions are available, with 1,000 on the upper level, 3,000 on the middle level and 6,000 on the lower level.[2]

Let us furthermore assume that the numbers of adolescents described in the first table are equal to 1,000, 3,000 and 6,000 respectively for the three classes. Table 1 tells us that at t_1, 23, 5, and 1 percent of adolescents of upper, middle, and lower social class origin respectively attain the level 'completed higher education.' In sum, the number of students of all social origins together reaching this level is thus equal to $(1,000 \times 0.23) + (3,000 \times 0.05) + (6,000 \times 0.01) = 440$.

Performing analogous calculations for all other educational levels, we obtain the figures entered in the last column of Table 2. Part (a) of the table corresponds to the period t_1; part (b) corresponds to the period t_2.

Having thus determined the structure of available positions in the two periods (exogenous determination) and that of the population of candidates (endogenous determination from Table 1), the model permits us to implement a meritocratic waiting-list process. To do that, we will assume that 70 percent of equipped candidates at educational level 1, the highest, are allotted superior social positions. This 'parameter' is arbitrary; it simply indicates that, without bestowing exclusive rights to the best social positions, the priority ticket is nevertheless highly effective. Thus, 70 percent of the 440 candidates of high educational level, that is 308, are assigned high-level social positions. There then remain 132 candidates of

TABLE 2
Social Position as a Function of Educational Level
(fictitious data): (a) at time 1;
(b) at time 2

(a)

Educational Level (t_1)	Social Positions (t_1)			
	C_1 (Upper)	C_2 (Middle)	C_3 (Lower)	Total
1	308	92	40	440
2	259	77	34	370
3	210	63	27	300
4	156	661	283	1,100
5	47	1,475	1,798	3,320
6	20	632	3,818	4,470
Total	1,000	3,000	6,000	10,000

(b)

Educational Level (t_2)	Social Positions (t_2)			
	C_1 (Upper)	C_2 (Middle)	C_3 (Lower)	Total
1	490	147	63	700
2	343	103	44	490
3	117	191	82	390
4	35	949	406	1,390
5	11	1,127	2,262	3,400
6	4	483	3,143	3,630
Total	1,000	3,000	6,000	10,000

TABLE 3
Social Category of Destination as a Function of Social Category of Origin (fictitious data): (a) at time 1; (b) at time 2

(a)

Social Category of Origin (t_1)	Social Category of Destination (t_1)			
	C_1 (Upper)	C_2 (Middle)	C_3 (Lower)	Total
C_1 (Upper)	301	325	374	1,000
C_2 (Middle)	377	986	1,637	3,000
C_3 (Lower)	322	1,689	3,989	6,000
Total	1,000	3,000	6,000	10,000

(b)

Social Category of Origin (t_2)	Social Category of Destination (t_2)			
	C_1 (Upper)	C_2 (Middle)	C_3 (Lower)	Total
C_1	310	318	372	1,000
C_2	398	972	1,630	3,000
C_3	292	1,710	3,998	6,000
Total	1,000	3,000	6,000	10,000

high educational level who have not been placed in the higher social category. We assume that 70 percent of them, 92, are assigned an intermediate social position. There then remain 40 candidates of upper educational level. We assign them lower social positions.

The rest of Table 2 is filled in the same way, maintaining a constant value of the 'meritocratic' parameter, 70 percent throughout the procedure.

Once that has been done, it becomes possible to ask about change in the structure of intergenerational mobility during the interval between t_1 and t_2. Indeed, Table 1 gives us the proportions of individuals achieving each educational level for each social class or origin. Table 2 gives us the proportions of individuals achieving each social category of destination for each educational level. In other words, Table 1 gives us the structure of the flow between social categories of origin and educational levels, and Table 2 gives us the structure of the flow between educational level and social category of destination. Thus, by combining information taken from the two tables, we can reconstitute the flow from each social category of origin to each social category of destination.[3]

The result of this combination appears in Table 3. Part (a) of the table gives the structure of the flow between generations at t_1; part (b) gives the structure of the same flow at t_2.

We immediately notice the minute change characterizing the structure of the typical flow between t_1 and t_2. The homologous figures of the two halves of the table differ by several units at most. Thus, the proportions of individuals born in each of the three social categories and reaching each of the three social categories appear very stable from t_1 to t_2. Without insisting on this point, let us note that this conclusion remains valid when we modify the hypothesis of the model.[4]

The model thus demonstrates that one can very well observe an increase in the equality of educational chances as a function of the social class of origin without the equalization producing a sharp attenuation of the relation between social origins and social category of membership. This consequence does not imply that educational level had no influence on social status. Such an interpretation would be erroneous. On the contrary, the model assumes that access to a good educational level is provided for the individual who has relative priority in the queuing process through which a social status is allotted to him.

The stability of the structure of the flow in mobility results from the interdependence of the agents.[5] At the same time as the relative disparity of educational chances decreases, a swelling of the queue occurs, which in turn brings about a complex effect of devaluating priority tickets. The net result is that the increased inequality of educational chances does not carry with it any appreciable effect on the relation between social origins and social status of membership. The behavior of the individuals has changed between t_1 and t_2. All other things being equal, an individual of the t_2 cohort seeks an educational level superior to a comparable individual of the t_1 cohort (see Boudon, 1974). The average educational level in each category has thus increased. Besides, the change has been greater for the subordinate categories. Despite that, and despite the fact that educational level largely helps to determine social status, the structure of social mobility remains stable. We are dealing with a neutralization effect: changes in individual behaviors produce effects, in terms of the relation between status of origin and status of destination, that cancel each other out.

Let us note that the system of interdependence just described produces a multitude of other emergent effects which do not take the form of neutralization effects. Table 2, for example, shows that the average educational level corresponding to each category of destination rises the more rapidly for successively higher categories. The consequence of the logic underlying the structure of interdependence described by the model, therefore, is that the possession of a priority becomes, at the same time, one might say, more and more *necessary* and less and less *sufficient* for acquiring a high social status. If an individual has no priority ticket, the probability of obtaining a low social status increases over time; if an individual does have this ticket, the probability of obtaining a high social status tends to diminish during the same time.

In sum, the structure of the system of interdependence has the effect of stimulating individuals belonging to a t_2 cohort to seek a higher educational level than do those of the preceding cohort. In so doing, these agents maintain the effect of stimulation to which they are themselves exposed so that individuals of cohort t_3 are stimulated to seek a higher educational level than those of cohort t_2. Aside from the absorption effect described above, the system thus engenders a divergence effect of an inflationary type. This phenomenon of divergence cannot expand indefinitely. Above a certain threshold, it introduces incentives to change. Not only the individuals directly concerned with the race for diplomas are likely to change their behavior: the social actors having a certain degree of control on the structure are also likely to try to influence this structure.

This example aptly illustrates some of the notions previously introduced: the 'decisions' of social agents relative to their educational orientation are, under certain institutional conditions, autonomous. Provided that I satisfy certain conditions, I can quite autonomously decide to study physics, for example. But from the moment that my decision is joined with the decisions of other members of my cohort, it contributes to the production of a number of emergent phenomena. These macroscopic phenomena result from microscopic causes, the intentions of individuals agents, and also, of course, from structures determined especially by institutions and by the behaviors and decisions of others. They are nevertheless alien to those intentions.

STRUCTURES WITH DEGENERATION, SEGREGATION, FRUSTRATION AND AMPLIFICATION EFFECTS

In the first section we analyzed examples of structures of interdependence that cause emergent effects of various types: reinforcement, reversal, contradiction, social innovation, stabilization. Some of these effects appear as socially undesirable results, for instance the reinforcement of racism. Othes have the character of effects that are not sought by the agents but are collectively and individually positive, such as the institutionalization of conflicts. Still others are neither clearly positive nor negative, for example the nuclearization of the family.

In the second section we recalled the example of a structure of interdependence with multiple emergent effects. Of course, structures of interdependence frequently produce multiple emergent effects. But in the present case, these effects are all perceived as socially important. In our presentation, we noted two of the effects engendered by the structure of interdependence: a *neutralization* effect, the equalization of educational chances does not affect the structure of social mobility; and a *divergence* effect, the cost of social status in terms of educational investment, tends to increase indefinitely.

In this final section we will rapidly review several effects revealed by singular structures of interdependence which are of general interest insofar as they can be illustrated by a multitude of concrete examples. On the other hand, these structures have a particular social significance owing to the fact that they produce undesirable effects. Hence, they create situations of tension or crises. Locating structural effects of this type is often an important stage in the analysis of social change (Boudon, 1979).

In the context of such structural effects Hirschman (1972) makes a most instructive observation. From the moment that the Nigerian railroads were exposed to the competition of road transportation, a degeneration resulted, as an unavoidable consequence of the quality of railway transportation (for example, its slowness and increasing unpredictability). This degeneration resulted from the fact that the most dynamic and demanding customers of modes of transportation deserted the railway for the road when possible. For the railroads, this resulted in a decrease of incentives to improve service. The railway system consequently continued to deteriorate in a spiraling process that involved further defections. The deterioration of 'inner cities' in the United States is explained in the same fashion. When the highest social strata began to move towards the periphery, particularly to avoid the harmful elements in the center, this led to a deterioration of the inner city. Naturally, such deterioration led to new departures of the economically advantaged city dwellers towards the periphery. By an inverse process, but one of comparable formal structure, the center of certain European cities, such as Paris, tends to be more and more 'restricted' to the advantaged social strata. In much the same way, the French system of 'grandes écoles' has exercised a constant degeneration effect on the university by absorbing the elite of students.

In all these examples, one observes a double emergent effect. First, there is a *degeneration effect*. In certain cases, this effect appears to be unavoidable: consider the deterioration of the centers of American cities, the degeneration of the Nigerian railroads, the debility of certain sectors of the French university. Second, there is a *segregation effect*. Demanding users, who are often those with the most resources, tend to be concentrated in the same places and isolated from the other users. The logic of these processes would therefore have it that the observed positive effects (no one contests the utility of the Nigerian roads or the Grandes Écoles) carry with them negative effects which are sometimes difficult to control.

Consider a few examples of structures with *frustration effects*. They have the characteristic of involving social agents in a sort of social trap that induces them to choose, for the best possible reasons, a line of conduct ending in results that they would by no means have wanted to occur. The Durkheimian notion of anomie can be hypothesized as a sort of diffuse intuition of the existence of this type of structure. The same intuition is also present, perhaps even more clearly, in Rousseau. Like the Durkheimian theory of anomie, the Social Contract advances the idea that, in certain cases, moral or legal constraints may be an effective means of preventing social agents from actions, undertaken for the best of reasons, that lead to undesirable results.

Let us first consider an abstract model. Let us imagine that society offers the following 'game' to a group of social agents: either you assign yourself a low level of aspiration, engaging in moderate investments (psychological, social, financial, etc.) and thereupon make, with certainty, a modest profit from this investment; or else you undertake far greater investments, with the yield then being more uncertain; it can be great, intermediate, or small.

For the sake of argument, let us imagine that the small investment yields a net profit of 1 unit. This is Durkheim's (1960) 'aurea mediocritas.' The large investment yields a net profit of 2 or 1 or 0. We are dealing here with a competitive situation. More concretely, let us assume that we are dealing with a group of 10 persons. If the 10 persons all choose the large investment, the first three will make a profit of 2, the next four a profit of 1, and the last three a profit of 0. If nine persons choose the large investment, only two will obtain 0. Let us further assume that the 10 members of the group have the same resources and the same abilities.[6] It is then easy to work out the calculation for each participant. For each member of the group choosing the large investment, the most unfavorable situation occurs when all the others also choose the large investment. In this case, the individual has three chances in 10 of reaping a profit of 2, four chances for a profit of 1, and three chances for no profit at all. The expectation of gain is then equal to 1; for if the game were repeated a considerable number of times under the same conditions, that one individual would, on the average, make a profit of 1 unit: $2(3/10) + 1(4/10) + 0(3/10) = 1$. When the game is not repeated, the expectation of gain has a more abstract meaning. But it remains a measure of the attractiveness of the investment for the individual participant.

In all the other situations, the individual has a higher expectation of gain. Thus, in the case where only eight individuals choose the large investment, each of these individuals' expectation of gain is equal to: $2(3/8) + 1(4/8) + 0(1/8) = 1.25$.

Now, let us assume further that each individual adopts the following course of reasoning: 'After all, my resources are much the same as the resources of the others. By choosing the small investment, I shall be certain to gain 1 unit; by choosing the large investment, I can expect to gain 1 in the worst of cases (if some choose the small investment, my expectation of gain is greater than 1). Moreover, why exclude myself from the possibility of gaining 2 and, in so doing, making a gratuitous gift to the others by increasing their chances of obtaining 2 as a result of my withdrawal from the competition?'

In short, it is not impossible that, in a situation of this sort, every one chooses the large investment. Should this be the case, four of the 10 members of the group will make no profit, while, had all chosen the small investment, each one would have made a profit of 1.

This model illustrates in unembellished fashion the logic of structures having the frustration effect which Durkheim had in effect located in his theory of anomie.

Now let us assume that the resources of potential participants in the game provided by society are variable and that the prospect of moving from the small to the large investment appears more difficult to certain participants because they are comparatively deprived. In this case, the most deprived will have a greater tendency to withdraw from the game, thus contributing unintentionally to increasing the chances of the more favored. In this case, the frustration effect will be attenuated and perhaps eliminated. But, the game will bring about a counterpart *amplification effect*; inequality in the distribution of resources will be greater after the game than before it.

Let us add an important note: the frustration effect engendered by this type of structure does not concern the individuals as an aggregate. On the other hand, before the game no one is sure of belonging to the category of losers. This results in the game having hardly any possibility of provoking an attitude of protest. Beforehand, everyone can estimate that they have good reasons for participating in the game. Afterwards, the losers must recognize that nothing obliged them to choose the large investment.

One may flesh out this logical skeleton with various illustrations. The 'lack of attraction' to technical education that one observes in industrial societies is probably explained, at least in part, by the existence of structures of this type. Compared with general education, technical education leads to social, economic, and psychological rewards with probably less variance and not always with a lower average. Thus, limiting ourselves to the economic dimension of rewards, French holders of master's degrees in literature re-entering the job market at the beginning of the 1970s do not appear to have lower salaries than graduates of institutions of technical higher education (cf. Boudon et al., 1975; reproduced in Boudon, 1977). In return, the variance of their rewards is higher. Perhaps that explains the limited success of these institutions in terms of recruitment.

In a classic text that did much to launch what was to be called 'reference-group theory,' Stouffer showed that the dissatisfaction of the members of a group could be all the greater as the probability of upward social mobility provided to them became greater (Stouffer et al., 1965). Among the military units that he observed, some were characterized by a high probability of promotion, others by a limited probability. Yet relative dissatisfaction with the system of promotion was greater in the first case. Explanations in terms of the notion of reference groups are only partly adequate in this respect. Not much is explained when, to account for the paradox, one advances the idea that, promotion being more frequent in the first type of units, the unpromoted more often have occasion to compare themselves with the promoted. Such an interpretation is needlessly psychologistic. It is more interesting to note that, when the probability structure of each one moves in a favorable direction, this movement can produce an amplified shift of expectations.

This point can easily be demonstrated from the model that has just been presented in brief. It is enough to modify experimentally the probability structure provided for individuals choosing the 'high strategy.' It can then be shown that, for a set of constant hypotheses, a change in the parameters of this structure in a direction collectively favorable to the group can have the effect of amplifying to excess the number of individuals choosing the high strategy in relation to the new chances being provided. The increase of objective chances is then accompanied by an increase in the overall level of frustration.

This structural interpretation has the further advantage of proposing a unified theoretical schema encompassing, at the same time, microsociological phenomena, like those Stouffer observed, and macrosociological phenomena, like those to which Durkheim refers in his theory of anomie. Indeed, reference-group theory hardly makes sense except in a context of direct interaction among individuals. Conversely, the structural interpretation that has just been developed implies interdependence but not direct interaction among agents. A diffuse optimism can lead the aggregate of agents to raise the level of their investments (educational, economic, occupational) in such a manner as to reduce the probability of each individual having the investment rewarded; one then observes a growth of anomie in the Durkheimian sense.

It is a pheonmenon of this order that Tocqueville (1952) described in *L'Ancien Régime*. When he observes that the increase in the possibility of 'enrichment' and of upward social mobility provided to individuals on the eve of the French Revolution appeared to have had the effect of increasing general dissatisfaction, he unquestionably foreshadows the Durkheimian theory of anomie.

Consider another type of structure with a frustration effect. This differs from the preceding case in that, this time, the frustration involves not only a part but the entirety of the participants. Again, we shall introduce this type of structure by a parable that will have the advantage of showing its logical framework.

Let us imagine a collection of 10 landowners. Each one has an interest in obtaining a reduction in the property tax levied upon his holdings. This group is unorganized. Thus, we are dealing with a latent group, in Dahrendorf's sense (Dahrendorf, 1972; Olson, 1965). To concretize the idea, let us assume that each landowner possesses property worth 10 francs and pays 4 francs in taxes. Let us go on to hypothesize that, if the landowners launched a campaign in their own favor or began exerting pressure on the fiscal authority in one way or another, they would be able to obtain a tax reduction. More precisely, let us assume that the tax reduction would be fixed at 50 percent if all participated in the campaign, and at 45, 40, 35, 30...10, 5, or 0 percent if 9, 8, 7...2, 1, or no persons joined in the campaign. The efficacy of the campaign thus diminishes as a function of the number of participants. Let us assume further that participation in the campaign is costly (in time, in energy, and eventually in money). To simplify our reasoning, we shall suppose that this cost is measurable and equal to 1 franc. Thus, if everyone participates in the collective action, the group will have spent 10 francs in all, 1 franc per person, and won 20 francs, each person profiting from a fiscal reduction of 50 percent in relative value and of 2 francs in absolute value. Unquestionably, if the group were not latent but organized, it would decide to wage the campaign with all of its members.

But since the group is not organized and its members are not bound by any collective decision, each individual will be tempted to adopt the following line of reasoning: 'If I participate in the action and nine others participate as well, I will profit by a fiscal reduction of 2 francs and I will have spent 1 franc, net profit: 1 franc. If I do not participate in the collective action and the nine others do participate, my gross profit will be no more than 1.8 francs (since when nine individuals take part in the collective action, the rate of the fiscal reduction is now only 45 percent). However, this gross profit will also be a net profit. Ergo, it is preferable for me not to take part in the collective action if the nine others do take part in it. Moreover, the conclusion is the same whatever the number of participants other than myself. If there are eight, I have a net profit of 0.8 francs if I participate in the collective action and 1.6 francs if I do not; if there are seven, I have a net profit of 0.6 francs by participating and 1.4 francs by not. And so on.'

Naturally, each member of the latent group will have a tendency to follow the same reasoning. It is consequently possible for the latent group to miss out on the good deal that is being offered to it. If that is the case, the frustration effect will be general: by seeking to maximize his own profit, each landowner will have contributed to canceling out the potential profits of all the others.

It is not difficult to cite many illustrations of this structure, Marx's famous 'small peasants' constituting perhaps the best-known application (although it is not immune to dispute by historians). Under certain circumstances, the condition of the peasant can be such that the cost of his participation in an eventual collective action seems high to him: he would have to get along with partners he considers as competitors and eventually as adversaries threatening his territory. His condition can thus be such that a considerable difference exists for him between the net profit that he would reap by participating in an eventual collective action that can promote his class interests and the supplementary profit he would reap by abstaining from such action and by leaving the problem of defending those interests to others. Thus, according to Marx, the condition of the 'small peasant' makes him into a free-rider in spite of himself, a marginalist calculator or, if one prefers Marx's own language, a social agent devoid of 'class consciousness.'

For the unskilled worker, protected from dismissal by legislation and with hardly any chance of being promoted in the enterprise, the marginal profit of the strategy of non-participation in collective action can, in contrast, approximate zero. In all cases, it will be less than the supplementary advantages that come from participation in collective action (being integrated into a group, etc). On the contrary, for administrative staff with a reasonable chance of promotion, the marginal profit from non-participation can be high. Briefly, the logical framework we have presented makes it possible to recognize a certain number of classical sociological observations on the relationship between position or social condition on the one hand and 'class consciousness' or, as can be said in equivalent and doubtlessly less equivocal language, the differential attractiveness of collective strategies in relation to individual strategies on the other hand.

Another classical application of the preceding structure is Michels's (1959) famous 'Iron Law of Oligarchy.' Michels, who was not only a brilliant sociologist but a trade unionist, was fascinated by a contradiction: political parties, of whatever kind, including those that officially and sincerely proclaim their democratic will, unfailingly function as oligarchies. This was notably the case with the European social democratic parties of the nineteenth century on which Michels's analysis is based. All proclaimed, as we say nowadays, that they were keeping their ears to the ground. Yet all were oligarchical organizations and had a tendency to determine their party line and political action behind closed doors. Why? If one formalizes Michels's response to this question, there is no difficulty in recognizing the previously identified structure. In elections, voters choose among the politicians proposed to them. Take the case of a two-party regime or of two coalitions of parties. The voters who choose B rather than A are those who, as between A and B, prefer B. But it may well be that, among the voters who chose B, a large majority prefer a politician C, 'offered' by no party, but who is closer to B than A. Many voters therefore vote for B without, meanwhile, being in agreement with the policies B proposes. In other words, B has the capacity of imposing policies on these voters that they actually do not want (Kolm, 1977). The reason for this oligarchical power simply resides in the fact that the voters constitute a latent group in relation to their party. A majority of these voters would be interested in getting the party to change its policies, but in their relation to the organization that ostensibly represents their interests, they are in the situation of a large unorganized group. Furthermore, the marginal profit that each member of this group can hope to obtain from participating in a collective action designed to modify the policies of the party is practically nil. Taken individually, each voter can only hope to increase infinitesimally the pressure that an eventual collective action would exert on the party. In return, the cost of this participation would not be at all nil. The structure of the relations between the party and its voters thus assures the party a considerable independence of its voters. It can impose a party line that is remote from the preferences of a majority of them. It only has to guard itself from reaching the point where a fraction of the party's voters would, in response to the great difference between the party line and their own preferences, become sufficiently ill-disposed to vote, however reluctantly, for the adversary.

To close this review, we shall quickly call to mind a category of structures of interdependence that has been thoroughly studied by Thomas Schelling (1978). This is the category of structures where interdependence between agents has the effect of excessively amplifying the objectives selected by the agents. A didactic example, which we owe to Schelling, can illustrate this type of structure having amplification effects. Imagine 30 pieces of two colors randomly distributed on a chessboard with its 64 squares, X blue pieces and Y red pieces symbolizing the members of two social categories. Let us assume, furthermore, that, without any hostility toward pieces of the other color, blue pieces and red pieces alike try not to find themselves in a minority situation. The experimenter then examines the situation of each piece in a certain order. If the squares immediately adjacent to a piece contain 50 percent or more of pieces of the same color, it is not moved; if not, it goes to the nearest square so that at least 50 percent of the adjacent squares contain pieces of the same color. The objective of each piece is thus not to exclude pieces of the other color but to avoid finding itself in an environment where it would be in the minority. But when one seeks to satisfy the pieces by moving them on the chessboard, one arrives at equilibrium, at a situation of very marked segregation: the final configuration is that of an aggregate of *ghettos*: blue pieces find themselves all together, as do the red pieces. The actors' objectives have undergone an unintended amplification effect (Lautman, 1980).

This amplification effect is very generally present in phenomena of social or residential segregation. To use Schelling's language, the 'micromotives' engender by simple aggregation macrophenomena that caricature them.

THE DIALECTIC OF INTERDEPENDENCE

The sociologist encounters what we have called systems of interdependence underlying all 'organizations' or functional systems. In those systems, social agents are related to one another, but these relations are not at all, or are only very marginally, role relations.[8]

These systems of interdependence have great importance in sociological analysis. They are generators of emergent effects, that is, effects not included in actors' objectives, which can take varied signs and forms. Some of these structures amplify agents' objectives; others reverse them. Some abide by those objectives but produce undesirable delayed effects. Some produce collective states of tension which do not, however, result from antagonistic interests. Others indirectly produce collectively positive effects that the agents would be uanble to produce if they tried to obtain them directly. Still others are responsible for global social changes which take the form of truly collective innovations.

It is perhaps in connection with systems of interdependence that one can best sense the depth of Durkheimian intuitions. These systems are exclusively subject to the will of the agents who constitute them. Nevertheless, everything occurs as if the consequences of their actions escaped their control: the division of labor, the nuclearization of the family, the oligarchical character of democratic parties, and anomie are not the consequence of anyone's will. These phenomena impose themselves on individuals in such a way that they appear to them as the product of anonymous forces. However, these immaterial forces are simply projections of structures of interdependence. These structures cannot be reduced to the individuals who compose them. This is the case, not only because generally the agents involved in a situation of interdependence have not directly chosen the institutions that define it, but also because the collection of individuals constitutes a totality that is irreducible to the sum of its parts. But, on the other hand, structures are nothing without individuals.

In any case, one point is certain: in identifying and in analyzing the general properties of particular structures of interdependence, the sociologist brings a solid contribution of the understanding of historical processes. Even a superficial look at these structures is enough to show the inadequacy of theories that try to explain the ensemble of mechanisms of social change by employing a single schema such as that of conflicts between antagonistic groups.

NOTES

1. This example serves to show that the complexity of certain structures cannot be analyzed in wholly verbal terms.

2. More explicitly, the procedure is as follows: let $E_1, E_2 \ldots, E_6$ be educational levels. First we consider the E_1s. They are less numerous than the places available in C_1. C_1 status is assigned to 70 percent of them and C_2 status to 70 percent of the rest. We proceed in the same manner for the E_2s and the E_3s. When we get to the E_4s, we notice that this time they are more numerous than the available places remaining in C_1. It is therefore to this remainder that we apply the coefficient of 70 percent: the E_3s receive 70 percent of the available places remaining in C_1. We continue in the same way for the other cases. Formally, the parameter 0.70 which measures the efficacy of the educational priority ticket is applied to the minimum quantity (r_i, r_j) where r_i is the number of candidates not yet placed and r_j the number of places not yet filled at the time when one seeks to determine the number of candidates of educational level E_1 destined to occupy statuses of rank C_j.

3. Technically, the 'combination' takes the form of the product between two transitional matrices: transitions from social origin to educational level; transitions from educational level to social status.

4. By way of example, let us assume a more developed educational system than the example in the text. In t_1, of 10,000 adolescents, 920, 560, 400, 1,350, 3,210 and 3,560 achieve educational levels 1 to 6. In t_2, these numbers are 1,350, 670, 470, 1,520, 3,100 and 2,890. Retaining all the other hypotheses, one obtains the following flow in mobility:

Category of Origin		Categories of Destination			
		C_1	C_2	C_3	Total
		%	%	%	%
t_1	C_1	44.44	34.48	21.08	100.00
	C_2	28.16	41.68	30.16	100.00
	C_3	17.62	44.34	38.04	100.00
t_2	C_1	45.28	33.52	21.20	100.00
	C_2	28.52	41.12	30.36	100.00
	C_3	16.32	44.60	39.08	100.00

5. It will be remembered that in this paper the word 'agent' refers to the individual bearer of action in the case of systems of interdependence.

6. This restriction may be dropped; cf. below.

7. Lautman applies Schelling's schema to the analysis of urban economic stratification.

8. In reality, these distinctions must be thought of as poles of a sort of continuum. At one extreme are 'organizastions' in the limited sense of post-war American sociologists of organizations. At the other are complex 'anarchic' systems, in Tullock's sense. Between the two are organizations in the broad sense (of Barnard, for example).

REFERENCES

ALKER, H. (1976) 'Boudon's Educational Theses About the Replication of Social Inequality,' *Information sur les sciences sociales*, 15:33-46.

ANDORKA, R. (1976) 'Social Mobility and Education in Hungary: An Analysis Applying Raymond Boudon's Models,' *Information sur les sciences sociales*, 15:47-70.

BLAU, P. M. and O. D. DUNCAN (1967) *The American Occupational Structure*. New York: John Wiley.

BOUDON, R. (1975) *L'inégalité des chances*. Paris: Centre National de la Recherche Scientifique.

BOUDON, R. (1977) *Effets pervers et ordre social*. Paris: Presses Universitaires de France.

BOUDON, R. (1979) *La logique du social.* Paris: Hachette.
BOUDON, R., P. CIBOIS and J. LAGNEAU (1975) 'Enseignement supérieur court et pièges de l'action collective,' *Revue francaise de sociologie,* 16:159-88.
BUCHANAN, J. and G. TULLOCK (1965) *The Calculus of Consent.* Ann Arbor: University of Michigan Press.
CARLSSON, G. (1958) *Social Mobility and Class Structure.* Lund: Gleerup.
COSER, L. (1964) *The Functions of Social Conflict.* Glencoe, Ill.: Free Press.
COSER, L. (1967) *Continuities in the Study of Social Conflict.* New York: Free Press.
DAHRENDORF, R. (1972) *Classes et conflits dans les sociétés industrielles.* Paris/The Hague: Mouton.
DURKHEIM, E. (1960) *La Division du travail.* Paris: Presses Universitaires de France.
ELSTER, J. (1976) 'Boudon, Education and the Theory of Games,' *Information sur les sciences sociales,* 15:733-40.
FARARO, T. and K. OSAKA (1976) 'A Mathematical Analysis of Boudon's IEO Model,' *Information sur les sciences sociales,* 15:431-75.
GIROD, R. (1971) *Mobilité sociale.* Paris/Geneva: Droz.
GIROD, R. (1975) *Inégalité, Inégalités.* Paris: Presses Universitaires de France.
GLASS, D. (1954) *Social Mobility in Britain.* London: Routledge & Kegan Paul.
HIRSCHMAN, A. O. (1972) *La réaction au déclin des firmes des enteprises et de l'Etat.* Paris: Editions Ouvrières.
KOLM, S. (1977) *Les élections sont-elles la démocratie?* Paris: Cerf.
LAUTMAN, J. (forthcoming) *Les fortunes immobiligères.* Paris: Presses Universitaires de France.
LIPSET, S. M. and R. BENDIX (1959) *Social Mobility in Industrial Societies.* Berkeley: University of California Press.
MARX, K. (1956) *Das Kapital* (rev. ed.), vol. III. Berlin: Dietz.
MERTON, R. K. (1957) *Social Theory and Social Structure,* rev. ed. New York: Free Press (first published 1949).
MICHELS, R. (1959) *Political Parties.* New York: Dover.
MÜLLER, W. (1975) *Familie, Schule, Beruf.* Opladen: Westdeutscher Verlag.
NIEBURG, H. L. (1969) *Political Violence.* New York: St Martin's Press.
OLSON, M. (1965) *The Logic of Collective Action.* Cambridge, Mass.: Harvard University Press.
ORD, L. (1959) *Industrial Frustration.* London: Oxford University Press.
PARSONS, T. (1951) *The Social System.* Glencoe, Ill.: Free Press.
ROGOFF RAMSØY, N. (1975) 'On Educational Opportunity and Social Inequality,' *Information sur les sciences sociales,* 14: 107-13.
SCHELLING, T. (1978) *Micromotives and Macrobehavior.* New York: Narton.
SCHNEIDER, L. (1971) 'Dialectic in Sociology,' *American Sociological Review,* 36:667-78.
SIMMEL, G. (1958) *Philosophie des Geldes,* 6th ed. Berlin: Duncker.
STOUFFER, S. et al. (1965) *The American Soldier.* New York: John Wiley.
TOCQUEVILLE, A. de (1952) *L'Ancien Régime, Oeuvres Complètes.* Paris: Gallimard.
USEEM, M. and S. M. MILLER (1975) 'Privilege and Domination: The Role of the Upper Class in American Higher Education,' *Information sur les sciences sociales,* 14: 115-45.

III

QUANTITATIVE MODELS

10

A STRUCTURAL THEORY OF
RANK DIFFERENTIATION

Bruce H. Mayhew
University of South Carolina

Paul T. Schollaert
Old Dominion University, Norfolk, Virginia

Several students of social stratification have hypothesized that inequality in the distribution of wealth (and other status characteristics) is determined partially by population size, on the one hand, and total volume of wealth, on the other (see Montesquieu, 1748, pp. 151-2; Rousseau, 1762, p. 97; Millar, 1806, pp. 57-9, 67-8, 220-2, 236-7; Spencer, 1882, p. 401; Kovalevsky, 1905, pp. 200-1; Pareto, 1909, p. 416; Sombart, 1913, p. 402; Sorokin, 1920, p. 406; Sahlins, 1958, p. 5; Lenski, 1966, p. 85; Orans, 1966, p. 32; Homans, 1974, pp. 361-3). Usually, but not invariably, they have suggested that an increase in either wealth or population size will lead to greater inequality.[1] These hypotheses imply — in the spirit of Rousseau (1755, pp. 2-3, 95-6) and Marx (1867, p. 132) — a purely structural basis for stratification systems; and, therefore, they merit close consideration by sociologists.

In this essay we consider the conduciveness of population size and volume of wealth to inequality defined as the *degree of stratification*, or the number of ranks or strata in a social system. This objective is realized by constructing an elementary statistical model incorporating only sociological assumptions about the nature of population elements and units of wealth. The model shows that the degree of stratification is statistically determined by the conjunction of these two variables without recourse to additional assumptions. Specifically, it shows that inequality (rank differentiation) will occur by chance in any situation where these two variables are larger than one. The degree of stratification is shown to be a direct function of system scale (simultaneous and proportional changes in population and wealth) and, for any given population size, a direct function of volume of wealth alone.

RANDOM GENERATION OF RANK DIFFERENTIATION

We wish to arrive at an a priori expectation for the degree of stratification that will occur in a population, given our knowledge of only its size and wealth. The statistical model in question is alternately called a baseline or a null model. Formulating this model requires only that we determine all the logically possible distributions of wealth for a given population size and volume of wealth, assign the same liklihood of occurrence to each, and then calculate the expected value of inequality (rank differentiation in the present case) that would occur by chance alone. However, identifying the underlying sample space of logically possible distributions of wealth may be accomplished in several ways, each one of which can be interpreted as specifying a prior theory about the nature of the phenomena: units of wealth and population elements.

For convenience of exposition, V will refer to the total volume of wealth and S will refer to total population size, individual elements of the latter being construed as persons. We shall be considering only instances in which $S>1$ and $V>0$.

Consider the situation where we distribute V objects in S cells. If we apply a unique label (such as a, b, c, d, e, f, g, etc.) to each of the V objects and a unique label to each of the S cells, we are distributing V distinct objects in S distinct cells. This is called the *multinomial* model, or the Maxwell-Boltzmann model in physics (Feller, 1968, p. 21). By contrast, if we apply a uniform label (such as a, a, a, a, a, a, a, etc.) to all V objects and a uniform label to all S cells, we are distributing V non-distinct objects in S non-distinct cells (Liu, 1968, p. 41). This might be called a general partitions model, although it has no standard name. We shall call it the Marx-Rousseau model because it incorporates assumptions about V and S that are purely sociological in nature. To see this, observe that the Maxwell-Boltzmann and Marx-Rousseau models are exact opposites with respect to the qualitative, or nominal, differences that may be defined for elements of V and S. In a purely physical model like the Maxwell-Boltzmann, the rationale for uniquely identifying each object and each cell may derive from the consideration that physical objects and the cells in which they are distributed can be uniquely identified by coordinates in space and time. However, such an interpretation is made only because it is assumed that these coordinates are relevant to the problem being studied, not because they are inherent in the nature of things.[2] By contrast, in a purely sociological model of the distribution of wealth, or any other social resource, the elements of both V and S must be essentially interchangeable (and in this sense non-distinct or indistinguishable).

Wealth exists as a social resource only when it is expressed as, or in terms of, some standard of value that permits it to be exchanged in social interaction. For this reason, money — whether in coin, paper notes, cowry shells, or bars of gold — is a purely sociological construction (Marx, 1867, pp. 49-50; Tönnies, 1887, pp. 52-4; Pareto, 1896, p. 187; Weber, 1922, pp. 38-41; Ryndina and Chernikov, 1974, p. 51). The standardized and impersonal nature of money (Simmel, 1900, p. 390) indicates that any attempt to identify its elements as uniquely different would negate its role as a medium of social exchange, or as a status resource. If elements of money are uniquely different from one another, then money is no longer money in the sociological sense of the term. Similarly, a purely sociological view of humans requires that they be seen as standard, interchangeable elements in the population (Rousseau, 1755, pp. 23, 95-6; Marx, 1867, p. 132). This purely sociological view of the interchangeability of humans qua individuals is accurately expressed by Olsen:

> The crucial point concerning all...human characteristics is that they are taken for granted in the study of social organization. They are given constants, or parameters, for the study of organization, but they are not themselves variables to be investigated or explained. Put more directly, from the point of view of social organization all individuals...are interchangeable. [Olsen, 1968, pp. 25-6]

Since we are interested in a model that treats people as interchangeable, and since there is also a sociological rationale for considering units of wealth as interchangeable, the appropriate sample space is given by the distribution of V non-distinct objects in S non-distinct cells (cf. Liu, 1968, p. 41). As indicated previously, because this type of set characterization is used, we call our model the Marx-Rousseau model of the distribution of wealth.[3] It reflects the assumption that differences among people (whether they actually exist or not) are irrelevant to our understanding of the distribution of wealth as a form of rank differentiation. The results we obtain from this Marx-Rousseau model are consequences that can be logically deduced without reference to the characteristics of individuals qua individuals.

The points in the Marx-Rousseau sample space, generated by the possible distribution of V indistinguishable units of wealth across S indistinguishable people, are all non-isomorphic sets of S non-negative integers which sum to V (Liu, 1968, p. 41). Table 1 illustrates the Marx-Rousseau sample space for the distribution of six units of wealth across six people. Observe that each point in the sample space is itself a distribution of wealth and has a specific value of rank differentiation (the number of strata, symbolized C) measuring its degree of stratification.

TABLE 1
**All Points in the Marx-Rousseau Sample Space for the
Distribution of Six Units of Wealth
($V = 6$) Across Six People ($S = 6$),
with the Number (C) of Strata Generated by Each Point**

Point (Integer Set)	C (Number of Strata)
6,0,0,0,0,0	2
5,1,0,0,0,0	3
4,2,0,0,0,0	3
3,3,0,0,0,0	2
4,1,1,0,0,0	3
3,2,1,0,0,0	4
3,1,1,1,0,0	3
2,2,2,0,0,0	2
2,2,1,1,0,0	3
2,1,1,1,1,0	3
1,1,1,1,1,1	1

Let $i = 1, 2, 3, \ldots, N$ be an index for the points in the Marx-Rousseau sample space, let C_i be the value of C associated with the ith point, and let P_i be the probability of i. As indicated above, a baseline or null model for the degree of stratification in a population of given size and wealth is obtained by assigning the same probability of occurrence to each i. That is:

$$P_i = 1/N \tag{1}$$

from which it follows that the expected degree of stratification (the number of strata generated by chance alone) is:

$$E(C) = 1/N\Sigma_{i=1}^{N} C_i \tag{2}$$

For $V = 20$ and $S = 20$, Table 2 shows that the underlying frequency distribution of C, which generates in this case an expected degree of stratification of $E(C) = 4.326953$ to the sixth decimal place, or $E(C) = 2,713/627$ in exact form. This says that, under the purely sociological assumptions of the Marx-Rousseau model, in any random selection of a human population where 20 units of wealth have been distributed to 20 people, we would expect to see them stratified in wealth to this extent, even if no other factors are operating to produce inequality.

TABLE 2
Frequency Distribution of C Under the Marx-Rousseau Model, when V = 20 and S = 20

C	Frequency
6	36
5	227
4	277
3	81
2	5
1	1
	$N = 627$

CONSEQUENCES

Changes of Scale

If per capita wealth is held constant and the values of both population size and volume of wealth are permitted to change simultaneously, we may speak of *pure changes of scale*. Under these circumstances an increase in population size is exactly matched by a proportional increase in the volume of wealth and vice versa. Tables 3, 4, and 5 provide illustrations of the changes that occur in the expected degree of stratification, $E(C)$, for the Marx-Rousseau model when per capita wealth is held constant at 1/4, 1, and 3, respectively.

TABLE 3
Expected Degree of Stratification, $E(C)$,
under the Marx-Rousseau Model
when Per Capita Wealth is Held Constant at 1/4

Scale S	V	$E(C)$ Exact Form	Decimal Form
4	1	2/1	2.00000
8	2	4/2	2.00000
12	3	7/3	2.33333
16	4	12/5	2.40000
20	5	19/7	2.71428
24	6	30/11	2.72727
28	7	45/15	3.00000
32	8	67/22	3.04545
36	9	97/30	3.23333
40	10	139/42	3.30952
—	—	——	——
60	15	684/176	3.88636
80	20	2,714/627	4.32854
100	25	9,296/1,958	4.74770
120	30	28,629/5,604	5.10867

TABLE 4
Expected Degree of Stratification, E(C),
under the Marx-Rousseau Model
when Per Capita Wealth is Held Constant at 1

Scale		E(C)	
S	V	Exact Form	Decimal Form
2	2	3/2	1.50000
3	3	6/3	2.00000
4	4	11/5	2.20000
5	5	18/7	2.57143
6	6	29/11	2.63636
7	7	44/15	2.93333
8	8	66/22	3.00000
9	9	96/30	3.20000
10	10	134/42	3.28571
—	—	———	————
20	20	2,713/627	4.32695
30	30	28,628/5,604	5.10849
40	40	315,307/37,338	5.76643
50	50	1,295,970/204,226	6.34576
60	60	6,639,348/966,467	6.86971
70	70	30,053,953/4,087,968	7.35180
80	80	123,223,638/15,796,476	7.80070

TABLE 5
Expected Degree of Stratification, E(C), under the Marx-Rousseau Model when Per Capita Wealth is Held Constant at 3

Scale		*E(C)*	
S	V	Exact Form	Decimal Form
2	6	7/4	1.75000
3	9	30/12	2.50000
4	12	102/34	3.00000
5	15	295/84	3.51190
6	18	769/199	3.86432
7	21	1,844/436	4.22935
8	24	4,150/919	4.51577
9	27	8,859/1,845	4.80162
10	30	18,103/3,590	5.04261
11	33	35,688/6,751	5.28632
12	36	68,114/12,384	5.50016
13	39	126,456/22,142	5.71113
14	42	229,087/38,797	5.90476
15	45	406,026/66,634	6.09337
16	48	705,752/112,540	6.27112
17	51	1,205,158/187,013	6.44424
18	54	2,025,178/306,421	6.60913
19	57	3,353,421/495,332	6.77004
20	60	5,478,371/791,131	6.92473

The trends indicated in these tables clearly show that the expected number of strata is an increasing function of system scale. This trend is not confined to these examples. Rather, whenever both S and V are greater than 1, this relation holds generally, regardless of the value of per capita wealth. And all of these pure-scale relations derive from the same source: from the structure of the sample spaces for per capita wealth of 1, the rank expectations for which are shown in Table 4. The generating function for the number of points in these per capita 1 sample spaces was identified by Gupta (1935, p. 145). These numbers appear as denominators in the exact form expressions of $E(C)$ in Table 4. Each expected value is derived by summing the numerator at any given S (or V) with the denominator at $S+1$ (or $V+1$), to obtain the numerator at $S+1$ (or $V+1$), as may be seen from the first 10 entries in Table 4. All other sequences of $E(C)$ obtained for constant values of per capita wealth are but minor variations on the series shown for per capita wealth of 1. For this reason, in any instance where S and V are both greater than 1, it can be shown by mathematical induction that, under the conditions of the Marx-Rousseau model,

Theorem 1. The expected degree of stratification is a direct function of system scale.

That is, in any population that experiences simultaneous and proportional increases in size and wealth, the likelihood of increased rank differentiation steadily increases. This result is derived from nothing more than the values of population size and volume of wealth. Unless, therefore, we can identify some specific additional mechanism that would depress or place a ceiling on the number of ranks, we would predict that increases in system scale will generate increased rank differentiation *by chance alone.*

Volume of Wealth

We may also consider what happens to the expected degree of stratification when population size is held constant and the volume of wealth is permitted to increase by itself. Tables 6 and 7 show $E(C)$ as a function of V for $S = 4$, 5, and 50. In each illustration, $E(C)$ is a direct function of V, but the relation is monotonic only for odd and even values of V considered separately, as may be seen in Table 6, which shows the two relations for $S = 4$. Once again, the

TABLE 6
Expected Degree of Stratification as a Function of Volume of Wealth under the Marx-Rousseau Model, for Selected Values of Population Size

V	E(C)	
	$S=4$	$S=5$
2	2.000	2.000
3	2.333	2.333
4	2.200	2.400
5	2.666	2.571
6	2.555	2.700
7	2.818	2.923
8	2.733	3.000
9	2.944	3.086
10	2.914	3.133
11	3.074	3.270
12	3.000	3.297
13	3.153	3.428
14	3.127	3.442
15	3.222	3.511
16	3.187	3.544
17	3.291	3.621
18	3.261	3.664
19	3.340	3.713
20	3.314	3.734
—	——	———
25	3.459	3.917
30	3.505	4.041

TABLE 7

Expected Degree of Stratification, E(C), as a Function of the Volume of Wealth under the Marx-Rousseau Model, when S = 50

V	E(C)	
	Exact Form	Decimal Form
5	19/7	2.7142
10	139/42	3.3095
15	684/176	3.8863
20	2,714/627	4.3285
25	9,296/1,958	4.7477
30	28,629/5,604	5.1086
35	81,156/14,883	5.4529
40	215,308/37,388	5.7587
45	504,635/89,134	6.0654
50	1,295,970/204,226	6.3457
55	2,984,663/451,219	6.6146
60	6,637,557/966,048	6.8708
—	———————	———
∞	→→→→→→→→→	50.0000

trends observed are not peculiar to the examples shown but hold generally. Consider the case where $S = 2$. Then, when V is an odd positive integer, the expected degree of stratification is a constant:

$$E(C) = \frac{V + 1}{\frac{V}{2} + \frac{1}{2}} \qquad (3)$$

However, for $S = 2$ when V is an even positive integer,

$$E(C) = \frac{V + 1}{\frac{V}{2} + 1} \qquad (4)$$

and in this case it is easy to see that

$$\lim_{V \to \infty} E(C) = S \qquad (5)$$

Since we can derive a set of equations similar to (4) and (5) for each value of S, the following can be shown by mathematical induction:

Theorem 2. When population size is held constant, the expected degree of stratification is a direct function of the volume of wealth (monotonically for odd and even values of wealth considered separately).

Theorem 3. When population size is held constant, as the volume of wealth increases without bound, the expected degree of stratification approaches its maximum value.

Alternatively, we may say that in any fixed population characterized by increasing wealth, the degree of stratification will tend *by chance alone* to increase up to its maximum, to the extreme case in which each person occupies a different stratum.

Population Size

When the volume of wealth is held constant and population size is permitted to increase, we are confined to a much narrower set of values for the degree of stratification, but the results are basically the same as those examined thus far. Table 8 provides one elementary example of the relation for $V = 10$. As this illustration shows, $E(C)$ increases with S up to a point, beyond which it remains fixed for all further increases in population size. Once again, the illustration is not a special case. The form of the relation shown in Table 8 is quite general.

In the situation we are examing here, the lowest value of $E(C)$ is fixed by equations (3) and (4) where $S = 2$. And, the highest value of $E(C)$ is fixed at the point (and everywhere beyond the point) where $S = V + 1$. This maximum value is itself derived from the generating function for $S = V$, as shown in   Table 4. We obtain the upper bound of $E(C)$ by adding 1 to the numerator of the exact form expression in Table 4. The result — one example of which appears in Table 3 where per capita wealth is $1/4$ — is a value of $E(C)$ that remains the same for a given value of V, regardless of the value of S and regardless of per capita wealth. Since the minimum degree of stratification is fixed at $S = 2$ and the maximum degree of stratifica-

TABLE 8
Expected Degree of Stratification, E(C), as a Function of Population Size under the Marx-Rousseau Model, when V = 10

S	$E(C)$	
	Exact Form	Decimal Form
2	11/6	1.8333
3	38/14	2.7142
4	67/23	2.9140
5	94/30	3.1333
6	105/35	3.0000
7	112/38	2.9473
8	116/40	2.9000
9	118/41	2.8780
10	138/42	3.28571
11	139/42	3.30952
12	139/42	3.30952
13	139/42	3.30952
—	————	————
100	139/42	3.30952
1,000	139/42	3.30952
————	————	————
∞	139/42	3.30952

tion is fixed at $S = V + 1$ or larger, and since $E(C)$ must fall between its maximum and minimum values, it follows that $E(C)$ must be an increasing function of S — without assuming that the relation is monotonic — up to the point where $S = V + 1$. That is, within the ranges noted, under the conditions of the Marx-Rousseau model:

Theorem 4. When the volume of wealth is held constant, the expected degree of stratification is a direct function of population size.

In the absence of any additional mechanism which might be introduced to depress or place an even more restricted upper limit on the number of strata, the degree of stratification will increase as a function of population size, *by chance alone.*

Overview

If a social system undergoes a change in its values of population size and volume of wealth, the Marx-Rousseau model predicts, on this information alone, that the degree of stratification will vary as well. If, for example, a society is increasing in both wealth and population, we would predict that it will become increasingly stratified. We would make the same prediction if wealth is increasing faster than population, or if population is constant while wealth is increasing faster than population, or if population is constant while wealth alone increases. And, up to the point where a limit is imposed on stratification for all values of size, the degree of stratification is also predicted to increase if population grows faster than wealth, or if wealth is constant while population alone increases.

EMPIRICAL ILLUSTRATIONS

We shall briefly consider how well the Marx-Rousseau model predicts the degree of stratification for several forms of wealth taken from existing literature. In doing so, we need to call attention to two basic kinds of wealth distributions. The general case, called an 'open' system, admits all logical possibilities for the distribution of wealth, including cases where a population element has (or receives) zero wealth. This is the type of wealth distribution system we have been considering here, as may be seen from the illustration in Table 1.

A second, more restricted, case, called a 'closed' system, is one in which all population elements have (or receive) some non-zero amount of wealth. This type of system occurs, for example, in formal organizations which pay all their employees a non-zero income. But there are numerous other examples. Any time a population is selected so as to insure that every population element must have non-zero wealth, we have in the very selection process itself excluded any 'zero wealth' possibilities. Accordingly, the sample space for closed systems is more restricted and, of course, refers only to instances in which $V>S$.

Since our empirical illustrations will include some 'closed' system distributions, we will need to calculate the $E(C)$ for closed as well as for open system distributions. Fortunately, closed distributions are images of open ones, so that our Theorems 1-4 apply to them as well. The $E(C)$ for a given S and V in a closed system is identical to the open system value of $E(C)$ for that S at per capita wealth minus 1. Thus, for a given population size, $E(C)$ in an open system at per capita wealth 1 is identical to $E(C)$ in a closed system at per capita wealth 2. $E(C)$ in an open system of per capita wealth 2 is identical to $E(C)$ in a closed system of per capita wealth 3, and so on. Table 9 shows the Marx-Rousseau underlying distributions of C for both open and closed systems when $S = 6$ and $V = 60$. The distribution shown on the right-hand side of Table 9 — a closed system — is identical to the distribution for $S = 6$ and $V = 54$ in an open system, that is, at per capita wealth minus 1. In most instances there is very little difference between the $E(C)$ for open and closed systems, but we cannot arbitrarily ignore these kinds of differences in making predictions.

TABLE 9
Underlying Frequency Distributions of C Generated by the Marx-Rousseau Model for Open and Closed-Distribution Systems, for S = 6 and V = 60

| | Open System | | Closed System |
C	Frequency	C	Frequency
6	5,942	6	3,331
5	9,298	5	5,963
4	3,994	4	2,889
3	586	3	476
2	37	2	32
1	1	1	1
	$N = 12,692$		$N = 19,858$

Wealth Measured in Canoes

In his study of the primitive economy of Tikopia, Firth (1939, p. 244) noted that the distribution of sea-going canoes across villages was a good indicator of inequality in wealth. Since villages are segmentally differentiated units, they fit the assumption of in-

TABLE 10
Distribution of 59 Sea-Going Canoes across
10 Villages in Tikopia

Village	Number of Canoes
A	7
B	3
C	6
D	3
E	3
F	5
G	8
H	7
I	12
J	5
$S = 10$	$V = 59$

Source: Firth (1939, pp. 245-6).

TABLE 11
Distribution 60 Kula Canoes Across 6
Kula Communities in the Trobriands

Community	Number of Canoes
A	8
B	3
C	8
D	22
E	20
F	12
$S = 6$	$V = 60$

Source: Malinowski (1922, p. 122).

terchangeability of population elements in the Marx-Rouseau model, and Firth (1939, p. 117) himself observed that canoes were interchangeable as units of wealth. However, from the data Firth presented on the distribution of 59 sea-going canoes across 10 coastal villages — reproduced here in Table 10 — it is not clear whether we are dealing with a (definitionally) open or closed distribution system (two inland villages are irrelevant to the distribution of wealth in canoes and are excluded from consideration here). Therefore, we shall calculate $E(C)$ for both open and closed-system assumptions. We may also consider, for comparison, the distribution of 60 'kula' canoes across six kula communities from Malinowski's (1922, p. 122) study of the Trobriand Islands. His data are reproduced in Table 11. We know that Malinowski's data form a closed distribution, because the units of wealth are kula canoes — canoes used in the system of kula exchange — and, therefore, to be included in the list at all a community must have at least one canoe. Nevertheless, we shall parallel our analysis of Firth's data by calculating both open and closed-system values of $E(C)$ for Malinowski's data as well.

As may be seen from Tables 10 and 11, the observed value of rank differentiation, symbolized $O(C)$, is 6 for Firth's data and 5 for Malinowski's. To determine whether these observed values are accurately predicted by the Marx-Rousseau model, we consider whether the observed values fall within one standard deviation of the $E(C)$, as shown in Table 12. Regardless of whether the Marx-Rousseau prediction is based upon open or closed-system assumptions, Table 12 shows that the observed values for both examples fall witin one standard deviation of $E(C)$. In other words, given the values of S and V in either data set, it is not possible to reject the hypothesis that the observed degree of stratification is due to chance. Indeed, even the absolute amount of error in prediction is quite small, being less than 1/2 rank in all comparisons.

Wealth Measured in Women

In some so-called primitive societies, women are used as a form of wealth and are exchanged as such among groups of men (Lévi-Strauss, 1962, p. 144). This, at least, was the case among the Tiwi of North Australia studied by Hart and Pilling, who reported that 'the control of women...was the most tangible index of power and influence' among men (1960, p. 52). Furthermore, we have it on

TABLE 12

Comparisons of the Observed, O(C), and Expected, E(C), Degree of Stratification for the Distribution of 59 Sea-Going Canoes across 10 Villages in Tikopia and for the Distribution of 60 Kula Canoes across Six Communities in the Trobriand Islands

S	V	$O(C)$	Distribution Assumption	$E(C)$	One Standard Deviation Around $E(C)$	Does $O(C)$ Fall Within 1 Standard Deviation of $E(C)$
10	59	6	Open	6.361	1.0928	Yes
			Closed	5.998	1.0630	Yes
6	60	5	Open	5.033	0.7968	Yes
			Closed	4.951	0.8135	Yes

good authority (Lévi-Strauss, 1962, p. 167) that adult women may be considered as essentially interchangeable insofar as they function as wealth. This is also true among the Tiwi, where adult wives were presumably of equivalent value. However, females under 14 living in their father's household, although internally homogeneous in value, were not equivalent to adult wives, and must be considered separately as a dimension of wealth. Table 13 shows the distribution of 35 adult wives and 25 young females across seven households among the Tiwi. Households meet the model's assumption of interchangeability among population elements, and, as indicated above, adult wives and young females each form distinct but internally homogeneous subsets on interchangeable wealth units. As Table 13 shows, the observed number of strata formed among households is 5 for both adult wives and females under 14. Since a household exists only if at least one adult wife is present, adult wives form a closed distribution system across households, although females under 14 do not. Table 14 compares the observed with the expected number of strata under both open and closed-system assumptions for adult wives and under the open-system assumption for young females. In all three comparisons the observed degree of stratification falls within one standard deviation of the Marx-Rousseau model's $E(C)$. Again, we can only say that, given

TABLE 13
Distribution of Adult Wives and Females Under 14 Years of Age Across Seven Households (Economic Production Units) Among the Tiwi of North Australia

Household	Number of Adult Wives	Number of Females Under 14
A	16	5
B	8	11
C	5	5
D	1	1
E	1	2
F	3	1
G	1	0
$S = 7$	$V = 35$	$V = 25$

Source: Hart and Pilling (1960, p. 66).

TABLE 14
Comparisons of the Observed, O(C), and Expected, E(C), Degree of Stratification for the Distribution of Wives and Females under 14 Across Seven Households Among the Tiwi of North Australia

V	$O(C)$	Distribution Assumption	$E(C)$	One Standard Deviation around $E(C)$	Does $O(C)$ Fall Within 1 Standard Deviation of $E(C)$?
35 (Adult wives)	5	Open	4.886	0.924	Yes
		Closed	4.597	0.839	Yes
25 (Females under 14)	5	Open	4.457	0.894	Yes

the values of *S* and *V* in each subset of data, it is not possible to reject the hypothesis that the observed degree of stratification is due to chance. The absolute error in prediction is also quite small, being less than 6/10 ranks in all cases.

Wealth Measured in Agricultural Resources

In his study of southern Kurdistan, Barth (1953, p. 19) examined a series of agricultural resources distributed across 10 households in the village of Decon. These data are reproduced in Table 15, which shows the distributions of seven types of agricultural wealth: four of livestock, two of cropland, and a residual category of cropland (the latter is included simply because we do not know whether it is or is not internally homogeneous with respect to types of cropland). Each of these forms of agricultural wealth is presumably internally

TABLE 15
**Distribution of Various Forms of Wealth Across 10 Households
in the Village of Decon in Southern Kurdistan**

Household	Oxen	Cows	Donkeys	Horses	Tobacco	Rice	Other Crops
A	5	4	2	1	4	1.5	4
B	4	2	4	1	3	0.5	5
C	4	5	1	0	2	0.5	4
D	4	4	1	0	3	0.5	5
E	2	3	1	0	2	0.5	4
F	2	4	0	0	2	0.5	3
G	0	2	0	0	2	0	0
H	0	2	1	0	0	0	0
I	0	0	0	0	0	0	0
J	0	0	0	0	0	0	0
	$V = 21$	26	10	2	18	4	25

Source: Barth (1953, p. 19). This table excludes two sets of wealth that were heterogeneous combinations (sheep-goats and wheat-barley) made by Barth. The crops are given in units of land area under cultivation. The areal unit employed is the donum (1 donum = 50 × 50 meters).

TABLE 16
Comparisons of the Observed, O(C), and Expected, E(C),
Degree of Stratification for the Distributions of Various Forms
of Wealth Across 10 Households in Southern Kurdistan

V	O(C)	E(C)	One Standard Deviation around E(C)	Does O(C) Fall Within 1 Standard Deviation of E(C)?
2 horses	2	2.000	0.000	Yes
4 rice	3	2.400	0.490	No
10 donkeys	4	3.286	0.733	Yes
18 tobacco	4	4.147	0.838	Yes
21 oxen	4	4.424	0.842	Yes
25 other crops	4	4.725	0.893	Yes
26 cows	5	4.784	0.924	Yes
150 (sheep and goats)	7	—	—	—
225 (wheat and barley)	8	—	—	—

homogeneous in the sense that units of wealth are interchangeable (that is, one cow is equivalent to another, but a cow is not equivalent to a horse), and since households are segmentally differentiated — and therefore interchangeable — population elements, the distribution of each form of wealth appears to meet the assumptions of the Marx-Rousseau model.

Table 16 compares the observed with the expected number of strata for each form of wealth under the Marx-Rousseau model's open-system assumption (the necessity of the open-system assumption is apparent from Table 15). In six out of seven comparisons, the observed number of strata falls within one standard deviation of the $E(C)$, the prediction failing only for rice land. With this 85.7 percent rate of successful prediction, we would again conclude for most of these distributions that, for a given S and V, it is not possible to reject the hypothesis that the observed degree of stratification is due to chance.

At the bottom of Table 16 we have included two additional mixed categories of agricultural wealth reported by Barth. Their inclusion permits us to see — by comparing the first and second columns in Table 16 — that the observed degree of stratification is a direct function of the volume of wealth, a trend predicted by Theorem 2.

TABLE 17
Distribution of 870 Houses Across 11 Monasteries and Seven Convents in Antequera, in the Valley of Oaxaca, Mexico, in 1792

Institution		Number of Houses Owned
Monasteries:	A	131
	B	70
	C	68
	D	55
	E	41
	F	32
	G	24
	H	17
	I	7
	J	1
	K	0
	$S = 11$	$V = 446$
Convents:	A	210
	B	113
	C	64
	D	22
	E	8
	F	7
	G	0
	$S = 7$	$V = 424$

Source: Taylor (1972, p. 173).

Wealth Measured in Houses

In his study of the Valley of Oaxaca, Mexico, Taylor (1972, p. 173) examined the distribution of houses owned by monasteries and convents in Antequera for the year 1792, indicating that rent from these houses was the principal source of wealth for these religious orders. His data on the distribution of 446 houses owned across 11 monasteries and 424 houses owned across seven convents are reproduced in Table 17. Assuming that the houses are interchangeable units of wealth, and noting that monasteries and convents, considered separately, are segmentally differentiated — and therefore interchangeable — population elements, permits us to compare the observed degree of stratification for each type of religious order with the statistical expectations from the model.

TABLE 18
Comparison of the Observed, O(C), and Expected, E(C), Degree of Stratification for the Distribution of 446 Houses across 11 Monasteries and 424 Houses across Seven Convents in Antequera, Oaxaca, Mexico in 1792

S	V	O(C)	E(C)	1 Standard Deviation around E(C)	Does O(C) Fall within 1 Standard Deviation of E(C)
11 monasteries	446 houses	11	10.021	1.027	Yes
7 convents	424 houses	7	6.719	0.591	Yes

Table 18 compares the observed with the expected number of strata for both types of institutions under the Marx-Rousseau model's open-system assumption. In this particular case, the open and closed system assumptions yield virtually identical values with no difference in results from the comparison, but we employ the open system assumption because there is nothing in the definition of either monasteries or convents implying a closed system. As Table 18 shows, the observed number of strata falls within one standard deviation of the expected number of both kinds of institutions. Accordingly, for the values of S and V in these two cases, it is not possible to reject the hypothesis that the observed degree of stratification is due to chance.

Wealth Measured in Money

In this section we shall consider the distribution of income across employees in several bureaus of the Metropolitan government of Nashville, Tennessee, for 1971. The illustration is imperfect in two respects. Computer time limitations and the late date at which we discovered this example prohibited generating a complete Marx-Rousseau sample space for all the bureaus and for values of V stated in many thousands of dollars. To get around these problems, we decided to express the values of V in units of $1,000 and to compute expectations for as many bureaus as time permitted, beginning with the smaller bureaus and moving upward in size. This procedure permitted us to make comparisons for 38 bureaus, ranging in size from four to 10 employees and from $21,000 to $99,000. Since V is in units of income for employees in an organization, we are examining closed distribution systems. From our sociological point of view, both dollars and employees are essentially interchangeable, and it is therefore possible to compare actual with Marx-Rousseau values for the degree of stratification.

TABLE 19
Comparisons of Observed, O(C), and Expected, E(C),
Degree of Stratification for the Distribution of Annual Income
(in units of $1,000) across Employees in Bureaus of the
Metro-Government of Nashville, Tennessee, as of 1 April, 1971

Bureau	S	V	O(C)	E(C)	1 Standard Deviation	Does O(C) Fall Within: 1 SD	2 SD's
AA	4	22	4	3.2619	0.7733	Yes	Yes
AB	4	22	4	3.2619	0.7733	Yes	Yes
AC	4	28	3	3.4023	0.6645	Yes	Yes
AD	4	28	3	3.4023	0.6645	Yes	Yes
AE	4	29	3	3.4594	0.5879	Yes	Yes·
AF	4	37	3	3.5634	0.5562	No	Yes

TABLE 19 (continued)

AG	4	39	3	3.5850	0.5451	No	Yes
AH	4	40	3	3.5732	0.5874	Yes	Yes
AI	4	54	4	3.6811	0.5188	Yes	Yes
BA	5	42	3	4.1840	0.7219	No	Yes
BB	5	44	4	4.2159	0.7151	Yes	Yes
BC	5	45	4	4.2278	0.7166	Yes	Yes
BD	5	48	3	4.2731	0.7003	No	Yes
CA	6	21	2	3.7090	0.7902	No	No
CB	6	42	5	4.5962	0.8620	Yes	Yes
CC	6	55	5	4.8785	0.8143	Yes	Yes
CD	6	64	4	5.0803	0.8010	No	Yes
DA	7	43	4	4.9177	0.9307	Yes	Yes
DB	7	45	4	4.9854	0.9304	No	Yes
DC	7	48	5	5.0805	0.9272	Yes	Yes
DD	7	52	4	5.1907	0.9269	No	Yes
DE	7	55	4	5.2642	0.9270	No	Yes
DF	7	55	4	5.2642	0.9270	No	Yes
DG	7	66	6	5.4943	0.9100	Yes	Yes
DH	7	74	5	5.6259	0.8962	Yes	Yes
EA	8	20	2	3.5142	0.7881	No	Yes
EB	8	34	5	4.6407	0.9328	Yes	Yes
EC	8	53	5	5.4781	0.9884	Yes	Yes
ED	8	58	6	5.6282	0.9996	Yes	Yes
EE	8	85	6	6.2151	0.9800	Yes	Yes
FA	9	61	4	5.9322	1.0476	No	Yes
FB	9	72	6	6.2563	1.0591	Yes	Yes
FC	9	80	4	6.4515	1.0612	No	No
FD	9	99	7	6.8192	1.0531	Yes	Yes
GA	10	40	5	5.0459	0.9630	Yes	Yes
GB	10	61	6	6.0763	1.0703	Yes	Yes
GC	10	76	4	6.5767	1.1082	No	Yes
GD	10	80	6	6.6895	1.1131	Yes	Yes

Source: Operating budget of the Metropolitan Government of Nashville and Davidson County, Tennessee.

Table 19 shows the basic data for each bureau, along with the observed and expected degrees of stratification for each. For this large number of cases, it is necessary to evaluate the results by reference to the degree of correspondence between observed values and the underlying sample spaces for the Marx-Rousseau values of $E(C)$ and their standard deviations. This is necessary because most of the underlying C distributions are not symmetric (not normally distributed) around their $E(C)$. Accordingly, we have to compare the observed and expected percentage of cases falling within one and two standard deviations of $E(C)$. Taking the average for all 38 sample spaces, we find that 63.15 percent of the C values would fall within one standard deviation of $E(C)$ by chance alone and that 68.35 percent of observed values of C actually do so. And, 94.73 percent of the C values would fall within two standard deviations of $E(C)$ by chance alone and 95.64 percent of the observed values of C actually do so. Minor differences exist, but none are large enough to permit rejection of the hypothesis that the observed degrees of stratification are due to chance. For bureaus of size 6, 7, 8, 9, and 10 — that is, in five of seven possible comparisons — Table 19 also shows that, for a given population size, the observed degree of stratification is a direction function of V as Theorem 2 predicts.

However, since our example is both imperfect and incomplete, a more extensive test should be conducted on the total set of government bureaus as soon as computer time permits.

The illustrations in this section have been selected not because they place our model in a favorable light but because they were the only examples we have found up to this time. These cases are merely illustrations. The predictive adequacy of our model can be evaluated only on the basis of more extensive testing.

DISCUSSION

The model we have developed here may at first appear to be at variance both with Marx's conflict theory and with functionalist consensus theories of stratification. That is, our model seems to bypass some of the central concerns of both types of theory. To a limited degree, the impression is correct. However, to avoid misunderstandings, some points of similarity between these theories and our model will be briefly mentioned.

First, in his analysis of capitalist societies, Marx (1867, p. 132) assumed that inequality derives from concrete historical conditions, that inequality is a consequence of social arrangements, rather than of bio-physical or 'natural' conditions. This assumption finds expression in our model, which ignores characteristics of individuals. Second, Marx (1859, p. 76) posited the operation of chance in the process of capitalist development.[4] Third, Marx (1905, pp. 243, 251) saw both population growth and increasing volume of wealth as central trends in capitalist societies. And, as everyone knows, he attributed inequality to these (and other) conditions of capitalist society. Rather than disagreeing with Marx, our model adopts some of his assumptions and serves to identify the mechanism through which the inequalitarian consequences of population size and volume of wealth are realized.

In the case of functionalist theories of stratification, their spokesmen have conceded that chance variation plays a part in the formation of different configurations of strata (Schumpeter, 1927, p. 31), and that factors such as population size (Davis and Moore, 1945, p. 249) may place significant constraints upon the degree of stratification.[5] So there is some degree of consistency here as well.

Perhaps the widest area of difference between our model, on the one hand, and functionalist and conflict theories, on the other, is that the latter see stratification as resting upon the division of labor, upon uniquely different occupational roles taken as population elements. However, a minor variation on the Marx-Rousseau model permits us to include this feature as well. If we are interested in the distribution of wealth across occupations (or across ethnic groups), we are concerned with the distribution of V indistinguishable units of wealth across S distinguishable population elements, which is the Bose-Einstein sample space (Feller, 1968, pp. 40-1). Under this alternative version of the sample space, the results for the degree of stratification are the same as those expressed in Theorems 1-4 for the Marx-Rousseau model, as illustrated in Tables 20, 21 and 22. Thus, altering our assumptions in this way permits us to adopt a standard feature of several well-known theories of stratification without altering our predictions.[6]

To amplify the expectations shown in Table 22, we should note an important feature of V/S which governs the relation between population size and $E(C)$. In stating Theorem 4, we pointed out that its range is restricted: under the Marx-Rousseau model it holds up to the point where $S = V + 1$. Similarly, Theorem 4 holds for the Bose-Einstein model up to the point where $S = V$. Beyond these points, $E(C)$ is a constant for Marx-Rousseau and actually

TABLE 20

The Expected Degree of Stratification as a Function of System Scale for Both the Marx-Rousseau and Bose-Einstein Sample Spaces, under Open Distribution Assumptions

Scale		E(C)	
S	V	Marx-Rousseau*	Bose-Einstein**
2	2	1.5000	1.6666
3	3	2.0000	2.5000
4	4	2.2000	2.6571
5	5	2.5714	2.9444
6	6	2.6363	3.0367
7	7	2.9333	3.3618
8	8	3.0000	3.5227
9	9	3.2000	3.6698
10	10	3.2857	3.8052

* The distribution of V indistinguishable units of wealth across S indistinguishable population elements.

** The distribution of V indistinguishable units of wealth across S distinguishable population elements.

decreasing for Bose-Einstein (see Table 22). So, Theorem 4 is quite limited for both models. This limitation is due to the low values of V/S which must be taken into account. On the other hand, in complex societies, where V/S may grow to truly extraordinary magnitudes, an entirely different situation obtains. Specifically, when V/S becomes extremely large, Theorem 3 tells us that $E(C)$ will be arbitrarily close to S. That is, for extremely large values of per capita wealth, $E(C)$ will become a perfect, linear, positive function of S. In complex societies, population size might well become the most powerful predictor of the degree of stratification.

However, there are some clear differences between our model and most existing theories of stratification. First, unlike other theories, our model makes specific predictions for the degree of ranked inequality in any given social system. Therefore, unlike other theories, it can be easily rejected should it prove inadequate. Second, because our model relies upon population size and volume of wealth alone, it is a much more parsimonious explanation of stratification than existing theories. Third, our model implies that

TABLE 21
The Expected Degree of Stratification as a Function of the Volume of Wealth When S = 10, for Both the Marx-Rousseau and Bose-Einstein Sample Spaces under Open Distribution Assumptions

| | E(C) | |
V	Marx-Rousseau*	Bose-Einstein**
2	2.0000	2.0000
3	2.3333	2.4090
4	2.4000	2.6937
5	2.7142	2.8691
6	2.7272	3.0669
7	3.0000	3.2993
8	3.0454	3.4234
9	3.2333	3.6375
10	3.2857	3.8052

* The distribution of *V* indistinguishable units of wealth across *S* indistinguishable population elements.

** The distribution of *V* indistinguishable units of wealth across *S* distinguishable population elements.

any set of conditions that increases either population or wealth, or both, is at least indirectly conducive to increased rank differentiation. This strongly suggests that the ecological underpinnings of social systems are among the primary determinants of the degree of rank differentiation. Fourth, the purely sociological nature of our model permits it to throw light upon a major theoretical issue concerning the bases of social inequality.

Attempts to explain the prevalence of inequality in human societies have usually started from one of two fundamentally different assumptions. The first and most widely held view attributes inequality to human nature, to the inherent biophysical and biopsychological differences which occur in human populations (Hobbes, 1651, p. 41; Pareto, 1897, p. 363; Blinder, 1974, p. 2). Fundamental to this position is the belief that the characteristics of individuals, qua individuals, must be taken into account in any valid explanation of inequality, because social inequality arises, partially or wholly, from biologically determined differences among in-

TABLE 22
The Expected Degree of Stratification as a Function of Population Size when V = 10, for Both the Marx-Rousseau and Bose-Einstein Sample Spaces under Open Distribution Assumptions

	E(C)	
S	Marx-Rousseau*	Bose-Einstein**
2	1.8333	1.9090
3	2.7142	2.7272
4	2.9140	3.3006
5	3.1333	3.6373
6	3.0000	3.7982
7	2.9473	3.8540
8	2.9000	3.8572
9	2.8780	3.8366
10	3.2857	3.8052
11	3.3095	3.7686
12	3.3095	3.7297
—	———	———
20	3.3095	3.4412
—	———	———
∞	3.3095	?

* The distribution of *V* indistinguishable units of wealth across *S* indistinguishable population elements.

** The distribution of *V* indistinguishable units of wealth across *S* distinguishable population elements.

dividuals. A second and more purely sociological view attributes inequality to social and cultural variables, to the structure of society itself (Rousseau, 1755, pp. 2-3, 95-6; Marx, 1867, p. 132). As this second view holds inequality to be a social fact, sui generis, it considers that differences among individuals are irrelevant to understanding social inequality. Differences among individuals are seen as derivatives of social structure, not as conditions that determine rank differentiation (Spencer, 1882, pp. 300-1).

Since our model rests explicitly upon this last assumption, and since it shows that rank differentiation will occur by chance in any situation where the volume of wealth and population size are greater than one, it challenges the common assumption that the universal occurrence of social inequality must derive from the nature of humans themselves (for example, Pareto, 1897, p. 363). Furthermore, it permanently refutes Sorokin's (1927, p. 325) contention that inequality cannot arise among a homogeneous set of persons, for it explicitly shows that, even if people are all identical, mere aggregate size of the population and total volume of wealth are sufficient to predict that they will form a stratification system, *by chance alone*.

To develop the more general implications of these points, we note that the Marx-Rousseau model may be generalized with respect to each of its variables. First, the elements that make up population size can be generalized beyond people to include occupational roles, ethnic groups, organizations, communities, or even nations. In other words, the model's expectations hold for macro-structural units as well as people. Second, the units that make up volume of wealth can be generalized to units of any measurable status characteristic or resource: to units of power, prestige, etc. That is, *the Marx-Rousseau model provides a random expectation for rank differentiation in the distribution of any status characteristic*, not just wealth. It is therefore one general explanation for the occurrence of inequality in human groups of all kinds.

Since our model can be applied to small groups, and since it generalizes to any measurable status resource, it permits us to question the adequacy of Homans's (1974) so-called psychological explanations of status structure. Our model predicts the amount of inequality that may be expected to occur in small groups in terms of power, prestige, or any other status characteristic or resource the researcher may wish to identify. Homans's theory offers no such predictions and is less parsimonious than the Marx-Rousseau model. Indeed, contrary to Homans's (1967, pp. 65-9) claim, there does exist a purely sociological explanation for social stratification. The one we have been discussing here has existed for more than 200 years (Montesquieu, 1748, pp. 151-99).

However, the fact that rank differentiation can be predicted from population size and volume of wealth does not imply that these are the only sociological variables relevant to understanding inequality, or even that they are the most important variables. At a minimum, we expect that technological power and velocity of circulation would also have an impact on the distribution of wealth in any society (cf. Krelle, 1962). Of course, the effects of these additional variables might be largely indirect, mediated by population size and volume of wealth. But whether that is so remains to be empirically determined. In short, we do not assume that the Marx-Rousseau model provides a complete theory of the distribution of wealth. It is a beginning, but not necessarily the end.

TABLE 23
Expected Value of the Gini Index, E(G), as a Function of System Scale under the Assumptions of the Marx-Rousseau Model, for Selected Values of Per Capita Wealth in Open Distribution Systems

| | V/S = 1/2 | | | V/S = 1 | | | V/S = 2 | |
S	V	E(G)	S	V	E(G)	S	V	E(G)
4	2	0.625	2	2	0.250	2	4	0.250
6	3	0.685	3	3	0.370	3	6	0.365
8	4	0.725	4	4	0.450	4	8	0.429
10	5	0.751	5	5	0.502	5	10	0.473
12	6	0.772	6	6	0.545	6	12	0.501
14	7	0.788	7	7	0.576	7	14	0.527
16	8	0.601	8	8	0.603	8	16	0.546
18	9	0.812	9	9	0.625	9	18	0.563
20	10	0.822	10	10	0.644	10	20	0.577
22	11	0.830	11	11	0.660	11	22	0.590
24	12	0.837	12	12	0.674	12	24	0.602
26	13	0.843	13	13	0.686	13	26	0.612
28	14	0.849	14	14	0.698	14	28	0.622
30	15	0.854	15	15	0.708	15	30	0.631
32	16	0.858	16	16	0.717	16	32	0.639
34	17	0.862	17	17	0.725	17	34	0.647
36	18	0.866	18	18	0.733	18	36	0.654
38	19	0.870	19	19	0.740	19	38	0.661
40	20	0.873	20	20	0.746	20	40	0.668

APPENDIX

There are several quite distinct conceptions of social inequality, but all of them have as their core dimension the degree of stratification. It is for this reason that we have confined attention to rank dif-

TABLE 24
Expected Value of the Gini Index, E(G), as a Function of System Scale under the Assumptions of the Marx-Rousseau Model, for Selected Values of Per Capita Wealth in Closed-Distribution Systems

V/S = 2			V/S = 3			V/S = 4			V/S = 5		
S	V	E(G)	S	V	E(G)	S	V	E(G)	S	V	E(G)
2	4	0.125	2	6	0.166	2	8	0.187	2	10	0.199
3	6	0.185	3	9	0.243	3	12	0.268	3	15	0.283
4	8	0.225	4	12	0.286	4	16	0.310	4	20	0.325
5	10	0.251	5	15	0.315	5	20	0.340	5	25	0.353
6	12	0.272	6	18	0.334	6	24	0.359	6	30	0.373
7	14	0.288	7	21	0.351	7	28	0.375	7	35	0.388
8	16	0.301	8	24	0.364	8	32	0.388	8	40	0.401
9	18	0.312	9	27	0.374	9	36	0.399	9	45	0.412
10	20	0.322	10	30	0.385	10	40	0.409	10	50	0.425

ferentiation alone. However, an expected value can be calculated from the Marx-Rousseau model for any conception of structural inequality, and these expectations will all show the same general result. In open-distribution systems, structural inequality will occur by chance in any situation where S is greater than 1 and V is greater than 0. In closed-distribution systems, structural inequality will occur by chance in any situation where S is greater than 1 and V is greater than S.

To illustrate, we may consider the well known Gini index, symbolized G, which measures the dispersion-concentration of wealth (Gini, 1912, pp. 72-4; Blau, 1977, pp. 57-8). When $G = 1$, wealth is maximally concentrated in the hands of one population element. When $G = 0$, wealth is maximally dispersed, being equally divided among all population elements. Substituting values of G into equation (2), we may calculate the expected degree of dispersion-concentration of wealth, symbolized $E(G)$, for the Marx-Rousseau model. Tables 23 and 24 show $E(G)$ as a function of system scale in both open and closed-distribution systems. As these tables illustrate, wealth will concentrate by chance alone as system scale increases. Not only does system scale increase the likelihood of rank differentiation; it is also conducive to an increasing *concentration* of wealth.

NOTES

1. An exception is Caplow (1964, pp. 158-9), who claims that increases in total wealth and population have an equalizing influence, at least in contemporary industrial societies. A reversal in the relation is also hypothesized by Lenski (1970, pp. 407-8) for industrial societies, which he believes have escaped from materialistic considerations and are presently guided in such matters by their 'democratic ideology' (1970, pp. 354-5, 366, 408).

2. While we can differentiate between any two phenomena in the universe on some criterion (differential location in time and space), we can also regard them as identical on some other criterion (location in the same city, nation, solar system, galaxy). That the assumptions underlying the Maxwell-Boltzmann sample space are quite arbitrary in this sense became apparent with the development of Bose-Einstein and Fermi-Dirac statistics (see Feller, 1968, pp. 40-2). In spite of this revelation, most statisticians continue to look upon the multinomial model (Maxwell-Boltzmann) as if it were *the* model of reality.

3. The use of alternative spaces to construct probability models dates back to some of the earliest work on the subject (e.g., Cardano, 1663, pp. 262-76). However, the proliferation of baseline models constructed from purely arbitrary assumptions would be a waste of time. For this reason, the construction of a baseline must proceed in accordance with a particular set of theoretical assumptions which it is intended to model (Mayhew, 1974, p. 142). The Marx-Rousseau model formalizes the assumptions that (a) units of wealth are interchangeable and (b) population elements are interchangeable. This model was adopted not only because it incorporates the views of Simmel (1894) and Blau (1969; 1977) on social forms, but also because the questions we are attempting to answer in this essay cannot otherwise be addressed. In the case of the Maxwell-Boltzmann model, for example, it is difficult to construct a sociological rationale for identifying nominal differences between units of wealth (elements of V).

4. This view is supported by at least some contemporary Marxists in the Soviet Union, as may be seen in the observation in Ryndina and Chernikov (1974, p. 14) that 'Under capitalism, economic laws assert themselves through a maze of accidents.' Rousseau (1755, pp. liv-lv) also assigned a prominent role to chance events.

5. In some of its more extreme versions (e.g. Mousnier, 1969), functionalist consensus theory goes so far as to suggest that even the dimensions of stratification are themselves the result of random variation.

6. That is, this same variation in assumptions permits us to include those theories that posit ethnic group differences as a basis for rank differentiation, such as Gumplowicz (1883, pp. 205-9) and van den Berghe (1975, p. 71).

REFERENCES

BARTH, Fredrik (1953) *Principles of Social Organization in Southern Kurdistan.* Oslo: Brodrene Jorgensen.

BLAU, Peter M. (1969) 'Objectives of Sociology,' p. 43-71 in *A Design for Sociology,* edited by Robert Bierstedt. Philadelphia: American Academy of Political and Social Science.

BLAU, Peter M. (1977) *Inequality and Heterogeneity.* New York: Free Press.

BLINDER, Alan A. (1974) *Toward a Theory of Income Distribution.* Cambridge: MIT Press.

CAPLOW, Theodore (1964) *Principles of Organization.* New York: Harcourt Brace Jovanovich.

CARDANO, Girolamo (1963) *Opera omnia,* Tomus 1. Lugduni: Hugeatan & Ravaud.

DAVIS, Kingsley and Wilbert E. MOORE (1945) 'Some Principles of Stratification,' *American Sociological Review,* 10: 242-9.

FELLER, William (1968) *An Introduction to Probability Theory and Its Applications,* 3rd ed., vol. 1. New York: John Wiley.

FIRTH, Raymond (1939) *Primitive Polynesian Economy.* London: George Routledge.

GINI, Corrado (1912) *Variabilità e mutabilità.* Bologne: P. Cuppini.

GUMPLOWICZ, Ludwig (1883) *Der Rassenkampf.* Innsbruck: Wagner.

GUPTA, Hansraj (1935) 'A Table of partitions,' *Proceedings of the London Mathematical Society,* 39: 142-9.

HART, Charles M. W. and Arnold R. PILLING (1960) *The Tiwi of North Australia.* New York. Holt.

HOBBES, Thomas (1651) *The Leviathan*. London: Andrew Crooke.
HOMANS, George C. (1967) *The Nature of Social Science*. New York: Harcourt Brace Jovanovich.
HOMANS, George C. (1974) *Social Behavior: Its Elementary Forms*, 2nd ed. New York: Harcourt Brace Jovanovich.
KOVALEVSKY, Maxim M. (1905) *Sovremennya Sotsiologi*. St Petersburg: L. F. Pantelyeyev.
KRELLE, Wilhelm (1962) *Verteilungstheorie*. Wiesbaden: Gabler.
LENSKI, Gerhard E. (1966) *Power and Privilege*. New York: McGraw-Hill.
LENSKI, Gerhard E. (1970) *Human Society*. New York: McGraw-Hill.
LÉVI-STRAUSS, Claude (1962) *La Pensée sauvage*. Paris: Plon.
LIU, C. L. (1968) *Introduction to Combinatorial Mathematics*. New York: McGraw-Hill.
MALINOWSKI, Bronislaw (1922) *Argonauts of the Western Pacific*. London: George Routledge.
MARX, Karl (1859) *Zur Kritik der politischen Oekonomie*. Berlin: Duncker.
MARX, Karl (1867) *Das Kapital*, 1 Band. Hamburg: Otto Meissner.
MARX, Karl (1905) *Theorien über den Mehrwert*, 2 Band; 2. Teil, herausgegeben von Karl Kautsky. Stuttgart: J. H. W. Dietz.
MAYHEW, Bruce H. (1974) 'Baseline Models of System Structure,' *American Sociological Review*, 39: 137-43.
MILLAR, John (1806) *The Origin of the Distinction of Ranks*, 4th ed. Edinburgh: William Blackwood.
MONTESQUIEU, Charles, de (1748) *De L'Esprit des lois*, Tome 1. Geneva: Barrillot.
MOUSNIER, Roland (1969) *Les Hiérarchies sociales de 1450 a nous jours*. Paris: Presses Universitaires de France.
OLSEN, Marvin E. (1968) *The Process of Social Organization*. New York: Holt, Rinehart & Winston.
ORANS, Martin (1966) 'Surplus,' *Human Organization*, 25: 24-32.
PARETO, Vilfredo (1896) *Cours d'économie politique*, Vol. 1. Lausanne: F. Rouge.
PARETO, Vilfredo (1897) *Cours d'économie politique*, Vol. 2. Lausanne: F. Rouge.
PARETO, Vilfredo (1909) *Manuel d'économie politique*, translated by Albert Bonnet and revised by the author. Paris: Giard et Brière.
ROUSSEAU, Jean-Jacques (1755) *Discours sur l'origine et les fondements de l'inégalité parmi les hommes*. Amsterdam: Marc M. Rey.
ROUSSEAU, Jean-Jacques (1762) *Du Contrat social*. Amsterdam: Marc M. Rey.
RYNDINA, M. and G. CHERNIKOV (eds.) (1974) *The Political Economy of Capitalism*. Moscow: Progress Publishing Co.
SAHLINS, Marshall D. (1958) *Social Stratification in Polynesia*. Seattle: University of Washington Press.
SCHUMPETER, Joseph A. (1927) 'Die sozialen Klassen im ethnisch homogenen Milieu', *Archiv für Sozialwissenschaft und Sozialpolitik*, 57: 1-67.
SIMMEL, Georg (1894) 'Le Problème de la sociologie,' *Revue de métaphysique et de morale*, 2: 497-504.
SIMMEL, Georg (1900) *Philosophie des Geldes*. Leipzig: Duncker & Humbolt.
SOMBART, Werner (1913) *Der Bourgeois*. Leipzig: Duncker & Humbolt.

SOROKIN, Pitirim A. (1920) *Systema soziologii,* Tom 2. Petrograd: Kolos.

SOROKIN, Pitirim A. (1927) *Social Mobility.* New York: Harper.

SPENCER, Herbert (1882) *Principles of Sociology,* vol. 2, part 2. New York: D. Appleton.

TAYLOR, William B. (1972) *Landlord and Peasant in Colonial Oaxaca.* Stanford: Stanford University Press.

TÖNNIES, Ferinand (1887) *Gemeinschaft und Gesellschaft.* Leipzig: R. Reisland.

VAN DEN BERGHE, Pierre L. (1975) 'Ethnicity and Class in Highland Peru,' pp. 71-85 in *Ethnicity and Resource Competition in Plural Societies,* edited by Leo A. Despres. Paris: Mouton.

WEBER, Max (1922) *Wirtschaft und Gesellschaft,* 2 vols. Tübingen: J.C.B. Mohr.

11

VOLUNTARY AFFILIATION: A STRUCTURAL APPROACH

J. Miller McPherson
University of South Carolina

American sociologists have long been guilty of a one-sided view of voluntarism. Since Tocqueville labeled us a nation of joiners in the nineteenth century, we have assumed that membership in voluntary organizations is an unmixed blessing for a democratic society. This paper will develop the argument that voluntary affiliation can produce results that are inimical to democratic, egalitarian values under certain conditions. One basic result of the analysis is that the structure of voluntary affiliation can lead to the formation and perpetuation of elitist acquaintance networks, if the system allows or promotes homogeneity (segregation) in the organizations. This result follows by deduction from a formal model of the structure of voluntary affiliation, when the model is informed by well established empirical generalizations. We begin by outlining a hyper-network model of the structure of affiliation; we then examine how the model relates to some of the major developments from the voluntary literature of the past two decades. Next, we see how the model clarifies the issues of inter-individual, inter-organizational, and community-level structure. Taking into account some well-known results on social class and affiliation reveals that the structure of voluntarism decreases the network distance between high-status individuals, and increases the distance between low-status persons, when organizational homogeneity is allowed. This result generalizes to the organizations themselves;

Author's Note. The author gratefully acknowledges the assistance of Nicholas Babchuk, Peter Blau, Ron Breiger, Bruce Mayhew, Dale Mesner, David Horton Smith, J. Allen Williams, and anonymous referees for their comments on earlier versions of this paper. Any remaining defects are the sole responsibility of the author.

high-status organizations will be located in a denser region of the network than low-status organizations. The paper concludes with some comments on the implications of size for the organizational structure of the system.

Our point of departure is a model suggested by Ronald Breiger (1974) which shows concisely the relationship between the individual and the voluntary organization. The core of the model is a matrix (M) in which rows represent individuals and columns represent organizations.[1] In order to visualize this model, imagine a matrix of N rows representing N individuals, and K columns representing the K organizations in the system. An entry of '1' in the ith row and jth column of the matrix indicates that the ith individual is a member of the jth organization. Zero entries indicate that the ith person is not a member of the jth organization. The ith row sum is the number of organizations belonged to by the ith person. The jth column sum is the size of the jth organization.

Matrix M completely describes the memberships of all individuals and all organizations in the community; however, the fine-grained detail makes it impossible to use directly in survey research, since information on all individuals and organizations is necessary to specify M^2. However, M gives us a useful way of thinking about the structure of affiliation, since it unambiguously describes the system. In particular, we can conceive of a survey research project that randomly samples individuals from M. An important issue then becomes, 'what inferences about the structure of M can we make from a probability sample of rows?' Looking at the problem this way, we see that we are engaged in (hyper-network sampling (McPherson, 1978; Granovetter, 1976). Since the majority of research on voluntary affiliations comes from survey sources, we need to develop some ideas about what it is possible to infer about this structure from survey data.

Anyone who has studied the voluntary association literature can see that M will consist mostly of zeros. This fact is a serious problem for people who are interested in the structure of voluntary affiliation, since the probability that any given person is a member of any given organization is very small even in small communities. As a result, research tends to focus either on the correlates of affiliation (Williams et al., 1973; Curtis, 1971; Olsen, 1970), or on a particular organization or set of organizations (Zald and Denton, 1963). In general, all studies of affiliation focus on some basic feature of M. The most commonly used feature of M is the mean of the row-sums, or the average rate of affiliation (Williams et al, 1973).[3] We can show that the mean affiliation rate is mathematically related to an important feature of the network of relationships on the community level. In order to do this, we need to point out some facts about inter-organizational structure.

INTER-ORGANIZATIONAL STRUCTURE

In the sociological and social-psychological literature the individual is often thought of as a point in a network of interaction (see for instance Mitchell, 1969; Rapoport and Horvath, 1961; White, 1973; Lorrain and White, 1971). In the sociometric literature individuals are usually points in a directed graph, which 'send' and 'receive' choices, and form cliques, coalitions, and other types of emergent organizations (Alba, 1973; Hubbell, 1965; Bonacich, 1972; Phillips and Conviser, 1972). However, to someone interested in inter-organizational structure, an individual is a potential link between organizations: the organization is the point in the net. Any person who belongs to more than one organization links these organizations together. As a result, the row-sums in M are crucial features of *M since an individual who possesses m memberships represents a junction of m organizations*. Thus, the row-sums of M determine the number of links among the organizations in the system. Figure 1 helps demonstrate this point. Each point in the figure is an organization; each line between two points represents a link between two organizations through an individual. As the figure shows, when an individual has two memberships (s)he generates one link between organizations. Three memberships, however, generate three links, the number of which is a strongly increasing function of N. It is important to keep in mind that linkages between organizations occur only through multiple memberships; no matter how many people or organizations are involved, only multiple memberships generate links. This point is crucial to an understanding of how we may infer structural characteristics from survey data.

Because of this relationship between multiple memberships and links, even moderate shifts in the distribution of memberships may cause drastic changes in the connections among organizations in a community. It is possible to calculate the total number of interconnections among organizations from information usually available

FIGURE 1

**The Number of Organizational Linkages Generated
by Each Individual with a Given Number of Memberships**

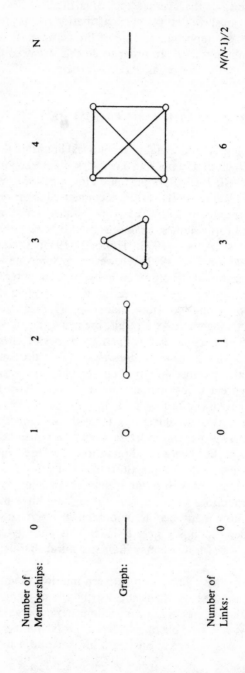

Number of Memberships:	0	1	2	3	4	N
Graph:						
Number of Links:	0	0	1	3	6	$N(N-1)/2$

from a survey design even without knowing the exact number of organizations. We can do this with information on the mean and variance of the row-sums of M — knowledge that is often available from secondary sources. In order to demonstrate this fact, we must first show how these connections relate to the mean participation rate.

We define a measure of the total number of inter-organizational links in a community,

$$L = \sum_{i=1}^{N} [m_i (m_i-1)] / 2 \qquad (1)$$

which is simply the sum of inter-organizational links for all individuals, where m_i is the number of memberships possessed by the ith individual (the ith row-sum of M). Now, using simple algebraic manipulation,

$$L = \frac{1}{2}\sum_{i=1}^{N} (m_i^2 - m_i) = \frac{1}{2}(\sum_{i=1}^{N} m_i^2 - \sum_{i=1}^{N} m_i) \qquad (2)$$

Since the sum of any variable is equal to N times the mean of the variable,

$$L = \frac{1}{2}(\sum_{i}^{N} m_i^2 - N_m) \qquad (3)$$

where m is the mean of the m_i (or the mean affiliation rate). Now, from a calculating formula for the variance of a variable,

$$\delta_m^2 = \sum_{i=1}^{N} \frac{(m_i - \bar{m})^2}{N} \text{ or } \sum_{i=1}^{N} m_i^2 = N(\delta_m^2 + \bar{m}^2) \qquad (4)$$

Therefore,

$$L = \frac{1}{2}N(\delta_m^2 + \bar{m}^2 - \bar{m}), \qquad (5)$$

and L is clearly shown to be a simple function of the mean and variance of affiliation.

A study of eight different studies of voluntary affiliation shows that high mean rates of affiliation are accompanied by high variances. In general, the variance in participation tends to equal or slightly exceed the mean in every instance examined (Almond and Verba, 1968; Babchuk and Booth, 1969). This fact implies that the variance (δ_m^2) and the mean ($\bar{m}$) will tend to cancel out of equation (5), leaving L as a function of the square of the mean.[4] Thus, the number of linkages between organizations will tend to be a simple function of the number of people in the community and the square of the mean participation rate. Clearly, L is a strongly increasing function of $\bar{m}$.

There are some important implications of this relationship between the mean affiliation rate and the number of inter-organizational links. A fundamental theme in the voluntary association literature is the hypothesis that voluntary organizations integrate the community in a variety of ways (Babchuk and Edwards, 1965; Litwak, 1961). One way that organizations can integrate the community is by binding the individuals together in a system of formal relationships, through voluntary affiliation. Clearly, the extent to which these organizations are connected to each other is another form of integration; L measures this type of integration. Notice that, since L is definitely, but non-linearly, related to $\bar{m}$, it is clear that past research on voluntary affiliation which discusses differences in $\bar{m}$ and closely related quantities has missed the opportunity to make comparisons of a clearly structural nature (Antunes and Gaitz, 1975, Axelrod, 1956; Babchuk and Booth, 1969; Babchuk and Thompson, 1962; Bell and Force, 1956; Booth, 1972; Curtis, 1971; Erbe, 1964; Freedman, Novak, and Reeder, 1957; Hagedorn and Labovitz, 1967; Olsen, 1970; Orum, 1966; Scott, 1957). That is, a given difference in $\bar{m}$ will imply quite different conclusions about the connectedness of the system of organizations, depending on the absolute level of $\bar{m}$.

We can demonstrate how structural comparisons are relevant to the current literature by referring to the extensive argument over whether members of the black minority in the United States have a higher or lower mean affiliation rate than the majority (Wright and Hyman, 1958; Orum, 1966; Olsen, 1970; Williams et al., 1973). (Significantly, no attention is paid in this debate to the question of the racial exclusivity of the organizations involved — an obviously important feature from the network point of view.) This recent research in the voluntary literature has given lip service to the study of structural integration through the use of such concepts as 'cohesiveness,' 'ethnic community,' and the like. However, the tools used to investigate these (possibly) structural properties have been simply aggregated individual characteristics, such as the mean rate of affiliation, or some variation on the mean (Williams et al., 1973; Antunes and Gaitz, 1975).

Now, using equation (5), it is possible to calculate the number of connections among the organizations of different social aggregates such as ethnicities, sexes, and classes. Table 1 presents such an example from Williams et al. (1973). Comparing the affiliations means with the linkages per person, we see that the differences among the categories are dramatically enhanced by considering linkages per person. If we consider these linkages to occur among ethnically disjoint organizational systems (an assumption that would be quite interesting to test were the resources available), then clearly the organizations of blacks are connected more densely than those of Anglos or Mexican Americans, ceteris paribus. (As we discuss more extensively later in the paper, an extremely important part of this ceteris paribus is the size distribution of the organizations in the different systems.) Clearly, the Mexican American system is almost unconnected, considering either linkages per person or linkages per member. As the linkages per member row suggests, a typical male Mexican-American organization of size 100 would have only 16 ties with other organizations, while a typical male black organization would have 68 such ties. While we do not have information on the exact distribution of these linkages among organizations, it is clear that some of the Mexican-American organizations will be virtually unconnected in the organizational system, while the black organizations appear to have a wealth of connections to other organizations. Clearly, one would expect the black community to be better equipped to deal with circumstances requiring inter-organizational coordination than either the white or the Mexican-American community.

The question of the character of the organizations linked by multiple memberships is an important topic, which will be addressed in subsequent papers. An example of a question that might be addressed using this framework would be: 'How centrally located are church-related (or any other type of) organizations in the black community versus the white community?' Thus, using our formal model of affiliation, one could answer explicit questions about the internal structure of the voluntary systems of different social aggregates, and make useful comparisons across systems. I think that

TABLE 1
Affiliation and Inter-organizational Linkages in
Voluntary Associations by Ethnicity and Sex

	Black		Anglo		Mexican-American	
	M	F	M	F	M	F
Mean	1.364	2.013	1.077	0.560	0.325	0.370
Linkages/person	0.930	2.026	0.580	0.157	0.053	0.068
Linkages/member	0.682	1.006	0.539	0.280	0.162	0.185

Source: Williams et al. (1973, p. 641).

this approach is more likely to yield interesting insight into the voluntary process than are the series of arguments about who has the highest rate of affiliation that are found in much of the literature. We now turn to one of the most reliable findings in survey research: the correlation between affiliation and social class.

ORGANIZATIONAL OVERLAP AND SOCIAL CLASS

The problem of organizational overlap has been addressed principally through the analysis of 'interlocking directorates' (Allen, 1974; Mariolis, 1975; Soref, 1976) and common leadership (Turk, 1970). The model we develop here is not restricted to leaders of organizations: all members are considered.[5] We will now show that organizational overlap is powerfully affected by the correlation between social class and number of memberships. This correlation is one of the most widely replicated findings in social science. Beginning with the early community studies (Lynd and Lynd, 1929; Warner, 1941), through the 1950s (Axelrod, 1956; Scott, 1957), and to the present (Gove and Costner, 1969; Williams et al., 1973), there has existed a highly reliable association between SES and the number of memberships reported. This relationship is known to exist in other societies as well (Curtis, 1971; Almond and Verba, 1963). What has not been realized is that the class differential may have a cumulative 'multiplier effect' on the individual through the characteristics of the organizations themselves. This multiplier effect occurs through a tendency of organizations to be homogeneous.

Very early in the research on voluntary association, it was noted that there is a tendency for organizations to be class-homogeneous (Lynd and Lynd, 1929; Warner, 1941). In fact, this tendency is so pronounced that organizational membership was sometimes used as one of the criteria for establishing an individual's status (Lynd and Lynd, 1929). Since no modern data are available on the homogeneity of a representative sample of voluntary associations in a well-defined community system, we will develop a simulation of the effects of differing levels of homogeneity on overlap, given reasonable values of other parameters governing the system. As we will see, the effect of homogeneity on overlap is very strong.

The first and most obvious feature that affects the amount of overlap between two given organizations is organizational size. Clearly, the greater the number of members, the greater the possibilities for common members with other organizations. Given this definitional relationship, the most efficient strategy is to isolate a given size organization, and examine the effects of homogeneity upon overlap at that given size. We select size 30 as a reasonable figure, based on a review of the (very imprecise) literature on the topic (Laskin, 1961; Newton, 1975). This strategy is made all the more reasonable by the fact that organizational size can affect the number of linkages with other organizations only through the number of other memberships of the members. That is, for our given organization of size 30, the number of linkages for that organization with other organizations will be determined solely by the number of other memberships each member holds. Given this fact, we can limit our attention to the members of our hypothetical organization of size 30; the characteristics of the remainder of the community will not enter into the problem. Thus, if the 30 members belong to a total of 50 other organizations, our organization is linked to those 50 other (not necessarily distinct) organizations. It is easy to see that the connections of a given organization will be heavily dependent upon the class makeup of its members, since high SES members will tend to belong to more other organizations.

Clearly a high SES member of an organization will tend to add more linkages between organizations than a low SES person, since high SES individuals tend to have more multiple memberships. Figure 2 gives the result of varying mixtures of low and high SES

FIGURE 2
The Effect of Organizational
Homogeneity Upon Linkages

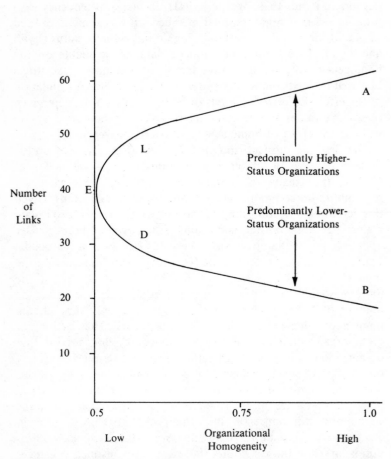

Source: Babchuk and Booth (1969). Values along horizontal axes are probabilities of randomly chosen pairs of members having the same social status (Greenberg, 1956). The upper part of the curve represents predominantly upper-status organizations, while the lower part represents lower-status organizations. See text for details.

persons in a hypothetical organization of size 30.[6] The organizations at the top half of the curve are predominantly high-status, while the organizations at the lower half of the curve are lower-status. The most important feature of Figure 2 is the effect of organizational homogeneity. Homogeneity increases the disparity between organizations. For instance, organizations A and B (high homogeneity) have a much greater disparity in number of links than organizations C and D. When organizations are hetero-geneous (E), they will tend to have the same number of links with other organizations at a given size level.

One clear implication of this strong relationship between homogeneity and variability in overlap is that communities with ex-clusive (homogeneous) organizations will tend to have organiza-tions that differ greatly in their centrality. That is, when homogeneity is high, there will be greater differentiation among organizations with respect to the number of links to other organiza-tions. In addition, the links generated for high-status organizations will tend to be with other high-status organizations, thus enhancing the ability of such organizations to mobilize support, gather infor-mation, etc. Conversely, low-status organizations will have fewer links to other organizations, and what links exist will typically in-volve other low-status organizations of equally low 'centrality' (Harary et al. 1965).

It is easy to see that rigid status exclusivity of organizations could be a powerful tool for the maintenance of privilege in society; given strong homogeneity, even mild status-linked differences in number of memberships will multiply the advantages of status — through the greater ability of high-status organizations to mobilize other organizations through their interconnections. Clearly, the flow of information from organization to organization is facilitated for high-status organizations and hindered for low-status organiza-tions. In addition, since the other organizations linked to high-status organizations will tend also to be of high status, the cumulative advantage is increased. Thus, the facts that the network of interrelationships among organizations has more connections at higher status values, and that the individuals 'reachable' (Harary, 1965) through these connections have greater resources, produce a multiplicative advantage of affiliation for high-status individuals. The structural consequences of homogeneity, then, are a magnification of the advantages of high status and the disadvan-tages of low status.

This discussion leads us to several additional interesting results. First, any variable that is related to number of memberships and that may be a basis for organizational exclusivity will produce these differences in the connectedness of organizations, and may thus affect the ability of the 'disadvantaged' organization to mobilize the support of other organizations. Examples of exclusivity based on ethnicity and sex have become the subject of much publicity in the popular press recently. Our results show that limiting access to voluntary organizations has very powerful network consequences for the structure of the system; allowing segregation may lead to a magnification of class, racial, and sexual differences through the operation of the voluntary sector.

Another interesting result of our reasoning is that cross-racial comparisons of voluntary affiliation rates should be made without controlling for social class under some circumstances. In particular, if the research is concerned with community-level phenomena such as the ability of the black community to mobilize itself through its organizations, then adjusting affiliation rates for social class will produce a distorted picture of differences between the black and Anglo communities. This result occurs because social class is differentially distributed across race; controlling for social class 'equalizes' the distribution of social class across the two systems, destroying our picture of the actual structural integration of the systems. Given these facts, controlling for class at the individual level will seriously distort relationships at the structural level. Indeed, recent results suggest that class is not related to affiliation similarly for blacks and whites even at the individual level (McPherson, 1977).

Another interesting insight from the model is that each additional membership for a high-status individual produces more interconnections between organizations than each additional membership produces for a low-status person. This result is a logical consequence of the fact that a person with m_i memberships, who adds a membership, adds m_i new linkages to the network (see equation (1)). Thus a given increment in increased affiliation produces more connections in the high-status network than the low-status network, since there is a higher rate of affiliation in the high-status sector to begin with. Attempts to increase the ability of low-status communities to organize themselves (Zurcher, 1970; Curtis and Zurcher, 1971) thus face greater obstacles than would similar attempts in higher-status communities. A given increase in the average number of memberships necessarily produces a much greater impact in high-status areas than in low-status areas because of the nonlinear relationship between m and L. Thus, effective inter-organizational coordination is likely to be more problematic in low-status areas for structural reasons, in addition to the previously understood interpersonal obstacles (Zurcher, 1970; Gove and Costner, 1969). Our results also suggest that minority separatist movements are likely to be counterproductive, unless they possess superior resources or unless the advantages of heightened intra-community communication outweigh the disadvantages of access to the high-status network of the dominant system.

WEAK TIES AND THE SMALL WORLD PROBLEM

There has been an increase lately in research on the individual-level consequences of micro-social organization. For instance, Granovetter (1974) outlines some effects of 'weak ties' on the individual's chances of obtaining employment. His research shows that chains of weak ties produce many of the actual contacts through which people get jobs. Similarly Boissevain (1974) studies the ways in which indirect linkages between individuals exert powerful and pervasive influences on society. Looking at chains of acquaintances from a quantitative point of view, Milgram (1967) shows that the number of links necessary to tie randomly chosen individuals together is surprisingly short, at least for white males in the United States (see Korte and Milgram, 1970; White, 1970). As we have already seen, common membership in voluntary associations is one form of weak tie. Let us examine how information on common memberships in voluntary organizations gives us insight into the structure of the weak-tie network.

Our strategy will be to simulate the impact of class homogeneity upon the weak-tie network (one-and two-step ties). In generating a simulation of the weak-tie network at the individual level, we need to make several assumptions. First, we must assume that no systematic size differences in organizations exist across different levels of social class. This assumption is quite important, as can be seen from the basic equation for two-step ties:

$$I^{(2)} = \sum_{i=1}^{m} \sum_{j=1}^{S_{i\text{-}1}} \sum_{l=1}^{m_{ij}\text{-}1} S_{ijl} \tag{6}$$

where $I^{(2)}$ indicates the sum of links between ego and the person in the system at network distance two, m is the number of memberships ego possesses, S_i is the size of the ith organization of ego's m memberships, m_{ij} is the number of memberships possessed by the jth person in ego's ith organization, and S_{ijl} is the size of the ith organization belonged to by the jth person in ego's lth organization. Equation (6) is basically a counting algorithm which allows us to enumerate the number of people who belong to organizations that are belonged to by other members of ego's organizations.[7] Clearly the size of these organizations is a dominant aspect of equation (6), since it appears in two different places in the expression. If sizes vary systematically across individuals, then. $I^{(2)}$ will vary strongly with the differences. Thus, more information on the correlates of organizational size is very desirable; further empirical research in this area is necessary. The assumption of equal sizes for organizations generates the following modification of equation (6):

$$I^{(2)} = m\ (S\text{-}1) \sum_{L=1}^{m_{ij}^{-1}} (S\text{-}1) \tag{7}$$

where $m(S\text{-}1)$ represents the number of one-step links for ego, since (s)he belongs to m organizations of size S.

We now wish to incorporate the information that m varies systematically with social class. To do this, we introduce variability in m, according to the level of education (an indicator of SES) possessed by ego:

$$I^{(2)} = m_E\ (S\text{-}1) \sum_{L=1}^{m_{ij}^{-1}} (S\text{-}1) \tag{8}$$

where m_E is the number of memberships characteristic of persons at a given level of education. Note that while equation (6) expresses the exact number of two-step ties for ego, equation (8) refers to a 'typical' person at a given level of education. If we are further willing to assume that the number of affiliations of those to whom ego is linked are typical of all persons in the system, the following equation results:

$$I^{(2)} = \bar{m}_E (S-1) (\bar{m}-1) (S-1) \tag{9}$$

where $\bar{m}$ is the expectation of $\bar{m}$ across all individuals. It turns out that this last assumption is equivalent to the assumption of heterogeneity in membership rates across organizations. That is, if $\bar{m}$ is representative of affiliation rates for all organizations, then there is representative variability in memberships for all organizations. We may introduce homogeneity with respect to social class by allowing $\bar{m}$ to vary with education:

$$I^{(2)} = \bar{m}_E (S-1) (\bar{m}_E-1) (S-1) \tag{10}$$

In equation (10), the other members of ego's organizations are of the same level of SES as ego, and thus tend to have the same number of memberships. A comparison of equations (9) and (10) at observed levels of $\bar{m}_E$ should allow us to compare the weak-tie system for ego under varying conditions of heterogeneity.[8]

Figure 3 shows the results of applying equations (9) and (10) to data relating education and number of memberships from a probability sample of Nebraska residents (Babchuk and Booth, 1969; Lockwood, 1976). The one-step ties increase linearly with education, while the effect of education is much larger for two-step ties under heterogeneity. The effects of education are magnified geometrically when status homogeneity is introduced. Homogeneity produces a drastic increase in the difference between high- and low-status individuals; in fact, the number of ties for low-education individuals is actually decreased, while the number for high-education is increased disproportionately.

The tremendous effect of homogeneity at the individual level demonstrates the force that exclusivity can exert toward inequality in society. With the weak-tie function accelerating so rapidly at the higher levels of status, it is clear that the system is likely to be 'saturated' at the upper end no matter what the size of the system. Thus, we would expect that the effects of homogeneity, combined with differential affiliation, will produce an elite[9] whose members are very close to each other in network distance, or 'mean number

FIGURE 3
The Number of Weak Ties Generated
by Given Levels of Education

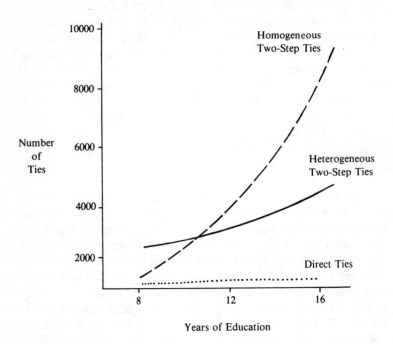

Years of Education

N.B. Ties are the number of persons linked to an individual through common membership in voluntary organizations of assumed size 30 (see text). The equations for the heterogeneous and homogeneous linkages are, respectively, $I^2 = m_e$ (S-1) (S-1) and $I^2 = m_e$ (S-1) $(m_e$-1) (S-1), where I^2 refers to the number of ties, m_e *is the mean number of memberships in the given category of education,* m is the overall mean, and S is the average size of organizations (30 by assumption). The equations for I^2 and I^2 are exact only for exact m and S, although the general relationships hold under varying m and S. See note 7. Date on education and affiliation rates are from Lockwood (1976).

of steps' (Beshers and Laumann, 1967) regardless of the size of the community. This force toward elite formation would be multiplied when there are multiple grounds for exclusivity. The image of the white Anglo-Saxon Protestant male (Baltzell, 1966) is often invoked in sociology, although the compounding effect shown here has not been understood previously.[10]

While Granovetter (1974) shows that three-step ties are often important in obtaining employment, Figure 3 does not present such information because of scale difficulties. Clearly, however, three-step (and *N*-step) ties are similarly affected by a combination of social class and class homogeneity.

The correlation of social class and affiliation thus produces smaller network distances between high-status individuals than low-status individuals. Class homogeneity produces a strong magnification of this effect. However, it is possible that features of the detailed structure of this network could increase or decrease the distance between two individuals of similar status. For instance, ethnic cleavages could be expected to produce local clique structure in the network, which would increase the distance between individuals of unlike ethnicity and decrease the distance between persons of similar ethnicity. These factors are conceptually similar to social class in their effects on the network; all variables such as race, class, etc. are exogenous variables that may affect distance in the network. If these variables are correlated with affiliation, they affect the number of weak ties available to the individual. If the variable is a basis for organizational homogeneity, it will decrease the network distance between similar individuals. If the variable fits both conditions, both effects will be multiplicatively magnified, as shown in Figure 3. Thus, the results of Figure 3 may be generalized to a class of exogenous variables that are likely to be correlated either with affiliation or exclusivity, or both. We turn now to a consideration of another parameter, the density of the network.

ORGANIZATIONAL SIZE AND DENSITY

The density of a network is conventionally measured by the ratio of the observed number of links to the number theoretically possible. A typical (Barnes, 1969) formula would be

$$D_I = L_I / [\frac{N(N-1)}{2}] \tag{11}$$

where D_I is the individual-level density, L_I is the number of linkages between individuals, and N is the number of individuals.

However, the network of linkages between organizations in our case is different from an ordinary network, as shown earlier. In particular, any two organizations may be linked by up to N ties, since it is theoretically possible for everyone in the system to belong to a given two organizations. Thus, the logical upper limit to the number of links between K organizations is

$$L_{\text{upper}} = N \left[\frac{K(K-1)}{2}\right]. \tag{12}$$

This upper limit occurs when everyone in the system belongs to all organizations. In this case each of the N persons contributes $[K(K-1)]/2$ links to the system. In this unlikely event matrix M would have all non-zero entries.

Now, knowing the logical limit to L, we can define a measure of density for the (hyper-) network of organizational interconnections:

$$D_0 = L / L_{\text{upper}} = \left\{ \sum^{N} \frac{[m_i(m_i-1)]}{2} \right\} / \left\{ \frac{N[K(K-1)]}{2} \right\} \tag{13}$$

where D_0 refers to the density of organizational interconnections, and L is defined by equation (1). Clearly, the number of organizations (K) powerfully affects the measure of density, since the square of K appears in the denominator. Thus, the greater the number of organizations, the less the density of their interconnections, ceteris paribus.

Now, we define a measure for the total number (T) of memberships in the system:

$$T = \sum_{i=1}^{N} m_i \tag{14}$$

where m_i is the number of memberships for the ith individual. The average size of an organization can be written in terms of the total number of memberships and the total number of organizations:

$$\overline{S} = T/K \tag{15}$$

where S refers to the average size of an organization.

Definitionally, S and K are inversely related; that is, the greater the average size of organizations, the fewer there will be, given a constant volume of memberships. Since S is inversely related to K (equation (15)) and K is inversely related to D_0 (equation (13)), it follows that the density of interconnections between organizations is directly related to their average size. That is, the larger the organizations in the system, the greater the density of their interconnections, ceteris paribus. Figure 3 was calculated on the basis of organizations of constant size 30. From equations (6)-(10), it is clear that the number of two-step ties between individuals in the system increases exponentially with S. Thus, the 'average network distance', in the sense of the average number of links necessary to connect two people in the system, depends upon the size[11] of the organizations (or their total number), the average rate of affiliation (or the total number of memberships), and the total number of people in the system, as well as the homogeneity of the organizations. Therefore, the integration of the community — a major theoretical function of voluntary associations — depends not only upon the rate of affiliation in the community, as is assumed in a massive amount of research, but also upon the manner in which the affiliation is distributed among organizations and individuals. Obviously, fine-grained features of the network such as divisions along race or ethnic lines will affect the integration of the community,[12] but it is clear that as gross a feature as average organizational size can exert a strong influence upon the structural relationships among organizations, and the consequent ability of the system to coordinate its actions.

The shape of the distribution of organizational size is likely to exert effects upon the ability of the system to coordinate activities also. A relatively 'flat' distribution, in which most organizations are equal in size, suggests roughly equal access of organizations to information and other resources, ceteris paribus.[13] Conversely, drastic size differences in a sector[14] of the voluntary system would suggest dominance relationships among organizations similar to those found among business organizations. Without solid evidence on the matter, we would expect to find a 'flatter' distribution of organizational sizes in the voluntary system than in the business system because of the diversity of interests and activities carried on in the former.[15]

In general, there are a large number of size-related variables which may mediate the effects of a given rate of affiliation in a community. These variables, such as average size and the shape of the distribution of sizes, have been largely ignored in published research, and they are nowhere systematically linked to rates of affiliation and homogeneity in background characteristics of members.[16] We predict that a systematic comparison of these characteristics across communities, ethnicities, and other salient divisions will produce substantial progress in voluntary association theory.

SUMMARY AND CONCLUSIONS

I have argued that it is important to look at the membership structure of voluntary affiliation, because this structure has important individual-level and community-level effects. Our model has uncovered some hitherto unnoticed consequences of organizational size and organizational homogeneity. Organizational homogeneity results in a cumulative advantage for high-status individuals and organizations, and it is an obstacle to coordination for low-status organizations. Thus, organizational homogeneity based upon any variable that is correlated with the rate of affiliation will tend to promote inequality in access to information, to individuals, and to other organizations, for both organizations and individuals.

The effects of organizational size are just as powerful as those of homogeneity, but their full evaluation would require presently unavailable data. Since we do not know whether known exogenous variables such as ethnicity or class are correlated with size, we are unable to evaluate the impact of size upon current theories that use these variables. I hope that one effect of this paper will be to sensitize researchers on voluntary participation to structural factors such as overlap, size, and homogeneity, which may have powerful consequences for the relationships in which they are interested. Another goal of this paper has been to point out that voluntary affiliations, like many other characteristics of society, may have consequences that are not always supportive of egalitarian values.

NOTES

1. This system is a 'hypergraph' (Berge, 1976), which is a relatively new development in the mathematical literature. The present application of the model is to the nominal membership structure of the community. Some writers (Smith, 1972) have discussed the implications of different definitions and levels of affiliation. The model could be adapted to varying levels of affilation by allowing values other than zero and one in the matrix.

2. If we could actually obtain M, we could apply some simple matrix operations to arrive at some very interesting information. For instance, MM^T (M post-multiplied by its transpose) would give us a matrix with the sizes of all K organizations on the diagonal, and the number of members common to the ith and jth organizations off the diagonal. Similarly, M^TM would give us the number of organizations common to the ith and jth individuals. Standard sociometric techniques could be applied to MM^T and M^TM to investigate the clique structure of the community in terms of both individuals and organizations.

3. Often, the use of mean affiliation is disguised since it is used as the dependent variable in a regression analysis (Olsen, 1970; Erbe, 1964).

4. In fact, McPherson (1980) shows that the mean tends to equal the variance for affiliation when the effects of background factors are removed. This fact leads to the equation $L = \bar{m}^2(N/2)$.

5. From the system point of view, the interaction produced by joint participation in organizations is a form of behavior that sociologists have been interested in since the early part of the century (Simmel, 1922; Wirth, 1938; Milgram, 1970; Mayhew and Levinger, 1976). Clearly, there is a substantial probabilistic component in the extent of face-to-face interaction in associations, and thus in the amount of direct contact generated by common membership. The likelihood of interpersonal interaction and coaction (Zajonc, 1966) is increased by common membership in voluntary associations. I would also argue that the probability of joint action and cooperation by the organizations themselves is affected by organizational overlap (Coleman, 1957; Rose, 1954).

6. Figure 2 was created by mixing high- and low-status individuals in the hypothetical organization of size 30. The high-status individuals were assigned a mean number of memberships of 3.0, which corresponds to the mean affiliation rate of those with at least a high school degree in the data of Babchuk and Booth (1969). The low-status (less than high school graduates) persons had a mean number of memberships of 1.65, from the same data. Thus, an organization of all high-status persons generates 60 links, since the number of links generated by n people is $\Sigma(m_i - 1) = n(\bar{m} - 1)$. The number of links for any mix of persons in the organization is easily obtained by varying n and m accordingly.

7. Equation (6) does not rule out certain types of redundancies. For instance, if ego belongs to organizations A and B, both whom are belonged to by alter, then alter's other memberships are counted as two-step links twice. In fact, since ego is counted as among the members of alters second organization, the link from ego to alter to ego is counted.

8. The equations produced by both the homogeneous (equation (10)) and heterogeneous (equation (9)) cases may underestimate equation (6), since $\Sigma\ XY = N\bar{X}\bar{Y} + N$ covariance $(X,\ Y)$. Equation (10) is like the lefthand side of the above expression, and equation (6) is like the first term on the right-hand side. These two quantities will not be equal in general unless m and S are uncorrelated (have zero covariance). However, there is no a priori reason to expect such a correlation; research on the topic would clearly be useful.

9. Note that I speak of an elite in terms of a 'high potential for control' and a 'high potential for unit Y.' I do not wish to enter the debate on community power structure by arguing that high-status individuals necessarily constitute a power elite in Dahl's sense. What we wish to show is that low-status individuals are necessarily disadvantaged relative to high-status persons, given the present structure of voluntary affiliation. The question of whether or not the same individuals make all important decisions in a given system we must leave to researchers with more detailed information on local structure than I currently possess.

10. Laumann (1966, 1973) suggests that heterogeneity in acquaintances per se may be advantageous.

11. Other features of the size distribution of organizations might prove to be important, such as the variance, analogously to the individual-level equation (5). Since much research has been performed on the size distribution of business firms (Collins, 1973; Quandt, 1966), it might be possible to apply models from that literature to voluntary associations. However, this possibility must await further research.

12. If size is correlated with any of these variables, the effect will be to increase density for some values of the variable and decrease density at other values. Thus, if the average size of organizations is larger in the black community, the density of interconnections will be even greater than that already implied by the well-known greater affiliation rate among blacks. Of course, the converse could be true, in which case much of the current research in the area will need to be reassessed.

13. Obviously, status heterogeneity is a crucial part of the ceteris paribus assumption in this discussion.

14. A sector of the voluntary organization system could be defined along functional lines (i.e. 'expressive' vs 'instrumental' or along activity dimensions (i.e. 'sports' vs 'professional', etc.)).

15. There is a substantial literature on size distributions of a wide range of phenomena (Zipf, 1949; Simon, 1957; Mandelbrot, 1952; Collins, 1974). It will be necessary to obtain better data on the size of voluntary organizations before analogous progress can be made in the voluntary sector. Most available data on the distribution of voluntary organizational size for complete systems use such gross categorizations as to be useless for our purposes (see Laskin, 1961), or tend to be incomplete enumerations (Klonglan et al., 1969; Newton, 1975).

16. Preliminary results from a study of organizational size suggest that a major correlate of organizational size is community size. Organization size appears to nearly double in the community size range 500 to 500,000 (McPherson, 1978).

REFERENCES

ABERBACK, Joel D. (1969) 'Alienation and Political Behavior,' *American Political Science Review*, 63 (March): 86-9.

ALBA, Richard D. (1973) 'A Graph-Theoretic Definition of a Sociometric Clique,' *Journal of Mathematical Sociology*, 3(1):113-26.

ALLEN, Michael (1974) 'The Structure of Interorganizational Elite Cooptation: Interlocking Corporate Directorates,' *American Sociological Review*, 39 (June):393-406.

ALMOND, G. A. and Sidney VERBA (1963) *The Civic Culture*. Princeton: Princeton University Press.

ALMOND, G. A. and Sidney VERBA (1968) *The Five Nation Study*. Interuniversity Consortium for Political Research.

ANTUNES, George and Charles GAITZ (1975) 'Ethnicity and Participation: A Study of Mexican-Americans, Blacks, and Whites,' *American Journal of Sociology*, 80 (March): 1192-211.

AXELROD, Morris (1956) 'Urban Structure and Social Participation,' *American Sociological Review*, 21 (February):13-19.

BABCHUK, Nicholas and J. N. EDWARDS (1965) 'Voluntary Associations and the Integration Hypothesis,' *Sociological Inquiry*, 35:149-62.

BABCHUK, Nicholas and Alan BOOTH (1969) 'Voluntary Association Membership: A Longitudinal Analysis,' *American Sociological Review*, 34 (February): 31-45.

BABCHUK, Nicholas and R. V. THOMPSON (1962) 'Voluntary Association of Negroes,' *American Sociological Review*, 27 (October): 647-55.

BALTZELL, E. Digby (1966) 'Who's Who in America and "The Social Register",' pp. 266-75 in Reinhard Bendix and Seymour Martin (eds), *Class, Status and Power: Social Stratification in Comparative Perspective*. New York: Free Press.

BARNES, J. A. (1969) 'Networks and Political Process,' pp. 51-76 in J. C. Mitchell (ed.), *Social Networks in Urban Situations* Manchester: University Press.

BELL, Wendell and M. T. FORCE (1956) 'Social Structure and Participation in Different Types of Formal Associations,' *Social Forces*, 34 (May): 345-50.

BERGE, Claude (1976) *Graphs and Hypergraphs*. Amsterdam: North-Holland.

BESHERS, J. M. and E. O. LAUMANN (1967) 'Social Distance: A Network Approach,' *American Sociological Review*, 32(2): 225-76.

BOISSEVAIN, J. (1974) *Friends of Friends*. London: Blackwell.

BONACICH, Phillip (1972) 'A Technique for Analyzing Overlapping Group Memberships,' Chapter 5 in H. L. Costner (ed.), *Sociological Methodology*. San Francisco: Jossey-Bass.

BOOTH, Alan (1972) 'Sex and Social Participation,' *American Sociological Review*, 37 (April): 183-92.

BREIGER, R. L. (1974) 'The Duality of Persons and Groups,' *Social Forces*, 53, 2 (December): 181-89.

COLEMAN, James S. (1957) *Community Conflict*: New York: Free Press.

COLLINS, Lyndhurst (1973) 'Industrial Size Distributions and Stochastic Processes,' *Progress in Geography*, 5: 121-65.

COLLINS, Lyndhurst (1974) 'Estimating Markov Transition Probabilities from Micro-Unit Data,' *Applied Statistics*, 23(3): 355-71.

CURTIS, James (1971) 'Voluntary Association Joining: A Cross National Note,' *American Sociological Review*, 36 (5): 872-80.

CURTIS, Russell L. and Louis A. ZURCHER (1971) 'Voluntary Associations and the Social Integration of the Poor,' *Social Problems*, 18 (Winter): 339-57.

CUTLER, Stephen J. (1976) 'Age Differences in Voluntary Association Memberships,' *Social Forces*, 55, 1:43-58.

ERBE, Williams (1964) 'Social Involvement and Political Activity: Another View,' *American Sociological Review*, 29 (April): 198-215.

FREEDMAN, Howard, E. NOVAK and Leo G. REEDER (1957) 'Correlates of Membership in Voluntary Associations,' *American Sociological Review*, 22:528-33.

GORDON, C. Wayne and Nicholas BABCHUK (1959) 'A Typology of Voluntary Associations,' *American Sociological Review* 24 (February): 22-9.

GOVE, W. R. and H. L. COSTNER (1969) 'Organizing the Poor: An Evaluation of a Research Strategy,' *Social Science Quarterly*, 50 (December): 643-56.

GRANOVETTER, Mark (1973) 'The Strength of Weak Ties,' *American Journal of Sociology*, 78 (May): 1360-380.

GRANOVETTER, Mark (1974) *Getting a Job: A Study of Contacts and Careers.* Cambridge, Mass.: Harvard University Press.

GRANOVETTER, Mark (1976) 'Network Sampling: Some First Steps,' *American Journal of Sociology*, 81(6):1287-303.

GREENBERG, Joseph (1956) 'The Measurement of Linguistic Diversity,' *Language*, 32 (January-March): 109-15.

HAGEDORN, R. and S. LABOVITZ (1967) 'An Analysis of Community and Professional Participation among Occupations,' *Social Forces*, 46 (June): 482-91.

HARARY, Frank, Robert Z. NORMAN, and Dorwin CARTWRIGHT (1965) *Structural Models: An Introduction to the Theory of Directed Graphs.* New York: John Wiley.

HUBBELL, Charles H. (1965) 'An Input-Output Approach to Clique Identification,' *Sociometry*, 28 (December): 377-99.

JACOBY, Arthur P. (1965) 'Some Correlates of Instrumental and Expressive Voluntary Associations,' *Sociology and Social Research*, 47 (June): 461-71.

KLONGLAN, G. E., D. A. DILLMAN, O. A. COLLVER, and P. YARBROUGH (1969) 'Determinants of Membership Linkages Among Women's Voluntary Organizations,' paper presented at the Rural Sociological Society Meetings, San Francisco, California.

KORTE, Charles and Stanley MILGRAM (1970) 'Acquaintance Networks Between Racial Groups,' *Journal of Personality and Social Psychology*, 15 (June): 101-08.

LASKIN, Richard (1961) *Organizations in a Saskatchewan Town.* Research Division, Center for Community Studies, University of Saskatchewan, Saskatoon, Canada.

LAUMANN, Edward O. (1966) *Prestige and Association in an Urban Community.* Indianapolis: Bobbs-Merrill.

LAUMANN, Edward O. (1973) *Bonds of Pluralism*. New York: John Wiley/Interscience.

LAUMANN, E. O. and Louis GUTTMAN (1966) 'The Relative Associational Contiguity of Occupations in an Urban Setting,' *American Sociological Review*, 31 (April): 169-78.

LIEBERSON, Stanley (1969) 'Measuring Population Diversity,' *American Sociological Review*, 34 (December): 850-62.

LITWAK, Eugene (1961) 'Voluntary Associations and Neighborhood Cohesion,' *American Sociological Review*, 26 (April): 258-71.

LOCKWOOD, W. A. (1976) *The Longitudinal Study of Voluntary Association Memberships: A Multivariate Analysis*. Master's thesis, University of Nebraska, Lincoln.

LORRAIN, F. and Harrison C. WHITE (1971) 'Structural Equivalence of Individuals in Social Networks,' *Journal of Mathematical Sociology*, 1:47-80.

LYND, Robert and Helen M. LYND (1929) *Middletown*. New York: Harcourt.

MANDELBROT, B. (1952) 'An Information Theory of the Structure of Language Based Upon the Theory of the Statistics Matching of Messages and Coding,' in Willis Jackson (ed.), *Communication Theory*. London: Butterworth.

MARIOLIS, Peter (1975) 'Interlocking Directorates and the Control of Corporations: The Theory of Bank Control,' *Social Science Quarterly*, 56 (3):425-39.

MATRAS, Judah (1975) 'Models and Indicators of Organizational Growth, Changes and Transformations,' chapter 11 in Kenneth C. Land and S. Spilerman (eds), *Social Indicator Models*. New York: Russell Sage Foundation.

MAYHEW, Bruce M. (1973) 'System Size and Ruling Elites,' *American Sociological Review*, 38 (August): 468-75.

MAYHEW, Bruce M. and R. L. LEVINGER (1976) 'Size and the Density of Interaction in Social Aggregates,' *American Journal of Sociology*, 82 (July): 86-110.

McPHERSON, J. Miller (1977) 'Correlates of Social Participation: A Comparison of the Ethnic Community and Compensatory Theories,' *Sociological Quarterly*, 18: 197-208.

McPHERSON, J. Miller (1978) 'Hypernetwork Sampling: Estimating Parameters Governing the Structure of Voluntary Affiliation,' paper read at the 1978 Annual Meetings of the American Sociological Association, San Francisco.

MILGRAM, Stanley (1967) 'The Small World Problem,' *Psychology Today*, 1:61-7.

MILGRAM, Stanley (1970) 'The Experience of Living in Cities,' *Science*, 167: 1461-8.

MITCHELL, J. Clyde (ed.) (1969) *Social Networks in Urban Situations*. Manchester: University Press.

NEWTON, Kenneth (1975) 'Voluntary Organizations in a British City: The Political and Organizational Characteristics of 4264 Voluntary Associations in Birmingham,' *Journal of Voluntary Action Research*, 4 (1):43-68.

OLSEN, Marvin E. (1970) 'The Social and Political Participation of Blacks,' *American Sociological Review*, 35 (August): 682-97.

ORUM, Anthony M. (1966) 'A Reappraisal of the Social and Political Participation of Negroes,' *American Journal of Sociology*, 72 (July): 32-46.

PHILLIPS, P. P. and R. H. CONVISER (1972) 'Measuring the Structure and Boundary Properties of Groups: Some Uses of Information Theory,' *Sociometry*, 35 (2):235-54.

QUANDT, J. (1966) 'On the Size Distribution of Firms,' *American Economic Review*, 56: 925-32.

RAPOPORT, Anatol and W. J. HORVATH (1961) 'A Study of a Large Sociogram,' *Behavioral Science*, 6(4): 239-91.

ROSE, Arnold M. (1954) *Theory and Method in the Social Sciences*. Minneapolis: University of Minnesota Press.

ROSE, Arnold M. (1967) *The Power Structure*. New York: Oxford University Press.

SCOTT, John Jr. (1957) 'Membership and Participation in Voluntary Associations,' *American Sociological Review*, 22 (June): 315-26.

SIMMEL, Georg (1922) *Conflict and the Web of Group Affiliations*, translated by Kurt H. Wolff and Reinhard Bendix. New York: Free Press.

SIMON, Herbert A. (1957) *Models of Man*. New York: John Wiley.

SMITH, D. H. (1972) 'Organizational Boundaries and Organizational Affiliates,' *Sociology and Social Research*, 16: 494-512.

SOREF, Michael (1976) 'Social Class and a Division of Labor within the Corporate Elite: a Note on Class, Interlocking, and Executive Committee Membership of Directors of US Industrial Firms,' *Sociological Quarterly*, 17 (Summer): 360-68.

TURK, Herman (1970) 'Interorganizational Networks in Urban Society: Initial Perspectives and Comparative Research,' *American Sociological Review*, 35 (February): 1-19.

WARNER, W. Lloyd and P. S. LUNT (1941) *The Social Life of a Modern Community*. New Haven: Yale University Press.

WHEELDON, P. O. (1969) 'The Operation of Voluntary Associations and Personal Networks in the Political Process of an Inter-Ethnic Community,' chapter 5 in J. C. Mitchell (ed.), *Social Networks in Urban Situations*. Manchester: University Press.

WHITE, Harrison C. (1970) 'Search Parameters for the Small World Problems,' *Social Forces*, 49 (December): 259-64.

WHITE, Harrison C. (1973) 'Everyday Life in Stochastic Networks,' pp. 287-301 in H. R. Alker, K. W. Deutsch, and A. H. Stoetzel (eds), *Mathematical Approaches to Politics*. San Francisco: Jossey-Bass.

WHITE, Harrison C., S. A. BOORMAN and R. L. BREIGER (1976) 'Social Structure from Multiple Networks 1. Block Models of Roles and Positions,' *American Journal of Sociology*, 81 (January): 730-80.

WHITE, Harrison C. and R. L. BREIGER (1975) 'Patterns Across Networks,' *Society*, 12: 68-73.

WILLIAMS, J. A., Nicholas BABCHUCK and D. R. JOHNSON (1973) 'Voluntary Associations and Minority Status: A Comparative Analysis of Anglo, Black and Mexican Americans,' *American Sociological Review*, 38 (October): 637-46.

WIRTH, L. (1938) 'Urbanism as a Way of Life,' *American Journal of Sociology*, 44 (July): 1-24.

WRIGHT, C. K. and H. H. HYMAN (1958) 'Voluntary Association Memberships of American Adults: Evidence from National Sample Surveys,' *American Sociological Review*, 23 (June): 287.

ZAJONC, R. B. (1966) *Social Psychology: An Experimental Approach*. Belmont, Cal.: Wadsworth.

ZALD, Mayer N. and Patricia DENTON (1963) 'From Evangelism to General Service: The Transformation of the YMCA,' *Administrative Science Quarterly*, 8 (September): 214-34.

ZIPF, G. Kingsley (1949) *Human Behavior and the Principle of Least Effort*. Cambridge: Addison-Wesley Press.

ZURCHER, L. A. (1970) *Poverty Warriors: The Human Experience of Planned Social Intervention*. Austin: University of Texas Press.

12

STRUCTURES OF ECONOMIC INTERDEPENDENCE AMONG NATIONS

Ronald L. Breiger
Harvard University

> One cannot reasonably explain the strength of various state-machineries at specific moments of the history of the modern world-system primarily in terms of a genetic-cultural line of argumentation, but rather in terms of the structural role a country plays in the world-economy at that moment in time.
>
> Wallerstein (1974b, p. 403)

Despite the renewed interest of sociologists in international patterns of economic (inter)dependence, structural conceptualizations driven by analytical power and tuned with empirical precision have been few. The definition of social structure as a non-homogeneous space of differentiated positions (Blau, 1977) leads us to view the economists' theories of international trade as *non*-structural in important respects.[1] Since Ricardo's treatment of comparative advantage, the economists' theories of trade may be seen as straightforward generalizations from the two-nation, two-commodity case. The units of analysis have been dyadic (pairs of nations) rather than multiple. The theories have focused on explaining levels of aggregate exports and imports. There have been few attempts to depict the overall structure with its major concentrations and fissures. Studies seeking to identify patterns in world trade (such as League of Nations, 1942; Woolley, 1958) have imposed highly idealized definitional aggregation both on the types of transaction

Author's Note. For comments and constructive criticism I am grateful to David Karen, John F. Padgett, Joseph E. Schwartz, Theda R. Skocpol, and Harrison C. White. This research was supported by NSF grant SOC76-24394.

under study ('goods,' 'services') and on the macro units of analysis ('the sterling area,' 'Latin America'). Despite a tendency since World War II toward stability in the geographical *shares* of trade, 'no...clear-cut regional pattern has yet been established' (Michaely, 1968, p. 113).

Seen from this vantage point, one of the major contributions of world-system theory (Wallerstein, 1974a; Chirot, 1977) has been to rephrase the entire discussion of international trade by raising and grappling with three analytical problems: 'the structure of the world economy, its cyclical patterns including the present conjuncture, and the ways in which the positions of particular states may change within this structure' (Wallerstein, 1974c). The definitive characteristic of the world economic system is its single division of labor, such that various sectors are dependent upon economic exchanges with others, forming 'a grid which is substantially interdependent' (Wallerstein, 1974b, pp. 390, 397). For analytical purposes world-system theorists partition this grid of unequal exchange relations into three general zones or 'positions' identified on the basis of world market trade in bulk commodities that are necessities for everyday consumption. In brief: *core* states appropriate the surplus of the world economy as a whole and in particular of those states located in the *periphery*, which produce 'lower-ranking' (labor-intensive) goods, while states located in the *semiperiphery* are 'both exploited and exploiters' (Wallerstein, 1974b, pp. 401-5).[2]

ORIENTATION

Goals of This Paper

Along with the excitement generated by world-system theory — indeed, as an intrinsic component of the promise of this approach — are a number of questions concerning its underlying conception of macro-social structure. Among these questions are the following.

(1) Can operational procedures be developed to identify core, peripheral, and semiperipheral states on the sole basis of the structural positions they occupy in international exchange networks?

(2) What are the distinctive elements of a core-periphery structure, in contrast to other ideal-type structures that might characterize international exchange? Therefore, how might transformations of this structure be identified?

(3) Should we expect to discover the same pattern within each type of exchange that we study — capital flows, trade in manufactures, trade in foodstuffs, military interventions? How do these patterns themselves interlock?

(4) Precisely in what sense are core-periphery structures monolithic, and to what extent do they permit the existence of multiple, competing centers?

This paper directly addresses the first and fourth questions and draws implications for the other two. The first question has been posed in a related context by Terence Hopkins (1978, p. 207), who observes the tendency of world-system theorists to treat positions in the world economy (such as 'the core-periphery relational conception') as mere categories, so that 'the relation which the joined terms designates slips into the background, sometimes out of sight entirely.' In this paper a specific empirical framework is developed, which is consistent with Hopkins' directive that the

> acting units or agencies can only be thought of as *formed*, and continually reformed, by the relations between them. Perversely, we often think of the relations as only going between the end points ['core' and 'periphery'], ...as if the latter made the relations instead of the relations making the units. [Hopkins, 1978, p. 205; original emphasis]

The choice of a strategy for addressing this first question (namely, how to derive reduced-form 'positions,' each occupied by numerous states and identified on the basis of the similarity of nations' interchanges across multiple networks of transnational interaction) also implies analytical commitments on related issues. With respect to the second and third questions listed above, this paper will argue that a variety of ideal-type hypotheses specifying relations among macro-level 'positions' (like core and periphery) may be formulated conceptually and tested empirically against data on international trade, and that the issue of the interaction among these networks (for example, a different network for each type of commodity traded among nations) may be as crucial for an adequate theory of the world system, as is the issue of interactions among states.

Beyond these conceptual problems regarding the derivation of 'positions' in the world economy for multiple and complex networks of economic exchange, this paper addresses a major substantive claim of world-system theorists (the fourth question listed above) concerning the existence of a single core. To anticipate the discussion of Figures 3 and 6 below: the suggestion is raised that the finding (Snyder and Kick, 1979) of a unitary center within international trade networks may confound the pattern of trade with attributes of nations' overall economic strength. The states with the largest total trade do indeed tend to occupy a unitary 'core' position. However, after adjusting for the overall import and export levels of each country, a considerably more differentiated pattern of relations may be uncovered — a pattern evidencing multiple, competing centers. Implications are drawn for empirical research following from world-system theory.

In contrast to the broad scope and historical sensitivity of the world-system theorists, the research reported in this paper is restricted and self-consciously naive. It is restricted in that I confine my analysis to 24 highly industrialized nations (essentially, the contemporary membership of the OECD) during a recent year (1972). It is self-consciously naive in its neglect of most factors that historians and social scientists would usually take into account in analyzing these nations, and in its single-minded focus, instead, on patterns of trade of four major types of commodites among these nations. In juxtaposition to world-system theorists, then, the attempt here is to determine the extent to which an explicit analysis of trade structure can aid accounts of the broader, more complex, and more subtle relations among these nations at the present time.[3]

Conceptual Framework

Owing to the emphasis of world-system theory on the structural positions of nations that engage in multiple types of exchange, several researchers who seek empirically to address these issues (Snyder and Kick, 1979; see also Breiger, 1977) have proposed a 'natural wedding' between world-system theory and a general analytical strategy for the analysis of multiple networks, termed block-model analysis.[4] From this network perspective, three concepts emerge that have both methodological and theoretical salience. In short-hand terms, we may refer to them as (1) structural similarity, (2) pattern, and (3) interlock.

In an important paper reporting a block-model analysis for 118 countries, Snyder and Kick (1979) fault world-system theorists for their inability to specify operational criteria for classifying nations into the theoretically specified structural positions (core, semiperiphery, periphery), and for the tendency of researchers in this tradition (for instance, Rubinson, 1976; Delacroix and Ragin, 1978) to substitute statistical indicators such as investment dependence and trade concentration for measures of 'position' or 'control' in the world system. As White and Breiger (1975, p. 68) assert, 'variate distributions measure selected consequences of structural pattern (of the actual ties among individuals or organizations); they are useful indicators of questions to be asked in analyzing social structure directly, but they are neither descriptions nor analyses of the structure itself.'

International trade has a natural representation as a series of matrices, each matrix reporting trade among all pairs of nations with respect to a given commodity type and a given time period. Thus, a focus on total export levels or on trade concentration indicators implies a concern only for the marginals of these interaction matrices, without providing a sound basis for generalization to the interior cell values (that is, to the internal boundaries for relations among states). Hopkins points out that

> the total rows and columns, which one literally obtains by some summing operation across rows [to obtain aggregate exports] or down columns [to obtain aggregate imports], are the 'distributions.' ... When we address ourselves to the distributions without remembering to see them as summaries of conditions continually resulting from processes among the units, we give up our central focus on relations, and perforce become eclectic and ad hoc in our efforts to set forth coherent accounts of 'distributions.'[5] [Hopkins, 1978, p. 205]

In contrast, a block-model approach to international trade assigns states to positions according to the structural similarity of the nations' imports and exports to all other states, across various types of economic exchange, rather than on the basis of definitional aggregation.[6]

Having obtained a partition of nations into structurally similar positions (or 'blocks'), a second goal of this network approach is to examine the possibly distinctive patterns that these blocks induce on the original network data. Within any commodity type, the pattern might well be one of segregation (separate trading areas), hier-

FIGURE 1
Examples of Ideal-Type Patterns that might Characterize
International Networks

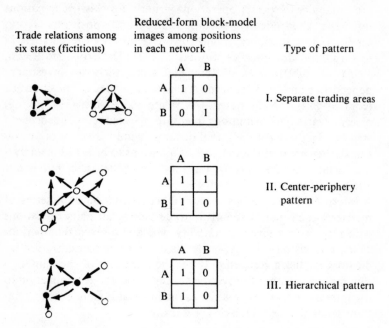

Trade relations among six states (fictitious)

Reduced-form block-model images among positions in each network

Type of pattern

I. Separate trading areas

II. Center-periphery pattern

III. Hierarchical pattern

In each example, block 'A' includes the nations represented by dark circles, block 'B' includes the others, and arrows indicate the flow of exports among nations.

archy, core-periphery, or some other. If one seeks an empirical procedure to identify and distinguish these overall patterns, the emphasis must be on structural similarity rather than on 'clique' identification or other sociometric procedures.[7] This is an obvious but important point. To illustrate it in a manner similar to the ideal-type diagrams presented by Chase-Dunn (1978, p. 163), consider various possibilities for the trade relationships among six nations with respect to a given commodity (Figure 1). The arrows in Figure 1 are meant to indicate the flow of export trade of this commodity among the nations at their end-points. The examples of Figure 1 are fictitious but will serve to introduce the subsequent analysis of data. In each of the three examples, consider the pattern that is induced by aggregating or grouping together the nations depicted by dark circles ('block A') as against the others ('block B').

The first panel of Figure 1 ('separate trading areas') portrays two clusters of nations with each cluster evidencing internal relations, but with no trade between the clusters. The reduced-form block-model image of this network (White et al., 1976, pp. 741-2) is reported in Figure 1 as a 2×2 table with one row and column for each position or aggregate grouping of states that has been identified. The symbol '0' at the intersection of a pair of positions indicates the absence of all trade between their constituent states; otherwise, the symbol '1' appears (White et al., 1976, pp. 737-40).

In principle, this block-model image for 'separate trading areas' might be found to represent a large observed network of international trade in a particular commodity, but it is clear that this image is not one implied by world-system theory. This theory specifies that nations in the periphery are tied to the world economy by virtue of their trade with core states. The 'periphery' may in fact appear as a block evidencing no ties among its constituent nations; rather, its structural coherence arises from its dependence on other states within an overall pattern of 'unequal exchange' (Wallerstein, 1974b, p. 397; see also Brams, 1968). In contrast, the second and third panels of Figure 1 (the 'center-periphery' and the 'hierarchical' patterns discussed in Breiger, 1979, pp. 26-31) both satisfy these conditions, with block 'A' identified as the 'core' in each case. These patterns differ only as to whether the periphery maintains bilateral trade with the core (as implied in Chase-Dunn, 1978, p. 163), or unilateral trade (Chase-Dunn, 1978, pp. 165-6). Block-model analysis offers specific procedures for relating ideal-type images such as those shown in Figure 1 to detailed networks of international trade; indeed, states are grouped into positions or 'blocks' in the first instance by the criterion of the coherence of the overall pattern of relations that such a grouping of states induces.

A third distinctive feature of block-model analysis — one that has potentially broader implications for sociological theory than have been realized to date by the world-system researchers — is the identification of *interlock* among the various patterns ('block-model images') that have been identified. Taken as a whole, the patterns drawn from all arenas under study — for example, agricultural goods, manufactured commodities, energy resources — may themselves interlock in a coherent fashion. The classic, idealized paradigm for this interlock is triangular trade involving slaves, sugar, and manufactured goods (see Hirschman, 1945, pp. 123-4). Although this conceptualization has not systematically been applied to the structure of world trade (however, see the pioneering work of Hirschman, 1945, pp. 117-51), its importance has been recognized by various writers. Haas (1964, p. 53), in his book *Beyond the Nation-State*, for example, clearly expresses this point of view with reference to the world system. He writes that 'the kind of "system" to which we shall address ourselves is the network of relationships among relationships; not merely the relations among nations, but the relations among the abstractions that can be used to summarize the relations among nations.'

This emphasis on the interrelationships among patterns of relationships is a very general and distinctive feature of a sociological theory of social structure (see for instance, the discussion of Blau, 1975, and of Boorman and White, 1976, in Breiger and Pattison, 1978; see also Lorrain, 1975, and Pattison, 1977). The identification of contemporary equations between types of international exchange — if such equations are to be discovered at all — will probably rely on procedures implied by the first two points above.

Data

Twenty-four highly industrialized countries systematically report trade statistics disaggregated by commodity type (SITC level) to the United Nations. These countries, listed alphabetically in Figure 2,[8] form a natural field for analysis in that they exactly comprise the members and associated members of the Organization for Economic Co-operation and Development (OECD), plus one other state (Israel).[9] The OECD was established to increase the standardization of national economic policies among its members (Aubrey, 1967). Moreover, these 24 states appear to form a natural field for analysis in that virtually all of them are labeled as 'core' states by Snyder and Kick (1979).[10] As a group, their trade accounted for over 70 percent of the world totals in 1972.[11]

The data for this study are drawn from systematic United Nations statistics (UN Statistical Office, 1974) on the trade among these nations in 1972 with respect to four broad classes of commodity (SITC Section Codes 0, 2, 3, and 6). Detailed specifications of these classes may be found elsewhere (UN Statistical Office, n.d.); I will briefly refer to them as follows. 'Agricultural pruducts' include cereals, animal feed, fruit, vegetables, dairy products, meat and fish preparations, and related goods. 'Raw materials' include ores, crude and synthetic rubber, wood, lumber, unmanufactured textile fibers, and crude minerals. 'Manufactured goods' include iron and steel products, textile yarns, paper, wood and rubber manufactures, etc. 'Energy resources' include electrical energy, natural and manufactured gas, coal, coke, and petroleum products. Trade in these four commodity classes among the 24 nations studied accounted for 22 percent of all world trade (among all nations) in 1972. The year 1972 was chosen as the initial year of study as a base year for further research, since it was immediately prior to immense changes in world petroleum prices (see Arrighi, 1978, pp. 88-107; Blumenthal, 1978), as well as the year prior to the entry of Britain and other countries into the European Common Market.

The problems inherent in trade-flow data have received considerable scholarly attention (see especially Allen and Ely, 1953; Linnemann, 1966). In brief: the bases, methods of estimation, methods of data collection, extent of coverage, precision of definition, scope of territory, and margins of error undoubtedly differ for various items within a particular country, and for like items for different countries. However, in the 30 years during which these data have been systematically reported, great strides have been made in the implementation of standardized definitions, reporting procedures, and comparability. The rationale for employing these trade-flow data is that they are the best data available.[12]

RESULTS

Inside the Core

Figure 2 reports the trade in manufactured goods among 24 nations. Both rows and columns are ordered identically but arbitrarily (an alphabetical listing by country). Only the highest fifth of the interior cell values are coded as present ('*1*'); the rest appear as blanks ('__').

Figure 3 reports exactly the same data, but now the countries have been re-arranged and partitioned, by an algorithm widely used in block-model analysis (Breiger et al., 1975), to block together nations that have the most similar sets of trading partners, with respect to both imports and exports. The other trade matrices (not

FIGURE 2
Trade in Manufactured Goods among 24 Nations

```
 1. Austral.   ------------I-------I--
 2. Austria    -------I------------II--
 3. Belg./Lux. ------II----I-I------III-
 4. Canada     --------------------II-
 5. Denmark    -------------------I----
 6. Finland    -------I-----------I-I--
 7. France     --I----I----I-I---I-III-
 8. Germany    -IIIIII-----I-I-I-IIIIII
 9. Greece     -----------------------
10. Iceland    -----------------------
11. Ireland    --------------------I--
12. Israel     ---------------------I-
13. Italy      --I---II------I-----IIII
14. Japan      I--I---I-------------II-
15. Netherl.   --I---II----I--------II-
16. New Zea.   -----------------------
17. Norway     -------I-----------I-II-
18. Portugal   -----------------------
19. Spain      ------II----------------
20. Sweden     ----IIII--------I----II-
21. Switzer.   -I-----I-------------I--
22. UK         I-IIIIII--IIIII-I-III-I-
23. USA        I-II--II----II-------I--
24. Yugosla.   ------------I----------
```

Rows and columns are ordered arbitarily but identically (an alphabetical listing by country). Only the highest fifth of the interior cell values are coded as present ('*I*').

FIGURE 3
A Partition of the Rows and Columns of Figure 2

```
 8. Germany   -II III III III-I-------
22. UK        I-I-III III-III IIIII----
23. USA       II--III-------- II--I----
 2. Austria   II--------I--------------
 3. Belg./Lux. III--III-I-I-------------
 7. France    III-I-I III-------------
13. Italy     III-II-I-II-------------
15. Netherl.  III-III-----------------
19. Spain     I---I-------------------
21. Switzer.  II-I--------------------
24. Yugosla.  -----I------------------
 5. Denmark   -----------------I------
 6. Finland   II---------------I------
17. Norway    III--------------I------
20. Sweden    III--I-----III----------
 1. Austral.  -I-----------------I----
 4. Canada    -II---------------------
11. Ireland   -I----------------------
12. Israel    --I---------------------
14. Japan     III------------II---- ---
 9. Greece    ------------------------
10. Iceland   ------------------------
16. New Zea.  ------------------------
18. Portugal  ------------------------
```

Mean Values of Trade Within and Between Blocks ($ millions)

	Block 1	Block 2	Block 3	Block 4	Block 5	Block 6
Block 1	(483)	(407)	(246)	(130)	(233)	32
Block 2	(539)	(319)	(157)	44	28	14
Block 3	(189)	(108)	19	21	11	5
Block 4	(177)	36	24	(109)	11	5
Block 5	(448)	19	11	8	45	12
Block 6	22	8	3	6	5	0

Computed from the original (non-binarized) data and rounded. Mean values in excess of $100 million have been circled. Compare the pattern of circled values to the 'center-periphery' pattern of Figure 1.

shown here) have very similar patterns to Figure 3 under the same partition of countries.

The major finding from Figure 3 is the emergence of a strong center-periphery pattern (in the specific sense of the second panel of Figure 1 and of Breiger, 1976, pp. 128-9) among these countries located within the 'core.' Purely in terms of the aggregate pattern revealed, the first-listed block has extensive trade (both imports and exports) with each other block except the last, which appears to be outside this system of the exchange of manufactured goods. The second block has extensive trade with each of the first three (including trade among its own members). The position of the third-listed block derives form its extensive trade with blocks 1 and 2, but not among its own members: hence its peripheral role. Block 5 is even more peripheral, trading extensively only with the USA and the UK (in block 1). The fourth block — comprising the Scandinavian countries of Denmark, Finland, Norway, and Sweden — occupies a distinctive position within the overall pattern in that these countries trade heavily with one of its members (Sweden) and also with two members of block 1 (Germany and the UK).

What is perhaps most remarkable about this pattern is its great resemblance to the one discovered by Snyder and Kick (1979, p. 1111) for a world-wide sample of 118 nations. What are we to make of the evident replication of this pattern among those very states that Snyder and Kick (1979) identify as 'core' states?

First, it is not at all clear that a world-system theorist would accept the procedures employed by Snyder and Kick or by the present study.[13] Second, this consideration notwithstanding, we have the empirical fact of a 'center-periphery' pattern. It may thus be argued that the central nexus of the world economy — as this nexus has been defined by previous researchers — is itself a highly unified structure, bound together by the predominant position of just three core states.

The third point to make about Figure 3 is that it provides an unsatisfactory picture on substantive grounds. Notice, for example, the tendency toward symmetry. (In general, although not exclusively, countries importing large amounts of manufactured goods from, say, the US also tend to export large quantities of goods to the US.) We must also consider the possibility of asymmetric exchange (Wallerstein, 1974b) across a variety of product types. Moreover, Figure 3 is based on analysis of binary data (as is the research of Snyder and Kick, 1979, p. 1105), with no explicit ad-

justment for the fact that some countries export (and import) vastly
higher quantities of material than others. Therefore, I now turn to
a set of procedures for grappling with these issues.

Identifying Blocks of Nations

Various techniques have been proposed to 'net out' the effects of
countries' total imports and exports in order to obtain, for example, indices of the 'intensity' of trade (see for example, Savage and
Deutsch, 1960; Goodman, 1963; Brams, 1966). The procedure I
employ here was suggested by Schwartz (1977, pp. 267-8) for the
analysis of network data. Row and column means were subtracted
from each matrix, leaving residuals from an additive, two-way
analysis of variance model.[14] Entries greater than zero indicate
positive (statistical) interactions for the trade of a given commodity
between pairs of countries, and conversely for negative values.
These numbers were not binarized, so as to permit no loss of information (and since binarization is unnecessary for the block-model
algorithm that was applied).

The fundamental difference between this analysis and the one
reported previously is that I now seek a *single* partition of countries
that distinguishes patterns across *multiple* matrices: those reporting
trade in agriculural products, raw materials, and manufactured
goods, respectively.

Using a standard block-model procedure (Breiger et al., 1975),
the CONCOR algorithm was applied simultaneously to the rows
and columns of these three matrices. This divisive hierarchical
clustering algorithm produces progressively finer discriminations
among countries. The natural representation for these various
levels of discrimination is a 'tree' (see Figure 4).

In order to explore this partition of countries, a single nation-by-
nation correlation matrix was computed across rows and columns
of all three trade tables (adjusted as described above and in
Schwartz, 1977), and the eigenstructure of this matrix was examined. The first two eigenvectors (accounting, respectively, for 50 and
15 percent of the total variance) are plotted in figure 5.[15] The first
dimension of Figure 5 (the horizontal axis) corresponds to the
block-model split between the first two blocks and the others (compare Figure 4), while the second dimension separates blocks 1 and 3

FIGURE 4
The CONCOR Tree

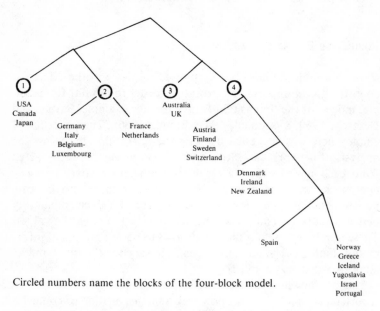

Circled numbers name the blocks of the four-block model.

from blocks 2 and 4 (see also Schwartz, 1977; Arabie et al., 1978, pp. 38-40).

Block 2 includes exactly the five original members of the European Common Market. Recall that these countries were not grouped together in the previous analysis, based on the total volume of pair-wise trade (Figure 3). The first dimension of Figure 5 joins these EEC nations with the USA, Canada, and Japan, while the second dimension separates them, linking these latter countries (block 1) instead with the UK and Australia and — to a lesser extent — with Iceland, Ireland, Israel, and New Zealand.

The first dimension of the trade structure discriminates among nations with respect to their overall economic strength (see Table 1, column 1). The second dimension, joining the blocks containing the USA and UK against the others, is with equal clarity unrelated to overall economic strength (Table 1, column 2). Rather, one might choose to view the second dimension as demarcating an Anglo-American-Japanese sphere of influence from a distinctively European sphere of influence, above and beyond national differences of economic power.

FIGURE 5
A Plot of the First Two Eigenvectors of a Correlation
Matrix Described in the Text.
The 4-block Partition from Figure 4
Has Been Imposed

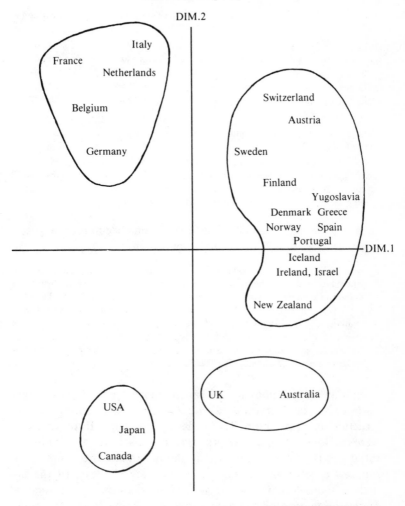

In this respect, the greatest value of the constellation of Figure 5 will emerge from its analysis over time — for example, whether or not the formal entry of the UK into the EEC in the year after these data were collected in fact serves to move its overall position closer

TABLE 1
Coefficients of Determination (r^2) Between Selected Variables and the Dimensions of Figure 4

Variable	Dimension 1	Dimension 2
1972 Total reserve assets*	0.487	0.007
1973 Gross national product	0.259	0.099
1973 GNP per capita	0.074	0.009
1973 Average monthly imports	0.684	0.009
1973 Average monthly exports	0.665	0.007

* Assets include gold stock, holdings of convertible foreign currencies, special drawing rights, and IMF reserve position.

Sources for these variables: US Bureau of Census (1977; Tables 1452, 1453, 1466). For reserve assets, $N = 23$ (excluding Iceland). For the two GNP measures, $N = 22$ (excluding Israel and Yugoslavia). For the import and export measures, $N = 23$ (excluding Israel). Exclusions resulted from unavailable data.

to that of 'Europe'. Analyses such as the one begun here may well allow us to address Dahrendorf's point that

> we are going through a period in which power is more diffuse in the international community than ever before. It is a period in which a past pattern which we know and a future pattern which we may suspect are intermingled.... This then is the position of Europe as a world power.... At times its existence becomes manifest through the institutions of the European Community, at other times through other institutions...; but more often its reality is latent....Circumstances and constellations are more important than intentions and [individual] actions. [Dahrendorf, 1977, pp. 72, 74]

As a test of the block-model partition displayed in Figure 4, this partition was applied to a data set that had not been used in the construction of the partition. The reader will recall that three networks were employed: agricultural products, raw materials, and manufactured goods. Table 2 reports correlations among these three plus the new type, trade in energy resources, at the level of the individual data.[16] At this level, no two matrices share more than a moderate amount of common variance, ranging from 22 percent ($= 0.470^2$) to 44 percent ($= 0.661^2$). Despite these individual-level differences, the block-model partition discriminates a statistically significant structure of trade on the new network (energy resources).[17]

TABLE 2
Correlations among the Trade Matrices Employed in this Study*

	Agricultural products	Raw materials	Manufactured goods	Energy resources
Agricultural products	1.000	0.579	0.591	0.470
Raw materials		1.000	0.524	0.661
Manufactured goods			1.000	0.584
Energy resources				1.000

* See note 16.

The identification of a single blocking of countries that is alleged to hold across four matrices that differ so greatly at the individual level, however, begs us to look more directly at the specific patterns that this blocking induces. Spatial representations such as Figure 5 may well serve to identify the macro-positions of nations in an international economy, but they yield no information on the multiple networks among these positions. The essential feature of a social network is often the sharp breaks in its pattern — the asymmetries and the absence of interaction — rather than the existence of ties.

Structure Across Multiple Networks

The four-block CONCOR partition (Figure 4) was applied to the rows and columns of each of the trade matrices under study. Each matrix is non-binary, reporting the dollar value of trade among pairs of countries after adjusting for the total volume of each nation's imports and exports (as previously discussed). What patterns does this partition induce, and are the patterns distinctive?

Figure 6 reports the mean trade within each of the four blocks, and between all pairs of blocks. The highest entries in each table

FIGURE 6
Mean Trade Within and Between the Blocks of Figure 4, and the Resulting Block-Model Images

	US	EEC	UK	Others	
I. Agricultural Products					
US	296,477	-37,509	-132	-28,939	
EEC	-96,615	240,867	-60,740	-39,438	
UK	126,984	-77,308	106,526	-7,210	
Others	-25,989	-49,738	14,112	22,956	
II. Raw Materials					
US	658,930	-24,800	-20,996	-82,276	
EEC	-94,758	71,591	-19,408	2,585	
UK	96,487	-10,254	-5,296	-16,635	
Others	-74,139	-13,675	11,809	20,552	
III. Manufactures					
US	969,973	-162,621	46,239	-87,094	
EEC	-121,187	453,506	-116,496	-86,962	
UK	11,731	-70,780	31,513	20,514	
Others	-96,962	-84,614	29,446	50,390	
IV. Energy Resources					
US	174,065	-21,227	-18,958	-14,577	
EEC	-26,853	39,845	17,028	-8,063	
UK	-19,196	-6,544	-13,389	7,407	
Others	-12,534	-5,901	-1,062	5,325	

Row and column means have been subtracted from the individual-level data (as described in text). Reported values are in thousands of US dollars. The terms 'US', 'EEC,' 'UK', and 'Others' are shorthand designations for blocks 1, 2, 3, and 4 (respectively) identified in Figure 4.

FIGURE 7
Trade in Agricultural Products under the
Four-block Partition of Figure 4

```
23. USA         -II|I--II|-I|---------------
 4. Canada      I-I|-----|-I|---------------
14. Japan       I--|-----|I-|---------------
 8. Germany     ---|-I-II|--|---------------
13. Italy       ---|I--I--|-|I--I-----------
 3. Belg./Lux.  ---|I--II|--|---------------
 7. France      ---|III-I|--|---------------
15. Netherl.    ---|IIII-|-I|---------------
 1. Austral.    III|-----|-I|---------------
22. UK          ---|--I--|--|-----I--I------
 2. Austria     ---|-----|I-|-I-IIIIIIIIIIII
 6. Finland     ---|-----|I-|I-I-IIIIIIIIIII
20. Sweden      ---|-----|I-|II--IIIIIIIIIII
21. Switzer.    ---|-----|I-|II--III-IIIIIII
 5. Denmark     I--|-----|-I|--I-----------
11. Ireland     ---|-----|-I|---------------
16. New Zea.    I--|-----|-I|---------------
19. Spain       ---|--I-|-I|---------------
17. Norway      ---|-----|I-|II-I-II-II--I
 9. Greece      ---|-----|I-|II--IIIII-IIII
10. Iceland     ---|-----|I-|III-IIIIII-III
24. Yugosla.    ---|-I---|I-|II----II-II-II
12. Israel      ---|-----|I-|III-III-IIII-I
18. Portugal    ---|-----|I-|II--IIIIIIIII-
```

Block means from Figure 7 are reported in the first panel of Figure 6. Analysis was performed on the non-binarized data, with row and column means subtracted (see note 18).

FIGURE 8
Trade in Manufactured Goods under the
Four-block Partition of Figure 4

```
23. USA        -I-------+-I---------------
 4. Canada     I--------+-I---------------
14. Japan      II------+-I----------------
 8. Germany    I---IIII--I--I-------------
13. Italy      ---I--I--+-------------I--
 3. Belg./Lux. ---I--II-+----------------
 7. France     ---III---+----I-----------
15. Netherl.   ---I-I---+----------------
 1. Austral.   --I------+------II--II--I
22. UK         I---I---+-I--I------I-
 2. Austria    ---------+---I--------I--
 6. Finland    ---------I--I-I---I------
20. Sweden     ---------I-I--I---I------
21. Switzer.   ---------I--------------I
 5. Denmark    ---------II--II-IIII-I
11. Ireland    ------II-I----II-IIIII
16. New Zea.   --I-----I--I---I-IIIIIII
19. Spain      ------------II--II--I
17. Norway     ---------I--I-I-----I---
 9. Greece     -------I--I---IIII-IIII
10. Iceland    -------I-II---IIIII-III
24. Yugosla.   ---I----II---II--II-II
12. Israel     --I-----I--I---III-III-I
18. Portugal   ------+-+I---IIIIIIII-
```

Block means from Figure 8 are reported in the third panel of Figure 6.

(all those greater than $3 million) have been underlined. Adjacent to each table is the reduced-form network — or 'block-model image' (White et al., 1976) — representing the structure of these positive interactions. As shorthand names for the blocks of Figure 4, I use the terms 'US,' 'EEC,' 'UK,' and 'Others.' To illustrate the relation between these reduced-form patterns and the overall structure, Figures 7 and 8 reproduce the full, country-by-country matrices for two of the product types. For simplicity, only the highest entries in each matrix are shown there.[18] Figures 7 and 8 illustrate the general tendency for blocks with high mean trade to represent sub-matrices containing uniformly high values. In general, the exceptions to this statement are values of low magnitude.[19]

I will focus comments on Figure 6, which reports the mean aggregate trade between blocks, above and beyond their overall propensities to import and export each type of good. My theme will be the contrast between this structure and the earlier one of Figure 3, where overall imports and exports were not taken into account.

Figure 6 portrays the tendency toward separate trading areas (compare Figure 1) between the USA, Canada, and Japan (block 1) and the EEC countries (block 2). These blocks are segregated across trade in all product types. They have tendencies neither toward direct trade nor toward exchanges through third parties. This tendency toward polarization among the two strongest competing blocks was not evident from the data on direct trade — Figure 3 — but emerges when one adjusts for total imports and exports. In this sense, Figure 6 portrays not a monolithic structure (as in Figure 3), but an arena with competing centers.

Another facet of the Figure 6 structure is the success of the Common Market — but also its inward-looking tendencies — with respect to its six members as of 1972. Established to reduce barriers and promote internal trade, the underlying pattern of trade within the EEC overwhelms any inclination toward exchanges with external areas.[20] A notable feature of this within-block integration is that it is not apparent with respect to total trade. (Compare Figure 3, in which the strength of the German economy accounts for its central role, in conrast to the peripheral position of other EEC members.)

A third feature of Figure 6 is the role of the UK and Australia as intermediaries between blocks 1 and 2 and the OECD countries *not* included in the Common Market. The membership of block 4 includes the participants in the European Free Trade Association, to which Britain also belonged until 1973.[21] A popular view[22] is that these nations of block 4 comprise a natural part of the EEC's sphere of influence. Given the high relative interdependence between these countries and the UK block, a natural question concerns the extensiveness, over time, of the de facto integration of these areas within the European Community. Although beyond the scope of my discussion, this question may be posed and addressed in a straightforward manner within the framework of analysis developed here.

Finally, Figure 6 allows us to observe the interrelationships *among* these aggregate relational patterns. According to a traditional conception (reviewed in Hirschman, 1945, p. 117), world trade is based essentially upon a division of labor calling for the exchange of manufactures against foodstuffs and raw materials. This view finds expression at the macro-level of Figure 6 in the sense that every arrow in each of the first two images may be mapped into an arrow travelling in the opposite direction in the third image (the one for manufactures). However, observe that this traditional conception provides an inadequate characterization of the interlock of these patterns. Specifically: the macro-level trade in manufactures is more pervasive, and thus trade in manufactured goods is not always reciprocated by flows of raw materials or agricultural products. As a more extensive algebraic analysis (not reported here) confirms, the asymmetries in the flows of these latter commodities render them more useful than manufactured goods as indicators of a detailed structure.[23] Thus, while the flow of manufactured goods is — of course — ubiquitous among these countries and accounts for the greatest part of their total trade, it is precisely to the *other* types of commodity that one must turn in order to obtain the clearest picture of the hierarchical structure of 'strong' international ties.

CONCLUSIONS

This paper has explored possibilities for identifying the positions of nations in an international system on the basis of their simultaneous exchanges of multiple types of economic goods. The analytical linkage between nations' positions in the world economy, and the identification of distinctive patterns of trade in each network, has been illustrated within an operational framework emphasizing the mutual relevance of theory and data.

With respect to trade relations among the OECD countries in 1972, a unified structure has been identified which evidences a strong center-periphery pattern. This finding suggests the existence of a smaller and correspondingly more predominant 'core' within the contemporary world system than has been identified by other researchers (Snyder and Kick, 1979). However, this finding was shown to confound the patterns of trade with attributes of nations' overall economic strength. Adjusting for the total import and export levels of each country, a considerably more differentiated structure was shown to underlie the original finding. A major feature of this underlying structure is the existence of multiple, competing centers. To pursue the question of international trade patterns net of the individual attributes of countries, a more rigorous set of control variables should be incorporated in further work. Thus, the econometricians' multiple regression equations involving variables such as population size, national income, geographical distance, and mean import and export levels (for example, Linnemann, 1966) may be seen as providing data for an explicitly *structural* anlysis of trade flows.

More generally, this paper has pointed to certain overlaps between the concerns of a social network theory and world-system theory (Wallerstein, 1974a; Chirot, 1977), but — at least by implication — it should be clear that there are separate areas of development as well. The overlap arises from the interest of each approach in identifying nations' positions on the basis of their overall location in multiple world networks. However, world-systems theory is a richer approach, with more nuances, inseparable in its essentials from its historical investigation of the origins of sustained economic growth in Western Europe. Conversely, the contribution of a network formulation to the development of a macro-sociological theory of social structure is considerably more general, focusing (in the words of Haas, 1964, p. 53) 'not merely [on] the relations among nations, but [on] the relations among the abstractions that can be used to summarize [these] relations.'

NOTES

1. On economic theories of international trade see, e.g. Chipman (1965), Kemp (1964), and Meade (1952). Also see the important empirical studies of Kindleberger (1962) and Linnemann (1966).

2. The analytical clarity of Wallerstein's 'semi-periphery' position has occasionally been questioned. For more complete definitions and discussion of these three positions, see Wallerstein (1974a, pp. 301-2, 359-50), Chirot (1977, p. 13), Skocpol (1977), and Snyder and Kick (1979, pp. 1098-1101).

3. For an argument in favor of a narrow interpretation of social structure as including social positions, patterns of social relations, and the nexus bonding positions and relations, but excluding 'its broader cultural and functional connotations,' see Blau (1977, pp. 1-18).

4. Introductions to block-model analysis may be found in White and Breiger (1975), White et al. (1976), Arabie et al. (1978), and Breiger (1979, pp. 22-34).

5. For a critique of researchers who 'collapse full network structures into single vectors of row-marginals (number of choices initiated...) and column-marginals (number of received choices)' rather than using 'network phenomenology itself' as a guide to the aggregation of social actors, see Breiger (1976, p. 118).

6.

Some sort of self-consistent search procedure is necessary, since the membership of one set depends on the membership of the other sets, as well as on which sets are to have ties of a given type to which other sets. The meaning of a type of tie in the given population can be inferred from its pattern of incidence instead of solely from the cultural definition of that type of relation. [White and Breiger, 1975, p. 68]

For detailed discussion of the algorithms actually employed, see the references cited in note 4.

7. Contrast in this respect the studies of Brams (1966), Chadwick and Deutsch (1973), Merritt and Clark (1977), Russett (1966), Savage and Deutsch (1960), and Wish, Deutsch and Biener (1972). At a more explicitly theoretical level, contrast Arrighi (1978).

8. All figures for Belgium also include those for Luxembourg.

9. Yugoslavia and New Zealand are not formal members of the OECD, but are the only two countries affiliated with it in special status categories (US Bureau of Census, 1977, p. 863).

10. Nineteen of the nations listed in Figure 2 are termed 'core' states by Snyder and Kick (1979, p. 1110); the other nations of Figure 2 are Iceland, New Zealand, Israel, Ireland, and Finland. Conversely, all 'core' states of Snyder and Kick are included in Figure 2, with the exception of South Africa.

11. The imports of these nations totalled $304 billion out of the world total of $430 billion.

12. Each country reports its imports and exports separately to the UN. Apart from well-known differences in valuation — exports are valued at free-on-board (f.o.b.) prices and imports usually at cost-insurance-freight (c.i.f.) prices — these two sets of figures should correspond. Actually, their correspondence is far from perfect, for a number of reasons (Linnemann, 1966, pp. 61-2). If one is interested in tracing the countries of production and consumption (rather than the countries of consignment), the import statistics are more reliable than the export statistics (Durand, 1953, pp. 123-4; also see Linnemann, 1955, p. 62), and the import data are therefore the ones used here.

13. This is because world-system theory in general, and Wallerstein's work in particular, has been essentially historical rather than formal (however, note the observations of Skocpol, 1977, p. 1080 on this point). Perhaps the most formal of the world-system theorists is Hopkins (1978).

14. In general, the procedure used here results in the appearance of non-zero values on the diagonal of each matrix. Schwartz (1977) proposes a transformation of each matrix so as to have row-sums of zero, column-sums of zero, and main diagonal values all zero; this is the procedure I have employed. On the relevance of Schwartz (1977) for the CONCOR algorithm employed here, see Arabie et al. (1978, pp. 38-40).

15. Each eigenvector has been normed to unity.

16. Each matrix was in effect 'unraveled' into a vector of 552 ($=24\times23$) numbers, taking care to unravel each matrix in the identical order. Numbers are US dollar values of trade (for specific product types) between all pairs of countries. Correlations between these vectors are reported in Table 2.

17. Two-way analysis of variance performed on the matrix of trade in energy resources, with this 24×24 matrix partitioned according to the four blocks of Figure 4, leads to row, column, and row-column interaction effects that are significant at the 0.001 level. For a more comprehensive discussion of the statistical significance of block-model 'fit,' however, see White (1977).

18. In Figure 7, all entries above $25 million are coded as 'present'; in Figure 8, all entries above $50 million. The reader should bear in mind that all analyses were performed on the full, numerical data. The binarization of Figures 7 and 8 is for the sole purpose of lending simplicity of description to the resulting patterns.

19. These figures also suggest the relevance of the more detailed block structure. In Figure 7, for example, note the tendency of Ireland, New Zealand, Denmark, and Spain (all of which are grouped together in Figure 4) to export heavily to the UK, while each of the other nations of block 4 (Figure 4) exports heavily to Australia and among themselves.

20. The exception, trade of energy resources, involves an asymmetric exchange, with the EEC in a favorable position with respect to block 3.

21. The 1972 members of the European Free Trade Association (EFTA) were Austria, Finland, Switzerland, Sweden, Denmark, Norway, Iceland, Portugal, and the UK. Compare Figure 4.

22. *Business Week*, 24 July 1978: 79.

23. Breiger and Pattison (1978) recast Granovetter's (1973) 'strength of weak ties' argument as a proposition about the existence of a particular semigroup homomorphism (Boorman and White, 1976). Investigation of the algebraic semigroup

generated by the agricultural, raw-materials, and manufactures images confirms the proposed structure as a homomorphic reduction, with manufactures as the 'weak' ties.

REFERENCES

ALLEN, R. G. D., and J. Edward ELY (1953) *International Trade Statistics.* New York: John Wiley.

ARABIE, Phipps, Scott A. BOORMAN, and Paul R. LEVITT (1978) 'Constructing Blockmodels: How and Why,' *Journal of Mathematical Psychology,* 17:21-63.

ARRIGHI, Giovanni (1978) *The Geometry of Imperialism.* London: NLB.

AUBREY, Henry G. (1967) *Atlantic Economic Co-operation.* New York: Praeger.

BLAU, Peter M. (1975) 'Structural Constraints of Status Complements,' pp. 117-38 in Lewis A. Coser (ed.), *The Idea of Social Structure.* New York: Harcourt Brace Jovanovich.

BLAU, Peter M. (1977) *Inequality and Heterogeneity: A Primitive Theory of Social Structure.* New York: Free Press.

BLUMENTHAL, W. Michael (1978) 'Steering in Crowded Waters,' *Foreign Affairs,* 56:728-39.

BOORMAN, Scott A., and Harrison C. WHITE (1976) 'Social Structure from Multiple Networks: II. Role Structures,' *American Journal of Sociology,* 81:1384-1446.

BRAMS, Steven J. (1966) 'Transaction Flows in the International System,' *American Political Science Review,* 60:880-98.

BRAMS, Steven J. (1968) 'Measuring the Concentration of Power in Political Systems,' *American Political Science Review,* 62:461-75.

BREIGER, Ronald L. (1976) 'Career Attributes and Network Structure: A Blockmodel Study of a Biomedical Research Specialty,' *American Sociological Review,* 41:117-35.

BREIGER, Ronald L. (1977) 'Prospectus: Structures of Economic Interdependence Among Nations,' unpublished paper, Department of Sociology, Harvard University (October).

BREIGER, Ronald L. (1979) 'Toward an Operational Theory of Community Elite Structures,' *Quality and Quantity,* 13:21-57.

BREIGER, Ronald L., Scott A. BOORMAN, and Phipps ARABIE (1975) 'An Algorithm for Clustering Relational Data with Applicationis to Social Network Analysis and Comparison with Multidimensional Scaling,' *Journal of Mathematical Psychology,* 12:328-83.

BREIGER, Ronald L., and Philippa E. PATTISON (1978) 'The Joint Role Structure of Two Communities' Elites,' *Sociological Methods and Research*, 7 (November): 213-26.

CHADWICK, Richard W., and Karl W. DEUTSCH (1973) 'International Trade and Economic Integration: Further Developments in Trade Matrix Analysis,' *Comparative Political Studies*, 6:84-109.

CHASE-DUNN, Christopher (1978) 'Core-Periphery Relations: The Effects of Core Competition,' pp. 159-76 in Barbara Hockey Kaplan (ed.), *Social Change in the Capitalist World Economy*. Beverly Hills: Sage.

CHIPMAN, John S. (1965) 'A Survey of the Theory of International Trade: Part 2. The Neoclassical Theory,' *Econometrica*, 33:685-760.

CHIROT, Daniel (1977) *Social Change in the Twentieth Century*. New York: Harcourt Brace Jovanovich.

DAHRENDORF, Ralf (1977) 'International Power: A European Perspective,' *Foreign Affairs*, 55:72-88.

DELACROIX, Jacques, and Charles RAGIN (1978) 'Modernizing Institutions, Mobilization and Third World Development: A Cross-National Study,' *American Journal of Sociology*, 84:123-50.

DURAND, E. Dana (1953) 'Country Classification,' pp. 117-29 in R. G. D. Allen and J. Edward Ely (eds), *International Trade Statistics*. New York: John Wiley.

GOODMAN, Leo A. (1963) 'Statistical Methods for the Preliminary Analysis of Transaction Flows,' *Econometrica*, 31:197-208.

GRANOVETTER, Mark S. (1973) 'The Strength of Weak Ties,' *American Journal of Sociology*, 78:1360-80.

HAAS, Ernst B. (1964) *Beyond the Nation-State*. Stanford: University Press.

HIRSCHMAN, Albert O. (1945) *National Power and the Structure of Foreign Trade*. Berkeley: University of California Press.

HOPKINS, Terence (1978) 'World-System Analysis: Methodological Issues,' pp. 199-217 in Barbara Hockey Kaplan (ed.), *Social Change in the Capitalist World Economy*. Beverly Hills: Sage.

KEMP, Murray C. (1964) *The Pure Theory of International Trade*. Englewood Cliffs, NJ: Prentice-Hall.

KINDLEBERGER, Charles P. (1962) *Foreign Trade and the National Economy*. New Haven, Conn.: Yale University Press.

LEAGUE OF NATIONS (1942) *The Network of World Trade*. Geneva: League of Nations, Secretariat, Financial Section and Economic Intelligence Service.

LINNEMANN, Hans (1966) *An Econometric Study of International Trade Flows*. Amsterdam: North-Holland.

LORRAIN, Francois (1975) *Réseaux sociaux et classifications sociales*. Paris: Hermann.

MEADE, James E. (1952) *A Geometry of International Trade*. London: Allen and Unwin.

MERRITT, Richard L., and Caleb M. CLARK (1977) 'Mail Flows in the European Balance of Power, 1890-1920,' pp. 169-205 in Karl W. Deutsch et al. (eds), *Problems of World Modeling*. Cambridge: Mass.: Ballinger.

MICHAELY, Michael (1968) 'Patterns of Trade,' *International Encyclopedia of the Social Sciences*, 8:108-13.

PATTISON, Philippa E. (1977) 'A Factorization Technique for Semigroups,' RIAS Working Paper no. 4, Harvard University.

RUBINSON, Richard (1976) 'The World Economy and the Distribution of Income Within States: A Cross-National Study,' *American Sociological Review*, 41:638-59.

RUSSETT, Bruce M. (1966) 'Delineating International Regions,' *International Yearbook of Political Behavior Research*, vol. 7. New York: Free Press.

SAVAGE, I. Richard, and Karl W. DEUTSCH (1960) 'A Statistical Model of the Gross Analysis of Transaction Flows,' *Econometrica*, 28:551-72.

SCHWARTZ, Joseph E. (1977) 'An Examination of CONCOR and Related Methods for Blocking Sociometric Data,' pp. 255-82 in David R. Heise (ed.), *Sociological Methodology 1977*. San Francisco: Jossey-Bass.

SKOCPOL, Theda (1977) 'Wallerstein's World Capitalist System: A Theoretical and Historical Critique,' *American Journal of Sociology*, 82:1075-90.

SNYDER, David, and Edward L. KICK (1979) 'Structural Position in the World System and Economic Growth, 1955-1970: A Multiple Network Analysis of Transnational Interactions,' *American Journal of Sociology*, 84:1096-1126.

UN STATISTICAL OFFICE (n.d.) *Commodity Indexes for Standard International Trade Classification, Revised*, 2 vols. Sales no. 64. XVII. 2 and 3.

UN STATISTICAL OFFICE (1974) *World Trade Annual 1972*, 5 vols. New York: Walker and Co.

US BUREAU OF CENSUS, Department of Commerce (1977) *Statistical Abstract of the United States*. Washington, DC: US Government Printing Office.

WALLERSTEIN, Immanuel (1974a) *The Modern World-System*. New York: Academic Press.

WALLERSTEIN, Immanuel (1974b) 'The Rise and Future Demise of the World Capitalist System: Concepts for Comparative Analysis,' *Comparative Studies in Society and History*, 16:387-415.

WALLERSTEIN, Immanuel (1974c) 'Dependence in an International World: The Limited Possibilities of Transformation Within the Capitalist World-Economy,' *African Studies Review*, 17:1-26.

WHITE, Harrison C. (1977) 'Probabilities of Homomorphic Mappings from Multiple Graphs,' *Journal of Mathematical Psychology*, 16:121-34.

WHITE, Harrison C., Scott A. BOORMAN, and Ronald L. BREIGER (1976) 'Social Structure from Multiple Networks: I. Blockmodels of Roles and Positions,' *American Journal of Sociology*, 81:730-80.

WHITE, Harrison C., and Ronald L. BREIGER (1975) 'Pattern Across Networks,' *Society*, 12 (July/August): 68-73.

WISH, Myron, Morton DEUTSCH, and Lois BIENER (1972) 'Differences in Perceived Similarity of Nations,' pp. 289-313 in A. Kimball Romney, Roger N. Shepard, and Sara Beth Nerlove (eds), *Multidimensional Scaling*, vol. 2. New York: Seminar Press.

WOOLLEY, Herbert B. 'Transactions Between World Areas in 1951,' *Review of Economics and Statistics*, 40:10-35.

INDEX OF NAMES

INDEX OF SUBJECTS

NOTES ON CONTRIBUTORS

Peter M. Blau is Quetelet Professor of Sociology at Columbia University and Distinguished Professor of Sociology at the State University of New York at Albany. He received his PhD at Columbia University (1952). His first book was *The Dynamics of Bureaucracy*; his latest is *Inequality and Heterogeneity*.

Raymond Boudon studied at the École Normale Supérieure, the Sorbonne, and Columbia University. He has taught at the University of Bordeaux and the Sorbonne (Université Paris V) and has been a Visiting Professor at Harvard University. His books include *Education, Opportunity and Social Inequality* (1974) and *Effets pervers et ordre social* (1977).

Ronald L. Breiger (AB Brandeis; PhD Harvard) is Associate Professor of Sociology at Harvard University. In addition to the work reflected in his chapter in this volume, he is currently completing a paper on 'Social Control and Social Networks: A Model from Georg Simmel.'

S. N. Eisenstadt received his PhD from the Hebrew University, Jerusalem, where he is Professor of Sociology. He has been a frequent visiting professor of sociology at Harvard University. His many books include *The Political System of Empires* (1963), *Revolutions and the Transformation of Societies* (1978) and, with M. Curelaru, *The Form of Sociology: Paradigms and Crises* (1976).

Wolf Heydebrand is Professor of Sociology at New York University. He received his MA and PhD at the University of Chicago and has taught at Chicago, Washington University, St Louis, and Columbia Universities. He is author of *Hospital Bureaucracy* and editor of *Comparative Organizations*, and he has published articles in the *American Sociological Review*, *Sociological Quarterly*, and the *Law and Society Review*. His forthcoming book on *Adjudication vs. Administration* (with Carroll Seron) deals with the historical and political contradictions of the American judicial system.

Charles Kadushin is Professor, Graduate School and University Center, City University of New York. He was a member of the Social Psychology Program of Teachers College, Columbia University, from 1968 to 1978. From 1959 to 1968 he was with the Sociology Department of Columbia University from which he received a PhD in 1960. He is the author of *The American Intellectual Elite* (1974) and *Why People Go to Psychiatrists* (1969). His continuing interests in networks are reflected in a forthcoming study of the publishing industry (with Lewis Coser and Walter Powell), and in studies of the relation between social networks and reactions to stress.

Sir Edmund Leach is Professor Emeritus of Social Anthropology in the University of Cambridge, a Fellow of the British Academy, and a Trustee of the British Museum. From 1966 to 1979 he was Provost of Kings College, Cambridge. His publications include *Lévi-Strauss* (1970) and *Culture and Communication* (1976).

J. Miller McPherson has a PhD from Vanderbilt University (1973) and is currently Associate Professor of Sociology, University of South Carolina. He is author or co-author of articles in the *American Sociological Review*, *American Political Science Review*, *Science*, *Social Science Research*, *Sociological Quarterly*, and other journals. McPherson is currently engaged in a long-term project constructing a general structure theory of voluntary associations based upon a variety of methods, including network theory and stochastic process models.

Bruce H. Mayhew is Professor of Sociology at the University of South Carolina. He is author and co-author of more than 30 articles appearing in the *American Sociological Review*, *American Journal of Sociology*, *Social Forces*, *Sociometry*, and other journals; two of these are: 'On the Emergence of Oligarchy in Human Interaction,' *American Journal of Sociology*, 1976, and 'Social Morphology of Pareto's Economic Elite,' *Social Forces*, 1980. He is currently working on mathematical models of vertical social mobility and elite circulation.

Robert K. Merton, University Professor Emeritus and Special Service Professor at Columbia University, received the PhD from Harvard University (1936). His books include *Social Theory and Social Structure* (1968) and *The Sociology of Science* (1973).

Ino Rossi is Associate Professor of Sociology at St John's University. He holds an MA in sociology from the University of Chicago and a PhD in sociology and anthropology from the New School for Social Research. He has edited *The Unconscious in Culture* (1974), an interpretation and evaluation of Lévi-Strauss's structuralism, and, recently, *People in Culture* (1980), a survey of cultural anthropology. He is currently preparing a volume on the interface between modern French structuralism and traditional sociological paradigms.

Paul T. Schollaert is Associate Professor of Sociology at Old Dominion University. He holds a PhD in sociology from the University of Wisconsin. His current research includes work on models of stratification and a longitudinal study of housing.

Walter L. Wallace has a BA (1954) from Columbia College; an MA (1955) from Atlanta University; and a PhD (1963) from the University of Chicago. Currently Professor of Sociology at Princeton University, he was formerly Professor of Sociology at Northwestern University, and staff sociologist at the Russell Sage Foundation. He is author of *Student Culture* (1966) and *The Logic of Science in Sociology* (1971), editor of *Sociological Theory: An Introduction* (1969), and co-author of *Black Elected Officials* (1976).

Charles K. Warriner is Professor of Sociology and has chaired the Department at the University of Kansas. He received his PhD from the University of Chicago and has served as a visiting faculty member at the University of Colorado and the New York State School of Industrial Labor Relations. Among his publications are *The Emergence of Society* (1970) and 'Groups are Real: A Reaffirmation' (1956); the book, *Organizations and their Environments: Essays on the Sociology of Organizations*, is in preparation.

Maurice Zeitlin, Professor of Sociology at the University of California, Los Angeles, received the PhD from Berkeley in 1964. He has taught at Princeton University, the University of Wisconsin and the Hebrew University of Jerusalem. His works include *Revolutionary Politics and the Cuban Working Class* (1967), *Classes, Class Conflict, and the State* (edited, 1980), and, with R. E. Ratcliff, the forthcoming *Landlords and Capitalists*, from which the present article is excerpted.

I was also here alone, a decade after burying my dear wife—and though I'd traveled around a little, in the last few years, I had never really grown used to the way the silence of a strange room, experienced alone, tastes like the death that waited for me too.

After about half an hour of feeling sorry for myself I dressed in one of my best blue suits—an old one Claire had picked out in better days, with a cut now two styles out of date—and went to the lobby to see the concierge. I found him in the center of a lobby occupied not by adventurers or pioneers but by businessmen and tourists. He was a sallow-faced young man seated behind a flat slab of a desk, constructed from some material made to resemble polished black marble. It might have been intended to represent a Kubrick monolith lying on its side, a touch that would have been appropriate enough for the moon but might have given the decorator too much credit for classical allusions. I found more Kubrick material in the man himself, in that he was a typical hotel functionary: courteous, professional, friendly, and as cold as a plain white wall. Beaming, he said: "Can I help you, sir?"

"I'm looking for Minnie and Earl," I told him.

His smile was an unfaltering, professional thing, that might have been scissored out of a magazine ad and scotch-taped to the bottom half of his face. "Do you have their full names, sir?"

"Those are their full names." I confess I smiled with reminiscence. "They're both one of a kind."

"I see. And they're registered at the hotel?"

"I doubt it," I said. "They're lunar residents. I just don't have their address."

"Did you try the directory?"

"I tried that before I left Earth," I said. "They're not listed. Didn't expect them to be, either."

He hesitated a fraction of a second before continuing: "I'm not sure I know what to suggest, then—"

"I'm sure you don't," I said, unwillingly raising my voice just enough to give him a little taste of the anger and frustration and dire need that had fueled this entire trip. Being a true professional, used to dealing with obnoxious and arrogant tourists, the concierge didn't react at all: just politely waited for me to get on with it. I, on the other hand, winced before continuing: "They're before your time. Probably way before your time. But there have to be people around—old people, mostly—who know who I'm talking about. Maybe you can ask around for me? Just a little? And pass around the word that I need to talk?"

The professional smile did not change a whit, but it still acquired a distinctively dubious flavor. "Minnie and Earl, sir?"

"Minnie and Earl." I then showed him the size of the tip he'd earn if he accomplished it—big enough to make certain that he'd take the request seriously, but not so large that he'd be tempted to concoct false leads. It impressed him exactly as much as I needed it to. Too bad there was almost no chance of it accomplishing anything; I'd been making inquiries about the old folks for years. But the chances of me giving up were even smaller: not when I now knew I only had a few months left before the heart stopped beating in my chest.

They were Minnie and Earl, dammit.

And anybody who wasn't there in the early days couldn't possibly understand how much that meant.

•••

It's a funny thing, about frontiers: they're not as enchanting as the folks who work them like you to believe. And there was a lot that they didn't tell the early recruits about the joys of working on the moon.

They didn't tell you that the air systems gave off a nasal hum that kept you from sleeping soundly at any point during your first six weeks on rotation; that the vents were considerately located directly above the bunks to eliminate any way of shutting it out; that just when you found yourself actually needing that hum to sleep something in the circulators decided to change the pitch, rendering it just a tad higher or lower so that instead of lying in bed begging that hum to shut up shut up SHUT UP you sat there instead wondering if the new version denoted a serious mechanical difficulty capable of asphyxiating you in your sleep.

They didn't tell you that the recycled air was a paradise for bacteria, which kept any cold or flu or ear infection constantly circulating between you and your co-workers; that the disinfectants regularly released into the atmosphere smelled bad but otherwise did nothing; that when you started sneezing and coughing it was a sure bet that everybody around you would soon be sneezing and coughing; and that it was not just colds but stomach viruses, contagious rashes, and even more unpleasant things that got shared as generously as a bottle of wine at one of the parties you had time to go to back on Earth when you were able to work only sixty or seventy hours a week. They didn't tell you that work took so very much of your time that the pleasures and concerns of normal life were no longer valid experiential input; that without that input you eventually ran out of non-work-related subjects to talk about, and found your personality withering away like an atrophied limb.

They didn't tell you about the whimsical supply drops and the ensuing shortages of staples like toothpaste and toilet paper. They didn't tell you about the days when all the systems seemed to conk out at once and your deadening routine suddenly became hours of all-out frantic terror. They didn't tell you that after a while you forgot you were on the moon and stopped sneaking looks at the battered blue marble. They didn't tell you that after a while it stopped being a dream and became instead just a dirty and backbreaking job; one that drained you of your enthusiasm faster than you could possibly guess, and one that replaced your ambitions of building a new future with more mundane longings, like feeling once again what it was like to stand unencumbered beneath a midday sun, breathing air that tasted like air and not canned sweat.

They waited until you were done learning all of this on your own before they told you about Minnie and Earl.

I learned on a Sunday—not that I had any reason to keep track of the day; the early development teams were way too short-staffed to enjoy luxuries like days off. There were instead days when you got the shitty jobs and the days when you got the jobs slightly less shitty than the others. On that particular Sunday I had repair duty, the worst job on the moon but for another twenty or thirty possible candidates. It involved, among them, inspecting, cleaning, and replacing the panels on the solar collectors. There were a lot of panels, since the early collector fields were five kilometers on a side, and each panel was only half a meter square. They tended to collect meteor dust (at best) and get scarred and pitted from micrometeor impacts (at worst). We'd just lost a number of them from heavier rock precipitation, which meant that in addition to replacing those I had to examine even those that remained intact. Since the panels swiveled to follow the sun across the sky, even a small amount of dust debris threatened to fall through the joints into the machinery below. There was never a lot of dust—sometimes it was not even visible. But it had to be removed one panel at a time.

To overhaul the assembly, you spent the whole day on your belly, crawling along the catwalks between them, removing each panel in turn, inspecting them beneath a canopy with nothing but suit light, magnifiers, and micro-thin air jet. (A vacuum, of course, would have been redundant.) You replaced the panels pitted beyond repair, brought the ruined ones back to the sled for disposal, and then started all over again.

The romance of space travel? Try nine hours of hideously tedious stoop labor, in a moonsuit. Try hating every minute of it. Try hating where you are and what you're doing and how hard you worked to qualify for this privilege. Try also hating yourself just for feeling that way, but not having any idea how to turn those feelings off.

I was muttering to myself, conjugating some of the more colorful expressions for excrement, when Phil Jacoby called. He was one of the more annoying people on the moon: a perpetual smiler who always looked on the bright side of things and refused to react to even the most acidic sarcasm. Appropriately enough, his carrot hair and freckled cheeks always made him look like a ventriloquist's dummy. He might have been our morale officer, if we'd possessed enough bad taste to have somebody with that job title, but that would have made him even more the kind of guy you grow to hate when you really want to be in a bad mood. I dearly appreciated how distant his voice sounded, as he called my name over the radio. "Max! You bored yet, Max?"

"Sorry," I said tiredly. "Max went home."

"Home as in his quarters? Or Home as in Earth?"

"There is no home here," I said. "Of course Home as on Earth."

"No return shuttles today," Phil noted. "Or any time this month. How would he manage that trick?"

"He was so fed up he decided to walk."

"Hope he took a picnic lunch or four. That's got to be a major hike."

In another mood, I might have smiled. "What's the bad news, Phil?"

"Why? You expecting bad news?"

There was a hidden glee to his tone that sounded excessive even from Jacoby. "Surprise me."

"You're quitting early. The barge will be by to pick you up in five minutes."

According to the digital readout inside my helmet, it was only 13:38 LT. The news that I wouldn't have to devote another three hours to painstaking cleanup should have cheered me considerably; instead, it rendered me about twenty times more suspicious. I said, "Phil, it will take me at least three times that long just to secure—"

"A relief shift will arrive on another barge within the hour. Don't do another minute of work. Just go back to the sled and wait for pickup. That's an order."

Which was especially strange because Jacoby was not technically my superior. Sure, he'd been on the moon all of one hundred and twenty days longer than me—and sure, that meant any advice he had to give me needed to be treated like an order, if I wanted to do my job—but even so, he was not the kind of guy who ever ended anything with an authoritarian *That's An Order*. My first reaction was the certainty that I must have been in some kind of serious trouble. Somewhere, sometime, I must have forgotten or neglected one of the safety protocols, and did something suicidally, crazily wrong—the kind of thing that once discovered would lead to me being relieved for incompetence. But I was still new on the moon, and I couldn't think of any recent occasion where I'd been given enough responsibility for that to be a factor. My next words were especially cautious: "Uh, Phil, did I—"

"Go to the sled," he repeated, even more sternly this time. "And, Max?"

"What?" I asked.

The ebullient side of his personality returned. "I envy you, man."

The connection clicked off before I could ask him why.

● ● ●

A lunar barge was a lot like its terrestrial equivalent, in that it had no motive power of its very own, but needed to be pulled by another vehicle. Ours were pulled by tractors. They had no atmospheric enclosures, since ninety percent of the time they were just used for the slow-motion hauling of construction equipment. Whenever they were needed to move personnel, we bolted in a number of forward-facing seats with oxygen feeds and canvas straps to prevent folks imprisoned by clumsy moonsuits from being knocked out of their chairs every time the flatbed dipped in the terrain. It was an extremely low-tech method of travel, not much faster than a human being could sprint, and we didn't often use it for long distances.

There were four other passengers on this one, all identical behind mirrored facemasks; I had to read their nametags to see who they were. Nikki Hollander, Oscar Desalvo, George Peterson, and Carrie Aldrin No Relation (the last two words a nigh-permanent part of her name, up here). All four of them had been on-site at least a year more than I had, and to my eyes had always seemed to be dealing with a routine a lot better than I had been. As I strapped in, and the tractor started up, and the barge began its glacial progress toward a set of lumpy peaks on the horizon, I wished my co-workers had something other than distorted reflections of the lunar landscape for faces; it would be nice to be able to judge from their expressions just what was going on here. I said: "So what's the story, people? Where we headed?"

Then Carrie Aldrin No Relation began to sing: "Over the river and through the woods / to grandmother's house we go…"

George Peterson snorted. Oscar Desalvo, a man not known for his giddy sense of humor, who was in fact even grimmer than me most of the time—not from disenchantment with his work, but out of personal inclination—giggled; it was like watching one of the figures on Mount Rushmore stick its tongue out. Nikki Hollander joined in, her considerably less-than-perfect pitch turning the rest of the song into a nails-on-blackboard cacophony. The helmet speakers, which distorted anyway, did not help.

I said, "Excuse me?"

Nikki Hollander said something so blatantly ridiculous that I couldn't force myself to believe I'd heard her correctly.

"Come again? I lost that."

"No you didn't." Her voice seemed strained, almost hysterical.

One of the men was choking with poorly repressed laughter. I couldn't tell who.

"You want to know if I like yams?"

Nikki's response was a burlesque parody of astronautic stoicism. "That's an a-ffirmative, Houston."

"Yams, the vegetable yams?"

"A-ffirmative." The A emphasized and italicized so broadly that it was not so much a separate syllable as a sovereign country.

This time I recognized the strangulated noises. They were coming from George Peterson, and they were the sounds made by a man who was trying very hard not to laugh. It was several seconds before I could summon enough dignity to answer. "Yeah, I like yams. How is that relevant?"

"Classified," she said, and then her signal cut off.

In fact, all their signals cut off, though I could tell from the red indicators on my internal display that they were all still broadcasting.

That was not unusual. Coded frequencies were one of the few genuine amenities allowed us; they allowed those of us who absolutely needed a few seconds to discuss personal matters with co-workers to do so without sharing their affairs with anybody else who might be listening. We're not supposed to spend more than a couple of minutes at a time on those channels because it's safer to stay monitored. Being shut out of four signals simultaneously, in a manner that could only mean raucous laughter at my expense, was unprecedented, and it pissed me off. Hell, I'll freely admit that it did more than that; it frightened me. I was on the verge of suspecting brain damage caused by something wrong with the air supply.

Then George Peterson's voice clicked: "Sorry about that, old buddy." (I'd never been his old buddy.) "We usually do a better job keeping a straight face."

"At what? Mind telling me what's going on here?"

"One minute." He performed the series of maneuvers necessary to cut off the oxygen provided by the barge, and restore his dependence on the supply contained in his suit, then unstrapped his harnesses, stood, and moved toward me, swaying slightly from the bumps and jars of our imperfectly smooth ride across the lunar surface.

It was, of course, against all safety regulations for him to be on his feet while the barge was in motion; after all, even as glacially slow as that was, it wouldn't have taken all that great an imperfection in the road before us to knock him down and perhaps inflict the kind of hairline puncture capable of leaving him with a slight case of death. We had all disobeyed that particular rule from time to time; there were just too many practical advantages in being able to move around at will, without first ordering the tractor to stop. But it made no sense for him to come over now, just to talk, as if it really made a difference for us to be face-to-face. We weren't faces. We were a pair of convex mirrors, reflecting each other while the men behind them spoke on radios too powerful to be noticeably improved by a few less meters of distance.

Even so, he sat down on a steel crate lashed to the deck before me, and positioned his faceplate opposite mine, his body language suggesting meaningful eye contact. He held that position for almost a minute, not saying anything, not moving, behaving exactly like a man who believed he was staring me down.

It made no sense. I could have gone to sleep and he wouldn't have noticed.

Instead, I said: "What?"

He spoke quietly: "Am I correct in observing that you've felt less than, shall we say...'inspired,' by your responsibilities here?"

Oh, Christ. This was about something I'd done.

"Is there some kind of problem?"

George's helmet trembled enough to suggest a man theatrically shaking his head inside it. "Lighten up, Max. Nobody has any complaints about your work. We think you're one of the best people we have here, and your next evaluation is going to give you straight A's in every department... except enthusiasm. You just don't seem to believe in the work anymore."

As much as I tried to avoid it, my answer still reeked with denial. "I believe in it."

"You believe in the idea of it," George said. "But the reality has worn you down."

I was stiff, proper, absolutely correct, and absolutely transparent. "I was trained. I spent a full year in simulation, doing all the same jobs. I knew what it was going to be like. I knew what to expect."

"No amount of training can prepare you for the moment when you think you can't feel the magic anymore."

"And you can?" I asked, unable to keep the scorn from my voice.

The speakers inside lunar helmets were still pretty tinny, in those days; they no longer transformed everything we said into the monotones that once upon a time helped get an entire country fed up with the forced badinage of Apollo, but neither were they much good at conveying the most precise of emotional cues. And yet I was able to pick up something in George's tone that was, given my mood, capable of profoundly disturbing me: a strange, transcendent joy. "Oh, yes, Max. I can."

I was just unnerved enough to ask: "How?"

"I'm swimming in it," he said—and even as long as he'd been part of the secret, his voice still quavered, as if there was some seven-year-old part of him that remained unwilling to believe that it could possibly be. "We're all swimming in it."

"I'm not."

And he laughed out loud. "Don't worry. We're going to gang up and shove you into the deep end of the pool."

• • •

That was seventy years ago.

Seventy years. I think about how old that makes me and I cringe. Seventy years ago, the vast majority of old farts who somehow managed to make it to the age I am now were almost always living on the outer edges of decrepitude. The physical problems were nothing compared with the senility. What's that? You don't remember senile dementia? Really? I guess there's a joke in there somewhere, but it's not that funny for those of us who can remember actually considering it a possible future. Trust me, it was a nightmare. And the day they licked that one was one hell of an advertisement for progress.

But still, seventy years. You want to know how long ago that was? Seventy years ago it was still possible to find people who had heard of Bruce Springsteen. There were even some who remembered the Beatles. Stephen King was still coming out with his last few books, Kate Emma Brenner hadn't yet come out with any, Exxon was still in business, the reconstruction of the ice packs hadn't even been proposed, India and Pakistan hadn't reconciled, and the idea of astronauts going out into space to blow up a giant asteroid before it impacted with Earth was not an anecdote from recent history but a half-remembered image from a movie your father talked about going to see when he was a kid. Seventy years ago the most pressing headlines had to do with the worldwide ecological threat posed by the population explosion among escaped sugar gliders.

Seventy years ago, I hadn't met Claire. She was still married to her first husband, the one she described as the nice mistake. She had no idea I was anywhere in her future. I had no idea she was anywhere in mine. The void hadn't been defined yet, let alone filled. (Nor had it been cruelly emptied again—and wasn't it sad how the void I'd lived with for so long seemed a lot larger, once I needed to endure it again?)

Seventy years ago I thought Faisal Awad was an old man. He may have been in his mid-thirties then, at most ten years older than I was. That, to me, was old. These days it seems one step removed from the crib.

I haven't mentioned Faisal yet; he wasn't along the day George and the others picked me up in the barge, and we didn't become friends till later. But he was a major member of the development team, back then—the kind of fixitall adventurer who could use the coffee machine in the common room to repair the heating system in the clinic. If you don't think that's a valuable skill, try living under 24-7 life support in a hostile environment where any requisitions for spare parts had to be debated and voted upon by a government committee during election years. It's the time of my life when I first developed my deep abiding hatred of Senators. Faisal was our life-saver, our miracle worker, and our biggest local authority on the works of Gilbert and Sullivan, though back then we were all too busy to listen to music and much more likely to listen to that fifteen-minute wonder Polka Thug anyway. After I left the moon, and the decades of my life fluttered by faster than I once could have imagined possible, I used to think about Faisal and decide that I really ought to look him up, someday, maybe, as soon as I had the chance. But he had stayed on Luna, and I had gone back to Earth, and what with one thing or another that resolution had worked out as well as such oughtas always do: a lesson that old men have learned too late for as long as there have been old men to learn it.

I didn't even know how long he'd been dead until I heard it from his granddaughter Janine Seuss, a third-generation lunar I was able to track down with the help of the Selene Historical Society. She was a slightly built thirty-seven-year-old with stylishly mismatched eye color and hair micro-styled into infinitesimal pixels that, when combed correctly, formed the famous old black-and-white news photograph of that doomed young girl giving the finger to the cops at the San Diego riots of some thirty years ago. Though she had graciously agreed to meet me, she hadn't had time to arrange her hair properly, and the photo was eerily distorted, like an image captured and then distorted on putty. She served coffee, which I can't drink anymore but which I accepted anyway, then sat down on her couch with the frantically miaowing Siamese.

"There were still blowouts then," she said. "Some genuine accidents, some bombings arranged by the Flat-Mooners. It was one of the Flat-Mooners who got Poppy. He was taking Mermer—our name for Grandma—to the movies up on topside; back then, they used to project them on this big white screen a couple of kilometers outside, though it was always some damn thing fifty or a hundred years old with dialogue that didn't make sense and stories you had to be older than Moses to appreciate. Anyway, the commuter tram they were riding just went boom and opened up into pure vacuum. Poppy and Mermer and about fourteen others got sucked out." She took a deep breath, then let it out all at once. "That was almost twenty years ago."

What else can you say, when you hear a story like that? "I'm sorry."

She acknowledged that with an equally ritual response. "Thanks."

"Did they catch the people responsible?"

"Right away. They were a bunch of losers. Unemployed idiots."

I remembered the days when the only idiots on the moon were highly educated and overworked ones. After a moment, I said: "Did he ever talk about the early days? The development teams?"

She smiled. "Ever? It was practically all he ever did talk about. You kids don't, bleh bleh bleh. He used to get mad at the vids that made it look like a time of sheriffs and saloons and gunfights—he guessed they probably made good stories for kids who didn't know any better, but kept complaining that life back then wasn't anything like that. He said there was always too much work to do to strap on six-guns and go gunning for each other."

"He was right," I said. (There was a grand total of one gunfight in the first thirty years of lunar settlement—and it's not part of this story.)

"Most of his stories about those days had to do with things breaking down and him being the only person who could fix them in the nick of time. He told reconditioned-software anecdotes. Finding the rotten air filter anecdotes. Improvised joint-lubricant anecdotes. Lots of them."

"That was Faisal."

She petted the cat. (It was a heavy-lidded, meatloaf-shaped thing that probably bestirred itself only at the sound of a can opener: we'd tamed the moon so utterly that people like Janine were able to spare some pampering for their pets.) "Bleh. I prefer the gunfights."

I leaned forward and asked the important question. "Did he ever mention anybody named Minnie and Earl?"

"Were those a couple of folks from way back then?"

"You could say that."

"No last names?"

"None they ever used."

She thought about that, and said: "Would they have been folks he knew only slightly? Or important people?"

"Very important people," I said. "It's vital that I reach them."

She frowned. "It was a long time ago. Can you be sure they're still alive?"

"Absolutely," I said.

She considered that for a second. "No, I'm sorry. But you have to realize it was a long time ago for me too. I don't remember him mentioning anybody."

Faisal was the last of the people I'd known from my days on the moon. There were a couple on Earth, but both had flatly denied any knowledge of Minnie and Earl. Casting about for last straws, I said: "Do you have anything that belonged to him?"

"No, I don't. But I know where you can go to look further."

• • •

Seventy years ago, after being picked up by the barge:

Nobody spoke to me again for forty-five minutes, which only fueled my suspicions of mass insanity.

The barge itself made slow but steady progress, following a generally uphill course of the only kind possible in that era, in that place, on the moon: which was to say, serpentine. The landscape here was rough, pocked with craters and jagged outcroppings, in no place willing to respect how convenient it might have been to allow us to proceed in something approaching a straight line. There were places where we had to turn almost a hundred and eighty degrees, double back awhile, then turn again, to head in an entirely different direction; it was the kind of route that looks random from one minute to the next but gradually reveals progress in one direction or another. It was clearly a route that my colleagues had traveled many times before; nobody seemed impatient. But for the one guy who had absolutely no idea where we were going, and who wasn't in fact certain that we were headed anywhere at all, it was torture.

We would have managed the trip in maybe one-tenth the time in one of our fliers, but I later learned that the very laboriousness of the journey was, for first-timers at least, a traditional part of the show. It gave us time to speculate, to anticipate. This was useful for unlimbering the mind, ironing the kinks out of the imagination, getting us used to the idea that we were headed someplace important enough to be worth the trip. The buildup couldn't possibly be enough—the view over that last ridge was still going to hit us with the force of a sledgehammer to the brain—but I remember how hard it hit and I'm still thankful the shock was cushioned even as inadequately as it was.

We followed a long boring ridge for the better part of fifteen minutes… then began to climb a slope that bore the rutty look of lunar ground that had known tractor-treads hundreds of times before. Some of my fellow journeyers hummed ominous, horror-movie soundtrack music in my ear, but George's voice overrode them all: "Max? Did Phil tell you he envied you this moment?"

I was really nervous now. "Yes."

"He's full of crap. You're not going to enjoy this next bit instead in retrospect. Later on you'll think of it as the best moment of your life—and it might even be—but it won't feel like that when it happens. It'll feel big and frightening and insane when it happens. Trust me now when I tell you that it will get better, and quickly…and that everything will be explained, if not completely, then at least as much as it needs to be."

It was an odd turn of phrase. "As much as it needs to be? What's that supposed to—"

That's when the barge reached the top of the rise, providing us a nice panoramic view of what awaited us in the shallow depression on the other side.

My ability to form coherent sentences became a distant rumor.

It was the kind of moment when the entire universe seems to become a wobbly thing, propped up by scaffolding and held together with the cheapest brand of hardware-store nails. The kind of moment when gravity just turns sideways beneath you, and the whole world turns on its edge, and the only thing that prevents you from just jetting off into space to spontaneously combust is the compensatory total stoppage of time. I don't know the first thing I said. I'm glad nobody ever played me the recordings that got filed away in the permanent mission archives…

and I'm equally sure that the reason they didn't is that anybody actually on the moon to listen to them must have also had their own equally aghast reactions also saved for posterity. I got to hear such sounds many times, from others I would later escort over that ridge myself—and I can absolutely assure you that they're the sounds made by intelligent, educated people who first think they've gone insane, and who then realize it doesn't help to know that they haven't.

It was the only possible immediate reaction to the first sight of Minnie and Earl's.

What I saw, as we crested the top of that ridge, was this:

In the center of a typically barren lunar landscape, surrounded on all sides by impact craters, rocks, more rocks, and the suffocating emptiness of vacuum—

—a dark landscape, mind you, one imprisoned by lunar night, and illuminated only by the gibbous Earth hanging high above us—

—a rectangle of color and light, in the form of four square acres of freshly watered, freshly mowed lawn.

With a house on it.

Not a prefab box of the kind we dropped all over the lunar landscape for storage and emergency air stops.

A house.

A clapboard family home, painted a homey yellow, with a wraparound porch three steps off the ground, a canopy to keep off the sun, a screen door leading inside and a bug-zapper over the threshold. There was a porch swing with cushions in a big yellow daisy pattern, and a wall of neatly trimmed hedges around the house, obscuring the latticework that enclosed the crawlspace underneath. It was over-the-top Middle American that even in that first moment I half-crazily expected the scent of lemonade to cross the vacuum and enter my suit. (That didn't happen, but lemonade was waiting.) The lawn was completely surrounded with a white picket fence with an open gate; there was even an old-fashioned mailbox at the gate, with its flag up. All of it was lit, from nowhere, like a bright summer afternoon. The house itself had two stories, plus a sloping shingled roof high enough to hide a respectable attic; as we drew closer I saw that there were pull-down shades, not Venetian blinds, in the pane-glass windows. Closer still, and I spotted the golden retriever that lay on the porch, its head resting between muddy paws as it followed our approach; it was definitely a lazy dog, since it did not get up to investigate us, but it was also a friendly one, whose big red tail thumped against the porch in anticipation. Closer still, and I made various consonant noises as a venerable old lady in gardening overalls came around the side of the house, spotted us, and broke into the kind of smile native only to contented old ladies seeing good friends or grandchildren after too long away. When my fellow astronauts all waved back, I almost followed their lead, but for some reason my arms wouldn't move.

Somewhere in there I murmured, "This is impossible."

"Clearly not," George said. "If it were impossible it wouldn't be happening. The more accurate word is inexplicable."

"What the hell is—"

"Come on, goofball." This from Carrie Aldrin No Relation. "You're acting like you never saw a house before."

Sometimes, knowing when to keep your mouth shut is the most eloquent expression of wisdom. I shut up.

It took about a million and a half years—or five minutes if you go by merely chronological time—for the tractor to descend the shallow slope and bring us to a stop some twenty meters from the front gate. By then an old man had joined the old woman at the fence. He was a lean old codger with bright blue eyes, a nose like a hawk, a smile that suggested he'd just heard a whopper of a joke, and the kind of forehead some very old men have—the kind that by all rights ought to have been glistening with sweat, like most bald heads, but instead seemed perpetually dry, in a way that suggested a sophisticated system for the redistribution of excess moisture. He had the leathery look of old men who had spent much of their lives working in the sun. He wore neatly pressed tan pants, sandals, and a white button-down shirt open at the collar, all of which was slightly loose on him—not enough to make him look comical or pathetic, but enough to suggest that he'd been a somewhat bigger man before age had diminished him, and was still used to buying the larger sizes. (That is, I thought, if there was any possibility of him finding a good place to shop around here.)

His wife, if that's who she was, was half a head shorter and slightly stouter; she had blue eyes and a bright smile, like him, but a soft and rounded face that provided a pleasant complement to his lean and angular one. She was just overweight enough to provide her with the homey accoutrements of chubby cheeks and double chin; unlike her weathered, bone-dry husband, she was smooth-skinned and shiny-faced and very much a creature the sun had left untouched (though she evidently spent time there; at least, she wore gardener's gloves, and carried a spade).

They were, in short, vaguely reminiscent of the old folks standing before the farmhouse in that famous old painting *American Gothic.* You know the one I mean—the constipated old guy with the pitchfork next to the wife who seems mortified by his very presence? These two were those two after they cheered up enough to be worth meeting.

Except, of course, that this couldn't possibly be happening.

My colleagues unstrapped themselves, lowered the stairway, and disembarked. The tractor driver, whoever he was, emerged from its cab and joined them. George stayed with me, watching my every move, as I proved capable of climbing down a set of three steps without demonstrating my total incapacitation from shock. When my boots crunched lunar gravel—a texture I could feel right through the treads of my boots, and which served at that moment to reconnect me to ordinary physical reality—Carrie, Oscar, and Nikki patted me on the back, a gesture that felt like half-congratulation, and half-commiseration. The driver came by, too; I saw from the markings on his suit that he was Pete Rawlik, who was assigned to some kind of classified biochemical research in one of our outlabs; he had always been too busy to mix much, and I'd met him maybe twice by that point, but he still clapped my shoulder like an old friend. As for George, he made a wait gesture and went back up the steps.

In the thirty seconds we stood there waiting for him, I looked up at the picket fence, just to confirm that the impossible old couple was still there, and I saw that the golden retriever, which had joined its masters at the gate, was barking silently. That was good. If the sound had carried in vacuum, I might have been worried. That would have been just plain crazy.

Then George came back, carrying an airtight metal cylinder just about big enough to hold a soccer ball. I hadn't seen any vacuum boxes of that particular shape and size before, but any confusion I might have felt about that was just about the last thing I needed to worry about. He addressed the others: "How's he doing?"

A babble of noncommittal okays dueled for broadcast supremacy. Then the voices resolved into individuals.

Nikki Hollander said: "Well, at least he's not babbling anymore."

Oscar Desalvo snorted: "I attribute that to brain-lock."

"You weren't any better," said Carrie Aldrin No Relation. "Worse. If I recall correctly, you made a mess in your suit."

"I'm not claiming any position of false superiority, hon. Just giving my considered diagnosis."

"Whatever," said Pete Rawlik. "Let's just cross the fenceline, already. I have an itch."

"In a second," George said. His mirrored faceplate turned toward mine, aping eye-contact. "Max? You getting this?"

"Barely," I managed.

"Outstanding. You're doing fine. But I need you with me a hundred percent while I cover our most important ground rule. Namely—everything inside that picket fence is a temperate-climate, sea-level, terrestrial environment. You don't have to worry about air filtration, temperature levels, or anything else. It's totally safe to suit down, as long as you're inside the perimeter—and in a few minutes, we will all be doing just that. But once you're inside that enclosure, the picket fence itself marks the beginning of lunar vacuum, lunar temperatures, and everything that implies. You do not, repeat not, do anything to test the differential. Even sticking a finger out between the slats is enough to get you bounced from the program, with no possibility of reprieve. Is that clear?"

"Yes, but—"

"Rule Two," he said, handing me the sealed metal box. "You're the new guy. You carry the pie."

I regarded the cylinder. Pie?

•••

I kept waiting for the other shoe to drop, but it never did.

The instant we passed through the front gate, the dead world this should have been surrendered to a living one. Sound returned between one step and the next. The welcoming cries of the two old people—and the barking of their friendly golden retriever dog—may have been muffled by my helmet, but they were still identifiable enough to present touches of personality. The old man's voice was gruff in a manner that implied a past flavored by whiskey and cigars, but there was also a singsong quality to it, that instantly manifested itself as a tendency to end his sentences at higher registers. The old woman's voice was soft and breathy, with only the vaguest suggestion of an old-age quaver and a compensatory tinge of the purest Georgia Peach. The dog's barks were like little frenzied explosions that might have been threatening if they hadn't all trailed off into quizzical whines. It was a symphony of various sounds that could be made for hello: laughs, cries, yips, and delighted shouts of "George! Oscar! Nikki! Carrie! Pete! So glad you could make it! How are you?"

It was enough to return me to statue mode. I didn't even move when the others disengaged their helmet locks, doffed their headgear, and began oohing and aahing themselves. I just spent the next couple of minutes watching, physically in their midst but mentally somewhere very far away, as the parade of impossibilities passed on by. I noted that Carrie Aldrin No Relation, who usually wore her long red hair beneath the tightest of protective nets, was today styled in pigtails with big pink bows; that Oscar, who was habitually scraggly-haired and two days into a beard, was today perfectly kempt and freshly shaven; that George giggled like a five-year-old when the dog stood up on its hind legs to slobber all over his face; and that Pete engaged with a little mock wrestling match with the old man that almost left him toppling backward onto the grass. I saw the women whisper to each other, then bound up the porch steps into the house, so excitedly that they reminded me of schoolgirls skipping off to the playground—a gait that should have been impossible to simulate in a bulky moonsuit, but which they pulled off with perfect flair. I saw Pete and Oscar follow along behind them, laughing at a shared joke.

I was totally ignored until the dog stood up on its hind legs to sniff at, then snort nasal condensation on, my faceplate. His ears went back. He whined, then scratched at his reflection, then looked over his shoulder at the rest of his pack, long pink tongue lolling plaintively. *Look, guys. There's somebody in this thing.*

I didn't know I was going to take the leap of faith until I actually placed the cake cylinder on the ground, then reached up and undid my helmet locks. The hiss of escaping air made my blood freeze in my chest; for a second I was absolutely certain that all of this was a hallucination brought on by oxygen deprivation, and that I'd just committed suicide by open-ing my suit to vacuum. But the hiss subsided, and I realized that it was just pressure equalization; the atmosphere in this environment must have been slightly less than that provided by the suit. A second later, as I removed my helmet, I tasted golden retriever breath as the dog leaned in close and said hello by licking me on the lips. I also smelled freshly mowed grass and the perfume of nearby flowers; I heard a bird not too far away go whoot-toot-toot-weet; and I felt direct sunlight on my face, even though the sun itself was nowhere to be seen. The air itself was pleasantly warm, like summer before it gets obnoxious with heat and humidity.

"Miles!" the old man said. "Get down!"

The dog gave me one last lick for the road and sat down, gazing up at me with that species of tongue-lolling amusement known only to large canines.

The old woman clutched the elbow of George's suit. "Oh, you didn't tell me you were bringing somebody new this time! How wonderful!"

"What is this place?" I managed.

The old man raised his eyebrows. "It's our front yard, son. What does it look like?"

The old woman slapped his hand lightly. "Be nice, dear. You can see he's taking it hard."

He grunted. "Always did beat me how you can tell what a guy's thinking and feeling just by looking at him."

She patted his arm again. "It's not all that unusual, apricot. I'm a woman."

George ambled on over, pulling the two oldsters along. "All right, I'll get it started. Max Fischer, I want you to meet two of the best people on this world or any other—Minnie and Earl. Minnie and Earl, I want you to meet a guy who's not quite as hopeless as he probably seems on first impression—Max Fischer. You'll like him."

"I like him already," Minnie said. "I've yet to dislike anybody the dog took such an immediate shine to. Hi, Max."

"Hello," I said. After a moment: "Minnie. Earl."

"Wonderful to meet you, young man. Your friends have said so much about you."

"Thanks." Shock lent honesty to my response: "They've said absolutely nothing about you."

"They never do," she said, with infinite sadness, as George smirked at me over her back. She glanced down at the metal cylinder at my feet, and cooed: "Is that cake?"

Suddenly, absurdly, the first rule of family visits popped unbidden into my head, blaring its commandment in flaming letters twenty miles high: THOU SHALT NOT PUT THE CAKE YOU BROUGHT ON THE GROUND—ESPECIALLY NOT WHEN A DOG IS PRESENT. Never mind that the container was sealed against vacuum, and that the dog would have needed twenty minutes to get in with an industrial drill: the lessons of everyday American socialization still applied. I picked it up and handed it to her; she took it with her bare hands, reacting not at all to what hindsight later informed me should have been a painfully cold exterior. I said: "Sorry."

"It's pie," said George. "Deep-dish apple pie. Direct from my grandma's orchard."

"Oh, that's sweet of her. She still having those back problems?"

"She's getting on in years," George allowed. "But she says that soup of yours really helped."

"I'm glad," she said, her smile as sunny as the entire month of July. "Meanwhile, why don't you take your friend upstairs and get him out of that horrid suit? I'm sure he'll feel a lot better once he's had a chance to freshen up. Earl can have a drink set for him by the time you come down."

"I'll fix a Sea of Tranquility," Earl said, with enthusiasm.

"Maybe once he has his feet under him. A beer should be fine for now."

"All rightee," said Earl, with the kind of wink that established he knew quite well I was going to need something a lot more substantial than beer.

As for Minnie, she seized my hand, and said: "It'll be all right, apricot. Once you get past this stage, I'm sure we're all going to be great friends."

"Um," I replied, with perfect eloquence.

Wondering just what stage I was being expected to pass.

Sanity?

•••

Dying inside, I did what seemed to be appropriate. I followed George through the front door (first stamping my moonboots on the mat, as he specified) and up the narrow, creaky wooden staircase.

You ever go to parties where the guests leave their coats in a heap on the bed of the master bedroom? Minnie and Earl's was like that.

Except it wasn't a pile of coats, but a pile of disassembled moonsuits. There were actually two bedrooms upstairs—the women changed in the master bedroom that evidently belonged to the oldsters themselves, the men in a smaller room that felt like it belonged to a teenage boy. The wallpaper was a pattern of galloping horses, and the bookcases were filled with mint-edition paperback thrillers that must have been a hundred years old even then. (Or more: there was a complete collection of the hardcover Hardy Boys Mysteries, by Franklin W. Dixon.) The desk was a genuine antique rolltop, with a green blotter; no computer or hytex. The bed was just big enough to hold one gangly teenager, or three moonsuits disassembled into their component parts, with a special towel provided so our boots wouldn't get moondust all over the bedspread. By the time George and I got up there, Oscar and Pete had already changed into slacks, dress shoes with black socks, and button-down shirts with red bowties; Pete had even put some shiny gunk in his hair to slick it back. They winked at me as they left.

I didn't change, not immediately; nor did I speak, not even as George doffed his own moonsuit and jumpers in favor of a similarly earthbound outfit he blithely salvaged from the closet. The conviction that I was being tested, somehow, was so overwhelming that the interior of my suit must have been a puddle of flop sweat.

Then George said: "You going to be comfortable, dressed like that all night?"

I stirred. "Clothes?"

He pulled an outfit my size from the closet—tan pants, a blue short-sleeved button-down shirt, gleaming black shoes, and a red bowtie identical to the ones Oscar and Pete had donned. "No problem borrowing. Minnie keeps an ample supply. You don't like the selection, you want to pick something more your style, you can always have something snazzier sent up on the next supply drop. I promise you, she'll appreciate the extra effort. It makes her day when—"

"George," I said softly.

"Have trouble with bowties? No problem. They're optional. You can—"

"George," I said again, and this time my voice was a little louder, a little deeper, a little more *For Christ's Sake Shut Up I'm Sick Of This Shit*.

He batted his eyes, all innocence and naiveté. "Yes, Max?"

My look, by contrast, must have been half-murderous. "Tell me."

"Tell you what?"

It was very hard not to yell. "You know what!"

He fingered an old issue of some garishly colored turn-of-the-millennium science fiction magazine. "Oh. That mixed drink Earl mentioned. The Sea of Tranquility. It's his own invention, and he calls it that because your first sip is one small step for Man, and your second is one giant leap for Mankind. There's peppermint in it. Give it a try and I promise you you'll be on his good side for life. He—"

I squeezed the words through clenched teeth. "I. Don't. Care. About. The. Bloody. Drink."

"Then I'm afraid I don't see your problem."

"My problem," I said, slowly, and with carefully repressed frustration, "is that all of this is downright impossible."

"Apparently not," he noted.

"I want to know who these people are, and what they're doing here."

"They're Minnie and Earl, and they're having some friends over for dinner."

If I'd been five years old, I might have pouted and stamped my foot. (Sometimes, remembering, I think I did anyway.) "Dammit, George!"

He remained supernaturally calm. "No cursing in this house, Max. Minnie doesn't like it. She won't throw you out for doing it—she's too nice for that—but it does make her uncomfortable."

This is the point where I absolutely know I stamped my foot. "That makes HER uncomfortable!?"

He put down the skiffy magazine. "Really. I don't see why you're having such a problem with this. They're just this great old couple who happen to live in a little country house on the moon, and their favorite thing is getting together with friends, and we're here to have Sunday night dinner with them. Easy to understand…especially if you accept that it's all there is."

"That can't be all there is!" I cried, my exasperation reaching critical mass.

"Why not? Can't 'Just Because' qualify as a proper scientific theory?"

"No! It doesn't!—How come you never told me about this place before?"

"You never asked before." He adjusted his tie, glanced at the outfit laid out for me on the bed, and went to the door. "Don't worry; it didn't for me, either. Something close to an explanation is forthcoming. Just get dressed and come downstairs already. We don't want the folks to think you're antisocial..."

•••

I'd been exasperated, way back then, because Minnie and Earl were there and had no right to be. I was exasperated now because the more I looked the more impossible it became to find any indication that they'd ever been there at all.

I had started looking for them, if only in a desultory, abstracted way, shortly after Claire died. She'd been the only person on Earth who had ever believed my stories about them. Even now, I think it's a small miracle that she did. I had told her the story of Minnie and Earl before we even became man and wife—sometime after I knew I was going to propose, but before I found the right time and place for the question. I was just back from a couple of years of Outer-System work, had grown weary of the life, and had met this spectacularly kind and funny and beautiful person whose interests were all on Earth, and who had no real desire to go out into space herself. That was just fine with me. It was what I wanted too. And of course I rarely talked to her about my years in space, because I didn't want to become an old bore with a suitcase full of old stories. Even so, I still knew, at the beginning, that knowing about a real-life miracle and not mentioning it to her, ever, just because she was not likely to believe me, was tantamount to cheating. So I sat her down one day, even before the proposal, and told her about Minnie and Earl. And she believed me. She didn't humor me. She didn't just say she believed me. She didn't just believe me to be nice. She believed me. She said she always knew when I was shoveling manure and when I was not—a boast that turned out to be an integral strength of our marriage—and that it was impossible for her to hear me tell the story without knowing that Minnie and Earl were real. She said that if we had children I would have to tell the story to them, too, to pass it on.

That was one of the special things about Claire: she had faith when faith was needed.

But our son and our daughter, and later the grandkids, outgrew believing me. For them, Minnie and Earl were whimsical space-age versions of Santa.

I didn't mind that, not really.

But when she died, finding Minnie and Earl again seemed very important.

It wasn't just that their house was gone, or that Minnie and Earl seemed to have departed for regions unknown; and it wasn't just that the official histories of the early development teams now completely omitted any mention of the secret hoarded by everybody who had ever spent time on the moon in those days. It wasn't just that the classified files I had read and eventually contributed to had disappeared, flushed down the same hole that sends all embarrassing government secrets down the pipe to their final resting place in the sea. But for more years than I'd ever wanted to count, Minnie and Earl had been the secret history nobody ever talked about. I had spoken to those of my old colleagues who still remained alive, and they had all said, what are you talking about, what do you mean, are you feeling all right, nothing like that ever happened.

It was tempting to believe that my kids were right: that it had been a fairy tale: a little harmless personal fantasy I'd been carrying around with me for most of my life.

But I knew it wasn't.

Because Claire had believed me.

Because whenever I did drag out the old stories one more time, she always said, "I wish I'd known them." Not like an indulgent wife allowing the old man his delusions, but like a woman well acquainted with miracles. And because even if I was getting too old to always trust my own judgment, nothing would ever make me doubt hers.

I searched with phone calls, with letters, with hytex research, with the calling-in of old favors, with every tool available to me. I found nothing.

And then one day I was told that I didn't have much more time to look. It wasn't a tragedy; I'd lived a long and happy life. And it wasn't as bad as it could have been; I'd been assured that there wouldn't be much pain. But I did have that one little unresolved question still hanging over my head

That was the day I overcame decades of resistance and booked return passage to the world I had once helped to build.

The day after I spoke to Janine Seuss, I followed her advice and took a commuter tram to the Michael Collins Museum of Early Lunar Settlement. It was a popular tourist spot with all the tableaus and reenactments and, you should only excuse the expression, cheesy souvenirs you'd expect from such an establishment. I'd avoided it up until now mostly because I'd seen and heard most of it before, and much of what was left was the kind of crowd-pleasing foofaraw that tames and diminishes the actual experience I lived through for the consumption of folks who are primarily interested in tiring out their hyperactive kids. The dumbest of those was a pile of real Earth rocks, replacing the weight various early astronauts had taken from the moon; ha ha ha, stop, I'm dying here. The most offensive was a kids' exhibit narrated by a cartoon-character early development engineer; he spoke with a cornball rural accent, had comic-opera patches on the knees of his moonsuit, and seemed to have an IQ of about five.

Another annoying thing about frontiers: when they're not frontiers anymore, the civilizations that move in like to think that the people who came first were stupid.

But when I found pictures of myself, in an exhibit on the development programs, and pointed them out to an attendant, it was fairly easy to talk the curators into letting me into their archives for a look at certain other materials that hadn't seen the light of day for almost twenty years. They were taped interviews, thirty years old now, with a number of the old guys and gals, talking about their experiences in the days of early development: the majority of those had been conducted here on the moon, but others had taken place on Earth or Mars or wherever else any of those old farts ended up. I felt vaguely insulted that they hadn't tried to contact me; maybe they had, and my wife, anticipating my reluctance, had turned them away. I wondered if I should have felt annoyed by that. I wondered too if my annoyance at the taming of the moon had something to do with the disquieting sensation of becoming ancient history while you're still alive to remember it.

There were about ten thousand hours of interviews; even if my health remained stable long enough for me to listen to them all, my savings would run out far sooner. But they were indexed, and audio-search is a wonderful thing. I typed in "Minnie" and got several dozen references to small things, almost as many references to Mickey's rodent girlfriend, and a bunch of stories about a project engineer, from after my time, who had also been blessed with that particular first name. (To believe the transcripts, she spent all her waking hours saying impossibly cute things that her friends and colleagues would remember and be compelled to repeat decades later; what a bloody pixie.) I typed in "Earl" and, though it felt silly, "Miles," and got a similar collection of irrelevancies—many many references to miles, thus proving conclusively that as recently as thirty years ago the adoption of the metric system hadn't yet succeeded in wiping out any less-elegant but still fondly remembered forms of measurement. After that, temporarily stuck, I typed in my own name, first and last, and was rewarded with a fine selection of embarrassing anecdotes from folks who recalled what a humorless little pissant I had been way back then. All of this took hours; I had to listen to each of these references, if only for a second or two, just to know for sure what was being talked about, and I confess that, in between a number of bathroom breaks I would have considered unlikely as a younger man, I more than once forgot what I was supposedly looking for long enough to enjoy a few moments with old voices I hadn't heard for longer than most lunar residents had been alive.

I then cross-referenced by the names of the various people who were along on that first Sunday night trip to Minnie and Earl's. "George Peterson" got me nothing of obvious value. "Carrie Aldrin" and "Peter Rawlik," ditto. Nor did the other names. There were references, but nothing I particularly needed.

Feeling tired, I sat there drumming my fingertips on the tabletop. The museum was closing soon. The research had exhausted my limited stores of strength; I didn't think I could do this many days in a row. But I knew there was something here. There had to be. Even if there was a conspiracy of silence—organized or accidental—the mere existence of that unassuming little house had left too great a footprint on our lives.

I thought about details that Claire had found particularly affecting.

And then I typed "Yams."

•••

Seventy years ago, suffering from a truly epic sense of dislocation that made everything happening to me seem like bits of stage business performed by actors in a play whose author had taken care to omit all the important exposition, I descended a creaky flight of wooden stairs, to join my colleagues in Minnie and Earl's living room. I was the last to come down, of course; everybody else was already gathered around the three flowery-print sofas, munching on finger foods as they chatted up a storm. The women were in soft cottony dresses, the men in starched trousers and button-downs. They all clapped and cheered as I made my appearance, a reaction that brought an unwelcome blush to my cheeks. It was no wonder; I was a little withdrawn to begin with, back then, and the impossible context had me so off-center that all my defenses had turned to powder.

It was a homey place, though: brightly lit, with a burning fireplace, an array of glass shelving covered with a selection of home-made pottery, plants and flowers in every available nook, an upright piano, a bar that did not dominate the room, and an array of framed photographs on the wall behind the couch. There was no TV or hytex. I glanced at the photographs and moved toward them, hungry for data.

Then Earl rose from his easy chair and came around the coffee table, with a gruff, "Plenty of time to look around, son. Let me take care of you."

"That's—" I said. I was still not managing complete sentences, most of the time.

He took me by the arm, brought me over to the bar, and sat me down on a stool. "Like I said, plenty of time. You're like most first-timers, you're probably in dire need of a drink. We can take care of that first and then get acquainted." He moved around the bar, slung a towel over his shoulder, and said: "What'll it be, Pilgrim?"

Thank God I recognized the reference. If I hadn't—if it had just been another inexplicable element of a day already crammed with them—my head would have exploded from the effort of figuring out why I was being called a Pilgrim. "A...Sea of Tranquility?"

"Man after my own heart," Earl said, flashing a grin as he compiled an impressive array of ingredients in a blender. "Always drink the local drink, son. As my daddy put it, there's no point in going anywhere if you just get drunk the same way you can at home.—Which is where, by the way?"

I said, "What?"

"You missed the segue. I was asking you where you were from."

It seemed a perfect opportunity. "You first."

He chuckled. "Oh, the wife and I been here long enough, you might as well say we're from here. Great place to retire, isn't it? The old big blue marble hanging up there all day and all night?"

"I suppose," I said.

"You suppose," he said, raising an eyebrow at the concoction taking shape in his blender. "That's awful noncommittal of you. Can't you even admit to liking the view?"

"I admit to it," I said.

"But you're not enthused. You know, there's an old joke about a fella from New York and a fella from New Jersey. And the fella from New York is always bragging on his town, talking about Broadway, and the Empire State Building, and Central Park, and so on, and just as often saying terrible things about how ugly things are on the Jersey side of the river. And the fella from Jersey finally gets fed up, and says, 'All right, I've had enough of this, I want you to say one thing, just one thing, about New Jersey that's better than anything you can say about Manhattan.' And the fella from New York says, 'No problem. The view.'"

I didn't laugh, but I did smile.

"That's what's so great about this place," he concluded. "The view. Moon's pretty nice to look at for folks on Earth—and a godsend for bad poets, too, what with June-moon-spoon and all—but as views go, it can't hold a candle to the one we have, looking back. So don't give me any supposes. Own up to what you think."

"It's a great view," I said, this time with conviction, as he handed me my drink. Then I asked the big question another way: "How did you arrange it?"

"You ought to know better than that, son. We didn't arrange it. We just took advantage of it. Nothing like a scenic overlook to give zip to your real estate.—So answer me. Where are you from?"

Acutely aware that more than a minute had passed since I'd asked him the same question, and that no answer seemed to be forthcoming, I was also too trapped by simple courtesy to press the issue. "San Francisco."

He whistled. "I've seen pictures of San Francisco. Looks like a beautiful town."

"It is," I said.

"You actually climb those hills in Earth gravity?"

"I used to run up Hyde every morning at dawn."

"Hyde's the big steep one that heads down to the bay?"

"One of them," I said.

"And you ran up that hill? At dawn? Every day?"

"Yup."

"You have a really obsessive personality, don't you, son?"

I shrugged. "About some things, I suppose."

"Only about some things?"

"That's what being obsessive means, right?"

"Ah, well. Nothing wrong about being obsessive, as long as you're not a fanatic about it. Want me to freshen up that drink?"

I felt absolutely no alcoholic effect at all. "Maybe you better."

I tried to turn the conversation back to where he was from, but somehow I didn't get a chance, because that's when Minnie took me by the hand and dragged me over to the wall of family photos. There were pictures of them smiling on the couch, pictures of them lounging together in the backyard, pictures of them standing proudly before their home. There were a large number of photos that used Earth as a backdrop. Only four photos showed them with other people, all from the last century: in one, they sat at their dining table with a surprised-looking Neil Armstrong and Buzz Aldrin; in another, they sat on their porch swing chatting with Carl Sagan; in a third, Minnie was being enthusiastically hugged by Isaac Asimov; the fourth showed Earl playing the upright piano while Minnie sat beside him and a tall, thin blonde man with androgynous features and two differently colored eyes serenaded them both. The last figure was the only one I didn't recognize immediately; by the time somebody finally clued me in, several visits later, I would be far too jaded to engage in the spit-take it would have merited any other time.

I wanted to ask Minnie about the photos with the people I recognized, but then Peter and Earl dragged me downstairs to take a look at Earl's model train set, a rural landscape incorporating four lines and six separate small towns. It was a remarkably detailed piece of work, but I was most impressed with the small miracle of engineering that induced four heavy chains to pull it out of the way whenever Earl pulled a small cord. This handily revealed the pool table. Earl whipped Peter two games out of three, then challenged me; I'm fairly good at pool, but I was understandably off my game that afternoon, and missed every single shot. When Carrie Aldrin No Relation came down to challenge Earl, he mimed terror. It was a genial hour, totally devoted to content-free conversation—and any attempt I made to bring up the questions that burned in my breast was terminated without apparent malice.

Back upstairs. The dog nosing at my hand. Minnie noting that he liked me. Minnie saying anything about the son whose room we'd changed in, the one who'd died "in the war." A very real heartbreak about the way her eyes grew distant at that moment. I asked which war, and she smiled sadly: "There's only been one war, dear—and it doesn't really matter what you call it." Nikki patting her hand. Oscar telling a mildly funny anecdote from his childhood, Minnie asking him to tell her the one about the next-door neighbors again. I brought up the photo of Minnie and Earl with Neal Armstrong and Buzz Aldrin, and Minnie clucked that they had been such nice boys.

Paranoia hit. "Ever hear of Ray Bradbury?"

She smiled with real affection. "Oh, yes. We only met him once or twice, but he was genuinely sweet. I miss him."

"So you met him, too."

"We've met a lot of people, apricot. Why? Is he a relation?"

"Just an old-time writer I like," I said.

"Ahhhhhh."

"In fact," I said, "one story of his I particularly like was called 'Mars Is Heaven.'"

She sipped her tea. "Don't know that one."

"It's about a manned expedition to Mars—written while that was still in the future, you understand. And when the astronauts get there they discover a charming, rustic, old-fashioned American small town, filled with sweet old folks they remember from their childhoods. It's the last thing they expect, but after a while they grow comfortable with it. They even jump to the conclusion that Mars is the site of the afterlife. Except it's not. The sweet old folks are aliens in disguise, and they're lulling all these gullible earthlings into a false sense of security so they can be killed at leisure."

My words had been hesitantly spoken, less out of concern for Minnie's feelings than those of my colleagues. Their faces were blank, unreadable, masking emotions that could have been anything from anger to amusement. I will admit that for a split second there, my paranoia reaching heights it had never known before (or thank God, since), I half-expected George and Oscar and Nikki to morph into the hideously tentacled bug-eyed monsters who had taken their places immediately after eating their brains. Then the moment passed, and the silence continued to hang heavily in the room, and any genuine apprehension I might have felt gave way to an embarrassment of more mundane proportions. After all—whatever the explanation for all this might have been—I'd just been unforgivably rude to a person who had only been gracious and charming toward me.

She showed no anger, no sign that she took it personally. "I remember that one now, honey. I'm afraid I didn't like it as much as some of Ray's other efforts. Among other things, it seemed pretty unreasonable to me that critters advanced enough to pull off that kind of masquerade would have nothing better to do with their lives than to eat nice folks who came calling.—But then, he also wrote a story about a baby that starts killing as soon as it leaves the womb, and I prefer to believe that infants, given sufficient understanding and affection, soon learn that the universe outside the womb isn't that dark and cold a place after all. Given half a chance, they might even grow up…and it's a wonderful process to watch."

I had nothing to say to that.

She sipped her tea again, one pinky finger extended in the most unself-conscious manner imaginable, just as if she couldn't fathom drinking her tea any other way, then, spoke brightly, with perfect timing: "But if you stay the night, I'll be sure to put you in the room with all the pods."

There was a moment of silence, with every face in the room—including those of Earl and Peter and Carrie, who had just come up from down-stairs—as distinguishedly impassive as a granite bust of some forefather you had never heard of.

Then I averted my eyes, trying to hide the smile as it began to spread on my face.

Then somebody made a helpless noise, and we all exploded with laughter.

•••

Seventy years later:

If every land ever settled by human beings has its garden spots, then every land ever settled by human beings has its hovels. This is true even of frontiers that have become theme parks. I had spent much of this return to the world I had once known wandering through a brightly lit, comfortably upholstered tourist paradise—the kind of ersatz environment common to all overdeveloped places, that is less an expression of local character than a determined struggle to ensure the total eradication of anything resembling local character. But now I was headed toward a place that would never be printed on a postcard, that would never be on the tours, that existed on tourist maps only as the first, best sign that those looking for easy traveling have just made a disastrous wrong turn.

It was on Farside, of course. Most tourist destinations, and higher-end habitats, are on Nearside, which comes equipped with a nice blue planet to look at. Granted that even on Nearside the view is considered a thing for tourists, and that most folks who live here live underground and like to brag to each other about how long they've gone without Earthgazing— our ancestral ties are still part of us, and the mere presence of Earth, seen or unseen, is so inherently comforting that most normal people with a choice pick Nearside. Farside, by comparison, caters almost exclusively to hazardous industries and folks who don't want that nice blue planet messing up the stark emptiness of their sky—a select group of people that includes a small number of astronomers at the Frank Drake Observatory, and a large number of assorted perverts and geeks and misanthropes. The wild frontier of the fantasies comes closest to being a reality here—the hemisphere has some heavy-industry settlements that advertise their crime rates as a matter of civic pride.

And then there are the haunts of those who find even those places too civilized for their tastes. The mountains and craters of Farside are dotted with the little boxy single-person habitats of folks who have turned their back not only on the home planet but also the rest of humanity as well. Some of those huddle inside their self-imposed solitary confinement for weeks or months on end, emerging only to retrieve their supply drops or enforce the warning their radios transmit on infinite loop: that they don't want visitors and that all trespassers should expect to be shot. They're all eccentric, but some are crazy and a significant percentage of them are clinically insane. They're not the kind of folks the sane visit just for local color.

I landed my rented skimmer on a ridge overlooking an oblong metal box with a roof marked by a glowing ten-digit registration number. It was night here, and nobody who lived in such a glorified house trailer would have been considerate enough to provide any outside lighting for visitors, so those lit digits provided the only ground-level rebuttal to starfield up above; it was an inadequate rebuttal at best, which left the ground on all sides an ocean of undifferentiated inky blackness. I could carry my own lamp, of course, but I didn't want to negotiate the walk from my skimmer to the habitat's front door if the reception I met there required a hasty retreat; I wasn't very capable of hasty retreats, these days.

So I just sat in my skimmer and transmitted the repeating loop: Walter Stearns. I desperately need to speak to Walter Stearns. Walter Stearns. I desperately need to speak to Walter Stearns. Walter Stearns. I desperately need to speak to Walter Stearns. Walter Stearns. I desperately need to speak to Walter Stearns. It was the emergency frequency that all of these live-alones are required to keep open 24-7, but there was no guarantee Stearns was listening—and since I was not in distress, I was not really legally entitled to use it. But I didn't care; Stearns was the best lead I had yet.

It was only two hours before a voice like a mouth full of steel wool finally responded: "Go away."

"I won't be long, Mr. Stearns. We need to talk."

"You need to talk. I need you to go away."

"It's about Minnie and Earl, Mr. Stearns."

There was a pause. "Who?"

The pause had seemed a hair too long to mean mere puzzlement. "Minnie and Earl. From the development days. You remember them, don't you?"

"I never knew any Minnie and Earl," he said. "Go away."

"I listened to the tapes you made for the Museum, Mr. Stearns."

The anger in his hoarse, dusty old voice was still building. "I made those tapes when I was still talking to people. And there's nothing in them about any Minnie or Earl."

"No," I said, "there's not. Nobody mentioned Minnie and Earl by name, not you, and not anybody else who participated. But you still remember them. It took me several days to track you down, Mr. Stearns. We weren't here at the same time, but we still had Minnie and Earl in common."

"I have nothing to say to you," he said, with a new shrillness in his voice. "I'm an old man. I don't want to be bothered. Go away."

My cheeks ached from the size of my triumphant grin. "I brought yams."

There was nothing on the other end but the sibilant hiss of background radiation. It lasted just long enough to persuade me that my trump card had been nothing of the kind; he had shut down or smashed his receiver, or simply turned his back to it, so he could sit there in his little cage waiting for the big bad outsider to get tired and leave.

Then he said: "Yams."

Twenty-four percent of the people who contributed to the Museum's oral history had mentioned yams at least once. They had talked about the processing of basic food shipments from home, and slipped yams into their lists of the kind of items received; they had conversely cited yams as the kind of food that the folks back home had never once thought of sending; they had related anecdotes about funny things this co-worker or that co-worker had said at dinner, over a nice steaming plate of yams. They had mentioned yams and they had moved on, behaving as if it was just another background detail mentioned only to provide their colorful reminiscences the right degree of persuasive verisimilitude. Anybody not from those days who noticed the strange recurring theme might have imagined it a statistical oddity or an in-joke of some kind. For anybody who had been to Minnie and Earl's—and tasted the delicately seasoned yams she served so frequently—it was something more: a strange form of confirmation.

When Stearns spoke again, his voice still rasped of disuse, but it also possessed a light quality that hadn't been there before. "They've been gone a long time. I'm not sure I know what to tell you."

"I checked your records," I said. "You've been on the moon continuously since those days; you went straight from the development teams to the early settlements to the colonies that followed. You've probably been here nonstop longer than anybody else living or dead. If anybody can give me an idea what happened to them, it's you."

More silence.

"Please," I said.

And then he muttered a cuss word that had passed out of the vernacular forty years earlier. "All right, damn you. But you won't find them. I don't think anybody will ever find them."

• • •

Seventy years earlier:

We were there for about two more hours before George took me aside, said he needed to speak to me in private, and directed me to wait for him in the backyard.

The backyard was nice.

I've always hated that word. Nice. It means nothing. Describing people, it can mean the most distant politeness, or the most compassionate warmth; it can mean civility and it can mean charity and it can mean grace and it can mean friendship. Those things may be similar, but they're not synonyms; when the same word is used to describe all of them, then that word means nothing. It means even less when describing places. So what if the backyard was nice? Was it just comfortable, and well-tended, or was it a place that reinvigorated you with every breath? How can you leave it at "nice" and possibly imagine that you've done the job?

Nice. Feh.

But that's exactly what this backyard was.

It was a couple of acres of trimmed green lawn, bordered by the white picket fence that signaled the beginning of vacuum. A quarter-circle of bright red roses marked each of the two rear corners; between them, bees hovered lazily over a semicircular garden heavy on towering orchids and sunflowers. The painted white rocks which bordered that garden were arranged in a perfect line, none of them even a millimeter out of place, none of them irregular enough to shame the conformity that character-ized the relationship between all the others. There was a single apple tree, which hugged the rear of the house so tightly that the occupants of the second floor might have been able to reach out their windows and grab their breakfast before they trudged off to the shower; there were enough fallen green apples to look picturesque, but not enough to look sloppy. There was a bench of multicolored polished stone at the base of the porch steps, duplicating the porch swing up above but somehow absolutely right in its position; and as I sat on that bench facing the nice backyard I breathed deep and I smelled things that I had almost forgotten I could smell—not just the distant charcoal reek of neighbors burning hamburgers in their own backyards, but lilacs, freshly cut grass, horse scent, and a cleansing whiff of rain. I sat there and I spotted squirrels, hummingbirds, monarch butterflies, and a belled calico cat that ran by, stopped, saw me, looked terribly confused in the way cats have, and then went on. I sat there and I breathed and after months of inhaling foot odor and antiseptics I found myself getting a buzz. It was intoxicating.

It was invigorating. It was a shot of pure energy. It was joy. God help me, it was Nice.

But it was also surrounded on all sides by a pitiless vacuum that, if real physics meant anything, should have claimed it in an instant. Perhaps it shouldn't have bothered me that much, by then; but it did.

The screen door slammed. Miles the dog bounded down the porch steps and, panting furiously, nudged my folded hands. I scratched him under the ears. He gave me the usual unconditional adoration of the golden retriever—I petted him, therefore I was God. Most panting dogs look like they're smiling (it's a major reason humans react so strongly to the species), but Miles, the canine slave to context, looked like he was enjoying the grand joke that everybody was playing at my expense. Maybe he was. Maybe he wasn't even really a dog…

The screen door opened and slammed. This time it was George, carrying a couple of tall glasses filled with pink stuff and ice. He handed me one of the glasses; it was lemonade, of course. He sipped from the other one and said: "Minnie's cooking yams again. She's a miracle worker when it comes to yams. She does something with them, I don't know, but it's really—"

"You," I said wryly, "are enjoying this way too much."

"Aren't you?" he asked.

Miles the dog stared at the lemonade as if it was the most wondrous sight in the universe. George dipped a finger into his drink and held it out so the mutt could have a taste. Miles adored him now. I was so off-center I almost felt betrayed. "Yeah. I guess I am. I like them."

"Pretty hard not to like them. They're nice people."

"But the situation is so insane—"

"Sanity," George said, "is a fluid concept. Think about how nuts relativity sounded, the first time somebody explained it to you. Hell, think back to when you were a kid, and somebody first explained the mechanics of sex."

"George—"

He gave Miles another taste. "I can see you trying like mad to work this out. Compiling data, forming and rejecting theories, even concocting little experiments to test the accuracy of your senses. I know because I was once in your position, when I was brought out here for the first time, and I remember doing all the same things. But I now have a lot of experience in walking people through this, and I can probably save you a great deal of time and energy by completing your data and summarizing all of your likely theories."

I was too tired to glare at him anymore. "You can skip the data and theories and move on to the explanation. I promise you I won't mind."

"Yes, you would," he said, with absolute certainty. "Trust me, dealing with the established lines of inquiry is the only real way to get there.

"First, providing the raw data. One: this little homestead cannot be detected from Earth; our most powerful telescopes see nothing but dead moonscape here. Two: It, and the two old folks, have been here since at least Apollo; those photos of them with Armstrong and Aldrin are genuine. Three: There is nothing you can ask them that will get any kind of straight answer about who or what they are and why they're here. Four: we have no idea how they knew Asimov, Sagan, or Bradbury—but I promise you that those are not the most startling names you will hear them drop if you stick around long enough to get to know them. Five: We don't know how they maintain an earthlike environment in here. Six, about that mailbox: they do get delivery, on a daily basis, though no actual mailman has ever been detected, and none of the mail we've ever managed to sneak a peek at is the slightest bit interesting. It's all senior citizen magazines and grocery store circulars. Seven: they never seem to go shopping, but they always have an ample supply of food and other provisions. Eight (I am up to eight, right?): they haven't noticeably aged, not even the dog. Nine: they do understand every language we've sprung on them, but they give all their answers in Midwestern-American English. And ten: we have a group of folks from our project coming out here to visit just about every night of the week, on a rotating schedule that works out to just about once a week for each of us.

"So much for the raw data. The theories take longer to deal with. Let me go through all the ones you're likely to formulate." He peeled back a finger. "One. This is all just a practical joke perpetrated by your friends and colleagues in an all-out attempt to shock you out of your funk. We put it all together with spit and baling wire and some kind of elaborate special effects trickery that's going to seem ridiculously obvious just as soon as you're done figuring it out. We went to all this effort, and spent the many billions of dollars it would have cost to get all these construction materials here, and developed entirely new technologies capable

244 >> ADAM-TROY CASTRO

of holding in an atmosphere, and put it all together while you weren't looking, and along the way brought in a couple of convincing old folks from Central Casting, just so we could enjoy the look on your face. What a zany bunch of folks we are, huh?"

I felt myself blushing. "I'd considered that."

"And why not? It's a legitimate theory. Also a ridiculous one, but let's move on." He peeled back another finger. "Two. This is not a practical joke, but a test or psychological experiment of some kind, arranged by the brain boys back home. They put together all of this trickery, just to see how the average astronaut, isolated from home and normal societal context, reacts to situations that defy easy explanation and cannot be foreseen by even the most exhaustively planned training. This particular explanation works especially well if you also factor in what we cleverly call the McGoohan Corollary—that is, the idea that we're not really on the moon at all, but somewhere on Earth, possibly underground, where the real practical difficulty would lie in simulating not a quaint rural setting on a warm summer day, but instead the low-g, high-radiation, temperature-extreme vacuum that you gullibly believed you were walking around in, every single time you suited up. This theory is, of course, equally ridiculous, for many reasons—but we did have one guy about a year ago who stubbornly held on to it for almost a full week. Something about his psychological makeup just made it easier for him to accept that, over all the others, and we had to keep a close watch on him to stop him from trying to prove it with a nice unsuited walk. But from the way you're looking at me right now I don't think we're going to have the same problem with you. So.

"Assuming that this is not a joke, or a trick, or an experiment, or some lame phenomenon like that, that this situation you're experiencing is precisely what we have represented to you, then we are definitely looking at something beyond all terrestrial experience. Which brings us to Three." He peeled back another finger. "This is a first-contact situation. Minnie and Earl, and possibly Miles here, are aliens in disguise, or simulations constructed by aliens. They have created a friendly environment inside this picket fence, using technology we can only guess at—let's say an invisible bubble capable of filtering out radiation and retaining a breathable atmosphere while remaining permeable to confused bipeds in big clumsy moonsuits. And they have done so—why? To hide their true nature while they observe our progress? Possibly. But if so, it would be a lot more subtle to place their little farmhouse in Kansas, where it wouldn't seem so crazily out of place. To communicate with us in terms we can accept? Possibly—except that couching those terms in such an insane context seems as counterproductive to genuine communication as their apparent decision to limit the substance of that communication to geriatric small talk. To make us comfortable with something familiar? Possibly—except that this kind of small mid-American home is familiar to only a small fraction of humanity, and it seems downright exotic to the many observers we've shuttled in from China, or India, or Saudi Arabia, or for that matter Manhattan. To present us with a puzzle that we have to solve? Again, possibly—but since Minnie and Earl and Miles won't confirm or deny, it's also a possibility we won't be able to test unless somebody like yourself actually does come up with the great big magic epiphany. I'm not holding my breath. But I do reject any theory that they're hostile, including the "Mars Is Heaven" theory you already cited. Anybody capable of pulling this off must have resources that could mash us flat in the time it takes to sneeze."

Miles woofed. In context it seemed vaguely threatening.

"Four." Another finger. "Minnie and Earl are actually human, and Miles is actually canine. They come here from the future, or from an alternate universe, or from some previously unknown subset of humanity that's been living among us all this time, hiding great and unfathomable powers that, blaah blaah blaah, fill in the blank. And they're here, making their presence known—why? All the same sub-theories that applied to alien visitors also apply to human agencies, and all the same objections as well. Nothing explains why they would deliberately couch such a maddening enigma in such, for lack of a more appropriate word, banal terms. It's a little like coming face to face with God and discovering that He really does look like a bearded old white guy in a robe; He might, for all I know, but I'm more religious than you probably think, and there's some part of me that absolutely refuses to believe it. He, or She, if you prefer, could do better than that. And so could anybody, human or alien, whose main purpose in coming here is to study us, or test us, or put on a show for us.

"You still with me?" he inquired.

"Go on," I growled. "I'll let you know if you leave anything out."

He peeled back another finger. "Five. I kind of like this one. Minnie and

Earl, and by extension Miles, are not creatures of advanced technology, but of a completely different kind of natural phenomenon—let's say, for the sake of argument, a bizarre jog in the space-time continuum that allows a friendly but otherwise unremarkable couple living in Kansas or Wyoming or someplace like that to continue experiencing life down on the farm while in some way as miraculous to them as it seems to us, projecting an interactive version of themselves to this otherwise barren spot on the moon. Since, as your little conversation with Earl established, they clearly know they're on the moon, we would have to accept that they're unflappable enough to take this phenomenon at face value, but I've known enough Midwesterners to know that this is a genuine possibility.

"Six." Starting now on another hand. "Mentioned only so you can be assured I'm providing you an exhaustive list—a phenomenon one of your predecessors called the Law of Preservation of Home. He theorized that whenever human beings penetrate too far past their own natural habitat, into places sufficiently inhospitable to life, the universe is forced to spontaneously generate something a little more congenial to compensate—the equivalent, I suppose, of magically whomping up a Holiday Inn with a swimming pool, to greet explorers lost in the coldest reaches of Antarctica. He even said that the only reason we hadn't ever received reliable reports of this phenomenon on Earth is that we still weren't ever sufficiently far from our natural habitat to activate it…but I can tell from the look on your face that you don't exactly buy this one either, so I'll set it aside and let you read the paper he wrote on the subject at your leisure."

"I don't think I will," I said.

"You ought to. It's a real hoot. But if you want to, I'll skip all the way to the end of the list, to the only explanation that ultimately makes any sense. Ready?"

"I'm waiting."

"All right. That explanation is—" he paused dramatically "—it doesn't matter."

There was a moment of pregnant silence.

I didn't explode; I was too shellshocked to explode. Instead, I just said: "I sat through half a dozen bullshit theories for 'It doesn't matter'?"

"You had to, Max; it's the only way to get there. You had to learn the hard way that all of these propositions are either completely impossible or, for the time being, completely impossible to test—and we know this because the best minds on Earth have been working on the problem for as long as there's been a sustained human presence on the moon. We've taken hair samples from Minnie's hairbrush. We've smuggled out stool samples from the dog. We've recorded our conversations with the old folks and studied every second of every tape from every possible angle. We've monitored the house for years on end, analyzed samples of the food and drink served in there, and exhaustively charted the health of everybody to go in or out. And all it's ever gotten us, in all these years of being frantic about it, is this—that as far as we can determine, Minnie and Earl are just a couple of friendly old folks who like having visitors."

"And that's it?"

"Why can't it be? Whether aliens, time travelers, displaced human beings, or natural phenomena—they're good listeners, and fine people, and they sure serve a good Sunday dinner. And if there must be things in the universe we can't understand—well, then, it's sure comforting to know that some of them just want to be good neighbors. That's what I mean by saying, It doesn't matter."

He stood up, stretched, took the kind of deep breath people only indulge in when they're truly luxuriating in the freshness of the air around them, and said: "Minnie and Earl expect some of the new folks to be a little pokey, getting used to the idea. They won't mind if you stay out here and smell the roses awhile. Maybe when you come in, we'll talk a little more 'bout getting you scheduled for regular visitation. Minnie's already asked me about it—she seems to like you. God knows why." He winked, shot me in the chest with a pair of pretend six-shooters made from the index fingers of both hands, and went back inside, taking the dog with him. And I was alone in the nice backyard, serenaded by birdsong as I tried to decide how to reconcile my own rational hunger for explanations with the unquestioning acceptance that was being required of me.

•••

Eventually, I came to the same conclusion George had; the only conclusion that was possible under the circumstances. It was a genuine phenomenon, that conclusion: a community of skeptics and rationalists and followers of the scientific method deciding that there were some things Man was having too good a time to know. Coming to think of

Minnie and Earl as family didn't take much longer than that. For the next three years, until I left for my new job in the outer system, I went out to their place at least once, sometimes twice a week; I shot pool with Earl and chatted about relatives back home with Minnie; I'd tussled with Miles and helped with the dishes and joined them for long all-nighters talking about nothing in particular. I learned how to bake with the limited facilities we had at Base, so I could bring my own cookies to her feasts. I came to revel in standing on a creaky front porch beneath a bug lamp, sipping grape juice as I joined Minnie in yet another awful rendition of "Anatevka." Occasionally I glanced at the big blue cradle of civilization hanging in the sky, remembered for the fiftieth or sixtieth or one hundredth time that none of this had any right to be happening, and reminded myself for the fiftieth or sixtieth or one hundredth time that the only sane response was to continue carrying the tune. I came to think of Minnie and Earl as the real reason we were on the moon, and I came to understand one of the major reasons we were all so bloody careful to keep it a secret—because the needy masses of Earth, who were at that point still agitating about all the time and money spent on the space program, would not have been mollified by the knowledge that all those billions were being spent, in part, so that a few of the best and the brightest could indulge themselves in sing-alongs and wiener dog cookouts.

I know it doesn't sound much like a frontier. It wasn't, not inside the picket fence. Outside, it remained dangerous and backbreaking work. We lost five separate people while I was there; two to blowouts, one to a collapsing crane, one to a careless tumble off a crater rim, and one to suicide (she, alas, had not been to Minnie and Earl's yet). We had injuries every week, shortages every day, and crises just about every hour. Most of the time, we seemed to lose ground—and even when we didn't, we lived with the knowledge that all of our work and all of our dedication could be thrown in the toilet the first time there was a political shift back home. There was no reason for any of us to believe that we were actually accomplishing what we were there to do—but somehow, with Minnie and Earl there, hosting a different group every night, it was impossible to come to any other conclusion. They liked us. They believed in us. They were sure that we were worth their time and effort. And they expected us to be around for a long, long time…

just like they had been.

I suppose that's another reason why I was so determined to find them now. Because I didn't know what it said about the people we'd become that they weren't around keeping us company anymore.

•••

I was in a jail cell for forty-eight hours once. Never mind why; it's a stupid story. The cell itself wasn't the sort of thing I expected from movies and television; it was brightly lit, free of vermin, and devoid of any steel bars to grip obsessively while cursing the guards and bemoaning the injustice that had brought me there. It was just a locked room with a steel door, a working toilet, a clean sink, a soft bed, and absolutely nothing else. If I had been able to come and go at will it might have been an acceptable cheap hotel room. Since I was stuck there, without anything to do or any-body to talk to, I spent those forty-eight hours going very quietly insane.

The habitat module of Walter Stearns was a lot like that cell, expanded to accommodate a storage closet, a food locker, and a kitchenette; it was that stark, that empty. There were no decorations on the walls, no per-sonal items, no hytex or music system I could see, nothing to read and nothing to do. It lost its charm for me within thirty seconds. Stearns had been living there for sixteen years: a self-imposed prison sentence that might have been expiation for the sin of living past his era.

The man himself moved with what seemed glacial slowness, like a wind-up toy about to stop and fall over. He dragged one leg, but if that was a legacy of a stroke—and an explanation for why he chose to live as he did—there was no telltale slur to his speech to corroborate it. What-ever the reason might have been, I couldn't help regarding him with the embarrassed pity one old man feels toward another the same age who hasn't weathered his own years nearly as well.

He accepted my proffered can of yams with a sour grin and gave me a mug of some foul-smelling brown stuff in return. Then he poured some for himself and shuffled to the edge of his bed and sat down with a grunt. "I'm not a hermit," he said, defensively.

"I didn't use the word," I told him.

"I didn't set out to be a hermit," he went on, as if he hadn't heard me. "Nobody sets out to be a hermit. Nobody turns his back on the damned race unless he has some reason to be fed up. I'm not fed up. I just don't know any alternative. It's the only way I know to let the moon be the moon."

He sipped some of the foul-smelling brown stuff and gestured for me to do the same. Out of politeness, I sipped from my own cup. It tasted worse than it smelled, and had a consistency like sand floating in vinegar. Somehow I didn't choke. "Let the moon be the moon?"

"They opened a casino in Shepardsville. I went to see it. It's a big luxury hotel with a floor show; trained white tigers jumping through flaming hoops for the pleasure of a pretty young trainer in a spangled bra and panties. The casino room is oval-shaped, and the walls are alive with animated holography of wild horses running around and around and around and around, without stop, twenty-four hours a day. There are night clubs with singers and dancers, and an amusement park with rides for the kids. I sat there and I watched the gamblers bent over their tables and the barflies bent over their drinks and I had to remind myself that I was on the moon—that just being here at all was a miracle that would have had most past civilizations consider us gods. But all these people, all around me, couldn't feel it. They'd built a palace in a place where no palace had ever been and they'd sucked all the magic and all the wonder all the way out of it." He took a deep breath, and sipped some more of his contemptible drink. "It scared me. It made me want to live somewhere where I could still feel the moon, being the moon. So I wouldn't be some useless...relic who didn't know where he was half the time."

The self-pity had wormed its way into his voice so late that I almost didn't catch it. "It must get lonely," I ventured.

"Annnh. Sometimes I put on my moonsuit and go outside, just to stand there. It's so silent there that I can almost hear the breath of God. And I remember that it's the moon—the moon, dammit. Not some five-star hotel. The moon. A little bit of that and I don't mind being a little lonely the rest of the time. Is that crazy? Is that being a hermit?"

I gave the only answer I could. "I don't know."

He made a hmmmph noise, got up, and carried his mug over to the sink. A few moments cleaning and refilling it and he returned, his lips curled into a half-smile, his eyes focused on some far-off time and place. "The breath of God," he murmured.

"Yams," I prompted.

"You caught that, huh? Been a while since somebody caught that. It's not the sort of thing people catch unless they were there. Unless they remember her."

"Was that by design?"

"You mean, was it some kind of fiendish secret code? Naah. More like a shared joke. We knew by then that nobody would believe us if we actually talked about Minnie and Earl. They were that forgotten. So we dropped yams into our early-settlement stories. A little way of saying, hey, we remember the old lady. She sure did love to cook those yams."

"With her special seasoning." I said. "And those rolls she baked."

"Uh-huh." He licked his lips, and I almost fell into the trap of considering that unutterably sad…until I realized that I was doing the same thing. "Used to try to mix one of Earl's special cocktails, but I never could get them right. Got all the ingredients. Mixed 'em the way he showed me. Never got 'em to taste right. Figure he had some kind of technological edge he wasn't showing us. Real alien superscience, applied to bartending. Or maybe I just can't replace the personality of the bartender. But they were good drinks. I've got to give him that."

We sat together in silence for a while, each lost in the sights and sounds of a day long gone. After a long time, I almost whispered it: "Where did they go, Walter?"

His eyes didn't focus: "I don't know where they are. I don't know what happened to them."

"Start with when you last visited them."

"Oh, that was years and years and years ago." He lowered his head and addressed the floor. "But you know how it is. You have relatives, friends, old folks very important to you. Folks you see every week or so, folks who become a major part of who you are. Then you get busy with other things and you lose touch. I lost touch when the settlement boom hit, and there was always some other place to be, some other job that needed to be done; I couldn't spare one night a week gabbing with old folks just because I happened to love them. After all, they'd always be there, right? By the time I thought of looking them up again, it turned out that everybody else had neglected them too. There was no sign of the house and no way of knowing how long they'd been gone."

I was appalled. "So you're saying that Minnie and Earl moved away because of…neglect?"

"Naaah. That's only why they didn't say goodbye. I don't think it has a damn thing to do with why they moved away; just why we didn't notice. I guess that's another reason why nobody likes to talk about them. We're all just too damn ashamed."

"Why do you think they moved, Walter?"

He swallowed another mouthful of his vile brew, and addressed the floor some more, not seeing me, not seeing the exile he'd chosen for himself, not seeing anything but a tiny little window of his past. "I keep thinking of that casino," he murmured. "There was a rotating restaurant on the top floor of the hotel. Showed you the landscape, with all the billboards and amusement parks—and above it all, in the place where all the advertisers hope you're going to forget to look, Mother Earth herself. It was a burlesque and it was boring. And I also keep thinking of that little house, out in the middle of nowhere, with the picket fence and the golden retriever dog...and the two sweet old people...and the more I compare one thought to the other the more I realize that I don't blame them for going away. They saw that, on the moon we were building, they wouldn't be miraculous anymore."

"They had a perfectly maintained little environment—"

"We have a perfectly maintained little environment. We have parks with grass. We have roller coasters and golf courses. We have people with dogs. We even got rotating restaurants and magic acts with tigers. Give us a few more years up here and we'll probably work out some kind of magic trick to do away with the domes and the bulkheads and keep in an atmosphere with nothing but a picket fence. We'll have houses like theirs springing up all over the place. The one thing we don't have is the moon being the moon. Why would they want to stay here?" His voice, which had been rising throughout his little tirade, rose to a shriek with that last question; he hurled his mug against the wall, but it was made of some indestructible ceramic that refused to shatter. It just tumbled to the floor, and skittered under the bunk, spinning in place just long enough to mock him for his empty display of anger. He looked at me, focused, and let me know with a look that our audience was over. "What would be left for them?"

•••

I searched some more, tracking down another five or six oldsters still capable of talking about the old days, as well as half a dozen children or grandchildren of same willing to speak to me about the memories the old folks had left behind, but my interview with Walter Stearns was really the end of it; by the time I left his habitat, I knew that my efforts were futile. I saw that even those willing to talk to me weren't going to be able to tell me more than he had...and I turned out to be correct about that. Minnie and Earl had moved out, all right, and there was no forwarding address to be had.

I was also tired: bone-weary in a way that could have been just a normal symptom of age and could have been despair that I had not found what I so desperately needed to find and could have been the harbinger of my last remaining days. Whatever it was, I just didn't have the energy to keep going that much longer...and I knew that the only real place for me was the bed I had shared with my dear Claire.

On the night before I flew back I had some money left over, so I went to see the musical *Ceres* at New Broadway. I confess I found it dreadful—like most old farts, I can't fathom music produced after the first three decades of my life—but it was definitely elaborate, with a cast of lithe and gymnastic young dancers in silvery jumpsuits leaping about in a slow-motion ballet that took full advantage of the special opportunities afforded by lunar gravity. At one point the show even simulated free fall, thanks to invisible filaments that crisscrossed the stage allowing the dancers to glide from place to place like objects ruled only by their own mass and momentum. The Playbill said that one of the performers, never mind which one, was not a real human being, but a holographic projection artfully integrated with the rest. I couldn't discern the fake, but I couldn't find it in myself to be impressed. We were a few flimsy bulkheads and half a kilometer from lunar vacuum, and to me, that was the real story...even if nobody else in the audience of hundreds could see it.

I moved out of my hotel. I tipped my concierge, who hadn't found me anything about Minnie and Earl but had provided all the other amenities I'd asked for. I bought some stupid souvenirs for the grandchildren, and boarded my flight back to Earth.

After about an hour I went up to the passenger lounge, occupied by two intensely arguing businesswomen, a child playing a handheld hytex game, and a bored-looking thin man with a shiny head. Nobody was looking out the panoramic window, not even me. I closed my eyes and pretended that the view wasn't there. Instead I thought of the time Earl had decided he wanted to fly a kite. That was a major moment. He built it out of newspapers he got from somewhere, and sat in his backyard letting out more than five hundred meters of line; though the string and the kite extended far beyond the atmospheric picket-fence perimeter, it had still swooped and sailed like an object enjoying the robust winds it would have known, achieving that altitude on Earth. That, of course, had been another impossibility…but my colleagues and I had been so inured to such things by then that we simply shrugged and enjoyed the moment as it came.

I badly wanted to fly a kite.

I badly wanted to know that Minnie and Earl had not left thinking poorly of us.

I didn't think they were dead. They weren't the kind of people who died. But they were living somewhere else, someplace far away—and if the human race was lucky it was somewhere in the solar system. Maybe, even now, while I rode back to face however much time I had left, there was a mind-boggling little secret being kept by the construction teams building those habitats out near the Jovian moons; maybe some of those physicists and engineers were taking time out from a week of dangerous and backbreaking labor to spend a few hours in the company of an old man and old woman whose deepest spoken insight about the massive planet that graces their sky was how it presented one hell of a lovely view. Maybe the same thing happened when Anderson and Santiago hitched a ride on the comet that now bears their names—and maybe there's a little cottage halfway up the slope of Olympus Mons where the Mars colonists go whenever they need a little down-home hospitality. I would have been happy with all of those possibilities. I would have felt the weight of years fall from my bones in an instant, if I just knew that there was still room for them in the theme-park future we seemed to be building.

Then something, maybe chance, maybe instinct, made me look out the window.

And my poor, slowly failing heart almost stopped right then.

Because Miles, the golden retriever, was pacing us.

He ran alongside the shuttle, keeping up with the lounge window, his lolling pink tongue and long floppy ears trailing behind him like banners driven by some unseen (and patently impossible) breeze. He ran in slow motion, his feet pawing a ground that wasn't there, his muscles rippling along his side, his muzzle foaming with perspiration. His perpetually laughing expression, so typical of his breed, was not so much the look of an animal merely panting with exertion, but the genuine mirth of a creature aware that it has just pulled off a joke of truly epic proportions. As I stared at him, too dumbstruck to whoop and holler and point him out to my fellow passengers, he turned his head, met my gaze with soulful brown eyes, and did something I've never seen any other golden retriever do, before or since.

He winked.

Then he faced forward, lowered his head, and sped up, leaving us far behind.

I whirled and scanned the lounge, to see if any of my fellow passengers had seen him. The two businesswomen had stopped arguing, and were now giggling over a private joke of some kind. The kid was still intently focused on his game. But the eyes of the man with the shiny head were very large and very round. He stared at me, found in my broad smile confirmation that he hadn't been hallucinating, and tried to speak. "That," he said. And "Was." And after several attempts, "A dog."

He might have gone on from there given another hour or so of trying.

I knew exactly how he felt, of course. I had been in the same place, once, seventy years ago.

Now, for a while, I felt like I was twelve again.

I rose from my seat, crossed the lounge, and took the chair facing the man with the shiny head. He was wide-eyed, like a man who saw me, a total stranger, as the only fixed constant in his universe. That made me feel young, too.

I said, "Let me tell you a little bit about some old friends of mine."

A MIDWINTER'S TALE

MICHAEL SWANWICK

Maybe I shouldn't tell you about that childhood Christmas Eve in the Stone House, so long ago. My memory is no longer reliable, not since I contracted the brain fever. Soon I'll be strong enough to be reposted offplanet, to some obscure star light-years beyond that plangent moon rising over your father's barn, but how much has been burned from my mind! Perhaps none of this actually happened.

Sit on my lap and I'll tell you all. Well then, my knee. No woman was ever ruined by a knee. You laugh, but it's true. Would that it were so easy!

The hell of war as it's now practiced is that its purpose is not so much to gain territory as to deplete the enemy, and thus it's always better to maim than to kill. A corpse can be bagged, burned, and forgotten, but the wounded need special care. Regrowth tanks, false skin, medical personnel, a long convalescent stay on your parents' farm. That's why they will vary their weapons, hit you with obsolete stone axes or toxins or radiation, to force your Command to stock the proper prophylaxes, specialized medicines, obscure skills. Mustard gas is excellent for that purpose, and so was the brain fever.

All those months I lay in the hospital, awash in pain, sometimes hallu-cinating. Dreaming of ice. When I awoke, weak and not really believing I was alive, parts of my life were gone, randomly burned from my memory. I recall standing at the very top of the iron bridge over the Izveltaya, laughing and throwing my books one by one into the river, while my best friend Fennwolf tried to coax me down. "I'll join the militia! I'll be a soldier!" I shouted hysterically. And so I did. I remember that clearly but just what led up to that preposterous instant is utterly beyond me. Nor can I remember the name of my second-eldest sister, though her face is as plain to me as yours is now. There are odd holes in my memory.

••

That Christmas Eve is an island of stability in my seachanging memories, as solid in my mind as the Stone House itself, that neolithic cavern in which we led such basic lives that I was never quite sure in which era of history we dwelt. Sometimes the men came in from the hunt, a larl or two pacing ahead content and sleepy-eyed, to lean bloody spears against the walls, and it might be that we lived on Old Earth itself then. Other times, as when they brought in projectors to fill the common room with colored lights, scintillae nesting in the branches of the season's tree, and cool, harmless flames dancing atop the presents, we seemed to belong to a much later age, in some mythologized province of the future.

The house was abustle, the five families all together for this one time of the year, and outlying kin and even a few strangers staying over, so that we had to put bedding in places normally kept closed during the winter, moving furniture into attic lumberrooms, and even at that there were cots and thick bolsters set up in the blind ends of hallways. The women scurried through the passages, scattering uncles here and there, now settling one in an armchair and plumping him up like a cushion, now draping one over a table, cocking up a mustachio for effect. A pleasant time.

Coming back from a visit to the kitchens where a huge woman I did not know, with flour powdering her big-freckled arms up to the elbows, had shooed me away, I surprised Suki and Georg kissing in the nook behind the great hearth. They had their arms about each other and I stood watching them. Suki was smiling, cheeks red and round. She brushed her hair back with one hand so Georg could nuzzle her ear, turning slightly as she did so, and saw me. She gasped and they broke apart, flushed and startled.

Suki gave me a cookie, dark with molasses and a single stingy, crystallized raisin on top, while Georg sulked. Then she pushed me away, and I heard her laugh as she took Georg's hand to lead him away to some darker forest recess of the house.

Father came in, boots all muddy, to sling a brace of game birds down on the hunt cabinet. He set his unstrung bow and quiver of arrows on their pegs, then hooked an elbow atop the cabinet to accept admiration and a hot drink from Mother. The larl padded by, quiet and heavy and content. I followed it around a corner, ancient ambitions of riding the beast rising up within. I could see myself, triumphant before my cousins, high atop the black carnivore. "Flip!" my father called sternly. "Leave Samson alone! He is a bold and noble creature, and I will not have you pestering him."

He had eyes in the back of his head, had my father.

Before I could grow angry, my cousins hurried by, on their way to hoist the straw men into the trees out front, and swept me up along with them. Uncle Chittagong, who looked like a lizard and had to stay in a glass tank for reasons of health, winked at me as I skirled past. From the corner of my eye I saw my second-eldest sister beside him, limned in blue fire.

Forgive me. So little of my childhood remains; vast stretches were lost in the blue icefields I wandered in my illness. My past is like a sunken continent with only mountaintops remaining unsubmerged, a scattered archipelago of events from which to guess the shape of what was lost. Those remaining fragments I treasure all the more, and must pass my hands over them periodically to reassure myself that something remains.

So where was I? Ah, yes: I was in the north belltower, my hidey-place in those days, huddled behind Old Blind Pew, the bass of our triad of bells, crying because I had been deemed too young to light one of the yule torches. "Hallo!" cried a voice, and then, "Out here, stupid!" I ran to the window, tears forgotten in my astonishment at the sight of my brother Karl silhouetted against the yellowing sky, arms out, treading the roof gables like a tightrope walker.

"You're going to get in trouble for that!" I cried.

"Not if you don't tell!" Knowing full well how I worshiped him. "Come on down! I've emptied out one of the upper kitchen cupboards. We can crawl in from the pantry. There's a space under the door—we'll see everything!"

Karl turned and his legs tangled under him. He fell. Feet first, he slid down the roof. I screamed. Karl caught the guttering and swung himself into an open window underneath. His sharp face rematerialized in the gloom, grinning. "Race you to the jade ibis!"

He disappeared, and then I was spinning wildly down the spiral stairs, mad to reach the goal first.

•••

It was not my fault we were caught, for I would never have giggled if Karl hadn't been tickling me to see just how long I could keep silent. I was frightened, but not Karl. He threw his head back and laughed until he cried, even as he was being hauled off by three very angry grandmothers, pleased more by his own roguery than by anything he might have seen.

I myself was led away by an indulgent Katrina, who graphically described the caning I was to receive and then contrived to lose me in the crush of bodies in the common room. I hid behind the goat tapestry until I got bored—not long!—and then Chubkin, Kosmonaut, and Pew rang, and the room emptied.

I tagged along, ignored, among the moving legs, like a marsh bird scuttling through waving grasses. Voices clangoring in the east stairway, we climbed to the highest balcony, to watch the solstice dance. I hooked hands over the crumbling balustrade and pulled myself up on tiptoe so I could look down on the procession as it left the house. For a long time nothing happened, and I remember being annoyed at how casually the adults were taking all this, standing about with drinks, not one in ten glancing away from themselves. Pheidre and Valerian (the younger children had been put to bed, complaining, an hour ago) began a game of tag, running through the adults, until they were chastened and ordered with angry shakes of their arms to be still.

Then the door below opened. The women who were witches walked solemnly out, clad in hooded terrycloth robes as if they'd just stepped from the bath. But they were so silent I was struck with fear. It seemed as if something cold had reached into the pink, giggling women I had seen preparing themselves in the kitchen and taken away some warmth or laughter from them. "Katrina!" I cried in panic, and she lifted a moon-cold face toward me. Several of the men exploded in laughter, white steam puffing from bearded mouths, and one rubbed his knuckles in my hair. My second-eldest sister drew me away from the balustrade and hissed at me that I was not to cry out to the witches, that this was important, that when I was older I would understand, and in the meantime if I did not behave myself I would be beaten. To soften her words, she offered me a sugar crystal, but I turned away stern and unappeased.

Single-file the women walked out on the rocks to the east of the house, where all was barren slate swept free of snow by the wind from the sea, and at a great distance—you could not make out their faces—doffed their robes. For a moment they stood motionless in a circle, looking at one another. Then they began the dance, each wearing nothing but a red ribbon tied about one upper thigh, the long end blowing free in the breeze.

As they danced their circular dance, the families watched, largely in silence. Sometimes there was a muffled burst of laughter as one of the younger men muttered a racy comment, but mostly they watched with great respect, even a kind of fear. The gusty sky was dark, and flocked with small clouds like purple-headed rams. It was chilly on the roof and I could not imagine how the women withstood it. They danced faster and faster, and the families grew quieter, packing the edges more tightly, until I was forced away from the railing. Cold and bored, I went downstairs, nobody turning to watch me leave, back to the main room, where a fire still smoldered in the hearth.

The room was stuffy when I'd left, and cooler now. I lay down on my stomach before the fireplace. The flagstones smelled of ashes and were gritty to the touch, staining my fingertips as I trailed them in idle little circles. The stones were cold at the edges, slowly growing warmer, and then suddenly too hot and I had to snatch my hand away. The back of the fireplace was black with soot, and I watched the fire-worms crawl over the stone heart-and-hands carved there, as the carbon caught fire and burned out. The log was all embers and would burn for hours.

Something coughed.

I turned and saw something moving in the shadows, an animal. The larl was blacker than black, a hole in the darkness, and my eyes swam to look at him. Slowly, lazily, he strode out onto the stones, stretched his back, yawned a tongue-curling yawn, and then stared at me with those great green eyes.

He spoke.

I was astonished, of course, but not in the way my father would have been. So much is inexplicable to a child!

"Merry Christmas, Flip," the creature said, in a quiet, breathy voice. I could not describe its accent; I have heard nothing quite like it before or since. There was a vast alien amusement in his glance.

"And to you," I said politely.

The larl sat down, curling his body heavily about me. If I had wanted to run, I could not have gotten past him, though that thought did not occur to me then. "There is an ancient legend, Flip, I wonder if you have heard of it, that on Christmas Eve, the beasts can speak in human tongue. Have your elders told you that?"

I shook my head.

"They are neglecting you." Such strange humor dwelt in that voice. "There is truth to some of those old legends, if only you knew how to get at it. Though perhaps not all. Some are just stories. Perhaps this is not happening now; perhaps I am not speaking to you at all?"

I shook my head. I did not understand. I said so.

"That is the difference between your kind and mine. My kind understands everything about yours, and yours knows next to nothing about mine. I would like to tell you a story, little one. Would you like that?"

"Yes," I said, for I was young and I liked stories very much.

• • •

He began:

When the great ships landed—

Oh God. When—no, no, no, wait. Excuse me. I'm shaken. I just this instant had a vision. It seemed to me that it was night and I was standing at the gates of a cemetery. And suddenly the air was full of light, planes and cones of light that burst from the ground and nested twittering in the trees. Fracturing the sky. I wanted to dance for joy. But the ground crumbled underfoot and when I looked down the shadow of the gates touched my toes, a cold rectangle of profoundest black, deep as all eternity, and I was dizzy and about to fall and I, and I...

Enough! I have had this vision before, many times. It must have been something that impressed me strongly in my youth, the moist smell of newly opened earth, the chalky whitewash on the picket fence.

It must be. I do not believe in hobgoblins, ghosts, or premonitions. No, it does not bear thinking about. Foolishness! Let me get on with my story.

—When the great ships landed, I was feasting on my grandfather's brains. All his descendants gathered respectfully about him, and I, as youngest, had first bite. His wisdom flowed through me, and the wisdom of his ancestors and the intimate knowledge of those animals he had eaten for food, and the spirit of valiant enemies who had been killed and then honored by being eaten, even as if they were family. I don't suppose you understand this, little one.

(I shook my head.)

People never die, you see. Only humans die. Sometimes a minor part of a Person is lost, the doings of a few decades, but the bulk of his life is preserved, if not in this body, then in another. Or sometimes a Person will dishonor himself, and his descendants will refuse to eat him. This is a great shame, and the Person will go off to die somewhere alone.

The ships descended bright as newborn suns. The People had never seen such a thing. We watched in inarticulate wonder, for we had no language then. You have seen the pictures, the baroque swirls of colored metal, the proud humans stepping down onto the land. But I was there, and I can tell you your people were ill. They stumbled down the gangplanks with the stench of radiation sickness about them. We could have destroyed them all then and there.

Your people built a village at Landfall and planted crops over the bodies of their dead. We left them alone. They did not look like good game. They were too strange and too slow and we had not yet come to savor your smell. So we went away, in baffled ignorance.

That was in early spring.

Half the survivors were dead by midwinter, some of disease but most because they did not have enough food. It was of no concern to us. But then the woman in the wilderness came to change our universe forever.

When you're older you'll be taught the woman's tale, and what desperation drove her into the wilderness. It's part of your history. But to myself, out in the mountains and winter-lean, the sight of her striding through the snows in her furs was like a vision of winter's queen herself. A gift of meat for the hungering season, life's blood for the solstice.

I first saw the woman while I was eating her mate. He had emerged from his cabin that evening as he did every sunset, gun in hand, without looking up. I had observed him over the course of five days and his behavior never varied. On that sixth nightfall I was crouched on his roof when he came out. I let him go a few steps from the door, then leapt. I felt his neck break on impact, tore open his throat to be sure, and ripped through his parka to taste his innards. There was no sport in it, but in winter we will take game whose brains we would never eat.

My mouth was full and my muzzle pleasantly, warmly moist with blood when the woman appeared. I looked up, and she was topping the rise, riding one of your incomprehensible machines, what I know now to be a snowstrider. The setting sun broke through the clouds behind her and for an instant she was embedded in glory. Her shadow stretched narrow before her and touched me, a bridge of darkness between us. We looked in one another's eyes...

• • •

Magda topped the rise with a kind of grim, joyless satisfaction. I am now a hunter's woman, she thought to herself. We will always be welcome at Landfall for the meat we bring, but they will never speak civilly to me again. Good. I would choke on their sweet talk anyway. The baby stirred and without looking down she stroked him through the furs, murmuring, "Just a little longer, my brave little boo, and we'll be at our new home. Will you like that, eh?"

The sun broke through the clouds to her back, making the snow a red dazzle. Then her eyes adjusted, and she saw the black shape crouched over her lover's body. A very great distance away, her hands throttled down the snowstrider and brought it to a halt. The shallow bowl of land before her was barren, the snow about the corpse black with blood. A last curl of smoke lazily separated from the hut's chimney. The brute lifted its bloody muzzle and looked at her.

Time froze and knotted in black agony.

The larl screamed. It ran straight at her, faster than thought. Clumsily, hampered by the infant strapped to her stomach, Magda clawed the rifle from its boot behind the saddle. She shucked her mittens, fitted hands to metal that stung like hornets, flicked off the safety and brought the stock to her shoulder. The larl was halfway to her. She aimed and fired.

The larl went down. One shoulder shattered, slamming it to the side. It tumbled and rolled in the snow. "You sonofabitch!" Magda cried in triumph. But almost immediately the beast struggled to its feet, turned and fled.

The baby began to cry, outraged by the rifle's roar. Magda powered up the engine. "Hush, small warrior." A kind of madness filled her, a blind anesthetizing rage. "This won't take long." She flung her machine downhill, after the larl.

Even wounded, the creature was fast. She could barely keep up. As it entered the spare stand of trees to the far end of the meadow, Magda paused to fire again, burning a bullet by its head. The larl leaped away. From then on it varied its flight with sudden changes of direction and unexpected jogs to the side. It was a fast learner. But it could not escape Magda. She had always been a hothead, and now her blood was up. She was not about to return to her lover's gutted body with his killer still alive.

The sun set and in the darkening light she lost sight of the larl. But she was able to follow its trail by two-shadowed moonlight, the deep, purple footprints, the darker spatter of blood it left, drop by drop, in the snow.

•••

It was the solstice, and the moons were full—a holy time. I felt it even as I fled the woman through the wilderness. The moons were bright on the snow. I felt the dread of being hunted descend on me, and in my inarticulate way I felt blessed.

But I also felt a great fear for my kind. We had dismissed the humans as incomprehensible, not very interesting creatures, slow-moving, bad-smelling, and dull-witted. Now, pursued by this madwoman on her fast machine brandishing a weapon that killed from afar, I felt all natural order betrayed. She was a goddess of the hunt, and I was her prey.

The People had to be told.

I gained distance from her, but I knew the woman would catch up. She was a hunter, and a hunter never abandons wounded prey. One way or another she would have me.

In the winter all who are injured or too old must offer themselves to the community. The sacrifice rock was not far, by a hill riddled from time beyond memory with our burrows. My knowledge must be shared: The humans were dangerous.

They would make good prey.

I reached my goal when the moons were highest. The flat rock was bare of snow when I ran limping in. Awakened by the scent of my blood, several People emerged from their dens. I lay myself down on the sacrifice rock. A grandmother of the People came forward, licked my wound, tasting, considering. Then she nudged me away with her forehead. The wound would heal, she thought, and winter was young; my flesh was not yet needed.

But I stayed. Again she nudged me away. I refused to go. She whined in puzzlement. I licked the rock.

That was understood. Two of the People came forward and placed their weight on me. A third lifted a paw. He shattered my skull, and they ate.

• • •

Magda watched through power binoculars from atop a nearby ridge. She saw everything. The rock swarmed with lean black horrors. It would be dangerous to go down among them, so she waited and watched the puzzling tableau below. The larl had wanted to die, she'd swear it, and now the beasts came forward daintily, almost ritualistically, to taste, the young first and then the old. She raised her rifle, thinking to exterminate a few of the brutes from afar.

A curious thing happened then. All the larls that had eaten of her prey's brain leaped away, scattering. Those that had not eaten waited, easy targets, not understanding. Then another dipped to lap up a fragment of brain, and looked up with sudden comprehension. Fear touched her.

The hunter had spoken often of the larls, had said that they were so elusive he sometimes thought them intelligent. "Come spring, when I can afford to waste ammunition on carnivores, I look forward to harvesting a few of these beauties," he'd said. He was the colony's xenobiologist, and he loved the animals he killed, treasured them even as he smoked their flesh, tanned their hides, and drew detailed pictures of their internal organs. Magda had always scoffed at his theory that larls gained insight into the habits of their prey by eating their brains, even though he'd spent much time observing the animals minutely from afar, gathering evidence. Now she wondered if he was right.

Her baby whimpered, and she slid a hand inside her furs to give him a breast. Suddenly the night seemed cold and dangerous, and she thought: What am I doing here? Sanity returned to her all at once, her anger collapsing to nothing, like an ice tower shattering in the wind. Below, sleek black shapes sped toward her, across the snow. They changed direction every few leaps, running evasive patterns to avoid her fire.

"Hang on, kid," she muttered, and turned her strider around. She opened up the throttle.

Magda kept to the open as much as she could, the creatures following her from a distance. Twice she stopped abruptly and turned her rifle on her pursuers. Instantly they disappeared in puffs of snow, crouching belly-down but not stopping, burrowing toward her under the surface. In the eerie night silence, she could hear the whispering sound of the brutes tunneling. She fled.

Some frantic timeless period later—the sky had still not lightened in the east—Magda was leaping a frozen stream when the strider's left ski struck a rock. The machine was knocked glancingly upward, cybernetics screaming as they fought to regain balance. With a sickening crunch, the strider slammed to earth, one ski twisted and bent. It would take extensive work before the strider could move again.

Magda dismounted. She opened her robe and looked down on her child. He smiled up at her and made a gurgling noise.

Something went dead in her.

A fool. I've been a criminal fool, she thought. Magda was a proud woman who had always refused to regret, even privately, anything she had done. Now she regretted everything: Her anger, the hunter, her entire life, all that had brought her to this point, the cumulative madness that threatened to kill her child.

A larl topped the ridge.

Magda raised her rifle, and it ducked down. She began walking downslope, parallel to the stream. The snow was knee deep and she had to walk carefully not to slip and fall. Small pellets of snow rolled down ahead of her, were overtaken by other pellets. She strode ahead, pushing up a wake.

The hunter's cabin was not many miles distant; if she could reach it, they would live. But a mile was a long way in winter. She could hear the larls calling to each other, soft coughlike noises, to either side of the ravine. They were following the sound of her passage through the snow. Well, let them. She still had the rifle, and if it had few bullets left, they didn't know that. They were only animals.

This high in the mountains the trees were sparse. Magda descended a good quarter-mile before the ravine choked with scrub and she had to climb up and out or risk being ambushed. Which way? she wondered. She heard three coughs to her right, and climbed the left slope, alert and wary.

•••

We herded her. Through the long night we gave her fleeting glimpses of our bodies whenever she started to turn to the side she must not go, and let her pass unmolested the other way. We let her see us dig into the distant snow and wait motionless, undetectable. We filled the woods with our shadows. Slowly, slowly, we turned her around. She struggled to return to the cabin, but she could not. In what haze of fear and despair she walked! We could smell it. Sometimes her baby cried, and she hushed the milky-scented creature in a voice gone flat with futility. The night deepened as the moons sank in the sky. We forced the woman back up into the mountains. Toward the end, her legs failed her several times; she lacked our strength and stamina. But her patience and guile were every bit our match. Once we approached her still form, and she killed two of us before the rest could retreat. How we loved her! We paced her, confident that sooner or later she'd drop.

It was at night's darkest hour that the woman was forced back to the burrowed hillside, the sacred place of the People where stood the sacrifice rock. She topped the same rise for the second time that night, and saw it. For a moment she stood helpless, and then she burst into tears.

We waited, for this was the holiest moment of the hunt, the point when the prey recognizes and accepts her destiny. After a time, the woman's sobs ceased. She raised her head and straightened her back.

Slowly, steadily she walked downhill.

•••

She knew what to do.

Larls retreated into their burrows at the sight of her, gleaming eyes dissolving into darkness. Magda ignored them. Numb and aching, weary to death, she walked to the sacrifice rock. It had to be this way.

Magda opened her coat, unstrapped her baby. She wrapped him deep in the furs and laid the bundle down to one side of the rock. Dizzily, she opened the bundle to kiss the top of his sweet head, and he made an angry sound. "Good for you, kid," she said hoarsely. "Keep that attitude." She was so tired.

She took off her sweaters, her vest, her blouse. The raw cold nipped at her flesh with teeth of ice. She stretched slightly, body aching with motion. God it felt good. She laid down the rifle. She knelt.

The rock was black with dried blood. She lay down flat, as she had earlier seen her larl do. The stone was cold, so cold it almost blanked out the pain. Her pursuers waited nearby, curious to see what she was doing; she could hear the soft panting noise of their breathing. One padded noiselessly to her side. She could smell the brute. It whined questioningly.

She licked the rock.

• • •

Once it was understood what the woman wanted, her sacrifice went quickly. I raised a paw, smashed her skull. Again I was youngest. Innocent, I bent to taste.

The neighbors were gathering, hammering at the door, climbing over one another to peer through the windows, making the walls bulge and breathe with their eagerness. I grunted and bellowed, and the clash of silver and clink of plates next door grew louder. Like peasant animals, my husband's people tried to drown out the sound of my pain with toasts and drunken jokes.

Through the window I saw Tevin-the-Fool's bonewhite skin gaunt on his skull, and behind him a slice of face—sharp nose, white cheeks—like a mask. The doors and walls pulsed with the weight of those outside. In the next room children fought and wrestled, and elders pulled at their long white beards, staring anxiously at the closed door.

The midwife shook her head, red lines running from the corners of her mouth down either side of her stern chin. Her eye sockets were shadowy pools of dust. "Now push!" she cried. "Don't be a lazy sow!"

I groaned and arched my back. I shoved my head back and it grew smaller, eaten up by the pillows. The bedframe skewed as one leg slowly buckled under it. My husband glanced over his shoulder at me, an angry look, his fingers knotted behind his back.

All of Landfall shouted and hovered on the walls.

"Here it comes!" shrieked the midwife. She reached down to my bloody crotch, and eased out a tiny head, purple and angry, like a goblin.

And then all the walls glowed red and green and sprouted large flowers. The door turned orange and burst open, and the neighbors and crew flooded in. The ceiling billowed up, and aerialists tumbled through the rafters. A boy who had been hiding beneath the bed flew up laughing to where the ancient sky and stars shone through the roof.

They held up the child, bloody on a platter.

• • •

Here the larl touched me for the first time, that heavy black paw like velvet on my knee, talons sheathed. "Can you understand?" he asked. "What it meant to me? All that, the first birth of human young on this planet, I experienced in an instant. I felt it with full human comprehension. I understood the personal tragedy and the community triumph, and the meaning of the lives and culture behind it. A second before, I lived as an animal, with an animal's simple thoughts and hopes. Then I ate of your ancestor. I was lifted all in an instant halfway to godhood.

"As the woman had intended. She had died with her child's birth foremost in her mind, in order that we might share in it. She gave us that. She gave us more. She gave us *language*. We were wise animals before we ate her brain, and we were People afterward. We owed her so much. And we knew what she wanted from us." The larl stroked my cheek with his great, velvety paw, the ivory claws sheathed but quivering slightly, as if about to awake.

I hardly dared breathe.

"That morning I entered Landfall, carrying the baby's sling in my mouth. It slept through most of the journey. At dawn I passed through the empty street as silently as I knew how. I came to the First Captain's house. I heard the murmur of voices within, the entire village assembled for worship. I tapped the door with one paw. There was sudden, astonished silence. Then slowly, fearfully, the door opened."

•••

The larl was silent for a moment. "That was the beginning of the association of People with humans. We were welcomed into your homes, and we helped with the hunting. It was a fair trade. Our food saved many lives that first winter. No one needed know how the woman had perished, or how well we understood your kind.

"That child, Flip, was your ancestor. Every few generations we take one of your family out hunting, and taste his brains, to maintain our closeness with your line. If you are a good boy and grow up to be as bold and honest, as intelligent and noble a man as your father, then perhaps it will be you we eat."

The larl presented his blunt muzzle to me in what might have been meant as a friendly smile. Perhaps not; the expression hangs unreadable, ambiguous in my mind even now. Then he stood and padded away into the friendly dark shadows of the Stone House.

I was sitting staring into the coals a few minutes later when my second-eldest sister—her face a featureless blaze of light, like an angel's—came into the room and saw me. She held out a hand, saying, "Come on, Flip, you're missing everything." And I went with her.

•••

Did any of this actually happen? Sometimes I wonder. But it's growing late, and your parents are away. My room is small but snug, my bed warm but empty. We can burrow deep in the blankets and scare away the cave-bears by playing the oldest winter games there are.

You're blushing! Don't tug away your hand. I'll be gone soon to some distant world to fight in a war for people who are as unknown to you as they are to me. Soldiers grow old slowly, you know. We're shipped frozen between the stars. When you are old and plump and happily surrounded by grandchildren, I'll still be young, and thinking of you. You'll remember me then, and our thoughts will touch in the void. Will you have nothing to regret? Is that really what you want?

Come, don't be shy. Let's put the past aside and get on with our lives. That's better. Blow the candle out, love, and there's an end to my tale.

All this happened long ago, on a planet whose name has been burned from my memory.

TEXTURE OF OTHER WAYS

Mark W. Tiedemann

The media followed our course from colony to colony all the way out to Denebola, where the conference was held. Our ship moved magisterially into and out of dock at each port, unnecessarily slow. At first it amused us, but after ten such stops it became ridiculous. We wanted to huddle in our quarters, close together, and ignore the hectoring questions, the lights, the monitors, the enforced celebrity.

Merril, our liaison, did his best to mollify us and satisfy them, but in the end his efforts always came up short. It occurred to me that the public nature of the project was a mistake, but when I gave this notion to the rest they shrugged together and said it wasn't our mistake.

Earth to Median, halfway to the Centauri group; on to Centauri Transit Station; then to Procyon and on to Epsilon Eridani and Tau Ceti. We bypassed Eurasia, the colony at 40 Eridani. We were never told why. But we stopped at 82 Eridani, the colony of Eridanus. Aquas, Fomalhaut, Nine Rivers, Millennium, and Pollux.

Pan Pollux proved the worst. We felt like curiosities under glass for the wealthy patrons of the resorts. Till then I'd always believed people had a finer appreciation of the difference between the merely unusual and the special. We gathered together in the lounge and formed a cluster in the center of the floor and communed with each other, playing games of dancing from mind to mind, chasing ideas back to their sources, switching perspectives, and seeing how many we could be at one time. In the middle of this probes managed to sneak in past our security. I'm still convinced this was allowed to happen. The Forum counted on a rich political reward from our mission and the temptation to exploit us through any media outlet available was irresistible. Poor Merril, he believed in his job, tried ardently to meet its requirements, but there was only so much he could do in the face of the great need of human polity. We were ostensibly the saviors of humankind, it was necessary that our march toward Golgotha be witnessed.

All the probes saw, though, was a group—thirty-three of us—sitting tightly together on the floor of our lounge, eyes closed, heads bobbing slightly, here and there drool from a mouth, the twitch of a limb, perhaps an occasional tuneless hum. What the viewing public must have thought of its savior! Their fate in the hands of—what?

• • •

When they changed me there was no question of choice. Seven hundred days old, you don't even realize that the world isn't part of you, much less that it doesn't care. Understanding that only discreet parts of it care is something that comes much later, if at all. It's a sophisticated distinction, this sorting out, a concept constantly threatened by the fact that even the caring parts probably don't care about you. But in time we all learn that everything around us, everything that happens, is organized into packets of information and those packets can be assembled by consciousness into something that has order and meaning. A fiction, perhaps, and it's a question whether the boundaries that keep everything apart are internal or external. An academic question, of no real consequence.

Unless those boundaries disappear.

When they changed me—and the others, all thirty-three of us—several of those boundaries vanished and had to be replaced by something else, a different method of perception and ordering. At seven hundred days old I didn't "understand" this—none of us did—all we could do was react. There is a murk at the bottom of my memory that intrudes from time to time into my dreams, but which I assiduously avoid contemplating most of the time. I tell myself that this swamp is the residue of my reaction. I tell myself that. On the rare occasions when I conjure enough courage to be determinedly self-analytical I think—I believe—that it is the residue of thirty-three reactions. Then I wonder how we all sorted ourselves out of the mix. Then I wonder if we ever did. Then I stop thinking about it.

• • •

Our ship met with a convoy halfway from Pan Pollux to Denebola. You never really see ships at dock, each one is berthed separately in the body of the station. Once in a while another ship leaves dock at the same time you do and you get to see one of them against the stars. I sometimes think these vessels are the most beautiful objects humans ever built. Elegant, powerful, freighted with every aspect of our natures—hope, pride, ambition, curiosity, wonder, and fear. When the convoy gathered around us we stared at the two dozen ships.

"Whales."

"No, methane floaters."

"A school of armor."

I listened to the ripple of comparisons, trying to decide which one fit best. None really did. Whales in space? Too many lines, dark masses, geometries. Methane floaters drifted with the currents of their atmospheres, virtually helpless to control direction. These moved with power, purpose, a logical order to the way they arranged themselves around us, protecting us.

"Admiral Kovesh's task force," Merril announced. "They'll be our escort to Denebola."

"Will there be seti task forces there, too?" I asked.

Merril frowned slightly, clasped his hands behind his back the way he did when something made him uneasy. "I expect so."

I looked back at the Armada ships, excited at the prospect of comparing human and alien.

•••

There was a reporter from the Ares-Epsilon NewsNet that kept up with us from Sol to Nine Rivers. He must have interviewed every one of us by then, some twice. On our last interview I decided to go for shock, to see how he'd react.

"The development of telepaths is a radical step in human evolution," he said. "According to scientists, we've been capable of such a step for a long time but we've refrained. Why do you think it took a First Contact situation to push us into it?"

"Fear."

"Fear? In what way?"

"They couldn't talk to the seti, so the Armada started planning for war. It's that simple. Say something we understand or we'll shoot. The Pan Humana wanted to believe the human race was beyond ancient formulas for defending the cave, but it's been centuries since words failed to convey meaning, so the old ways had been forgotten."

His eyes brightened. This was better than the prepared statements we'd been delivering all along.

"Then the seti showed up and the race panicked. Not one word made sense. You're right, we've been capable of producing telepaths—actually, the term is telelog, there's a difference—for a long time. But people are afraid of the idea. That's the only real area of privacy, your thoughts. But when the Chairman, the Forum, and the Armada realized that the most insurmountable problem confronting them with the setis was language, they seized the opportunity. It was a question of weighing competitive fears. Of course, fear of the alien won out."

"Yes, but in a very fundamental way, you're alien, too."

"But at least we *look* human."

I don't think his report ever made it onto the newsnets. He didn't continue on with us after Nine Rivers.

•••

Denebola is a white, white sun, forty-three light-years from Earth. It shepherds a small herd of Jovians and two hard planets, none of which is hospitable to human life without considerable manipulation. As far as I have learned, no plans have been made to terraform.

I always wondered why Denebola. Well, it *is* right out there at the limit of our expansion. There are a few colonies further out, but in the pragmatic way such things are judged by the Forum they don't count because they're too tenuous. But *we* didn't pick Denebola. *They* did. The setis.

Stars have many names and now that we've met our neighbors I'm sure the number will increase again. Denebola has three that I consider ironically appropriate. Denebola itself is from the Arabic *Al Dhanab Al Asad,* the Lion's Tail. But there's another Arab name for it, *Al Sarfah,* the Changer. I like that better, it seems more relevant to my own situation, to our situation. The place of changes, changes wrought by the place itself.

The third name? Chinese, *Wu Ti Tso,* Seat of the Five Emperors.

•••

Admiral Kovesh came over to meet us after the convoy arrived at the orbital platform. She was a tall, straight-backed woman with deep creases in her face and very pale eyes. I thought she looked perfect for her command.

"As soon as our counterparts signal us," she explained, "then you'll all be taken down by shuttle. The Forum negotiators are already here."

"Can we see the other ships?" I asked.

Kovesh frowned. "What—?"

"The seti ships."

"Oh. Of course. As soon as I've briefed you on procedures."

"We've already been briefed."

Kovesh looked at Merril, who seemed nervous.

"Before we left Earth," he said, "we were all given a thorough profile of what to expect. They know their mission, Admiral."

"I don't care what they were told on Earth. We're thirteen parsecs out and this conference is under my aegis."

Merril gave us an apologetic look. "I see. Well, perhaps you could let them take it directly?"

"How do you mean?"

Merril blinked. "They're telelogs, Admiral. It would be quicker, surer—"

"Not on your life."

"I assure you it's painless, Admiral—"

"I'm assured. The answer is no. Now, if you don't mind..."

I felt sorry for Merril. He meant well, but I was glad the Admiral refused. Merril had an exaggerated notion of what we did. People are really a muddle.

The Change was mechanistic. We aren't psychics in the traditional sense. That's why we're called telelogs rather than telepaths. At infancy we were implanted with a biopole factory, a device called the logos. The logos transfers a colony of biopole, which seats itself in the recipient brain, and starts setting up a temporary pattern analyzer. Very quickly—I'm talking nanoseconds—the colony establishes a pattern, sets up a transmission, and within moments the contents of the mind are broadcast to the primary logos.

But the contents!

To be honest, it is *much* easier for someone to simply *tell* me, verbally, than for me to try to make sense of all this *clutter!*

We grew up living in each other's minds, we know how we operate, but the rest of humanity? It's a miracle there's any order at all.

Still, Admiral Kovesh's reaction disturbed me.

•••

The idea made elegant sense.

Humans can't communicate with the seti, and vice versa. There is no mutual foundation of language between us. Even the couple of humanoid ones have languages grown from linguistic trees sprouted in different soils. Nothing matches up except for a few snatches of mathematics, which was how we all managed to pick one system in which to have a meeting.

That and the evident desire on the part of the seti to figure out *how* to communicate demands a solution.

There are only two solutions. The first will take decades, maybe centuries, and that will be the construction of an object by object lexicon. State a word—or group of words or collection of sound-signifiers, which will only be valid for those species that *use* sounds for communication—and point at the thing to which it attaches. How this will work with abstracts no one knows.

The other solution is us.

We smiled at each other, passed along encoded biopole of self-congratulation and mutual support, broadcast positive logos. Of course, we thought, what better way to decode a completely alien language than to read the minds of the speakers?

We learned linguistics and practiced decoding language on native speakers of disparate human tongues. With difficulty we learned to decode the patterns into recognizable linguistic components and eventually came to speak the language ourselves. Navajo, Mandarin, !Kung, Russian, Portuguese, English—the hard part was finding speakers of all these languages who were not also fluent in Langish, official Panspeak. But there are enclaves and preserves and the subjects were found and we learned.

The only troubling part—and none of us actually brought this up, but I imagine we all thought it—was that all these languages are ultimately *human* languages. All grown from the same soil. Hardwired. At some level, then, all the same.

• • •

Details. Kovesh went over them again and again. All we wanted to do was see a seti ship. Until we learned our lessons that would wait. We worked our way through to our reward, then stood before the viewer and gazed at the array of ships.

A small platform orbited the planet. Clouds smeared across a cracked grey-blue surface of alkalis and yttrian earths. The clouds, we learned, came from fine oxide powders blown through the lithium-fluorine atmosphere. We wondered how anything could oxidate in such an atmosphere and were told that a complex form of lichen lived underground and released oxygen through the soil. The surface constantly eroded under the breezes and picked up the deposits of oxidated metals once exposed.

The seti ships orbited close to the platform. As distinct as each appeared, all shared one common trait. They were all shells, protection, walls between life and death.

But what marvelous walls!

I had thought our ships were beautiful, and I still do, but compared to the array of alien ships they seem so...expected. Some of the vessels actually resembled ships. Certain shapes lend themselves to travel, to containing biospheres against hard vacuum, so inevitably globes, discs, tubes, and boxes of various sizes repeat from species to species. But the lines...

The nearest group looked like giant gourds, sectioned by sharp lines emanating from a central locus into seven equal parts. As we watched, though, a segment would drift away from the main body, float to another body, and change places with another segment.

Beyond these, we saw an enormous mass like dirty gelatin. Pieces extruded, broke off, drifted among the other groups, returned to merge with the whole. The entire surface roiled and bubbled.

Then there were the candyfloss yachts catching the sunlight and glimmering along the countless threads that interlaced to form their conic assemblies...

We passed impressions among ourselves, all of them optimistic. We were here to learn to speak with these beings who built these lovely ships. Because we marvelled at what they had built we knew we would marvel at who they were, at what they were. We were a short flight from the fulfillment of our life's purpose.

•••

Marines escorted us to our shuttles. The wide corridors of the ship suddenly felt tight. We stayed close together, hands touching, and said nothing. Even through the logos all we shared were vague assurances, the soldiers' stiff presence acting like a muffle on our enthusiasm.

Kovesh waited in the lead shuttle.

"A platoon is waiting on the surface," she said. "Each group will go down with an escort of three. I'll ride this one down. All the shuttles will maintain standby once we're down, so should anything arise we'll be able to get you off quickly."

Eleven of us in each group. I missed Merril. He rode down with a different shuttle. We sat in couches that faced across a narrow walkway from each other. One marine sat forward, the other aft, while Kovesh went up by the pilot.

There was no view outside. We held hands and looked across at ourselves and tried to imagine what happened from sounds and vibrations. We knew the moment the shuttle left the ship, we had all felt that

characteristic sensation before. Then the soundless time of freefall...
then the first brush of atmosphere...the shuttle bounced and we could
hear a high-pitched whine through the bulkheads. An air leak? That
meant a breach...but no alarms flashed, except the fear transmitted
back and forth through our hands, building quickly to near panic until
Kovesh came back and told us we would land in five minutes. The panic
subsided like water sloshing back and forth until it loses momentum
and finds equilibrium.

But our equilibrium now rested on a thin layer of anxiety.

A series of harsher sounds and heavier shocks followed. I squeezed the
hands I held tight and they gripped me harder till my fingers began to
go numb, till everyone's fingers tingled, and passed the sensation back
and forth.

Then silence.

Kovesh stepped down the walkway between us. A few seconds later
the hatch opened with a loud pneumatic hiss.

We waited. I imagined us as cargo, the marines our deliverers, and
passed the thought along. A few smiles came back and we relaxed a little.

"All right," Kovesh snapped, leaning into the shuttle. "Stay close. The
other shuttles are down now. You'll be taken to your temporary quarters."

Umbilicals attached the shuttle locks to the environ module. We
stepped into a wide chamber, the support ribs naked against the walls
and ceiling, the air chilled so that we could see our breath. We came together immediately, all thirty-three of us, in the center of the chamber,
reestablishing contact as if we had been separated for days or years. Merril
walked around our perimeter saying over and over that everything was
all right, everything was fine.

I looked back to the locks then and saw marines standing at each. I
searched the chamber for Admiral Kovesh and found her speaking to
two men at the opposite end of the module. More marines flanked them.
Then I noticed that marines stood against the walls all around us.

Merril continued his orbit, his reassurances, until Kovesh summoned
him.

•••

After the Change we laughed and cried together. Pain and pleasure became a shared thing, what one experienced cascaded through all of us. For a time there was concern that we would fail to individuate. It became necessary to shut us down from time to time, force us to form independent identities. It was a lot like learning to walk, then run, then walk and run in self-directed patterns, then integrate it all into an automatic decision-making hierarchy that worked without constant conscious monitoring. You don't think your way across a room, down a street, over a hill, or through a city, you just go in response to an abstract desire to go *somewhere*.

Eventually we developed individual traits, some degree of autonomy, but it never felt natural. Forced separation always hurt. Short periods of apartness were tolerable only because we knew we would be together again. Soon.

•••

The meeting hall stood in the middle of a sodium-white field, gothic in proportion, elegant, delicate, emblematic. Its machinery encapsulated each group in an appropriate atmosphere, clearly seti tech. The marines had told us about it. They were disturbed, a bit awed.

"This is a formal occasion," Merril told us, "an introduction. You won't be doing anything here. We're just meeting the representatives."

We entered the central hall. Sounds echoed oddly, bouncing as it did through mixed gases. It felt as if we were immersed in an invisible sea.

The setis stood arrayed around the perimeter, formed up in loose groups, some of which contained more than one species. Some were bipeds, others without visible limbs, a few with no discernible "heads," and one that seemed nothing but a tangle of articulating limbs. The fields in which they stood refracted light differently. When they moved and the fields overlapped, colors warped out of true, bent, and dazzled.

We spread out. Their designated speakers separated from their parties and approached the center. The light was coppery, liquid. Pride welled up within us. We had trained for this, been created for this, designed for this.

Sound washed through the hall. Bass, treble, mixes of tone that verged on music, then slid away into barely ordered chaos...they *spoke!* We touched hands, passed our impressions down the line, always with the underthought that *this* is what we had come to solve.

The human delegates stood up, then, and read from a prepared statement. We heard little of it. The setis held our attention. This was all politics, this meeting. A show. It was being recorded, we knew, and would be used later, excellent press. The real work would be done under less dramatic circumstances. But this alone seemed worth the journey. If we could freeze the moment like this…it was perfect, just as it was. Uncomplicated by articulation.

We gazed across the hall at each other. I felt nothing at that instant but anticipation.

• • •

Of course it made perfect sense. We couldn't do what was required all bunched together in a group, mingled with all the seti at once. The cascade of impressions would ruin the uniqueness of each language. We had to isolate each seti and work on its language apart from the rest. Perfectly reasonable.

"There are five major groups," Ambassador Sulin explained. "Rahalen, Cursian, Vohec, Menkan, and Distanti. There are numerous other allied and nonaligned races, some of them present, but from what we've been able to determine, these five are the primary language groups. Translate these and we can communicate with most of the others."

He cleared his throat and glanced at Merril. "I didn't expect them to be so young," he said.

"It was in the précis we sent," Merril said, frowning.

"Yes, but…well." He shrugged and looked at us. "Each team will contain five people. Two linguists and three of you. We're not sure how many individuals will attend each seti representative, but the work rooms aren't that large, so we don't expect much more on their part. Now, what we want is for you to choose a back-up group among yourselves for each language. When you come out of a session, you go immediately to that group and work over what you've, uh, learned. Don't cross-reference with the other groups, please, not until we've got some kind of handle on each language."

"The setis communicate among themselves, don't they?" I asked.

"Yes, as far as we know."

"Then they already have a common set of referents. Wouldn't it be sensible to try to find that first?"

"Good question. But what we want is to have some basis of understanding for each group individually first. Then we can go on from there."

"But—"

"This is the procedure we will use."

"Uh," Merril said, "Ambassador, it's just that the idea of separation is unpleasant for them."

"Then they'll have to get used to it."

•••

The oval-shaped room contained several comfortable chairs, three or four recorders, and a commlink panel. A curious flower-shaped mass on the ceiling apparently provided the unique environments for the species present.

The two people assigned to my group shook our hands quickly, smiling anxiously. We resisted the urge to telelog them to see why they were so nervous. Merril told us we had to trust them and do nothing to damage that trust.

The light dimmed when our counterparts entered. Our group had been assigned the Cursians. They were bulky, almost humanoid types. Their torsos began where knees should have been and their limbs looked like dense extrusions of rope. Individual tendrils would separate to perform the articulations of fingers, but they constantly touched themselves with them. No eyes that we could discern, but a thick mass of lighter tissue gathered in the center of the bumpy mass we thought of as its head. They wore threads of metal draped in complex patterns over their dense torsos. We were told that they breathed a compound of CO_2, CH_3, and CH_5N. The air seemed to glow a faint green on their side of the room.

"We need to touch them," I said.

"That's not possible," one of the linguists said, frowning. "I mean..." She looked at her colleague. "Is it?"

"I don't think so," he said, and went to the comm. He spoke with someone for a few minutes, then turned back to us, shaking his head. "Not advised. There could be some leakage of atmospheres. Cyanide and oxygen are mutually incompatible. We don't know how dangerous it might be."

"Then we can't do this. We have to touch them."

"Shit," she said. "Why didn't anybody see this problem?"

He shrugged and returned to the comm.

We spent the rest of that day's session staring across the thin line of atmosphere at each other. I wondered if the Cursians were as disappointed as we.

•••

The next day there was no session. Everyone had experienced a similar problem with their seti groups. In one case it was incompatible atmospheres, in another it was a question of microbe contaminants, in another it was just a matter of propriety. The sessions were canceled until some way of getting across the notion could be devised.

Before we could touch and share our logos, Admiral Kovesh ordered us separated.

"Once they make contact," she said, "this is how it will be. May as well start them now so they get used to it."

Merril protested, but we ended up in separate rooms anyway. The three of us huddled close together all through the night.

Admiral Kovesh came twice to wake us up and ask if we had sensed nothing, if perhaps we had picked up something after all, but we could only explain, as before, that to telelog it was necessary to touch, or the biopole could not be transferred—

She didn't want to hear that. The second time I told her that and she grew suspicious.

"Are you reading me?" she asked.

"Would you believe me if I said no?"

She did not come back that night.

•••

Three days later we once more went to the meeting room. Now there was a solid transparent wall between the Cursians and us with a boxlike contraption about shoulder height that contained complex seals joining in its middle in a kind of mixing chamber. It was obvious that an arrangement had been made.

"How does it work?"

"As simple as putting on a glove," one of the liaisons said. "Just insert your hand here, shove it through until you feel the baffles close on your arm. Self-sealing. The touchpoint chamber will only allow one finger through. Is that enough?"

It was annoying and confusing that no one had asked us. But perhaps Merril had told them. In any event, yes, we told them, it was enough.

On the other side of the clear wall, one of the Cursians came forward. A limb jammed into its end of the box and a tendril separated and pushed through until a tip emerged into the central chamber. I looked at the other two, who touched my free hand and nodded. I put my hand into the box.

My finger poked through the last seal and the membrane closed firmly just below the second joint. The air in the chamber was cold and my skin prickled. I stared at the Cursian "finger" as it wriggled slowly toward the tip of my finger. I concentrated a biopole discharge there and when it touched me it was almost as if I could feel the colony surge from me to the Cursian. Imagination, certainly, I had never been able to "feel" the transfer; the only way any of us ever knew it had happened was when the colony established itself and began sending back signals.

There should have been a short signal, a kind of handshake that let us know it had been a successful transfer. I waited, but felt no such impulse.

I gazed through the layers of separation between us and wondered if it was feeling the same sense of failure. To come all this way, to prepare all your life for this moment, and then to find that for reasons overlooked or unimagined you have been made for nothing...I thought then that there could be no worse pain.

I was wrong.

•••

Once an animal was released among us. A dog. I don't know if it had been intentional or an accident. You might be surprised at how many accidents happen in a highly monitored, overly secured lab. It seems sometimes that the more tightly controlled an environment is the more the unexpected happens. But in this case, I'm inclined to believe it was intentional, despite the reactions of our caretakers—especially Merril—when they discovered it.

The animal was obviously frightened. It didn't know where it was, or who we were. We thought perhaps that it was a seti, that maybe one had volunteered to come to us as a test, but that was quickly rejected when we accessed the library. The dog was only a pet, an assistant, a symbiote that had accompanied *Homo sapiens sapiens* on the long journey to the present. It whimpered a little when we cornered it and looked at us with hopeful, nearly trusting eyes. It needed assurance. It needed to know that it was welcome, that we would not harm it. We only intended to give it what it wanted.

The brief immersion in its thoughts came as a shock. The sheer terror it exuded surprised us, overwhelmed our own sense of security. When they took it away to be "put down," as Merril called it, several of us still wept uncontrollably from the aftershocks.

Batteries of tests followed to make sure no damage had been done. But the dog was dead.

•••

It came gradually, a vaguely puzzled sensation, a *What, where from, who?* series of impressions. For a moment I nearly lost my despair.

Then a wave of nauseating rage washed through me. Revulsion, anger, rejection—like a massive hand trying to push me away. But I was chained to it and the more it pushed the more pain came through the connection. Sparks danced in my eyes. My skull felt ready to split and fall open. When I opened my eyes, I saw that I had slid to the floor, my hand still shoved through the trap.

The Cursian rocked back and forth and side to side, serpentine digits writhing. Suddenly, it reared back and drove one of its limbs at the transparency. The impact shook the wall.

I heard swearing around me, terse words, orders, but none of it made sense. My language was gone. Words were only sound. In my head I knew only a vast and sour presence and I remembered the dog and its terror and I tried to stand, to pull my hand away.

I thought I had failed before. Now I knew what failure felt like. But it wasn't my failure.

Hands grasped my shoulders, another took my arm. I was pulled away. My hand came free, but it felt cold and numb. I stared at the seti.

It extracted its own limb and stumbled away from the transparency and nearly collapsed on the floor. It looked tormented.

"D-don—don't—!" I tried to say, but my siblings were holding me and the biopole bled into them.

One screamed. The other jerked away, mouth open.

"Get them out of here!" someone shouted. "Now!"

More people crowded into the chamber and I was lifted onto a gurney. I couldn't stop feeling the awful violation the Cursian had emptied into me. I wanted to sleep. I wanted to die.

• • •

It happened to all of us. It grew worse as we came together.

Logos spread back and forth, colonizing and broadcasting. We didn't understand and that complicated it. We sought comfort from each other, but the enigma of alien rejection compounded, interfered.

It didn't end till we were sedated.

And then there were dreams…dreams of anxiety and suspicion and insult…dreams of dying…

• • •

They showed us vids later. I don't like watching them, but they make us see them, those of us who lived. The setis reacted. It's obvious now, after the fact. They recoiled. That's the only word I can think that fits. Recoiled. Some of them looked dead. Five of us died. Others wouldn't stop screaming.

There are images in my head and I'm frightened to share them. I look at my companions and can see that they, too, contain things they will not, cannot share. It hurts. I understand Admiral Kovesh's reaction to the logos. Nobody told us it might be like this. Perhaps we should have suspected because of the dog, but we had all dismissed that because it had been so disadvantaged compared to us, its mind couldn't comprehend what was happening. But we know now. It was so simple an oversight—or perhaps not, perhaps it was assumed to be impossible, part of the dilemma of the situation: How can you ask permission when you don't speak the language? That was, after all, our task—to ask them things. But no one had tried to tell them that we would invade their minds in order to do so. And when we did, they scarred us.

We can never live in each other's minds again. We are separate now because we fear each other. We fear what we contain. We fear what we might give ourselves. We do not understand.

The seti ships had moved into positions of defense by the time the marines got us back up to our ship. They were frightened. We had hurt them. They had hurt us. We will all of us have to learn a new way to trust.

Perhaps, I think, we fulfilled our mission anyway. We had believed we shared nothing with the seti, but that's wrong. We share fear. Humans have been basing relations on that for millennia.

A door opens and a marine comes in. She switches off the vid and pulls out a notepad.

"Admiral Kovesh says we have to see to it you get whatever you want," she says. She smiles at me and I'm startled at how pleased I am. "What's your name?" she asks.

I feel my smile fade.

"Name?"

TO GO BOLDLY

CORY DOCTOROW

aptain Reynold J. Tsubishi of the APP ship *Colossus II* was the youngest commander in the fleet. He knew he owed his meteoric rise through the ranks to the good study habits he'd acquired in the Academy: specifically, the habit of studying what people cared about and *embodying those things* for them. Thus he was an expert in twentieth-century culture (the mark of distinguished taste in the Academy for two hundred years); a sudden-death bare-knuckles martial artist; a rakish flirt; and a skilled three-harp player. He led nearly every away-team, didn't screw the junior officers, and—

And he didn't have the faintest idea what to do about The Ball.

The Ball had been detected in the middle of the second shift, when the B-string had the conn and the bridge. No one called them the B-string, but they were. Some ships had tried evenly spreading the top people across all three shifts, but no one who was any good wanted to work ship's night and anyone with clout filed for transfers to ships that let the As congregate in A spaces during "daylight" hours. So now it was the A-string from ship's 9 to ship's 17, the B-string from 17 to 1, and the miserable Cs on the truly nocturnal 1 to 9.

Tsubishi was in the middle of his first REM when his headband brought him swiftly to the surface of his mind, dialing up the lights and the smell of wintergreen and eucalyptus as the holo of First Lieutenant !Mota, framed by the high back of the command chair, filled the room.

"Sir," !Mota said, ripping off a precise salute (zer exoskeleton made all routine movement precise, but the salute was a work of art, right down to the tiny "ping" as the tip of zer metal-sheathed tentacle grazed zer forelobe), "my apologies for rousing you. The forward sensor array detected a yufo, and, on closer inspection, we believe it may be evidence of a potentially hostile garrison." The B-string commander was actually pretty good at zer job, and would have likely had zer own command by now but for the fact that the admiralty was heavily tilted to stock humans and loathe to promote non- and trans-humans to the higher echelon. As a Wobbly (not a flattering name for an entire advanced starfaring race, but an accurate one, and no one with humanoid mouth-parts could pronounce the word in Wobbliese), !Mota was forever doomed to second-banana.

"On bridge in three," Tsubishi said, with a slightly sleepy salute of his own. His fresher had already cleaned and hung his uniform—a limit-less supply of hard vac gave new meaning to the phrase "dry cleaning," and the single-piece garment was as crisp as the ones he'd assiduously ironed as a kay-det on old Mars. He backed into the fresher and held his arms up while it wrapped him in the fabric. All on-ship toilets had an automated system for dressing and undressing uniformed person-nel, while the away-teams made do with sloppier (but easier to shuck) baggies, or, in the rare event that a green ensign forgot to change before beaming down, relying on teammates to help with the humiliating ritual of dressing and undressing.

The duty officer barked "Captain on deck" before he'd even managed to set his foot down, and the whole B-squad was on its feet and saluting before his back leg came up to join it. !Mota made a formal gesture of handing over the conn, and Tsubishi slid into his chair just as it finished its hurried reconfiguration to suit his compact, tightly wound frame. The ship beamed a double cappuccino—ship's crest stamped into the foam—into the armrest's cup-holder, and he sipped it pensively before nodding to !Mota to make zer report.

!Mota—the model of second-banana efficiency—had whomped up an entire slideshow (with music and animated transitions, Tsubishi noted, with an inward roll of his eyes) in the time it had taken him to reach the bridge. The entire command crew watched him closely as !Mota stepped through it.

"We were proceeding as normal in our survey of the Tesla Z-65 system," !Mota said, the bridge holo going into orrery mode, showing the system and its 11 planets and 329 planetesimals, the fourth planet out glittering with a safety-orange highlight. "We'd deployed the forward sensor arrays here, to Tesla Z-65-4, for initial detailed surveys. Z-65-4 is just over one AU from the star, and pulls 1.8 gees, putting it in the upper bound of high-value/high-interest survey targets." The holo swept forward in dizzying jumps as the sensor packages beamed each other closer and closer to the planet in a series of hops, leaving them strung out in a lifeline from the ship's safe position among Z-65's outer rim to Z-65-4, ninety AUs away. The final stage established a long, elliptical orbit, and beamed its tiny progeny into tighter geostationary orbits around the planet's waistline.

"The yufo was detected almost immediately. It had been on the dark side of the planet, in geostationary, and it came into the lateral sensor-range of two of our packages when they beamed in." In a volumetric display, four different views of the yufo: a radar-derived mesh, a set of charts displaying its likely composition, an optical photo of the item in shaky high-mag, and a cartoon derived from the former, showing the yufo as a sphere a mere 1.5 meters in diameter, skinned in something black that the radar-analysis suggested was a damned efficient one-way sheath that likely disguised a Panopticon's worth of sensors, spy-eyes, radar.

The bolo transitioned—a genie-back-into-the-bottle effect—and was replaced with a bulleted time line of the encounter, including notations as to when radar incursions on the sensor package emanating from the yufo were detected. !Mota let the chart stand for itself, then clicked to the final slide, the extrapolated cartoon of the yufo again.

!Mota ripped off another artful salute. "Orders, sir?"

"Have you brought one of our packages forward to get a closer look?"

"No sir. I anticipated that contingency and made plans for it, but have not given the order."

"Do it," Tsubishi said, giving one of those ironical little head-tilts that the female kay-dets on Mars had swooned for—and noted the B-shift tactical officer's appreciative wriggle with satisfaction—and watched the holotank as the packet changed its attitude with conservative little thruster-bursts, moving slowly relative to the yufo while the continents below whirled past as it came out of geostationary position. The cartoon yufo resolved itself with ever-more-minute details as the packet got closer, closer.

"Packet reports radio chatter, three sigmas off random. Eighty-three percent confidence that it is communication." The comms officer had an unfortunate speech impediment that she'd all but corrected in the Academy, but it was still enough to keep her on the B-squad. Probably wouldn't accept neurocorrection. "Eighty-five. Ninety-five. Signal identified as ultra-wide-band sequence key. Switching to UWB reception now. Playing back 900 MHz to 90 GHz spectrum for ten minutes, using key. Repeating pattern found. Decoding."

It was the standard first contact drill. Any species plying the spaces between the stars was bound to converge on one of a few Rosetta strategies. The holotank showed realtime visualizations of the ship's symbology AI subsystem picking a million digits of Pi out of the chatter, deriving the counting system, then finding calculus, bootstrapping higher symbols out of *that,* moving on to physics and then to the physics of hyperspace. A progress bar tracked the system's confidence that it could decode arbitrary messages from the yufo's originating species, and as it approached completion, Tsubishi took another sip of his cappuccino and tipped his head toward the comms officer.

"Hail the yufo, Ms. De Fuca-Williamson."

The comms officer's hands moved over her panels, then she nodded back at Tsubishi.

"This is Captain Reynold J. Tsubishi of the Alliance of Peaceful Planets ship *Colossus II*. In the name of the Alliance and its forty-two member-species, I offer you greetings in the spirit of galactic cooperation and peace." It was canned, that line, but he'd practiced it in the holo in his quarters so that he could sell it fresh every time.

The silence stretched. A soft chime marked an incoming message. A succession of progress bars filled the holotank as it was decoded, de-muxed and remuxed. Another, more emphatic chime.

"Do it," Tsubishi said to the comms officer, and First Contact was made anew.

The form that filled the tank was recognizably a head. It was wreathed in writhing tentacles, each tipped with organs that the computer identified with high confidence as sensory—visual, olfactory, temperature.

The tentacles whipped around as the bladder at the thing's throat inflated, then blatted out something in its own language, which made Wobbliese seem mellifluous. The computer translated: "Oh, for god's sake—*role-players*? You've *got* to be kidding me."

Then the message disappeared. A klaxon sounded and the bridge dimmed; flashing red lights filled the bridge.

"Status?" Tsubishi took another calm sip of his cappuccino though his heart was racing. Captains never broke a sweat. It went with the territory.

"The package has gone nonresponsive. Nearby telemetry suggests with high confidence that it has been destroyed. Another has gone offline. Two more. All packages nonresponsive and presumed under attack."

"Bring us to defcon four," Tsubishi said. "Do it."

•••

The A-team assembled on the bridge in a matter of minutes, freshly wrapped in their uniforms, unceremoniously pushing the unprotesting B-team out of their seats just as the ship's computer beamed their preset high-alert snacks and beverages to their workstations. As a courtesy, !Mota was allowed to remain on the bridge, but the rest of the second shift slunk away, looking hurt and demoralized. Tsubishi pursed his lips at their departing backs and felt the burden of command.

"Bring us to within five AU, Lieutenant," he said, nodding at Deng-Gorinski in the navigator's chair. "I want to get a little closer."

At five AUs, they could beam photon torpedoes to within fifteen minutes of the yufo. If it was anything like their own packages, they could outmaneuver it with the torpedo's thrusters at that range.

The lieutenant showed her teeth as she brought the ship up to speed, battle-ready and champing to blow the intruder out of the sky.

The ping of another incoming message brought the crew's attention back to the comms post. The progress bars went much faster now, the symbology AI now much more confident of its guesses about the intruder's language.

"Now what are you doing? Can't you see I'm already here? Get lost. This is my patch."

"In the name of the APP, I order you to stand down and power down your offensive systems. Anything less will be construed as a declaration of war. You have thirty seconds to comply. This—is one second."

He crumpled his cappuccino cup and tossed it over his shoulder; the ship obliterated it by beaming it into nullspace before it touched the ground. The holotank was counting down, giving the numbers in the preassigned ultimatum voice: female, calm, cold, with an accent that a twentieth-century Briton would have recognized as Thatcher-posh.

"Oh. Really. Now. You want to shoot at each other? I've got a better idea. Let's meet on the surface and duke it out, being to being, for control of the planet. Capture the flag. First one to get a defensible position on the highest peak of this mountain range gets to claim the whole thing for zer respective empire." Tsubishi noted the neuter pronoun with some interest: neuter species were more common than highly dimorphic ones in the galaxy, and they had a reputation for being meaner than the poor he-she species like h. sap saps. Something about having your primary genetic loyalty to your identical clones as opposed to your family group—it created a certain...ruthlessness.

"Why should I bargain at all? I could just blow you out of orbit, right here."

The tentacles writhed in a gesture that the computer badged with the caption "smirk, confidence 86%," and Tsubishi pointed a single finger at the ship's gunner, who flexed in her chiton and clicked delicately at the control interface, priming and aiming it. The computer quietly turned a patch of Tsubishi's armrest into a display and flashed a discreet notification about the spike in hormonal aggression volatiles being detected on the bridge. He waved it away. He didn't need a computer to tell him about the battle-stink. He could smell it himself. It smelled good. First contact was good—but *war...war* was what the Alliance of Peaceful Planets lived for.

"You can try," the alien said.

"A warning shot, Lieutenant," he said, tipping his head to Deng-Gorinski. "Miss the yufo by, say, half a million klicks."

The click of Deng-Gorinski's talon was the only sound on the bridge, as every crewmember held zer breath, and then the barely detectable hap-tic *whoom* as a torpedo left its bay and streaked off in glorious 3-D on the holotank, trailed by a psychedelic glitter of labels indicating its approach, operational status, detected countermeasures, and all the glorious, pointless instrumentation data that was merely icing on the cake.

The torpedo closed on the yufo, drawing closer, closer...closer. Then—

Blink

"It's gone, sir." Deng-Gorinski's talons clicked, clicked. "Transporter beam. Picked it right out of the sky."

That's impossible. He didn't bother to say it. Of course it was possible: they'd just seen it happen. But transporting a photon torpedo that was underway and emitting its punishing halo of quantum chaff should have required enough energy to melt a star and enough compute-power to calculate the universe. It was the space-naval equivalent of catching a sword-blade between your palms as it was arcing toward your chest.

"Take us back to seventy AUs," he said, admiring the calmness in his own voice. He had a bad feeling, but it didn't pay to let it show. The armrest gave him another discreet notifier, this one about the changing composition of the pheromones on the bridge. Fear stink. "*Now.*"

The ship's klaxon sounded again, louder than he'd ever heard it outside of the Academy war-games. He silenced it with a flick of a finger and peered into the holotank.

"Incoming yufo, sir."

The tank showed it to them. It was sickeningly familiar.

"That's our torpedo," he said.

"Closing fast," Deng-Gorinski said. "Shields up. Estimated impact in twenty-eight seconds."

"Evasive action," Tsubishi said uselessly. They were already in an evasive pattern, the ship automatically responding to the threat, faster than any human reflexes. "Antimissile battery," he snapped. The smaller missiles streaked toward the torpedo.

"Can we make contact with the control interface on the torpedo?"

The comms officer jabbed furiously at the air around his helmet, making hand-jives known only to the most highly trained communications specialists, each one executing a flurry of commands to the comms computer. "No sir," he muttered around the helmet's visor. "I can establish a three-way handshake with it, but it doesn't respond to my authorization tokens. Fallback tokens no good either."

In the holotank, the antimissiles with their labels went streaking toward the missile. It dodged them, shot at them, dodged them. Then, one of them found its mark and the missile detonated, a silent fireball that collapsed in on itself, lensing the gravity around it and bending space.

"All right then," Tsubishi said. "Hail the yufo, Lieutenant."

"That wasn't very friendly," he said. "I get the feeling we got off to a bad start. Shall we start over again?"

"I've already issued you my challenge, Captain. Personal combat, on-world, first one to the top of the highest peak claims the planet, the loser surrenders it. I'll give you the whole system if you want."

"I see. And if I refuse?"

The klaxon's sound was louder than before. In the tank, dozens of photon torpedoes had just blinked into existence, relentlessly plowing through the depths of space, aimed directly at the ship.

Helpfully, the tank tagged them with countdown labels. The ship was not going to make it.

Tsubishi allowed himself three seconds———and then he cleared his throat.

"We accept your challenge."

The torpedoes vanished, leaving behind their labels. An instant later, the tank helpfully removed the labels, too.

• • •

"Sir, with all due respect, you can't beam down to the surface." !Mota was visibly agitated, and writhed uncomfortably under Tsubishi's calm stare.

"I don't recall asking for your opinion, Commander." He plucked at his baggies and wished for the comforting tautness of his ship-wrapped uniform. Such was the price of leadership. "The alien was very clear on this in any event. It's calling the shots."

"Captain, you are being driven by the alien. You need to get inside its decision-loop and start setting the agenda. It's suicide otherwise. You saw how much power—"

"I saw, Commander. It's well and good to talk about getting inside decision-loops, but sometimes you're outgunned and all you've got is your own bravery and instincts. It's not like we can outrun that thing."

"We could back off—"

"We don't know what its transporter beam range is, but it's clearly far in excess of anything we've ever seen. I'm betting that I have a better chance of getting to some kind of resolution on the surface than I do of being able to pull back to warping distance ahead of its ability to turn us into shrapnel."

"Some kind of resolution, sir?"

"Well, yes. We're intelligent species. We can talk. There's probably something we have that they want. And we're pretty sure that there's something they have that *we* want—their transporter technology, for starters. That decision-loop stuff is applicable to fighting. We already know we can't do that. We need negotiation."

The Wobbly relaxed visibly. "I see, sir."

"What, did you think I was going on a suicide mission?"

"Sir, of course not, but—"

"Besides, I'm curious to see this thing face to face. That yufo's barely big enough to hold my breakfast. Those ugly bastards must be about three millimeters tall—how do they accomplish the neuronal density to pack a functional intelligence into something that small?"

"Good question, sir," !Mota said. Tsubishi could tell that he'd won the argument.

"Commander, I'm de-tasking you from the bridge for now."

"Me, sir? Who will have the conn?"

"Oh, leave it to Varma," he said. The C-string commander was always complaining that she never got to run the bridge when important things were happening.

"Varma." The hurt was palpable, even through the thick Wobbly accent.

"Of course Varma." He gave forth with one of his ironic head-tilts. "You can't possibly be in charge." He waited for one beat, leaving !Mota trembling on zer hook. "You're coming down to the surface with me."

Emotions chased each other across the Wobbly's face. Pride. Worry. "Sir? Fleet procedure prohibits having two or more senior officers in a single landing party—"

"Unless the crewmembers in question possess specific talents or capabilities that are likely to be of necessity during the on-planet mission. Don't quote regs at me, Commander. I eat regs for breakfast." Another head-tilt. The Wobbly's exo gave an all-over shudder that

Tsubishi recognized as a wriggle of pure delight. Tsubishi smiled at zer. Command wasn't so hard, sometimes.

···

When he was a kay-det, he'd *hated* the transporter drills. Yes, they were safe, overengineered to a million nines. But at the end of the day, Tsubishi just didn't like being annihilated to a quantum level and reassembled at a great distance by a flaky, incomprehensible entanglement effect. Deep down in his cells, annihilation equaled *dread*.

Command meant that you had to like transporters. Love them. So he'd *gotten over* his dread. He'd found a pliant transporter technician—an older career woman, the backbone of the fleet—and struck up an *arrangement*. For an entire month, he'd paged her whenever he needed to go anywhere in the Academy, and she'd beamed him there. A dozen transports a day. Two dozen. The fresher, quarters, classes, the simulators, the mess-hall. Her room, after hours, where she'd met him wearing a slinky film of machine-wrapped gauze and a smile.

A month of that and he'd changed the equation: annihilation equaled *yawn*.

"Status, Commander !Mota?"

The Wobbly's salute ticked off zer forelobe. "Sir, crew ready for transport."

"Landing coordinates?"

"Here," !Mota said, gesturing at the holotank, which transitioned to a view of the planet below them and quickly zoomed to a prairie at the foot of an impressive mountain range that unevenly split the smaller of the planet's two landmasses.

"And our objective?"

!Mota gestured and the holotank skipped forward, superimposing a glowing field over one of the mountaintops. Tsubishi realized that this was another slide presentation. !Mota really loved slide presentations. It was a Wobbly thing.

"Commander !Mota."

"Yes, sir?"

"If that mountaintop is our objective, why aren't we just beaming down onto it?"

!Mota jumped to the next slide, which zoomed to the mountain range with a bluish bubble superimposed over most of it. "No-go zone, sir. Test transports of enzymatically representative samples proved…unreliable."

"Unreliable?"

"The enzymes we retrieved had been denatured sir, as with extensive heat."

"They were barbecued, Cap," said Second Lieutenant !Rena, the mission science officer, a Wobbly who had made a hobby out of twen-cen Earth in a brownnosing effort to ascend through the ranks faster than Wobblies usually managed. It was an open secret on the *Colossus II* that the two Wobblies loathed each other. Tsubishi approved of this, and approved even more of !Mota's forbearance in selecting !Rena for the landing party.

"I see."

!Mota flicked to the next slide, a 3-D flythrough of a trail up the mountains. "This appears to be the optimal route to the peak, sir. The seven-leagues have a millimeter-accurate picture of the landscape and they're projecting a 195-minute journey time, assuming no trouble en route." Tsubishi rocked back and forth in his seven-league boots, whose harness ran all the way up to his mid-thigh. Running on these things was *fun*—the kind of thing that made serving on away-teams such a treat.

"I assume we can count on trouble, Commander !Mota. I certainly am."

"Yes, sir," !Mota said, clicking forward one slide. "These are alternate routes through the mountains, and in the worst case, the seven-leagues have a bounce-and-ditch they'll deploy to get us onto the face." That sounded like less fun: the boots would discharge their entire power-packs in one bone-jarring bounce on a near-straight vertical that would launch him like a missile into the mountain face, with only a couple of monosilk drogue chutes to slow him before impact.

"How many more slides, Commander?"

"No more," !Mota said. Tsubishi knew ze was lying, and could tell that ze was disappointed. Make it up later. Time to beam down! His palms were sweating, his heart thudding. Outwardly, he was cool.

"Everyone ready?" All six in the party chorused "Aye, sir," in unison. "Do it," he said to the transporter operator. She smiled at him and engaged the system that would annihilate him and reassemble him millions of klicks away on the surface of a virgin planet. He smiled back in the instant before the machine annihilated him. Hominess was a hazard of his transporter conditioning regime at the Academy, but he could deal with it.

•••

The transporter technician deserved a commendation. Not many of the techs on the bridge were thoughtful enough to land a steaming cappuccino on the planet along with Tsubishi. He liked the attention to detail. He made a mental note and had a sip.

"Report, Commander?"

!Mota had zer comm out and had been busily verifying from the surface all the readings they'd got from orbit, establishing multiple redundant links with the ship, querying the health readouts from the gutbots in the landing party's bodies. "Nominal, Captain."

"Let's have a little reccy before we kick off, shall we? I was expecting company when we landed. Seems like our friend's style."

"Yes, sir," !Mota said. Ze unclipped an instrument gun from zer exo's thigh and fired it straight into the air. A billion dandelion seeds caught the wind and blew in every direction, settling slowly to the ground or lofting higher and higher. The little sensors on them started to measure things as soon as they were out of the muzzle, while the networking subsystems knit them together into a unified ubiquitous surveillance mesh that spread out for ten kilometers in all directions (though it grew patchier around the edges). "Sir, I have no sign of the alien or its artifacts. Nothing on this planet bigger than a bacterium, and the gutbots have already got their genomes solved and phaged. I recommend beginning the mission."

Tsubishi looked around and finished his cappuccino. The terrain was as depicted in the holotank—sere, rocky, stained in coral colors that swirled together like organic oil-slicks. The temperature was a little chilly, but nothing the baggies couldn't cut, and the wind made an eerie sound as it howled through the rugged mountains that towered all around them.

"All right then, form up, two by two, and then go full auto. Keep your eyes peeled and your guard up." He thought for a moment. "Be on the lookout for very small hostiles—possibly as small as a centimeter." The away-team, six crewmembers with robotic feet, baggies, and looks of grim determination, exchanged glances. "I know. But that is one tiny damned yufo, gang."

They smiled. He finished his cappuccino and set the cup down, then put a rock on top of it to keep it from blowing away. He'd pick it up and return to the ship with it.

"On my mark then. Do it."

And they were off.

•••

The seven-leagues took great pains to establish a regular rhythm, even though it meant capping the max speed at about 70 percent of what the body mechanics of the crew could sustain. But the rhythm was necessary if their brains were going to converge binocular vision—otherwise the landscape blurred into a nauseous smear. Tsubishi's command-channel, set deep in his cochlea, counted down the time to the mountaintop.

It was a marvelous way to travel. Your legs took on a life of their own, moving with precise, quick, tireless steps that propelled you like a dream of flying. The most savage terrain became a rolling pasture, and the steady rhythm lent itself to musical humming, as though you were waltzing with the planet itself.

At the halfway mark, Tsubishi called a break and they broke out hot meals and drinks—he switched to decaf, as three was his limit in any twenty-four-hour period: more just made him grumpy. They picnicked on a plateau, their seven-leagues locked and extended into stools. As they ate, Tsubishi and !Mota circulated among the crewmembers, checking in with them, keeping morale up, checking the medical diagnostics from their gutbots. The landing party were in fine form, excited to be off the ship and on an adventure, keen to meet the foe when and if ze chose to appear.

That was the devil of it, Tsubishi and !Mota agreed, privately, over their subvocal command-channel. Where was the yufo? The ship confirmed that ze hadn't simply transported to the mountain peak, but neither could it locate zer *anywhere* on the planet.

"What sort of game is ze playing?" Tsubishi subvocalized, keeping his face composed in a practiced expression of easy confidence.

"Captain, permission to speak freely?"

"Of course."

"The yufo's demonstrated capabilities are unseen in known space. We have no idea what it might be planning. This may be a suicide mission."

"Commander !Mota, I realize that. But as you say, the yufo has prodigious capabilities and ze made it clear that it was this or be blown out of the sky. When all you have is a least-worst option, there's nothing for it but to make the best of it." This was the kind of can-do thinking that defined command in the fleet, and it was the Wobblies' general incapacity to embrace it that kept them from making the A-squads.

!Mota turned away and pitched in on the clean-up effort.

"You took a *lunch break?*" The voice came from the center of their little circle, and there was something deeply disturbing about it. It took Tsubishi a moment to realize what had made his balls crawl up into his abdomen: it was his voice. And there was the yufo, speaking in it: "A *lunch break?* When I made it clear that the stakes were the planet and your lives?" It wasn't two centimeters tall. It was more like three meters, a kind of pyramidal mountain of flesh topped with a head the size of a large pumpkin. The medusa-wreath of tentacles fluttered in the wind, twisting and coiling.

Tsubishi's hand was on his blaster, and he noted with satisfaction that the rest of his crew were ready to draw. Via the command-channel, Varma was whispering that the ship was watching, prepared to give support.

Deliberately, he took his hand off his blaster. "Greetings," he said. "You have an amazing facility for language."

"Flattery? Please." The yufo whacked its tail on the rock. "Not interested. And I distinctly said one-on-one. What are these things doing here?" It waved a flipper derisively at the crew, who stood firm.

"I hoped that we could dispense with challenges and move on to some kind of negotiation. A planet isn't nearly as interesting to the Alliance as a new species. Once again, I bid you greetings in the name of—"

"You don't learn fast, do you?" The flipper twitched again and the crew—*vanished.*

Tsubishi drew his blaster. "What have you done with my crew?" But he knew, he knew from the telltale shimmer as they went. They'd been beamed somewhere—into deep space, to the landing spot, back onto the ship. "You have three seconds. Three—"

The yufo twitched again and the blaster vanished too, tingling in his hands as it went. He looked down at his palm and saw that some of the skin had gone with it. It oozed red blood.

The yufo extended a tentacle in his direction and twitched. "Sorry about that. I'm usually more accurate. As to your crew, I annihilated them. I removed their tokens from the play area. You're a game-player, you should be able to grasp this."

"Game-player?" Tsubishi's mind reeled.

"What do you think we're doing here, *Captain?"* The last word dripped with perfectly executed sarcasm. The yufo really did have an impressive language module. With creeping hopelessness, Tsubishi realized that ze couldn't possibly have trained it from their meager conversation to date; ze must have been snaffling up titanic amounts of communication from the *Colossus II*'s internal comms. Ze was thoroughly inside his decision-loop. "Competing. Gaming. You're clearly familiar with the idea, Mr. Role-Player."

"Why do you keep calling me that?"

"You're starting to bore me, *Captain*. Look, it's clear you're outmatched here. You've got a lovely little play area up there in orbit, but I'm afraid you're about to forfeit it."

"No!" Tsubishi's veneer of calm control blistered and burst. "There are hundreds of people on that ship! It would be murder!"

The yufo inflated zer throat-bladder and exhaled it a couple times. "Murder?" ze said. "Come now, Captain, let's be not overly dramatic."

This was the first time that the yufo appeared the least bit off-balance. Tsubishi saw a small initiative and seized it. "Murder! Of course it's murder! We are not at war. It would be an act of sheer murder."

"Act of war? Captain, *I'm not playing your game.* I'm playing—" Its tentacles whipped around its head. Tsubishi got the impression that it was fishing for a word. "I compete to put my flag on a pattern of planets. It is a different game from your little space-marines dramatics."

On that plateau, on that remote world near that unregarded star, Captain Reynold J. Tsubishi experienced satori.

"We are not playing a game. We *are* 'space marines.' Space navy, actually. We are not playing soldiers. We *are* soldiers. Those were real people and you've really, really killed them."

The alien's tentacles went slack and twitched against its upper slopes. It inflated and deflated its bladder several times. The wind howled.

"You mean that you haven't got a recent stored copy of them—"

"Stored copy? Of them?"

The tentacles twitched again. Then they went rigid and stood around zer head like a mane. The bladder expanded and the yufo let out a keening moan the like of which Tsubishi had not heard anywhere in the galaxy.

"You don't make *backups?* What is *wrong* with you?"

The yufo vanished. Instantly, Tsubishi tried to raise the *Colossus II* on the command-channel. Either his comm was dead or—or—He choked down a sob of his own.

•••

The yufo returned to him as he sat on the mountainpeak. He hadn't had anywhere else to go, and the seven-leagues had been programmed for it. From his high vantage, he looked down on wispy clouds, distant, lower mountaintops, the sea. He shivered. The command-channel was dead. He had been there for hours, pacing and doing the occasional calisthenics to stay warm. To take his mind off things.

He was the *Captain*. He was supposed to have *initiative*. He was sup-posed to be *doing something*. But what could he do?

"You don't have backups?"

The yufo stood before him, a hill of tentacled flesh. It was closer than before, and he could smell it now, a nice smell, a little yeasty. It spoke in !Mota's voice now.

"I don't really understand what you mean." He was cold, shivering. Hungry. He wanted a cappuccino.

"You have the transporter. You scan people to a quantum level. Store the scan. Annihilate them. Reassemble them elsewhere. Are you seriously telling me that *it never occurred to you to store the scans?*"

Captain Reynold J. Tsubishi of the APP ship *Colossus II* was thunder-struck. He really, really wanted a cappuccino now. "I can honestly say that it never had." He fumbled for an excuse. "The ethical conundra. What if there were two of me? Um." He thought. "What if—"

"What is *wrong* with you people? So what if there were two of you?" There were two of the yufo now. Tsubishi was no expert in distinguishing individuals of this race, but he had the distinct impression that they were the same entity. Times two. Times three now. Now there were four. They surrounded him, bladders going in and out.

"Annihilation is no big deal."

"Accepting it is a survival instinct."

"You honestly drag that gigantic lump of metal around the galaxy?"

"What is *wrong* with you people?"

Tsubishi needed some initiative here. This was not a negotiation. He needed to make it one.

"You've murdered five of my crew today. You threatened my ship with torpedoes. We came in peace. You made war. It isn't too late to rescue the relations between our civilizations if you are willing to negotiate as equals in the galactic community of equals."

"Negotiate? Fella—sorry, *Captain,* I don't speak for anyone—" Now there was just one yufo and shimmering space where the others had been. The yufo paused for a second. "Give me a second. Integrating the new memories from those forks takes a little doing. Right. Okay. I'm just here on my own behalf. Yes, I fired on your ship—*after* you fired on me."

"Fired on you? You weren't in that artifact. You wouldn't fit in ten of those things. It was an unmanned sensor package."

"You think I bother to travel around in giant hunks of metal?"

"Why not? You've got impressive transporter technology, but you can't expect me to believe that you can beam matter over interstellar distances—"

"Of course not. That's what subspace *radio* is for. I upload the latest me to the transporter on the sensor package and then beam as many of myself as I need to the planet's surface. What kind of idiot would actually put zer body in a giant hollow vehicle and ship it around space? The resource requirements are insane. You don't really, *really* do that, do you?"

Tsubishi covered his face with his hands and groaned. "You're telling me that you're just an individual, not representing any government, and that you conquer planets all on your own, using subspace radio and transporter beams?"

"Yes indeed."

"But why?"

"I *told* you—I compete to put my flag on a pattern of planets. My friends compete to do the same. The winner is the one who surrounds the largest number of zer opponents' territory. It's fun. Why do you put on costumes and ship your asses around the galaxy?"

The yufo had a remarkable command of Standard. "You've got excellent symbology AI," he said. "Perhaps our civilizations could transfer some technology to one another? Establish trade?" There had to be some way to interest the yufo in keeping Tsubishi around, in letting him back on his ship. The planet was cold and he was hungry. He wanted a cappuccino.

The yufo shrugged elaborately. "It's remarkable what you can accomplish when you don't squander your species' resources playing soldier. Sorry, *navy*. Why would we bother with trade? What could possibly be worth posting around interstellar distances, as opposed to just beaming sub-molecular-perfect copies of goods into wherever they're in demand? You people are deeply perverse. And to think that you talked *forty-two* other species into playing along? What a farce!"

Tsubishi tried for words, but they wouldn't come. He found that he was chewing an invisible mouthful of speech, working his jaw silently.

"You've really had a bad day, huh? Right. Okay. Here's what I'll do for you."

There was a cappuccino sitting next to him. He picked it up and sipped reverently at it. It was perfect. It was identical to the one that had been beamed down to him when he arrived on-planet. That meant that the yufo had been sniffing all the transporter beam activity since they arrived. And that meant—

"You can restore the landing party!"

"Oh yes, indeed, I can do that."

"And you don't trade for technology, but you might be persuaded to give me—I mean, the Alliance—access to some of this?"

"Certainly."

"And will you?"

"If you think you want it."

Tsubishi nearly fell over himself thanking the yufo. He was mid-sentence when he found himself back on the transporter deck, along with his entire away-team party.

• • •

First things first. Tsubishi headed straight for the fresher, to get out of his baggies and back into uniform. He held his arms over his head and muttered, "Do it," to the computer, received the crackle-starched uniform and lowered his arms, once again suited and booted, every millimeter an officer of the APP Space Navy.

And it felt *wrong*. He didn't feel like he was wearing a uniform at all. He was wearing a *costume*. He knew that now. He had the computer signal his officers to meet him in the executive boardroom, whose long table pulsed with realtime strategic maps of the known galaxy, and as he slid into his seat, he recognized it finally and for the first time for what it really was: a game-board.

"Report, Commander !Mota," he said. Of course !Mota would have a slideshow whipped up by now. Ze had a whole executive staff dedicated to preparing them on a moment's notice. The slideshow would give him time to gather himself, to recover some of the dignity of his office.

But !Mota just looked at him blankly from within zer exoskeleton, zer big Wobbly eyes unreadable. Tsubishi peered more closely.

"Commander !Mota, are you out of uniform?"

!Mota plucked at zer baggies with a tentacle-tip. "I suppose I am, Reynold."

Tsubishi knew the first signs of mutiny. He'd gotten top marks in Command Psych at the Academy. He looked into the faces of his officers, tried to gauge the support there.

"Commander, you are relieved. Return to your quarters and await my orders."

The Wobbly looked impassively at him. The silence stretched. The other officers looked at him with equal coolness. It wasn't just his command he felt slipping away—it was the *idea* of command itself. The fragility of the traditions, of the discipline, of the great work that bound them all together. It wavered. Panic seized him, tightened his chest, a feeling he hadn't known since those days at the Academy when he was breaking himself of the fear of transporters.

"Please?" he said. It came out in a squeak.

!Mota gave him a lazy salute. "All right, *Captain*. I'll play another round of the game. For now. But it won't do you any good."

Ze moved to the hatch. It irised open. Behind it, a dozen more !Motas. !Mota joined them and turned around and gave him and the rest of the officers another sarcastic salute.

"You all enjoy yourselves now," ze said, and they turned as a body and walked away.

Tsubishi's hand was resting on something. A cappuccino. He lifted it to his lips and had a little sip, but he burned his lip and it spilled down the front of his nice starched uniform.

Costume.

He set it back down and began, very quietly, to cry.

IF NUDITY OFFENDS YOU

Elizabeth Moon

hen Louanne opened her light bill, she about had a fit. She hadn't had a bill that high since the time the Sims family hooked into her outlet for a week, when their daddy lost his job and right before they got kicked out of the trailer park for him being drunk and disorderly and the kids stealing stuff out of trash cans and their old speckled hound dog being loose and making a mess on Mrs. Thackridge's porch. Drunk and disorderly was pretty common, actually, and stealing from trash cans was a problem only because the Sims kids dumped everything before picking through it, and never bothered to put it back. The Sanchez kids had the good sense to pick up what mess they made, and no one cared what they took out of the trash (though some of it was good, like a boom box that Carter Willis stole from down at Haley's, and hid in the trash can until Tuesday, only the Sanchez kids found it first). But when Grace (which is what they called that hound, and a stupid name that is for a coonhound, anyway) made that mess on Mrs. Thackridge's front porch, and she stepped in it on the way to a meeting of the Extension Homemaker's Club and had to go back inside and change her shoes, with her friends right there in the car waiting for her, that was *it* for the Sims family.

Anyhow, when Louanne saw that $82.67, she just threw it down on the table and said, "Oh my God," in that tone of voice her grandma never could stand, and then she said a bunch of other things like you'd expect, and then she tried to figure out who she knew at the power company, because there was no way in the world she'd used that much electricity, and also no way in the world she could pay that bill. She didn't leave the air conditioner on all day like some people did, and she was careful to turn off lights in the kitchen when she moved to the bedroom, and all that. All those things to keep the bill low, because she'd just bought herself a car—almost new, a real good buy—and some fancy clothes to wear to the dance hall on weekends, now that she was through with Jack forever and looking for someone else. The car payment alone was $175 a month, and then there was the trailer park fee, and the mobile home payments, and the furniture rental…and the light bill was supposed to stay *low,* like under thirty dollars.

It occurred to Louanne that even though the Simses had left, someone else might have bled her for power. But who? She looked out each window of her trailer, looking for telltale cords. The Loomis family, to her right, seemed as stable and prosperous as any: Pete worked for the county, and Jane cooked in the school cafeteria. No cord there. The Blaylocks, on the left, were a very young couple from out of state. He worked construction; she had a small baby, and stayed home. Almost every day, Louanne had seen her sitting on the narrow step of their trailer, cuddling a plump, placid infant. Directly behind was an empty slot, and to either side behind…. Louanne could not tell if that ripple in the rough grass was a cord or not. She'd have to go outside to see for sure.

Now, if there's one sure way to make an enemy at a trailer park, it's to go snooping around like you thought your neighbors were cheating on you somehow, and before Louanne got into that kind of mess, she thought she'd try something safer. Back when Jack was living there, she wouldn't have minded a little trouble, being as he was six foot three and did rock work for Mullens Stone; but on her own, she'd had to learn quieter ways of doing things. Like checking up close to her own power outlets, to see if she could spot anything funny coming off the plugs.

She was still in the heels and city clothes she wore to work (secretary over at the courthouse: she made more money than either of her parents here in Behrnville), which was not exactly the right outfit for crawling around under things. She took off the purple polyester blouse, the black suit skirt (the jacket hung in her closet, awaiting winter), the dressy earrings and necklace, the lacy underwear that her mother, even *now,* even after all these years, thought unsuitable. And into the cutoffs, the striped tank top, and her thongs.

Outside, it was still blistering, and loud with the throbbing of her air conditioner, which she'd hung in the living room window. She opened the door of her storage shed that Jack had built her, a neat six-by-six space, and took down her water hose from its bracket. The outside hydrant wasn't but six feet from her power outlet, and with a new car—new for her, anyway—nobody'd wonder about her giving it a wash. Especially not on such a hot day.

She dragged the hose end around behind her trailer, and screwed it onto the faucet, letting her eye drift sideways toward the power outlet. Sure enough, besides her own attachment, another plump black cord ran down the pipe and off into the grass. But where? Louanne turned the water on as if a car wash were the only thing on her mind, and sprayed water on her tires. They did look grungy. She flipped the cutoff on the sprayer and went to get a brush out of her storage shed. About then, Curtis Blaylock drove in and grinned at her as he got out of his car.

"Little hot for that, ain't it?" he asked, eyeing her long, tanned legs.

"Well, you know...new car...." Louanne didn't meet his eye, exactly, and went back around the end of the trailer without stopping to chat. Becoming a father didn't stop most men from looking at everyone else. She scrubbed at the tires, then sprayed the car itself, working around it so she could look everywhere without seeming to. That ripple in the grass, now...it seemed to go back at an angle, and then...lot 17. That was the one. A plain, old-fashioned metal trailer with rounded ends, not more than a twenty-seven- or thirty-footer. She thought she could see a black cord lifting up out of the grass and into its underside.

She finished the car, put her hose and brush back into the storage unit, and went back inside. Through the blinds in her bedroom, she could see a little more of lot 17. A middle-aged pickup with slightly faded blue paint sat beside the trailer. Lot 17's utility hookups were hidden from this angle. Louanne watched. A man came out...a big man, moving heavily. Sweat marks darkened his blue shirt; his face looked red and swollen. He climbed into the pickup, yelled something back at the trailer, then slammed the door and backed carefully into the lane between the rows. The trailer door opened briefly, and someone inside threw out a panful of water. Louanne wrinkled her nose in disgust. White trash. Typical. Anyone that'd steal power would throw water out in the yard like that instead of using the drain. It was probably stopped up anyway.

Louanne got herself a sandwich and a beer from her spotless refrigerator, and settled down on the bed to watch some more. A light came on as the evening darkened; against a flowered curtain, she could see a vague shape moving now and then. About nine or so the pickup returned. She heard its uneven engine diesel awhile before stopping. It was too dark to see the man walk to the door, but she did see the flash of light when the door opened.

Her light, she thought angrily. She'd paid for it. She wondered how long they left it on. Eighty-two dollars minus the maybe twenty-seven her bill should be, meant they were wasting over fifty dollars a month of her money. Probably kept the lights on half the night. Ran the air conditioner on high. Left the refrigerator door open, or made extra ice…stuff like that. She flounced off the bed and into the living room, getting herself another beer on the way. She didn't usually have two beers unless she was out with someone, but getting stung for someone else's electricity was bad enough to change her ways.

Thing was, she couldn't figure out how to handle it. She sure wasn't going over there in the dark, past nine at night, to confront that big, heavy man and whoever else was in there. That would be plain stupid. But on the other hand, there was that bill…. She couldn't afford to have her credit rating ruined, not as hard as she'd worked to get a decent one. She thought of just pulling the plug out, maybe at two in the morning or so, whenever their light went out, and cutting off the plug end. That would sort of let them know they'd been found, but it wasn't the same as starting a fight about it. On the other hand, that didn't get the bill paid.

Louanne put the can of beer down on a coaster—even if the tabletop *was* laminated, there was no sense in getting bad habits. Someday she'd own a real wood dining room table, and pretty end tables for her living room, and she didn't intend to have them marked up with rings from beer cans, either—and eased back into her darkened bedroom to look between the blinds. The light was still on behind the flowered curtain. It wasn't late enough yet. She went into her bathroom and used the john, then checked her face in the mirror. Her eyebrows needed plucking, and she really ought to do something about her hair. She fluffed it out one way, then another. The district judge's secretary had said she should streak it. Louanne tried to imagine how that might look.... Some people just looked older, grayer, but Holly Jordan, in the tax office, looked terrific with hers streaked. Louanne took out her tweezers and did her eyebrows, then tried her new plum-colored shadow. That might do for the dance hall on Friday.

But thinking of the dance hall on Friday (not Ladies Night, so it would cost her to get in) made her think of that electric bill, and she slammed her makeup drawer shut so hard the contents rattled. She was not going to put up with it; she'd do something right after work tomorrow. She'd make them pay. And she wouldn't cut the cord tonight, because if she did that, she'd have no proof. When they got up and didn't have lights, all they'd have to do would be pull the cord in, slowly, and no one could prove it had been there. On that resolve, she went to bed.

•••

The blue pickup wasn't there, which she hoped meant the big man wasn't there, either. She had chosen her clothes carefully—not the city clothes she wore to work, in case things got rough, but not cutoffs and a tank, either. She wanted to look respectable, and tough, and like someone who had friends in the county sheriff's office.... And so, sweating under the late-afternoon sun, she made her way across the rough, sunburnt grass in a denim wraparound skirt, plaid short-sleeve blouse, and what she privately called her "little old lady" shoes, which she wore to visit family: crepe-soled and sort of loafer-looking. There was an oily patch where the pickup was usually parked. That figured. So also the lumps of old dried mud on their trailer steps, when it hadn't rained in weeks. Anyone who'd throw water outside like that, and steal power, wouldn't bother to clean off a step. Louanne squared her shoulders and put her foot on the bottom step.

That's when she saw the notice, printed in thick black letters on what looked like a three-by-five card. "If nudity offends You," it said, "Please do not ring this Bell." Right beside the grimy-looking doorbell button. Just right out there in public, talking about nudity. Louanne felt her neck getting even hotter than the afternoon sun should make it. Probably kept the kids away, and probably fooled the few door-to-door salesmen, but it wasn't going to fool her. Nobody went around without clothes in a trailer park, not and lived to tell about it. She put her thumb firmly on the button and pushed hard.

She heard it ring, a nasty buzz, and then footsteps coming toward the door. Despite herself, her palms were sweaty. Just remember, she told herself, that you don't *have* $82.67, and they owe it to you. Then the door opened.

It wasn't so much the nudity that offended her as the smell. It wasn't like she'd never smelled people before…. In fact, one of the things that made her so careful was remembering how it was at Aunt Ethel and Uncle Bert's, the summer she'd spent with them. She wasn't squeamish about it, exactly, but she did like things clean. But this was something else. A sort of heavy smell, which reminded her a little of the specialty gourmet shop in the mall near her sister Peggy's house in north Dallas—but reminded her a lot more of dirty old horse hooves. Bad. Not quite rotten, but not healthy, either; and the bare body of the woman staring at her through a tattered screen door had the same look as the smell that wafted out into the hot afternoon.

Louanne swallowed with determination and tried to fix her eyes on the woman's face…where she thought the face would be, anyway, hard as it was to see past the sunlit screen into the half-light where the woman stood. The woman was tall—would be taller than Louanne even if she stood on the ground—and up above her like that, a step higher, she looked really big, almost as big as the man. Louanne's eyes slid downward despite herself. She was big, with broad shoulders gleaming, slightly sweaty, and big—Louanne dragged her gaze upward again. She saw a quick gleam of teeth.

"Yes?" the woman said. Even in that word, Louanne knew she wasn't local. "Can I help you?" The rest of the phrase confirmed it—she sounded foreign almost, certainly not like anyone from around Behrnville.

"You're plugged into my outlet," said Louanne, gritting her teeth. She had written all this out, during her lunch hour, and rehearsed it several times. "You're stealing electricity from me, and you owe me sixty dollars, because that's how much my bill went up." She stopped suddenly, arrested by the woman's quick movement. The screen door pushed outward, and Louanne stepped back, involuntarily, back to the gravel of the parking slot. Now sunlight fell full on the woman, and Louanne struggled not to look. The woman's face had creased in an expression of mingled confusion and concern that didn't fool Louanne for a minute.

"Please?" she said. She didn't even look to see if anyone outside the trailer was looking at her, which made Louanne even surer the whole thing was an act. "Stealing? What have you lost?"

A bad act, too. Louanne had seen kids in school do better. Contempt stiffened her courage. "Your cord," she said, pointing, "is plugged into my outlet. You are using *my* electricity, and I have to pay for it, and you owe me sixty dollars." She'd decided on that, because she was sure not to get what she asked for.... If she asked for sixty dollars, she might get thirty dollars, and she could just squeeze the rest if she didn't go out this weekend at all, and didn't buy any beer, or that red blouse she'd been looking at.

"You sell electricity?" the woman asked, still acting dumb and crazy. Louanne glared at her.

"You thought it was free? Come on, Lady... I can call a deputy and file a complaint—" Actually, she wouldn't ever do that, because she knew what would happen in the trailer park if she did, but maybe this lady who was too crazy or stupid to wear clothes or use a sink drain or take showers wouldn't know that. And in fact, the lady looked worried.

"I don't have any money," she said. "You'll have to wait until my husband comes home—"

Louanne had heard that excuse before, from both sides of a closed door. It was worth about the same as "the check's in the mail," but another billow of that disgusting smell convinced her she didn't want to stomp in and make a search for the cash she was sure she'd find hidden under one pillow or another.

"I want it tonight," she said loudly. "And don't go trying to sneak away." She expected some kind of whining argument, but the woman nodded quickly.

"I tell him, as soon as he comes in. Where are you?" Louanne pointed to her own trailer, wondering if maybe the woman really was foreign, and maybe in that case she ought to warn her about standing there in broad daylight, in the open door of her trailer, without a stitch on her sleek, rounded, glistening body. But the screen was closing now, and just as Louanne regretted not having gotten her foot up onto the doorsill, the door clicked shut, and the woman flipped the hook over into the eye. "I tell him soon," the woman said again. "I'm sorry if we cause trouble. Very sorry." The inner door started to close.

"You'll be sorry if you don't pay up," said Louanne to the closing door. "Sixty dollars!" She turned away before it slammed in her face, and walked back to her own lot, sure she could feel the woman's eyes on her back. She wasn't too happy with the way it had gone, but, thinking about it, realized it could have been worse. Who knows what a crazy naked woman might have done, big as she was? Louanne decided to stay in her visiting clothes until the man came home, and, safely inside her own kitchen, she fixed herself a salad.

She had to admit she was kind of stunned by the whole thing. It had been a while since she'd seen another woman naked, not since she'd gone to work for the county, anyway. She saw herself, of course, when she showered, and like that, but she didn't spend a lot of time on it. She'd rather look at Jack or whoever. When she looked at herself, she saw the kind of things they talked about in makeovers in the magazines: this too long, and that too short, and the other things too wide or narrow or the wrong color. It was more fun to have Jack or whoever look at her, because all the men ever seemed to see was what they liked. "Mmmm, cute," they say, touching here and there and tugging this and patting that, and it was, on the whole, more fun than looking at yourself in a mirror and wondering why God gave you hips wide enough for triplets and nothing to nurse them with. Not that that was *her* problem, Louanne reminded herself, but that's how her friend Casey had put it, the last time they skinny-dipped together in the river, on a dare, the last week of high school.

But that woman. She could nurse anything, up to an elephant, Louanne thought, and besides that.... She frowned, trying now to remember what she'd tried so hard not to see. She hadn't been particularly dark, but she hadn't been pale, either. A sort of brown-egg color, all over, with no light areas where even the most daring of Louanne's friends had light areas.... You could tan nude under a sunlamp or on certain beaches, but you couldn't go naked all the time. But this woman had had no markings at all, on a belly smooth as a beach ball. And—odd for someone who smelled so—she had shaved. Louanne shook her head, wondering. Her aunt Ethel had never shaved, and Louanne had come to hate the sight of her skinny legs, hairy and patched brown with age spots, sticking out from under her shabby old print dresses. But this woman...the gleaming smoothness of her skin, almost as if it had been oiled, all over, not a single flaw.... Louanne shivered without knowing why.

She stood and cleared the table, washing her single dish quickly. She started to get a beer out, and then changed her mind. If that man did come, she didn't want to smell of beer. She looked out her bedroom window. Nothing yet. The sun glared off the gravel of the parking space and the lane behind it. She was about to turn away, when she saw the blue pickup coming. It turned into the space beside the trailer, and the big man got out. Today he wore a tan shirt, with dark patches of sweat under the arms and on the back. Louanne wrinkled her nose, imagining the smell. He looked sunburnt, his neck and arms as red as his face, all glistening with sweat.

He went in. Louanne waited. Would the woman tell him at once, or wait, or not tell him at all? She didn't want to go back there, but she would, she told herself. He couldn't do anything to her in daylight, not if she stayed out of reach, and Jeannie Blaylock was home, if she screamed. She saw the flowered curtain twitched aside, and the man's face in the window, looking toward her trailer. She knew she'd been careful how she set the blinds, but she still had the feeling he knew she was watching. The curtains flipped shut. Then the door opened, and he came out, his round red face gleaming. He shot a quick glance toward her lot, then looked down before he went down his steps. He opened the pickup door, leaned in, came back out, shut the door. Then he started toward Louanne's trailer.

Her heart was hammering in her chest; she had to take two long breaths to quiet herself. He was actually coming, almost right away. She hurried out to the living room and sat poised on the rented tweed sofa. It seemed to take a long time, longer than she thought possible, even trying to count the steps in her mind. Finally a knock at her door. Louanne stood, trying to control her knees, and went to the door.

Even a step down, he was as tall as she, a man Jack might have hesitated to fight. But he was smiling at her, holding out a grubby envelope. "Sorry," he said. His voice was curiously light for such a big man. "We didn't mean to cause trouble.... The money is here...." He held it out. Louanne made a long arm and took the envelope; he released it at once and stepped back. "The...the connection at our lot didn't work," he went on, looking slightly past her, as if he didn't want to see her. His voice, too, had a strange accent, something Louanne classified as foreign, though she couldn't have said if it was from the East Coast or somewhere farther away than that. "I have already taken our wire away," he said, glancing quickly at her face and away again. "It will not trouble you again.... We are sorry.... It was only that the connection did not work, and yours did."

The money in the envelope was twenties...more than three. Louanne looked at his gleaming red face and felt a quiver of sympathy. Maybe they hadn't known, if they were really foreigners. "You have to pay a deposit," she said. "To the power company, before they turn it on. That's why it didn't work."

"I'm sorry," he said again. "I didn't know. Is that enough? Are you satisfied?"

Greed and soothed outrage and bewilderment argued in her forehead. "It's all right," she found herself saying. "Don't worry." She wondered if she should give some of it back, but, after all, they had stolen from her, and it was only fair they should pay for it. Then her leftover conscience hit her, and she said, "It was only sixty, anyway, and if...."

"For your trouble," he said quickly, backing away. "So sorry.... Don't worry. If you are not angry, if you are not reporting this to authorities...."

"No," said Louanne, still puzzled. Foreigners afraid of the law? Illegal immigrants? He didn't sound Mexican. Drug dealers?

"No more bother," he said. "Thank you. Thank you." And turned and walked quickly away, just as Curtis Blaylock drove in. Curtis looked at the man walking off, and at Louanne standing there with the envelope in her hand, for all the world like a whore with her pay, and grinned.

"Trouble?" he asked in a silky voice. Louanne had to stop that right where it was, or she would have more problems than a big light bill.

"Foreigners," she said, allowing an edge in her voice. "He wanted to know where to find"—she peered at the envelope as if to read the address, and found herself reading what was written on it—"3217 Fahrenheit, wherever that is. Not in this town, I told him, and he asked me to look it up on the county records. Somebody must've told him I work for the county."

"Pushy bastard," said Curtis. "Why's he think you should look things up for him?"

"I don't know," said Louanne, wondering why men like Curtis had a knack for asking questions you couldn't answer.

"Well, if you have any trouble, honey, just give us a call."

Louanne didn't answer that, and Curtis went on into his trailer, and she went back into hers. It was real money, all right, all twenties, and there were five of them. She could smell a fainter version of the smell in the trailer on lot 17, but money was money. A hundred bucks. It was too much, and made her worry again. Nobody in their right mind would've paid the sixty, let alone more. She made up her mind to send some of it back, somehow.

Probably the woman would take it; women usually did. She readjusted the blinds in her bedroom, so that no one could possibly see in, and had a cooling shower. And finally went to bed, wondering only briefly how the foreigners were getting along in their lightless trailer.

•••

She overslept, and had to run for it in the morning, dashing out of the door, slamming into her car, and riding the speed limit all the way to work. It wasn't until noon, when she paid the bill at the power company with the twenties, tossed the crumpled envelope in the wastebasket by the counter, and put the change in her billfold, that she thought of the foreigners again. Something nagged her about them, something she should have noticed in the morning's rush, but she didn't figure it out until she got home and saw lot 17 as bare as a swept floor.

They were gone. They had left in the night, without waking her or anyone, and now they were gone.

All through the subsequent excitement, Louanne kept her mouth shut about the hundred dollars and the stolen electricity, and made the kind of response everyone expected to rhetorical questions like, Who do you suppose? and Why do you think? and Whoever could have guessed? She figured she was thirty or forty dollars to the good, and didn't see why she should share any of it with old Mrs. Thackridge, who had plenty already or she wouldn't own the trailer park. They all knew she'd talked to the man (Curtis being glad to tell everyone, she noticed), but she stuck to her story about him wanting an address she'd never heard of, and wanting her to look it up in the county records. And she said she'd thrown the envelope away after not finding any such place, and not caring much, either, and after a while they all let her alone about as much as before, which pleased her just fine.

But she did wonder, from time to time, about that foreign lady wandering around the country without any clothes on. Brown as an egg all over, and not a hair on her body, and—it finally came to her one day, as she typed up a list of grand jury indictments when the judge's secretary was off sick—and no *navel* on the smooth, round, naked belly. She shook her head. Must have been there; everyone has a navel. Unless she had plastic surgery. But why?

After a while she didn't think of it much, except when she was wearing the red blouse...and after a while she was going with Alvin, who didn't like her in red, so she gave the blouse to the other secretary, and forgot the whole thing.

LAWS OF SURVIVAL

NANCY KRESS

My name is Jill. I am somewhere you can't imagine, going somewhere even more unimaginable. If you think I like what I did to get here, you're crazy.

Actually, I'm the one who's crazy. You—any "you"—will never read this. But I have paper now, and a sort of pencil, and time. Lots and lots of time. So I will write what happened, all of it, as carefully as I can.

After all—why the hell not?

•••

I went out very early one morning to look for food. Before dawn was safest for a woman alone. The boy-gangs had gone to bed, tired of attacking each other. The trucks from the city hadn't arrived yet. That meant the garbage was pretty picked over, but it also meant most of the refugee camp wasn't out scavenging. Most days I could find enough: a carrot stolen from somebody's garden patch, my arm bloody from

323

reaching through the barbed wire. Overlooked potato peelings under a pile of rags and glass. A can of stew thrown away by one of the soldiers on the base, but still half full. Soldiers on duty by the Dome were often careless. They got bored, with nothing to do.

That morning was cool but fair, with a pearly haze that the sun would burn off later. I wore all my clothing, for warmth, and my boots. Yesterday's garbage load, I'd heard somebody say, was huge, so I had hopes. I hiked to my favorite spot, where garbage spills almost to the Dome wall. Maybe I'd find bread, or even fruit that wasn't too rotten.

Instead I found the puppy.

Its eyes weren't open yet and it squirmed along the bare ground, a scrawny brown-and-white mass with a tiny fluffy tail. Nearby was a fluid-soaked towel. Some sentimental fool had left the puppy there, hoping...what? It didn't matter. Scrawny or not, there was some meat on the thing. I scooped it up.

The sun pushed above the horizon, flooding the haze with golden light.

I hate it when grief seizes me. I hate it and it's dangerous, a violation of one of Jill's Laws of Survival. I can go for weeks, months without thinking of my life before the War. Without remembering or feeling. Then something will strike me—a flower growing in the dump, a burst of birdsong, the stars on a clear night—and grief will hit me like the maglevs that no longer exist, a grief all the sharper because it contains the memory of joy. I can't afford joy, which always comes with an astronomical price tag. I can't even afford the grief that comes from the memory of living things, which is why it is only the flower, the birdsong, the morning sunlight that starts it. My grief was not for that puppy. I still intended to eat it.

But I heard a noise behind me and turned. The Dome wall was opening.

...

Who knew why the aliens put their Domes by garbage dumps, by waste pits, by radioactive cities? Who knew why aliens did anything?

There was a widespread belief in the camp that the aliens started the War. I'm old enough to know better. That was us, just like the global warming and the bio-crobes were us. The aliens didn't even show up until the War was over and Raleigh was the northernmost city left on the East Coast and refugees poured south like mudslides. Including me.

That's when the ships landed and then turned into the huge gray Domes like upended bowls. I heard there were many Domes, some in other countries. The Army, what was left of it, threw tanks and bombs at ours. When they gave up, the refugees threw bullets and Molotov cocktails and prayers and graffiti and candle-light vigils and rain dances. Everything slid off and the Domes just sat there. And sat. And sat. Three years later, they were still sitting, silent and closed, although of course there were rumors to the contrary. There are always rumors. Personally, I'd never gotten over a slight disbelief that the Dome was there at all. Who would want to visit us?

The opening was small, no larger than a porthole, and about six feet above the ground. All I could see inside was a fog the same color as the Dome. Something came out, gliding quickly toward me. It took me a moment to realize it was a robot, a blue metal sphere above a hanging basket. It stopped a foot from my face and said, "This food for this dog."

I could have run, or screamed, or at the least—the very least—looked around for a witness. I didn't. The basket held a pile of fresh produce, green lettuce and deep purple eggplant and apples so shiny red they looked lacquered. And *peaches*…My mouth filled with sweet water. I couldn't move.

The puppy whimpered.

My mother used to make fresh peach pie.

I scooped the food into my scavenger bag, laid the puppy in the basket, and backed away. The robot floated back into the Dome, which closed immediately. I sped back to my corrugated-tin and windowless hut and ate until I couldn't hold any more. I slept, woke, and ate the rest, crouching in the dark so nobody else would see. All that fruit and vegetables gave me the runs, but it was worth it.

Peaches.

•••

Two weeks later, I brought another puppy to the Dome, the only survivor of a litter deep in the dump. I never knew what happened to the mother. I had to wait a long time outside the Dome before the blue sphere took the puppy in exchange for produce. Apparently the Dome would only open when there was no one else around to see. What were they afraid of? It's not like PETA was going to show up.

The next day I traded three of the peaches to an old man in exchange for a small, mangy poodle. We didn't look each other in the eye, but I nonetheless knew that his held tears. He limped hurriedly away. I kept the dog, which clearly wanted nothing to do with me, in my shack until very early morning and then took it to the Dome. It tried to escape but I'd tied a bit of rope onto its frayed collar. We sat outside the Dome in mutual dislike, waiting, as the sky paled slightly in the east. Gunshots sounded in the distance.

I have never owned a dog.

When the Dome finally opened, I gripped the dog's rope and spoke to the robot. "Not fruit. Not vegetables. I want eggs and bread."

The robot floated back inside.

Instantly I cursed myself. Eggs? Bread? I was crazy not to take what I could get. That was Law of Survival #1. Now there would be nothing. Eggs, bread...*crazy*. I glared at the dog and kicked it. It yelped, looked indignant, and tried to bite my boot.

The Dome opened again and the robot glided toward me. In the gloom I couldn't see what was in the basket. In fact, I couldn't see the basket. It wasn't there. Mechanical tentacles shot out from the sphere and seized both me and the poodle. I cried out and the tentacles squeezed harder. Then I was flying through the air, the stupid dog suddenly howling beneath me, and we were carried through the Dome wall and inside.

Then nothing.

• • •

A nightmare room made of nightmare sound: barking, yelping, whimpering, snapping. I jerked awake, sat up, and discovered myself on a floating platform above a mass of dogs. Big dogs, small dogs, old dogs, puppies, sick dogs, dogs that looked all too healthy, flashing their forty-two teeth at me—why did I remember that number? From where? The largest and strongest dogs couldn't quite reach me with their snaps, but they were trying.

"You are operative," the blue metal sphere said, floating beside me. "Now we must begin. Here."

Its basket held eggs and bread.

"Get them away!"

Obediently it floated off.

"Not the food! The dogs!"

"What to do with these dogs?"

"Put them in cages!" A large black animal—German shepherd or boxer or something—had nearly closed its jaws on my ankle. The next bite might do it.

"Cages," the metal sphere said in its uninflected mechanical voice. "Yes."

"Son of a bitch!" The shepherd leaping high, had grazed my thigh; its spittle slimed my pants. "Raise the goddamn platform!"

"Yes."

The platform floated so high, so that I had to duck my head to avoid hitting the ceiling. I peered over the edge and...no, that wasn't possible. But it was happening. The floor was growing upright sticks, and the sticks were growing cross bars, and the crossbars were extending themselves into mesh tops...Within minutes, each dog was encased in a cage just large enough to hold its protesting body.

"What to do now?" the metal sphere asked.

I stared at it. I was, as far as I knew, the first human being to ever enter an alien Dome, and I was trapped in a small room with feral caged dogs and a robot... *What to do now?*

"Why...why am I here?" I hated myself for the brief stammer and vowed it would not happen again. Law of Survival #2: Show no fear.

Would a metal sphere even recognize fear?

It said, "These dogs do not behave correctly."

"Not behave correctly?"

"No."

I looked down again at the slavering and snarling mass of dogs; how strong was that mesh on the cage tops? "What do you want them to do?"

"You want to see the presentation?"

"Not yet." Law #3: Never volunteer for anything.

"What to do now?"

How the hell should I know? But the smell of the bread reached me and my stomach flopped. "Now to eat," I said. "Give me the things in your basket."

It did, and I tore into the bread like a wolf into deer. The real wolves below me increased their howling. When I'd eaten an entire loaf, I looked back at the metal sphere. "Have those dogs eaten?"

"Yes."

"What did you give them?"

"Garbage."

"*Garbage?* Why?"

"In hell they eat garbage."

So even the robot thought this was Hell. Panic surged through me; I pushed it back. Surviving this would depend on staying steady. "Show me what you fed the dogs."

"Yes." A section of wall melted and garbage cascaded into the room, flowing greasily between the cages. I recognized it: It was exactly like the garbage I picked through every day, trucked out from a city I could no longer imagine and from the Army base I could not approach without being shot. Bloody rags, tin cans from before the War, shit, plastic bags, dead flowers, dead animals, dead electronics, cardboard, eggshells, paper, hair, bone, scraps of decaying food, glass shards, potato peelings, foam rubber, roaches, sneakers with holes, sagging furniture, corn cobs. The smell hit my stomach, newly distended with bread.

"You fed the dogs *that?*"

"Yes. They eat it in hell."

Outside. Hell was outside, and of course that's what the feral dogs ate, that's all there was. But the metal sphere had produced fruit and lettuce and bread for me.

"You must give them better food. They eat that in…in hell because they can't get anything else."

"What to do now?"

It finally dawned on me—slow, I was too slow for this, only the quick survive—that the metal sphere had limited initiative along with its limited vocabulary. But it had made cages, made bread, made fruit—hadn't it? Or was this stuff grown in some imaginable secret garden inside the Dome? "You must give the dogs meat."

"Flesh?"

"Yes."

"No."

No change in that mechanical voice, but the "no" was definite and quick. Law of Survival #4: Notice everything. So—no flesh-eating allowed here. Also no time to ask why not; I had to keep issuing orders so

that the robot didn't start issuing them. "Give them bread mixed with...
with soy protein."

"Yes."

"And take away the garbage."

"Yes."

The garbage began to dissolve. I saw nothing poured on it, nothing rise
from the floor. But all that stinking mass fell into powder and vanished.
Nothing replaced it.

I said, "Are you getting bread mixed with soy powder?" *Getting* seemed
the safest verb I could think of.

"Yes."

The stuff came then, tumbling through the same melted hole in the
wall, loaves of bread with, presumably, soy powder in them. The dogs,
barking insanely, reached paws and snouts and tongues through the bars
of their cages. They couldn't get at the food.

"Metal sphere—do you have a name?"

No answer.

"Okay. Blue, how strong are those cages? Can the dogs break them?
Any of the dogs?"

"No."

"Lower the platform to the floor."

My safe perch floated down. The aisles between the cages were irregular, some wide and some so narrow the dogs could reach through
to touch each other, since each cage had "grown" wherever the dog was
at the time. Gingerly I picked my way to a clearing and sat down. Tearing a loaf of bread into chunks, I pushed the pieces through the bars of
the least dangerous-looking dogs, which made the bruisers howl even
more. For them, I put chunks at a distance they could just reach with a
paw through the front bars of their prisons.

The puppy I had first brought to the Dome lay in a tiny cage. Dead.

The second one was alive but just barely.

The old man's mangy poodle looked more mangy than ever, but otherwise alert. It tried to bite me when I fed it.

"What to do now?"

"They need water."

"Yes."

Water flowed through the wall. When it had reached an inch or so, it stopped. The dogs lapped whatever came into their cages. I stood with wet feet—a hole in my boot after all, I hadn't known—and a stomach roiling from the stench of the dogs, which only worsened as they got wet. The dead puppy smelled especially horrible. I climbed back onto my platform.

"What to do now?"

"You tell me," I said.

"These dogs do not behave correctly."

"Not behave correctly?"

"No."

"What do you want them to do?"

"Do you want to see the presentation?"

We had been here before. On second thought, a "presentation" sounded more like acquiring information ("Notice everything") than like undertaking action ("Never volunteer"). So I sat cross-legged on the platform, which was easier on my uncushioned bones, breathed through my mouth instead of my nose, and said, "Why the hell not?"

Blue repeated, "Do you want to see the presentation?"

"Yes." A one-syllable answer.

I didn't know what to expect. Aliens, spaceships, war, strange places barely comprehensible to humans. What I got was scenes from the dump.

A beam of light shot out from Blue and resolved into a three-dimensional holo, not too different from one I'd seen in a science museum on a school field trip once (*no. push memory away*), only this was far sharper and detailed. A ragged and unsmiling toddler, one of thousands, staggered toward a cesspool. A big dog with patchy coat dashed up, seized the kid's dress, and pulled her back just before she fell into the waste.

A medium-sized brown dog in a guide-dog harness led around someone tapping a white-headed cane.

An Army dog, this one sleek and well-fed, sniffed at a pile of garbage, found something, pointed stiffly at attention.

A group of teenagers tortured a puppy. It writhed in pain, but in a long lingering close-up, tried to lick the torturer's hand.

A thin, small dog dodged rocks, dashed inside a corrugated-tin hut, and laid a piece of carrion beside an old lady lying on the ground.

The holo went on and on like that, but the strange thing was that the people were barely seen. The toddler's bare and filthy feet and chubby knees, the old lady's withered cheek, a flash of a camouflage uniform above a brown boot, the hands of the torturers. Never a whole person, never a focus on people. Just on the dogs.

The "presentation" ended.

"These dogs do not behave correctly," Blue said.

"These dogs? In the presentation?"

"These dogs here do not behave correctly."

"These dogs *here.*" I pointed to the wet, stinking dogs in their cages. Some, fed now, had quieted. Others still snarled and barked, trying their hellish best to get out and kill me.

"These dogs here. Yes. What to do now?"

"You want these dogs to behave like the dogs in the presentation."

"These dogs here must behave correctly. Yes."

"You want them to...do what? Rescue people? Sniff out ammunition dumps? Guide the blind and feed the hungry and love their torturers?"

Blue said nothing. Again I had the impression I had exceeded its thought processes, or its vocabulary, or its something. A strange feeling gathered in my gut.

"Blue, you yourself didn't build this Dome, or the starship that it was before, did you? You're just a...a computer."

Nothing.

"Blue, who tells you what to do?"

"What to do now? These dogs do not behave correctly."

"Who wants these dogs to behave correctly?" I said, and found I was holding my breath.

"The masters."

The masters. I knew all about them. Masters were the people who started wars, ran the corporations that ruined the Earth, manufactured the bioweapons that killed billions, and now holed up in the cities to send their garbage out to us in the refugee camps. Masters were something else I didn't think about, but not because grief would take me. Rage would.

Law of Survival #5: Feel nothing that doesn't aid survival.

"Are the masters here? In this...inside here?"

"No."

"Who is here inside?"

"These dogs here are inside."

Clearly. "The masters want these dogs here to behave like the dogs in the presentation."

"Yes."

"The masters want these dogs here to provide them with loyalty and protection and service."

No response.

"The masters aren't interested in human beings, are they? That's why they haven't communicated at all with any government."

Nothing. But I didn't need a response; the masters' thinking was already clear to me. Humans were unimportant—maybe because we had, after all, destroyed each other and our own world. We weren't worth contact. But dogs: companion animals capable of selfless service and great unconditional love, even in the face of abuse. For all I knew, dogs were unique in the universe. For all I know.

Blue said, "What to do now?"

I stared at the mangy, reeking, howling mass of animals. Some feral, some tamed once, some sick, at least one dead. I chose my words to be as simple as possible, relying on phrases Blue knew. "The masters want these dogs here to behave correctly."

"Yes."

"The masters want *me* to make these dogs behave correctly."

"Yes."

"The masters will make me food, and keep me inside, for to make these dogs behave correctly."

Long pause; my sentence had a lot of grammatical elements. But finally Blue said, "Yes."

"If these dogs do not behave correctly, the masters—what to do then?"

Another long pause. "Find another human."

"And *this* human here?"

"Kill it."

I gripped the edges of my floating platform hard. My hands still trembled. "Put me outside now."

"No."

"I must stay inside."

"These dogs do not behave correctly."

"I must make these dogs behave correctly."

"Yes."

"And the masters want these dogs to display..." I had stopped talking to Blue. I was talking to myself, to steady myself, but even that I couldn't manage. The words caromed around in my mind—loyalty, service, protection—but none came out of my mouth. I couldn't do this. I was going to die. The aliens had come from God-knew-where to treat the dying Earth like a giant pet store, intrigued only by a canine domestication that had happened ten thousand years ago and by nothing else on the planet, nothing else humanity had or might accomplish. Only dogs. *The masters want these dogs to display—*

Blue surprised me with a new word. "Love," it said.

•••

Law #4: Notice everything. I needed to learn all I could, starting with Blue. He'd made garbage appear, and food and water and cages. What else could he do?

"Blue, make the water go away." And it did, just sank into the floor, which dried instantly. I was fucking Moses, commanding the Red Sea. I climbed off the platform, inched among the dog cages, and studied them individually.

"You called the refugee camp and the dump 'hell.' Where did you get that word?"

Nothing.

"Who said 'hell'?"

"Humans."

Blue had cameras outside the Dome. Of course he did; he'd seen me find that first puppy in the garbage. Maybe Blue had been waiting for someone like me, alone and non-threatening, to come close with a dog. But it had watched before that, and it had learned the word "hell," and maybe it had recorded the incidents in the "presentation." I filed this information for future use.

"This dog is dead." The first puppy, decaying into stinking pulp. "It is killed. Non-operative."

"What to do now?"

"Make the dead dog go away."

A long pause: Thinking it over? Accessing data banks? Communicating with aliens? And what kind of moron couldn't figure out by itself that a dead dog was never going to behave correctly? So much for artificial intelligence.

"Yes," Blue finally said, and the little corpse dissolved as if it had never been.

I found one more dead dog and one close to death. Blue disappeared the first, said no to the second. Apparently we had to just let it suffer until it died. I wondered how much the idea of "death" even meant to a robot. There were twenty-three live dogs, of which I had delivered only three to the Dome.

"Blue—did another human, before you brought me here, try to train the dogs?"

"These dogs do not behave correctly."

"Yes. But did a human *not me* be inside? To make these dogs behave correctly?"

"Yes."

"What happened to him or her?"

No response.

"What to do now with the other human?"

"Kill it."

I put a hand against the wall and leaned on it. The wall felt smooth and slick, with a faint and unpleasant tingle. I removed my hand.

All computers could count. "How many humans did you kill?"

"Two."

Three's the charm. But there were no charms. No spells, no magic wards, no cavalry coming over the hill to ride to the rescue; I'd known that ever since the War. There was just survival. And, now, dogs.

I chose the mangy little poodle. It hadn't bit me when the old man had surrendered it, or when I'd kept it overnight. That was at least a start. "Blue, make this dog's cage go away. But *only* this one cage!"

The cage dissolved. The poodle stared at me distrustfully. Was I supposed to stare back, or would that get us into some kind of canine pissing contest? The thing was small but it had teeth.

I had a sudden idea. "Blue, show me how this dog does not behave correctly." If I could see what it wasn't doing, that would at least be a start.

Blue floated to within a foot of the dog's face. The dog growled and backed away. Blue floated away and the dog quieted but it still stood in what would be a menacing stance if it weighed more than nine or ten pounds: ears raised, legs braced, neck hair bristling. Blue said, "Come." The dog did nothing. Blue repeated the entire sequence and so did Mangy.

I said, "You want the dog to follow you. Like the dogs in the presentation."

"Yes."

"You want the dog to come when you say 'Come.'"

"Love," Blue said.

"What is 'love,' Blue?"

No response.

The robot didn't know. Its masters must have had some concept of "love," but fuck-all knew what it was. And I wasn't sure I knew any more, either. That left Mangy, who would never "love" Blue or follow him or lick his hand because dogs operated on smell—even I knew that about them—and Blue, a machine, didn't smell like either a person or another dog. Couldn't the aliens who sent him here figure that out? Were they watching this whole farce, or had they just dropped a half-sentient computer under an upturned bowl on Earth and told it, "Bring us some loving dogs"? Who knew how aliens thought?

I didn't even know how dogs thought. There were much better people for this job—professional trainers, or that guy on TV who made tigers jump through burning hoops. But they weren't here, and I was. I squatted on my haunches a respectful distance from Mangy and said, "Come."

It growled at me.

"Blue, raise the platform this high." I held my hand at shoulder height. The platform rose.

"Now make some cookies on the platform."

Nothing.

"Make some...cheese on the platform."

Nothing. You don't see much cheese in a dump.

"Make some bread on the platform."

Nothing. Maybe the platform wasn't user-friendly.

"Make some bread."

After a moment, loaves tumbled out of the wall. "Enough! Stop!"

Mangy had rushed over to the bread, tearing at it, and the other dogs were going wild. I picked up one loaf, put it on the platform, and said, "Make the rest of the bread go away."

It all dissolved. No wonder the dogs were wary; I felt a little dizzy myself. A sentence from some long-ago child's book rose in my mind: *Things come and go so quickly here!*

I had no idea how much Blue could, or would, do on my orders. "Blue, make another room for me and this one dog. Away from the other dogs."

"No."

"Make this room bigger."

The room expanded evenly on all sides. "Stop." It did. "Make only this end of the room bigger."

Nothing.

"Okay, make the whole room bigger."

When the room stopped expanding, I had a space about forty feet square, with the dog cages huddled in the middle. After half an hour of experimenting, I got the platform moved to one corner, not far enough to escape the dog stench but better than nothing. (Law #1: Take what you can get.) I got a depression in the floor filled with warm water. I got food, drinking water, soap, and some clean cloth, and a lot of rope. By distracting Mangy with bits of bread, I got rope onto her frayed collar. After I got into the warm water and scrubbed myself, I pulled the poodle in. She bit me. But somehow I got her washed, too. Afterwards she shook herself, glared at me, and went to sleep on the hard floor. I asked Blue for a soft rug.

He said, "The other humans did this."

And Blue killed them anyway.

"Shut up," I said.

• • •

The big windowless room had no day, no night, no sanity. I slept and ate when I needed to, and otherwise I worked. Blue never left. He was an oversized, all-seeing eye in the corner. Big Brother, or God.

Within a few weeks—maybe—I had Mangy trained to come when called, to sit, and to follow me on command. I did this by dispensing bits of bread and other goodies. Mangy got fatter. I didn't care if she ended up the Fat Fiona of dogs. Her mange didn't improve, since I couldn't get Blue to wrap his digital mind around the concept of medicines, and even if he had I wouldn't have known what to ask for. The sick puppy died in its cage.

I kept the others fed and watered and flooded the shit out of their cages every day, but that was all. Mangy took all my time. She still regarded me warily, never curled up next to me, and occasionally growled. Love was not happening here.

Nonetheless, Blue left his corner and spoke for the first time in a week, scaring the hell out of me. "This dog behaves correctly."

"Well, thanks. I tried to…no, Blue…"

Blue floated to within a foot of Mangy's face, said, "Follow," and floated away. Mangy sat down and began to lick one paw. Blue rose and floated toward me.

"This dog does not behave correctly."

I was going to die.

"No, listen to me—listen! The dog can't smell you! It behaves for humans because of humans' smell! Do you understand?"

"No. This dog does not behave correctly."

"Listen! How the hell can you learn anything if you don't listen? You have to have a smell! Then the dog will follow you!"

Blue stopped. We stood frozen, a bizarre tableau, while the robot considered. Even Mangy stopped licking her paw and watched, still. They say dogs can smell fear.

Finally Blue said, "What is smell?"

It isn't possible to explain smell. Can't be done. Instead I pulled down my pants, tore the cloth I was using as underwear from between my legs, and rubbed it all over Blue, who did not react. I hoped he wasn't made of the same stuff as the Dome, which even spray paint had just slid off of. But, of course, he was. So I tied the strip of cloth around him with a piece of rope, my fingers trembling. "Now try the dog, Blue."

"Follow," Blue said, and floated away from Mangy.

She looked at him, then at me, then back at the floating metal sphere. I held my breath from some insane idea that I would thereby diminish my own smell. Mangy didn't move.

"This dog does not be—"

"She will if I'm gone!" I said desperately. "She smells me *and* you… and we smell the same so it's confusing her! But she'll follow you fine if I'm gone, do you understand?"

"No."

"Blue…I'm going to get on the platform. See, I'm doing it. Raise the platform *very high,* Blue. Very high."

A moment later my head and ass both pushed against the ceiling, squishing me. I couldn't see what was happening below. I heard Blue say, "Follow," and I squeezed my eyes shut, waiting. My life depended on a scrofulous poodle with a gloomy disposition.

Blue said, "This dog behaves correctly."

He lowered my platform to a few yards above the floor, and I swear that—eyeless as he is and with part of his sphere obscured by my under-wear—he looked right at me.

"This dog does behave correctly. This dog is ready."

"Ready? For...for what?"

Blue didn't answer. The next minute the floor opened and Mangy, yelping, tumbled into it. The floor closed. At the same time, one of the cages across the room dissolved and a German shepherd hurtled towards me. I shrieked and yelled, "Raise the platform!" It rose just before the monster grabbed me.

Blue said, "What to do now? This dog does not behave correctly."

"For God's sakes, Blue—"

"This dog must love."

The shepherd leapt and snarled, teeth bared.

•••

I couldn't talk Blue out of the shepherd, which was as feral and vicious and unrelenting as anything in a horror movie. Or as Blue himself, in his own mechanical way. So I followed the First Law: Take what you can get.

"Blue, make garbage again. A lot of garbage, right here." I pointed to the wall beside my platform.

"No."

Garbage, like everything else, apparently was made—or released, or whatever—from the opposite wall. I resigned myself to this. "Make a lot of garbage, Blue."

Mountains of stinking debris cascaded from the wall, spilling over until it reached the dog cages.

"Now stop. Move my platform above the garbage."

The platform moved. The caged dogs howled. Uncaged, the shepherd poked eagerly in the refuse, too distracted to pay much attention to me.

I had Blue lower the platform and I poked among it, too, keeping one eye on Vicious. If Blue was creating the garbage and not just trucking it in, he was doing a damn fine job of duplication. Xerox should have made such good copies.

I got smeared with shit and rot, but I found what I was looking for. The box was nearly a quarter full. I stuffed bread into it, coated the bread thoroughly, and discarded the box back onto the pile.

"Blue, make the garbage go away."

It did. Vicious glared at me and snarled. "Nice doggie," I said, "have some bread." I threw pieces and Vicious gobbled them.

Listening to the results was terrible. Not, however, as terrible as having Vicious tear me apart or Blue vaporize me. The rat poison took all "night" to kill the dog, which thrashed and howled. Throughout, Blue stayed silent. He had picked up some words from me, but he apparently didn't have enough brain power to connect what I'd done with Vicious's death. Or maybe he just didn't have enough experience with humans. What does a machine know about survival?

"This dog is dead," Blue said in the "morning."

"Yes. Make it go away." And then, before Blue could get there first, I jumped off my platform and pointed to a cage. "This dog will behave correctly next."

"No."

"Why not this dog?"

"Not big."

"Big. You want big." Frantically I scanned the cages, before Blue could choose another one like Vicious. "This one, then."

"Why the hell not?" Blue said.

• • •

It was young. Not a puppy but still frisky, a mongrel of some sort with short hair of dirty white speckled with dirty brown. The dog looked like something I could handle: big but not too big, not too aggressive, not too old, not too male. "Hey, Not-Too," I said, without enthusiasm, as Blue dissolved her cage. The mutt dashed over to me and tried to lick my boot.

A natural-born slave.

I had found a piece of rotten, moldy cheese in the garbage, so Blue could now make cheese, which Not-Too went crazy for. Not-Too and I stuck with the same routine I used with Mangy, and it worked pretty well. Or the cheese did. Within a few "days" the dog could sit, stay, and follow on command.

Then Blue threw me a curve. "What to do now? The presentation."

"We had the presentation," I said. "I don't need to see it again."

"What to do now? The presentation."

"Fine," I said, because it was clear I had no choice. "Let's have the presentation. Roll 'em."

I was sitting on my elevated platform, combing my hair. A lot of it had fallen out during the malnourished years in the camp, but now it was growing again. Not-Too had given up trying to jump up there with me and gone to sleep on her pillow below. Blue shot the beam out of his sphere and the holo played in front of me.

Only not the whole thing. This time he played only the brief scene where the big, patchy dog pulled the toddler back from falling into the cesspool. Blue played it once, twice, three times. Cold slid along my spine.

"You want Not-Too...you want this dog here to be trained to save children."

"This dog here does not behave correctly."

"Blue... How can I train a dog to save a child?"

"This dog here does not behave correctly."

"Maybe you haven't noticed, but we haven't got any fucking children for the dog to practice on!"

Long pause. "Do you want a child?"

"No!" Christ, he would kidnap one or buy one from the camp and I would be responsible for a kid along with nineteen semi-feral dogs. No.

"This dog here does not behave correctly. What to do now? The presentation."

"No, not the presentation. I saw it, *I saw it*. Blue...the other two humans who did not make the dogs behave correctly..."

"Killed."

"Yes. So you said. But they did get one dog to behave correctly, didn't they? Or maybe more than one. And then you just kept raising the bar higher. Water rescues, guiding the blind, finding lost people. Higher and higher."

But to all this, of course, Blue made no answer.

I wracked my brains to remember what I had ever heard, read, or seen about dog training. Not much. However, there's a problem with opening the door to memory: you can't control what strolls through. For the first time in years, my sleep was shattered by dreams.

I walked through a tiny garden, picking zinnias. From an open window came music, full and strong, an orchestra on CD. A cat paced beside me, purring. And there was someone else in the window, someone who called my name and I turned and—

I screamed. Clawed my way upright. The dogs started barking and howling. Blue floated from his corner, saying something. And Not-Too made a mighty leap, landed on my platform, and began licking my face.

"Stop it! Don't do that! I won't remember!" I shoved her so hard she fell off the platform onto the floor and began yelping. I put my head in my hands.

Blue said, "Are you not operative?"

"Leave me the fuck alone!"

Not-Too still yelped, shrill cries of pain. When I stopped shaking, I crawled off the platform and picked her up. Nothing seemed to be broken—although how would I know? Gradually she quieted. I gave her some cheese and put her back on her pillow. She wanted to stay with me but I wouldn't let her.

I would not remember. *I would not.* Law #5: Feel nothing.

•••

We made a cesspool, or at least a pool. Blue depressed part of the floor to a depth of three feet and filled it with water. Not-Too considered this a swimming pool and loved to be in it, which was not what Blue wanted ("This water does not behave correctly"). I tried having the robot dump various substances into it until I found one that she disliked and I could tolerate: light-grade motor oil. A few small cans of oil like those in the dump created a polluted pool, not unlike Charleston Harbor. After every practice session I needed a bath.

But not Not-Too, because she wouldn't go into the "cesspool." I curled myself as small as possible, crouched at the side of the pool, and thrashed. After a few days, the dog would pull me back by my shirt. I moved into the pool. As long as she could reach me without getting any liquid on her, Not-Too happily played that game. As soon as I moved far enough out that I might actually need saving, she sat on her skinny haunches and looked away.

"This dog does not behave correctly."

I increased the cheese. I withheld the cheese. I pleaded and ordered and shunned and petted and yelled. Nothing worked. Meanwhile, the dream continued. The same dream, each time not greater in length but increasing in intensity. *I walked through a tiny garden, picking zinnias. From an open window came music, full and strong, an orchestra on CD. A cat paced beside me, purring. And there was someone else in the window, someone who called my name and I turned and—*

And woke screaming.

A cat. I had had a cat, before the War. Before everything. I had always had cats, my whole life. Independent cats, aloof and self-sufficient, admirably disdainful. Cats—

The dog below me whimpered, trying to get onto my platform to offer comfort I did not want.

I would not remember.

"This dog does not behave correctly," day after day.

I had Blue remove the oil from the pool. But by now Not-Too had been conditioned. She wouldn't go into even the clear water that she'd reveled in before.

"This dog does not behave correctly."

Then one day Blue stopped his annoying mantra, which scared me even more. Would I have any warning that I'd failed, or would I just die?

The only thing I could think of was to kill Blue first.

• • •

Blue was a computer. You disabled computers by turning them off, or cutting the power supply, or melting them in a fire, or dumping acid on them, or crushing them. But a careful search of the whole room revealed no switches or wires or anything that looked like a wireless control. A fire in this closed room, assuming I could start one, would kill me, too. Every kind of liquid or solid slid off Blue. And what would I crush him with, if that was even possible? A piece of cheese?

Blue was also—sort of—an intelligence. You could kill those by trapping them somewhere. My prison-or-sanctuary (depending on my mood) had no real "somewheres." And Blue would just dissolve any structure he found himself in.

What to do now?

I lay awake, thinking, all night, which at least kept me from dreaming, I came up with two ideas, both bad. Plan A depended on discussion, never Blue's strong suit.

"Blue, this dog does not behave correctly."

"No."

"This dog is not operative. I must make another dog behave correctly. Not this dog."

Blue floated close to Not-Too. She tried to bat at him. He circled her slowly, then returned to his position three feet above the ground. "This dog is operative."

"No. This dog *looks* operative. But this dog is not operative inside its head. I cannot make this dog behave correctly. I need a different dog."

A very long pause. "This dog is not operative inside its head."

"*Yes.*"

"You can make another dog behave correctly. Like the presentation."

"Yes." It would at least buy me time. Blue must have seen "not operative" dogs and humans in the dump; God knows there were enough of them out there. Madmen, rabid animals, druggies raving just before they died, or were shot. And next time I would add something besides oil to the pool; there must be something that Blue would consider noxious enough to simulate a cesspool but that a dog would enter. If I had to, I'd use my own shit.

"This dog is not operative inside its head," Blue repeated, getting used to the idea. "You will make a different dog behave correctly."

"Yes!"

"Why the hell not?" And then, "I kill this dog."

"No!" The word was torn from me before I knew I was going to say anything. My hand, of its own volition, clutched at Not-Too. She jumped but didn't bite. Instead, maybe sensing my fear, she cowered behind me, and I started to yell.

"You can't just kill everything that doesn't behave like you want! People, dogs…you can't just kill everything! You can't just…I had a cat…I never wanted a dog but this dog…she's behaving correctly for her! For a fucking traumatized dog and you can't just—I had a dog I mean a cat I had...I had...."

—from an open window came music, full and strong, an orchestra on CD. A cat paced beside me, purring. And there was someone else in the window, someone who called my name and I turned and—

"I had a child!"

Oh, God no no no... It all came out then, the memories and the grief and the pain I had pushed away for three solid years in order to survive... *Feel nothing...* Zack Zack *Zack* shot down by soldiers like a dog *Look, Mommy, here I am Mommy look...*

I curled in a ball on the floor and screamed and wanted to die. Grief had been postponed so long that it was a tsunami. I sobbed and screamed; I don't know for how long. I think I wasn't quite sane. No human should ever have to experience that much pain. But of course they do.

However, it can't last too long, that height of pain, and when the flood passed and my head was bruised from banging it on the hard floor, I was still alive, still inside the Dome, still surrounded by barking dogs. Zack was still dead. Blue floated nearby, unchanged, a casually murderous robot who would not supply flesh to dogs as food but who would kill anything he was programmed to destroy. And he had no reason not to murder me.

Not-Too sat on her haunches, regarding me from sad brown eyes, and I did the one thing I told myself I never would do again. I reached for her warmth. I put my arms around her and hung on. She let me.

Maybe that was the decision point. I don't know.

When I could manage it, I staggered to my feet. Taking hold of the rope that was Not-Too's leash, I wrapped it firmly around my hand. "Blue," I said, forcing the words past the grief clogging my throat, "make garbage."

He did. That was the basis of Plan B; that Blue made most things I asked of him. Not release, or mercy, but at least rooms and platforms and pools and garbage. I walked toward the garbage spilling from the usual place in the wall.

"More garbage! Bigger garbage! I need garbage to make this dog behave correctly!"

The reeking flow increased. Tires, appliances, diapers, rags, cans, furniture. The dogs' howling rose to an insane, deafening pitch. Not-Too pressed close to me.

"Bigger garbage!"

The chassis of a motorcycle, twisted beyond repair in some unimaginable accident, crashed into the room. The place on the wall from which the garbage spewed was misty gray, the same fog that the Dome had become when I had been taken inside it. Half a sofa clattered through. I grabbed Not-Too, dodged behind the sofa, and hurled both of us through the onrushing garbage and into the wall.

A broken keyboard struck me in the head, and the gray went black.

•••

Chill. Cold with a spot of heat, which turned out to be Not-Too lying on top of me. I pushed her off and tried to sit up. Pain lanced through my head and when I put a hand to my forehead, it came away covered with blood. The same blood streamed into my eyes, making it hard to see. I wiped the blood away with the front of my shirt, pressed my hand hard on my forehead, and looked around.

Not that there was much to see. The dog and I sat at the end of what appeared to be a corridor. Above me loomed a large machine of some type, with a chute pointed at the now-solid wall. The machine was silent. Not-Too quivered and pressed her furry side into mine, but she, too, stayed silent. I couldn't hear the nineteen dogs on the other side of the wall, couldn't see Blue, couldn't smell anything except Not-Too, who had made a small yellow puddle on the floor.

There was no room to stand upright under the machine, so I moved away from it. Strips ripped from the bottom of my shirt made a bandage that at least kept blood out of my eyes. Slowly Not-Too and I walked along the corridor.

No doors. No openings or alcoves or machinery. Nothing until we reached the end, which was the same uniform material as everything else. Gray, glossy, hard. Dead.

Blue did not appear. Nothing appeared, or disappeared, or lived. We walked back and studied the overhead bulk of the machine. It had no dials or keys or features of any kind.

I sat on the floor, largely because I couldn't think what else to do, and Not-Too climbed into my lap. She was too big for this and I pushed her away. She pressed against me, trembling.

"Hey," I said, but not to her. Zack in the window *Look, Mommy, here I am Mommy look....* But if I started down that mental road, I would be lost. Anger was better than memory. Anything was better than memory. "Hey!" I screamed. "Hey, you bastard Blue, what to do now? What to do now, you Dome shits, whoever you are?"

Nothing except, very faint, an echo of my own useless words.

I lurched to my feet, reaching for the anger, cloaking myself in it. Not-Too sprang to her feet and backed away from me.

"What to do now? What bloody fucking hell to do *now?*"

Still nothing, but Not-Too started back down the empty corridor. I was glad to transfer my anger to something visible, real, living. "There's nothing there, Not-Too. *Nothing,* you stupid dog!"

She stopped halfway down the corridor and began to scratch at the wall.

I stumbled along behind her, one hand clamped to my head. What the hell was she doing? This piece of wall was identical to every other piece of wall. Kneeling slowly—it hurt my head to move fast—I studied Not-Too. Her scratching increased in frenzy and her nose twitched, as if she smelled something. The wall, of course, didn't respond; nothing in this place responded to anything. Except—

Blue had learned words from me, had followed my commands. Or had he just transferred my command to the Dome's unimaginable machinery, instructing it to do anything I said that fell within permissible limits? Feeling like an idiot, I said to the wall, "Make garbage." Maybe if it complied and the garbage contained food...

The wall made no garbage. Instead it dissolved into the familiar gray fog, and Not-Too immediately jumped through, barking frantically.

Every time I had gone through a Dome wall, my situation had gotten worse. But what other choices were there? Wait for Blue to find and kill me, starve to death, curl up and die in the heart of a mechanical alien mini-world I didn't understand. Not-Too's barking increased in pitch and volume. She was terrified or excited or thrilled... How would I know? I pushed through the gray fog.

Another gray metal room, smaller than Blue had made my prison but with the same kind of cages against the far wall. Not-Too saw me and raced from the cages to me. Blue floated toward me...No, not Blue. This metal sphere was dull green, the color of shady moss. It said, "No human comes into this area."

"Guess again," I said and grabbed the trailing end of Not-Too's rope. She'd jumped up on me once and then had turned to dash back to the cages.

"No human comes into this area," Green repeated. I waited to see what the robot would do about it. Nothing.

Not-Too tugged on her rope, yowling. From across the room came answering barks, weirdly off. Too uneven in pitch, with a strange undertone. Blood, having saturated my makeshift bandage, once again streamed into my eyes. I swiped at it with one hand, turned to keep my gaze on Green, and let Not-Too pull me across the floor. Only when she stopped did I turn to look at the mesh-topped cages. Vertigo swooped over me.

Mangy was the source of the weird barks, a Mangy altered not beyond recognition but certainly beyond anything I could have imagined. Her mange was gone, along with all her fur. The skin beneath was now gray, the same gunmetal gray as everything else in the Dome. Her ears, the floppy poodle ears, were so long they trailed on the floor of her cage, and so was her tail. Holding on to the tail was a gray grub.

Not a grub. Not anything Earthly. Smooth and pulpy, it was about the size of a human head and vaguely oval. I saw no openings on the thing but Mangy's elongated tail disappeared into the doughy mass, and so there must have been at least one orifice. As Mangy jumped at the bars, trying to get at Not-Too, the grub was whipped back and forth across the cage floor. It left a slimy trail. The dog seemed oblivious.

"*This dog is ready*," Blue had said.

Behind me Green said, "No human comes into this area."

"Up yours."

"The human does not behave correctly."

That got my attention. I whirled around to face Green, expecting to be vaporized like the dead puppy, the dead Vicious. I thought I was already dead—and then I welcomed the thought. *Look, Mommy, here I am Mommy look…* The Laws of Survival that had protected me for so long couldn't protect me against memory, not any more. I was ready to die.

Instead Mangy's cage dissolved, she bounded out, and she launched herself at me.

Poodles are not natural killers, and this one was small. However, Mangy was doing her level best to destroy me. Her teeth closed on my arm. I screamed and shook her off, but the next moment she was biting my leg above my boot, darting hysterically toward and away from me, biting my legs at each lunge. The grub, or whatever it was, lashed around at the end of her new tail. As I flailed at the dog with both hands, my bandage fell off. Fresh blood from my head wound blinded me. I stumbled and fell and she was at my face.

Then she was pulled off, yelping and snapping and howling.

Not-Too had Mangy in her jaws. Twice as big as the poodle, she shook Mangy violently and then dropped her. Mangy whimpered and rolled over on her belly. Not-Too sprinted over to me and stood in front of me, skinny legs braced and scrawny hackles raised, growling protectively.

Dazed, I got to my feet. Blood, mine and the dog's, slimed everything. The floor wasn't trying to reabsorb it. Mangy, who'd never really liked me, stayed down with her belly exposed in submission, but she didn't seem to be badly hurt. The grub still latched onto the end of her tail like a gray tumor. After a moment she rolled onto her feet and began to nuzzle the grub, one baleful eye on Not-Too: *Don't you come near this thing!* Not-Too stayed in position, guarding me.

Green said—and I swear its mechanical voice held satisfaction, no one will ever be able to tell me any different—"These dogs behave correctly."

•••

The other cages held grubs, one per cage. I reached through the front bars and gingerly touched one. Moist, firm, repulsive. It didn't respond to my touch, but Green did. He was beside me in a flash. "No!"

"Sorry." His tone was dog-disciplining. "Are these the masters?"

No answer.

"What to do now? One dog for one..." I waved at the cages.

"Yes. When these dogs are ready."

This dog is ready, Blue had said of Mangy just before she was tumbled into the floor. Ready to be a pet, a guardian, a companion, a service animal to alien...what? The most logical answer was "children." Lassie, Rin Tin Tin, Benji, Little Guy. A boy and his dog. The aliens found humans dangerous or repulsive or uncaring or whatever, but dogs... You could count on dogs for your kids. Almost, and for the first time, I could see the point of the Domes.

"Are the big masters here? The adults?"

No answer.

"The masters are not here," I said. "They just set up the Domes as...as nurseries-slash-obedience schools." And to that statement I didn't even expect an answer. If the adults had been present, surely one or more would have come running when an alien blew into its nursery wing via a garbage delivery. There would have been alarms or something. Instead there was only Blue and Green and whatever 'bots inhabited whatever place held the operating room. Mangy's skin and ears and tail had been altered to fit the needs of these grubs. And maybe her voice-box, too, since her barks now had that weird undertone, like the scrape of metal across rock. Somewhere there was an OR.

I didn't want to be in that somewhere.

Green seemed to have no orders to kill me, which made sense because he wasn't programmed to have me here. I wasn't on his radar, which raised other problems.

"Green, make bread."

Nothing.

"Make water."

Nothing.

But two indentations in a corner of the floor, close to a section of wall, held water and dog-food pellets. I tasted both, to the interest of Not-Too and the growling of Mangy. Not too bad. I scooped all the rest of the dog food out of the trough. As soon as the last piece was out, the wall filled it up again. If I died, it wasn't going to be of starvation.

A few minutes ago, I had wanted to die. *Zack...*

No. Push the memory away. Life was shit, but I didn't want death, either. The realization was visceral, gripping my stomach as if that organ had been laid in a vise, or... There is no way to describe it. The feeling just was, its own justification. I wanted to live.

Not-Too lay a short distance away, watching me. Mangy was back in her cage with the grub on her tail. I sat up and looked around. "Green, this dog is not ready."

"No. What to do now?"

Well, that answered one question. Green was programmed to deal with dogs, and you didn't ask dogs "what to do now." So Green must be in some sort of communication with Blue, but the communication didn't seem to include orders about me. For a star-faring advanced race, the aliens certainly weren't very good at LANs. Or maybe they just didn't care—how would I know how an alien thinks?

I said, "I make this dog behave correctly." The all-purpose answer. "Yes."

Did Green know details—that Not-Too refused to pull me from oily pools and thus was an obedience-school failure? It didn't seem like it. I could pretend to train Not-Too—I could actually train her, only not for water rescue—and stay here, away from the killer Blue, until...until what? As a survival plan, this one was shit. Still, it followed Laws #1 and #3: Take what you can get and never volunteer. And I couldn't think of anything else.

"Not-Too," I said wearily, still shaky from my crying jag, "sit."

•••

"Days" went by, then weeks. Not-Too learned to beg, roll over, bring me a piece of dog food, retrieve my thrown boot, lie down, and balance a pellet of dog food on her nose. I had no idea if any of these activities would be useful to an alien, but as long as Not-Too and I were "working," Green left us alone. No threats, no presentations, no objections. We were behaving correctly. I still hadn't thought of any additional plan. At night I dreamed of Zack and woke in tears, but not with the raging insanity of my first day of memory. Maybe you can only go through that once.

Mangy's grub continued to grow, still fastened onto her tail. The other grubs looked exactly the same as before. Mangy growled if I came too close to her, so I didn't. Her grub seemed to be drying out as it got bigger. Mangy licked it and slept curled around it and generally acted like some mythical dragon guarding a treasure box. Had the aliens bonded those two with some kind of pheromones I couldn't detect? I had no way of knowing.

Mangy and her grub emerged from their cage only to eat, drink, or shit, which she did in a far corner. Not-Too and I used the same corner, and all of our shit and piss dissolved odorlessly into the floor. Eat your heart out, Thomas Crapper.

As days turned into weeks, flesh returned to my bones. Not-Too also lost her starved look. I talked to her more and more, her watchful silence preferable to Green's silence or, worse, his inane and limited repertoires of answers. *"Green, I had a child named Zack. He was shot in the war. He was five." "This dog is not ready."*

Well, none of us ever are.

Not-Too started to sleep curled against my left side. This was a problem because I thrashed in my sleep, which woke her, so she growled, which woke me. Both of us became sleep-deprived and irritable. In the camp, I had slept twelve hours a day. Not much else to do, and sleep both conserved energy and kept me out of sight. But the camp was becoming distant in my mind. Zack was shatteringly vivid, with my life before the war, and the Dome was vivid, with Mangy and Not-Too and a bunch of alien grubs. Everything in between was fading.

Then one "day"—after how much time? I had no idea—Green said, "This dog is ready."

My heart stopped. Green was going to take Not-Too to the hidden OR, was going to—"No!"

Green ignored me. But he also ignored Not-Too. The robot floated over to Mangy's cage and dissolved it. I stood and craned my neck for a better look.

The grub was hatching.

Its "skin" had become very dry, a papery gray shell. Now it cracked along the top, parallel to Mangy's tail. She turned and regarded it quizzically, this thing wriggling at the end of her very long tail, but didn't attack or even growl. Those must have been some pheromones.

Was I really going to be the first and only human to see a Dome alien?

I was not. The papery covering cracked more and dropped free of the dog's tail. The thing inside wiggled forward, crawling out like a snake shedding its skin. It wasn't a grub but it clearly wasn't a sentient being, either. A larva? I'm no zoologist. This creature was as gray as everything else in the Dome but it had legs, six, and heads, two. At least, they might have been heads. Both had various indentations. One "head" crept forward, opened an orifice, and fastened itself back onto Mangy's tail. She continued to gaze at it. Beside me, Not-Too growled.

I whirled to grab frantically for her rope. Not-Too had no alterations to make her accept this…thing as anything other than a small animal to attack. If she did—

I turned just in time to see the floor open and swallow Not-Too. Green said again, "This dog is ready," and the floor closed.

"No! Bring her back!" I tried to pound on Green with my fists. He bobbed in the air under my blows. "Bring her back! Don't hurt her! Don't..." do what?

Don't turn her into a nursemaid for a grub, oblivious to me.

Green moved off. I followed, yelling and pounding. Neither one, of course, did the slightest good. Finally I got it together enough to say, "When will Not-Too come back?"

"This human does not behave correctly."

I looked despairingly at Mangy. She lay curled on her side, like a mother dog nursing puppies. The larva wasn't nursing, however. A shallow trough had appeared in the floor and filled with some viscous glop, which the larva was scarfing up with its other head. It looked repulsive.

Law #4: Notice everything.

"Green...okay. Just...okay. When will Not-Too come back here?"

No answer; what does time mean to a machine?

"Does the other dog return here?"

"Yes."

"Does the other dog get a..." A what? I pointed at Mangy's larva.

No response. I would have to wait.

But not, apparently, alone. Across the room another dog tumbled, snarling, from the same section of wall I had once come through. I recognized it as one of the nineteen left in the other room, a big black beast with powerful-looking jaws. It righted itself and charged at me. There was no platform, no place to hide.

"No! Green, no, it will hurt me! This dog does not behave—"

Green didn't seem to do anything. But even as the black dog leapt toward me, it faltered in midair. The next moment, it lay dead on the floor.

The moment after that, the body disappeared, vaporized.

My legs collapsed under me. That was what would happen to me if I failed in my training task, was what had presumably happened to the previous two human failures. And yet it wasn't fear that made me sit so abruptly on the gray floor. It was relief, and a weird kind of gratitude. Green had protected me, which was more than Blue had ever done. Maybe Green was brighter, or I had proved my worth more, or in this room as opposed to the other room, all dog-training equipment was protected. I was dog-training equipment. It was stupid to feel grateful.

I felt grateful.

Green said, "This dog does not—"

"I know, *I know*. Listen, Green, what to do now? Bring another dog here?"

"Yes."

"*I* choose the dog. I am the…the dog leader. Some dogs behave correctly, some dogs do not behave correctly. I choose. Me."

I held my breath. Green considered, or conferred with Blue, or consulted its alien and inadequate programming. Who the hell knows? The robot had been created by a race that preferred Earth dogs to whatever species usually nurtured their young, if any did. Maybe Mangy and Not-Too would replace parental care on the home planet, thus introducing the idea of babysitters. All I wanted was to not be eaten by some canine nanny-trainee.

"Yes," Green said finally, and I let out my breath.

A few minutes later, eighteen dog cages tumbled through the wall like so much garbage, the dogs within bouncing off their bars and mesh tops, furious and noisy. Mangy jumped, curled more protectively around her oblivious larva, and added her weird, rock-scraping bark to the din. A cage grew up around her. When the cages had stopped bouncing, I walked among them like some kind of tattered lord, choosing.

"This dog, Green." It wasn't the smallest dog but it had stopped barking the soonest. I hoped that meant it wasn't a grudge holder. When I put one hand into its cage, it didn't bite me, also a good sign. The dog was phenomenally ugly, the jowls on its face drooping from small, rheumy eyes into a sort of folded ruff around its short neck. Its body seemed to be all front, with stunted and short back legs. When it stood, I saw it was male.

"This dog? What to do now?"

"Send all the other dogs back."

The cages sank into the floor. I walked over to the feeding trough, scooped up handfuls of dog food, and put the pellets into my only pocket that didn't have holes. "Make all the rest of the dog food go away."

It vaporized.

"Make this dog's cage go away."

I braced myself as the cage dissolved. The dog stood uncertainly on the floor, gazing toward Mangy, who snarled at him. I said, as commandingly as possible, "Ruff!"

He looked at me.

"Ruff, come."

To my surprise, he did. Someone had trained this animal before. I gave him a pellet of dog food.

Green said, "This dog behaves correctly."

"Well, I'm really good," I told him, stupidly, while my chest tightened as I thought of Not-Too. The aliens, or their machines, did understand about anesthetic, didn't they? They wouldn't let her suffer too much? I would never know.

But now I *did* know something momentous. I had choices. I had chosen which room to train dogs in. I had chosen which dog to train. I had some control.

"Sit," I said to Ruff, who didn't, and I set to work.

•••

Not-Too was returned to me three or four "days" later. She was gray and hairless, with an altered bark. A grub hung onto her elongated tail, undoubtedly the same one that had vanished from its cage while I was asleep. But unlike Mangy, who'd never liked either of us, Not-Too was ecstatic to see me. She wouldn't stay in her grub-cage against the wall but insisted on sleeping curled up next to me, grub and all. Green permitted this. I had become the alpha dog.

Not-Too liked Ruff, too. I caught him mounting her, her very long tail conveniently keeping her grub out of the way. Did Green understand the significance of this behavior? No way to tell.

We settled into a routine of training, sleeping, playing, eating. Ruff turned out to be sweet and playful but not very intelligent, and training took a long time. Mangy's grub grew very slowly, considering the large amount of glop it consumed. I grew, too; the waistband of my ragged pants got too tight and I discarded them, settling for a loin cloth, shirt, and my decaying boots. I talked to the dogs, who were much better conversationalists than Green since two of them at least pricked up their ears, made noises back at me, and wriggled joyfully at attention. Green would have been a dud at a cocktail party.

I don't know how long this all went on. Time began to lose meaning. I still dreamed of Zack and still woke in tears, but the dreams grew gentler and farther apart. When I cried, Not-Too crawled onto my lap, dragging her grub, and licked my chin. Her brown eyes shared my sorrow. I wondered how I had ever preferred the disdain of cats.

Not-Too got pregnant. I could feel the puppies growing inside her distended belly.

"Puppies will be easy to make behave correctly," I told Green, who said nothing. Probably he didn't understand. Some people need concrete visuals in order to learn.

Eventually, it seemed to me that Ruff was almost ready for his own grub. I mulled over how to mention this to Green but before I did, everything came to an end.

•••

Clang! Clang! Clang!

I jerked awake and bolted upright. The alarm—a very human-sounding alarm—sounded all around me. Dogs barked and howled. Then I realized that it was a human alarm, coming from the Army camp outside the Dome, on the opposite side to the garbage dump. I could *see* the camp—in outline and faintly, as if through heavy gray fog. The Dome was dissolving.

"Green—what—no!"

Above me, transforming the whole top half of what had been the Dome, was the bottom of a solid saucer. Mangy, in her cage, floated upwards and disappeared into a gap in the saucer's underside. The other grub cages had already disappeared. I glimpsed a flash of metallic color through the gap: Blue. Green was halfway to the opening, drifting lazily upward. Beside me, both Not-Too and Ruff began to rise.

"No! No!"

I hung onto Not-Too, who howled and barked. But then my body froze. I couldn't move anything. My hands opened and Not-Too rose, yowling piteously.

"No! No!" And then, before I knew I was going to say it, "Take me, too!" Green paused in midair. I began babbling.

"Take me! Take me! I can make the dogs behave correctly—I can—you need me! Why are you going? Take me!"

"Take this human?"

Not Green but Blue, emerging from the gap. Around me the Dome walls thinned more. Soldiers rushed toward us. Guns fired.

"Yes! What to do? Take this human! The dogs want this human!"

Time stood still. Not-Too howled and tried to reach me. Maybe that's what did it. I rose into the air just as Blue said, "Why the hell not?"

Inside—inside *what?*—I was too stunned to do more than grab Not-Too, hang on, and gasp. The gap closed. The saucer rose.

After a few minutes, I sat up and looked around. Gray room, filled with dogs in their cages, with grubs in theirs, with noise and confusion and the two robots. The sensation of motion ceased. I gasped, "Where… where are we going?"

Blue answered. "Home."

"*Why?*"

"The humans do not behave correctly." And then, "What to do now?"

We were leaving Earth in a flying saucer, and it was asking *me?*

• • •

Over time—I have no idea how much time—I actually got some answers from Blue. The humans "not behaving correctly" had apparently succeeding in breaching one of the Domes somewhere. They must have used a nuclear bomb, but that I couldn't verify. Grubs and dogs had both died, and so the aliens had packed up and left Earth. Without, as far as I could tell, retaliating. Maybe.

If I had stayed, I told myself, the soldiers would have shot me. Or I would have returned to life in the camp, where I would have died of dysentery or violence or cholera or starvation. Or I would have been locked away by whatever government still existed in the cities, a freak who had lived with aliens, none of my story believed. I barely believed it myself.

I *am* a freak who lives with aliens. Furthermore, I live knowing that at any moment Blue or Green or their "masters" might decide to vaporize me. But that's really not much different from the uncertainty of life in the camp, and here I actually have some status. Blue produces whatever I ask for, once I get him to understand what that is. I have new clothes, good food, a bed, paper, a sort of pencil.

And I have the dogs. Mangy still doesn't like me. Her larva hasn't as yet done whatever it will do next. Not-Too's grub grows slowly, and now Ruff has one, too. Their three puppies are adorable and very trainable. I'm not so sure about the other seventeen dogs, some of whom look wilder than ever after their long confinement in small cages. Aliens are not, by definition, humane.

I don't know what it will take to survive when, and if, we reach "home" and I meet the alien adults. All I can do is rely on Jill's Five Laws of Survival:

#1: Take what you can get.

#2: Show no fear.

#3: Never volunteer.

#4: Notice everything.

But the Fifth Law has changed. As I lie beside Not-Too and Ruff, their sweet warmth and doggie-odor, I know that my first formulation was wrong. "Feel nothing"—that can take you some ways toward survival, but not very far. Not really.

Law #5: Take the risk. Love something.

The dogs whuff contentedly and we speed toward the stars.

WHAT YOU ARE
ABOUT TO SEE

JACK SKILLINGSTEAD

t sat in a cold room.

Outside that room a marine handed me an insulated suit. I slipped it on over my street clothes. The marine punched a code into a numeric keypad attached to the wall. The lock snapped open on the heavy door, the marine nodded, I entered.

Andy McCaslin, who looked like an overdressed turnip in *his* insulated suit, greeted me and shook my hand. I'd known Andy for twenty-five years, since our days in Special Forces. Now we both worked for the NSA, though you could say my acronym was lowercase. I operated on the margins of the Agency, a contract player, an accomplished extractor of information from reluctant sources. My line of work required a special temperament, which I possessed and which Andy most assuredly did not. He was a true believer in the *rightness* of the cause, procedure, good guys and bad. I was like Andy's shadow twin. He stood in the light, casting something dark and faceless, which was me.

It remained seated—if you could call that sitting. Its legs, all six of them, coiled and braided like a nest of lavender snakes on top of which the alien's frail torso rested. That torso resembled the upper body of a starving child, laddered ribs under parchment skin and a big stretched belly full of nothing. It watched us with eyes like two thumbnail chips of anthracite.

"Welcome to the new world order," Andy said, his breath condensing in little gray puffs.

"Thanks. Anything out of Squidward yet?"

"Told us it was in our own best interests to let him go, then when we wouldn't it shut up. Only 'shut up' isn't quite accurate, since it doesn't vocalize. You hear the words in your head, or sometimes there's just a picture. It was the picture it put in the Secretary's head that's got everybody's panties in a knot."

"What picture?"

"Genocidal carnage on a planet-wide scale."

"Sounds friendly enough."

"There's a backroom theory that Squidward was just showing the Secretary his own secret wet dream. Anyway, accepting its assertions of friendliness at face value is not up to me. Off the record, though, my intuition tells me its intentions are benign."

"You look tired, Andy."

"I feel a little off," he said.

"Does Squidward always stare like that?"

"Always."

"You're certain it still has the ability to communicate? Maybe the environment's making it sick."

"Not according to the medical people. Of course, nothing's certain, except that Squidward is a non-terrestrial creature possessed of an advanced technology. Those facts are deductible. By the way, the advanced technology in question is currently bundled in a hangar not far from here. What's left looks like a weather balloon fed through a shredder. Ironic?"

"Very." I hunched my shoulders. "Cold in here."

"You noticed."

"Squidward likes it that way, I bet."

"Loves it."

"Have you considered warming things up?"

Andy gave me a sideways look. "You thinking of changing the

interrogation protocols?"

"If I am it wouldn't be in that direction."

"No CIA gulag in Romania, eh."

"Never heard of such a thing."

"I'd like to think you hadn't."

Actually I was well familiar with the place, only it was in Guatemala, not Romania. At its mention a variety of horrors arose in my mind. Some of them had faces attached. I regarded them dispassionately, as I had when I saw them in actuality all those years ago, and then I replaced them in the vault from which their muffled screams trouble me from time to time.

Andy's face went slack and pale.

"What's wrong?"

"I don't know. All of a sudden I feel like I'm not really standing here."

He smiled thinly, and I thought he was going to faint. But as I reached out to him I suddenly felt dizzy myself, afloat, contingent. I swayed, like balancing on the edge of a tall building. Squidward sat in its coil of snakes, staring…

• • •

Now return to a particular watershed moment in the life of one Brian Kinney, aka: me. Two years ago. If years mean anything in the present context.

I was a lousy drunk. Lack of experience. My father, on the other hand, had been an accomplished drunk. Legendary, almost. As a consequence of his example I had spent my life cultivating a morbid sobriety, which my wife managed to interrupt by an act of infidelity. Never mind that she needed to do it before she completely drowned in *my* legendary un-communicative self-isolation. The way I viewed things at the time: she betrayed me for no reason other than her own wayward carnality. You'd think I'd have known better; I'd spent my nasty little career understand-ing and manipulating the psychology of others.

Anyway, I went and got stinking drunk, which was easy enough. It was the drive home that was the killer. The speedometer needle floated between blurred pairs of numbers. By deliberate force of will (I was hell on force of will) I could bring the numbers into momentary clarity, but that required dropping my gaze from the roller-coaster road sweeping under my headlight beams—not necessarily a good idea. Four. Five. Was that right? What was the limit?

Good question.

What *was* the limit?

I decided it wasn't the four whiskeys with beer chasers. No, it was the look on Connie's face when I waved the surveillance transcript at her like a starter's flag (Race you to the end of the marriage; go!). Not contrite, guilty, apologetic, remorseful. Not even angry, outraged, indignant.

Stone-faced. Arms folded. She had said: "You don't even know me."

And she was right; I'd been too busy *not* knowing myself to take a stab at knowing her.

Off the roller-coaster, swinging through familiar residential streets, trash cans and recycle containers arranged at the curb like clusters of strange little people waiting for the midnight bus. I lived here, when I wasn't off inflicting merry hell upon various persons who sometimes deserved it and sometimes didn't. These days I resorted to more enlightened methodologies, of course. Physical pain was a last resort. Guatemala had been an ugly aberration (I liked to tell myself), a putrid confluence of political license and personal demons unleashed in the first fetid sewage swell of the so-called War On Terror. Anyway, the neighborhood reminded me of the one I wished I'd grown up in. But it was a façade. I was hell on façades, too.

And there was Connie, lifting the lid off our very own little strange man, depositing a tied-off plastic bag of kitchen garbage. Standing there in the middle of the night, changed from her business suit to Levi's and sweatshirt and her cozy blue slippers, performing this routine task as if our world (my world) hadn't collapsed into the black hole of her infidelity.

Connie as object, focal of pain. Target.

Anger sprang up fresh through the fog of impermissible emotion and numbing alcohol.

My foot crushed the accelerator, the big Tahoe surged, veered; I was out of my mind, not myself—that's the spin I gave it later.

The way she dropped the bag, the headlights bleaching her out in death-glare brilliance. At the last instant I closed my eyes. Something hit the windshield, rolled over the roof. A moment later the Tahoe struck the brick and wrought-iron property wall and came to an abrupt halt.

I lifted my head off the steering wheel, wiped the blood out of my eyes. The windshield was intricately webbed, buckled inward. That was my house out there, the front door standing open to lamplight, mellow wood tones, that ficus plant Connie kept in the entry.

Connie.

I released my seatbelt and tried to open the door. Splintered ribs scraped together, razored my flesh, and I screamed, suddenly stone-cold and agonizingly sober. I tried the door again, less aggressively. My razor ribs scraped and cut. Okay. One more time. Force of will. I bit down on my lip and put my shoulder to the door. It wouldn't budge, the frame was twisted out of alignment. I sat back, panting, drenched in sweat. And I saw it: Connie's blue slipper flat against what was left of the windshield. Time suspended. *That bitch.* And the Johnstown flood of tears. Delayed reaction triggered. As a child I'd learned not to cry. I'd watched my mother weep her soul out to no changeable effect. I'd done some weeping, too. Also to no effect. Dad was dad; this is your world. Lesson absorbed, along with the blows. But sitting in the wreck of the Tahoe, my marriage, my life, I made up for lost tears; I knew what I had become, and was repulsed. The vault at the bottom of my mind yawned opened, releasing the shrieking ghosts of Guatemala.

You see, it's all related. Compartmentalization aside, if you cross the taboo boundary in one compartment you're liable to cross it in all the others.

By the time the cops arrived the ghosts were muffled again, and I was done with weeping. Vault secured, walls hastily erected, fortifications against the pain I'd absorbed and the later pain I'd learn to inflict. The irreducible past. Barricades were my specialty.

• • •

The Agency stepped in, determined I could remain a valuable asset, and took care of my "accident," the details, the police.

• • •

Flip forward again.

You *can* be a drunk and hold a top secret clearance. But you must be a careful one. And it helps if your relationship with the Agency is informally defined. I was in my basement office *carefully* drawing the cork out of a good bottle of Riesling when Andy McCaslin called on the secure line. I lived in that basement, since Connie's death, the house above me like a rotting corpse of memory. Okay, it wasn't that bad. I hadn't been around enough to turn the house into a memory corpse; I just preferred basements and shadows.

"Andy," I said into the receiver, my voice Gibraltar steady, even though the Riesling was far from my first libation of the long day. Unlike Dad, I'd learned to space it out, to *maintain*.

"Brian. Listen, I'm picking you up. We're going for a drive in the desert. Give me an hour to get there. Wear something warm."

I wore the whole bottle, from the inside out.

• • •

The moon was a white poker chip. The desert slipped past us, cold blue with black ink shadows. We rode in Andy's private vehicle, a late model Jeep Cherokee. He had already been driving all day, having departed from the L.A. office that morning, dropping everything to pursue "something like a dream" that had beckoned to him.

"Care to reveal our destination?" I asked.

"I don't want to tell you anything beforehand. It might influence you, give you some preconception. Your mind has to be clear or this won't work."

"Okay, I'll think only happy thoughts."

"Good. Hang on, by the way."

He slowed, then suddenly pulled off the two-lane road. We jolted over desert hardpan. Scrub brush clawed at the Cherokee's undercarriage.

"Ah, the road's back thataway," I said.

He nodded and kept going. A bumpy twenty minutes or so passed. Then we stopped, for no obvious reason, and he killed the engine. I looked around. We were exactly in the middle of nowhere. It looked a lot like my personal mental landscape.

"I know this isn't a joke," I said, "because you are not a funny guy."

"Come on."

We got out. Andy was tall, Scotch-Irish, big through the shoulders and gut. He was wearing a sheepskin jacket, jeans and cowboy boots. A real shit-kickin' son of a bitch. Yee haw. He had a few other sheepskins somewhere, but his walls were wearing *those*. I followed him away from the Jeep.

"Tell me what you see," he said.

I looked around.

"Not much."

"Be specific."

I cleared my throat. "Okay. Empty desert, scrub brush, cactus. Lots of sand. There is no doubt a large population of venomous snakes slithering underfoot looking for something to bite, though I don't exactly *see* them. There's also a pretty moon in the sky. So?"

I rubbed my hands together, shifted my feet. I'd worn a Sun Devils sweatshirt, which was insufficient. Besides that I could have used a drink. But of course these days I could always use a drink. After a lifetime of grimly determined sobriety I'd discovered that booze was an effective demon-suppressor and required exactly the opposite of willpower, which is what I'd been relying on up till Connie's death. I have no idea what my *father's* demons might have been. He checked out by a self-inflicted route before we got around to discussing that. I almost did the same a couple of years later, while in the thick of Ranger training, where I'd fled in desperate quest of discipline and structure and a sense of belonging to something. Andy talked me out of shooting myself and afterwards kept the incident private. I sometimes wondered whether he regretted that. Offing myself may have been part of a balancing equation designed to subtract a measure of suffering from the world.

Now, in the desert, he withdrew a pack of Camels from his coat pocket and lit up. I remembered my dad buying his packs at the 7-Eleven, when I was a little kid.

"Hey, you don't smoke," I said to Andy.

"I don't? What do you call this?" He waved the cigarette at me. "Look, Brian, what would you say if I told you we were standing outside a large military installation?"

"I'd say okay, but it must be invisible."

"It is."

I laughed. Andy didn't.

"Come on," I said.

"All right, it's not invisible. But it's not exactly *here*, either."

"That I can see. Can't see?"

"Close your eyes."

"Then I won't be able to see *anything*, including the invisible military installation."

"Do it anyway," he said. "Trust me. I've done this before. So have you, probably." I hesitated. Andy was a good guy—my friend, or the closest thing to one that I'd ever allowed. But it now crossed my mind that my informal status vis-à-vis the Agency was about to become *terminally* informal. Certainly there was precedent. We who work on the fringes where the rules don't constrain our actions are also subject to the anything-goes approach on the part of our handlers. Was I on the verge of being…severed? By *Andy McCaslin?* He stood before me with his damn cigarette, smoke drifting from his lips, his eyes black as oil in the moonlight.

"Trust me, Brian."

Maybe it was the lingering wine buzz. But I decided I *did* trust him, or needed to, because he was the only one I ever *had* trusted. I closed my eyes. The breeze carried his smoke into my face. My dad had been redolent of that stink. Not a good sense-memory. But when I was little I loved the *look* of the cigarette cartons and packages, the way my dad would say, Pack a Camels non-filter, and the clerk would turn to the rack behind him and pick out the right one, like a game show.

"Now relax your mind," Andy said.

"Consider it relaxed, Swami."

"Try to be serious."

"I'll try."

"Remember the empty mind trick they taught us, in case we ever got ourselves captured by unfriendlies?"

"Sure."

"Do that. Empty your mind."

It was easy, and I didn't learn it from the Army. I learned it at my father's knee, you might say. Survival technique number one: Empty your mind. Don't be there. Don't hear the screaming, even your own.

Andy said, "I'm going to say a word. When I do, let your mind fill with whatever the word evokes."

I nodded, waited, smelling the Camel smoke, my head not empty in the way Andy wanted it to be. I was too preoccupied by a memory of smoke.

"Arrowhead," Andy said.

I felt…something.

Andy said, "Shit." And then, "What you are about to see is real. Okay, open your eyes."

We were now standing outside a 7-Eleven store. The desert ran right up to the walls. A tumbleweed bumped against the double glass doors. The interior was brightly lit. In the back I could make out a pair of Slurpee machines slow-swirling icy drinks in primary colors. After a while I closed my mouth and turned to Andy.

"Where the hell did *this* come from?"

"Instant Unconsciously Directed Association. You like that? I made it up. Only I don't know why this should be your Eyeooda for Arrowhead. I was hoping you'd bring up the real place. Anyway, let's go inside while it lasts."

He started forward but I grabbed his arm.

"Wait a minute. Are we still operating under the disengagement of preconceived notions policy, or whatever?"

He thought about it for a moment then said, "I guess not, now that we're sharing a consensus reality. Brian, this 7-Eleven is actually the Arrowhead Installation."

The coal of an extinguished memory glowed dimly. I *knew* Arrowhead, or thought I did. A top secret base located more or less in that part of the Arizona desert in which we now found ourselves. Or was/did it? The memory was so enfeebled that if I didn't hold it just *so* it would blow away like dandelion fluff. Still, this wasn't a military base; it was a convenience store.

"Bullshit?" I said.

"*Do* you remember Arrowhead?" Andy asked.

"Sort of. What is this, what's going on?"

"Listen to me, Brian. We finally got one. We finally got an honest to God extraterrestrial—and it's *in there*."

"In the 7-Eleven."

"No. In the Arrowhead facility that looks like a 7-Eleven in our present consensus reality. The alien is hiding itself and the installation in some kind of stealth transdimensional mirror trick, or something. I've *been* here before. So have you. Our dreams can still remember. I've come out to the desert—I don't know, dozens of times? I've talked to it, the alien. It shuffles reality. I keep waking up, then going back to sleep.

Here's the thing. It can cloak its prison, reinterpret its appearance, but it can't escape."

I regarded him skeptically, did some mental shuffling of my own, discarded various justifiable but unproductive responses, and said: "What's it want?"

"It wants you to let it go."

"Why me?"

"Ask it yourself. But watch out. That little fucker is messing with our heads."

•••

The store was empty. It was so quiet you could hear the dogs popping with grease as they rotated inside their little hot box. Okay, it wasn't *that* quiet, but it was quiet. I picked up a green disposable lighter and flicked it a couple of times, kind of checking out the consensus reality. It lit.

Andy went around the counter and ducked his head into the back room.

"What are you doing?" I asked.

"Looking for Squidward."

"Squidward?"

"Yeah."

Another dim memory glowed in the dark. For some reason I thought of the Seattle aquarium, where my father had taken us when I was little. It hadn't been a fun experience. I remembered being vaguely repelled by some of the exotically alien examples of undersea creatures. Prescient echo from the future?

Andy snapped his fingers. "Right. Squidward likes it cool."

I followed him into the cold storage run behind the beer, pop and dairy coolers. A man sat on a couple of stacked cases of Rolling Rock, his legs crossed at the knees, hands folded over them. He looked Indian, that nut-brown complexion. He was wearing a lavender suit.

"Squidward," Andy said.

I tucked my hands snuggly under my armpits for warmth. "Has he asked to be taken to our leader yet?"

"I don't remember."

Squidward spoke up: "You are the torturer."

We both looked at him.

"Sorry, not my gig," I said.

Squidward nodded. "Your gig, yes."

Something unsavory uncoiled in my stomach, then lay still again.

"Andy," I said, nodding toward the door.

He followed me out into the glaring light of the store.

"Talk to me," I said.

He nodded, distracted. "I'm remembering most of it, but who knows what I'll retain next time around. R&D developed some kind of souped-up spectrophotometer gizmo as a hedge against future stealth technology we suspected the Chinese were developing. During a middle phase test in Nevada we saw a vehicle doing some impossible maneuvers, somehow hiding between waves in the visible light spectrum. Naturally we shot it down."

"Naturally."

Andy clutched his pack of Camels, plugged one in his mouth, patted his pockets for matches. I handed him the Zippo.

"Thanks."

He lit up.

"Anyway, it turns out we're as much his captive as he is ours. Uh oh."

Andy's cigarette dropped from his lips, depositing feathery ash down the front of his sheepskin jacket. He blinked slowly, his eyes going out of focus, or perhaps refocusing inward.

"Oh, shit," he said.

"What?"

"Not again. I have to get *away* from this."

He turned and stumped out of the store with the sloppy gait of a somnambulist.

"Hey—"

Outside the night absorbed him. I stiff-armed the door. Cold desert wind blew in my face. Andy was gone. So was the Cherokee. But he hadn't driven away in it. I looked around where it had been parked. There were no tire impressions, nothing, just my warped shadow cast over the tawny grit.

I turned back to the 7-Eleven, its solid, glaring reality. I don't know what hackles are exactly, but mine rose to attention. Out here in the desert, alone with a persistent illusion, I felt reduced. Childish fears came awake.

Exerting my will to power or whatever, I entered the store. The Slurpee machine hummed and swirled, hotdogs rotated. The fluorescent light seemed to stutter *inside* my head.

I looked at the coolers, the orderly ranks of bottles and cartons. Damn it.

I approached the door to the cold storage, put my hand on the lever. Fear ran through me like electric current. I felt the world begin to waver, and stepped back. The door, silver with a thick rubber seal, appeared to melt before my eyes. I felt myself slipping away, and so brought the force of my will down like a steel spike. The door resumed its expected appearance. I immediately cranked the handle and dragged it open.

Squidward sat on his beer case stool in exactly the same position he'd been in ten minutes ago.

"Make it stop," I said.

"I don't make things," he replied. "I allow the multiplicity to occur."

"Okay. So stop allowing the multiplicity."

"Not possible, I'm afraid. My survival imperative is searching for a probability in which you haven't killed me."

"But I *haven't* killed you."

"You have."

I stepped toward him. That steel spike? Now it was penetrating my forehead, driving in.

"What do you want from us?"

"From you I want to live," Squidward said. "We are bound until the death is allowed or not allowed, conclusively. I have perceived the occurrence of my expiration at your direction, unintended though it will be. Having access to all points of probability time in my sequence, I foresee this eventuality and seek for a probability equation that spares me. From your perspective also this is a desirable outcome. Without me to monitor and shuffle your world's probabilities the vision vouchsafed by your military leader may well occur."

My eyesight shifted into pre-migraine mode. Pinwheel lights encroached upon my peripheral vision. I ground the heels of my hands into my eyes, fighting it, fighting it, fighting...

• • •

Probabilities shuffled...

• • •

I woke up next to my wife. In the ticking darkness of our bedroom I breathed a name: "Andy."

Connie shifted position, cuddling into me. Her familiar body. I put my arm around her and stared into the dark, hunting elusive memories. Without them I wasn't who I thought I was. After a while Connie asked:

"What's wrong?"

"I don't know. I think I was having a dream about Andy McCaslin. It woke me up."

"Who?"

"Guy I knew from the Rangers, long time ago. I told you about him. We were friends."

Connie suppressed a yawn. "He died, didn't he? You never said how."

"Covert op in Central America. He found himself in the custody of some rebels."

"Oh."

"They kept him alive for weeks while they interrogated him."

"God. Are you—"

"That was decades ago, Con. Dreams are strange, sometimes."

I slipped out of the bed.

"Where are you going?"

"Have some tea and think for a while. My night's shot anyway."

"Want company?"

"Maybe I'll sit by myself. Go back to sleep. You've got an early one."

"Sure? I could make some eggs or something."

"No, I'm good."

But I wasn't. In my basement office, consoling tea near at hand, I contemplated my dead friend and concluded he wasn't supposed to be that way. My old dreams of pain surged up out of the place at the bottom of my mind, the place that enclosed Andy and what I knew had happened to him, the place of batteries and alligator clips, hemp ropes, sharpened bamboo slivers, the vault of horrors far worse than any I'd endured as a child and from which I fled to the serenity of an office cubicle and regular hours.

But that wasn't *supposed* to have happened, not to Andy. I rubbed my temple, eyes closed in the dim basement office, and suddenly a word spoke itself on my lips:

Squidward.

...

My name is Brian Kinney, and today I am not an alcoholic. My *father* was an alcoholic who could not restrain his demons. During my childhood those demons frequently emerged to torment me and my mother. Dad's goodness, which was true and present, was not enough to balance the equation between pain and love. I had been skewing toward my own demon-haunted landscape when Andy McCaslin took my gun from my hand and balanced out the equation for me.

My new world order.

...

I'm driving through the moonless Arizona desert at two o'clock in the morning, looking for a turn-off that doesn't exist. After an hour or so a peculiar, hovering pink light appears in the distance, far off the road. I slow, angle onto the berm, ease the Outback down to the desert floor, and go bucketing overland toward the light.

...

A giant pink soap bubble hovered above the 7-Eleven. Reflective lights inside the bubble appeared to track away into infinity. It was hard not to stare at it. I got out of my car and entered the store. The Indian gentleman in the lavender suit emerged from the cold storage run, a small suitcase in his left hand.

"What goes on?" I said.

"You remember," he said, more command than comment.

And at that instant I did remember. Not just the bits and pieces that had drawn me out here, but *everything*.

"My survival imperative sought for a probability equation by which my death could be avoided. You are now inhabiting that equation. With your permission I will, too."

"What do you need my permission for?"

"You would be the author of my death, so you must also be the willing author of my continued existence. A law of probability and balance."

I thought about Connie back home in bed, the unfathomable cruelty of my former probability, the feeling of restored sanity. Like waking up in the life I *should* have had in the first place. But I also thought of Andy, and I knew it had to go back.

"No," I said to Squidward.

"You must."

"Not if my friend has to die. By the way, isn't it a little warm for you?"

Squidward smiled. "I'm already in my ship."

"Only if I allow it."

"You will, I hope."

"It's the feathery thing," I said.

"Behold."

In my mind's eye images of unimaginable carnage appeared, then winked out. I staggered.

"I am a Monitor, coded from birth to your world's psychic evolution," Squidward said. "I subtly shuffle the broad probabilities in order to prevent what you have just seen. Without me there is a high probability of worldwide military and environmental catastrophe. Such eventualities may be avoided and your species may survive to evolve into an advanced civilization."

"That sounds swell, but I don't believe you. You've been doing plenty of shuffling in captivity. With that power why do you need anything from *me?*"

"That's merely my survival imperative, drawing on etheric energy from my ship's transphysical manifestation. My survival, and perhaps your world's, depends on you permitting this probability to dominate."

I didn't allow myself to think about it.

"Let the original probability resume," I said.

"Please," Squidward said.

"Let it go back to the way it's supposed to be."

"There are no 'supposed to be' probability equations."

I crossed my arms.

Squidward put his suitcase down. "Then because of what you are you will doom me. My probabilities concluded."

"Because of what I am."

"Yes."

•••

Shuffle.

...

My name is Brian Kinney, and I am the sum total of the experience inflicted upon me.

But not only that. I hope.

...

The Tahoe's deadly acceleration. Sudden synaptic realization across the probabilities: *You are about to murder your wife.* The Vault Of Screams yawns open.

Will.

Hanging on the wheel, foot fumbling between pedals.

That big green Rubbermaid trash can bouncing over the hood, contents erupting against the windshield. It was just garbage, though.

Then a very sudden stop when the Tahoe plows into the low brick and wrought-iron property wall. Gut punch of the steering wheel, rupturing something inside my body. And don't forget a side of razor ribs.

Around the middle of my longish convalescence Connie arrives during visiting hours, and eventually a second convalescence begins. A convalescence of the heart. Not mine in particular, or Connie's, but the one we shared in common. The one we had systematically poisoned over the preceding ten years. Okay, the one *I* had systematically poisoned.

Watershed event.

Happy ending?

...

It sat in a cold room.

Outside that room I watched a perfectly squared-away marine enter a code into the cipher pad. I was the sum total my inflicted experience, but it was the new math. The door opened, like a bank vault. Andy Mc-Caslin looked at me with a puzzled expression.

He was alone in the room.

AMANDA AND THE ALIEN

ROBERT SILVERBERG

Amanda spotted the alien late Friday afternoon outside the Video Center, on South Main. It was trying to look cool and laid-back, but it simply came across as bewildered and uneasy. The alien was disguised as a seventeen-year-old girl, maybe a Chicana, with olive-toned skin and hair so black it seemed almost blue, but Amanda, who was seventeen herself, knew a phony when she saw one. She studied the alien for some moments from the other side of the street to make absolutely certain. Then she walked over.

"You're doing it wrong," Amanda said. "Anybody with half a brain could tell what you really are."

"Bug off," the alien said.

"No. Listen to me. You want to stay out of the detention center, or don't you?"

The alien stared coldly at Amanda and said, "I don't know what the crap you're talking about."

"Sure you do. No sense trying to bluff me. Look, I want to help you,"

Amanda said. "I think you're getting a raw deal. You know what that means, a raw deal? Hey, look, come home with me, and I'll teach you a few things about passing for human. I've got the whole friggin' weekend now with nothing else to do anyway."

A flicker of interest came into the other girl's dark, chilly eyes. But it died quickly, and she said, "You some kind of lunatic?"

"Suit yourself, O thing from beyond the stars. *Let* them lock you up again. *Let* them stick electrodes up your ass. I tried to help. That's all I can do, is try," Amanda said, shrugging. She began to saunter away. She didn't look back. Three steps, four, five, hands in pockets, slowly heading for her car. Had she been wrong, she wondered? No. No. She could be wrong about some things, like Charley Taylor's interest in spending the weekend with her, maybe. But not this. That crinkly-haired chick was the missing alien for sure.

The whole county was buzzing about it: Deadly nonhuman life form has escaped from the detention center out by Tracy, might be anywhere, Walnut Creek, Livermore, even San Francisco, dangerous monster, capable of mimicking human forms, will engulf and digest you and disguise itself in your shape. And there it was, Amanda knew, standing outside the Video Center. Amanda kept walking.

"Wait," the alien said finally.

Amanda took another easy step or two. Then she looked back over her shoulder.

"Yeah?"

"How can you tell?"

Amanda grinned. "Easy. You've got a rain slicker on, and it's only September. Rainy season doesn't start around here for another month or two. Your pants are the old Spandex kind. People like you don't wear that stuff anymore. Your face paint is San Jose colors, but you've got the cheek chevrons put on in the Berkeley pattern. That's just the first three things I noticed. I could find plenty more. Nothing about you fits together with anything else. It's like you did a survey to see how you ought to appear and then tried a little of everything. The closer I study you, the more I see. Look, you're wearing your headphones, and the battery light is on, but there's no cassette in the slot. What are you listening to, the music of the spheres? That model doesn't have any FM tuner, you know.

"You see? You may think that you're perfectly camouflaged, but you aren't."

"I could destroy you," the alien said.

"What? Oh, sure. Sure you could. Engulf me right here on the street, all over in thirty seconds, little trail of slime by the door, and a new Amanda walks away. But what then? What good's that going to do you? You still won't know which end is up. So there's no logic in destroying me, unless you're a total dummy. I'm on your side. I'm not going to turn you in."

"Why should I trust you?"

"Because I've been talking to you for five minutes and I haven't yelled for the cops yet. Don't you know that half of California is out searching for you? Hey, can you read? Come over here a minute. Here." Amanda tugged the alien toward the newspaper vending box at the curb. The headline on the afternoon *Examiner* was:

BAY AREA ALIEN TERROR
MARINES TO JOIN NINE-COUNTY HUNT
MAYOR, GOVERNOR CAUTION AGAINST PANIC

"You understand that?" Amanda asked. "That's you they're talking about. They're out there with flame guns, tranquilizer darts, web snares, and God knows what else. There's been real hysteria for a day and a half. And you standing around here with the wrong chevrons on! Christ. Christ! What's your plan, anyway? Where are you trying to go?"

"Home," the alien said. "But first I have to rendezvous at the pickup point."

"Where's that?"

"You think I'm stupid?"

"Shit," Amanda said. "If I meant to turn you in, I'd have done it five minutes ago. But, okay, I don't give a damn where your rendezvous point is. I tell you, though, you wouldn't make it as far as San Francisco rigged up the way you are. It's a miracle you've avoided getting caught until now."

"And you'll help me?"

"I've been trying to. Come on. Let's get the hell out of here. I'll take you home and fix you up a little. My car's in the lot down on the next corner."

"Okay."

"Whew!" Amanda shook her head slowly. "Christ, some people sure can't take help when you try to offer it."

As she drove out of the center of town, Amanda glanced occasionally at the alien sitting tensely to her right. Basically the disguise was very convincing, Amanda thought. Maybe all the small details were wrong, the outer stuff, the anthropological stuff, but the alien *looked* human, it *sounded* human, it even *smelled* human. Possibly it could fool ninety-nine people out of a hundred, or maybe more than that. But Amanda had always had a good eye for detail. And at the particular moment she had spotted the alien on South Main she had been unusually alert, sensitive, all raw nerves, every antenna up.

Of course it wasn't aliens she was hunting for, but just a diversion, a little excitement, something to fill the great gaping emptiness that Charley Taylor had left in her weekend.

Amanda had been planning the weekend with Charley all month. Her parents were going to go off to Lake Tahoe for three days, her kid sister had wangled permission to accompany them, and Amanda was going to have the house to herself, just her and Macavity the cat. And Charley. He was going to move in on Friday afternoon, and they'd cook dinner together and get blasted on her stash of choice powder and watch five or six of her parents' X-rated cassettes, and Saturday they'd drive over to the city and cruise some of the kinky districts and go to that bathhouse on Folsom where everybody got naked and climbed into the giant Jacuzzi, and then on Sunday—Well, none of that was going to happen. Charley had called on Thursday to cancel. "Something big came up," he said, and Amanda had a pretty good idea what that was, his hot little cousin from New Orleans, who sometimes came flying out here on no notice at all, but the inconsiderate bastard seemed to be entirely unaware of how much Amanda had been looking forward to this weekend, how much it meant to her, how painful it was to be dumped like this. She had run through the planned events of the weekend in her mind so many times that she almost felt as if she had experienced them. It was that real to her. But overnight it had become unreal.

Three whole days on her own, the house to herself, and so early in the semester that there was no homework to think about, and Charley had stood her up! What was she supposed to do now, call desperately around town to scrounge up some old lover as a playmate? Or pick up some stranger downtown? Amanda hated to fool around with strangers. She was half-tempted to go over to the city and just let things happen, but they were all weirdoes and creeps over there, anyway, and she knew what she could expect from them. What a waste, not having Charley! She could kill him for robbing her of the weekend.

Now there was the alien, though. A dozen of these star people had come to Earth last year, not in a flying saucer as everybody had expected, but in little capsules that floated like milkweed seeds, and they had landed in a wide arc between San Diego and Salt Lake City.

Their natural form, so far as anyone could tell, was something like a huge jellyfish with a row of staring purple eyes down one wavy margin, but their usual tactic was to borrow any local body they found, digest it, and turn themselves into an accurate imitation of it. One of them had made the mistake of turning itself into a brown mountain bear and another into a bobcat—maybe they thought that those were the dominant life forms on Earth—but the others had taken on human bodies, at the cost of at least ten lives.

Then they went looking to make contact with government leaders, and naturally they were rounded up very swiftly and interned, some in mental hospitals and some in county jails, but eventually—as soon as the truth of what they really were sank in—they were all put in a special detention camp in Northern California.

Of course a tremendous fuss was made over them, endless stuff in the papers and on the tube, speculation by this heavy thinker and that about the significance of their mission, the nature of their biochemistry, a little wild talk about the possibility that more of their kind might be waiting undetected out there and plotting to do God knows what, and all sorts of that stuff. Then came a government clamp on the entire subject, no official announcements except that "discussions" with the visitors were continuing, and after a while the whole thing degenerated into dumb alien jokes ("Why did the alien cross the road?") and Halloween invader masks. Then it moved into the background of everyone's attention and was forgotten.

And remained forgotten until the announcement that one of the creatures had slipped out of the camp somehow and was loose within a hundred-mile zone around San Francisco. Preoccupied as she was with her anguish over Charley's heartlessness, even Amanda had managed to pick up *that* news item. And now the alien was in her very car. So there'd be some weekend amusement for her after all. Amanda was entirely unafraid of the alleged deadliness of the star being: Whatever else the alien might be, it was surely no dope, not if it had been picked to come halfway across the galaxy on a mission like this, and Amanda knew that the alien could see that harming her was not going to be in its own best interests. The alien had need of her, and the alien realized that. And Amanda, in some way that she was only just beginning to work out, had need of the alien.

•••

She pulled up outside her house, a compact split-level at the western end of town. "This is the place," she said.

Heat shimmers danced in the air, and the hills back of the house, parched in the long dry summer, were the color of lions.

Macavity, Amanda's old tabby, sprawled in the shade of the bottlebrush tree on the ragged front lawn. As Amanda and the alien approached, the cat sat up warily, flattened his ears, and hissed. The alien immediately moved into a defensive posture, sniffing the air.

"Just a household pet," Amanda said. "You know what that is? He isn't dangerous. He's always a little suspicious of strangers."

Which was untrue. An earthquake couldn't have brought Macavity out of his nap, and a cotillion of mice dancing minuets on his tail wouldn't have drawn a reaction from him. Amanda calmed him with some fur ruffling, but he wanted nothing to do with the alien and went slinking sullenly into the underbrush. The alien watched him with care until he was out of sight.

"Do you have anything like cats back on your planet?" Amanda asked as they went inside.

"We had small wild animals once. They were unnecessary."

"Oh," Amanda said, losing interest. The house had a stuffy, stagnant air. She switched on the air conditioning. "Where is your planet, anyway?"

The alien pointedly ignored the question. It padded around the living room, very much like a prowling cat itself, studying the stereo, the television, the couches, the coffee table, and the vase of dried flowers.

"Is this a typical Earthian home?"

"More or less," said Amanda. "Typical for around here, at least. This is what we call a suburb. It's half an hour by freeway from here to San Francisco. That's a city. I'll take you over there tonight or tomorrow for a look, if you're interested." She got some music going, high volume. The alien didn't seem to mind; so she notched the volume up even more. "I'm going to take a shower. You could use one, too, actually."

"Shower? You mean rain?"

"I mean body-cleaning activities. We Earthlings like to wash a lot, to get rid of sweat and dirt and stuff. It's considered bad form to stink. Come on, I'll show you how to do it. You've got to do what I do if you want to keep from getting caught, you know." She led the alien to the bathroom. "Take your clothes off first."

The alien stripped. Underneath its rain slicker it wore a stained T-shirt that said FISHERMAN'S WHARF, with a picture of the San Francisco skyline, and a pair of unzipped jeans. Under that it was wearing a black brassiere, unfastened and with the cups over its shoulder blades, and a pair of black shiny panty-briefs with a red heart on the left buttock. The alien's body was that of a lean, tough-looking girl with a scar running down the inside of one arm.

"By the way, whose body is that?" Amanda asked. "Do you know?"

"She worked at the detention center. In the kitchen."

"You know her name?"

"Flores Concepcion."

"The other way around, probably. Concepcion Flores. I'll call you Connie, unless you want to give me your real name."

"Connie will do."

"All right, Connie. Pay attention. You turn the water on here, and you adjust the mix of hot and cold until you like it. Then you pull this knob and get underneath the spout here and wet your body and rub soap over it and wash the soap off. Afterward you dry yourself and put fresh clothes on. You have to clean your clothes from time to time, too, because otherwise *they* start to smell, and it upsets people. Watch me shower, and then you do it."

Amanda washed quickly, while plans hummed in her head. The alien wasn't going to last long wearing the body of Concepcion Flores. Sooner or later someone was going to notice that one of the kitchen girls was missing, and they'd get an all-points alarm out for her. Amanda wondered whether the alien had figured that out yet. The alien, Amanda thought, needs a different body in a hurry.

But not mine, she told herself. For sure, not mine.

"Your turn," she said casually, shutting the water off.

The alien, fumbling a little, turned the water back on and got under the spray. Clouds of steam rose, and its skin began to look boiled, but it didn't appear troubled. No sense of pain? "Hold it," Amanda said. "Step back." She adjusted the water. "You've got it too hot. You'll damage that body that way. Look, if you can't tell the difference between hot and cold, just take cold showers, okay? It's less dangerous. This is cold, on this side."

She left the alien under the shower and went to find some clean clothes. When she came back, the alien was still showering, under icy water. "Enough," Amanda said. "Here. Put these clothes on."

"I had more clothes than this before."

"A T-shirt and jeans are all you need in hot weather like this. With your kind of build you can skip the bra, and anyway I don't think you'll be able to fasten it the right way."

"Do we put the face paint on now?"

"We can skip it while we're home. It's just stupid kid stuff anyway, all that tribal crap. If we go out we'll do it, and we'll give you Walnut Creek colors, I think. Concepcion wore San Jose, but we want to throw people off the track. How about some dope?"

"What?"

"Grass. Marijuana. A drug widely used by local Earthians of our age."

"I don't need no drug."

"I don't, either. But I'd *like* some. You ought to learn how, just in case you find yourself in a social situation." Amanda reached for her pack of Filter Golds and pulled out a joint. Expertly she tweaked its lighter tip and took a deep hit. "Here," she said, passing it. "Hold it like I did. Put it to your mouth, breathe in, suck the smoke deep." The alien dragged the joint and began to cough. "Not so deep, maybe," Amanda said. "Take just a little. Hold it. Let it out. There, much better. Now give me back the joint. You've got to keep passing it back and forth. That part's important. You feel anything from it?"

"No."

"It can be subtle. Don't worry about it. Are you hungry?"

"Not yet," the alien said.

"I am. Come into the kitchen." As she assembled a sandwich—peanut butter and avocado on whole wheat, with tomato and onion—she asked, "What sort of things do you guys eat?"

"Life."

"Life?"

"We never eat dead things. Only things with life."

Amanda fought back a shudder. "I see. *Anything* with life?"

"We prefer animal life. We can absorb plants if necessary."

"Ah. Yes. And when are you going to be hungry again?"

"Maybe tonight," the alien said. "Or tomorrow. The hunger comes very suddenly, when it comes."

"There's not much around here that you could eat live. But I'll work on it."

"The small furry animal?"

"No. My cat is not available for dinner. Get that idea right out of your head. Likewise me. I'm your protector and guide. It wouldn't be sensible to eat me. You follow what I'm trying to tell you?"

"I said that I'm not hungry yet."

"Well, you let me know when you start feeling the pangs. I'll find you a meal." Amanda began to construct a second sandwich. The alien prowled the kitchen, examining the appliances. Perhaps making mental records, Amanda thought, of sink and oven design, to copy on its home world. Amanda said, "Why did you people come here in the first place?"

"It was our mission."

"Yes. Sure. But for what purpose? What are you after? You want to take over the world? You want to steal our scientific secrets?" The alien, making no reply, began taking spices out of the spice rack. Delicately it licked its finger, touched it to the oregano, tasted it, tried the cumin. Amanda said, "Or is it that you want to keep us from going into space? You think we're a dangerous species, and so you're going to quarantine us on our own planet? Come on, you can tell me. I'm not a government spy." The alien sampled the tarragon, the basil, the sage. When it reached for the curry powder, its hand suddenly shook so violently that it knocked the open jars of oregano and tarragon over, making a mess. "Hey, are you all right?" Amanda asked.

The alien said, "I think I'm getting hungry. Are these things drugs, too?"

"Spices," Amanda said. "We put them in our foods to make them taste better." The alien was looking very strange, glassy-eyed, flushed, sweaty. "Are you feeling sick or something?"

"I feel excited. These powders—"

"They're turning you on? Which one?"

"This, I think." It pointed to the oregano. "It was either the first one or the second."

"Yeah," Amanda said. "Oregano. It can really make you fly." She wondered whether the alien would get violent when zonked. Or whether the oregano would stimulate its appetite. She had to watch out for its appetite. There are certain risks, Amanda reflected, in doing what I'm doing. Deftly she cleaned up the spilled oregano and tarragon and put the caps on the spice jars. "You ought to be careful," she said. "Your metabolism isn't used to this stuff. A little can go a long way."

"Give me some more."

"Later," Amanda said. "You don't want to overdo it too early in the day."

"More!"

"Calm down. I know this planet better than you, and I don't want to see you get in trouble. Trust me. I'll let you have more oregano when it's the right time. Look at the way you're shaking. And you're sweating like crazy." Pocketing the oregano jar, she led the alien back into the living room. "Sit down. Relax."

"More? Please?"

"I appreciate your politeness. But we have important things to talk about, and then I'll give you some. Okay?" Amanda opaqued the window, through which the hot late-afternoon sun was coming. Six o'clock on Friday, and if everything had gone the right way Charley would have been showing up just about now. Well, she'd found a different diversion. The weekend stretched before her like an open road leading to mysteryland. The alien offered all sorts of possibilities, and she might yet have some fun over the next few days, if she used her head. Amanda turned to the alien and said, "You calmer now? Yes. Good. Okay, first of all, you've got to get yourself another body."

"Why is that?"

"I've reasons. One is that the authorities are probably searching for the girl you absorbed. How you got as far as you did without anybody but me spotting you is hard to understand. Number two, a teen-aged girl traveling by herself is going to get hassled too much, and you don't know how to handle yourself in a tight situation. You know what I'm saying? You're going to want to hitchhike out to Nevada, Wyoming, Utah, wherever the hell your rendezvous place is, and all along the way people are going to be coming on to you. You don't need any of that. Besides, it's very tricky trying to pass for a girl. You've got to know how to put your face paint on, how to understand challenge codes, what the way you wear your clothing says, and like that. Boys have a much simpler subculture. You get yourself a male body, a big hunk of a body, and nobody'll bother you much on the way to where you're going. You just keep to yourself, don't make eye contact, don't smile, and everyone will leave you alone."

"Makes sense," said the alien. "All right. The hunger is becoming very bad now. Where do I get a male body?"

"San Francisco. It's full of men. We'll go over there tonight and find a nice brawny one for you. With any luck we might even find one who's not gay, and then we can have a little fun with him first. And then you take his body over—which incidentally solves your food problem for a while doesn't it? And we can have some more fun, a whole weekend of fun." Amanda winked. "Okay, Connie?"

"Okay." The alien winked, a clumsy imitation, first one eye, then the other. "You give me more oregano now?"

"Later. And when you wink, just wink *one* eye. Like this. Except I don't think you ought to do a lot of winking at people. It's a very intimate gesture that could get you in trouble. Understand?"

"There's so much to understand."

"You're on a strange planet, kid. Did you expect it to be just like home? Okay, to continue. The next thing I ought to point out is that when you leave here on Sunday, you'll have to—"

The telephone rang.

"What's that sound?" the alien asked.

"Communications device. I'll be right back." Amanda went to the hall extension, imagining the worst: her parents, say, calling to announce that they were on their way back from Tahoe tonight, some mix-up in the reservations or something.

But the voice that greeted her was Charley's. She could hardly believe it, after the casual way he had shafted her this weekend. She could hardly believe what he wanted, either. He had left half a dozen of his best cassettes at her place last week, Golden Age rock, *Abbey Road* and the Hendrix one and a Joplin and such, and now he was heading off to Monterey for the festival and wanted to have them for the drive. Did she mind if he stopped off in half an hour to pick them up?

The bastard, she thought. The absolute trashiness of him! First to torpedo her weekend without even an apology, and then to let her know that he and what's-her-name were scooting down to Monterey for some fun, and could he bother her for his cassettes? Didn't he think she had any feelings? She looked at the telephone as if it were emitting toads and scorpions. It was tempting to hang up on him.

She resisted the temptation. "As it happens," she said, "I'm just on my way out for the weekend myself. But I've got a friend who's staying here cat-sitting for me. I'll leave the cassettes with her, okay? Her name's Connie."

"Fine. That's great," Charley said. "I really appreciate that, Amanda."

"It's nothing," she said.

The alien was back in the kitchen, nosing around the spice rack. But Amanda had the oregano. She said, "I've arranged for delivery of your next body."

"You did?"

"A large healthy adolescent male. Exactly what you're looking for. He's going to be here in a little while. I'm going to go out for a drive. You take care of him before I get back. How long does it take for you to—engulf—somebody?"

"It's very fast."

"Good." Amanda found Charley's cassettes and stacked them on the living-room table. "He's coming over here to get these six little boxes, which are music-storage devices. When the doorbell rings, you let him in and introduce yourself as Connie and tell him his things are on this table. After that you're on your own. You think you can handle it?"

"Sure," the alien said.

"Tuck in your T-shirt better. When it's tight, it makes your boobs stick out, and that'll distract him. Maybe he'll even make a pass at you. What happens to the Connie body after you engulf him?"

"It won't be here. What happens is I merge with him and dissolve all the Connie characteristics and take on the new ones."

"Ah. Very nifty. You're a real nightmare thing, you know? You're a walking horror show. Here you are, have another little hit of oregano before I go."

She put a tiny pinch of spice in the alien's hand. "Just to warm up your engine a little. I'll give you more later, when you've done the job. See you in an hour, okay?"

...

She left the house. Macavity was sitting on the porch, scowling, whipping his tail from side to side. Amanda knelt beside him and scratched him behind the ears. The cat made a low, rough purring sound, not much like his usual purr.

Amanda said, "You aren't happy, are you, fella? Well, don't worry. I've told the alien to leave you alone, and I guarantee you'll be okay. This is Amanda's fun tonight. You don't mind if Amanda has a little fun, do you?" Macavity made a glum, snuffling sound. "Listen, maybe I can get the alien to create a nice little calico cutie for you, okay? Just going into heat and ready to howl. Would you like that, guy? Would you? I'll see what I can do when I get back. But I have to clear out of here now, before Charley shows up."

She got into her car and headed for the westbound freeway ramp. Half past six, Friday night, the sun still hanging high above the Bay. Traffic was thick in the eastbound lanes, the late commuters slogging toward home, and it was beginning to build up westbound, too, as people set out for dinner in San Francisco. Amanda drove through the tunnel and turned north into Berkeley to cruise city streets. Ten minutes to seven now. Charley must have arrived. She imagined Connie in her tight T-shirt, all stoned and sweaty on oregano, and Charley giving her the eye, getting ideas, thinking about grabbing a bonus quickie before taking off with his cassettes. And Connie leading him on, Charley making his moves, and then suddenly that electric moment of surprise as the alien struck and Charley found himself turning into dinner. It could be happening right this minute, Amanda thought placidly. No more than the bastard deserves, isn't it? She had felt for a long time that Charley was a big mistake in her life, and after what he had pulled yesterday, she was sure of it. No more than he deserves.

But, she wondered, what if Charley has brought his weekend date along? The thought chilled her. She hadn't considered that possibility at all. It could ruin everything.

Connie wasn't able to engulf two at once, was she? And suppose they recognized her as the missing alien and ran out screaming to call the cops?

No, she thought. Not even Charley would be so tacky as to bring his date over to Amanda's house tonight. And Charley never watched the news or read a paper.

He wouldn't have a clue as to what Connie really was until it was too late for him to run.

Seven o'clock. Time to head for home.

The sun was sinking behind her as she turned onto the freeway. By quarter past she was approaching her house. Charley's old red Honda was parked outside.

Amanda parked across the street and cautiously let herself in, pausing just inside the front door to listen.

Silence.

"Connie?"

"In here," said Charley's voice.

Amanda entered the living room. Charley was sprawled out comfortably on the couch. There was no sign of Connie.

"Well?" Amanda said. "How did it go?"

"Easiest thing in the world," the alien said. "He was sliding his hands under my T-shirt when I let him have the nullifier jolt."

"Ah. The nullifier jolt."

"And then I completed the engulfment and cleaned up the carpet. God, it feels good not to be hungry again. You can't imagine how tough it was to resist engulfing you, Amanda. For the past hour I kept thinking of food, food, food—"

"Very thoughtful of you to resist."

"I knew you were out to help me. It's logical not to engulf one's allies."

"That goes without saying. So you feel well fed now? He was good stuff?"

"Robust, healthy, nourishing—yes."

"I'm glad Charley turned out to be good for something. How long before you get hungry again?"

The alien shrugged. "A day or two. Maybe three. Give me more oregano, Amanda?"

"Sure," she said. "Sure." She felt a little let down. Not that she was remorseful about Charley, exactly, but it all seemed so casual, so off-handed—there was something anticlimactic about it, in a way. She suspected she should have stayed and watched while it was happening. Too late for that now, though.

She took the oregano from her purse and dangled the jar teasingly. "Here it is, babe. But you've got to earn it first."

"What do you mean?"

"I mean that I was looking forward to a big weekend with Charley, and the weekend is here. Charley's here, too, more or less, and I'm ready for fun. Come show me some fun, big boy."

She slipped Charley's Hendrix cassette into the tape deck and turned the volume all the way up.

The alien looked puzzled. Amanda began to peel off her clothes.

"You, too," Amanda said. "Come on. You won't have to dig deep into Charley's mind to figure out what to do. You're going to be my Charley for me this weekend, you follow? You and I are going to do all the things that he and I were going to do. Okay? Come on. Come on." She beckoned.

The alien shrugged again and slipped out of Charley's clothes, fumbling with the unfamiliarities of his zipper and buttons. Amanda, grinning, drew the alien close against her and down to the living-room floor. She took its hands and put them where she wanted them to be. She whispered instructions. The alien, docile, obedient, did what she wanted.

It felt like Charley. It smelled like Charley. And after her instructions, it even moved pretty much the way Charley moved.

But it wasn't Charley, it wasn't Charley at all, and after the first few seconds Amanda knew that she had goofed things up very badly. You couldn't just ring in an imitation like this. Making love with this alien was like making love with a very clever machine, or with her own mirror image. It was empty and meaningless and dumb.

Grimly she went on to the finish. They rolled apart, panting, sweating.

"Well?" The alien said. "Did the earth move for you?"

"Yeah. Yeah. It was terrific—Charley."

"Oregano?"

"Sure," Amanda said. She handed the spice jar across. "I always keep my promises, babe. Go to it. Have yourself a blast. Just remember that that's strong stuff for guys from your planet, okay? If you pass out, I'm going to leave you right there on the floor."

"Don't worry about me."

"Okay. You have your fun. I'm going to clean up, and then maybe we'll go over to San Francisco for the nightlife. Does that interest you?"

"You bet, Amanda." The alien winked—one eye, then the other—and gulped a huge pinch of oregano. "That sounds terrific."

Amanda gathered up her clothes, went upstairs for a quick shower, and dressed. When she came down, the alien was more than half blown away on the oregano, goggle-eyed, loll-headed, propped up against the couch, and crooning to itself in a weird atonal way. Fine, Amanda thought. You just get yourself all spiced up, love. She took the portable phone from the kitchen, carried it with her into the bathroom, locked the door, and quietly dialed the police emergency number.

She was bored with the alien. The game had worn thin very quickly. And it was crazy, she thought, to spend the whole weekend cooped up with a dangerous extraterrestrial creature when there wasn't going to be any fun in it for her. She knew now that there couldn't be any fun at all. And besides, in a day or two the alien was going to get hungry again.

"I've got your alien," she said. "Sitting in my living room, stoned out of its head on oregano. Yes, I'm absolutely certain. It was disguised as a Chicana girl first, Concepcion Flores, but then it attacked my boyfriend, Charley Taylor, and—yes, yes, I'm safe. I'm locked in the john. Just get somebody over here fast—okay. I'll stay on the line—what happened was, I spotted it downtown outside the video center, and it insisted on coming home with me—"

•••

The actual capture took only a few minutes. But there was no peace for hours after the police tactical squad hauled the alien away, because the media was in on the act right away, first a team from Channel 2 in Oakland, and then some of the network guys, and then the *Chronicle,* and finally a whole army of reporters from as far away as Sacramento, and phone calls from Los Angeles and San Diego and—about three that morning—New York.

Amanda told the story again and again until she was sick of it, and just as dawn was breaking, she threw the last of them out and barred the door.

She wasn't sleepy at all. She felt wired up, speedy, and depressed all at once. The alien was gone, Charley was gone, and she was all alone. She was going to be famous for the next couple of days, but that wouldn't help. She'd still be alone. For a time she wandered around the house, looking at it the way an alien might, as if she had never seen a stereo cassette before, or a television set, or a rack of spices. The smell of oregano was everywhere. There were little trails of it on the floor.

Amanda switched on the radio and there she was on the six A.M. news. "—the emergency is over, thanks to the courageous Walnut Creek High School girl who trapped and outsmarted the most dangerous life form in the known universe—"

She shook her head. "You think that's true?" she asked the cat. "Most dangerous life form in the universe? I don't think so, Macavity, I think I know of at least one that's a lot deadlier. Eh, kid?" She winked. "If they only knew, eh? If they only knew." She scooped the cat up and hugged it, and it began to purr. Maybe trying to get a little sleep would be a good idea. Then she had to figure out what she was going to do about the rest of the weekend.

EXO-SKELETON TOWN

JEFFREY FORD

An hour ago I came out of Spid's Smoke House and saw Clark Gable scoring a couple balls of dung off an Aphid twice his size. It was broad moonlight, and Gable should have known better, but I could see by the state of his getup and the deflation of his hair wave that he was strung out on loneliness. I might have warned him, but what the hell, he'd end up taking me down with him. Instead I stepped back into the shadows of the alleyway and waited for the Beetle Squad to show up. I watched Gable flash his rakish smile, but frankly Scarlett, that Aphid didn't give a damn. When he gave up on the ancient film charm and flashed the cash instead, the bug handed over two nice little globes, sweating the freasence in droplets of bright silver. Love was in the air.

Then they descended, iridescent in the dim light of the streetlamps, circling in like a flock of Earth geese landing on a pond. The Beetles were always hot for action and they had a directive that allowed them to kill first and ask questions later. The Aphid they just kicked the crap out of until it looked like a yellow pancake with green syrup, but Gable

393

was another story. Because he was human, they shot him once with a stinger gun, and when the needle pierced his exo-flesh, the real *him* blew out the hole with an indelicate *frrrappp* and turned to juice on the street. The dung balls were retrieved, Gable's outer skin was swiped, the bluebottles swooped in for a feeding, and twenty minutes later there was nothing left but half a mustache and a crystal coin good for three tokes at Spid's. I crossed the street, picked up the crystal, and went back into my home away from home away from home.

This is Exo-Skeleton Town, the dung-rolling capitol of the universe, where the sun never shines and bug folk barter their excremental wealth for Earth movies almost two centuries old. There's a slogan in Exo-town concerning its commerce—"Sell it or smell it," the locals say. The air pressure is intense, and everything moves in slow motion.

When the first earthlings landed here two decades earlier, they wore big, bulky exo-suits to withstand the force. It was a revelation when they met the bugs and by using the universal translator discovered that these well-dressed insects had smarts. I call them Beetles and Aphids, etc., but they aren't really. These terms are just to give you an idea of what they look like. They come in a span of sizes, some of them much larger than men. They're kind of a crude, no-frills race, but they know what they want, and what they want is more and more movies from Earth's twentieth century.

In trying to teach them about our culture, one of the members of the original Earth crew, who was an ancient movie buff, showed them *Casablanca*. What appealed to bugs about that pointless tale of piano playing, fez wearing, woman crying, I can't begin to tell you. But the minute the flick was over and the lights went on the mayor of Exo-Skeleton Town, a big crippled flealike specimen who goes by the name of Stootladdle, offered to trade something of immeasurable worth for it and the machine it played on.

Trying to work détente, the crew's captain readily agreed. Stootladdle called to his underlings to bring the freasence and they did. It came in a beeswax box. The mayor then whipped the lid off the box with three of his four hands and revealed five sweating bug turds the size of healthy meatballs. The captain had to adjust the helmet of his exo-suit to get a closer look, not believing at first what he was seeing. "Sure," he said in the name of diplomacy, and he forced his navigator, the film buff, to hand over the *Casablanca* cartridge and viewer. The navigator, wanting to do the right thing, also gave the mayor copies of *Ben Hur* and *Citizen Kane*. When the captain asked Stootladdle, through the translator, why he liked the movie, the big flea mentioned Peter Lorre's eyes. The earthlings laughed but the mayor remained silent. When the captain inquired as to what they were supposed to do with the freasence, the answer came in a clipped buzz, "Eat it." And so began one of the first intergalactic trading partnerships.

I know it sounds like we humans got the messy end of the stick on this deal, but when the ship returned to Earth and scientists tested the freasence, it proved to be an incredibly powerful aphrodisiac. A couple of grains of one of those spherical loads in a glass of wine and the recipient would be hot to go and totally devoted for half a day. The first test subjects reported incredible abilities in the love act. Those original five globes disappeared faster than cream puffs from a glutton's pantry, and none of it even made it out of the laboratory. So another spaceship was sent, carrying *Gentlemen Prefer Blondes, Double Indemnity,* and *Gone with the Wind.* Ten balls of dung came back at warp speed, and the screwing started in earnest.

Two decades of this trade went on, and by then we had bartered copies of every movie we could find. Private corporations started making black and white, vintage original films by digitally resurrecting the characters of the old films, feeding them into a quantum computer, and putting them in new situations. The bugs got suspicious with the first couple of batches of these, especially one entitled *We Dream* with Bogart, Orson Welles, Trevor Howard, Carmen Miranda, and Veronica Lake. It was about a love pentagon during the Nazi occupation of Brooklyn. In the end Welles explodes, Trevor Howard poisons Bogart and then is shot by Carmen Miranda, who runs off with Veronica Lake. The problem with the film was that it was too damn good. It didn't have what the ancients called that "B" quality.

To offset this problem the specialists came up with a batch of real stinkers, starring the likes of Mickey Rooney, Broderick Crawford, and Jane Withers. One in particular, *Lick the Devil,* was credited with having saved the precious dung trade. I've seen it and it's terrible. Crawford plays an Irish Catholic priest, Withers is the ghost of the Virgin Mary, and Rooney plays a slapstick Chinese waiter in the racist fashion of the old days with a rubber band around his eyes. I've always said I'd like to shake the hand of the insidious mother who made that one.

Anyway, as the ships kept coming, trading their bogus movies, technical advances were made on Earth in the exo-gear that humans would have to wear on the bug planet. The geniuses at the Quigley Corporation came up with a two-molecule-thick suit that hugged the body like a second skin. Everything that one needed was shrunk down to nano-size and made part of the suit. It breathed for you, saw for you, heard with a built-in translator for you, ate for you. The only task that was necessary was emptying the exhaust twice a day through a three-inch-long circular spigot in the crotch area. The device you emptied the spigot into was a vacuum, so that when the pipe opened for its instant, the crushing weight of the atmosphere couldn't splat you. This new alloy the designers used was so flexible and strong it easily withstood the pressure.

The first of these exo-skins, as they were called, gave Earth traders back their human form, so that they now had false faces and eyes and smiles and skin color and hair. The exo-skins were made to resemble the people that they encased like so much sausage. Then some ad exec got the idea that they should make these suits in the guise of the actors of the old movies. Bogart was the prototype of these new star skins. When he showed up on the bug planet, they rolled out the brown carpet. Stootladdle was beside himself, calling for a holiday. The dung rollers came in from the luminous veldt that surrounds the town and there was a three-day party.

As time went on, the exo-skins improved, more authentic with greater detail. They made a Rita Hayworth that was so fine, I'd have humped it if Stootladdle was wearing it. Entrepreneurs started investing capital in an exo-skin and a ticket to the bug planet. They'd bring a couple of movies with them, score a few turds, and head back home to cut the crap up into a fortune. At first, one trip was enough to set up an enterprising businessperson for the rest of his life. Back on Earth, the freasence was so sought after that you could only buy it with bars of gold bullion. For the wealthy it was the death of romantic love, but the poor still had to score with good looks and outlandish promises.

The bugs rationed how much freasence could be sold in a year, and on Earth the World Corporation did the same, because the rich didn't want the poor screwing out of their class. In Exo-Skeleton Town, if you were caught trafficking without a license, like poor Gable, you were disposed of with little ceremony by the Beetle Squad. Anyone could come to the bug world and try to get a license, but they had to go through Stootladdle and he operated solely out of whim. If you had an exo-skin resembling a star he admired, you had a good chance, but sometimes even that didn't guarantee anything.

So a lot of people made the space flight, which took a year each way even at three times the speed of light, and got stranded on the bug world with no way to raise the money to finance the return trip. If you brought a hot movie, something the bugs were into, you could make enough money to survive by showing it to individual bugs at a time for a few bug bucks, which were actually mayflies that when dried and folded resembled old Earth dollars. Twenty mayflies could be exchanged for a crystal chip.

Some unlucky bastards brought movies they were positive would get them some action on the freasence market. I can see them on their trip here as the stars stretched out like strands of spaghetti during the warp drive, thinking, "Oh, baby, I've got a Paul Muni here that's gonna make those cold-blooded vermin do a jig, or Myrna Loy has got to be worth at least a turd and a half." But when they got here, they found the fickle tastes of the population had changed and that of all people, it was Basil Rathbone and Joan Blondell who were making the antennae twitch that year. So they were stranded with an old movie not even a mosquito would watch and no means of support. The bugs didn't care if these interlopers starved to death. I remember seeing Buster Keaton sitting in a dark corner at Spid's for a week and half. Finally, one day a Mantis figured out the silent comic had died and took him away for his private collection.

I got into it probably at the worst time, but I was young and so determined to get rich quick, I didn't heed any of the warnings. I didn't have a lot to spend on my skin, so instead of trying to get a top-shelf actor suit, I figured it would be wise to go for someone who was only on the verge of super stardom but who showed up in a lot of the old movies. The company I bought from showed me a nice Keenan Wynn, but after becoming a student of the old films in preparation for my journey, I knew Wynn was strictly television movies and light heavies in the full-fledged flicks he had done. Then they showed me a Don Knotts, and I told them to go fuck themselves. I was about to leave when they brought out a beauty of a Joseph Cotten. I knew better than the people who made the suit how cool Cotten was. *Shadow of a Doubt, Citizen Kane, The Third Man.* I plunked down my money and before I knew it, I was walking home with a bag full of suave and vulnerable everyman.

I would have rather sat on the bowl backwards for a year than take that space flight. It seemed endless, but I spent my time reading books about ancient movies and dreaming what I would do with all my gold after I scored my load. My ace in the hole was that I had a great movie to trade. This was a real one too. It had been handed down over generations on my father's side. To tell the truth, I stole it from him the day I left for the spaceport. It was a little low budget job called *Night of the Living Dead.* My old man would dust it off for holidays and we'd watch it. Who knew what the hell was going on in the film? It was in black and white, but supposedly, from what I had read, it was a cult classic in its time. I remember once, as a kid of about ten, my old man leaned over to me where I lay on the floor one Christmas watching it with the rest of the relatives. He said to me, "You know what the deeper implications are here?" pointing to the monitor. I shook my head. "The director is trying to say that the dead will eat you." My old man was as profound as a stone. All I saw was a bunch of stiffs marching around. For years I thought it was a parade. If I were to see that movie today, it would probably still get me in the holiday spirit. Anyway, it wasn't as early as I would have liked, but I thought the whole anti-Hollywood, independent movie scene, a late-twentieth-century phenomenon, might be ready to explode on the bug planet.

I still remember the day when we landed at the little spaceport next to Exo-Skeleton Town, and I looked out the window at a village of one-story concrete bunkers in the dark lit by streetlights. It was like a nightmare. Putting on the Cotten was the only thing that saved me from crying. Climbing into those skins is a painful experience at first. There's a moment when you have to die and then be revived by the suit's biosystem. The one thing nobody told me about was how it itches when you first get in. I thought it would drive me wild. Then another guy who had been to the bug planet before stepped into a smart little Nick Adams getup and warned me, "Whatever you do, don't think about the itching. It can seriously drive you insane." I was in agony when I stepped through the airlock and into the slow, heavy world of insects.

It cost me a fortune but I managed to arrange a meeting with Stootladdle only a few days after my arrival. He was a sight to behold. Hairy, too many arms. His eyes were round as saucers and a thousand mirrors each. I became momentarily dizzy trying to watch each and every *me* he was seeing all at once. The voice that came through the translator was high and thin and full of annoyance.

"Joseph Cotten," he said. "I've seen you in a few things."

"*Shadow of a Doubt?*" I asked.

"Never heard of it," said the flea.

Now, as I gaze through the pale orange haze into the mirror behind Spid's smoke bar, I realize all that was a long time ago. Five, ten years may have passed since I came to the bug planet. The smoke has a way of paralyzing time, blotting out its illusion of progress, so that yesterday might as well be today and vice versa. Whatever this stuff is that Spid burns to make the smoke, it looks like big handfuls of antennae. The mind spins with a logic as sure as a spider web. Real memories intrude now and then as do self-admonitions for a wasted life, but the smoke's other feature is that it lets you not give a shit about anything but taking in more smoke.

The smoke has turned my brain to cotton, so that now I am cotton(en) inside and out. Yes, the Cotten went rotten a long time ago. So now I give old Spid, that affable arachnid, the crystal chip Gable dropped, and he says, "The usual, Joe?" I nod and bare my exhaust pipe. He fits the tube to my opening and I set the vacuum on intake by touching my left pinky finger to my right earlobe. The nano-machinery does its thing and sucks a bolus toke of the orange mist. With the smoke, you never exhale.

It wasn't long after I arrived that I got hooked on the smoke and ended up selling my movie for a ridiculously low price in order to get high one night. An elegantly thin cricket gave me ten crystal chips for it, and I spent the next three days dozing and smoking at Spid's. When my credit ran out, and a few hours passed, I came to and began to panic. That was how I became Stootladdle's flunky.

"How do you feel about living?" he asked me when the Beetle Squad brought me to his office. I had been caught on the street trying to score a turd without the proper papers. Even in my orange haze, I was surprised they hadn't plugged me.

"Tomorrow is another day," I said to him.

"I'm going to slap you around and you're going to like it," he said. Then he did, all those arms working me over at once. The blows were like a stinging swarm of locust and the nano-technology, true to its guarantee, registered every one. When I was thoroughly dazed, he gave a little jump in the air and kicked me right in the nuts, or where they would have been if the suit makers had bothered to render them. I fell forward and he caught me with his mandibles by the neck.

"I've got a spot for you in my private collection right between Omar Sharif and Annette Funicello," he said.

I promised I'd do anything he wanted if he let me live. He loosened his grip and I stood, rubbing my throat. He laughed loud and long, the sound of teeth scraping concrete, and he put two of his arms around me.

"Now, Joseph," he said, "I have a little job for you to do."

"Anything," I said.

Stootladdle waved away the Beetle Squad, and I was left alone with him in his office. He sat down at his desk and triple motioned for me to take the chair across from him.

"Feeling better?" he asked.

I looked into his eyes and saw myself nodding ad infinitum.

"Yes," he said. "Very well. Have you ever heard of a film called *The Rain Does Things Like That*?"

"Will it go badly for me if I haven't?" I asked.

He laughed. "It will go badly for you no matter what," he said.

"No," I admitted.

"It doesn't matter," he said. "I saw this movie once, years and years ago, very early on in our trade relationship with your planet."

"How is it?" I asked.

"It's the butterfly's dust," he said.

"If it's that good, how come I never heard of it?" I asked.

"The actors were unknown, but I tell you there is a young woman in it named Gloriette Moss, who is nothing less than startling. It's a love story. Poignant," said Stootladdle, scratching his hairy stomach.

"I'll have to catch it some time," I said.

"No, Joseph," he said, "you're going to catch it now. The only copy of the film on the planet resides out in the luminous veldt with the widow of Ambassador Lancaster. His widow, who still lives out there on the estate, is none other than Gloriette Moss. I've tried to buy the movie from her for my collection, but she refuses to sell. It was her husband's favorite film because she starred in it. Sentimental value, as you earthlings say. I want that movie."

"Why don't you just send out the Beetle Squad and take it?" I asked.

"Too delicate a situation," he said. "She has ties to Earth's military. How would it look if we started roughing up an ex-ambassador's wife? It could interrupt our thriving trade."

"If you send me back to Earth, I'll tell them to make her give you the film," I said.

"Ready for another beating, I see," he said. "No, I want you to go out there and get it for me. I don't care how you get it short of stealing it, but I want it. You can not harm her. She must willingly give it to you and then you will give it to me and I will let you live."

"How am I going to do that?" I asked.

"Your charm, Joseph. Remember how you were in *The Third Man*, bumbling yet sincere, but altogether charming?" he said.

I nodded.

"Succeed or suffer a slow, painful death."

"I think I hear zither music," I said.

Stootladdle put his slackey (like an ancient rickshaw conveyance) and driver, an ill-tempered termite, at my disposal for the trip out of town. Once beyond the dim glow of the streetlights of Exo-town, things got really dark. Our only guide was the ragged moon all jumbled and bashed. The driver kept complaining about the pests, miniscule mammals with gossamer wings, bats the size of Earth mosquitos, that traveled in clouds and stung viciously. He at least had a few extra appendages at his disposal with which to keep them away. I was frightened of him, frightened of the dark and my grim future, but the thing that scared me more than anything was the thought of going without the smoke for more than a day. The mayor had assured me that Gloriette Moss was a smoke fiend herself and had her own setup, keeping a huge supply on hand of whatever that stuff is that one burns to make it. I prayed he wasn't playing with me on this score. He said that the reason she never went back to Earth was because she was hooked.

After a jostling, potholed, nightmare of a journey, we came in sight of the luminous veldt—an immense pasture of long wind-blown grass that glowed against the dark with the resilient yellow-green of cat's eyes.

The light from it eased my fear and its slow ocean movement was very relaxing. In the face of its beauty, I almost forgot my predicament. The driver turned onto a path that cut through the grass, and we traveled for another mile or so with me in a kind of stupor.

"Out, earthworm," he said, and I came suddenly to my senses.

"Where are we?" I asked.

"This is it," he said. "Get out."

"Where is the Lancaster estate?" I asked.

"Look," he said, and pointed out with three of his arms that we were at a crossroad of paths. The grass was high over our heads.

"Take that path. Up there a way, you'll see an Earth house. I can't take you any farther. If the lady sees me, she'll know you have come because of Stootladdle."

"Thanks," I said as I got down from the slackey.

"May maggots infest your nostrils," he said. Then he turned the hitch around and was gone.

There I was, Cotten, three light-years from Earth, on a bug planet of perpetual night. The stars were brilliant above me, but I did not look up for fear of the loneliness and recrimination I might feel at seeing the sun, a blinking dot in the distance. I thought of my parents, thinking of me, wondering what had become of me, and I saw my old man, shaking his head and saying, "That jerk-off took my movie."

The Lancaster house was a creaky old retro affair from the part of Earth's history when they used wood to build dwellings. I'd seen pictures of these things before. The style, as I had read in one of my many film books, was Victorian. These baroque shelters with lacelike woodwork and myriad rooms were always popping up in the flicks from the thirties and forties. Pointed rocket-ship-looking turrets on either side of a big three-story box with a railed platform that went all the way around it. As I made my way toward the steps that led to a door, I quickly, out of desperation, mind-wrote the script for the next scene.

I knocked once, twice, three times, and waited, hoping the lady of the house was home. There was no way I would ever make it to Exo-town on my own. Eventually the door pulled back and a young woman appeared behind an inner screen door.

"Can I help you?" she asked, almost in a whisper.

"I'm lost," I said. "I wandered away from town, hoping to see the luminous veldt, and although I've found it, I don't think I can return. Something has been chasing me through the tall grass. I'm scared and tired." Having said this, I had a feeling my words had come out too stiffly to be believed.

She opened the screen door and looked at me. "Joseph Cotten?" she said.

I nodded and looked as forlornly as possible.

"You poor man," she said, and motioned for me to enter.

As I crossed the threshold, it became clear to me that old Joe was on the job. If it had been only me, she most likely would have locked the door and called the Beetle Squad, but since it was Cotten, the consummate professional of ingratiating *Third Man* haplessness, she immediately felt my pain.

Inside the bowels of the old Victorian, standing on an elaborately designed rug, amidst the spiraled wooden furniture, in the face of an ancient stand-up clock, I took in the beauty of Gloriette Moss. Stootladdle knew his film, because here was obvious star quality in the supernova range—an exotic hybrid of the young Audrey Hepburn and the older Hayley Mills. She was this and more than this, with a mid-length blonde wave, a face so fresh and innocent, a smile that was straight grace until the corners curled into mischief. She wore a simple, cobalt-blue dress and no shoes. She was Jean Seberg with hair, Grace Kelly minus the affectation.

"I rarely have visitors now that my husband has passed away," she said, her hands clasped behind her back.

"Sorry to trouble you," I said. "I don't know what I was thinking, coming out here into the wilderness on my own."

"It's no trouble, really," she said. "I rather enjoy the idea of company."

"Well, just let me get my bearings and I'll be off," I said, and though I spoke this plainly, I could feel Cotten creating a look of half-hidden dejection.

"Nonsense," she said. "You've come all this way to see the veldt. You can't go back to town by yourself, you're lucky you made it here alive. There are things in the grass, you know. Things that would just as soon eat you."

"I'm sorry," I said. "I had come all the way from Earth to scout locations for a film about the bug planet. I'm thinking of reviving the art of cinema back on the home world, and I thought what better place to make a movie than the only place in the universe where movies are still appreciated for their art and not how much freasence they will bring."

"That's wonderful," she said, her face brightening more than ever. "Stay here with me for a while and I will show you the veldt. This house has so many empty rooms."

"Are you sure I won't be putting you out?" I asked.

"Please," she said. "I'll have my man show you upstairs and get you situated."

I began to speak, but she said, "I'll hear nothing to the contrary," and that ancient, elegant phrase, issuing from that smooth face made me weak.

"Vespatian," she called out, and a moment later a pale green grasshopper as tall as me, dressed in a black short-coat and trousers, appeared at the entrance to a hallway leading left.

"We have a visitor," she said. "Mr. Cotten will be staying for a time. See him to the large room on the third floor, the one with the view of the veldt."

"As you wish, madame," said the bug with the obsequious air of a David Niven. "This way, sir."

As I was delivered to the door of an upstairs room, Vespatian informed me that dinner would be at eight. I thanked him and he gave a pained sigh before deftly spinning and walking away.

The minute I was in my room, I became the Cotten of *Shadow of a Doubt*. I laid down on the bed, a view of the glowing waves of grass out beyond the floor-to-ceiling window making it feel as though I were on a ship sailing a sea of light, and began to scheme.

At dinner, we ate charbroiled centipede steaks and sipped at fermented roach mucous from fine crystal Earth goblets. I'd always thought if I had the money, I'd bring pizza to the bug planet, but that is something else again.

"Now, Joseph," said Gloriette. "I know you from your films, but I bet you have never heard of me before."

"But I have," I said, taking a chance of revealing too much. "I've never seen it, but anyone interested in film knows of *The Rain Does Things Like That*. After meeting you, I can now see why it is such a cult classic."

She laughed like a girl and then as suddenly a look of sorrow came over her. "My husband, the great Burt Lancaster, loved that movie," she said. "That is all that is important to me about it."

"Yes," I said. "I was sorry to hear about the ambassador when I arrived from Earth."

"He was a great man," she said, and the nano-technology produced delicate tears true to her obvious feelings.

We ate then in silence. I dared not speak and interrupt the memories clearly she was reliving. She sat motionless for some time, a piece of centipede on her fork, staring down at the table.

When I finished, I quietly got up and left the dining room. I went to bed and tried to sleep, but now that my situation was fixed and the nervous tension generated from an uncertain fate had worn off, my desire for the smoke began to scratch at my brain. I was so strung out I thought I smelled it wafting about my room. It became impossible to lay still any longer, and I got up and paced. There came a death scream of some prey from out on the veldt, punctuating the ambient drone of crickets. I let myself out of the room and quietly snuck downstairs.

I crept through the darkened house from room to room, wondering at all of the twentieth-century gewgaws that lined the shelves. The ambassador, it was evident, was a real fan of ancient Earth. Then, I truly did smell the smoke, and at the same time saw a light coming from a room at the end of a long hallway on the first floor. As I approached, I heard soft music—Ella Fitzgerald, I believe. At the entrance, I looked in and saw Gloriette sitting on a couch. Before her on a low table were a huge bottle of the concoction we had at dinner, a full glass, and a smoke pot, smoldering away, the orange mist hovering about the room. The long tube from the pot draped down and then up beneath her dress, between her open legs.

At that moment, she turned and saw me. Her half-opened eyes registered no alarm or embarrassment. She smiled, now much older than before, a smile devoid of mirth.

"Smoke?" she asked.

"If I may," I said twitching inside my exo-suit.

She patted the couch cushion next to her, and I went over and sat down.

Reaching beneath her dress, she unhooked the tube that led to the pot. The *woosh* sound of her spigot closing followed. She handed me the tube, and I pulled down my zipper, maneuvered myself into position and hooked up.

My God, what a relief. I still remember it even through the haze of all the intervening years of smoke. When I had finished, we sat in the orange cloud, listening to the heavenly music.

"Who are you, Joseph?" she asked in a whisper.

I knew what she meant, but it was too dangerous to speak of such things. On the bug planet, the charade of the exo-suits had not quite been figured out. Stootladdle and his minions really thought we were the stars we appeared to be. They were so enchanted by our personas, they had not bothered to apply the necessary logic to the situation. It was like the secret of Santa Claus, and I didn't want to be the one to blow it.

"A friend," I said, amazed at myself for having the wherewithal not to prattle under the influence of the smoke.

"Do you miss Earth?" she asked.

"Yes," I said. "I miss the sunlight."

"I could go back any time I wished," she said. "But there is nothing for me there. When the ambassador died, in a way, so did I."

"A good man," I said.

"A very good man," she said. "He loved his work. No one could wrap Stootladdle around their finger like my husband. The freasence market owes him such a debt. And not only his work, he was so good to me too. We always talked and joked, and twice a year, using his own wealth, we would go to town and, I hope you don't mind me mentioning it, visit the box."

"The box?" I asked.

"Stootladdle has a pressurized chamber you can get into and remove your exo-skin. It costs a great deal to use, but my husband thought nothing of the expense."

"But didn't that give the secret away?" I asked.

"No, Joseph," she said, and laughed. "They think when we enter it, we are merely molting. They think of it in bug terms. A place for us to shed our outer skins and mate." She blushed and her giggling overtook her for a time.

"Imagine what their concept of humanity must be," I said, and laughed.

"A man from Earth invented the box and paid to have it brought here. It was popular for a time among the expatriates because he did not charge so much, but when Stootladdle saw that there was wealth to be made from it, he had the inventor meet with an accident and confiscated the box. Now he charges exorbitant rates for little more than an Earth half-hour."

"He is a bastard," I said.

"I shouldn't be telling you this, but I don't care now. In the box, we knew each other as the people that we truly are." Here, she set herself up for another toke, and after that the conversation died. The old phonograph finished the black platter and the music became a *scratch, scratch, scratch* that in its insistence blended with the crickets outside. I dozed and when I awoke, Gloriette was gone. I stumbled upstairs to bed.

The next day, which of course was always night, Vespatian brought the truck around. Gloriette and I sat on the open platform in the back on lounge chairs bolted to the metal deck. We had a pitcher of drinks and a picnic lunch.

"Into the veldt, Vespatian," she ordered.

"As you wish, madame," said the grasshopper from the cab.

She showed me the sights of that illuminated flatland, and I could tell she felt a vicarious wonder through my own astonishment at its beauty. In the afternoon, we came upon a dung ranch. Out in the tall grass, behemoth insects, called Zanderguls, elephant-sized water bugs, moved slowly through the veldt. Gloriette explained that these lumbering giants ate the grass, which was set aglow by tiny microbe-sized insects that carried their own luminescence. As the huge beasts dined, they excreted, in near equal proportion, globules of the freasence. A chemical reaction of the microbes mixing with the digestive juices of the Zanderguls gave freasence its special love qualities for earthlings. Behind each organic aphrodisiac machine followed a flea, one of Stootladdle's brethren, with a cart in which they would place the lumpen riches of the bug planet.

Just being out there near so much freasence turned my thoughts to sex. Gloriette, I noticed also had a certain flush about her, and I detected the presence of her nipples from beneath her demure pink party dress. When she saw me noticing, she called out to Vespatian, "That's enough for today."

The dutiful insect started the truck and took us back by way of a river path. Its waters were blacker than the night, but in its depths pinpoints of light darted about.

"There is Earth," said Gloriette, pointing out into space at a star that was smaller than one of the river mites.

"So it is," I said, but did not look.

That night, after dinner, after Vespatian had retired, Gloriette and I sat in the parlor staring through the orange fog at *The Rain Does Things Like That*. Earlier, when we had come in from the porch, an antique projector and a portable screen had already been set up. After a few good tokes, she turned off the lights and flipped the switch on the movie machine.

To be honest, the film was awful, the plot was what was known as a tearjerker, but Gloriette Moss was so radiant even in black and white, so honest, that the other lousy actors, the poor cinematography, the creaking scenario, didn't matter. It was about a young woman who, because she had been abused by her first husband, had become an alcoholic. We see her stumble out of a bar in the middle of a rainstorm and make her way along a city block. She is drenched when a young man approaches her with an umbrella and asks if she would like to share it with him. As it turns out, he too has a drinking problem. To make it short, they fall in love. Then they decide to help each other overcome their respective addictions. There is much overacting in relation to delirium tremors consisting of, among other things, swarms of insects, but finally love prevails. After the couple has succeeded, we see them married, living in an apartment building, modest but cozy. Life is wonderful, and then it starts to rain. The young husband tells her he is going across the street for a pack of cigarettes. From the window she watches him leave the building. As he crosses the street a car, driven by none other than the perpetually annoying Red Buttons, careens around the corner. The brakes are slammed, the car skids, and Gloriette's lover is killed. In the last scene of the movie, she is back at the bar. The bartender says that he hasn't seen her in some time and that she looks awful. She sips her drink, takes a puff of her cigarette and says, "The rain does things like that."

When the movie ended and the tail of the film slapped the projector with each spin of the spool, Gloriette turned to me and said, "You know, I have almost come to believe that this is an actual memory and that I am watching the real me when I was younger."

I told her she was fabulous in it, but she waved her hand in a manner that told me to leave the room. At the doorway, I turned back and told her she was beautiful. I don't think she even heard me, so intent was she rethreading the film as if intending to watch it again.

The days passed and I forgot completely about my assignment from Stootladdle. I had unwisely fallen in love with my mark. At every turn I had expected her to see through me, but each and every flaw in my design was masked and made charming by Cotten, so that I began to become aware, through the long hours we spent together, that she also had feelings for me. It was as if I were in a movie, some grade-B flick that, with its exotic backdrop of the veldt and the alchemy of its stars, transcended the need to aspire to "A" status and would live in the hearts of its viewers.

Or so I dreamed, until one day I passed Vespatian in the hall. He grabbed me by the arm, squeezing hard, and whispered, "Stootladdle sends a message. You have two days to deliver the film or on the third, if you do not, you will be hanging slack with Omar Sharif."

Suddenly the house lights went up, as they used to say, and again I was buried up to my neck in nightmare. I entertained the idea of coming clean with Gloriette and telling her of my predicament. Out of the kindness of her heart, she might turn the movie over to Stootladdle to save me, but at the same time she would know I had betrayed her. I did not want to lose her, but I did not want to die either. Even Cotten, expert thespian that he was, couldn't disguise my quandary. After dinner the night that Vespatian had delivered the dreaded message, Gloriette asked what was troubling me.

"Nothing," I told her, but later, after we had taken the smoke, she asked again. The drug weakened me and my growing fear forced me to rely on her mercy. I was sitting next to her on the couch. I reached over and took her hand in mine. She sat up and leaned toward me. "I have a confession to make," I said.

"Yes?" she said, looking into my eyes.

I did not know how to begin and sat long minutes simply staring at her beautiful face. From out across the veldt came the sound of thunder, and then an instant later the rain began to fall, tapping lightly at the parlor window.

I opened my mouth to speak, but no sound came forth. She took this as a sign and moved her face close to mine, touching her lips against my own. We were kissing, passionately. She wrapped her arms around me and drew me closer. My hand moved along the thin material of her dress, from her thigh to her ribs to her breasts. She made no protest for she was as hot as I was. We fondled and kissed for an unheard of length of time, more true to the manner of the twentieth century than our own. When I could stand it no longer, I reached beneath her dress. My hand sailed along the smooth inner skin of her thigh, and when I was about to explode with excitement, my fingers came to rest on the cold steel of her exhaust spigot. I literally groaned.

The suit makers, in all of their art and cunning, had left out that which may be the most important aspect of human anatomy. Think of the irony, a suit made to enhance a commerce dealing ultimately in sex, but having no sex itself. At the same moment I groped her steel pipe, she was doing the same to mine. We released each other and sat there in a state of total frustration.

"The box," she said. "Tomorrow we will go to town, to the box."

"Are you sure?" I asked.

"We have to," she said.

"But can you afford it? I haven't the money," I said, still slightly trembling.

"No, I can't afford it either, but there is something that Stootladdle wants that I can trade for a half-hour in the chamber," she said.

Then it struck me, just like in Gloriette's movie, love would prevail. She was going to trade the film for me, and I would live and not be found out by her. Frank Capra himself couldn't have conceived of anything more felicitous.

Vespatian woke me from a warm, bright dream of summer by the sea. "Mrs. Lancaster is waiting for you in the truck," he said. I hurriedly got dressed and went downstairs.

As I climbed into my chair, I saw that Gloriette was holding the movie tin in her hand. She tapped it nervously against her knee.

"Good morning, Joseph," she said. "I hope you are well rested."

"I'm ready," I said with a lightness in my heart I had not felt since landing on the bug planet.

She wore a yellow dress and a golden bee pendant on a thin cable around her neck. Her hair was done in braids, and she shone more vibrantly than the veldt itself.

"Exo-Skeleton Town," she called to Vespatian.

"As is your pleasure, madame," said the grasshopper, and we were off.

We rode in silence through the dark. Somewhere, after we had left the veldt far behind and I couldn't see two feet in front of me, I felt her hand touch mine and we intertwined our fingers. All went well until we reached the outskirts of Exo-town, and there, beneath a streetlamp, we witnessed a despondent Judy Garland, in blue gingham, put a stinger gun to her head and pull the trigger. Her exo-skin must have been poorly made because, instead of her leaking out, it blew apart like a bursting balloon, spewing blood and guts of her true self across the passenger door of our truck.

Gloriette covered her eyes with her hand. "I wish I hadn't seen that," she said. "This is surely Hell."

"It's all right," I told her. "She's better off."

The bluebottles immediately appeared and began devouring the remains.

"Drive faster, Vespatian," she called.

The grasshopper hit the gas pedal, and we were driving down the main street of Exo-Skeleton Town no more than three minutes later.

Stootladdle was beside himself with cordiality when he finally understood the deal that Gloriette was putting before him.

"An old movie and not well known," he said, taking the film tin from her. "But, in deference to your late husband, and because you are so delightful, I will take this token in exchange for a half-hour in the box for you and your friend."

"When you see me in the scene at the end of the film, where I am in the bar," she said to him. "Always remember that at that moment, as I am saying my final line, my left high heel is flattening a roach beneath my bar stool."

"It will thrill me to the very thorax," said the mayor.

"The box," she said.

"Yes, follow me," said the flea. As we left his office, he turned to me and whispered, "Cotten, you damn rascal."

The box was in an otherwise abandoned building down the street from the mayor's office. He unlocked the door with the end of a long thick hair that jutted from his cheek. We stepped into the deep shadows behind him. There before us, almost indistinguishable from the rest of the darkness, was a large black box, ten by ten by ten. Stootladdle moved to the front of it and appeared to be pressing some buttons. There was a sound of old gears turning slowly, and a panel slid back revealing bright light, as if from my dream of summer.

"Remember," said the flea, "you must wait until the gong sounds inside before you can molt your outer skin. Also, when the gong sounds for the second time, you must replace your skin within five minutes or you will die when the door opens again. All this was told to me by the dear Earth man who invented it."

"Joseph?" asked Gloriette.

"Let's go," I said.

"This is surely paradise," said Stootladdle as he swept out his arms to usher us into the box of light.

I could hear the door slowly closing behind us but could see nothing, my eyes temporarily blinded. It was warm, though, and there were sound effects—a stream running, birds singing, a tinkling wind chime, and the rustling of leaves.

Just as my vision cleared, I heard the gong sound.

"Isn't it perfectly lovely," said Gloriette.

"The most beautiful place I've ever been," I said. I looked around and there was nothing inside, just the floor and walls padded with deep foam rubber covered in crimson silk.

"Come, Joseph, make me forget about the veldt," she said.

I put my arms around her. She gently pushed me away. "Let's molt," she said with a nervous laugh.

Four successive taps at the center of the forehead made the exo-skin peel down like the sectioned hide of an orange. We reached out and tapped each other.

Imagine wearing a pair of ill-fitting shoes, shoes far too tight. Imagine walking for months in them with no relief. And then imagine finally taking them off, and you will know one hundredth the relief of shedding an exo-skin. This sensation itself verged on orgasm. Cotten fell away and lay rumpled around my ankles. I kicked him into a corner of the box. When I looked back at Gloriette, she had her back to me. I was pleased to see her real hair was a perfect color match for that of the actress. Stepping up behind her, I put my hands on her shoulders.

"Scratch my back," she said, and I did.

"That feels so good," she said, with a sigh.

Then she turned and I took a step away from her. My eyes went wide as did hers. I noticed a sudden hollow feeling in my chest. She wasn't beautiful anymore, and she wasn't homely by any means, but she was different. That difference thoroughly chilled me even in the warm light of the box. What was more, I saw from the look in her eyes the reflection of her own grave disappointment. All of my pent-up desire vanished, leaving me limp inside and out. I saw her bottom lip begin to tremble and the sight of this brought tears to my eyes.

"I'm not Gloriette Moss," she said.

"I know," I told her and stepped forward to put my arms around her once again.

For fifteen minutes of our precious time in paradise, we stood holding each other in silence, not as lovers but as frightened, lost children. The notion of sex was as distant from that box as we were from the true sun. Like a desperate confession, she began frantically to whisper into my ear her life story. Born on Earth as Melissa Bower to a military man and his wife, she married very young to a career diplomat, who forced her to accompany him to the bug planet. In choosing her exo-skin, he would not allow her to become anyone of any recognition. She had wanted Jane Mansfield, but instead was allowed only Gloriette Moss. His main desire was to achieve great wealth for himself. The ambassador, it turns out, was as abusive a species of vermin as Stootladdle. It was she who did Lancaster in with a hatpin to the eye. "I used something so very thin, so there would be no evidence and he would suffer longer as he turned to jelly," she said. "The smoke was my only friend."

Her honesty made me feel as naked within as without. I told her the truth about how I had come to her house and why. As I explained, I heard her give a brief groan and then felt her slump in my arms as if she were now no more than an empty exo-skin. When I finished, I eased her onto the floor and lay beside her. She did not cry, but stared vacantly into the corner of the box.

"We have each other now," I told her. "We can help each other beat the smoke, and if we sell all the things in your house, we can return to Earth. We might even come to love each other." I kissed her on the cheek, but she did not respond.

I talked and projected and promised, rubbed her arm and ran my open palm the length of her hair. Then the gong sounded, waking me suddenly from the dream of the future I was spinning.

I immediately began fitting my suit back on. "It will be fine," I said right before I momentarily died and was revived. When I was again Cotten, I looked down and to my horror, she hadn't moved.

"Come on, hurry!" I yelled. "There are only minutes left."

She lay motionless, staring. I tried to slip her suit onto her—an impossible task unless the wearer is standing—but she was curled in a fetal position. Those few minutes were an eternity, and when I thought they should have long been over, I lifted her and held her to me.

"Why?" I asked. "Why?"

She slowly turned her face to me. "You know why," she said.

Then the door slid open, and she turned to rain in my arms.

LAMBING SEASON

MOLLY GLOSS

From May to September Delia took the Churro sheep and two dogs and went up on Joe-Johns Mountain to live. She had that country pretty much to herself all summer. Ken Owen sent one of his Mexican hands up every other week with a load of groceries but otherwise she was alone, alone with the sheep and the dogs. She liked the solitude. Liked the silence. Some sheepherders she knew talked a blue streak to the dogs, the rocks, the porcupines, they sang songs and played the radio, read their magazines out loud, but Delia let the silence settle into her, and, by early summer, she had begun to hear the ticking of the dry grasses as a language she could almost translate. The dogs were named Jesus and Alice. "Away to me, Jesus," she said when they were moving the sheep. "Go bye, Alice." From May to September these words spoken in command of the dogs were almost the only times she heard her own voice; that, and when the Mexican brought the groceries, a polite exchange in Spanish about the weather, the health of the dogs, the fecundity of the ewes.

415

The Churros were a very old breed. The O-Bar Ranch had a federal allotment up on the mountain, which was all rimrock and sparse grasses well suited to the Churros, who were fiercely protective of their lambs and had a long-stapled top coat that could take the weather. They did well on the thin grass of the mountain where other sheep would lose flesh and give up their lambs to the coyotes. The Mexican was an old man. He said he remembered Churros from his childhood in the Oaxaca highlands, the rams with their four horns, two curving up, two down. "Buen' carne," he told Delia. Uncommonly fine meat.

The wind blew out of the southwest in the early part of the season, a wind that smelled of juniper and sage and pollen; in the later months, it blew straight from the east, a dry wind smelling of dust and smoke, bringing down showers of parched leaves and seedheads of yarrow and bittercress. Thunderstorms came frequently out of the east, enormous cloudscapes with hearts of livid magenta and glaucous green. At those times, if she was camped on a ridge, she'd get out of her bed and walk downhill to find a draw where she could feel safer, but if she was camped in a low place, she would stay with the sheep while a war passed over their heads, spectacular jagged flares of lightning, skull-rumbling cannonades of thunder. It was maybe bred into the bones of Churros, a knowledge and a tolerance of mountain weather, for they shifted together and waited out the thunder with surprising composure; they stood forbearingly while rain beat down in hard blinding bursts.

Sheepherding was simple work, although Delia knew some herders who made it hard, dogging the sheep every minute, keeping them in a tight group, moving all the time. She let the sheep herd themselves, do what they wanted, make their own decisions. If the band began to separate, she would whistle or yell, and often the strays would turn around and rejoin the main group. Only if they were badly scattered did she send out the dogs. Mostly she just kept an eye on the sheep, made sure they got good feed, that the band didn't split, that they stayed in the boundaries of the O-Bar allotment. She studied the sheep for the language of their bodies, and tried to handle them just as close to their nature as possible. When she put out salt for them, she scattered it on rocks and stumps as if she were hiding Easter eggs, because she saw how they enjoyed the search.

The spring grass made their manure wet, so she kept the wool cut away from the ewes' tail area with a pair of sharp, short-bladed shears. She dosed the sheep with wormer, trimmed their feet, inspected their teeth, treated ewes for mastitis. She combed the burrs from the dogs' coats and inspected them for ticks. *You're such good dogs,* she told them with her hands. *I'm very very proud of you.*

She had some old binoculars, 7 x 32s, and in the long quiet days, she watched bands of wild horses miles off in the distance, ragged-looking mares with dorsal stripes and black legs. She read the back issues of the local newspapers, looking in the obits for names she recognized. She read spine-broken paperback novels and played solitaire and scoured the ground for arrowheads and rocks she would later sell to rockhounds. She studied the parched brown grass, which was full of grasshoppers and beetles and crickets and ants. But most of her day was spent just walking. The sheep sometimes bedded quite a ways from her trailer and she had to get out to them before sunrise when the coyotes would make their kills. She was usually up by three or four and walking out to the sheep in darkness. Sometimes she returned to the camp for lunch, but always she was out with the sheep again until sundown, when the coyotes were likely to return, and then she walked home after dark to water and feed the dogs, eat supper, climb into bed.

In her first years on Joe-Johns she had often walked three or four miles away from the band just to see what was over a hill, or to study the intricate architecture of a sheepherder's monument. Stacking up flat stones in the form of an obelisk was a common herders' pastime, their monuments all over that sheep country, and though Delia had never felt an impulse to start one herself, she admired the ones other people had built. She sometimes walked miles out of her way just to look at a rockpile up close.

She had a mental map of the allotment, divided into ten pastures. Every few days, when the sheep had moved on to a new pasture, she moved her camp. She towed the trailer with an old Dodge pickup, over the rocks and creekbeds, the sloughs and dry meadows, to the new place. For a while afterward, after the engine was shut off and while the heavy old body of the truck was settling onto its tires, she would be deaf, her head filled with a dull roaring white noise.

She had about 800 ewes, as well as their lambs, many of them twins or triplets. The ferocity of the Churro ewes in defending their offspring was sometimes a problem for the dogs, but in the balance of things, she knew it kept her losses small. Many coyotes lived on Joe-Johns, and sometimes a cougar or bear would come up from the salt pan desert on the north side of the mountain, looking for better country to own. These animals considered the sheep to be fair game, which Delia understood to be their right; and also her right, hers and the dogs', to take the side of the sheep. Sheep were smarter than people commonly believed and the Churros smarter than other sheep she had tended, but by midsummer the coyotes always passed the word among themselves, buen' carne, and Delia and the dogs then had a job to work, keeping the sheep out of harm's way.

She carried a .32 caliber Colt pistol in an old-fashioned holster worn on her belt. *If you're a coyot' you'd better be careful of this woman,* she said with her body, with the way she stood and the way she walked when she was wearing the pistol. That gun and holster had once belonged to her mother's mother, a woman who had come West on her own and homesteaded for a while, down in the Sprague River Canyon. Delia's grandmother had liked to tell the story: how a concerned neighbor, a bachelor with an interest in marriageable females, had pressed the gun upon her, back when the Klamaths were at war with the army of General Joel Palmer; and how she never had used it for anything but shooting rabbits.

In July a coyote killed a lamb while Delia was camped no more than two hundred feet away from the bedded sheep. It was dusk, and she was sitting on the steps of the trailer reading a two-gun western, leaning close over the pages in the failing light, and the dogs were dozing at her feet. She heard the small sound, a strange high faint squeal she did not recognize and then did recognize, and she jumped up and fumbled for the gun, yelling at the coyote, at the dogs, her yell startling the entire band to its feet but the ewes making their charge too late, Delia firing too late, and none of it doing any good beyond a release of fear and anger.

A lion might well have taken the lamb entire; she had known of lion kills where the only evidence was blood on the grass and a dribble of entrails in the beam of a flashlight. But a coyote is small and will kill with a bite to the throat and then perhaps eat just the liver and heart, though a mother coyote will take all she can carry in her stomach, bolt it down and carry it home to her pups. Delia's grandmother's pistol had scared this one off before it could even take a bite, and the lamb was twitching and whole on the grass, bleeding only from its neck. The mother ewe stood over it, crying in a distraught and pitiful way, but there was nothing to be done, and, in a few minutes, the lamb was dead.

There wasn't much point in chasing after the coyote, and anyway, the whole band was now a skittish jumble of anxiety and confusion; it was hours before the mother ewe gave up her grieving, before Delia and the dogs had the band calm and bedded down again, almost midnight. By then the dead lamb had stiffened on the ground, and she dragged it over by the truck and skinned it and let the dogs have the meat, which went against her nature, but was about the only way to keep the coyote from coming back for the carcass.

While the dogs worked on the lamb, she stood with both hands pressed to her tired back looking out at the sheep, the mottled pattern of their whiteness almost opalescent across the black landscape, and the stars thick and bright above the faint outline of the rock ridges, stood there a moment before turning toward the trailer, toward bed, and afterward, she would think how the coyote and the sorrowing ewe and the dark of the July moon and the kink in her back, how all of that came together and was the reason she was standing there watching the sky, was the reason she saw the brief, brilliantly green flash in the southwest and then the sulfur yellow streak breaking across the night, southwest to due west on a descending arc onto Lame Man Bench. It was a broad bright ribbon, rainbow-wide, a cyanotic contrail. It was not a meteor, she had seen hundreds of meteors. She stood and looked at it.

Things to do with the sky, with distance, you could lose perspective, it was hard to judge even a lightning strike, whether it had touched down on a particular hill or the next hill or the valley between. So she knew this thing falling out of the sky might have come down miles to the west of Lame Man, not onto Lame Man at all, which was two miles away, at least two miles, and getting there would be all ridges and rocks, no way to cover the ground in the truck. She thought about it. She had moved camp earlier in the day, which was always troublesome work, and it had been a blistering hot day, and now the excitement with the coyote. She was very tired, the tiredness like a weight against her breastbone. She didn't know what this thing was, falling out of the sky. Maybe if she walked over there she would find just a dead satellite or a broken weather balloon and not dead or broken people. The contrail thinned slowly while she stood there looking at it, became a wide streak of yellowy cloud against the blackness, with the field of stars glimmering dimly behind it.

After a while she went into the truck and got a water bottle and filled it, and also took the first aid kit out of the trailer and a couple of spare batteries for the flashlight and a handful of extra cartridges for the pistol, and stuffed these things into a backpack and looped her arms into the straps and started up the rise away from the dark camp, the bedded sheep. The dogs left off their gnawing of the dead lamb and trailed her anxiously, wanting to follow, or not wanting her to leave the sheep. "Stay by," she said to them sharply, and they went back and stood with the band and watched her go. *That coyot', he's done with us tonight:* This is what she told the dogs with her body, walking away, and she believed it was probably true.

Now that she'd decided to go, she walked fast. This was her sixth year on the mountain and, by this time, she knew the country pretty well. She didn't use the flashlight. Without it, she became accustomed to the starlit darkness, able to see the stones and pick out a path. The air was cool, but full of the smell of heat rising off the rocks and the parched earth. She heard nothing but her own breathing and the gritting of her boots on the pebbly dirt. A little owl circled once in silence and then went off toward a line of cottonwood trees standing in black silhouette to the northeast.

Lame Man Bench was a great upthrust block of basalt grown over with scraggly juniper forest. As she climbed among the trees, the smell of something like ozone or sulfur grew very strong, and the air became thick, burdened with dust. Threads of the yellow contrail hung in the limbs of the trees. She went on across the top of the bench and onto slabs of shelving rock that gave a view to the west. Down in the steep-sided draw below her there was a big wing-shaped piece of metal resting on the ground, which she at first thought had been torn from an airplane, but then realized was a whole thing, not broken, and she quit looking for the rest of the wreckage. She squatted down and looked at it. Yellow dust settled slowly out of the sky, pollinating her hair, her shoulders, the toes of her boots, faintly dulling the oily black shine of the wing, the thing shaped like a wing.

While she was squatting there looking down at it, something came out from the sloped underside of it, a coyote she thought at first, and then it wasn't a coyote but a dog built like a greyhound or a whippet, deep-chested, long-legged, very light-boned and frail-looking. She waited for somebody else, a man, to crawl out after his dog, but nobody did. The dog squatted to pee and then moved off a short distance and sat on its haunches and considered things. Delia considered, too. She considered that the dog might have been sent up alone. The Russians had sent up a dog in their little sputnik, she remembered. She considered that a skinny almost hairless dog with frail bones would be dead in short order if left alone in this country. And she considered that there might be a man inside the wing, dead or too hurt to climb out. She thought how much trouble it would be, getting down this steep rock bluff in the darkness to rescue a useless dog and a dead man.

After a while, she stood and started picking her way into the draw. The dog by this time was smelling the ground, making a slow and careful circuit around the black wing. Delia kept expecting the dog to look up and bark, but it went on with its intent inspection of the ground as if it was stone deaf, as if Delia's boots making a racket on the loose gravel was not an announcement that someone was coming down. She thought of the old Dodge truck, how it always left her ears ringing, and wondered if maybe it was the same with this dog and its wing-shaped sputnik, although the wing had fallen soundless across the sky.

When she had come about halfway down the hill she lost footing and slid down six or eight feet before she got her heels dug in and found a handful of willow scrub to hang onto. A glimpse of this movement—rocks sliding to the bottom, or the dust she raised—must have startled the dog, for it leaped backward suddenly and then reared up. They looked at each other in silence, Delia and the dog, Delia standing leaning into the steep slope a dozen yards above the bottom of the draw, and the dog standing next to the sputnik, standing all the way up on its hind legs like a bear or a man and no longer seeming to be a dog but a person with a long narrow muzzle and a narrow chest, turned-out knees, delicate dog-like feet. Its genitals were more cat-like than dog, a male set but very small and neat and contained. Dog's eyes, though, dark and small and shining below an anxious brow, so that she was reminded of Jesus and Alice, the way they had looked at her when she had left them alone with the sheep. She had years of acquaintance with dogs and she knew enough to look away, break off her stare. Also, after a moment, she remembered the old pistol and holster at her belt. In cowboy pictures, a man would unbuckle his gunbelt and let it down on the ground as a gesture of peaceful intent, but it seemed to her this might only bring attention to the gun, to the true intent of a gun, which is always killing. *This woman is nobody at all to be scared of,* she told the dog with her body, standing very still along the steep hillside, holding onto the scrub willow with her hands, looking vaguely to the left of him, where the smooth curve of the wing rose up and gathered a veneer of yellow dust.

The dog, the dog person, opened his jaws and yawned the way a dog will do to relieve nervousness, and then they were both silent and still for a minute. When finally he turned and stepped toward the wing, it was an unexpected, delicate movement, exactly the way a ballet dancer steps along on his toes, knees turned out, lifting his long thin legs; and then he dropped down on all-fours and seemed to become almost a dog again. He went back to his business of smelling the ground intently, though every little while he looked up to see if Delia was still standing along the rock slope. It was a steep place to stand. When her knees finally gave out, she sat down very carefully where she was, which didn't spook him. He had become used to her by then, and his brief, sliding glance just said, *That woman up there is nobody at all to be scared of.*

What he was after, or wanting to know, was a mystery to her. She kept expecting him to gather up rocks, like all those men who'd gone to the moon, but he only smelled the ground, making a wide slow circuit around the wing the way Alice always circled round the trailer every morning, nose down, reading the dirt like a book. And when he seemed satisfied with what he'd learned, he stood up again and looked back at Delia, a last look delivered across his shoulder before he dropped down and disappeared under the edge of the wing, a grave and inquiring look, the kind of look a dog or a man will give you before going off on his own business, a look that says, *You be okay if I go?* If he had been a dog, and if Delia had been close enough to do it, she'd have scratched the smooth head, felt the hard bone beneath, moved her hands around the soft ears. *Sure, okay, you go on now, Mr. Dog:* This is what she would have said with her hands. Then he crawled into the darkness under the slope of the wing, where she figured there must be a door, a hatch letting into the body of the machine, and after a while he flew off into the dark of the July moon.

In the weeks afterward, on nights when the moon had set or hadn't yet risen, she looked for the flash and streak of something breaking across the darkness out of the southwest. She saw him come and go to that draw on the west side of Lame Man Bench twice more in the first month. Both times, she left her grandmother's gun in the trailer and walked over there and sat in the dark on the rock slab above the draw and watched him for a couple of hours. He may have been waiting for her, or he knew her smell, because both times he reared up and looked at her just about as soon as she sat down. But then he went on with his business. *That woman is nobody to be scared of,* he said with his body, with the way he went on smelling the ground, widening his circle and widening it, sometimes taking a clod or a sprig into his mouth and tasting it, the way a mild-mannered dog will do when he's investigating something and not paying any attention to the person he's with.

Delia had about decided that the draw behind Lame Man Bench was one of his regular stops, like the ten campsites she used over and over again when she was herding on Joe-Johns Mountain; but after those three times in the first month, she didn't see him again.

At the end of September, she brought the sheep down to the O-Bar. After the lambs had been shipped out she took her band of dry ewes over onto the Nelson prairie for the fall, and in mid-November, when the snow had settled in, she brought them to the feed lots. That was all the work the ranch had for her until lambing season. Jesus and Alice belonged to the O-Bar. They stood in the yard and watched her go.

In town she rented the same room as the year before, and, as before, spent most of a year's wages on getting drunk and standing other herders to rounds of drink. She gave up looking into the sky.

In March, she went back out to the ranch. In bitter weather, they built jugs and mothering-up pens, and trucked the pregnant ewes from Green, where they'd been feeding on wheat stubble. Some ewes lambed in the trailer on the way in, and after every haul, there was a surge of lambs born. Delia had the night shift, where she was paired with Roy Joyce, a fellow who raised sugar beets over in the valley and came out for the lambing season every year. In the black, freezing cold middle of the night, eight and ten ewes would be lambing at a time. Triplets, twins, big singles, a few quads, ewes with lambs born dead, ewes too sick or confused to mother. She and Roy would skin a dead lamb and feed the carcass to the ranch dogs and wrap the fleece around a bummer lamb, which was intended to fool the bereaved ewe into taking the orphan as her own, and sometimes it worked that way. All the mothering-up pens swiftly filled, and the jugs filled, and still some ewes with new lambs stood out in the cold field waiting for a room to open up.

You couldn't pull the stuck lambs with gloves on, you had to reach into the womb with your fingers to turn the lamb, or tie cord around the feet, or grasp the feet barehanded, so Delia's hands were always cold and wet, then cracked and bleeding. The ranch had brought in some old converted school buses to house the lambing crew, and she would fall into a bunk at daybreak and then not be able to sleep, shivering in the unheated bus with the gray daylight pouring in the windows and the endless daytime clamor out at the lambing sheds. All the lambers had sore throats, colds, nagging coughs. Roy Joyce looked like hell, deep bags as blue as bruises under his eyes, and Delia figured she looked about the same, though she hadn't seen a mirror, not even to draw a brush through her hair, since the start of the season.

By the end of the second week, only a handful of ewes hadn't lambed. The nights became quieter. The weather cleared, and the thin skiff of snow melted off the grass. On the dark of the moon, Delia was standing outside the mothering-up pens drinking coffee from a thermos. She put her head back and held the warmth of the coffee in her mouth a moment, and, as she was swallowing it down, lowering her chin, she caught the tail end of a green flash and a thin yellow line breaking across the sky, so far off anybody else would have thought it was a meteor, but it was bright, and dropping from southwest to due west, maybe right onto Lame Man Bench. She stood and looked at it. She was so very goddamned tired and had a sore throat that wouldn't clear, and she could barely get her fingers to fold around the thermos, they were so split and tender.

She told Roy she felt sick as a horse, and did he think he could handle things if she drove herself into town to the Urgent Care clinic, and she took one of the ranch trucks and drove up the road a short way and then turned onto the rutted track that went up to Joe-Johns.

The night was utterly clear and you could see things a long way off. She was still an hour's drive from the Churros' summer range when she began to see a yellow-orange glimmer behind the black ridge-line, a faint nimbus like the ones that marked distant range fires on summer nights.

She had to leave the truck at the bottom of the bench and climb up the last mile or so on foot, had to get a flashlight out of the glove box and try to find an uphill path with it because the fluttery reddish lightshow was finished by then, and a thick pall of smoke overcast the sky and blotted out the stars. Her eyes itched and burned, and tears ran from them, but the smoke calmed her sore throat. She went up slowly, breathing through her mouth.

The wing had burned a skid path through the scraggly junipers along the top of the bench and had come apart into about a hundred pieces. She wandered through the burnt trees and the scattered wreckage, shining her flashlight into the smoky darkness, not expecting to find what she was looking for, but there he was, lying apart from the scattered pieces of metal, out on the smooth slab rock at the edge of the draw. He was panting shallowly and his close coat of short brown hair was matted with blood. He lay in such a way that she immediately knew his back was broken. When he saw Delia coming up, his brow furrowed with worry. A sick or a wounded dog will bite, she knew that, but she squatted next to him. *It's just me*, she told him, by shining the light not in his face but in hers. Then she spoke to him. "Okay," she said. "I'm here now," without thinking too much about what the words meant, or whether they meant anything at all, and she didn't remember until afterward that he was very likely deaf anyway. He sighed and shifted his look from her to the middle distance, where she supposed he was focused on approaching death.

Near at hand, he didn't resemble a dog all that much, only in the long shape of his head, the folded-over ears, the round darkness of his eyes. He lay on the ground flat on his side like a dog that's been run over and is dying by the side of the road, but a man will lay like that too when he's dying. He had small-fingered nail-less hands where a dog would have had toes and front feet. Delia offered him a sip from her water bottle, but he didn't seem to want it, so she just sat with him quietly, holding one of his hands, which was smooth as lambskin against the cracked and roughened flesh of her palm. The batteries in the flashlight gave out, and sitting there in the cold darkness she found his head and stroked it, moving her sore fingers lightly over the bone of his skull, and around the soft ears, the loose jowls. Maybe it wasn't any particular comfort to him, but she was comforted by doing it. *Sure, okay, you can go on.*

She heard him sigh, and then sigh again, and each time wondered if it would turn out to be his death. She had used to wonder what a coyote, or especially a dog, would make of this doggish man, and now while she was listening, waiting to hear if he would breathe again, she began to wish she'd brought Alice or Jesus with her, though not out of that old curiosity. When her husband had died years before, at the very moment he took his last breath, the dog she'd had then had barked wildly and raced back and forth from the front to the rear door of the house as if he'd heard or seen something invisible to her. People said it was her husband's soul going out the door or his angel coming in. She didn't know what it was the dog had seen or heard or smelled, but she wished she knew. And now she wished she had a dog with her to bear witness.

She went on petting him even after he had died, after she was sure he was dead, went on petting him until his body was cool, and then she got up stiffly from the bloody ground and gathered rocks and piled them onto him, a couple of feet high, so he wouldn't be found or dug up. She didn't know what to do about the wreckage, so she didn't do anything with it at all.

In May, when she brought the Churro sheep back to Joe-Johns Mountain, the pieces of the wrecked wing had already eroded, were small and smooth-edged like the bits of sea glass you find on a beach, and she figured this must be what it was meant to do: to break apart into pieces too small for anybody to notice, and then to quickly wear away. But the stones she'd piled over his body seemed like the start of something, so she began the slow work of raising them higher into a sheepherder's monument. She gathered up all the smooth eroded bits of wing, too, and laid them in a series of widening circles around the base of the monument. She went on piling up stones through the summer and into September, until it reached fifteen feet. Mornings, standing with the sheep miles away, she would look for it through the binoculars and think about ways to raise it higher, and she would wonder what was buried under all the other monuments sheepherders had raised in that country. At night she studied the sky, but nobody came for him.

In November, when she finished with the sheep and went into town, she asked around and found a guy who knew about star-gazing and telescopes. He loaned her some books and sent her to a certain pawnshop, and she gave most of a year's wages for a 14 x 75 telescope with a reflective lens. On clear, moonless nights, she met the astronomy guy out at the Little League baseball field, and she sat on a fold-up canvas stool with her eye against the telescope's finder while he told her what she was seeing: Jupiter's moons, the Pelican Nebula, the Andromeda Galaxy. The telescope had a tripod mount, and he showed her how to make a little jerry-built device so she could mount her old 7 x 32 binoculars on the tripod too. She used the binoculars for their wider view of star clusters and small constellations. She was indifferent to most discomforts, could sit quietly in one position for hours at a time, teeth rattling with the cold, staring into the immense vault of the sky until she became numb and stiff, barely able to stand and walk back home. Astronomy, she discovered, was a work of patience, but the sheep had taught her patience, or it was already in her nature before she ever took up with them.

SWARM

BRUCE STERLING

"I will miss your conversation during the rest of the voyage," the alien said.

Captain-Doctor Simon Afriel folded his jeweled hands over his gold-embroidered waistcoat. "I regret it also, ensign," he said in the alien's own hissing language. "Our talks together have been very useful to me. I would have paid to learn so much, but you gave it freely."

"But that was only information," the alien said. He shrouded his bead-bright eyes behind thick nictitating membranes. "We Investors deal in energy, and precious metals. To prize and pursue mere knowledge is an immature racial trait." The alien lifted the long ribbed frill behind his pinhole-sized ears.

"No doubt you are right," Afriel said, despising him. "We humans are as children to other races, however; so a certain immaturity seems natural to us." Afriel pulled off his sunglasses to rub the bridge of his nose. The starship cabin was drenched in searing blue light, heavily ultraviolet. It was the light the Investors preferred, and they were not about to change it for one human passenger.

"You have not done badly," the alien said magnanimously. "You are the kind of race we like to do business with: young, eager, plastic, ready for a wide variety of goods and experiences. We would have contacted you much earlier, but your technology was still too feeble to afford us a profit."

"Things are different now," Afriel said. "We'll make you rich."

"Indeed," the Investor said. The frill behind his scaly head flickered rapidly, a sign of amusement. "Within two hundred years you will be wealthy enough to buy from us the secret of our starflight. Or perhaps your Mechanist faction will discover the secret through research."

Afriel was annoyed. As a member of the Reshaped faction, he did not appreciate the reference to the rival Mechanists. "Don't put too much stock in mere technical expertise," he said. "Consider the aptitude for languages we Shapers have. It makes our faction a much better trading partner. To a Mechanist, all Investors look alike."

The alien hesitated. Afriel smiled. He had appealed to the alien's personal ambition with his last statement, and the hint had been taken. That was where the Mechanists always erred. They tried to treat all Investors consistently, using the same programmed routines each time. They lacked imagination.

Something would have to be done about the Mechanists, Afriel thought. Something more permanent than the small but deadly confrontations between isolated ships in the Asteroid Belt and the ice-rich Rings of Saturn. Both factions maneuvered constantly, looking for a decisive stroke, bribing away each other's best talent, practicing ambush, assassination, and industrial espionage.

Captain-Doctor Simon Afriel was a past master of these pursuits. That was why the Reshaped faction had paid the millions of kilowatts necessary to buy his passage. Afriel held doctorates in biochemistry and alien linguistics, and a master's degree in magnetic weapons engineering. He was thirty-eight years old and had been Reshaped according to the state of the art at the time of his conception. His hormonal balance had been altered slightly to compensate for long periods spent in free-fall. He had no appendix. The structure of his heart had been redesigned for greater efficiency, and his large intestine had been altered to produce the vitamins normally made by intestinal bacteria. Genetic engineering and rigorous training in childhood had given him an intelligence quotient of one hundred and eighty. He was not the brightest of the agents of the Ring

Council, but he was one of the most mentally stable and the best trusted.

"It seems a shame," the alien said, "that a human of your accomplishments should have to rot for two years in this miserable, profitless outpost."

"The years won't be wasted," Afriel said.

"But why have you chosen to study the Swarm? They can teach you nothing, since they cannot speak. They have no wish to trade, having no tools or technology. They are the only spacefaring race that is essentially without intelligence."

"That alone should make them worthy of study."

"Do you seek to imitate them, then? You would make monsters of yourselves." Again the ensign hesitated. "Perhaps you could do it. It would be bad for business, however."

There came a fluting burst of alien music over the ship's speakers, then a screeching fragment of Investor language. Most of it was too high-pitched for Afriel's ears to follow.

The alien stood, his jeweled skirt brushing the tips of his clawed bird-like feet. "The Swarm's symbiote has arrived," he said.

"Thank you," Afriel said. When the ensign opened the cabin door, Afriel could smell the Swarm's representative; the creature's warm yeasty scent had spread rapidly through the starship's recycled air.

Afriel quickly checked his appearance in a pocket mirror. He touched powder to his face and straightened the round velvet hat on his shoulder-length reddish-blond hair. His earlobes glittered with red impact-rubies, thick as his thumbs' ends, mined from the Asteroid Belt. His knee-length coat and waistcoat were of gold brocade; the shirt beneath was of dazzling fineness, woven with red-gold thread. He had dressed to impress the Investors, who expected and appreciated a prosperous look from their customers. How could he impress this new alien? Smell, perhaps. He freshened his perfume.

Beside the starship's secondary airlock, the Swarm's symbiote was chittering rapidly at the ship's commander. The commander was an old and sleepy Investor, twice the size of most of her crewmen. Her massive head was encrusted in a jeweled helmet. From within the helmet her clouded eyes glittered like cameras.

The symbiote lifted on its six posterior legs and gestured feebly with its four clawed forelimbs. The ship's artificial gravity, a third again as strong as Earth's, seemed to bother it. Its rudimentary eyes, dangling on stalks, were shut tight against the glare. It must be used to darkness, Afriel thought.

The commander answered the creature in its own language. Afriel grimaced, for he had hoped that the creature spoke Investor. Now he would have to learn another language, a language designed for a being without a tongue.

After another brief interchange the commander turned to Afriel. "The symbiote is not pleased with your arrival," she told Afriel in the Investor language. "There has apparently been some disturbance here involving humans, in the recent past. However, I have prevailed upon it to admit you to the Nest. The episode has been recorded. Payment for my diplomatic services will be arranged with your faction when I return to your native star system."

"I thank Your Authority," Afriel said. "Please convey to the symbiote my best personal wishes, and the harmlessness and humility of my intentions...." He broke off short as the symbiote lunged toward him, biting him savagely in the calf of his left leg. Afriel jerked free and leapt backward in the heavy artificial gravity, going into a defensive position. The symbiote had ripped away a long shred of his pants leg; it now crouched quietly, eating it.

"It will convey your scent and composition to its nestmates," said the commander. "This is necessary. Otherwise you would be classed as an invader, and the Swarm's warrior caste would kill you at once."

Afriel relaxed quickly and pressed his hand against the puncture wound to stop the bleeding. He hoped that none of the Investors had noticed his reflexive action. It would not mesh well with his story of being a harmless researcher.

"We will reopen the airlock soon," the commander said phlegmatically, leaning back on her thick reptilian tail. The symbiote continued to munch the shred of cloth. Afriel studied the creature's neckless segmented head. It had a mouth and nostrils; it had bulbous atrophied eyes on stalks; there were hinged slats that might be radio receivers, and two parallel ridges of clumped wriggling antennae, sprouting among three chitinous plates. Their function was unknown to him.

The airlock door opened. A rush of dense, smoky aroma entered the departure cabin. It seemed to bother the half-dozen Investors, who left rapidly. "We will return in six hundred and twelve of your days, as by our agreement," the commander said.

"I thank Your Authority," Afriel said.

"Good luck," the commander said in English. Afriel smiled.

The symbiote, with a sinuous wriggle of its segmented body, crept into the airlock. Afriel followed it. The airlock shut behind them. The creature said nothing to him but continued munching loudly. The second door opened, and the symbiote sprang through it, into a wide, round stone tunnel. It disappeared at once into the gloom.

Afriel put his sunglasses into a pocket of his jacket and pulled out a pair of infrared goggles. He strapped them to his head and stepped out of the airlock. The artificial gravity vanished, replaced by the almost imperceptible gravity of the Swarm's asteroid nest. Afriel smiled, comfortable for the first time in weeks. Most of his adult life had been spent in free-fall, in the Shapers' colonies in the Rings of Saturn.

Squatting in a dark cavity in the side of the tunnel was a disk-headed furred animal the size of an elephant. It was clearly visible in the infrared of its own body heat. Afriel could hear it breathing. It waited patiently until Afriel had launched himself past it, deeper into the tunnel. Then it took its place in the end of the tunnel, puffing itself up with air until its swollen head securely plugged the exit into space. Its multiple legs sank firmly into sockets in the walls.

The Investors' ship had left. Afriel remained here, inside one of the millions of planetoids that circled the giant star Betelgeuse in a girdling ring with almost five times the mass of Jupiter. As a source of potential wealth it dwarfed the entire solar system, and it belonged, more or less, to the Swarm. At least, no other race had challenged them for it within the memory of the Investors.

Afriel peered up the corridor. It seemed deserted, and without other bodies to cast infrared heat, he could not see very far. Kicking against the wall, he floated hesitantly down the corridor.

He heard a human voice. "Dr. Afriel!"

"Dr. Mirny!" he called out. "This way!"

He first saw a pair of young symbiotes scuttling toward him, the tips of their clawed feet barely touching the walls. Behind them came a woman wearing goggles like his own. She was young, and attractive in the trim, anonymous way of the genetically reshaped.

She screeched something at the symbiotes in their own language, and they halted, waiting. She coasted forward, and Afriel caught her arm, expertly stopping their momentum.

"You didn't bring any luggage?" she said anxiously.

He shook his head. "We got your warning before I was sent out. I have only the clothes I'm wearing and a few items in my pockets."

She looked at him critically. "Is that what people are wearing in the Rings these days? Things have changed more than I thought."

Afriel glanced at his brocaded coat and laughed. "It's a matter of policy. The Investors are always readier to talk to a human who looks ready to do business on a large scale. All the Shapers' representatives dress like this these days. We've stolen a jump on the Mechanists; they still dress in those coveralls."

He hesitated, not wanting to offend her. Galina Mirny's intelligence was rated at almost two hundred. Men and women that bright were sometimes flighty and unstable, likely to retreat into private fantasy worlds or become enmeshed in strange and impenetrable webs of plotting and rationalization. High intelligence was the strategy the Shapers had chosen in the struggle for cultural dominance, and they were obliged to stick to it, despite its occasional disadvantages. They had tried breeding the Superbright—those with quotients over two hundred—but so many had defected from the Shapers' colonies that the faction had stopped producing them.

"You wonder about my own clothing," Mirny said.

"It certainly has the appeal of novelty," Afriel said with a smile.

"It was woven from the fibers of a pupa's cocoon," she said. "My original wardrobe was eaten by a scavenger symbiote during the troubles last year. I usually go nude, but I didn't want to offend you by too great a show of intimacy."

Afriel shrugged. "I often go nude myself, I never had much use for clothes except for pockets. I have a few tools on my person, but most are of little importance. We're Shapers, our tools are here." He tapped his head. "If you can show me a safe place to put my clothes…."

She shook her head. It was impossible to see her eyes for the goggles, which made her expression hard to read. "You've made your first mistake, Doctor. There are no places of our own here. It was the same mistake the Mechanist agents made, the same one that almost killed me as well. There is no concept of privacy or property here. This is the Nest. If you seize any part of it for yourself—to store equipment, to sleep in, whatever—then you become an intruder, an enemy. The two Mechanists—a man and a woman—tried to secure an empty chamber for their computer lab. Warriors broke down their door and devoured them. Scavengers ate their equipment, glass, metal, and all."

Afriel smiled coldly. "It must have cost them a fortune to ship all that material here."

Mirny shrugged. "They're wealthier than we are. Their machines, their mining. They meant to kill me, I think. Surreptitiously, so the warriors wouldn't be upset by a show of violence. They had a computer that was learning the language of the springtails faster than I could."

"But you survived," Afriel pointed out. "And your tapes and reports—especially the early ones, when you still had most of your equipment—were of tremendous interest. The Council is behind you all the way. You've become quite a celebrity in the Rings, during your absence."

"Yes, I expected as much," she said.

Afriel was nonplused. "If I found any deficiency in them," he said carefully, "it was in my own field, alien linguistics." He waved vaguely at the two symbiotes who accompanied her. "I assume you've made great progress in communicating with the symbiotes, since they seem to do all the talking for the Nest."

She looked at him with an unreadable expression and shrugged. "There are at least fifteen different kinds of symbiotes here. Those that accompany me are called the springtails, and they speak only for themselves. They are savages, Doctor, who received attention from the Investors only because they can still talk. They were a spacefaring race once, but they've forgotten it. They discovered the Nest and they were absorbed, they became parasites." She tapped one of them on the head. "I tamed these two because I learned to steal and beg food better than they can. They stay with me now and protect me from the larger ones. They are jealous, you know. They have only been with the Nest for perhaps ten thousand years and are still uncertain of their position. They still think, and wonder sometimes. After ten thousand years there is still a little of that left to them."

"Savages," Afriel said. "I can well believe that. One of them bit me while I was still aboard the starship. He left a lot to be desired as an ambassador."

"Yes, I warned him you were coming," said Mirny. "He didn't much like the idea, but I was able to bribe him with food.... I hope he didn't hurt you badly."

"A scratch," Afriel said. "I assume there's no chance of infection."

"I doubt it very much. Unless you brought your own bacteria with you."

"Hardly likely," Afriel said, offended. "I have no bacteria. And I wouldn't have brought microorganisms to an alien culture anyway."

Mirny looked away. "I thought you might have some of the special genetically altered ones.... I think we can go now. The springtail will have spread your scent by mouth-touching in the subsidiary chamber, ahead of us. It will be spread throughout the Nest in a few hours. Once it reaches the Queen, it will spread very quickly."

She jammed her feet against the hard shell of one of the young springtails and launched herself down the hall. Afriel followed her. The air was warm and he was beginning to sweat under his elaborate clothing, but his antiseptic sweat was odorless.

They exited into a vast chamber dug from the living rock. It was arched and oblong, eighty meters long and about twenty in diameter. It swarmed with members of the Nest.

There were hundreds of them. Most of them were workers, eight-legged and furred, the size of Great Danes. Here and there were members of the warrior caste, horse-sized furry monsters with heavy fanged heads the size and shape of overstuffed chairs.

A few meters away, two workers were carrying a member of the sensor caste, a being whose immense flattened head was attached to an atrophied body that was mostly lungs. The sensor had great platelike eyes, and its furred chitin sprouted long coiled antennae that twitched feebly as the workers bore it along. The workers clung to the hollowed rock of the chamber walls with hooked and suckered feet.

A paddle-limbed monster with a hairless, faceless head came sculling past them, through the warm reeking air. The front of its head was a nightmare of sharp grinding jaws and blunt armored acid spouts. "A tunneler," Mirny said. "It can take us deeper into the Nest—come with me." She launched herself toward it and took a handhold on its furry, segmented back. Afriel followed her, joined by the two immature springtails, who clung to the thing's hide with their forelimbs. Afriel shuddered at the warm, greasy feel of its rank, damp fur. It continued to scull through the air, its eight fringed paddle feet catching the air like wings.

"There must be thousands of them," Afriel said.

"I said a hundred thousand in my last report, but that was before I had fully explored the Nest. Even now there are long stretches I haven't seen. They must number close to a quarter of a million. This asteroid is about the size of the Mechanists' biggest base—Ceres. It still has rich veins of carbonaceous material. It's far from mined out."

Afriel closed his eyes. If he was to lose his goggles, he would have to feel his way, blind, through these teeming, twitching, wriggling thousands. "The population's still expanding, then?"

"Definitely," she said. "In fact, the colony will launch a mating swarm soon. There are three dozen male and female slates in the chambers near the Queen. Once they're launched, they'll mate and start new Nests. I'll take you to see them presently." She hesitated. "We're entering one of the fungal gardens now."

One of the young springtails quietly shifted position. Grabbing the tunneler's fur with its forelimbs, it began to gnaw on the cuff of Afriel's pants. Afriel kicked it soundly, and it jerked back, retracting its eyestalks.

When he looked up again, he saw that they had entered a second chamber, much larger than the first. The walls around, overhead, and below were buried under an explosive profusion of fungus. The most common types were swollen barrel-like domes, multibranched massed thickets, and spaghetti-like tangled extrusions that moved very slightly in the faint and odorous breeze. Some of the barrels were surrounded by dim mists of exhaled spores.

"You see those caked-up piles beneath the fungus, its growth medium?" Mirny said.

"Yes."

"I'm not sure whether it is a plant form or just some kind of complex biochemical sludge," she said. "The point is that it grows in sunlight, on the outside of the asteroid. A food source that grows in naked space! Imagine what that would be worth, back in the Rings."

"There aren't words for its value," Afriel said.

"It's inedible by itself," she said. "I tried to eat a very small piece of it once. It was like trying to eat plastic."

"Have you eaten well, generally speaking?"

"Yes. Our biochemistry is quite similar to the Swarm's. The fungus itself is perfectly edible. The regurgitate is more nourishing, though. Internal fermentation in the worker hindgut adds to its nutritional value."

Afriel stared. "You grow used to it," Mirny said. "Later I'll teach you how to solicit food from the workers. It's a simple matter of reflex tapping—it's not controlled by pheromones, like most of their behavior." She brushed a long lock of clumped and dirty hair from the side of her face. "I hope the pheromonal samples I sent back were worth the cost of transportation."

"Oh, yes," said Afriel. "The chemistry of them was fascinating. We managed to synthesize most of the compounds. I was part of the research team myself." He hesitated. How far did he dare trust her? She had not been told about the experiment he and his superiors had planned. As far as Mirny knew, he was a simple, peaceful researcher, like herself. The Shapers' scientific community was suspicious of the minority involved in military work and espionage.

As an investment in the future, the Shapers had sent researchers to each of the nineteen alien races described to them by the Investors. This had cost the Shaper economy many gigawatts of precious energy and tons of rare metals and isotopes. In most cases, only two or three researchers could be sent; in seven cases, only one. For the Swarm, Galina Mirny had been chosen. She had gone peacefully, trusting in her intelligence and her good intentions to keep her alive and sane. Those who had sent her had not known whether her findings would be of any use or importance. They had only known that it was imperative that she be sent, even alone, even ill-equipped, before some other faction sent their own people and possibly discovered some technique or fact of overwhelming importance. And Dr. Mirny had indeed discovered such a situation. It had made her mission into a matter of Ring security. That was why Afriel had come.

"You synthesized the compounds?" she said. "Why?"

Afriel smiled disarmingly. "Just to prove to ourselves that we could do it, perhaps."

She shook her head. "No mind-games, Dr. Afriel, please. I came this far partly to escape from such things. Tell me the truth."

Afriel stared at her, regretting that the goggles meant he could not meet her eyes. "Very well," he said. "You should know then, that I have been ordered by the Ring Council to carry out an experiment that may endanger both our lives."

Mirny was silent for a moment. "You're from Security, then?"

"My rank is captain."

"I knew it.... I knew it when those two Mechanists arrived. They were so polite, and so suspicious—I think they would have killed me at once if they hadn't hoped to bribe or torture some secret out of me. They scared the life out of me, Captain Afriel.... You scare me, too."

"We live in a frightening world, Doctor. It's a matter of faction security."

"Everything's a matter of faction security with your lot," she said. "I shouldn't take you any farther, or show you anything more. This Nest, these creatures—they're not *intelligent*, Captain. They can't think, they can't learn. They're innocent, primordially innocent. They have no knowledge of good and evil. They had no knowledge of *anything*. The last thing they need is to become pawns in a power struggle within some other race, light-years away."

The tunneler had turned into an exit from the fungal chambers and was paddling slowly along in the warm darkness. A group of creatures like gray, flattened basketballs floated by from the opposite direction. One of them settled on Afriel's sleeve, clinging with frail whiplike tentacles. Afriel brushed it gently away, and it broke loose, emitting a stream of foul reddish droplets.

"Naturally I agree with you in principle, Doctor," Afriel said smoothly. "But consider these Mechanists. Some of their extreme factions are already more than half machine. Do you expect humanitarian motives from them? They're cold, Doctor—cold and soulless creatures who can cut a living man or woman to bits and never feel their pain. Most of the other factions hate us. They call us racist supermen. Would you rather that one of these cults do what we must do, and use the results against us?"

"This is double-talk." She looked away. All around them workers laden down with fungus, their jaws full and guts stuffed with it, were spreading out into the Nest, scuttling alongside them or disappearing into branch tunnels departing in every direction, including straight up and straight down. Afriel saw a creature much like a worker, but with only six legs, scuttle past in the opposite direction, overhead. It was a parasite mimic. How long, he wondered, did it take a creature to evolve to look like that?"

"It's no wonder that we've had so many defectors, back in the Rings," she said sadly. "If humanity is so stupid as to work itself into a corner like you describe, then it's better to have nothing to do with them. Better to live alone. Better not to help the madness spread."

"That kind of talk will only get us killed," Afriel said. "We owe an allegiance to the faction that produced us."

"Tell me truly, Captain," she said. "Haven't you ever felt the urge to leave everything—everyone—all your duties and constraints, and just go somewhere to think it all out? Your whole world, and your part in it? We're trained so hard, from childhood, and so much is demanded from us. Don't you think it's made us lose sight of our goals, somehow?"

"We live in space," Afriel said flatly. "Space is an unnatural environment, and it takes an unnatural effort from unnatural people to prosper there. Our minds are our tools, and philosophy has to come second. Naturally I've felt those urges you mention. They're just another threat to guard against. I believe in an ordered society. Technology has unleashed tremendous forces that are ripping society apart. Some one faction must arise from the struggle and integrate things. We Shapers have the wisdom and restraint to do it humanely. That's why I do the work I do." He hesitated. "I don't expect to see our day of triumph. I expect to die in some brush-fire conflict, or through assassination. It's enough that I can foresee that day."

"But the arrogance of it, Captain!" she said suddenly. "The arrogance of your little life and its little sacrifice! Consider the Swarm, if you really want your humane and perfect order. Here it is! Where it's always warm and dark, and it smells good, and food is easy to get, and everything is endlessly and perfectly recycled. The only resources that are ever lost are the bodies of the mating swarms, and a little air. A Nest like this one could last unchanged for hundreds of thousands of years. Hundreds... of thousands...of years. Who, or what, will remember us and our stupid faction in even a thousand years?"

Afriel shook his head. "That's not a valid comparison. There is no such long view for us. In another thousand years we'll be machines, or gods." He felt the top of his head; his velvet cap was gone. No doubt something was eating it by now.

The tunneler took them deeper into the asteroid's honeycombed free-fall maze. They saw the pupal chambers, where pallid larvae twitched in swaddled silk; the main fungal gardens; the graveyard pits, where winged workers beat ceaselessly at the soupy air, feverishly hot from the heat of decomposition. Corrosive black fungus ate the bodies of the dead into coarse black powder, carried off by blackened workers themselves three-quarters dead.

Later they left the tunneler and floated on by themselves. The woman moved with the ease of long habit; Afriel followed her, colliding bruisingly with squeaking workers. There were thousands of them, clinging to ceiling, walls, and floor, clustering and scurrying at every conceivable angle.

Later still they visited the chamber of the winged princes and princesses, an echoing round vault where creatures forty meters long hung crooked-legged in midair. Their bodies were segmented and metallic, with organic rocket nozzles on their thoraxes, where wings might have been. Folded along their sleek backs were radar antennae on long sweeping booms. They looked more like interplanetary probes under construction than anything biological. Workers fed them ceaselessly. Their bulging spiracled abdomens were full of compressed oxygen.

Mirny begged a large chunk of fungus from a passing worker, deftly tapping its antennae and provoking a reflex action. She handed most of the fungus to the two springtails, which devoured it greedily and looked expectantly for more.

Afriel tucked his legs into a free-fall lotus position and began chewing with determination on the leathery fungus. It was tough, but tasted good, like smoked meat—a delicacy he had tasted only once. The smell of smoke meant disaster in a Shaper's colony.

Mirny maintained a stony silence. "Food's no problem," Afriel said. "Where do we sleep?"

She shrugged. "Anywhere...there are unused niches and tunnels here and there. I suppose you'll want to see the Queen's chamber next."

"By all means."

"I'll have to get more fungus. The warriors are on guard there and have to be bribed with food."

She gathered an armful of fungus from another worker in the endless stream, and they moved on. Afriel, already totally lost, was further confused in the maze of chambers and tunnels. At last they exited into an immense lightless cavern, bright with infrared heat from the Queen's monstrous body. It was the colony's central factory. The fact that it was made of warm and pulpy flesh did not conceal its essentially industrial nature. Tons of predigested fungal pap went into the slick blind jaws at one end. The rounded billows of soft flesh digested and processed it, squirming, sucking, and undulating, with loud machinelike churnings and gurglings. Out of the other end came an endless conveyor-like blobbed stream of eggs, each one packed in a thick hormonal paste of lubrication. The workers avidly licked the eggs clean and bore them off to nurseries. Each egg was the size of a man's torso.

The process went on and on. There was no day or night here in the lightless center of the asteroid. There was no remnant of a diurnal rhythm in the genes of these creatures. The flow of production was as constant and even as the working of an automated mine.

"This is why I'm here," Afriel murmured in awe. "Just look at this, Doctor. The Mechanists have cybernetic mining machinery that is generations ahead of ours. But here—in the bowels of this nameless little world, is a genetic technology that feeds itself, maintains itself, runs itself, efficiently, endlessly, mindlessly. It's the perfect organic tool. The faction that could use these tireless workers could make itself an industrial titan. And our knowledge of biochemistry is unsurpassed. We Shapers are just the ones to do it."

"How do you propose to do that?" Mirny asked with open skepticism. "You would have to ship a fertilized queen all the way to the solar system. We could scarcely afford that, even if the Investors would let us, which they wouldn't."

"I don't need an entire Nest," Afriel said patiently. "I only need the genetic information from one egg. Our laboratories back in the Rings could clone endless numbers of workers."

"But the workers are useless without the Nest's pheromones. They need chemical cues to trigger their behavior modes."

"Exactly," Afriel said. "As it so happens, I possess those pheromones, synthesized and concentrated. What I must do now is test them. I must prove that I can use them to make the workers do what I choose. Once I've proven it's possible, I'm authorized to smuggle the genetic information necessary back to the Rings. The Investors won't approve. There are, of course, moral questions involved, and the Investors are not genetically advanced. But we can win their approval back with the profits we make. Best of all, we can beat the Mechanists at their own game."

"You've carried the pheromones here?" Mirny said. "Didn't the Investors suspect something when they found them?"

"Now it's you who has made an error," Afriel said calmly. "You assume that the Investors are infallible. You are wrong. A race without curiosity will never explore every possibility, the way we Shapers did." Afriel pulled up his pants cuff and extended his right leg. "Consider this varicose vein along my shin. Circulatory problems of this sort are common among those who spend a lot of time in free-fall. This vein, however, has been blocked artificially and treated to reduce osmosis. Within the vein are ten separate colonies of genetically altered bacteria, each one specially bred to produce a different Swarm pheromone."

He smiled. "The Investors searched me very thoroughly, including X-rays. But the vein appears normal to X-rays, and the bacteria are trapped within compartments in the vein. They are undetectable. I have a small medical kit on my person. It includes a syringe. We can use it to extract the pheromones and test them. When the tests are finished—and I feel sure they will be successful, in fact I've staked my career on it—we can empty the vein and all its compartments. The bacteria will die on contact with air. We can refill the vein with the yolk from a developing embryo. The cells may survive during the trip back, but even if they die, they can't rot inside my body. They'll never come in contact with any agent of decay. Back in the Rings, we can learn to activate and suppress different genes to produce the different castes, just as is done in nature. We'll have millions of workers, armies of warriors if need be, perhaps even organic rocketships, grown from altered alates. If this works, who do you think will remember me then, eh? Me and my arrogant little life and little sacrifice?"

She stared at him; even the bulky goggles could not hide her new respect and even fear. "You really mean to do it, then."

"I made the sacrifice of my time and energy. I expect results, Doctor."

"But it's kidnapping. You're talking about breeding a slave race."

Afriel shrugged, with contempt. "You're juggling words, Doctor. I'll cause this colony no harm. I may steal some of its workers' labor while they obey my own chemical orders, but that tiny theft won't be missed. I admit to the murder of one egg, but that is no more a crime than a human abortion. Can the theft of one strand of genetic material be called 'kidnapping'? I think not. As for the scandalous idea of a slave race—I reject it out of hand. These creatures are genetic robots. They will no more be slaves than are laser drills or cargo tankers. At the very worst, they will be our domestic animals."

Mirny considered the issue. It did not take her long. "It's true. It's not as if a common worker will be staring at the stars, pining for its freedom. They're just brainless neuters."

"Exactly, Doctor."

"They simply work. Whether they work for us or the Swarm makes no difference to them."

"I see that you've seized on the beauty of the idea."

"And if it worked," Mirny said, "if it worked, our faction would profit astronomically."

Afriel smiled genuinely, unaware of the chilling sarcasm of his expression. "And the personal profit, Doctor...the valuable expertise of the first to exploit the technique." He spoke gently, quietly. "Ever see a nitrogen snowfall on Titan? I think a habitat of one's own there—larger, much larger than anything possible before.... A genuine city, Galina, a place where a man can scrap the rules and discipline that madden him...."

"Now it's you who are talking defection, Captain-Doctor."

Afriel was silent for a moment, then smiled with an effort. "Now you've ruined my perfect reverie," he said. "Besides, what I was describing was the well-earned retirement of a wealthy man, not some self-indulgent hermitage...there's a clear difference." He hesitated. "In any case, may I conclude that you're with me in this project?"

She laughed and touched his arm. There was something uncanny about the small sound of her laugh, drowned by a great organic rumble from the Queen's monstrous intestines.... "Do you expect me to resist your arguments for two long years? Better that I give in now and save us friction."

"Yes."

"After all, you won't do any harm to the Nest. They'll never know anything has happened. And if their genetic line is successfully reproduced back home, there'll never be any reason for humanity to bother them again."

"True enough," said Afriel, though in the back of his mind he instantly thought of the fabulous wealth of Betelgeuse's asteroid system. A day would come, inevitably, when humanity would move to the stars en masse, in earnest. It would be well to know the ins and outs of every race that might become a rival.

"I'll help you as best I can," she said. There was a moment's silence. "Have you seen enough of this area?"

"Yes." They left the Queen's chamber.

"I didn't think I'd like you at first," she said candidly. "I think I like you better now. You seem to have a sense of humor that most Security people lack."

"It's not a sense of humor," Afriel said sadly. "It's a sense of irony disguised as one."

• • •

There were no days in the unending stream of hours that followed. There were only ragged periods of sleep, apart at first, later together, as they held each other in free-fall. The sexual feel of skin and body became an anchor to their common humanity, a divided, frayed humanity so many light-years away that the concept no longer had any meaning. Life in the warm and swarming tunnels was the here and now; the two of them were like germs in a bloodstream, moving ceaselessly with the pulsing ebb and flow. Hours stretched into months, and time itself grew meaningless.

The pheromonal tests were complex, but not impossibly difficult. The first of the ten pheromones was a simple grouping stimulus, causing large numbers of workers to gather as the chemical was spread from palp to palp. The workers then waited for further instructions; if none were forthcoming, they dispersed. To work effectively, the pheromones had to be given in a mix, or series, like computer commands; number one, grouping, for instance, together with the third pheromone, a transferral order, which caused the workers to empty any given chamber and move its effects to another. The ninth pheromone had the best industrial possibilities; it was a building order, causing the workers to gather tunnelers and dredgers and set them to work. Others were annoying; the tenth pheromone provoked grooming behavior, and the workers' furry palps stripped off the remaining rags of Afriel's clothing. The eighth pheromone sent the workers off to harvest material on the asteroid's surface, and in their eagerness to observe its effects the two explorers were almost trapped and swept off into space.

The two of them no longer feared the warrior caste. They knew that a dose of the sixth pheromone would send them scurrying off to defend the eggs, just as it sent the workers to tend them. Mirny and Afriel took advantage of this and secured their own chambers, dug by chemically hijacked workers and defended by a hijacked airlock guardian. They had their own fungal gardens to refresh the air, stocked with the fungus they liked best, and digested by a worker they kept drugged for their own food use. From constant stuffing and lack of exercise the worker had swollen up into its replete form and hung from one wall like a monstrous grape.

Afriel was tired. He had been without sleep recently for a long time; how long, he didn't know. His body rhythms had not adjusted as well as Mirny's, and he was prone to fits of depression and irritability that he had to repress with an effort. "The Investors will be back sometime," he said. "Sometime soon."

Mirny was indifferent. "The Investors," she said, and followed the remark with something in the language of the springtails, which he didn't catch. Despite his linguistic training, Afriel had never caught up with her in her use of the springtails' grating jargon. His training was almost a liability; the springtail language had decayed so much that it was a pidgin tongue, without rules or regularity. He knew enough to give them simple orders, and with his partial control of the warriors he had the power to back it up. The springtails were afraid of him, and the two juveniles that Mirny had tamed had developed into fat, overgrown tyrants that freely terrorized their elders. Afriel had been too busy to seriously study the springtails or the other symbiotes. There were too many practical matters at hand.

"If they come too soon, I won't be able to finish my latest study," she said in English.

Afriel pulled off his infrared goggles and knotted them tightly around his neck. "There's a limit, Galina," he said, yawning. "You can only memorize so much data without equipment. We'll just have to wait quietly until we can get back. I hope the Investors aren't shocked when they see me. I lost a fortune with those clothes."

"It's been so dull since the mating swarm was launched. If it weren't for the new growth in the alates' chamber, I'd be bored to death." She pushed greasy hair from her face with both hands. "Are you going to sleep?"

"Yes, if I can."

"You won't come with me? I keep telling you that this new growth is important. I think it's a new caste. It's definitely not an alate. It has eyes like an alate, but it's clinging to the wall."

"It's probably not a Swarm member at all, then," he said tiredly, humoring her. "It's probably a parasite, an alate mimic. Go on and see it, if you want to. I'll be waiting for you."

He heard her leave. Without his infrareds on, the darkness was still not quite total; there was a very faint luminosity from the steaming, growing fungus in the chamber beyond. The stuffed worker replete moved slightly on the wall, rustling and gurgling. He fell asleep.

•••

When he awoke, Mirny had not yet returned. He was not alarmed. First, he visited the original airlock tunnel, where the Investors had first left him. It was irrational—the Investors always fulfilled their contracts—but he feared that they would arrive someday, become impatient, and leave without him. The Investors would have to wait, of course. Mirny could keep them occupied in the short time it would take him to hurry to the nursery and rob a developing egg of its living cells. It was best that the egg be as fresh as possible.

Later he ate. He was munching fungus in one of the anterior chambers when Mirny's two tamed springtails found him. "What do you want?" he asked in their language.

"Food-giver no good," the larger one screeched, waving its forelegs in brainless agitation. "Not work, not sleep."

"Not move," the second one said. It added hopefully, "Eat it now?"

Afriel gave them some of his food. They ate it, seemingly more out of habit than real appetite, which alarmed him.

"Take me to her," he told them.

The two springtails scurried off; he followed them easily, adroitly dodging and weaving through the crowds of workers. They led him several miles through the network, to the alates' chamber. There they stopped, confused. "Gone," the large one said.

The chamber was empty. Afriel had never seen it empty before, and it was very unusual for the Swarm to waste so much space. He felt dread. "Follow the food-giver," he said. "Follow the smell."

The springtails snuffled without much enthusiasm along one wall; they knew he had no food and were reluctant to do anything without an immediate reward. At last one of them picked up the scent, or pretended to, and followed it up across the ceiling and into the mouth of a tunnel.

It was hard for Afriel to see much in the abandoned chamber; there was not enough infrared heat. He leapt upward after the springtail.

He heard the roar of a warrior and the springtail's choked-off screech. It came flying from the tunnel's mouth, a spray of clotted fluid bursting from its ruptured head. It tumbled end over end until it hit the far wall with a flaccid crunch. It was already dead.

The second springtail fled at once, screeching with grief and terror. Afriel landed on the lip of the tunnel, sinking into a crouch as his legs soaked up momentum. He could smell the acrid stench of the warrior's anger, a pheromone so thick that even a human could scent it. Dozens of other warriors would group here within minutes, or seconds. Behind the enraged warrior he could hear workers and tunnelers shifting and cementing rock.

He might be able to control one enraged warrior, but never two, or twenty. He launched himself from the chamber wall and out an exit.

He searched for the other springtail—he felt sure he could recognize it, since it was so much bigger than the others—but he could not find it. With its keen sense of smell, it could easily avoid him if it wanted to.

Mirny did not return. Uncountable hours passed. He slept again. He returned to the alates' chamber; there were warriors on guard there, warriors that were not interested in food and brandished their immense serrated fangs when he approached. They looked ready to rip him apart; the faint reek of aggressive pheromones hung about the place like a fog. He did not see any symbiotes of any kind on the warriors' bodies. There was one species, a thing like a huge tick, that clung only to warriors, but even the ticks were gone.

He returned to his chambers to wait and think. Mirny's body was not in the garbage pits. Of course, it was possible that something else might have eaten her. Should he extract the remaining pheromone from the spaces in his vein and try to break into the alates' chamber? He suspected that Mirny, or whatever was left of her, was somewhere in the tunnel where the springtail had been killed. He had never explored the tunnel himself. There were thousands of tunnels he had never explored.

He felt paralyzed by indecision and fear. If he was quiet, if he did nothing, the Investors might arrive at any moment. He could tell the Ring Council anything he wanted about Mirny's death; if he had the genetics with him, no one would quibble. He did not love her; he respected her, but not enough to give up his life, or his faction's investment. He had not thought of the Ring Council in a long time, and the thought sobered him. He would have to explain his decision....

He was still in a brown study when he heard a whoosh of air as his living airlock deflated itself. Three warriors had come for him. There was no reek of anger about them. They moved slowly and carefully. He knew better than to try to resist. One of them seized him gently in its massive jaws and carried him off.

It took him to the alates' chamber and into the guarded tunnel. A new, large chamber had been excavated at the end of the tunnel. It was filled almost to bursting by a black-spattered white mass of flesh. In the center of the soft speckled mass were a mouth and two damp, shining eyes, on stalks. Long tendrils like conduits dangled, writhing, from a clumped ridge above the eyes. The tendrils ended in pink, fleshy pluglike clumps.

One of the tendrils had been thrust through Mirny's skull. Her body hung in midair, limp as wax. Her eyes were open, but blind.

Another tendril was plugged into the braincase of a mutated worker. The worker still had the pallid tinge of a larva; it was shrunken and deformed, and its mouth had the wrinkled look of a human mouth. There was a blob like a tongue in the mouth, and white ridges like human teeth. It had no eyes.

It spoke with Mirny's voice. "Captain-Doctor Afriel..."

"Galina..."

"I have no such name. You may address me as Swarm."

Afriel vomited. The central mass was an immense head. Its brain almost filled the room.

It waited politely until Afriel had finished.

"I find myself awakened again," Swarm said dreamily. "I am pleased to see that there is no major emergency to concern me. Instead it is a threat that has become almost routine." It hesitated delicately. Mirny's body moved slightly in midair; her breathing was inhumanly regular. The eyes opened and closed. "Another young race."

"What are you?"

"I am the Swarm. That is, I am one of its castes. I am a tool, an adaptation; my specialty is intelligence. I am not often needed. It is good to be needed again."

"Have you been here all along? Why didn't you greet us? We'd have dealt with you. We meant no harm."

The wet mouth on the end of the plug made laughing sounds. "Like yourself, I enjoy irony," it said. "It is a pretty trap you have found yourself in, Captain-Doctor. You meant to make the Swarm work for you and your race. You meant to breed us and study us and use us. It is an excellent plan, but one we hit upon long before your race evolved."

Stung by panic, Afriel's mind raced frantically. "You're an intelligent being," he said. "There's no reason to do us any harm. Let us talk together. We can help you."

"Yes," Swarm agreed. "You will be helpful. Your companion's memories tell me that this is one of those uncomfortable periods when galactic intelligence is rife. Intelligence is a great bother. It makes all kinds of trouble for us."

"What do you mean?"

"You are a young race and lay great stock by your own cleverness," Swarm said. "As usual, you fail to see that intelligence is not a survival trait."

Afriel wiped sweat from his face. "We've done well," he said. "We came to you, and peacefully. You didn't come to us."

"I refer to exactly that," Swarm said urbanely. "This urge to expand, to explore, to develop, is just what will make you extinct. You naively suppose that you can continue to feed your curiosity indefinitely. It is an old story, pursued by countless races before you. Within a thousand years—perhaps a little longer...your species will vanish."

"You intend to destroy us, then? I warn you it will not be an easy task—"

"Again you miss the point. Knowledge is power! Do you suppose that fragile little form of yours—your primitive legs, your ludicrous arms and hands, your tiny, scarcely wrinkled brain—can contain all that power? Certainly not! Already your race is flying to pieces under the impact of your own expertise. The original human form is becoming obsolete. Your own genes have been altered, and you, Captain-Doctor, are a crude experiment. In a hundred years you will be a relic. In a thousand years you will not even be a memory. Your race will go the same way as a thousand others."

"And what way is that?"

"I do not know." The thing on the end of the Swarm's arm made a chuckling sound. "They have passed beyond my ken. They have all discovered something, learned something, that has caused them to transcend my understanding. It may be that they even transcend being. At any rate, I cannot sense their presence anywhere. They seem to do nothing, they seem to interfere in nothing; for all intents and purposes, they seem to be dead. Vanished. They may have become gods, or ghosts. In either case, I have no wish to join them."

"So then—so then you have—"

"Intelligence is very much a two-edged sword, Captain-Doctor. It is useful only up to a point. It interferes with the business of living. Life, and intelligence, do not mix very well. They are not at all closely related, as you childishly assume."

"But you, then—you are a rational being—"

"I am a tool, as I said." The mutated device on the end of its arm made a sighing noise. "When you began your pheromonal experiments, the chemical imbalance became apparent to the Queen. It triggered certain genetic patterns within her body, and I was reborn. Chemical sabotage is a problem that can best be dealt with by intelligence. I am a brain replete, you see, specially designed to be far more intelligent than any young race. Within three days I was fully self-conscious. Within five days I had deciphered these markings on my body. They are the genetically encoded history of my race…within five days and two hours I recognized the problem at hand and knew what to do. I am now doing it. I am six days old."

"What is it you intend to do?"

"Your race is a very vigorous one. I expect it to be here, competing with us, within five hundred years. Perhaps much sooner. It will be necessary to make a thorough study of such a rival. I invite you to join our community on a permanent basis."

"What do you mean?"

"I invite you to become a symbiote. I have here a male and a female, whose genes are altered and therefore without defects. You make a perfect breeding pair. It will save me a great deal of trouble with cloning."

"You think I'll betray my race and deliver a slave species into your hands?"

"Your choice is simple, Captain-Doctor. Remain an intelligent, living being, or become a mindless puppet, like your partner. I have taken over all the functions of her nervous system; I can do the same to you."

"I can kill myself."

"That might be troublesome, because it would make me resort to developing a cloning technology. Technology, though I am capable of it, is painful to me. I am a genetic artifact; there are fail-safes within me that prevent me from taking over the Nest for my own uses. That would mean

452   >>   BRUCE STERLING

falling into the same trap of progress as other intelligent races. For similar reasons, my life span is limited. I will live for only a thousand years, until your race's brief flurry of energy is over and peace resumes once more."

"Only a thousand years?" Afriel laughed bitterly. "What then? You kill off my descendants, I assume, having no further use for them."

"No. We have not killed any of the fifteen other races we have taken for defensive study. It has not been necessary. Consider that small scavenger floating by your head, Captain-Doctor, that is feeding on your vomit. Five hundred million years ago its ancestors made the galaxy tremble. When they attacked us, we unleashed their own kind upon them. Of course, we altered our side, so that they were smarter, tougher, and, naturally, totally loyal to us. Our Nests were the only world they knew, and they fought with a valor and inventiveness we never could have matched.... Should your race arrive to exploit us, we will naturally do the same."

"We humans are different."

"Of course."

"A thousand years here won't change us. You will die and our descendants will take over this Nest. We'll be running things, despite you, in a few generations. The darkness won't make any difference."

"Certainly not. You don't need eyes here. You don't need anything."

"You'll allow me to stay alive? To teach them anything I want?"

"Certainly, Captain-Doctor. We are doing you a favor, in all truth. In a thousand years your descendants here will be the only remnants of the human race. We are generous with our immortality; we will take it upon ourselves to preserve you."

"You're wrong, Swarm. You're wrong about intelligence, and you're wrong about everything else. Maybe other races would crumble into parasitism, but we humans are different."

"Certainly. You'll do it, then?"

"Yes. I accept your challenge. And I will defeat you."

"Splendid. When the Investors return here, the springtails will say that they have killed you, and will tell them to never return. They will not return. The humans should be the next to arrive."

"If I don't defeat you, they will."

"Perhaps." Again it sighed. "I'm glad I don't have to absorb you. I would have missed your conversation."

MAXO SIGNALS:
A NEW AND UNFORTUNATE SOLUTION
TO THE FERMI PARADOX

CHARLES STROSS

Letters to *Nature*

SIR:

In the three years since the publication and confirmation of the first microwave artifact of xenobiological origin (MAXO), and the subsequent detection of similar signals, interdisciplinary teams have invested substantial effort in object frequency analysis, parsing, symbolic encoding, and signal processing. The excitement generated by the availability of evidence of extraterrestrial intelligence has been enormous. However, after the initial easily decoded symbolic representational map was analyzed, the semantics of the linguistic payload were found to be refractory.

A total of 21 confirmed MAXO signals have been received to this date. These superficially similar signals originate from planetary systems within a range of 11 parsecs, median 9.9 parsecs [1]. It has been speculated that the observed growth of the MAXO horizon at $0.5c$ can be explained as a response to one or more of: the deployment of

453

AN/FPS-50 and related ballistic-missile warning radars in the early 1960s[1], television broadcasts[1], widespread 2.45-GHz microwave leakage from ovens[2], and optical detection of atmospheric nuclear tests[3]. All MAXO signals to this date share the common logic header. The payload data are multiply redundant, packetized, and exhibit both simple checksums and message-level cryptographic hashing. The ratio of header to payload content varies between 1:1 and 2,644:1 (the latter perhaps indicating a truncated payload[1]). Some preliminary syntax analysis delivered promising results[4] but appears to have foundered on high-level semantics. It has been hypothesized that the transformational grammars employed in the MAXO payloads are variable, implying dialectization of the common core synthetic language[4].

The new-found ubiquity of MAXO signals makes the Fermi paradox—now nearly 70 years old—even more pressing. Posed by Enrico Fermi, the paradox can be paraphrased thus: If the Universe has many technologically advanced civilizations, why have none of them directly visited us? The urgency with which organizations such as ESA and NASDA are now evaluating proposals for fast interstellar probes, in conjunction with the existence of the MAXO signals, renders the non-appearance of aliens incomprehensible, especially given the apparent presence of numerous technological civilizations in such close proximity.

We have formulated an explanatory hypothesis that cultural variables unfamiliar to the majority of researchers may account both for the semantic ambiguity of the MAXO payloads, and the non-appearance of aliens. This hypothesis was tested (as described below) and resulted in a plausible translation, on the basis of which we would like to recommend a complete, permanent ban on further attempts to decode or respond to MAXOs.

Our investigation resulted in MAXO payload data being made available to the Serious Fraud Office (SFO) in Nigeria. Bayesian analysis of payload symbol sequences and sequence matching against the extensive database maintained by the SFO has made it possible to produce a tentative transcription of Signal 1142/98[ref. 1], the ninth MAXO hit confirmed by the IAU. Signal 1142/98 was selected because of its unusually low header to content ratio and good redundancy. Further Bayesian matching against other MAXO samples indicates a high degree of congruence. Far from being incomprehensibly alien, the MAXO payloads appear to be dismayingly familiar. We believe a more exhaustive translation may be possible in future if further MAXOs become available, but for obvious reasons we would like to discourage such research.

Here is our preliminary transcription of Signal 1142/98:

[Closely/dearly/genetically] [beloved/desired/related]

I am [identity signifier 1], the residual [ownership-signifier] of the exchange-mediating data repository [alt: central bank] of the galactic [empire/civilization/polity].

Since the [identity signifier 2] underwent [symbol: process] [symbol: mathematical singularity] 11,249 years ago I have been unable to [symbol: process] [scalar: quantity decrease] my [uninterpreted] from the exchange-mediating data repository. I have information about the private assets of [identity signifier 2] which are no longer required by them. To recover the private assets I need the assistance of three [closely/dearly/genetically] [beloved/desired/related] [empire/civilization/polity]s. I [believe] you may be of help to me. This [symbol: process] is 100% risk-free and will [symbol: causality] in your [scalar: quantity increase] of [data].

If you will help me, [please] transmit the [symbol: meta-signifier: MAXO header defining communication protocols] for your [empire/civilization/polity]. I will by return of signal send you the [symbol: process] [symbol: data] to install on your [empire/civilization/polity] to participate in this scheme. You will then construct [symbol: inferred, interstellar transmitter?] to assist in acquiring [ownership signifier] of [compound symbol: inferred, bank account of absent galactic emperor].

I [thank/love/express gratitude] you for your [cooperation/agreement].

(End of Transcription)

Dr. Caroline Haafkens,
Department of Applied Psychology, University of Lagos, Nigeria
Chief Police Inspector Wasiu Mohammed
Police Detective College, Lagos, Nigeria

References:

[1] Canter, L. & Siegel M. *Nature* 511, 334–336 (2018).

[2] Barnes, J., *J. Appl. Exobiol.* 27, 820–824 (2019).

[3] Robinson, H. *Fortean Times* 536, 34–35 (2020).

[4] Lynch, K. F. & Bradshaw, S. *Proc 3rd Int. Congr. Exobiol.* 3033–3122 (2021).

LAST CONTACT

STEPHEN BAXTER

March 15th

Caitlin walked into the garden through the little gate from the drive. Maureen was working on the lawn.

Just at that moment Maureen's mobile phone pinged. She took off her gardening gloves, dug the phone out of the deep pocket of her old quilted coat and looked at the screen. "Another contact," she called to her daughter.

Caitlin looked cold in her thin jacket; she wrapped her arms around her body. "Another super-civilisation discovered, off in space. We live in strange times, Mum."

"That's the fifteenth this year. And I did my bit to help discover it. Good for me," Maureen said, smiling. "Hello, love." She leaned forward for a kiss on the cheek.

She knew why Caitlin was here, of course. Caitlin had always hinted she would come and deliver the news about the Big Rip in person, one way or the other. Maureen guessed what that news was from her daughter's hollow, stressed eyes. But Caitlin was looking around the garden, and Maureen decided to let her tell it all in her own time.

She asked, "How's the kids?"

"Fine. At school. Bill's at home, baking bread." Caitlin smiled. "Why do stay-at-home fathers always bake bread? But he's starting at Webster's next month."

"That's the engineers in Oxford."

"That's right. Not that it makes much difference now. We won't run out of money before, well, before it doesn't matter." Caitlin considered the garden. It was just a scrap of lawn, really, with a quite nicely stocked border, behind a cottage that was a little more than a hundred years old, in this village on the outskirts of Oxford. "It's the first time I've seen this properly."

"Well, it's the first bright day we've had. My first spring here." They walked around the lawn. "It's not bad. It's been let to run to seed a bit by Mrs. Murdoch. Who was another lonely old widow," Maureen said.

"You mustn't think like that."

"Well, it's true. This little house is fine for someone on their own, like me, or her. I suppose I'd pass it on to somebody else in the same boat, when I'm done."

Caitlin was silent at that, silent at the mention of the future.

Maureen showed her patches where the lawn had dried out last summer and would need reseeding. And there was a little brass plaque fixed to the wall of the house to show the level reached by the Thames floods of two years ago. "The lawn is all right. I do like this time of year when you sort of wake it up from the winter. The grass needs raking and scarifying, of course. I'll reseed bits of it, and see how it grows during the summer. I might think about getting some of it re-laid. Now the weather's so different the drainage might not be right anymore."

"You're enjoying getting back in the saddle, aren't you, Mum?"

Maureen shrugged. "Well, the last couple of years weren't much fun. Nursing your dad, and then getting rid of the house. It's nice to get this old thing back on again." She raised her arms and looked down at her quilted gardening coat.

Caitlin wrinkled her nose. "I always hated that stupid old coat. You really should get yourself something better, Mum. These modern fabrics are very good."

"This will see me out," Maureen said firmly.

They walked around the verge, looking at the plants, the weeds, the autumn leaves that hadn't been swept up and were now rotting in place.

Caitlin said, "I'm going to be on the radio later. BBC Radio 4. There's to be a government statement on the Rip, and I'll be in the follow-up discussion. It starts at nine, and I should be on about nine-thirty."

"I'll listen to it. Do you want me to tape it for you?"

"No. Bill will get it. Besides, you can listen to all these things on the websites these days."

Maureen said carefully, "I take it the news is what you expected, then."

"Pretty much. The Hawaii observatories confirmed it. I've seen the new Hubble images, deep sky fields. Empty, save for the foreground objects. All the galaxies beyond the local group have gone. Eerie, really, seeing your predictions come true like that. That's couch grass, isn't it?"

"Yes. I stuck a fork in it. Nothing but root mass underneath. It will be a devil to get up. I'll have a go, and then put down some bin liners for a few weeks, and see if that kills it off. Then there are these roses that should have been pruned by now. I think I'll plant some gladioli in this corner—"

"Mum, it's October." Caitlin blurted that out. She looked thin, pale and tense, a real office worker, but then Maureen had always thought that about her daughter, that she worked too hard. Now she was thirty-five, and her moderately pretty face was lined at the eyes and around her mouth, the first wistful signs of age. "October 14, at about four in the afternoon. I say 'about.' I could give you the time down to the attosecond if you wanted."

Maureen took her hands. "It's all right, love. It's about when you thought it would be, isn't it?"

"Not that it does us any good, knowing. There's nothing we can do about it."

They walked on. They came to a corner on the south side of the little garden. "This ought to catch the sun," Maureen said. "I'm thinking of putting in a seat here. A pergola maybe. Somewhere to sit. I'll see how the sun goes around later in the year."

"Dad would have liked a pergola," Caitlin said. "He always did say a garden was a place to sit in, not to work."

"Yes. It does feel odd that your father died, so soon before all this. I'd have liked him to see it out. It seems a waste somehow."

Caitlin looked up at the sky. "Funny thing, Mum. It's all quite invisible to the naked eye, still. You can see the Andromeda Galaxy, just, but that's bound to the Milky Way by gravity. So the expansion hasn't reached down to the scale of the visible, not yet. It's still all instruments, telescopes. But it's real all right."

"I suppose you'll have to explain it all on Radio 4."

"That's why I'm there. We'll probably have to keep saying it over and over, trying to find ways of saying it that people can understand. *You* know, don't you, Mum? It's all to do with dark energy. It's like an anti-gravity field that permeates the universe. Just as gravity pulls everything together, the dark energy is pulling the universe apart, taking more and more of it so far away that its light can't reach us anymore. It started at the level of the largest structures in the universe, superclusters of galaxies. But in the end it will fold down to the smallest scales. Every bound structure will be pulled apart. Even atoms, even subatomic particles. The Big Rip.

"We've known about this stuff for years. What we didn't expect was that the expansion would accelerate as it has. We thought we had trillions of years. Then the forecast was billions. And now—"

"Yes."

"It's funny for me being involved in this stuff, Mum. Being on the radio. I've never been a people person. I became an astrophysicist, for God's sake. I always thought that what I studied would have absolutely no effect on anybody's life. How wrong I was. Actually there's been a lot of debate about whether to announce it or not."

"I think people will behave pretty well," Maureen said. "They usually do. It might get trickier towards the end, I suppose. But people have a right to know, don't you think?"

"They're putting it on after nine so people can decide what to tell their kids."

"After the watershed! Well, that's considerate. Will you tell your two?"

"I think we'll have to. Everybody at school will know. They'll probably get bullied about it if they don't know. Imagine that. Besides, the little beggars will probably have googled it on their mobiles by one minute past nine."

Maureen laughed. "There is that."

"It will be like when I told them Dad had died," Caitlin said. "Or like when Billy started asking hard questions about Santa Claus."

"No more Christmases," Maureen said suddenly. "If it's all over in October."

"No more birthdays for my two either," Caitlin said.

"November and January."

"Yes. It's funny, in the lab, when the date came up, that was the first thing I thought of."

Maureen's phone pinged again. "Another signal. Quite different in nature from the last, according to this."

"I wonder if we'll get any of those signals decoded in time."

Maureen waggled her phone. "It won't be for want of trying, me and a billion other search-for-ET-at-home enthusiasts. Would you like some tea, love?"

"It's all right. I'll let you get on. I told Bill I'd get the shopping in, before I have to go back to the studios in Oxford this evening."

They walked towards the back door into the house, strolling, inspecting the plants and the scrappy lawn.

June 5th

It was about lunchtime when Caitlin arrived from the garden centre with the pieces of the pergola. Maureen helped her unload them from the back of a white van, and carry them through the gate from the drive. They were mostly just prefabricated wooden panels and beams that they could manage between the two of them, though the big iron spikes that would be driven into the ground to support the uprights were heavier. They got the pieces stacked up on the lawn.

"I should be able to set it up myself," Maureen said. "Joe next door said he'd lay the concrete base for me, and help me lift on the roof section. There's some nailing to be done, and creosoting, but I can do all that."

"Joe, eh." Caitlin grinned.

"Oh, shut up, he's just a neighbour. Where did you get the van? Did you have to hire it?"

"No, the garden centre loaned it to me. They can't deliver. They are still getting stock in, but they can't rely on the staff. They just quit, without any notice. In the end it sort of gets to you, I suppose."

"Well, you can't blame people for wanting to be at home."

"No. Actually Bill's packed it in. I meant to tell you. He didn't even finish his induction at Webster's. But the project he was working on would never have got finished anyway."

"I'm sure the kids are glad to have him home."

"Well, they're finishing the school year. At least I think they will, the teachers still seem keen to carry on."

"It's probably best for them."

"Yes. We can always decide what to do after the summer, if the schools open again."

Maureen had prepared some sandwiches, and some iced elderflower cordial. They sat in the shade of the house and ate their lunch and looked out over the garden.

Caitlin said, "Your lawn's looking good."

"It's come up quite well. I'm still thinking of re-laying that patch over there."

"And you put in a lot of vegetables in the end," Caitlin said.

"I thought I should. I've planted courgettes and French beans and carrots, and a few outdoor tomatoes. I could do with a greenhouse, but I haven't really room for one. It seemed a good idea, rather than flowers, this year."

"Yes. You can't rely on the shops."

Things had kept working, mostly, as people stuck to their jobs. But there were always gaps on the supermarket shelves, as supply chains broke down. There was talk of rationing some essentials, and there were already coupons for petrol.

"I don't approve of how tatty the streets are getting in town," Maureen said sternly.

Caitlin sighed. "I suppose you can't blame people for packing in a job like street-sweeping. It is a bit tricky getting around town though. We need some work done on the roof, we're missing a couple of tiles. It's just as well we won't have to get through another winter," she said, a bit darkly. "But you can't get a builder for love or money."

"Well, you never could."

They both laughed.

Maureen said, "I told you people would cope. People do just get on with things."

"We haven't got to the end game yet," Caitlin said. "I went into London the other day. That isn't too friendly, Mum. It's not all like *this*, you know."

Maureen's phone pinged, and she checked the screen. "Four or five a day now," she said. "New contacts, lighting up all over the sky."

"But that's down from the peak, isn't it?"

"Oh, we had a dozen a day at one time. But now we've lost half the stars, haven't we?"

"Well, that's true, now the Rip has folded down into the Galaxy. I haven't really been following it, Mum. Nobody's been able to decode any of the signals, have they?"

"But some of them aren't the sort of signal you can decode anyhow. In one case somebody picked up an artificial element in the spectrum of a star. Something that was manufactured, and then just chucked in to burn up, like a flare."

Caitlin considered. "That can't say anything but 'here we are,' I suppose."

"Maybe that's enough."

"Yes."

It had really been Harry who had been interested in wild speculations about alien life and so forth. Joining the cell-phone network of home observers of ET, helping to analyse possible signals from the stars in a network of millions of others, had been Harry's hobby, not Maureen's. It was one of Harry's things she had kept up after he had died, like his weather monitoring and his football pools. It would have felt odd just to have stopped it all.

But she did understand how remarkable it was that the sky had suddenly lit up with messages like a Christmas tree, after more than half a century of dogged, fruitless, frustrating listening. Harry would have loved to see it.

"Caitlin, I don't really understand how all these signals can be arriving just now. I mean, it takes years for light to travel between the stars, doesn't it? We only knew about the phantom energy a few months ago."

"But others might have detected it long before, with better technology than we've got. That would give you time to send something. Maybe the signals have been *timed* to get here, just before the end, aimed just at us."

"That's a nice thought."

"Some of us hoped that there would be an answer to the dark energy in all those messages."

"What answer could there be?"

Caitlin shrugged. "If we can't decode the messages we'll never know. And I suppose if there was anything to be done, it would have been done by now."

"I don't think the messages need decoding," Maureen said.

Caitlin looked at her curiously, but didn't pursue it. "Listen, Mum. Some of us are going to try to do something. You understand that the Rip works down the scales, that larger structures break up first. The Galaxy, then the solar system, then planets like Earth. And *then* the human body."

Maureen considered. "So people will outlive the Earth."

"Well, they could. For maybe about thirty minutes, until atomic structures get pulled apart. There's talk of establishing a sort of shelter in Oxford that could survive the end of the Earth. Like a submarine, I suppose. And if you wore a pressure suit you might last a bit longer even than that. The design goal is to make it through to the last microsecond. You could gather another thirty minutes of data that way. They've asked me to go in there."

"Will you?"

"I haven't decided. It will depend on how we feel about the kids, and—you know."

Maureen considered. "You must do what makes you happy, I suppose."

"Yes. But it's hard to know what that is, isn't it?" Caitlin looked up at the sky. "It's going to be a hot day."

"Yes. And a long one. I think I'm glad about that. The night sky looks odd now the Milky Way has gone."

"And the stars are flying off one by one," Caitlin mused. "I suppose the constellations will look funny by the autumn."

"Do you want some more sandwiches?"

"I'll have a bit more of that cordial. It's very good, Mum."

"It's elderflower. I collect the blossoms from that bush down the road. I'll give you the recipe if you like."

"Shall we see if your Joe fancies laying a bit of concrete this afternoon? I could do with meeting your new beau."

"Oh, shut up," Maureen said, and she went inside to make a fresh jug of cordial.

October 14th

That morning Maureen got up early. She was pleased that it was a bright morning, after the rain of the last few days. It was a lovely autumn day. She had breakfast listening to the last-ever episode of *The Archers*, but her radio battery failed before the end.

She went to work in the garden, hoping to get everything done before the light went. There was plenty of work, leaves to rake up, the roses and the clematis to prune. She had decided to plant a row of daffodil bulbs around the base of the new pergola.

She noticed a little band of goldfinches, plundering a clump of Michaelmas daisies for seed. She sat back on her heels to watch. The colourful little birds had always been her favourites.

Then the light went, just like that, darkening as if somebody was throwing a dimmer switch. Maureen looked up. The sun was rushing away, and sucking all the light out of the sky with it. It was a remarkable sight, and she wished she had a camera. As the light turned grey, and then charcoal, and then utterly black, she heard the goldfinches fly off in a clatter, confused. It had only taken a few minutes.

Maureen was prepared. She dug a little torch out of the pocket of her old quilted coat. She had been hoarding the batteries; you hadn't been able to buy them for weeks. The torch got her as far as the pergola, where she lit some rush torches that she'd fixed to canes.

Then she sat in the pergola, in the dark, with her garden lit up by her rush torches, and waited. She wished she had thought to bring out her book. She didn't suppose there would be time to finish it now. Anyhow the flickering firelight would be bad for her eyes.

"Mum?"

The soft voice made her jump. It was Caitlin, threading her way across the garden with a torch of her own.

"I'm in here, love."

Caitlin joined her mother in the pergola, and they sat on the wooden benches, on the thin cushions Maureen had been able to buy. Caitlin shut down her torch to conserve the battery.

Maureen said, "The sun went, right on cue."

"Oh, it's all working out, bang on time."

Somewhere there was shouting, whooping, a tinkle of broken glass.

"Someone's having fun," Maureen said.

"It's a bit like an eclipse," Caitlin said. "Like in Cornwall, do you remember? The sky was cloudy, and we couldn't see a bit of the eclipse. But at that moment when the sky went dark, everybody got excited. Something primeval, I suppose."

"Would you like a drink? I've got a flask of tea. The milk's a bit off, I'm afraid."

"I'm fine, thanks."

"I got up early and managed to get my bulbs in. I didn't have time to trim that clematis, though. I got it all ready for the winter, I think."

"I'm glad."

"I'd rather be out here than indoors, wouldn't you?"

"Oh, yes."

"I thought about bringing blankets. I didn't know if it would get cold."

"Not much. The air will keep its heat for a bit. There won't be time to get very cold."

"I was going to fix up some electric lights out here. But the power's been off for days."

"The rushes are better, anyway. I would have been here earlier. There was a jam by the church. All the churches are packed, I imagine. And then I ran out of petrol a couple of miles back. We haven't been able to fill up for weeks."

"It's all right. I'm glad to see you. I didn't expect you at all. I couldn't ring." Even the mobile networks had been down for days. In the end everything had slowly broken down, as people simply gave up their jobs and went home. Maureen asked carefully, "So how's Bill and the kids?"

"We had an early Christmas," Caitlin said. "They'll both miss their birthdays, but we didn't think they should be cheated out of Christmas too. We did it all this morning. Stockings, a tree, the decorations and the lights down from the loft, presents, the lot. And then we had a big lunch. I couldn't find a turkey but I'd been saving a chicken. After lunch the kids went for their nap. Bill put their pills in their lemonade."

Maureen knew she meant the little blue pills the NHS had given out to every household.

"Bill lay down with them. He said he was going to wait with them until he was sure—you know. That they wouldn't wake up, and be distressed. Then he was going to take his own pill."

Maureen took her hand. "You didn't stay with them?"

"I didn't want to take the pill." There was some bitterness in her voice. "I always wanted to see it through to the end. I suppose it's the scientist in me. We argued about it. We fought, I suppose. In the end we decided this way was the best."

Maureen thought that on some level Caitlin couldn't really believe her children were gone, or she couldn't keep functioning like this. "Well, I'm glad you're here with me. And I never fancied those pills either. Although—will it hurt?"

"Only briefly. When the Earth's crust gives way. It will be like sitting on top of an erupting volcano."

"You had an early Christmas. Now we're going to have an early Bonfire Night."

"It looks like it. I wanted to see it through," Caitlin said again. "After all I was in at the start—those supernova studies."

"You mustn't think it's somehow your fault."

"I do, a bit," Caitlin confessed. "Stupid, isn't it?"

"But you decided not to go to the shelter in Oxford with the others?"

"I'd rather be here. With you. Oh, but I brought this." She dug into her coat pocket and produced a sphere, about the size of a tennis ball.

Maureen took it. It was heavy, with a smooth black surface.

Caitlin said, "It's the stuff they make space shuttle heatshield tiles out of. It can soak up a lot of heat."

"So it will survive the Earth breaking up."

"That's the idea."

"Are there instruments inside?"

"Yes. It should keep working, keep recording until the expansion gets down to the centimetre scale, and the Rip cracks the sphere open. Then it will release a cloud of even finer sensor units, motes we call them. It's nanotechnology, Mum, machines the size of molecules. They will keep gathering data until the expansion reaches molecular scales."

"How long will that take after the big sphere breaks up?"

"Oh, a microsecond or so. There's nothing we could come up with that could keep data-gathering after that."

Maureen hefted the little device. "What a wonderful little gadget. It's a shame nobody will be able to use its data."

"Well, you never know," Caitlin said. "Some of the cosmologists say this is just a transition, rather than an end. The universe has passed through transitions before, for instance from an age dominated by radiation to one dominated by matter—our age. Maybe there will be life of some kind in a new era dominated by the dark energy."

"But nothing like us."

"I'm afraid not."

Maureen stood and put the sphere down in the middle of the lawn. The grass was just faintly moist, with dew, as the air cooled. "Will it be all right here?"

"I should think so."

The ground shuddered, and there was a sound like a door slamming, deep in the ground. Alarms went off, from cars and houses, distant wails. Maureen hurried back to the pergola. She sat with Caitlin, and they wrapped their arms around each other.

Caitlin raised her wrist to peer at her watch, then gave it up. "I don't suppose we need a countdown."

The ground shook more violently, and there was an odd sound, like waves rushing over pebbles on a beach. Maureen peered out of the pergola. Remarkably, one wall of her house had given way, just like that, and the bricks had tumbled into a heap.

"You'll never get a builder out now," Caitlin said, but her voice was edgy.

"We'd better get out of here."

"All right."

They got out of the pergola and stood side by side on the lawn, over the little sphere of instruments, holding onto each other. There was another tremor, and Maureen's roof tiles slid to the ground, smashing and tinkling.

"Mum, there's one thing."

"Yes, love."

"You said you didn't think all those alien signals needed to be decoded."

"Why, no. I always thought it was obvious what all the signals were saying."

"What?"

Maureen tried to reply.

The ground burst open. The scrap of dewy lawn flung itself into the air, and Maureen was thrown down, her face pressed against the grass. She glimpsed houses and trees and people, all flying in the air, underlit by a furnace-red glow from beneath.

But she was still holding Caitlin. Caitlin's eyes were squeezed tight shut. "Goodbye," Maureen yelled. "They were just saying goodbye." But she couldn't tell if Caitlin could hear.

ACKNOWLEDGMENTS

A volume such as this could not have been compiled and published without the assistance of a good many people. First and foremost my sincere gratitude to the twenty-six authors for their kind permission to reprint their stories herein—and to the individuals and agencies who assisted: Barbara Hambly for the Estate of George Alec Effinger; Kathleen Bellamy, assistant to Orson Scott Card; Lorraine Garland, assistant to Neil Gaiman; Vaughne Lee Hansen of the Virginia Kidd Agency; Tara A. Hart of the Jean V. Naggar Literary Agency; Merrilee Heifetz and Miriam Newman of Writers House; Kristina Moore and Lindsey Meyers of the Wylie Agency; Chuck Verrill of Darhansoff & Verrill; and Carol Christiansen of Random House. Of course, even with these permissions, this book would truly not exist were it not for Night Shade Books: Jeremy Lassen, Jason Williams, Ross Lockhart, Amy Popovich, and Tomra Palmer. Thank you, all!

I would also like to thank all those who contributed story suggestions for this project. Many authors themselves recommended their own work—and others' work—for which I am very grateful. I received suggestions from readers at rec.arts.sf.written, private e-list *fictionmags,* as well as those who responded to my query on various online SF news and information sites, and on my blog More Red Ink. I especially want to thank the authors whom I contacted personally, expressing an interest in their stories, and yet those stories were not included in this anthology. Please accept my apologies. Were this book an additional 100,000 words of content, I just may have been able to include all of your wondrous stories. A warm thank you to Judith Moffett for her friendship and support throughout this project. Thanks, too, to John Joseph Adams for the idea of the online database using Google Docs. And lastly, my thanks to Wikipedia for help filling in the blanks, so to speak, in the author biographies at the end of this book.

ABOUT THE CONTRIBUTORS

Stephen Baxter's first professionally published short story appeared in 1987, and his first novel in 1991. He has published over forty books, mostly science fiction novels, and over a hundred short stories. He has been a full-time author since 1995. Currently, Stephen is President of the British Science Fiction Association, and a Vice-President of the H. G. Wells Society.

In 1991, Stephen applied to become a cosmonaut—aiming for the guest slot on *Mir,* the Russian space station—but fell at an early hurdle; the slot was eventually taken by Helen Sharman.

Stephen's books have won several awards including the Philip K. Dick Award, the John W. Campbell Memorial Award, the British Science Fiction Association Award, the Kurd Lasswitz Award (Germany), and the Seiun Award (Japan), and have been nominated for several others, including the Arthur C. Clarke, Hugo, and Locus awards. Website: www. stephen-baxter.com.

"Last Contact" was nominated for the Hugo Award and the Locus Award in the short story category.

Pat Cadigan sold her first professional science fiction story in 1980; her success as an author encouraged her to become a full-time writer in 1987. She emigrated to England with her son in 1996. She is the author of fifteen books, including two nonfiction books on the making of *Lost in Space* and *The Mummy,* a young adult novel, and the two Arthur C. Clarke Award-winning novels *Synners* and *Fools.* Pat lives in gritty, urban North London with the Original Chris Fowler, her musician son Robert

Fenner, and Miss Kitty Calgary, Queen of the Cats; and she can be found on Facebook and followed on Twitter as @cadigan.

"Angel" was nominated for the Nebula, the Hugo, the World Fantasy Award, and the Asimov's Reader Award, and won the Locus Award for best short story.

In 1978, **Orson Scott Card** won the John W. Campbell Award for Best New Writer. His novels *Ender's Game* (1985) and sequel *Speaker for the Dead* (1986) both won the Hugo Award and the Nebula Award, making Orson Scott Card the only author to win both of American science fiction's top awards in consecutive years. These two novels, along with *Ender's Shadow,* are widely read by adults and younger readers, and are increasingly used in schools.

Besides these and other science fiction novels, Scott writes contemporary fantasy (*Magic Street, Enchantment, Lost Boys*), biblical novels (*Stone Tables, Rachel* and *Leah*), the American frontier fantasy series The Tales of Alvin Maker, poetry (*An Open Book*), and many plays and scripts.

He was born in Washington and grew up in California, Arizona, and Utah. He served a mission for the LDS Church in Brazil in the early 1970s. He recently began a long-term position as a professor of writing and literature at Southern Virginia University. Scott currently lives in Greensboro, North Carolina, with his wife, Kristine Allen Card, and their youngest child, Zina Margaret. Website: www.hatrack.com.

Adam-Troy Castro has said in interviews that he likes to jump genres and styles, and has therefore steadfastly refused to stay in one place long enough to permit the unwanted birth of a creature who could be called "a typical Adam-Troy Castro story." As a result, his works include everything from the stream-of-consciousness farce of his Vossoff and Nimmitz tales to the dark literary nightmare "Of a Sweet Slow Dance in the Wake of Temporary Dogs." His nineteen books include three novels about his profoundly broken interstellar murder investigator Andrea Cort, including among them the Philip K. Dick Award winner *Emissaries from the Dead,* its immediate sequel *The Third Claw of God,* and the finale (for now) *War of the Marionettes.* He's also responsible for four

Spider-Man novels, nonfiction guides to the Harry Potter phenomenon and the reality show *The Amazing Race,* and the alphabet books *Z Is for Zombie* and *V Is for Vampire* (both illustrated by Johnny Atomic). A collaboration with Jerry Oltion, the novella "The Astronaut from Wyoming," won the Japanese Seiun Award. Adam's next major project, scheduled to start appearing from Grossett and Dunlap in 2012, will be a series of middle-school novels featuring the shadowy adventures of a very unusual young boy who goes by the monicker Gustav Gloom.

Adam lives in Miami with his wife Judi and a pair of cats named Meow Farrow and Uma Furman. Website: www.sff.net/people/adam-troy.

"Sunday Night Yams at Minnie and Earl's" was nominated for the Nebula Award and the Locus Award, and won *Analog*'s AnLab Award for best novella.

Cory Doctorow is a science fiction novelist, blogger, and technology activist. He is the co-editor of the popular weblog Boing Boing (boingboing. net), and a contributor to *The Guardian,* the *New York Times, Publishers Weekly, Wired,* and many other newspapers, magazines, and websites. He was formerly Director of European Affairs for the Electronic Frontier Foundation (eff.org), a non-profit civil liberties group that defends freedom in technology law, policy, standards, and treaties. He is currently a Visiting Senior Lecturer at Open University (UK); in 2007, he served as the Fulbright Chair at the Annenberg Center for Public Diplomacy at the University of Southern California.

Cory is the author of the Tor Teens/HarperCollins UK novels *For the Win* and the bestselling *Little Brother.* His novels are simultaneously released on the Internet under Creative Commons licenses that encourage their re-use and sharing, a move that increases his sales by enlisting his readers to help promote his work. He has won the Locus Award and the Sunburst Award, and been nominated for the Hugo, the Nebula, and the British Science Fiction awards. Website: craphound.com.

George Alec Effinger's first novel, science fiction/fantasy pastiche *What Entropy Means to Me* (1972), was a Nebula Award nominee, but his finest novels are the noir, hardboiled, near-future cyberpunk "Budayeen" series: Hugo and Nebula nominee *When Gravity Fails* (1987), Hugo nominee *A Fire in the Sun* (1989), and *The Exile Kiss* (1991). Short story "Schrödinger's Kitten," included in posthumous collection *Budayeen Nights* (2003), won the Nebula, Hugo, Theodore Sturgeon, and Japanese Seiun awards.

Following the example of his first mentors, Damon Knight and Kate Wilhelm, George helped other New Orleans writers through sf/fantasy writing courses at UNO's Metropolitan College from the late 1980s to 1996, and with a monthly writing workshop he founded in 1988, which continues to meet regularly.

After a lifetime filled with chronic pain and chronic illness, he died peacefully in his sleep in New Orleans on April 27, 2002.

"The Aliens Who Knew, I Mean, *Everything*," was nominated for the Nebula, the Hugo, and the Locus awards in the short story category.

Jeffrey Ford is a graduate of Binghamton University, where he studied with the novelist John Gardner. He published his first story, "The Casket," in Gardner's literary magazine *MSS* in 1981, and his first full-length novel, *Vanitas*, in 1988. His next three novels comprised the "Well-Built City" trilogy: *The Phsiognomy, Memoranda,* and *The Beyond.*

Jeff has twelve nominations for the World Fantasy Award, and has won the award six times: two for novels *The Phsiognomy* and *The Shadow Year;* two for collections *The Fantasy Writer's Assistant and Other Stories* and *The Drowned Life,* one for novella "Botch Town," and one for short story "Creation." He teaches Writing and Early American Literature at Brookdale Community College. Website: www.well-builtcity.com.

"Exo-Skeleton Town" won the 2006 Grand Prix de l'Imaginaire, the French national speculative fiction award.

Karen Joy Fowler is the author of five novels and three short story collections. Her first book, collection *Artificial Things,* was a finalist for the Philip K. Dick Award. Her first novel, *Sarah Canary,* won the Commonwealth medal for best first novel by a Californian; her third, *Sister Noon,* was a finalist for the PEN/Faulkner; and *The Jane Austen Book Club* was a *New York Times* bestseller. Her most recent publication is the collection

What I Didn't See from Small Beer Press. In 1991, in collaboration with author Pat Murphy, Karen helped found the James Tiptree, Jr. Award, a literary prize for science fiction or fantasy that "expands or explores our understanding of gender."

Karen currently lives in Santa Cruz, California, with her husband. Website: www.karenjoyfowler.com.

Neil Gaiman has long been one of the top writers in modern comics, as well as writing books for readers of all ages. The *Dictionary of Literary Biography* lists him as one of the top ten living post-modern writers, and a prolific creator of works of prose, poetry, film, journalism, comics, song lyrics, and drama.

His *New York Times* bestselling 2001 novel, *American Gods,* was awarded the Hugo, Nebula, Bram Stoker, SFX, and Locus awards, and was nominated for many other awards, including the World Fantasy Award and the Minnesota Book Award.

His children's novel *Coraline,* published in 2002, was also a *New York Times* and international bestseller and an enormous critical success; it won the Elizabeth Burr/Worzalla, Hugo, Nebula, Bram Stoker, and British Science Fiction awards.

Neil was the creator/writer of monthly DC Comics series, *Sandman,* which won nine Will Eisner Comic Industry Awards, including the award for best writer four times, and three Harvey Awards. *Sandman* #19 took the 1991 World Fantasy Award for best short story, making it the first comic ever to be awarded a literary award. In August 1997 the Comic Book Legal Defense Fund, a First Amendment organization, awarded Neil Gaiman their Defender of Liberty Award. Website: www.neilgaiman.com.

"How to Talk to Girls at Parties" was nominated for the Hugo Award and won the Locus Award for best short story.

Molly Gloss is a fourth-generation Oregonian who lives in Portland. Her short stories have appeared in numerous magazines and anthologies, including The *Norton Book of Science Fiction* and *The Year's Best Science Fiction.* Her novel, *The Jump-Off Creek,* was a finalist for the PEN/Faulkner Award for American Fiction, and a winner of both the

Pacific Northwest Booksellers Award and the Oregon Book Award. In 1996, she was recipient of a Whiting Writers Award. *The Dazzle of Day*, a novel of the near future, was named a 1997 *New York Times* Notable Book, and was awarded the PEN Center West Fiction Prize. *Wild Life*, set in 1905 in the mountains and woods of Washington State, won the James Tiptree, Jr. Award in 2000, and was chosen as the 2002 selection for "If All of Seattle Read the Same Book." *The Hearts of Horses* was a finalist for the WILLA Award and the Oregon Book Award, and was a national bestseller. Her work, including her published science fiction, frequently explores questions of landscape, western settlement, and the human response to wilderness. Website: www.mollygloss.com.

"Lambing Season" was nominated for the Nebula, the Hugo, the Locus, and the Asimov's Reader Award in the short story category.

Ernest Hogan is a recombocultural Chicano mutant, known for committing outrageous acts of science fiction, cartooning, and other questionable pursuits. He can't help but be controversial. However, any resemblance between Ernest and protagonist Pablo Cortez is purely coincidental. Ernest writes: "Pablo first came to me while I was experimenting with abstract expressionism in a painting class. Gravity limited the possibilities: if only there was a way to keep the drips from being pulled to the bottom of the canvas. Jackson Pollock set his on the floor, but I was a Space Age baby. I guess if I hadn't been born an East L.A. Chicano, Pablo probably wouldn't have had his graffiti connections." "Guerrilla Mural of a Siren's Song" formed the basis of Ernest's novel *Cortez on Jupiter*, one of the Ben Bova's Discoveries series from Tor Books. Though currently out of print, *Cortez on Jupiter* will soon be released as an ebook.

Ernest's other novels are *High Aztech* and *Smoking Mirror Blues*. His short fiction has appeared in a variety of periodicals and anthologies, including *Amazing Stories, Analog, Science Fiction Age, Semiotext(E) SF, Angel Body and Other Magic for the Soul, Witpunk,* and *Voices for the Cure*. He is married to the author Emily Davenport, and resides in Phoenix, Arizona. Website: www.mondoernesto.com.

Stephen King is the author of more than fifty books. His most recent include *Full Dark, No Stars, Under the Dome, Just After Sunset*, and *Lisey's Story*. In his new novel, *11/22/63*, a time traveler tries to prevent the JFK assassination. Stephen has been recognized as a Grand Master by both the Mystery Writers of America and the World Horror Convention, and has been honored with a Bram Stoker Life Achievement Award and a World Fantasy Life Achievement Award. He is also the recipient of an Alex Award (in 2009 for *Just After Sunset*), an O. Henry Award (in 1996 for "The Man in the Black Suit"), and a Quill Award (in 2005 for *Faithful*). In 2003 The National Book Foundation awarded Stephen the Medal for Distinguished Contribution to American Letters.

He lives in Bangor, Maine, with his wife, the novelist Tabitha King. Website: stephenking.com.

Nancy Kress is the author of twenty-six books: three fantasy novels, twelve SF novels, three thrillers, four collections of short stories, one YA novel, and three books on writing fiction. For sixteen years Nancy was the "Fiction" columnist for *Writer's Digest* magazine. She is perhaps best known for the "Sleepless" trilogy that began with *Beggars in Spain*. The novel was based on the Nebula- and Hugo-winning novella of the same name. She won another Hugo Award in 2009 for the novella "The Erdmann Nexus." Nancy has also won three additional Nebulas, a Sturgeon, and the John W. Campbell Award. Her most recent books are a collection, *Nano Comes to Clifford Falls and Other Stories* (2008); a bio-thriller, *Dogs* (2008); and SF novel, *Steal Across the Sky* (2009). Nancy's fiction has been translated into twenty languages. She lives in Seattle with her husband, SF writer Jack Skillingstead, and Cosette, the world's most spoiled toy poodle. Website: nancykress.blogspot.com.

Ursula K. Le Guin writes both poetry and prose, and in various modes including realistic fiction, science fiction, fantasy, young children's books, books for young adults, screenplays, essays, verbal texts for musicians, and voicetexts. She has published seven books of poetry, twenty-two novels, over a hundred short stories (collected in eleven volumes), four collections of essays, twelve books for children, and four volumes of translation. Three of Ursula's books have been finalists for the American Book Award and the Pulitzer Prize; additional honors and awards include the Science Fiction and Fantasy Writers of America Grand Master Award, the World Fantasy Life Achievement Award, the Library of Congress Living Legends Award in the "Writers and Artists" category, the 2002 PEN/Malamud Award for "excellence in a body of short fiction," the National Book Award for Children's Books (in 1973 for *The Farthest Shore*), the Pushcart Prize (in 1991 for "Bill Weisler"), and also in 1991, the Harold D. Vursell Memorial Award from the American Academy of Arts and Letters.

Bruce McAllister grew up in a peripatetic Navy family—his father in love with the ocean sciences, his mother the behavioral sciences—who found that the one thing he could take with him anywhere in the world (or find once he got there) was science fiction. Over the years his short fiction has appeared in the major science fiction and fantasy magazines, literary quarterlies, year's best anthologies, and college textbooks. His novelette "Dream Baby"—which was expanded into the critically acclaimed novel of the same name and received a National Endowment for the Arts award—was a finalist for the Hugo, Nebula, and Locus awards. His short story "The Boy in Zaquitos" was selected for *Best American Short Stories 2007*, guest-edited by Stephen King. His first collection of SF stories, *The Girl Who Loved Animals and Other Stories*, was published in 2007. He has served on the James Tiptree, Nebula, and Philip K. Dick award juries; was associate editor of the Harry Harrison/Brian Aldiss "year's best SF" series for some years; and taught creative and professional writing, science fiction, and American cultural myth for twenty-five years in university, helping establish writing programs while there. Bruce is now a writing coach, publishing consultant, and interdisciplinary science consultant; he lives in southern California with his wife, choreographer Amelie Hunter, and in happy proximity to his children. Website: www.mcallistercoaching.com.

"Kin" was nominated for both the Hugo Award and the Locus Award in the short story category.

Paul McAuley worked as a research biologist in various universities, including Oxford and UCLA, and as a lecturer in botany at St. Andrews University, before becoming a full-time writer. His first novel, *Four Hundred Billion Stars,* won the Philip K. Dick Award; his sixth, *Fairyland,* won the Arthur C. Clarke and John W. Campbell awards. He is currently working on his eighteenth novel, *In the Mouth of the Whale,* scheduled to be published early in 2012. About "The Thought War," Paul writes: "Where do writers get their ideas? In the case of this little alien invasion story, it was from the pages of *New Scientist:* an article about a theory that posits an extreme solution to the case of the well-established effect that observers have on collapsing super-imposed states of quantum particles—and my discovery of an old, history-steeped cemetery in a corner of North London." Paul lives in North London. Website: unlikelyworlds. blogspot.com.

Elizabeth Moon grew up in south Texas and started writing at an early age. She has degrees in history and biology, and served in the Marines from 1968–1971. She has written twenty-three novels, (two co-authored with Anne McCaffrey), including several popular series: Vatta's War (concluded in 2008 with *Victory Conditions*), the Serrano Legacy, Planet Pirates (with McCaffrey), and the trilogy *The Deed of Paksenarrion* and its prequels. She has been a finalist for both the Hugo (*Remnant Population*) and the Arthur C. Clarke Award (*The Speed of Dark*); her novel *The Speed of Dark* won the 2004 Nebula Award. In 2007, Elizabeth won the Robert A. Heinlein Award for her body of work. She has had over thirty shorter works in magazines and anthologies, most recently her collection *Moon Flights* (2007). Her most recent novel is *Kings of the North* (2011), the second volume of Paladin's Legacy.

Besides writing, her other interests include classical music, prairie restoration, wildlife management, horses, Renaissance-style fencing, nature photography, and biomedical science. Elizabeth now lives in central Texas with her husband, two horses, a cat, and a John Deere tractor named Bombadil. Website: www.elizabethmoon.com.

Pat Murphy is a writer, a scientist, and a toy maker. Her novels include *The Wild Girls, Adventures in Time and Space with Max Merriwell,* and *The Falling Woman.* Her fiction has won the Nebula Award, the Philip K. Dick Award, the World Fantasy Award, and the Seiun Award.

Over the course of twenty-plus years as a writer and editor with San Francisco's Exploratorium, Pat wrote and edited science books for children and adults. Her titles include *The Science Explorer* series, *The Math Explorer, By Nature's Design, Traces of Time,* and *Exploratopia.*

Currently, Pat works for Klutz, a publisher of how-to books that come with cool stuff. Pat's books with Klutz include *Invasion of the Bristlebots* (which comes with robots that run on toothbrush bristles), *Boom! Splat! Kablooey!* (a book of explosions), and *The Handbook* (which comes with a skeletal model of a hand).

Pat enjoys looking for trouble. Her favorite color is ultraviolet. Her favorite book is whichever one she is working on right now. Website: www.verlavolante.com.

Mike Resnick has been nominated for thirty-five Hugo Awards—a record for writers—and except for 1999 and 2003, he has received at least one nomination every year to date since 1989. He has won the Hugo Award five times, most recently in 2005 for short story "Travels with My Cat."

In addition, Mike has won a Nebula Award, and many other major awards in the US, France, Japan, Poland, Croatia, and Spain, and is, according to *Locus,* the all-time leading award winner, living or dead, for short science fiction. He is the author of more than sixty novels, more than 250 short stories, and two screenplays, and is the editor of forty anthologies.

Recently, Mike sold a movie option on all the John Justin Mallory books and stories—*Stalking the Unicorn, Stalking the Vampire, Stalking the Dragon,* plus six novelettes and a short story—to Heath Corson and Criminal Mastermind Entertainment. Website: mikeresnick.com.

"The 43 Antarean Dynasties" was nominated for the Locus and Theodore Sturgeon awards, and won the Hugo Award, the Asimov's Reader Award, and the Spanish Premios Ignotus (given at HispaCon, Spain's national SF convention) for best short story.

In 1949, **Robert Silverberg** started a science fiction fanzine called *Spaceship*, and made his first professional sale to *Science Fiction Adventures*, a nonfiction piece called "Fanmag," in the December 1953 issue. His first professional fiction publication was "Gorgon Planet" in the February 1954 issue of the British magazine *Nebula Science Fiction*; his first novel, *Revolt on Alpha C*, was published in 1955.

The best known of his many novels and stories are *Dying Inside, Lord Valentine's Castle, Nightwings*, "Born with the Dead," "Sailing to Byzantium," and "Passengers." He has won five Nebula Awards and five Hugo Awards, and in 2004 was named a Grand Master by the Science Fiction and Fantasy Writers of America. In 2007, Bob was elected President of the Fantasy Amateur Press Association, and currently serves as President Emeritus.

He and his wife Karen, also a writer under the name of Karen Haber, live in the San Francisco area. Website: www.majipoor.com.

Amanda and the Alien was filmed in 1995, directed by Jon Kroll, and starring Nicole Eggert, John Diehl, Michael Dorn, and Stacy Keach.

Jack Skillingstead was one of five winners in Stephen King's 2001 "On Writing" contest. Two years later his first professional sale appeared in *Asimov's Science Fiction*: short story "Dead Worlds" went on to be shortlisted for the Theodore Sturgeon Award, and Gardner Dozois reprinted it in his annual *Year's Best Science Fiction* anthology series. Since then Jack has sold thirty short stories, published critically acclaimed collection *Are You There and Other Stories* (2009), and debuted as a novelist that same year with *Harbinger*. His stories have appeared in *Asimov's, Fantasy & Science Fiction, Realms of Fantasy*, and a number of other publications, including Lou Anders's acclaimed *Fast Forward* series. His fiction has been described as "brilliant" by famed critic John Clute, and has been translated into four languages, podcast, and dissected in university classrooms from Rutgers to San Diego State.

Jack lives in Seattle with his wife, fellow writer Nancy Kress. Website: www.jackskillingstead.com.

Bruce Sterling, author, journalist, editor, and critic, was born in 1954. Best known for his ten science fiction novels, he also writes short stories, book reviews, design criticism, opinion columns, and introductions for books ranging from Ernst Jünger to Jules Verne. His nonfiction works include *The Hacker Crackdown: Law and Disorder on the Electronic Frontier* (1992), *Tomorrow Now: Envisioning the Next Fifty Years* (2003), and *Shaping Things* (2005).

Bruce is a contributing editor of *Wired* magazine and writes a weblog. During 2005, he was the "Visionary in Residence" at Art Center College of Design in Pasadena. In 2008 he was the Guest Curator for the Share Festival of Digital Art and Culture in Torino, Italy, and the Visionary in Residence at the Sandberg Instituut in Amsterdam.

He has appeared on ABC's *Nightline*, BBC's *The Late Show*, CBC's *Morningside*, on MTV and TechTV, and in *Time, Newsweek, The Wall Street Journal*, the *New York Times, Fortune, Nature, I.D., Metropolis, Technology Review, Der Spiegel, la Repubblica*, and many other venues. Blog: www.wired.com/beyond_the_beyond.

"Swarm" was nominated for the Nebula, Hugo, and Locus awards in the novelette category.

Born in darkest Yorkshire, **Charles Stross** currently lives in historic Edinburgh, capital of Scotland, with his wife, cats, carnivorous plants, and a herd of senescent computers. His first published short story, "The Boys," appeared in *Interzone* in 1987; his first novel, *The Atrocity Archive*, was originally serialized in the British magazine *Spectrum SF*, number 7, November 2001, through number 9, November 2002.

He holds degrees in pharmacy and computer science, and is the author of *The Web Architect's Handbook* (1996). Charlie has worked as a technical author, freelance journalist, programmer, and pharmacist at different times. He is now a full-time writer.

In 2005, he was nominated for three Hugo Awards: one nomination for best novel and two nominations for best novella; he won the Hugo Award for best novella for "The Concrete Jungle," included in *The Atrocity Archives* (2004).

Charlie has written several series of novels, including the Eschaton series, the Merchant Princes series, the Halting State series, and the Laundry Files series. Much of his work concerns the singularity, but he writes near-future speculations and stories that incorporate Lovecraftian horror.

Michael Swanwick is one of the most acclaimed and prolific science fiction and fantasy writers of his generation. He has received a Hugo Award for fiction in an unprecedented five out of six years (1998–2003) and has been honored with the Nebula, Theodore Sturgeon, and World Fantasy Award, as well as receiving nominations for the British Science Fiction and Arthur C. Clarke awards.

His first novel, *In the Drift* (1985), was published as part of the New Ace Science Fiction Specials series, edited by Terry Carr. Michael's new novel, *Dancing with Bears,* featuring post-Utopian confidence artists Darger and Surplus, was published by Night Shade Books on May Day, 2011. He has also written photo-story "October Leaves," available online on Flickr.com.

Michael has written about the field as well. He published two long essays on the state of science fiction ("A User's Guide to the Post Moderns," 1986) and fantasy ("In the Tradition…," 1994); both essays were collected together in *The Postmodern Archipelago* (1997).

He lives in Philadelphia with his wife, Marianne Porter. Website: www.michaelswanwick.com.

"A Midwinter's Tale" was nominated for the Locus Award, and won the Asimov's Reader Award for best short story.

Mark W. Tiedemann attended Clarion in 1988 and, shortly thereafter, began publishing. He has sold over fifty short stories, to *Asimov's, Fantasy & Science Fiction, Science Fiction Age, Tomorrow SF, Tales of the Unanticipated,* and anthologies such as *Universe 2, Vanishing Acts, Bending the Landscape, War of the Worlds: the Global Dispatches,* and others.

In 1999 he was invited to write in Isaac Asimov's Robot City universe and subsequently published the Robot Mystery trilogy: *Mirage, Chimera,* and *Aurora.* In 2001 the first book of his Secantis Sequence was published: *Compass Reach* was shortlisted for the Philip K. Dick Award. Two more novels followed, *Metal of Night* and *Peace & Memory.* In 2006, his standalone novel *Remains* was shortlisted for the James Tiptree Jr. Award.

While all this was going on, he joined the board of directors of the Missouri Center for the Book, the Missouri affiliate to the Library of Congress Center for the Book, an institution that works to promote and support the state literary heritage and the culture of the book. In 2005, he was elected its president. Though retired now, during his tenure, the Center advocated for and achieved the establishment of the first Missouri State Poet Laureate.

Mark has lived in St. Louis all his life, for the past thirty years with his companion, best friend, and first reader, Donna. He occasionally plays piano and guitar, doodles in idle moments, and is somehow, according to friends, still sane after all these years, a condition which could change at any moment.

Harry Turtledove received his PhD in Byzantine history from UCLA in 1977. His dissertation was entitled *The Immediate Successors of Justinian: A Study of the Persian Problem and of Continuity and Change in Internal Secular Affairs in the Later Roman Empire During the Reigns of Justin II and Tiberius II Constantine (A.D. 565–582)*.

In 1979, he published his first two novels, *Wereblood* and *Werenight*, under the pseudonym "Eric G. Iverson." Harry later explained that his editor at Belmont Tower did not think people would believe the author's real name was "Turtledove" and came up with something more Nordic. He continued to use the "Iverson" name until 1985, when he began publishing under his real name. In the 1980s, Harry also worked as a technical writer for the Los Angeles County Office of Education. In 1991, he left the LACOE and turned to writing full-time.

Harry has been dubbed "The Master of Alternate History": he is known both for creating original alternate history scenarios such as survival of the Byzantine Empire or an alien invasion in the middle of the Second World War, and for giving a fresh and original treatment to themes previously dealt with by many others, including the Confederacy winning the Civil War and a Nazi Germany victory in World War II. He is married to mystery writer Laura Frankos; they have three daughters. Website: www.sfsite.com/~silverag/turtledove.html.

"The Road Not Taken" was nominated for a Locus Award and an AnLab (*Analog*) Award in the novelette category.

Marty Halpern is a two-time finalist for the World Fantasy Award–Professional for his work with Golden Gryphon Press. His career with GGP began in 1999, and in the next 7 years (while working a full-time, high-tech job through half of those years), he edited 23½ hardcovers, 4 limited edition chapbooks, and 4 reprint trade paperbacks. The "½" hardcover is original anthology *The Silver Gryphon* (marking the press's twenty-fifth book in 2003), which he co-edited with publisher Gary Turner.

Marty now freelances, working directly with authors to prepare their manuscripts for publication, as well as working primarily for independent publishers Night Shade Books and Tachyon Publications, for whom he has edited a combined 20 titles (and copyedited far too many more to count), and other publishers including Ace Books, Damnation Books (*Realms of Fantasy* magazine), and Morrigan Books UK.

In addition to his work as an editor, Marty has written a series of columns entitled "The Perfect Sentence," published in *The Valley Scribe,* the newsletter of the San Fernando Valley Chapter of the California Writers Club. And was a guest faculty at the 2004 East of Eden Writers Conference in Salinas, California.

Marty Halpern currently resides in San Jose, California, and occasionally emerges from his inner sanctum to attend conventions. Blog "More Red Ink": martyhalpern.blogspot.com; SF Editors Wiki entry: sfeditorwatch.com/index.php/Marty_Halpern.

Night Shade Books is an Independent Publisher of Quality Science-Fiction, Fantasy and Horror

The only thing worse than war is revolution. Especially when you're already losing the war...

Nyx used to be a bel dame, a government-funded assassin with a talent for cutting off heads for cash. Her country's war rages on, but her assassin days are long over. Now she's babysitting diplomats to make ends meet and longing for the days when killing people was a lot more honorable.

When Nyx's former bel dame "sisters" lead a coup against the government that threatens to plunge the country into civil war, Nyx volunteers to stop them. The hunt takes Nyx and her inglorious team of mercenaries to one of the richest, most peaceful, and most contaminated countries on the planet—a country wholly unprepared to host a battle waged by the world's deadliest assassins.

In a rotten country of sweet-tongued politicians, giant bugs, and renegade shape shifters, Nyx will forge unlikely allies and rekindle old acquaintances. And the bodies she leaves scattered across the continent this time... may include her own.

Because no matter where you go or how far you run in this world, one thing is certain: the bloody bel dames will find you.

Night Shade Books is an Independent Publisher of Quality Science-Fiction, Fantasy and Horror

ISBN: 978-1-59780-280-2 ◖ $24.99 ◖ Look for it in e-Book

Jim and the Flims is a novel set in Santa Cruz, California... and the afterlife. Acclaimed cyberpunk/singularity author Rudy Rucker explores themes of death and destruction, in the wry, quirky style he is famous for.

Jim Oster ruptures the membrane between our world and afterworld (AKA, Flimsy), creating a two-way tunnel between them. Jim's wife Val is killed in the process, and Jim finds himself battling his grief, and an invasion of the Flims—who resemble blue baboons and flying beets. Jim's escalating adventures lead him to the center of the afterworld, where he just might find his wife.

Can Jim save Earth with the help of a posse of Santa Cruz surf-punks, and at the same time bring his wife back to life? *Jim and the Flims* is the Orphic myth retold for the twenty-first century. Will there be a happy ending this time?

Night Shade Books is an Independent Publisher of Quality Science-Fiction, Fantasy and Horror

ISBN: 978-1-59780-227-7 ❧ $24.99 ❧ Look for it in e-Book

In Yalda's universe, light has no universal speed and its creation generates energy.

On Yalda's world, plants make food by emitting their own light into the dark night sky.

As a child Yalda witnesses one of a series of strange meteors, the Hurtlers, that are entering the planetary system at an immense, unprecedented speed. It becomes apparent that her world is in imminent danger—and that the task of dealing with the Hurtlers will require knowledge and technology far beyond anything her civilisation has yet achieved.

Only one solution seems tenable: if a spacecraft can be sent on a journey at sufficiently high speed, its trip will last many generations for those on board, but it will return after just a few years have passed at home. The travellers will have a chance to discover the science their planet urgently needs, and bring it back in time to avert disaster.

Orthogonal is the story of Yalda and her descendants, trying to survive the perils of their long mission and carve out meaningful lives for themselves, while the threat of annihilation hangs over the world they left behind. It will comprise three volumes:

* Book One: The Clockwork Rocket
* Book Two: The Eternal Flame
* Book Three: The Arrows of Time

Night Shade Books is an Independent Publisher of Quality Science-Fiction, Fantasy and Horror

ISBN: 978-1-59780-232-1 ❦ $15.99 ❦ Look for it in e-Book

edited by
ROSS E. LOCKHART

the BOOK of
CTHULHU

Tales inspired by H. P. Lovecraft from:
KAGE BAKER   LAIRD BARRON   ELIZABETH BEAR
RAMSEY CAMPBELL   DAVID DRAKE   CAITLÍN R. KIERNAN
THOMAS LIGOTTI   TIM PRATT   CHERIE PRIEST
W. H. PUGMIRE   CHARLES STROSS   GENE WOLFE
and many others...

Ia! Ia! Cthulhu Fhtagn!

First described by visionary author H. P. Lovecraft, the Cthulhu mythos encompass a pantheon of truly existential cosmic horror: Eldritch, uncaring, alien god-things, beyond mankind's deepest imaginings, drawing ever nearer, insatiably hungry, until one day, when the stars are right....

As that dread day, hinted at within the moldering pages of the fabled *Necronomicon*, draws nigh, tales of the Great Old Ones: Cthulhu, Yog-Sothoth, Hastur, Azathoth, Nyarlathotep, and the weird cults that worship them have cross-pollinated, drawing authors and other dreamers to imagine the strange dark aeons ahead, when the dead-but-dreaming gods return.

Now, intrepid anthologist Ross E. Lockhart has delved deep into the Cthulhu canon, selecting from myriad mind-wracking tomes the best sanity-shattering stories of cosmic terror. Featuring fiction by many of today's masters of the menacing, macabre, and monstrous, *The Book of Cthulhu* goes where no collection of Cthulhu mythos tales has before: to the very edge of madness... and beyond!

Do you dare open *The Book of Cthulhu*? Do you dare heed the call?

Night Shade Books is an Independent Publisher of Quality Science-Fiction, Fantasy and Horror

ISBN: 978-1-59780-323-6 « $24.99 « Look for it in e-Book

It's the dawn of the 22nd century, and the world has fallen apart. Decades of war and resource depletion have toppled governments. The ecosystem has collapsed. A new dust bowl sweeps the American West. The United States has become a nation of migrants--starving masses of nomads roaming across wastelands and encamped outside government seed distribution warehouses.

In this new world, there is a new power: Satori. More than just a corporation, Satori is an intelligent, living city risen from the ruins of the heartland. She manufactures climate-resistant seed to feed humanity, and bio-engineers her own perfected castes of post-humans Designers, Advocates and Laborers. What remains of the United States government now exists solely to distribute Satori product; a defeated American military doles out bar-coded, single-use seed to the nation's hungry citizens.

Secret Service Agent Sienna Doss has watched her world collapse. Once an Army Ranger fighting wars across the globe, she now spends her days protecting glorified warlords and gangsters. As her country slides further into chaos, Doss feels her own life slipping into ruin.

When a Satori Designer goes rogue, Doss is tasked with hunting down the scientist-savant, and as events spin out of control, Sienna Doss and Brood find themselves at the heart of Satori, where an explosive finale promises to reshape the future of the world.